PATTI SMITH
ON PATTI SMITH

OTHER BOOKS IN THE MUSICIANS IN THEIR OWN WORDS SERIES

Bowie on Bowie: Interviews and Encounters with David Bowie
The Clash on the Clash: Interviews and Encounters
Cobain on Cobain: Interviews and Encounters
Coltrane on Coltrane: The John Coltrane Interviews
Dolly on Dolly: Interviews and Encounters with Dolly Parton
Fleetwood Mac on Fleetwood Mac: Interviews and Encounters
George Harrison on George Harrison: Interview and Encounters
Hendrix on Hendrix: Interviews and Encounters with Jimi Hendrix
Joni on Joni: Interviews and Encounters with Joni Mitchell
Judy Garland on Judy Garland: Interviews and Encounters
Keith Richards on Keith Richards: Interviews and Encounters
Led Zeppelin on Led Zeppelin: Interviews and Encounters
Lennon on Lennon: Conversations with John Lennon
Leonard Cohen on Leonard Cohen: Interviews and Encounters
Miles on Miles: Interviews and Encounters with Miles Davis
Springsteen on Springsteen: Interviews, Speeches, and Encounters
Tom Waits on Tom Waits: Interviews and Encounters
The Who on the Who: Interviews and Encounters

PATTI SMITH
ON PATTI SMITH

interviews and encounters

EDITED BY AIDAN LEVY

CHICAGO
REVIEW
PRESS

Published by Chicago Review Press Incorporated
814 North Franklin Street
Chicago, Illinois 60610

ISBN 978-0-912777-00-9

Library of Congress Control Number: 2020941426

A list of credits and copyright notices for the individual pieces in this collection can be found on pages 521–526.

Interior design: Jonathan Hahn

Printed in the United States of America
5 4 3 2 1

To Kaitlin and Diana,
The life in your fingers unwound my existence
Dead to the world alive I awoke

CONTENTS

Acknowledgments   xi

Preface: Patti's Labyrinth   xiii

Part I · 1972–1979: Gloria in Excelsis Deo

The Poetry of Performance: An Interview with Patti Smith │ VICTOR BOCKRIS

    August 15, 1972 │ Red Room Books.   3

Patti Smith: Somewhere, Over the Rimbaud │ SUSIN SHAPIRO

    December 1975 │ *Crawdaddy*.   23

Patti Smith: Poetry in Motion │ ROBIN KATZ

    December 13, 1975 │ *Sounds*   30

Patti Smith: Her Horses Got Wings, They Can Fly │ DAVE MARSH

    January 1976 │ *Rolling Stone*.   38

Interview with Patti Smith │ MICK GOLD

    May 10, 1976 │ Interview Transcript   53

Patti Smith: Misplaced Joan of Arc │ MICHAEL GROSS

    August 1976 │ *Blast*.   70

Patti Smith: Patti Cracks Noggin, Raps On Regardless │ VIVIEN GOLDMAN

    February 5, 1977 │ *Sounds*.   80

Delicate Delinquent │ LEGS MCNEIL (TRANSCRIBED BY STEVE TAYLOR)

    February 1977 │ *Punk*   83

ZigZag Articles │ JOHN TOBLER

    April and June 1978 │ *ZigZag*.   96

It's Hot: A Patti Smith Interview │ PEGGY THOMPSON

    May 12–19, 1978 │ *Georgia Straight* (Canada)   108

Guest Deejay Patti Smith │ HOWIE KLEIN

    May 14, 1978 │ *KSAN*   113

Patti Smith: Straight, No Chaser │ NICK TOSCHES

    September 1978 │ *Creem*.   123

The Patti Smith Group | ANDY SCHWARTZ

June 1979 | *New York Rocker*................................... 129

When Patti Rocked | WILLIAM S. BURROUGHS

March 1979, published April 1988 | *Spin* 147

Part II · 1988–1996: Dream of Life

Patti Smith Resurfaces | JIM SULLIVAN

August 27, 1988 | *Boston Globe*................................ 161

**Patti Smith: The Power and the Glory,
the Resurrection and the Life** | GERRIE LIM

July 1995 | *BigO* (Singapore) 167

Patti Smith | THURSTON MOORE

Winter 1996 | *Bomb*... 182

Patti Smith: She Is Risen | HOLLY GEORGE-WARREN

May 1996 | *Option*.. 197

The ATN Q&A: Patti Smith (Parts 1 and 2) | MICHAEL GOLDBERG AND JAAN UHELSZKI

June 1996 | *Addicted to Noise* 205

The Rebel: Patti Smith | BEN EDMONDS

August 1996 | *MOJO*.. 223

John Cale and Patti Smith: How We Met | LUCY O'BRIEN

August 25, 1996 | *Independent* 239

Part III · 1997–2009: Blakean Years

In These Viral Times: An Exclusive Interview with Patti Smith | LAURIE FITZPATRICK

November 1997 | *A&U*.. 247

The Progressive Interview: Patti Smith | JOHN NICHOLS

December 1997 | *Progressive* 257

Patti Smith Returns to Ground Zero | FRED MILLS

January 30, 1998 | *Goldmine*................................... 269

Patti Smith Talks About *Gung Ho* | JODY DENBERG

January 21, 2000 | KGSR 283

Patti Smith on Allen Ginsberg | JERRY ARONSON

    February 15, 2001 | *The Life and Times of Allen Ginsberg*.......... 302

Patti Smith Strikes a Strong Note for a Peaceable Kingdom | ED MASLEY

    June 6, 2004 | *Pittsburgh Post-Gazette* 307

An Interview with Patti Smith on *Auguries of Innocence* | LAWRENCE FRENCH

    November 2005 | KUSF 312

Patti Smith Discusses *Twelve* on *Words and Music* | RITA HOUSTON

    April 11, 2007 | WFUV.. 329

Exit Interview: Patti Smith | RICHARD RYS

    July 22, 2008 | *Philadelphia* 342

Patti Smith and Steven Sebring on *Patti Smith: Dream of Life* | ANTHONY DECURTIS

    December 29, 2009 | *POV* 345

Part IV · 2010–2018: Devotion

Jonathan Lethem and Patti Smith | JONATHAN LETHEM

    November 3, 2010 | PEN America 365

Patti Smith: Warrior Poet | PAUL ZOLLO

    January/February 2011 | *American Songwriter*.................... 373

Patti Smith Discusses *Banga* on *Words and Music* | ERIC HOLLAND

    June 5, 2012 | WFUV 380

Patti Smith: I Will Always Live Like Peter Pan | CHRISTIAN LUND

    August 24, 2012 | Louisiana Channel........................... 395

Patti Smith: Making the Past Present | DANIEL DAVID BAIRD

    March 2013 | *Border Crossings* (Canada)........................ 414

Patti Smith's Eternal Flame | ALAN LIGHT

    Conducted 2007, published February 12, 2015 | *Medium Cuepoint*.... 423

Patti Smith Says *M Train* Is the Roadmap to Her Life | SHADRACH KABANGO

    October 15, 2015 | *q*, Canadian Broadcasting Corporation......... 430

Patti Smith Looks Back on Life Before She Became the Godmother of Punk | TERRY GROSS

    October 23, 2015 | *Fresh Air* 440

Patti Smith on *Devotion* | MARGERY EAGAN AND JIM BRAUDE

    September 28, 2017 | *Boston Public Radio*, WBGH................ 455

Patti Smith on Climate Change and the One
Thing Donald Trump Is Afraid Of | KRISTIN IVERSEN
October 18, 2017 | *Nylon* (US) 465

All the Poets (Musicians on Writing): Patti Smith | SCOTT TIMBERG
September 29, 2017 | *LA Review of Books*........................ 473

Patti Smith on "Because the Night" at 40: How Her Bruce Springsteen
Collaboration Is "A Whole Life in a Song" | HILARY HUGHES
June 21, 2018 | *Billboard*...................................... 488

About the Contributors 507
Credits 521
Index......................... 527

ACKNOWLEDGMENTS

Patti Smith was born in Chicago at Grant Hospital during a blizzard in 1946 and grew up a block from Logan Square, so Chicago Review Press is a fitting home for this book. It would not have been possible without the support of Yuval Taylor, who shepherded so many of the Musicians in Their Own Words series books and retired as senior editor at Chicago Review Press in 2019 after twenty-one years. Yuval, a venerable writer himself, edited my first book, *Dirty Blvd.: The Life and Music of Lou Reed*, and I thank him for his ongoing support and friendship. He left the editing of this book in the capable hands of Kara Rota, who has been a joy to work with from the moment we met. The entire Chicago Review Press team—publisher Cynthia Sherry, Ben Krapohl, Alex Granato, and Jon Hahn—did an impeccable job shepherding the manuscript through the editing process. I am grateful to Jeff Burger, who has edited many of the books in the series, for guidance at the outset. I would like to thank my literary agent, Russell Galen, for being a tireless advocate for my often-tireless work.

As for the contents of this book, I would first like to thank prolific author, critic, and rock advocate Barney Hoskyns, the editor of *Rock's Backpages*, for creating an invaluable service to researchers and rock aficionados and aiding immeasurably in the licensing process. I am grateful for the help of Janice Braun, the director of the library and special collections at the F.W. Olin Library at Mills College, who supplied scans from the Patti Smith Collection of many of the interviews as they originally appeared. This book really would not have been possible without the perceptive insights of the contributors. I came of age idolizing many of them, and I have so much respect for the body of work they have collectively produced—for spreading the rock gospel, which is sometimes a thankless job. It is a true honor to present their work in rock journalism within these pages. Since I began work on this project, two contributors have passed away—Nick Tosches and Scott Timberg. Both were inspirations to me, and I am honored to reprint their work here posthumously and to keep their restless intellectual spirit alive.

Of course, this book could not exist without the wisdom of Patti Smith, who for the past five decades has helped us all think more critically, feel more deeply, live more passionately, and err with greater humanity. If I have erred here, please forgive me.

During the process of researching, compiling, and editing this book, I welcomed my first child, Diana, into the world. She has been the joy of my life—worth losing sleep over. I would like to thank her in advance for sacrificing some of her infancy to this project. Still, I took Patti Smith's advice from the pages of this book, and worked before Diana woke up, from 5:00 to 8:00 AM, much to my cat Jody's delight. Thank you always to my family for help and solidarity in whatever I do. Finally, boundless gratitude to my partner, the brilliant, beautiful, and hilarious Dr. Kaitlin Mondello, for agreeing to come through this labyrinth with me, and for all the laughter. I worked in the morning . . . because the night belongs to you.

PREFACE: PATTI'S LABYRINTH

I met Patti Smith only once. It was 2011, and I was working my first job after college, on *Law & Order: Criminal Intent*, as the construction department production assistant, affectionately known as the "shop PA." Smith, a longtime watcher and first-time player, had a guest-starring role on the final season in an episode called "Icarus." She played Columbia University mythology professor Cleo Alexander, who was called on by Vincent D'Onofrio's gimlet-eyed Detective Goren to help unravel an actor's mysterious death on the fictional Broadway production *Icarus: Fly to the Light*. In Smith's show-stealing scene, Goren goes to Columbia to interview Alexander in her office:

Cleo Alexander: Icarus—my favorite metaphor for failed ambition! Hubris. Here it is—the clew, uh, C-L-E-W, a ball of thread or yarn.

Goren: Right, a ball of yarn that Daedalus gave to Theseus to help him escape from the labyrinth, which angered King Minos, who then imprisoned Daedalus and Icarus in the same labyrinth.

Alexander: Are you sure you need my help?

Goren: I do need your help. Tell me more about the labyrinth.

Alexander: Well, the word is pre-Greek in origin, Minoan.

Goren: I saw this in her office. The classical labyrinth, circular in pattern, unicursal.

Alexander: Single path.

Goren: Going in circles, but one path, not difficult to navigate.

Alexander: You know, in some versions of the myth, it's more of a maze—multicursal, like a puzzle, with choices of direction.

It's Smith's perfect detective show cameo. Her life as an artist has been multicursal—beyond her five-decade career in rock, she has been a visual artist, a poet, a photographer, all the while "still the girl that can put her foot through the amplifier." And in navigating her own personal labyrinth, she has improvised her way through some surprising choices of direction. And as for failed ambition, Patti Smith is the antithesis. She set out to bring blood back to what she called "performance poetry," and as a young poet reading at the Poetry Project with Lenny Kaye, she did it; she set out to "wake people up," and starting with her first, self-produced single, "Piss Factory," she did it; she set out to "do the great record, write the great book," and in *Horses* and *Just Kids*, she did it; she set out to "get back to the Tower of Babel," to one universal language, and through her art, she did it. Patti Smith transcended, and every time she did, she just kept on going toward scaling the next height. She is Icarus—she flew too close to the sun, but she survived.

It's also perfect that her cameo in *Criminal Intent* would seize on the power of the word—in this case the etymology of the labyrinth itself. When Smith wrote the ad copy for *Horses*, her iconic debut album, this is how she defined it: "three chords merged with the power of the word." The word, with its intoxicating rhythm, its signifying potential, its capacity to really communicate. Patti Smith is the word made flesh.

An interview, to use an old definition from the Oxford English Dictionary, means a "looking into" or "a view, glance, glimpse (of a thing)." It can also mean a "mutual view (of each other)," coming from the French *entrevoir*—"to have a glimpse of." It seems apropos that Patti Smith would typify a concept stemming from the French, when the French literary avant-garde—Rimbaud, Baudelaire, Genet, Camus—have exerted such a formative influence on her work.

All interviews have an investigative quality to them; there is a kind of detective work being done. There are interviews where the interviewer is only seeking information, and then there are personal interviews. All interviews of the latter sort start with the same basic question: Who is the subject? And they all, in one way or another, seek the truth. To this end, an interviewer might ask someone they've never met probing questions they would not dare ask a close friend, and the interviewee might provide an honest answer. It was no coincidence that Plato chose the dialogue to reveal the greatest truths. That back-and-forth or call-and-response often gets at something deeper than one voice talking—it's a dynamic collaboration or pursuit. We might think of Socrates as the greatest interviewer of all. And Patti Smith is one of the greatest interviewees.

The rock interview as a subgenre has been characterized in part by a kind of self-mythologizing or decadent self-fashioning—and bending the truth—but Smith seems to have turned the genre on its head. Like her lacerating, stripped-down brand of rock-poetry, a fiery riposte to the excesses of glam-rock that had descended on stadiums when she burst onto the scene in the '70s, Smith's interviews bespeak a radical, often brutal honesty. Think of the black tie and white shirt, the iconic cover photo of *Horses* that launched Robert Mapplethorpe's career, as a kind of habit. From the moment Patti Smith came on the mic, chanting "Jesus died for somebody's sins but not mine," the irreverent opening line to "Gloria," it was obvious this voice was searching for something deeper. Reading a Patti Smith interview can feel like stepping into the other side of the confession booth.

Smith's interview persona eschews the standard palaver some journalists had come to expect from lesser rock gods. Hers was an odd performance of the self that is part artful evasion, sardonic derision, rapier wit, gutter wisdom, and truth laid bare—all improvised—in which, through searching, near-religious rapture, she invites her interlocutors into the inner sanctum of her soul. Simply put, Patti Smith elevated the interview to an art form. In the canon of rock journalism, it could be said that an interview with Patti Smith came closer to the Platonic ideal than anything.

So who is Patti Smith? The best interviews don't provide a definitive answer. This book certainly won't tell you, but it will get you closer to the truth, and you might learn something about a life lived dancing barefoot along the way. It will transport you to places she's been—to William Burroughs's bunker; to Jack Kerouac's grave site with Thurston Moore; to the Portobello Hotel in London, where she rhapsodized for hours with a gaggle of reporters on her first European tour; to the legendary Record Plant Studios in New York, behind the scenes of what became *Radio Ethiopia*; to the gritty studio of KSAN, which Greil Marcus once called the "heart of rock 'n' roll radio in America"; to the beach at English Bay in Vancouver, where she shared some Fudgsicles on a hot spring day in 1978. It will also take you to quieter places—to the Chelsea loft she shared with Robert Mapplethorpe for her very first interview, with Victor Bockris in 1972; to moving discussions with Jonathan Lethem and Terry Gross decades after Mapplethorpe's passing of her relationship with her friend and soulmate, the subject of her National Book Award–winning memoir, *Just Kids*; deep into her songwriting process; and to her lifelong obsession with great books. This labyrinth is not just multicursal, but recursive. She tells and retells some of the same stories over and over again—in response to the same questions—but they evolve with each retelling. And if you read carefully, there are quite a few she tells only once. This is her mythology, but unlike Greek myth, it's pretty clear that it's all true.

Yet the truth can be slippery. What we see in this collection of interviews spanning her entire career is a series of glimpses, a view from many different angles. There is the godmother of punk, the voracious reader, the memoirist, the poet, the torch singer, the performance artist, the mother, the enfant terrible, the lapsed Jehovah's Witness, the improviser par excellence, the comedian, the fashion icon, the Detroit housewife, the Top 40 hit maker, the modern-day Joan of Arc, the Philly girl, the "bad girl," the visionary, the mystic, the shaman, the recluse, the laundress, the lover, the political activist, the environmentalist, the guest deejay, the documentary subject, the unrepentant daydreamer, the patron saint of outsiders everywhere. Patti Smith is all these things and more. She is so deeply personal in these interviews that we may feel like we know her, but we don't; no one interview captures her restless spirit, nor could it. For Patti Smith, to quote Walt Whitman, contains multitudes. And in being larger than life, she somehow reminds us that so do we.

Back to *my* Patti Smith—an idle moment in the spring of 2011 on the set of *Law & Order: Criminal Intent*. I was walking bleary-eyed to check inventory and make yet another pot of coffee in the crew kitchen, which was behind the Major Case squad room and the holding cell where we used to take naps. And on my way, Patti Smith walked by. The production still photographer stopped me, and I couldn't imagine why. "Don't you want a photo with Patti Smith?" she said. I was dumbfounded. Why would Patti Smith want to waste a second on me, this backstage twentysomething outsider factotum? But as the photographer snapped the shot, I cracked a smile. And Patti did, too. When I think back on it, I remember her smile, the glint in her eyes—Patti Smith was *alive*. And she thanked me.

Unlike the other guest stars who came through Chelsea Piers, where the show was filmed, Smith decided to wander around the set introducing herself to the crew. It wasn't necessary, but it made sense; the daughter of a factory worker and a waitress who grew up in rural South Jersey, she has always been of the people. I don't have the photo, but I don't need it—the memory is vivid. I was sleepwalking through that soundstage, but for a moment, I woke up. She was just so present. And within three years, I had shifted course dramatically; I started taking my writing more seriously and became a doctoral student at Columbia, where I met my own Cleo Alexander. Meeting Patti on one random afternoon may have had nothing to do with any of that, but you never know. In hindsight, maybe her pausing in that dark hallway—just the fact that she saw me—awakened something long dormant. It is this generosity of spirit, this overwhelming presence of creative energy, that has defined Smith's career, and has made her such a candid interview subject. Waking people up is what Patti Smith has been doing her whole life, and I am confident this book will rouse a few sleepers.

Smith was not involved in the creation of this book. It is intended as a tribute for her fans, as a reference text, as a supplement to her own art, as equipment for living—as a clue or *clew* to the labyrinth of her life, and maybe to yours. There is no substitute for her own work—the endlessly inspiring volumes of poetry, albums, performances, and the ruminative, heart-wrenching, and ultimately joyful books *Just Kids*, *M Train*, *Devotion*, and most recently, *The Year of the Monkey*. There will always be more room on my bookshelf for another book by Patti Smith.

In this volume, Smith imparts hard-earned life lessons about loss, resilience, passion, devotion, and how to live with a full heart. She teaches us to keep on dancing, singing, making, laughing, and working, no matter what life throws at us. She has walked through fire but was not burned. "What matters is to know what you want and to pursue it and understand that it's gonna be hard because life is really difficult," she told Christian Lund, the director of the Louisiana Literature Festival in Humlebæk, Denmark, in 2012:

> You're gonna lose people you love, you're gonna suffer heart-break, sometimes you'll be sick, sometimes you'll have a really bad toothache, sometimes you'll be hungry, but on the other end you'll have the most beautiful experiences. Sometimes just the sky, sometimes, you know, a piece of work that you do that feels so wonderful, or you find somebody to love, or your children. There's beautiful things in life. So when you're suffering, just, you know, it's part of the package. You look at it—we're born and we also have to die. We know that. So it makes sense that we're gonna be really happy and things are gonna be really fucked up, too. Just ride with it. You know, it's like a roller-coaster ride. It's never gonna be perfect; it's gonna have perfect moments and rough spots, but it's all worth it. Believe me.

In editing this collection, I have learned so much from Patti Smith, wisdom born of lived experience which I can't pretend to fully comprehend and will be grappling with for years to come. I hope she will do the same for you.

Oh I'll send you a telegram
Send it deep in the heart of you
Deep in the heart of your brain is a lever
Oh deep in the heart of your brain is a switch

Patti Smith has been pulling that lever and flipping that switch since before she recorded these lines on "Radio Ethiopia," the title track to her underappreciated second studio album. In a 1978 interview collected here, she calls it "my favoritest cut of anything that we've ever done, and it's never gotten airplay." Well, Patti, if you're listening, I'm playing it here.

—AIDAN LEVY

PART I
1972–1979
Gloria in Excelsis Deo

THE POETRY OF PERFORMANCE: AN INTERVIEW WITH PATTI SMITH

Victor Bockris | August 15, 1972 | Red Room Books

It was a balmy Tuesday—August in New York—and a twenty-five-year-old Patti Smith was meeting Victor Bockris in the loft she shared with Robert Mapplethorpe, down the block from the legendary Chelsea Hotel. *Seventh Heaven*, her first book of poems, was published earlier that year by Telegraph Books, the independent publisher Bockris cofounded with poets Aram Saroyan and Andrew Wylie. Smith was enmeshed in the city's bohemian demimonde. In 1971, she had begun performing poetry with guitarist Lenny Kaye at the Poetry Project at St. Mark's Church on East 10th Street, penned a review of a Lotte Lenya anthology for *Rolling Stone*, and acted in *Cowboy Mouth*, the play she conceived of and cowrote with Sam Shepard. But she had never been the subject of an interview, and a palpable sense of self-discovery for interviewer and interviewee alike suffused the dialogue.

Bockris, who was born in England in 1949 and graduated from the University of Pennsylvania in 1971, was not yet the beat-punk chronicler he was destined to become; Smith was not yet the "Godmother of Punk." The week before they met, Smith had been to the Rolling Stones show at Madison Square Garden. That day, her sister Linda was there to witness the electric energy, inspired by Mapplethorpe's edgy art, which hung on the walls. "This was the first occasion on which I realized I had some talent as an interviewer," wrote Bockris, "and I imagine Patti must have realized she was an outstanding interviewee."

This historic interview, which Bockris called "one of the top ten interviews of my life," is Smith's first. It was originally published in September 1972 by Jeff Goldberg's Philadelphia-based Red Room Books and is reproduced here in its entirety. The original typescript had little punctuation or capitalization. Bockris added it in when it was anthologized in his collection *Beat Punks: New York's Underground Culture from the Beat Generation to the Punk Explosion* (New York: Open Road, 2016). That version is presented here, with several minor additions restored from the original text. —Ed.

INTRODUCTION

ONE

Writing is a physical experience. I have seen Andrew Wylie write a poem with nine words in it. His body concentrates. The tiny scrap of paper becomes the centre of the room. I speak to him. He doesn't hear.

Patti Smith sits among the debris of her room. Scattered around her are ornaments and filth. Patti Smith sits on the edge of her bed with the typewriter. The spot vibrates. The room is clean.

Writing is a physical expression. We destroy our tools. Our houses and cloths become backgrounds. We reach the centre of ourselves.

A writer is a falling star.

TWO

The poet is a performer. Poets are public property. Science can't reach them. Poetry is secret. None of us know where we came from.

Victor Bockris

Victor Bockris: Would you consider yourself to be the greatest poet in New York City?

Patti Smith: Um, the greatest poet in New York City? Um, shit. I can't think of what to say. I don't think I'm a great poet at all. I don't even think I'm a good poet. I just think I write neat stuff.

Bockris: Why does it sell well?

Smith: 'Cause I sell. 'Cause you know I got a good personality and people really like me. When people buy my book you know they're really buying a piece of Patti Smith. That book is autobiographical. It sheds the light of my heroes on it. No good poet thinks they're good. Blaise Cendrars said he was a bad poet.

Bockris: How does it work in relation to people who don't know you? People in Omaha?

Smith: Because I think I'm a good writer. I'm a good writer in the same way Mickey Spillane or Raymond Chandler or James M. Cain is a good writer. There's a lot of American rhythms. I mean I can seduce people. I got good punchlines, you know. I got all the stuff that Americans like. Some of it's dirty. There's a lot of good jokes. I mean I write to entertain. I write to make people laugh. I write to give a double take. I write to seduce a chick. I wrote "Girl Trouble" about Anita Pallenberg. Anita Pallenberg would read it and think twice and think maybe she'd invite me over to the south of France and have a little nookie or something. Everything I write has a motive behind it. I write to have somebody. I write the same way I perform. I mean you only perform because you want people to fall in love with you. You want them to react to you.

Bockris: John Wieners said to me yesterday that he figured he'd only just become a poet. He's thirty-eight and he figured this latest book of his [*Selected Poems*] was his first book. And it took him seventeen years to get there. What do you feel about that?

Smith: The other day I reread my book and figured I had written my last book. I don't think that has anything to do with anything. Rimbaud wrote his last book when he was twenty-two and sometimes I figure I did my best work as an artist from post-adolescent energy.

Bockris: Do you think you're a genius?

Smith: I'm not very intelligent.

Bockris: But genius is something else. So you agree, right?

Smith: Yeah, yeah. It's like when I was a little kid I always knew that I had some special kind of thing inside me. I mean I wasn't very attractive. I wasn't very verbal. I wasn't very smart in school. I wasn't anything that showed physically to the world that I was something special but I had this tremendous hope all the time, you know, I had this tremendous spirit that kept me going no matter how fucked up I was. Just had this kind of light inside me that kept spurring me on.

Bockris: Why don't you take us back there to New Jersey in those days when you were a teenager beginning the great trail out? I mean, tell us when you first started to write and everything. How it happened.

Smith: Well, I always wrote. After I was seven when I read *Little Women* I wanted to be like Louisa May Alcott. The whole thing to me was in *Little Women*. Jo was the big move. It seems silly but Jo in *Little Women* with all those fairy tales and plays introduced me to the writer as performer. She would write those plays and perform them and get her sisters laughing even in the face of death so I wanted to be a chick like her, you know, who wrote and performed what I wrote and so I used to write these dumb little plays and then I wrote these banal little short stories but I wasn't good. I showed no promise and then when I went to high school I used to write these really dramatic poems just like any other kid writes. About everything I didn't know about. I was a virgin. I had never faced death. I had never faced war and pestilence and of course I read about sex, pestilence, disease, malaria, I read about everything but I never . . .

Bockris: What year is this?

Smith: '62–'63. Then in '64 you know I started really getting involved in the lives of people. You know, it was like around '63–'64 I got seduced by people's lifestyles, like you know Modigliani, Soutine, Rimbaud.

Bockris: How did you get in touch with Rimbaud?

Smith: Well, I was working in a factory and I was inspecting baby-buggy bumper beepers and it was my lunch break and there was this genius sausage sandwich that the guy in the little cart would bring and I really wanted one. They were like $1.45 but the thing is the guy only brought two a day and the two ladies who ruled the factory, named Stella Dragon and Dotty Hook, took these sausage sandwiches. They were really a wreck, they had no teeth and everything.

So there was nothing else I wanted. You get obsessed with certain tastes. My mouth was really dying for this hot sausage sandwich so I was real depressed. So I went across the railroad tracks to this little bookstore. I was roaming around there and I was looking for something to read and I saw *Illuminations*, you know, the cheap paperback of *Illuminations*. I mean, every kid had it. Rimbaud looks so genius. There's that grainy picture of Rimbaud and I thought he was so neat looking and I instantly snatched it up and I didn't even know what it was about, I just thought Rimbaud was a neat name. I probably called him Rimbald and I thought he was so cool. So I went back to the factory. And I was reading it. It was in French on one side and English on the other and this almost cost me my job 'cause Dotty Hook saw that I was reading something that had foreign language and she said, "What are you reading that foreign stuff for?" and I said "It's not foreign," and she said, "It's foreign—it's communist—anything foreign is communist." So then she said it so loud that everybody thought I was reading *The Communist Manifesto* or something and they all ran up and, of course, complete chaos, and I just left the factory in a big huff and I went home. So of course I attached a lot of importance to that book before I had even read it and I just really fell in love with it. It was gracious son of Pan that I fell in love with it 'cause it was so sexy.

Bockris: At what point in this stage did you figure out and begin to understand what you were doing?

Smith: Not until a few months ago.

Bockris: Why then?

Smith: Well, see, what happened is I didn't really fall in love with writing as writing. I fell in love with writers' lifestyles: Rimbaud's lifestyle—I was in love with Rimbaud for being a mad angel and all that shit. And then I became friends with Janet [Hamill] and she was a writer, there was all these writers in New Jersey. There was just like this little scene. I was secretly writing. I was doing a lot of art. People knew me as an artist and so, like, I was secretly ashamed of my writing because all my best friends were great writers. So I didn't have no confidence in myself. I used to write stuff mostly about girls getting rid of their virginity and I used to write like Lorca. I wrote this one thing about this brother raping his cold sister under the white moon. It was called "The Almond Tree."

While his father raped the young stepmother and she died and he was
. . . He looked at her cadaver and he said, "You are cold in death[,] even
colder to me than you were in life."

Bockris: What do you find are the major problems you have as a writer
at this point?

Smith: When I was a kid? Well, I had no understanding of language. I
was so romantic and I thought all you had to do is expel the romance.
I had no idea the romance of language was a whole thing in itself. I had
no idea of what to do with language. I mean, all I had was I used to
record my dreams. I had no conception of style of words.

Bockris: Tell me how *Seventh Heaven* got put together. It's a 48-page
book. That's a lot of work.

Smith: Right before I met Telegraph Books[,] I started in the last two
years reorganizing my style. I started feeling confidence in my writing. I
just realized what language was. You know, I started seeing language as
magic. Two things happened that really liberated me. The major thing
was reading Mickey Spillane. Because I wanted to move out of . . . I was
starting to get successful in writing these long almost rock and roll poems.
And I liked to perform them but I suddenly realized that though they
were great performed, they weren't such hot shit written down. I'm not
saying I didn't stand behind them, but there's a certain kind of poetry
that's performance poetry. It's like the American Indians weren't writing
conscious poetry, they were making chants. They were making ritual language and the language of ritual is the language of the moment. But as far
as being frozen on a piece of paper is concerned, they weren't inspiring.
You can do anything when you perform, you can say anything you want
as long as you're a great performer, you know you can repeat a word over
and over and over as long as you're a fantastic performer. You know you
never understand what Mick Jagger is saying except "Let It Boogie" [*It's
unclear which song Smith is referring to here.* —Ed.] or "Jumping Jack
Flash" but it's always so powerful 'cause he's such a fantastic performer.

Bockris: Well how do you deal with that problem? That's a central problem in your work. Tony Glover says in his review of *Seventh Heaven*.

He talks about the poetry of performance. I feel that's a central thing we're dealing with at the moment. How to get it down so you can have a book that people can read, but that you can also perform.

Smith: That book to me represents me on the tightrope between writing and performing. I was writing stuff like "Mary Jane" or the Joan of Arc stuff, which is total performance poetry but, you know, I think they were worthy of being printed because their content is important. The Joan of Arc poem is almost total rhythm masturbation but it puts Joan of Arc in a new light, it puts her forth as a virgin with a hot pussy who realizes that she's gonna get knocked off before she gets a chance to come. So there is a concept there that made the rhythm worth[y] of being frozen. But like I said, I was reading Mickey Spillane. I couldn't get into prose 'cause I don't talk that well. I'm not good in grammar. I can't spell. I have lousy sentence structure. I don't know how to use commas so I just get very intimidated when I write something that isn't completely vertical. So I started reading Mickey Spillane, you know, and Mike Hammer, his hammer language: I ran, I ran fast down the alley. And back again. I mean he wrote like that. Three-word sentences and they're like a chill and they're real effective and I got real seduced by his speed and at the same time I started reading Céline 'cause it's just too intellectual but the idea that he could freeze one word and put a period. He dared put one word—yellow—and follow it by forty other words like forty movements, also like some kind of concerto or something. He's not as seducing to me as Mickey Spillane but I juggled the two.

And then the third thing: I was reading Michaux. He's so funny. He wrote this thing called *The Adventure of Phene* [*Smith refers here to the "Plume Travels" vignette in Henri Michaux's* A Certain Plume —*Ed.*] and it's about this guy who's totally paranoid. He's so paranoid he goes to Rome and wants to see the Coliseum and the travel guide says, "Stay away from the Coliseum. It's in bad enough shape already without a guy like you poking around it." And Phene says, "Oh, I'm so sorry. Well, could I at least have a postcard?" And he says, "Don't be ridiculous." And he says, "Oh, I never really meant to have a postcard. I don't even know why I came to this country." And he leaves. So I mean I got three things. I got speed, humor, the holiness of the single word. So I just mixed them all up.

Bockris: Mostly European influences, Rimbaud, Cendrars, Céline, Michaux.

Smith: Well, it used to be totally European. I had no interest in American writing at all.

Bockris: Why?

Smith: It's because of biographies. I was mostly attracted to lifestyles and there just were not any great biographies of genius American lifestyles except the cowboys. And I'm a girl and I was interested in the feminineness of men.

Bockris: What you're trying to do in your writing is create a lifestyle. *Seventh Heaven* is a lifestyle.

Smith: If I didn't think so much of myself I'd think I was a name-dropper, but there's a difference. You can read my book and who do you get out of it? Edie Sedgwick, Marianne Faithfull, Joan of Arc, Frank Sinatra . . . all people I really like. But I'm not doing it to drop names. I'm doing it to say this is another piece of who I am. You know, I am an American. It's ironic I should be so involved with the French because I'm absolutely an American. I'm shrouded in the lives of my heroes.

Bockris: Would you find anybody in America now who you think influences you a lot?

Smith: It's mostly dead people.

Bockris: Anybody alive?

Smith: Dylan. You can't reject Dylan. But Dylan seduced me when he had a fantastic lifestyle. I'll always love Dylan all my life[,] but Dylan was a big thing to me when he was BOB DYLAN. Now he's whatever he is[,] but when he was there and had America in the grip of his fist, then I got so excited about him. As far as anybody living.

Bockris: I find the position of a writer is a fairly isolated one. It's fairly lonely task. Do you find that?

Smith: No, 'cause I don't have the balls to say I'm a writer. I don't think I'm good enough. See, I love my works. I think I've written some really good things. I think "Judith" is just as good as anything ever written, but I couldn't sit down and do it all the time. Oh, Sam Shepard. I admire him.

Bockris: Do you find you learn from him?

Smith: Sure, I learn from Sam because Sam is one of the most magic people I've ever met. Sam is really the most true American man I've ever met in as far as he's also hero-oriented. He has a completely western romance mind. He loves gangsters, he loves cowboys, he's totally physical. He loves bigness. You know Americans love bigness. In his plays there's always a huge Cadillac or a huge breast or a huge monster. His whole life moves on rhythms. He's a drummer. I mean, everything about Sam is so beautiful and has to do with rhythm. That's why Sam and I successfully collaborated because he didn't know that he was . . . intuitively he worked with the rhythm. I do it conceptually. I work with being a thematic writer. He just does it because he's got rhythm in his blood. I do it intellectually. He does it from the heart. And so we were able to establish a really deep communion that way.

Bockris: You're not working with him at the moment, are you?

Smith: No.

Bockris: You don't associate with many writers?

Smith: Well, my best friends are writers. I never collaborate.

Bockris: I wasn't thinking so much of collaborations. People I feel more comfortable with tend to be writers nowadays because they tend to recognize me and I tend to recognize them.

Smith: No, I don't think I have the modern writer's lifestyle.

Bockris: You don't take yourself seriously?

Smith: Ultimately, I don't take anything serious and I can take everything seriously. I'm too much of a cynic to take anything serious. If I'm in a good, pure, relaxed state I can look at certain of my works and like them. But most of the time I look at my stuff and say, Ah, this is a load of shit. Mick Jagger listens to his albums and says they're shit. Bob

Dylan listens to his albums and says they're shit. It hurts me to read an interview where Bob Dylan says he hates *Nashville Skyline*. But I know how I feel. The best work to me is the work in progress. Which is why I produce. . . . I almost hate to see my work go out. I'm more guilty of not being published than any publisher because I'm always in progress. I didn't like to finish my drawings. Yeats was like that. How many versions of "Leda and the Swan" did he do? It's so difficult 'cause it means it's dead. De Kooning did twenty-eight dead women under *Women I* because you know he couldn't stand to say that she was done. It's like you know when a woman has a baby, she created it. It's just begun. But when an artist does a piece of work, as soon as he does the last brushstroke or the last period, it's finished.

Bockris: How did you feel when *Seventh Heaven* came out?

Smith: I carried it around with me for weeks.

Bockris: Did it catalyze anything in your head about writing?

Smith: I stopped writing for a while. I was like a kid at first. I didn't understand it. I saw it. It was in front of me. I liked to carry it on buses and hope people would recognize it was me on the cover. I stopped seeing the poetry as soon as it was printed. The only poem . . . I'll stand behind that book, I think it's a damn good book, but the only two poems I like the best are the two last ones which are the most recent ones. I think "Judith" is the best thing I ever writ.

Bockris: Would you say anything about the difference between being a man and a woman in relation to writing?

Smith: I don't feel it that much.

Bockris: You write about it a lot.

Smith: Being a writer?

Bockris: No, you're a woman. You used the image a few minutes ago of giving birth to a child. It rang a bell in my mind. . . .

Smith: I don't consider myself a female poet. It's only lately that I've been able to consider myself a female artist. I don't think I hold any sex.

I think I have both masculine and feminine rhythms in my work. In the same sense I don't think Mick Jagger is just a masculine performer.

Bockris: You're bisexual.

Smith: Completely heterosexual.

Bockris: You talk as if you were bisexual.

Smith: Most of my poems are written to women because women are most inspiring. Who are most artists? Men. Who do they get inspired by? Women. The masculinity in me gets inspired by female. I get, you know, I fall in love with men and they take me over. I ain't no women's lib chick. So I can't write about a man because I'm under his thumb but a woman I can be male with. I can use her as my muse. I tried to make it with a chick once and I thought it was a drag. She was too soft. I like hardness. I like to feel a male chest. I like bone. I like muscle. I don't like all that soft breast.

Bockris: You find women inspiring from a distance. Anita Pallenberg, Joan of Arc, Marianne Faithfull, Edie Sedgwick, you know. . . .

Smith: No, I don't know any of the girls I wrote about. I wrote about Judy, one of my best friends, but I could only write about her when she was away from me for a year. Then all of a sudden she became a muse. I don't like women close up because they're attainable. It's like I met Edie Sedgwick a few times and she had nothing to do with me. Who was I? But I thought she was swell, she was one of my first heroines. Vali's a perfect example. Vali's one of the only chicks I've ever attained and she didn't go in my book. Vali has been a heroine of mine since I was fourteen years old. She was my original heroine. And when I met her she tattooed my knee. We kissed and all that. She suddenly vanished as one of my great muses. I didn't put her in the book and she's the one chick who deserved it because we touched.

Bockris: Tell me about the writing of a poem for you.

Smith: Let me get the book out. I'll take "Judith." Most of my poems I write in two ways. I write them from first writing a letter to someone who will never receive the letter or I write recording a dream. "Skunk

Dog" was a complete dream. Judy was a girl I was in love with in the brain. I'm in love with her because we have similar brain energy. We can travel through time. We have this fantastic way of communicating. But she doesn't let me touch her. She's one girl that maybe I would have like to have done something to. At one point I was really obsessed with her and she wouldn't let me and at one point she went away to Nepal and right before she left she grabbed me and kissed me and I was so shocked I pushed her away and she said, "You blew it" just 'cause I was too chicken-shit. As long as she acted real tough . . . but as soon as she reached out for me I got scared. I'm a phony. So anyway Judy was away and I loved her so much that I couldn't stand it. I started dreaming of her. So I was trying to write her a letter, but when you really love someone it's almost impossible to write them. It's people you love the most who you can't communicate with verbally. I had such a strong mental contact with this girl that I couldn't talk to her. So I was at the typewriter. It's made writing a much more physical thing. I write with the same fervor as Jackson Pollock used to paint. And all the things that we had, like, we loved the movie *Judex*, I started writing down in a line, just words but, you know, words that were perfect, words like "kodak," "radiant," "jellybitch," and I just tried writing these words.

Bockris: You built the rest of the poem around the central words?

Smith: Yeah. I had these words. I was trying to write her a letter but I had no idea where she was, so obviously it was a piece of narcissism. I was just trying to write this thing. Sort of jacking off. I was trying to project with words and language a photograph of Judy. So, anyway, I had all these words and they laid around for a couple of days and I looked at them and they were almost a perfect square and that's just how it is. I stretched them, put a few periods in. I go through a real process of elimination. What I did to this is I spread it out, made it into a two page thing of which maybe one and a half pages were shit, so I eliminate the page and a half, then I extend what is left.

Bockris: How long did it take you to write that poem?

Smith: About two and a half days. I think it's perfect. Another reason I like this poem is it explains our relationship through words like "jewel," "angelfood," "avocado," it illustrates our personal aesthetic, then it illustrates our problem because it says she would not let me touch her. The other thing is it has my love for punchline. My favorite thing in it is "ah spansule." That's another thing. I love words. I heard some guy say "spansule" as I was writing this. I said, "That's a neat word, what does it mean?" He said, "Spansule, gelatin, a hollow pill." I love definitions. I wrote that down and I like it so much and I wanted to put it in this poem but what was my motive for putting it in this poem? So I said, "Ah spansule a hollow pill what's in it for me." That's joke enough, but I kept carrying it, for love of Judy Judy Judy punch punch punch[,] which . . . I think that's funny.

Bockris: Well, why do you find most other writers in America boring?

Smith: I think I'm a timeless writer.

Bockris: You're a writer in the middle of a literary scene and you're totally ignoring the literary scene around you. How long can you keep going on your own?

Smith: I can keep going because I'm constantly stimulated by earth's glitter. I'm constantly stimulated. I'm not at any loss for material.

Bockris: Are you satisfied with holding on to the same style?

Smith: No, I write totally differently.

Bockris: What are you writing now?

Smith: Back to Rimbaud again. "Judith" is really a left-handed part of *Illuminations* and I'm writing more like that now. I'm allowing myself to get more obscure. I've always been against that. I like people to say what they mean. But what I'm moving into now is sort of the style of the *Illuminations* but more describing situations that have not happened. Like that thing I told you called "Parade." I like to talk casually about things like I say, "Regard I've popped out my eye, there it lies on the ground like some sick kodak. I pick it up and throw it in the face of an unsuspecting grandma, a pedestrian." I like writing like a news reporter about more obscure events. In other words my writing is much more didactic. Documentaries of fantasies. That gives me a chance to get really obscure in terms of actions but it gives the reader a chance because it's written so rigidly they don't know something really bizarre is happening.

Bockris: Do you know what you're doing or is it hit and miss?

Smith: I know what I'm doing. I was never an egomaniac . . .

Bockris: You're not?

Smith: . . . until lately because I know what I'm doing.

Bockris: When did that moment come?

Smith: It came when I started writing things like "Judith." I know that's a good poem. I know it'll be a good poem in ten years from now. To me when I am both inspired and have light emitting from me and feel real natural and intuitive but also at the same time clearly walk into my brain and look around.

Bockris: Before we get on to talking about things in the present let's clear up a few things in the past. Tell me about Blaise Cendrars and his influence on you and how that came about.

Smith: I was working at Scribner's. I discovered Blaise Cendrars because of packaging. I should have discovered him years ago but people are so jealous and want Apollinaire to be the big spirit of the twenties and Blaise has really been sucked in the mud, you know. So I was working at Scribner's and Doubleday published *Moravagine*. It was beautifully packaged, had a drawing on it very similar to how I draw which immediately seduced me. I saw the drawing on the cover, it looked just like one of my drawings, I looked on the back and it said something about insanity and a collective consciousness. . . .

Bockris: Do you write when you're traveling?

Smith: Right now I've been in this room in this city for so long I don't see it any more and I'm not being stimulated. Lately I've just been doing a lot of cleaning inside my brain. My eyes are not seeing anything around me. So I've been dreaming a lot, recording dreams and trying to look within, but I'm not worried about it. I'm just waiting for the moment when I'll get to take a train or plane someplace and I know I'll spurt out because I've just got to see new things. I think Rimbaud said he needs new scenery and a new noise and I need that.

Bockris: Does the fact that you don't find any younger writers you learn from depress you?

Smith: Their lifestyles don't attract me. I think I'm ballsier, a better performer. I think they can learn from me.

Bockris: So you feel the people you can learn from are the rock and roll scene?

Smith: Yeah, in the sixties it was Jim Morison [sic], Bob Dylan, now it's still the Rolling Stones. There was Smokey Robinson. I can still get excited about Humphrey Bogart. I like people who are bigger than me. I'm not interested in meeting poets or a bunch of writers who I don't think are bigger than life. I'm a hero worshipper, I'm not a fame fucker, but I am a hero worshipper. I've always been in love with heroes, that's what seduced me into art. You know Modigliani, Jackson Pollock, de Kooning, people that were hot shit, you know. I want to know heroes, not eighth-class writers.

Bockris: Let's get into the poetry of performance. I've just finished as [sic] essay called "The Poet Is a Performer." So that seems to me to be where it's at. What does it mean to you?

Smith: Poets have been, I think, part of it is because of Victorian England or something or how they crucified Oscar Wilde or something, but poets have become simps. There's this new thing: the poet is a simp, the sensitive young man always away in the attic, but it wasn't always like that. It used to be that the poet was a performer and I think the energy of Frank O'Hara started to re-inspire that. In the sixties there was all that happening stuff. Then Frank O'Hara died and it sort of petered out and then Dylan and Allen Ginsberg revitalized it, but then it got all fucked up again because instead of people learning from Dylan and Allen Ginsberg and realizing that a poet was a performer, they thought that a poet was a social protester. So it got fucked up. I ain't into social protesting.

Bockris: You obviously have a real belief in the possibility of poetry becoming a big public art again, which I really dig. But exactly how to [sic] you think that can happen?

Smith: I've found it has more to do with the physical presence. Physical presentation in performing is more important than what you're saying, quality comes through of course, but if your quality of intellect is high and your love of the audience is evident and you have a strong physical presence you can get away with anything. I mean Billy Graham is a great performer even though he is a hunk of shit. Adolph Hitler was a fantastic performer. He was a black magician. And I learned from that. You can seduce people into mass consciousness.

Bockris: Don't you think you're directly competing with the Rolling Stones and how can you possibly win?

Smith: It's not that I want to win. It's just that I think the Rolling Stones aren't always around, you know. I think Mick Jagger is one of the greatest living performers. The other thing that gave me hope for the future of poetry is the Rolling Stones concert at Madison Square Gardens because Jagger was real tired and fucked up. It was Tuesday, he had done two concerts and he was just really on the brink of collapse but the kind of collapse that transcends into magic. He was so tired that he needed the energy of the audience. And he was not a rock and roll singer Tuesday night, he was closer to a poet than he ever has been. Because he was tired he could hardly sing. I love the music of the Rolling Stones, but what was foremost was not the music but the performance, the naked performance. And it was like his naked performance, his rhythm, his movement, his talk. He was so tired he was saying things like "very warm here warm warm warm it's very hot here hot hot New York New York New York bang bang bang." I mean none of that stuff is genius but it was his presence and his power to hold the audience in his palm. There was electricity. If the Rolling Stones had walked off that night and left Mick Jagger alone he was as great as any great poet that night. He could've spoken some of his best lyrics and had the audience just as magnetized. Maybe just with Charlie's drum, Charlie's drums and Mick (I'm not renouncing the others, I love Keith Richards to death). Just the drum beat rhythm and Mick's words or refrains that are always magic could have been very powerful and could have I believe held the audience. And that excited me so much I almost blew apart because I saw almost a complete future of poetry. I really saw it, I really felt it. I got so excited I could hardly stand being in my skin and, like, I believe in that. That's given me faith to keep going.

Bockris: In as much as there is the possibility of poets becoming public figures, what is the public function of the poet?

Smith: All I try to do is entertain. Another thing I do is give people breathing room. In other words . . . I don't mean any of the stuff I say. When I say that bad stuff about God or Christ, I don't mean that stuff. I don't know what I mean, it's just it gives somebody a new view, a new way to look at something. I like to look at things from ten or fifteen different angles, you know. So it gives people a chance to be blasphemous through me. The other thing is that through performance I reach such states in which my brain feels so open, so full of light, it feels huge. It feels as big as the Empire State Building and if I can develop a communication with an audience, a bunch of people, when my brain is that big and very receptive, imagine the energy and the intelligence and all the things I can steal from them.

Bockris: Would you give up writing tomorrow if you could continue performing in some other way?

Smith: No, I can't give it up. I have no choice.

Bockris: Is that really true?

Smith: I wanted to be an artist, I worked to be an artist for maybe six years and so as soon as I became a good artist all of a sudden I couldn't draw because in 1969 it began that I put my piece of paper and my canvas in front of me and I could see the finished product before I even touched the paper and it was frightening to me. I like to work. I like that anguish you go through when you're writing something. I like to battle with language. When I started being able to see the finished product before I got a chance to work it out, it had no interest for me. I'm not interested in the finished product; I'm interested in creating the moment. I mean the finished product is for the people who buy the stuff, you know. And I'm not interested in doing stuff so other people can get their rocks off only. I gave up art just like that in one day after putting seven years into it. And I was fucking good and then I wrote and now what happens is I became so good at writing those vertical poems, those performing poems, they're no longer a challenge.

Bockris: So what did you do?

Smith: I stopped.

Bockris: Are you in a transition phase?

Smith: Yeah. Transition phases are very hard for me. They usually come in the summer and last about three months and they're usually the worst three months of my life. This one wasn't 'cause I happened to be in love. They usually come when I'm most fucked up. My brain is hungrier than it ever has been in my whole life but my pussy is being fed so I can . . . So I'm not as fucked up as I could be. Last year when this happened I just wanted to kill myself. I thought I wasn't learning, I wasn't developing.

Bockris: Are you self-critical?

Smith: Extremely self-critical. So much as I love my work, I hate it.

Bockris: If I was to offer you a reading tour with three other poets, who would you choose as the three other poets?

Smith: Jim Carroll, Bernadette Mayer, and Muhammad Ali.

Bockris: Why?

Smith: Because they're all good performers. Ali's a good performer. He's got great rhythms. He's a good writer in a certain frame of reference. He's entertaining. Bernadette Mayer because I like what she does conceptually. She's a real speed-driven poet. Sometimes I don't like her because she's overly political and too influenced by St. Mark's, but she's also a good performer. Jim Carroll because I think he's one of the best poets in America. At least he was when he was writing; I don't know if he still writes. Jim Carroll is one of America's true poets. I mean, he is a true poet. It kills me he's twenty-three, he wrote all his best poems the same year of his life as Rimbaud did. He had the same intellectual quality and bravado as Rimbaud. He's a junkie. He's bisexual. He's been fucked by every male and female genius in America. He's been fucked over by all those people. He lives all over. He lives a disgusting life. Sometimes you have to pull him out of a gutter. He's been in prison. He's a total fuck-up. But what great poet wasn't? I think the St. Mark's poets are so namby-pamby they're frauds. They write about "Today at 9:15 I shot speed with Brigid, sitting in the such and such." They're real cute about putting it in a poem but if Jim Carroll comes into the church and throws up that's not a poem to them, that's not cool. If you could play with it in your poetry that's okay but if you're really with it, that's something else. They don't want to face it. I think he's got all the characteristics of a great poet. He was St. Mark's chance to have something real among them. And they blackballed him because he fucked up. I mean, he didn't come to his poetry reading. He was in jail. Good for him. "Oh, well, we can't ask him to do poetry readings anymore." That's ridiculous.

Bockris: Do you read Pound or Olson?

Smith: I like some of Pound. I'd rather read Eliot. I like pieces of Pound. I like Jules Laforgue better than either of them. I like Pound when he uses ditties same as Eliot, but I don't understand much of what they're saying. My intelligence is really dubious. I memorized "Prufrock" when I was a teenager. I thought it was beautiful. It had a lot to do with instilling in me a love of flowing rhythms but I don't know what that poem's about.

Bockris: Do you find you learn a lot from Warhol?

Smith: I used to think he was real cool in the sixties 'cause I like his lifestyle, I like the people he surrounded himself with and there was a lot of energy in the Factory. It paralleled with Bob Dylan but I think his whole family has gotten a lot tackier. But every time I want to say something about Andy Warhol I don't trust him. Socially, you know, I've met him a lot of times and he's always very nice. I don't know how to take him. . . . Let me just say one nice thing about Andy Warhol: he gave Stevie Wonder a camera, which was really cool, which is also what a good hustler he is. He has the ability to zoom in on the heart of things. Such an action reveals the two moods of Andy.

Bockris: Are you interested in interviewing people?

Smith: I'd like to talk with Mick Jagger, mostly because I'd like to talk about performing. I'd like to talk to Dylan if he was in a certain mood, but that's why I stopped doing rock writing. I started interviewing people like Rod Stewart who I admire but because of my ego and my faith in my own work I don't like meeting people on unequal terms, so I figured I'd stop doing that and would wait until they discovered me and we can meet on equal grounds. I couldn't wait to meet Rod Stewart and then when I met him I didn't want to ask him anything. I wanted to tell him stuff. I didn't want to ask Rod Stewart about his work. I wanted to show him mine, that's because right now I'm into performing. I'm into extending myself rather than putting other people into me. I've spent half to three quarters of my life sucking from other people and now I'd like to give some.

Bockris: Do you think you're really a phony?

Smith: When I say that I mean it totally endearingly, I say it with love, you know. I just think I get a kick out of myself. I act tough. I act like a bitch, a motherfucker, it's like when I'm doing this interview I act real tough and then my boyfriend comes in and I apologize to him and say, "I'll be finished quick, baby." I'm like a chameleon, I'm not a phony. I'm like a chameleon. I can fall into the rhythm of almost any situation as it calls for me. If I'm supposed to be a motherfucker I can be a motherfucker, if I'm supposed to be a sissy or a pansy I'll be that too. I'll be a sexpot, I'll be a waif. It doesn't mean I'm phony, it just means I'm flexible. I can marry the moment.

PATTI SMITH: SOMEWHERE, OVER THE RIMBAUD

Susin Shapiro | December 1975 | *Crawdaddy* (US)

This interview took place at Electric Lady Studios in Greenwich Village, during a recording session for Patti Smith's debut studio album—what would become *Horses*. John Cale, who had gone onto a successful solo career after leaving the Velvet Underground, was producing, and Clive Davis had recently signed Smith to his new label, Arista Records, after seeing her perform at a private showcase.

In 1974, the Patti Smith Group had self-released their debut single, "Hey Joe" and "Piss Factory," on their own Mer label, with Robert Mapplethorpe bankrolling the studio time at Electric Lady. Now, as Smith moved to a major label, *Crawdaddy*—which was founded a year before *Rolling Stone* in 1966 and was "the first magazine to take rock music seriously," as *New York Times* critic John Rockwell once put it—was betting that her cerebral punk aesthetic would catch on. So was Bob Dylan, who gave Smith his blessing backstage when he came out to see her perform the summer of '75 at The Other End, the short-lived rebranding of legendary West Village club The Bitter End. There was a lot of buzz around Patti Smith, who had made waves as a downtown poet and habitue of the legendary scene at CBGB on the Bowery. But still, when Susin Shapiro interviewed her that fall at Electric Lady, it wasn't clear whether she would be "an overnight sensation . . . or an exotic flash in the pan."

The ghost of Jimi Hendrix hung heavy that day in the studio, which had been designed for him in 1970; Electric Lady opened just a month before his death on September 18. Smith recorded "Elegie," which would close *Horses*, on the fifth anniversary of Hendrix's death. As the album came together piece by piece, guitarist Lenny Kaye, bassist Ivan Kral, pianist Richard Sohl, and drummer Jay Dee Daugherty were "all squeezing this piece of coal," as Smith put it. We all know how it turned out. —Ed.

NEW YORK—It's 8:30 AM on a fog-soup Friday, an indecent hour to be conducting an interview, much less making a record.

I tiptoe through oil-slicked puddles and into Electric Lady Studios, with its wallpapered basement and carpet of silences broken by the occasional ping of a pinball game in progress. By the time this print hits the fans, Patti Smith will either be an overnight sensation (after four years) or an exotic flash in the pan; but no matter which, something is happening here. The air is thickly momentous as some tentative mixes filter through what is in the process of becoming her debut album, four sleepless weeks in the making.

I've been waiting for this ever since Patti first stuffed her amphetamine semantics into my brain at a now-defunct cafe; the endless outpouring of verse accompanied by a band that played traveling music for her flights into fantasy and raw imagery, punch-drunk fists waving wildly, leaning on one thin hip in black suit jacket and jeans, word-crazed and crooning, a cross between Keith Richards and Mia Farrow; an omnisexual high priestess careening freely between the genders, elevating rock 'n' roll into incantation.

She sits down next to me on the purple corduroy couch, slouching at a 45-degree angle. This dynamic, jet-haired, finely-etched, still dressed in black and ballet slippers with soles, almost-apparition rock musician Patti Smith is sitting down! Ready to jump up when producer John Cale calls in to say there's something to hear. Electric Ladyland is fitting atmosphere for the godchild-of-Jimi-Hendrix, and Patti resurrects him more than once.

She lops off the g's at the ends of words, says dese, dem and dose, has a voice of Vaseline mixed with sand, goes tight-lipped and mute when she doesn't want to answer a question. Mostly, she speaks haltingly and with clarity.

"It drives me nuts when someone comes in and says, 'Tell me your life story.' Do you have questions? I love questions, they always have the element of surprise!" (I stutter in admiration for the eight books of poetry she's published.) [*Smith published five books before recording her first album*: Seventh Heaven, A Useless Death, Kodak, Early Morning Dream, *and* Witt. —*Ed.*] "My push is to get beyond the word into something that's more fleshy, that's why I like performing. The Word is just for me, when I'm alone late at night and I'm jerkin' off, you know, pouring out streams of words. That's a very one-to-one process, but I'm interested in communicatin'. I'm another instrument in the band.

"I started out as a missionary, but I couldn't find a religion which didn't promise things to some people to the exclusion of others. The personal voyage into some kind of light shouldn't be denied to anybody. I got into painting after that; was turned on to anything that projected a body in motion, like Picasso's blue period. I was a skinny, graceless girl and Picasso was able to take the human form and make it into something graceful. I was taught by art that no matter what you were, if you levitated yourself to your highest form you would be graceful." (She is no longer graceless, but still skinny.)

"Instead of being just a puny outcast, I started walking tall because I was close to the blue period. I got into sculpture too—Brancusi, for example; anything that had to do with purity of form. Then I began to feel the limitation of a piece of paper or the canvas. I got hung up with the idea that museums were sort of like zoos. . . . I decided that the highest place an artist could go would be to get hung up on a wall in a museum. The piece of art doesn't transform itself any more once it's done. The viewer may go through a transformation . . . it's a very subtle thing, how it actually hits people. The move into poetry wasn't accidental. The calligraphic, like Arabian writing, always appealed to me. I got into letters, words, the rhythm of certain words together, and gradually started writing poems that were songs because of my obsession with rhythm. I love writing because there's acoustic-type typewriters and electric ones. It's a physical act, but the word is still trapped on the page. The neat thing about performing is it keeps the act of creation alive. I love the process of creation, although the end product in itself is a necessary evil. Still, I'm glad it's there, otherwise I wouldn't have Rolling Stones records and William Burroughs books to enjoy."

Patti has crept into the higher regions of Rimbaud, the French poet, constantly soliloquizing about him in her poems. As a pedestrian, I expect to hear in detail about the meaning of his literature. "The first thing I got from Rimbaud was the power of the outer image: his face. I was a teenage girl, didn't have a boyfriend, I looked at *Illuminations*, he was a good-looking guy! He even had long hair before the Beatles. It was that simple . . . nothing cosmic. He sorta looked like Dylan. When I got his book I was into rock 'n' roll; I didn't give a shit about poetry. But what has always attracted me has been perfection, whether it's a diamond or a Smokey Robinson song. Rimbaud's poetry was perfection on the page, like glittering graphite. I don't really understand poetry. I never even understood Dylan, or 'Mr. Jones' either. [*Smith refers here to Bob Dylan's "Ballad of a Thin Man," as in "Because something is happening here but you don't know what it is / Do you, Mr. Jones?" –Ed.*] I just hear Dylan and the words don't seem to matter. Dylan's delivery, his phrasing, his physical image, his energy. Same thing when I met him. He's a very physical guy. And he has the highest integrity, like Jimi Hendrix." (She looks around the room, acknowledging his ghost.) "I think Dylan recognized the same things in me. We didn't really talk about nothin' but the feelings were there . . . the way he said my name, the way we looked at each other. . . . It was very real." (Dylan paid a widely publicized visit to Patti after her performance at the Other End and seemed well pleased to be there.)

I want to know why all her heroes are men, are all her heroes men? "Most of my heroes are men simply because most of the heaviest people in the world have been men. There hasn't been a woman who has done what Jimi Hendrix did. I don't blame that on anything; if a woman wanted to do it, she'd do it. If I wanted to do what Hendrix had done, I should have learned to play the guitar ten years ago. Too bad I didn't have the discipline. Actually, I like women. One of my biggest heroes is Jeanne Moreau. She has perfected all the moves, the high art of smoking a cigarette . . . or walking with a straight skirt. Perfecting those kinds of rhythms are, to me, just as worthy of worship as somebody's playin' a great harmonica. It's completely coincidental that most people I admire are guys.

"I admire Anna Magnani too. Actually, I'm nuts about women, you know? Women are narcissistic and so am I. I'd much rather look at pictures of women than men. *Brenda Starr*'s my favourite comic, *Vogue* is my favorite magazine. Anyway, nobody—man, woman or horse—has topped what Jimi Hendrix has done. His gender is totally beside the point; the real question is, what planet did he come from?"

Questions are popcorn in my mind. What about your record? How do you like the mixes so far? I fight the urge to put my ear to the thick wood studio door. She resists telling me, seems offended.

"I don't feel any kind of pressure . . . commercial or financial. Arista doesn't expect me to be a singles artist. They just want me to be successful. I want to be successful. Jesus wanted to be successful too. . . . He wanted everybody to see the light. If I had wanted to live in a garret somewhere I'da stayed in Pitman [New Jersey]. I didn't decide to do a record out of the blue; I've been deliberating for many years. I'm not interested in having a family. My creative instincts are with art, poetry and music. I don't have any other motivation than to do something really great; I mean, I wouldn't want to do a Captain & Tennille record. I'd rather be a housewife, and a good housewife, admired by all the other housewives in the area, than be a mediocre rock singer. The only crime in art is to do lousy art. I'm going to promote myself exactly as I am, with all my weak points and my strong ones. My weak points are that I'm self-conscious and often insecure, and my strong point is that I don't feel any shame about it.

"People like to look at me as this tough, punky shit-kicker. Well, I am like that . . . but I'm also very fragile. It's important that people know that; I couldn't stand being just some leather boy. There are masculine and feminine rhythms in me. We're all made up of opposites, and they often crucify us, but I deal with that by accepting the bad stuff. I don't feel guilty or stupid because of my weaknesses. On my record, I'm trying to reveal as much about myself as I can. Sometimes I sing great, and sometimes I sacrifice great singing for very human moments. I have to let people know I am as weak as I am strong, or I'm never gonna make it. . . .

"All the cuts are long ones, except 'Elegy for Jimi Hendrix,' which is 2:35 [*Released as "Elegie"* —*Ed.*]. I got the idea for 'Birdland' when I read this book by Peter Reich called *Book of Dreams*. . . . There's a passage in it about when he was little and his father [the maverick psychiatrist, Wilhelm] died. He kept going out into the fields hoping his father would pick him up in a spaceship, or a UFO. He saw all these UFOs coming at him and inside one was his father, glowing and shining. Then the air force planes came in and chased the UFOs away and he was left there crying: No! Daddy! Come back! It really moved me. Another song, 'Break it Up,' started with a dream I had about Jim Morrison. I went into this clearing and he was lying on a marble slab. He was human but his wings were made of stone. He was struggling to get free but the stone wings imprisoned him. I was standing there, sort of like a little boy, or a child, screaming 'Break it up! Break it up!' and finally his wings broke and he was free to fly away. So I wrote this song with Tom Verlaine called 'Break it Up.'" (Tom Verlaine is the lead guitarist for a New York rock group, Television.)

"We recorded 'Elegy' on Sept. 18th, the anniversary of Hendrix's death. I also wrote a song about my 18-year-old sister, Kimberly, and rewrote the Van Morrison song 'Gloria,' and 'Land of a Thousand Dances' with an improvisational middle about the Sea of Possibilities . . . a boy slashing his throat and tearing out his vocal cords.

"How am I getting along with John Cale? It's like *A Season in Hell*. He's a fighter and I'm a fighter so we're fightin'. Sometimes fightin' produces a champ. It's a real honour makin' a record. If I do a great record, it sort of helps me pay back the debt to all the other great records that came to me . . . the Wailers, Minnie Riperton, Stevie, James Brown. . . . I mean, they've inspired me throughout the years. I would love to do a record that had just three minutes on it that inspired Smokey Robinson.

"There's great chemistry between me and the guys in the band [which includes rock-critic/guitarist Lenny Kaye; bassist Ivan Kral; piano man Richard Sohl; and drummer Jay Daugherty]. I'll sit down with them and say 'play some simple chords' and I'll start daydreaming and talking over the music, spilling poetry and they'll keep me going by playing a certain way or changing the chord structure . . . and it just grows from there.

When I'm onstage, they never know what I'm going to do in 'Birdland.' They give me as much celluloid as I need for my film.

"I control the band only to the point where they get enough freedom to control me. One night Lenny will be hot and I'll just do poetry to his guitar solo. Another night I'll be my piano player; another night they keep up with me. I have my throat, they have their instruments. We're all squeezing this piece of coal and I can see the shoots of light starting to come out, the beginnings of a diamond."

PATTI SMITH: POETRY IN MOTION

Robin Katz | December 13, 1975 | *Sounds*

Horses was released the day this article ran, and Patti Smith simultaneously became a major label artist and landed her first major magazine cover, in the December 13, 1975, issue of the British publication *Sounds*. Prolific rock journalist Robin Katz was fresh off touring with Bruce Springsteen on the *Born to Run* tours when she fell into the orbit of the black-clad punk poet, who was suddenly exerting an ineluctable gravitational pull on the scene she was rapidly coming to define. Katz attempted the impossible feat of capturing Smith's effervescent cadence of speech, complete with stage directions to show when she paused to come up for air.

"There are millions of things I want to be—a jazz singer, a movie star," Smith said. "When I get older as I get all of this stuff down, I want to be a fantastic storyteller." Yet at twenty-nine years old, she already was. —Ed.

Patti Smith cannot compromise. She functions on her very own level of stratosphere, creating poetry, writing songs, lapping up the more elusive statics of life. She describes herself as "an energy eater" and has the magnetic kind of personality that makes anyone walking within fifty yards of her an automatic piece of iron. Swish. One second you're minding your own business, the next you're listening to her rattle out a story with your mouth hanging open and your concentration pivoting on one point.

On stage this spindly little creature pants, screams, whines, wimpers, whispers and punctuates the heavy air with her punching, gyrating fists.

She wails with the commitment of both Van Morrison and Connie Francis (the lump of tears in the throat).

When Patti communicates, she makes fanzine a form of art, moves poetry to become the rhythm section of rock, and switches outspoken sensuality from the traditional male throne to the descendants of Adam's rib.

Her charisma as an artist stems from the very fact that she will not appeal to everyone. Another Lou Reed, Nikki Giovanni, or Laura Nyro to be preciously cherished, absorbed and emulated.

A lithe figure, you first notice an almost white face in contrast to an uncombed straw swatch of jet black (dyed) hair. Her usually black clothing hangs off her like a crinkled raincoat on an upright coat rack.

She talks in rough cut New Yorkese (though she's from south Jersey), dropping "writing" and "singing" to "writin'" and "singin'."

She can talk for five minutes without grabbing a breath and will side track a point for twenty minutes before returning to the original question. Take, for instance, Ms. Smith on her earliest musical influence.

"The first record I ever heard was '[The] Girl Can't Help It,' when I was around six. This boy I knew had an RCA Victor Victrola with one of those big round spindles. He said, 'Listen to this.' I remember it had a maroon label.

"The first record I ever owned was Jerry Lewis singing 'Rockabye Your Baby With A Dixie Melody' and Harry Belafonte's 'Shrimp Boats' *(breath). [Harry Belafonte never recorded "Shrimp Boats." It was recorded in 1951 by Jo Stafford. —Ed.]*

"But my favourite was 'Come Josephine On Your Flying Machine' by Les Paul and Mary Ford. [*Les Paul and Mary Ford never recorded this song, but did record "Josephine" in 1951 as the B-side to "I Wish I Had Never Seen Sunshine." —Ed.*] That was like the first drug song. I wanted to do it on my album like Hendrix. But when this boy put on 'The Girl Can't Help It,' and when you're that little and someone puts on Little Richard . . . I just stood there *(breath)*. I didn't know what to do.

"Now, when I heard Mick Jagger I knew what to do. Drop my pants."

Smith is committed to Jagger, Hendrix and Dylan. There are several of her favourite recurring themes. There is even the instance during one of her shows when guitar player Lenny Kaye was having extended technical trouble.

"I don't really mind," Smith told the crowd. "I mean, Mick would wait all night for Keith."

"Little Richard," she continued, "was a big part of my life as a kid. It was really important especially in high school 'cause I was a great dancer. One of the reasons I was so bad in school was because I was up all night dancing, mimicking.

"I can mimic every Marvelettes record. I got all their hand gestures down. (She goes into an enthusiastic 'Don't Mess with Bill' complete with pseudo-coy vocals and determined batting eyelashes). That's where I got a lot of the stage motions I use now. Boxing gestures in little space, *(breath)*.

"I remember when Ben E. King played at the Airport Drive In and taught me and 400 other kids how to do The Monkey. He introduced us to Little Stevie Wonder. He carried him onstage like a little monkey on his back, and everyone went nuts. Smokey Robinson did 'Mickey's Monkey' and Ben E. King, who had done 'Spanish Harlem,' started doing this dance. And like the next day, The Monkey had wiped out South Jersey.

"At that time, it was all James Brown, all black. I didn't like white music. It was either John Coltrane or Smokey Robinson. We didn't have no time for the Beach Boys or the Beatles. 'Cept when Jagger came out. Then, I was happy to be white. There was nothing like him.

"I was into James Brown and Smokey but I didn't want to fuck them. All of a sudden I looked at Jagger and I knew.

"Dylan was the same. There was this whole new consciousness. Lou Reed too.

"Hey," she sidetracks, "we're doing this song where we sing 'Pale Blue Eyes' *(she sings)* and then it goes into 'Louie Louie.'

So, Patti Smith, survivor of scarlet fever and willing carrier of Stones fever, grew out of a rocky adolescence in the pits of South Jersey. Patti's supersonic metabolism needed an outlet and in true student prince fashion, she took to art.

She followed the sewers to New York City where she found an artist/boyfriend named Robert Mapplethorpe and hung around Pratt Institute for Art to try to pick up on the smells of creativity.

But Patti Smith's muse was about to identify itself. She found out the hard way, that her love for Dylan and Rimbaud was not just fanfare. It was the essence of her own greatest gift. Psychic poetry.

"It used to be," she rambled almost as bewildered at her own discovery as any listener would be, "that I'd have my piece of paper, and I'd improvise. Then it got to the point where the drawin' (pronounced by Patti as "drawlin") would flash in front of the piece of paper and all I'd have to do is follow the lines. It wasn't fast enough.

"So then I made a transition. I'd draw (drawl) a figure, then the figure would be saying something. So I'd write down the words. I got into calligraphy. Then the whole piece of paper was just in my way. It became a material object that I had to take care of. Taking care of the words is much easier than taking care of the art of the word. It's a slow transition.

"In a space of a year I moved from the character to the balloon. Then I'm the words in the balloon. Then the words get bigger and they obliterate the balloon. Like words in the air became my new hallucination.

"I began to see language: Mary Jane, heart, wing, plane, tunnel of love. I began to get these phrases just like the train rhythms and that started haunting me.

"I'd go to a party and I just wanted to have a good time. And these crazy rhythms started and I thought, 'I'm going to write a poem,' and I would rebel and say, 'I'm not going to write it.' And so it started getting louder in my ear. So I had to start carrying a notepad with me all the time."

At this time, there are some people who are going to pinch themselves and wonder if Patti Smith is really a woman under the influence of genius, or is just a raving nutter like other people they know.

Patti knows. She's had to live with her mutant-ness long enough. She laughs about it more than you would give such a deep character credit for.

"All my friends who were takin' acid wouldn't let me have any. They said, 'You're too weird. You'll have us all committing suicide.' So they'd be on acid and I'd be on nothing and I'd be the most stoned person in the room. Eatin' energy again," she deduced.

"They'd have to ask me to leave. But that's when I discovered Hendrix. And do you know why I loved him? Because everyone always wanted him to talk about black is beautiful. But he'd talk about how Mars is beautiful."

And then there's the trip to Paris with best friend and younger sister Kimberly. In the midst of trying to decide which road art would take, Smith began having nightmares. The Stones were about to split and each night she'd see Brian Jones drowning in his own soup.

Patti even created a chant: "Brian, Brian / I'm not lyin' / I'm just tryin' to reach you." But she didn't reach him in time. Jones' death added more kindling to the fire under her rock poetry.

More than ever, Patti Smith became determined to search for the universal language of telepathy we all spoke before the stake out at the Tower of Babel.

"We've got to find the lost tongue. And we're getting closer. And the first lead is right there," she cried pointing to the poster from the film, *Ladies and Gentlemen, The Rolling Stones.*

"Ever since I was a kid I've been looking for the lost tongue and look at that logo. The Stones are one of the most important things of this century. It's no accident that after following Dylan as a young girl, we're friends now. We influence each other, discuss poetry together. It had to happen because we're looking for the same thing.

"We can help each other and this whole line between artist and fan will have to be erased because we all have to move faster to reach some illuminated moment."

On return to New York, five years ago, Patti Smith slowly but surely began to get her lightning quick ideas into solid form. Gravitating to the Chelsea Hotel, much frequented home away from home of groups like The Airplane and The Doors, Smith began reciting her poetry to an audience of performers.

"I had to tell 'em good," she smiles proudly, "'cause when your audience is performers you gotta be right in there. And if there's a guy in the room who's foxy, I'm going to do my best."

It was a woman, however, Jane Friedman, who gave Patti her first regular stint as the opening act for anyone at the Mercer Arts Centre, a conglomerate building in the Village that simultaneously housed three off-Broadway plays, small rock concerts and a coffee shop.

The only thing ancient to be seen, (or not seen) were the building's support beams which collapsed a couple of years ago taking the building with them. Friedman became Smith's manager and it was time to find a new place to play.

"At Mercer I'd have no microphone. I'd do poems about car crashes, mama's boys having to prove themselves, tributes to Hendrix and Jones. Whatever propelled me into physical action I did."

Rock journalist Lenny Kaye turned guitarist for her, and pianist Richard Sohl a.k.a. D.N.V. (Death in Venice) rounded out the mini-band. Smith describes Kaye as "a fellow fan" and Sohl as "a hustler who loves sailors, the seamier Dorian Grey [sic] side of life with a Genet sense of existence."

"One of the reasons the club scene underground happened is because bands like us and Television had to create them. There was no place to play. Jane would push to have us open anywhere, Max's for Phil Ochs, Reno Sweeney (a nauseatingly pseudo trendy club). It was hard but I started gettin' a following and good reviews."

By '74 Patti was able to give up her job as a book clerk for Scribner's, was living with Alan Lanier of Blue Oyster Cult and had released a single called 'Piss Factory.' It was privately financed by Robert Mapplethorpe.

Smith unearthed CBGB's, a tiny bar in the derelict Bowery where the owner's pet afghan gives the room a permanent odor of dog shit and neon beer ads brighten the loo-like walls. Jim Wolcott of the *Village Voice* found Smith's energy likened to that of a "Wild Mustang," and she returned the astute observation by following his advice and adopting the horse as her motto and album title.

When Dylan caught her show, Wolcott reported: "She was positively playing to Dylan . . . and he, being an expert at gamesmanship sat there crossing and uncrossing his legs, playing back." The article was dubbed "Tarantula Meets Mustang." [*"Tarantula Meets Mustang: Dylan Calls on Patti Smith,"* Village Voice, *July 7, 1975* —Ed.] And this is the electricity that heroines are made of.

The static from CBGB's filtered down to a record contract with the newly formed Arista Records, in uncharacteristic form, president Clive

Davis eagerly awaited Patti's first album without pushing for a single as part of the parcel. By this time Smith added another guitarist, Ivan Kral.

"It was like when Keith Moon joined The Who," said Patti in another energy rush.

"He just came in and said he was going to play with us and we said all right. He looks the most like me, or Keith Richards. He wears all black and likes the 'Privilege' concept of a rock messiah taking over the world."

And just as they headed for the studios, Jay Dee Daugherty became their drummer. John Cale became their producer. And in a very harried, haggard and hurried fortnight they produced *Horses*. The album to split threeds [*sic*] between the rumours and the real thing. Define your own idea of strangeness. Poetry in Motion/Rimbaud with too much pepper. Obsessive, compelling, disjointed and disturbing.

"The record is a document of a group becoming a group," testified Patti.

"Not only is it a document of where we were at, for the last two years, but it's the document of the group all coming together.

"Our next record is going to be the first record we do as a group. This record to me is a magnet. I think of the group as a magnet.

"The thing with Cale is that we fought constantly. It was fantastic. The thing is, he's intense and I'm intense and I'm relentless. I wanted it to be that our record would not sound like anyone else's. And he wanted to help but we had different ways of approaching things.

"I think things should happen fast. I don't believe in overdub and all that mixing. I believe in doing it and just doing it right. Spontaneity . . .

"I just don't look at anything in the future to fix up what's happening in the present. I don't like the idea of doing scratch vocals. Why can't I do it great at this moment?"

Smith scratches her head and the creative process takes off once more. She dismisses any talk of androgynous appeal by citing Jagger as rock's first two-way trouble shooter and jumps into words from a poem called 'Beyond Gender.'

"I'm totally vulnerable as a girl," she admitted. "But when you're doing art you have no time for divisions. I don't want to start with exclusions. It's like Marley and Rasta. You know white people aren't surprised that black people do great stuff. Why should black people be surprised that white people aren't all stupid? And the Mormons, and their belief that you have to be white to get to God. We're all conspiring for the same thing, to get back to the Tower of Babel.

"Like I don't want to be anything yet. People say, are you a rock poetess, a girl singer, a rock singer? I'm not anything.

"I don't want to be anything. As soon as I find out, it's over. Then I can die or go onto the next stage of life. I want to stay alive as long as possible, probably because I was such a late bloomer.

"I think Hendrix was one of the heaviest people of the twentieth century, but I don't want to be dead. I am like my father, a constant student. Except now, I'm like a rock and roll star student.

"There are millions of things I want to be—a jazz singer, a movie star. When I get older as I get all of this stuff down, I want to be a fantastic storyteller.

"It's no accident that the greatest storyteller in history was a woman. Scheherazade, right? It doesn't matter if a man wrote them. And for the future, I won't need grammar.

"What I need grammar for is poetry. Don't ever put grammar down. You don't know how much I struggle with every poem I do. I struggle for hours, days, months. I don't know how to write it down. I don't know how to write a sentence or put in tenses.

"I was a speed reader, too, which means I don't read sentences, I read the essence of a sentence. That's cool, but I can't make my poetry diamond-hard like Rimbaud.

"I'm teaching myself. I'm 29 and I'm teaching myself all that stupid stuff I should have learned as a kid (*breath and turn next corner*).

"Hendrix as a kid got his chords down. He got all that out of his way when he was young. And when he got older he could be totally free like jazz guys. They got all that virtuoso crap down and then they can go anywhere.

"I'm still like the reaper who uses the sickle."

PATTI SMITH: HER HORSES GOT WINGS, THEY CAN FLY

Dave Marsh | **January 1976** | *Rolling Stone*

When this piece was published, *Horses* had already made an impact, but the question still remained as to whether Patti Smith could land her cerebral brand of punk poetry "outside the coasts." *Creem* cofounder Dave Marsh, one of Lester Bangs's only critical sparring partners who could go toe to toe with him, first encountered Smith at a party in 1971, the same year he was credited by some with coining the term "punk rock." Then, "taking your eyes off her wasn't impossible," he wrote, "but it was pretty goddamned unlikely." Marsh was an early booster, he wrote me, "the first person who wanted to publish her poetry, and the first who did." Though he had his reservations about the hype, he knew Smith, who claimed to have grown up "in a tougher part of Jersey than Bruce Springsteen," was resilient enough to outlast her critics.

The piece is not without its edges. Marsh had little interest in separating the myth from the reality of her rock origin story—"I'd rather not know," he wrote. But he does push back on some of her ideas, the kind of intellectual challenge that produced *Horses*, and in this case, a scintillating profile of an artist on the rise. "I am fairly sure she didn't like the story," Marsh wrote, reflecting on it more than 40 years later. "I think it was after that one that she said, 'You know, you're an asshole even when you're right,' or something along that line." Not shying away from conflict, cultures in collision, makes Smith a quintessentially American original, and she expounds on her ideology here, what Marsh describes as "her firm belief that it all tied together at its core, rock & roll and High Art." She had the temerity to take on a system that insisted "nobody's going to sign a poet," a system that wanted to turn her into a "leather Liza Minnelli," and by being Patti Smith, proved them all wrong. As Marsh attested, she silenced the hecklers in the end, "often by heckling back." —Ed.

I was a little loose in the attic. When I was a kid I tied do-rags
around my head tight. I was scared my soul would fly out at night.
Scared my vital breath would make the big slip. some ventriloquist.
So I steered from drugs and threw myself in full frenzied dance.

—Patti Smith 1973

She'd been dancing awhile when I first saw her. She walked into that Upper West Side party like a Jersey urchin who'd just inherited Manhattan. All in black—turtleneck and tight black slacks. She seemed more frail than she really was, but not fragile, though you could have counted her ribs, and her jet black hair straggled like waterlogged yarn. Her skin so pale it was nearly translucent, cheeks drawn so tight and thin I was tempted to pull her aside and offer her a decent meal. If only her teeth had been half rotted, she would have passed for Keith Richards' waif sister.

Taking your eyes off her wasn't impossible. But it was pretty goddamned unlikely.

She glided across the room easy as any rock & roll queen in her beat-up Mary Janes, full of sex and innocence; every eye was pulled her way, every blabbing mouth set off in unison. All the women hated her then—the solidarity of sisterhood was not so firm in 1971—but the men were awed.

Even before the party, I had known who she was. Steve Paul, the blue velvet Winter brothers impresario, had stopped by my home in Detroit a few months earlier with a tape of a poetry reading. I didn't care much about poems, but Lenny Kaye, a fellow critic, was her backup guitar. Mostly I was intrigued by the idea of a girl Steve who was a ringer for Keith.

have you seen
dylans dog
it got wings
it can fly

I don't remember what else she read, but she took me right over. In her voice were not simply references but the very rhythms of rock & roll. I wanted to know more, maybe publish a few of her poems in the magazine I was editing. Steve thought bigger—he was gonna make her a rock & roll star.

> *Sixteen and time to pay off. I get this job in a Piss Factory inspectin' pipe. 40 hours, $36 a week, but it's a paycheck Jack. It's so hot in here, hot like Sahara, I couldn't think for the heat. But these bitches are too lame to understand, too goddamn grateful to get this job to realize they're gettin' screwed up the ass.*
>
> —"Piss Factory," 1974

Patti Smith grew up in Pitman, a town in South Jersey, near Philly and Camden, whose principal industry is a Columbia Records pressing plant. Her father, a former tap dancer, worked in a factory; her mother, who gave up singing to raise a family, was a waitress.

As the oldest of four children, Patti took much responsibility for her two sisters, Kimberly and Linda, and a brother, Todd, about whom she doesn't talk much now. ("He's a butcher or something like that in Philadelphia now, I'm pretty sure," says her manager, Jane Friedman.) To keep the kids interested, Patti made up stories and acted out plays. When she was seven, she had a siege of scarlet fever, during which she lay hallucinating in front of the "amoebic, jewel-shaped indigo flame" of a coal stove. Her imagination improved.

"When I was young, what we read was the Bible and UFO magazines. Just like I say I'm equal parts Balenciaga and Brando, well, my dad was equal parts God and Hagar the Spaceman for Mega City. My mother taught me fantasy; my mother's like a real hip Scheherazade. Between the two of 'em, I developed a sensibility."

The high school Patti went to was "sort of experimental. We had geniuses and epileptics all mixed in." This may be less metaphorical than it seems: Pitman is in the Pines, a swamp area that lies between the Jersey Shore to the east and the industrial flatlands to the west. It is regarded as a backwater by the rest of the state. Its residents, called Pineys, are known for such rustic practices as inbreeding, guaranteed to produce such genetic sports as epilepsy. Patti told a friend that the incidence of epilepsy was so high that all the kids carried popsicle sticks in their pockets to use as tongue depressors in case of a classmate's sudden grand or petit mal seizure. Patti's family weren't Pineys—they were originally from Chicago and Philadelphia. But coupled with her fevered coal stove visions and the UFO magazines, not to mention the Bible, it must have been a hell of a place to live.

"I grew up in a tougher part of Jersey than Bruce Springsteen," Patti says. "I wasn't horrified by Altamont, it seemed natural to me. Every high-school dance I went to, somebody was stabbed." Her first boyfriend was a black Jamaican twin, but her parents didn't mind. "My father was busy trying to get God to make the next move on the chessboard. What's he care about a 16-year-old boy?"

At the time, Patti was completely infatuated with black music, black style. Her fondest adolescent memory seems to have been harmonizing to early soul records in the back of a high-school bus, or dancing to them in someone's basement. "I was just one of a million girls who could do Ronettes records almost as good as the Ronettes."

Her rock & roll breakout began on a Sunday evening: "My father always watched Ed Sullivan, and he screamed at me, 'Look at these guys!' I was totally into black stuff, I didn't wanna see this Rolling Stones crap. But my father acted so nuts, it was like, he was so cool, for him to react so violently attracted me." As she wrote in 1973, "they put the touch on me. I was blushing jelly, this was no mamas boy music. it was alchemical. I couldn't fathom the recipe but I was ready. Blind love for my father was the first thing I sacrificed to Mick Jagger."

But the recipe was more complicated. One day, when Patti was still in high school, Patti and her mother had a fight. To make up, Mrs. Smith brought home two Bob Dylan albums, "because he dresses just like you." Like most of us, Patti discovered in Dylan a passion for social justice, a madness for language and a personal style. But Patti learned more. Like Dylan's, the myth of Patti Smith's origins is intricately constructed and endlessly fascinating. Unlike him, she has managed to keep most parts of it straight through several retellings. No one knows how much is invented, how much flat fact. Maybe it all happened, maybe none of it. I'd rather not know—either way.

Unlike Dylan, or rock's other Westchester rebels, Patti was a true working-class girl. When she worked in a factory during and after high school, it was for the cash, not experience. (The experience did provide the basis of her epic "Piss Factory", though.) Still, in a tough lower-class town, she was strange, and so was everything about her from her family and ideas to her body itself. It was reedy and breastless even then, as much a boy's as a woman's. Patti knew it; maybe she even exploited it: "Even since I felt the need to choose I'd choose male. I felt boy rythums [*sic*] when I was in knee pants. So I stayed in pants. I sobbed when I had to use the public ladies room. My undergarments made me blush. Every feminine gesture I affected from my mother humiliated me," she wrote in her 1967 poem called "Female."

Then she got pregnant. The circumstances don't matter—she was in junior college at the time—but she had the baby without getting married and gave it up for adoption. Teenage pregnancies weren't uncommon in South Jersey; in fact, they are just the sort of thing which happens to normal, well-adjusted girls everywhere. But to Patti, the overwhelmingly female sensation of pregnancy was revolting and made her feel defiled. She wrote: "bloated. pregnant. I crawl thru the sand. like a lame dog. like a crab. pull my fat baby belly to the sea. pure edge. pull my hair out by the roots. roll and drag and claw like a bitch. like a bitch. like a bitch."

But underneath it all, she thought she was still an ordinary teenage girl. "There was nothing different between me and Dot Hook or whoever. Nothing different except the desire to get the fuck out of there. I was just one of a million girls. Ain't nothing illuminated about me."

The pregnancy did change her, though, made her realize just how completely out of place she was. "It developed me as a person, made me start to value life, to value chance, that I'm not down in South Jersey on welfare with a nine-year-old kid. 'Cause every other girl in South Jersey who got in trouble at the time is down there."

After she had the baby, she came to New York in 1967, hanging around Pratt, the Brooklyn art college. She claims she was driven to the city by "Light My Fire," the Doors hit that summer. Maybe she was. A little earlier, in the factory, she had discovered *Illuminations*, by Arthur Rimbaud, the French poet who wrote all his poetry before he was 20. She spotted his face on the cover of a book and took off. "He looked just like Dylan," she still says with a sense of wonder.

At Pratt, she met Robert Mapplethorpe, an artist "who looked like George Harrison. I was drawing. And he encouraged me to do bigger drawings and then write on my drawings and then I was writing these poems on the drawings. And he loved the poems. I was so nebulous when I came to New York, I had this total maniac energy and my *Don't Look Back* walk. And I met Robert and he helped me take all this totally nebulous energy and put it in a form."

She wanted to go to Paris to study art. With her younger sister, Linda, she left. "Then I thought, fuck art, I want to be a traveler. And you have to travel with all these paints and shit. And I like to be free. Sometimes, I think I'm a singer so I don't have to carry a drum kit around."

Paris was lonely for two girls who spoke no French. "Our only touch with anything was to find something good on a jukebox." They hooked up with a street troupe, singers and a fire eater, who she claims taught her to pass the hat and, when time and finances were right, pick the pocket. Then Godard's *One Plus One*, featuring the Rolling Stones recording "Sympathy for the Devil," was released.

"Oh God, we were there night and day. We'd come in the morning and watch it over and over and over again, for five days running. It was May and then I started having all this weird stuff happen to me. First of all, I got an English rock paper and it said that Brian Jones might leave the Stones. God! Wasn't that a heavy thing!"

The Smith sisters and the street troupe moved to a farm outside Paris, Le Puits, the Wishing Well. *One Plus One* plus the newspaper item created a strange disjunction in her night life: Patti Smith began to dream of Brian Jones.

"They were so real, and every one was the same. The first one, I was riding in this old Victorian carriage with Mick and Keith and they were talking to each other in this funny language. They kept talking about ritual, it reminded me of voodoo, Haiti or something. And Anita

Pallenberg was sitting there real nervous, clutching her hands. I kept saying, 'Where's Brian? Where'd Brian go?' They'd say, 'Never mind.' Then I thought I saw him pass by in this big picture hat, like a Victorian duchess or something. It was one of these art dreams, like some Renoir movie with all these pastel colors. And then the rain started coming down, like Noah's rain. I got this weird feeling and I got out of the carriage and it was all Victorian, all English. And I looked and there was water rising about four feet and he was floating in this old Catherine the Great black Victorian dress and this big picture hat.

"So I told my sister about it and I forgot it. Then the next night the same thing happened. Now I don't even remember the dreams. I remember the second one was more Kenneth Anger, more homosexual, with switchblades. At the end, I came into the bathroom and his head was in the toilet. It was always water, you know?

"Then this big pot of boiling water spilled on me. In reality, I was in a lotta pain, had second degree burns or something, all over me, so they gave me belladonna and morphine. I went to sleep and I had this dream that I was crawling in the grass. And there was a whirlpool, rocks and river and ocean and whirlpool, and we were slipping, it was me and Brian, he had my ankle and he was holding on. I was clutching the grass and I felt really sick, and I was banging, banging the grass. I remember the grass being cool and wet. I grabbed something and it was a hem, I looked up and it was Brian. He said, 'Throw up.' He's saying, 'Spit it out. Spit it out.' He grabbed my hair and he says, 'Spit it out.' And I remember this white hem, like a Moroccan djellaba, grabbing it and spitting up.

"I woke up. I was throwing up, and it was like I woulda . . . You know how they say Jimi Hendrix died? Well, that dream really blew my mind. I said to my sister, 'Let's go back to Paris.' Maybe we could call up—but I didn't know any rock people then, I didn't even know Bobby Neuwirth. That was the whole tragedy, that I was just totally nobody, I had no connections. I had no money, I couldn't fly to London. And I felt like I had this information that Brian Jones was gonna die. So we went back to Paris and the next day, I couldn't even find it in English, it just said, 'Brian Jones Mort.'"

She began to dream of her father now, about his heart. She and Linda decided to go home. When they arrived, her father was in bed. He'd had a heart attack.

She stayed in Pitman only briefly, then moved back to New York, into the Chelsea Hotel with Mapplethorpe. She was trying to write a requiem for Brian Jones. "That's when my life really blew apart. In a cool way." In the lobby of the Chelsea, she met Bobby Neuwirth, who had played Guildenstern to Bob Dylan's Rosencrantz throughout the middle Sixties. As Patti tells it, Neuwirth accosted her and asked where she had learned to walk. She replied, "From *Don't Look Back*," the Dylan movie in which Neuwirth was a principal, and the friendship was formed.

"He didn't really understand the whole Brian Jones thing," Patti explains. "But the thing was, he recognized something within the pieces, something that I didn't see. I didn't know what I was doing. I wasn't trying to create art or change the world, I was trying to rid myself of my guilt, my mania about it, my obsession." Neuwirth protected her, telling friends she wasn't a groupie, demanding they keep their hands off.

It was a heady time to be at the Chelsea. Throughout 1970, select parts of the Andy Warhol crowd were living there, as were William Burroughs, the Jefferson Airplane and Janis Joplin. So was playwright Sam Shepard. "He saw in me some other kinda thing. Sam liked the way I walked. He always inspired me to start fights in bars. He always pushed this other thing in me." Shepard's vision of her must have been perverse—*The Tooth of Crime,* the rock play he later wrote, is rather transparently based on Patti, although the protagonist is male. It is a sadistic work, filled with intimations of murder and defeat, set on a stark stage. Shepard, a leading figure just then in the off-Broadway theater, and Patti co-wrote a book of plays, *Mad Dog Blues.* But she and Sam didn't last.

At first she worked as a clerk in Scribner's Fifth Avenue bookstore, for $75 a week. Later, as she became better known, she wrote for a number of publications (including this one), scuffling for a living. She was willing to do a lot of work (she was a staff writer at *Rock* magazine for a time) but she always did it her own way. (She lost the *Rock* job after an interview with Eric Clapton where, according to the myth, she asked only one question: What are your six favorite colors?) Patti never forgot who the star was. And she kept writing.

Gerard Malanga, the Warhol acolyte (he rubber-stamped the signatures on the Warhol electric chair lithographs), invited her to share a reading at St. Mark's in the Bowery with him; with the encouragement of the Chelsea crowd, particularly rock critic Lenny Kaye who backed her on guitar, she gave it a try. It won her a small cult, and the scene makers, ever aware of new faces, courted her avidly for a while. St. Mark's also won the interest of Steve Paul, the former club owner (the Scene, on West 46th Street, had been the biggest rock club in the city in the mid-Sixties), publicist (for the Peppermint Lounge, at 17) and now manager of Johnny and Edgar Winter. She aroused his entrepreneurial instinct as no one since the blues brothers.

But Patti wasn't malleable. Steve wanted her to drop the poetry and start singing, perhaps with Edgar Winter. Although she was attracted by rock & roll, she wanted her poetry, too. "I've known I was gonna be a big shot since I was four," she said. "I just didn't know it had anything to do with my throat."

Then as now, her heroes were more far ranging than rock stars. While she was fascinated by Lou Reed, Jimi Hendrix, Janis Joplin—who had befriended her at the Chelsea, too—and particularly Jim Morrison, she equated them with her high cultural idols, William Burroughs, Edith Piaf, Baudelaire and, of course, Rimbaud.

"Steve was one of the prime people who said, 'You'll never make it with the poetry, take it out of the act.' He wanted me to be a sort of leather Liza Minnelli, I think," she says. "But the whole thing that Steve did for me, he made me fight for what I believed in. Because he was so adamant, I got adamant. We parted with me saying, 'I ain't never gonna do this shit, I ain't never gonna do a record unless they let me do exactly what I want to do.'"

Utterly unbroken, she delved deeper into poetry, though she still wrote occasional criticism and a few song lyrics for Blue Oyster Cult albums. (She and BOC keyboardist Allen Lanier have had a longtime on-and-off living arrangement.) Three volumes of her poetry appeared: *Seventh Heaven*, late in 1971, published by a small Berkeley house; Middle

Earth Press put out *Kodak* in 1972; and in 1973, the Gotham Book Mart published *Witt* (pronounced white). Sales were small, but steady.

She and Kaye remained in touch—although he spent much of 1973 in Europe—getting together for readings which were slowly evolving into concerts.

In early 1973, the Mercer Arts Center began to function as a focal point for glitter rock bands such as the New York Dolls. Patti hung around; she knew many of the musicians and business people from her Village haunts. And she was reintroduced to Jane Friedman, an acquaintance from the Chelsea days and a partner in the Wartoke publicity firm, which had been responsible for coordinating press for Woodstock (as it later would be for Watkins Glen). Friedman was booking rock acts into one of the Mercer rooms and she let Patti open for them. Patti read without a mike or instrumentalist, bellowing through cupped hands or a megaphone at kids who liked to heckle; but both she and Friedman say Patti always won them over in the end, often by heckling back.

Finally, Patti, explaining that Friedman had always been present at the most crucial moments in her career, asked Jane to manage her. Presuming that she had a poet on her hands again—she had worked at the Gaslight in Greenwich Village during the era of beat poetry readings—Jane agreed.

Born to be. born to be me. just the right dark glasses.

—"Balance" 1973

In 1974, it all fell together. Friedman's effect began to be felt—she's no hard-nosed businessperson, but she has the practical sensibility Patti lacks. And she knew how to push her. Together with Allen Lanier, Jane convinced Patti to try singing, first at home at the piano, then on the stage.

What Patti Smith was about to attempt had been pulled off by no one before her. She fits no female rock stereotype, not the suppliant lover Joni Mitchell epitomizes nor Janis Joplin's brassy but vulnerable 'Little Girl Blue.' To get the total adulation she wanted, Patti would have to be as much her own creation as the greatest male stars. Like all of them—Jagger, Dylan, Bowie, Stewart—intense sexuality was sped along by gender ambiguity. This fascination with androgynous creativity and her own ability to exchange sexual roles influenced her early works. The aggressive lesbian imagery of her first book, *Seventh Heaven,* gave way to aggressive heterosexual fantasies. But the material was still outrageous enough to prompt Jim Delehant, A&R director at Atlantic, the company where Patti felt she most belonged ("After all, I am the last white [*n*-word]"), to characterize "Piss Factory" as too filthy to be considered.

In mid-1974, she and her band went into the studio to record a single on Mer Records, a label that had been invented and financed for the purpose by Lenny Kaye, Robert Mapplethorpe and Wartoke. The 45 contained her two key performance pieces, "Piss Factory" and "Hey Joe." The latter began as a sort of toast to Patty Hearst—"I was wonderin' were you gettin' it every night from a black revolutionary man and his woman," she said in the introductions, calling forth the sort of deep racial fears that inspired rock in the first place—and exploded into joyous cacophony. The cult grew more intense as a result, even if the booking agents and major record company A&R men didn't respond.

Somewhere, Patti firmly believed, there was a place where Rimbaud's intense aesthetic lust met the Ronettes' boyfriend's stud passion. Surer than ever, she began to locate it, not just in her poetry but in her music—discovering ways to rework raunch classics like "Gloria," "Hey Joe" and "Land of a Thousand Dances" to fit her style—and in the look on her audience's face.

She found it at Max's Kansas City, where she and her trio played for several weeks, in the rhythmic grooves the band imagined with her; she found out that it connected with the uninitiated in San Francisco, where she went with a booking at a tiny Berkeley record store for a reading and wound up singing at Winterland, Bill Graham's Fillmore surrogate. Part of it was her firm belief that it all tied together at its core, rock & roll and High Art. Part of it was simply inevitable: "Of course I wanted to work in the rock & roll tradition. I didn't know any other tradition existed."

Throughout the winter, the band played CBGB, a tiny Bowery bar which featured many of the acts displaced by the folding of Mercer and Max's. Their confidence grew with their repertoire and a few of the braver record company A&R people began to express an interest. Stephen Holden of RCA went so far as to record a demo tape in the Sixth Avenue RCA studio in February 1975. John Rockwell found out and wrote a column about it in the *New York Times.*

Suddenly, interest sprang up in another quarter. Clive Davis, president of Arista Records and formerly of CBS, was on the phone. Davis maintains that his interest had been piqued by Patti's friend Lou Reed; Rockwell's column, he insists, had nothing to do with it. Others are more skeptical about the coincidence.

In a way, it was a perfect matchup. All of Smith's benefactors have had a parental bent and Davis is the Great White Father of the record industry. His stars aren't signed so much as courted and wedded. Today, there is obviously great affection between the two: he, concerned not to push too fast, she, respectful of his care.

Signing had one immediate result: At a May date at the Other End, Bob Dylan showed up. (Davis said that he went as a personal favor.) "It was neat that I got to see Dylan, got to spend any time with him before I did my record. I never discussed nothing. We never discussed nothing. We never talked. I mean we talked. . . . You know how I felt? I been talking to him in my brain for 12 years, and now I don't have nothing to say to him. I feel like we should have telepathy by now. Me and my sister don't talk."

Suddenly Johnny gets the feelin' he's bein' surrounded by horses horses horses
Comin' in in all directions, white, shinin' silver studs with their noses all in flames . . .
Do you know how to Pony?

—Patti Smith, "Land of a Thousand Dances"

Through spring and half the summer, Patti sought a producer. Finally, she settled on John Cale. "My picking John was about as arbitrary as picking Rimbaud. I saw the cover of *Illuminations* with Rimbaud's face, y'know, he looked so cool, just like Bob Dylan. So Rimbaud became my favorite poet. I looked at the cover of *Fear* [Cale's 1974 solo record] and I said, 'Now there's a set of cheekbones.' The thing is I picked John . . . in my mind I picked him because his records sounded good. But I hired the wrong guy. All I was really looking for was a technical person. Instead, I got a total maniac artist. I went to pick out an expensive watercolor painting and instead I got a mirror. It was really like *A Season in Hell,* for both of us. But inspiration doesn't always have to be someone sending me half a dozen American Beauty roses. There's a lotta inspiration going on between the murderer and the victim. And he had me so nuts I wound up doing this nine-minute cut ['Birdland'] that transcended anything I ever did before."

It was the culmination of a dream. "Everybody always says no, you can't, you'll never be able to do it. Nobody's going to sign a poet. You'll never be able to get the kind of record you want. It's really easy—all you have to do is know what you want and be strong. Clive Davis never argued with me once about the material on the record. It wasn't any big sweat; he trusted us." (This may be slightly off the mark; Davis did ask that two songs have portions remixed.)

But the central issue, to Patti, remains clear. "People are so sure of the impossibility of things that it's like in 'Land of a Thousand Dances'—they don't see the sea of possibility. All I know is I got to do exactly what I wanted to do. It took me four years to get it but it was worth the wait."

Recording *Horses* pushed Patti even further into the scarlet fever fantasy she had inhabited since childhood. And when her sense of mission becomes confused with her sense of fantasy, problems can arise. "I'm into rock & roll right now because there's a place for me. I don't think it's no accident that Bob Marley and me should be coming up at the same time. Not because I have anything to do with Bob Marley—I just feel like a whole new thing's happening. It's time to figure out what happened in the Sixties. What we can get from the Sixties is that people got so far out that old concepts were really dead. Everything that keeps us apart is really old news, man. People don't know it yet, but future generations will figure it out. That's why I'm working on a link—to keep it going."

This is excellent rhetoric but there are some fearsome contradictions in Smith's specific application of her fantasy to reality. Talking about Jimi Hendrix's reasons for operating in the white idiom, she remarks: "He had to become white because it's a white tradition to do high art and Jimi was really into poetry. And Rimbaud was totally into black people, Rimbaud believed totally that he was part [n-word], because of the Ethiopians being a totally relentless physical race. Jimi Hendrix had to be like that because of synthesizing." Or speaking of how reggae has led her to a fascination with Rastafarianism, the Jamaican religion: "So many kids are getting into it, they're gonna have to change the rules. It's not a black thing anymore; it's not even Jamaican. It belongs to us now."

Those fantasies are like nothing so much as Norman Mailer's White Negro [*Norman Mailer's* The White Negro, *originally published in a 1957 special issue of* Dissent *and later that year by City Lights. —Ed.*], the ultimate cultural usurper; worse, they are reminiscent of Mailer's championing of Charles Manson, another white man who wanted to appropriate black revolution for his own purposes.

Some of Patti's theories are more charming. Her perspective on women is illuminating: "I don't like categorizing stuff, but women's roles all through history have been to act as hierophant or someone who's guarded the secrets or guarded the temple. I'm a girl doing what guys usually did, the way that I look, the goals and kinds of things I want to help achieve through rock. It's more heroic stuff and heroic stuff has been traditionally male. Like Hendrix and Jim Morrison and all those people. I mean, Jim Morrison was trying to elevate the word; he was the poet in rock & roll before me. He was an *academic* poet. Lou Reed—another academic poet. I'm more like down-to-earth than them guys."

But what if everything fails? In mid-November, *Horses,* manufactured at the Pitman Columbia plant, was released by Arista and in January Patti goes on her first, full-scale tour outside the coasts. If she is as fragile as some think, she will break and run at the first sign of rejection. If she's as tough as I think, she'll find a way. But what if it all falls through, no more records, no more songs? "The cornerstone of the little temple Jane and I built is poetry. I always had that. It's like in Hollywood, if you've got good tits. So Russ Meyer'll take you. It's the one thing you've got. You can get Lloyd's of London to insure 'em, but at least you've got your tits."

But some have thought beyond that point of failure, to complete success. "My father," Patti laughed one day, riding down to the Village from her Broadway rehearsal hall in a taxi, "has already put in his order for a car."

A Mercedes, a Bentley, a Lincoln?

"Oh I don't know. A Corolla or something? Is that the name?"

Or, as she wrote about a dream of the return of Brian Jones two years ago:

I can't help it. I cry out. How are you? Have you been all right. He smiles. He turns away and says: 'I have everything under control.'

INTERVIEW WITH PATTI SMITH

Mick Gold | May 10, 1976 | Interview Transcript

In May 1976 Smith was on her first European tour on the back of *Horses*. Smith was in London for her UK debut, playing the Roundhouse May 16 and 17 with opening act the Stranglers, who opened for the Ramones' UK debut two months later. Some believed the hype; others were skeptical; everyone was intrigued. This interview took place on May 10 in Patti's room on the fourth floor of the Portobello Hotel, the Victorian-era haunt in posh Notting Hill, where Lou Reed, Van Morrison, and the Sex Pistols once stayed. Patti wore a white button-down, black slacks, and a black tie as she puffed on a cigarette during this marathon two-hour session, punctuated by click of cameras shuttering and the phone ringing in constant syncopation. Journalists wandered in and out—mostly unidentified, other than *New York Times* critic and Bob Dylan biographer Robert Shelton—but twenty-eight-year-old rock writer Mick Gold stayed. He was there to take it all in and decide for himself.

Smith was in an "expansive mood that day," Gold recalled, animated by the discovery that the B-side to her single, "Gloria," a live recording of "My Generation" done in Cleveland on January 26, 1976, had been bleeped:

> *People try to put us down*
> *Just because we get around*
> *I don't need that fucking shit*
> *Hope I die because of it*

She was incensed, and she pulled no punches with the defensive British Arista representative, who was also there. The conversation was peppered with colorful anecdotes: Rimbaud in Ethiopia, her relationship with Bob Dylan, being invited on stage by Fred "Sonic" Smith, whom she had recently met at Detroit's Lafayette Coney Island. But Smith devoted much of this uncensored interview to censorship—of Brancusi, on the radio, or of her inexhaustible, irrepressible self—and this excerpt focuses on that central issue. Lenny Kaye is there too with a pithy retort or a well-timed one-liner whenever the situation calls for it. The interview ended with a confrontation with Steve Lake, the critic who wrote a caustic review in the December 13, 1975, issue of *Melody Maker* with the headline "Poet and a No-Man Band," with a caption underneath Smith's photo: "Her head must roll." It was hanging on the wall of the hotel room.

Yet if Gold had any doubts going in, he emerged a convert to what might be called the church of Patti. "She simply cannot be labeled," he wrote in the resulting profile for *Street Life*. "I have no simple verdict, except that I believe in her." —Ed.

Patti Smith: Does any of you guys know the story on, uh . . . I hear that our single's been released here with bleeps in it.

Unidentified: It certainly has.

Smith: Well I can tell you what. You want to write something in your paper?

Mick Gold: Mm-hmm.

Smith: You tell the kids that I say not to buy it.

Unidentified: Hmm . . .

Gold: Yeah?

Smith: You tell them that it's against my wishes and that, like, I'm gonna do everything I can to get it . . . to get it pulled back, and like, first of all, it was supposed to be put out . . . the whole point of doing a single to me is to give people somethin' new. Somethin' different than the album, some new fresh approach, which is why . . . and make it exciting, which is why I labored and paid, paid with my own money for that picture sleeve, because kids dig picture sleeves. There was nothin' to me more exciting than gettin' a picture sleeve on a single. They should have the picture sleeve, and I fought and fought for the song not to be censored. And England is much more progressive than America, I feel. In fact, Canada, they play it uncensored. They don't—they play it on the *radio*.

Unidentified: Do they not play it on the radio in the States?

Smith: No.

Unidentified: They don't?

Smith: Just on some underground stations.

Unidentified: Let me just say, by the way, that the single that Patti is talking about, the track that Patti's talking about, is the B-side of the new single, "My Generation," which is the old Pete Townshend song.

Smith: Yeah, we did it live in Cleveland, and it has this line, "I don't need no fuckin' shit, hope I die because of it." 'Cause it was live, and they bleeped it. They didn't bleep it in America, and that's not how it's supposed to be, and it was against my wishes. And like one of the things that our group is really fighting for is to break censorship in rock 'n' roll, because to me, rock 'n' roll, or whatever it's called—say rock 'n' roll, so a simple way so I can communicate—is, like, my art. I've like shifted from poetry to painting and rock 'n' roll; I have the same commitment as all of them. They're all art to me. Like I said, art has to be redefined. And there's no censorship. The government or record companies and all cannot, do not have . . . they just don't have the right nor the sophistication to assume to censor an artist. And just like the American government censoring the *Bird in Space* [*In 1926, Romanian sculptor Constantin Brancusi's* Bird in Space *sculptures were charged the tariff for manufactured goods when customs officials refused to believe it was art, resulting in a court battle —Ed.*], they wanted to throw it away as scrap metal. They said, "This isn't art." Brancusi had to fight and fight and fight to, like, prove that it was art. Government doesn't know shit, you know, whether it's art or not.

Unidentified: But it's not the record company you're hitting by saying "Don't buy it."

Smith: No, it's me, because I get the dough, and first of all, if the record company—I don't know who bleeped it. I'm not going to accuse because I don't know. Whether it was the government, or whether it was the record company, whoever did it, did it against my wishes. It's everything I stand against, and I don't want kids buying it, which, when it comes down to it, only hurts me, you know? But I feel like I'm gonna work, do everything I can while I'm here, to have the record rereleased as planned, with its picture sleeve and with the uncensored version. I'm ashamed of it. I'm ashamed of the fact that it was censored, and I'm ashamed that it doesn't have its sleeve, and I don't want people to buy it.

[*Indistinct comment from unidentified reporter.*]

Arista Representative: This situation is as far as the . . . By the way, the record you have, that I put in all the press kits, is the American copy, which has a sleeve and is uncensored, anyway. The reason that we had to bleep it, bleep the B-side, was that we were, our distributors, EMI, would not have released the record unless we had. Now that was, so, the decision—

Smith: But see, you should have, right away you should have called me up, because I would have given you something else for the B-side. I would have done a poem, I would have gone out of my way to like . . . I should have been informed. The record company must keep its artists informed.

Arista Representative: Well, certainly, it was done with, I mean, for what it's worth, it was done with Clive's full understanding, because obviously—

Smith: See, Clive [*Arista head Clive Davis —Ed.*] told me he didn't know a thing about it. Clive told me—all right, so right away, here's the thing—Clive said that he didn't know a thing about it. It was done behind his back.

Arista Representative: We obviously, I mean, Christ, it's a far too strong a thing for us to have wanted not to put it out, so we were in a [*indistinct*]. Either it was not going to go out at all, the record wasn't going to go out at all, because there's, see, there's no . . . The way we're structured—

Unidentified: It doesn't make any sense. I mean, EMI distributed John Lennon's stuff with "fuck" on it—

Arista Representative: Well, I mean, all I know is that we didn't even mention it. We just put it through, and it got up—

Smith: OK, so here's another thing that shows. I have always stood behind my record company. I stand behind my record company because they've stood behind me. I always say, you know, that they believe in me and stand behind me and don't repress me as an artist. But here is one example of, like, how you—an artist cannot stand behind his company unless the company stands behind the artist. It must be mutual. I was told by Clive. . . . And I respect Clive, and Clive has done a lot for me. He let me release my album untouched, uncensored. He let me do my single. But also, the fact of the matter is, when I went to Clive about this, when my management went to Clive, he said he didn't know a thing about it and that England did it all on their own. So, England, you're exonerated [*laughs*]—

Unidentified: You're put on the—

Smith: But I still don't want, I still feel, unless they have to have it, you know—and I'll tell another thing—if the kids buy, if they have to have it, what they can do is, my management company is on the back of the record. They send a letter to the management company; I'll send them something. I'll send them a . . . I'll send them something to help make up for it. I don't know what else I can say, but I'm like, I can't tell you how, like, much this hurt me, you know, because I feel like any time I do something that shows a loss of integrity, it's gonna ruin my credibility as an artist. An artist doesn't mean—

Arista Representative: Paul Simon, Paul Simon's A-side in England had a, had a, had it—

Unidentified: [*to Arista representative*] But surely, you haven't, I mean, surely you wouldn't have done this for distribution. It's still distributed, but you wouldn't get any airplay.

Arista Representative: No, we—no, no, no, it wouldn't get distributed!

Smith: Well, the B-side isn't supposed to get airplay!

Arista Representative: No, we weren't anticipating any—well, we weren't promoting that side. So no, simply, it was [*indistinct*] the issue that we wouldn't have had any record if we had let it go as it was.

Unidentified: They wouldn't put it out just because it's got "fuckin' shit" on it?

Smith: That's hard to believe.

Lenny Kaye: The way we feel is if they want to censor it, then we'd rather not put it out.

Smith: We would have put something else out. I would have done a rap about censorship on the back. Really, I would have said, "My generation is in blah blah blah," and I would've talked about it and tried to get people to rise against it. How can I get kids, how can we promote change if, like, we're like, if the rug is pulled out under us? I mean, I'm willing to make less money. I don't give a shit about the money. Makin' money is cool because it means that I can run off to Ethiopia and finish my book about Rimbaud. Or, you know, I can give, I can give an underground group some amps or something. But we don't really, that's not how we started, you know. And as far as I'm concerned, Lenny Kaye made more money being a rock writer than he does being my guitar player. He doesn't give a shit. 'Cause this was the thing that I wanted to talk about the most, you know. It was like—

Unidentified: When do you leave?

Unidentified: Yeah, "that's the track that eventually made it, let's take it over." [*Indistinct.*] It's ironic.

Smith: And yeah, I mean, yeah. I mean, can you imagine? Can you imagine like how, I mean we create it. "Let's take it over in the middle of it." You know, you're letting yourself . . . I mean, I just want people, the kids to be aware that, that I was not aware that this happened. The only reason I found out about it is one of your writers called me up in America and said, you know, said . . . I mean it's just like something, I just feel like I don't want anybody to think that I copped out. I mean, the only way I can like remedy it is to like show how much I'm serious by telling people that they should, you know, boycott the record, or order it from America, you know? I mean, I-I would rather see somebody *bootleg* my American version and somebody else get the money, just so it's out the way it should be. I mean, it's not like, you know, like I'm some philanthropist that doesn't give a shit about money. It's just that, you know, it's like blood money to me if I get it, you know. We fought so hard. I mean, we didn't just get that handed to us. We fought and fought and fought to get that single out. And you know, the way I look at it, I got really pissed off at my country [*laughs*] because you know, it's like, there are two very important American slang terms. They're nothing but slang. They've been abstracted from the physical act. When people say "fuckin' shit," they don't think of a big turd, or two people makin' it anymore, it's just words, you know. It's like, you know, I mean it's like, we've gone beyond that. It's American slang. It's in dictionaries, and it's like some of the famous lines in the world. You know, you can go in the part of pygmy country and I'll bet you'll find some guy goin' [*in a deep, rumbling voice*] "*fuck.*" [*Unidentified laughter.*] And it's like, I think that especially in our bicentennial time, you know, that we should rise up and, like, stand behind our stuff, you know. Good and bad, you know? That's why I was so proud of Canada. I couldn't believe deejays in Canada, especially Montreal, they play the whole thing. This guy from Montreal said, he played it for me, he said, "Live over the radio." I said, "How can you do that? You're not even American? What're you takin' this risk for?" He said, "I'll fight them, I don't care. You're an artist. I'll fight 'em. I hope they try." I was so proud of him. You know, I was really proud of him. Boy, it just, like . . . that, to me, I started crying, I thought it was so great. You know, and then I come here and I find out *that* happened, and it makes me feel, you know, just so like if I can get it across to the kids that I didn't do it, you know, and I'm doin' everything I can to like remedy it.

Kaye: Censorship is one of the worst evils in the world because it's somebody telling you what to do, and the problem with this world is that everybody's got their nose up your ass.

Smith: I mean, look, to me one of the greatest crimes of, like, the twentieth century is that the Rolling Stones, the most important, the top rock 'n' roll band in the world, in the history of the universe, had to like change "Let's spend the night together" to "Let's spend some time together." I cried when that happened. I actually cried, I was so hurt that the Rolling

Stones after doin' all this kind of stuff, for not only our economy and our consciousnesses and, you know, for like lonely nights, I mean, givin' us all this stuff—they had to fuckin' change, you know, their song. I mean, really, I mean, how much can you . . . how much . . . Like I said, artists always suffer, you know? Artists always go through it.

Arista Representative: They didn't have to change it here.

Smith: No, they had to change it in America. You know, they had to change it on the *Ed Sullivan Show* or something, I dunno.

Kaye: They had to change it [*indistinct*].

Smith: Yeah, that's right. [*Laughs.*]

Unidentified: But really, in a way, that's been censorship by Arista Records, self-censorship. I mean, you didn't even fight it—

Smith: It's EMI or something. I don't know who it is, you know. My manager, that's managerial stuff. I'll have her take care of it. [*A journalist laughs.*] That's what she's great at. My manager fought—I mean you should have heard her, she was great, man—she fought to get it not censored. That's how, you know, we fought for a sleeve, we fight for everything, you know. I mean, that's the whole thing. Rock 'n' roll is still warfare. Total warfare all the time. You're always fightin'. You're always fightin'. But see, one thing you must say about Arista, like here, even if they did it, I have to like say another thing is, like . . . I keep forgettin' your name, it doesn't matter.

Arista Representative: Howard.

Smith: Howard. He's not a *yes man*, huh? We're not tryin' to get him in any trouble or anything, because he's got answers, he tries to supply me with the answers, but like he's not, he's like a guy like who seems really into like— [*Unidentified speaker makes a muffled comment to Smith.*] I don't have any more. Oh, I'll take some vitamins, yeah . . . [Howard] seems to really be into like what we're doing, or like explore what we're doing, and takin' the bad aspects of us as well as the good. You think some other record company guy would sit there and let some artist, you know, say that kind of shit in an interview? They'd have a heart attack.

Unidentified: Well they'd be saying, "Would you like another drink, Ken?" [*Laughter.*]

Smith: I mean, that's also important, so I don't want you to get a bad attitude about [the] English area of Arista. I mean, I think they're pretty hip out here, you know.

Unidentified: *Now* would you like another drink, Ken?

[*Laughter.*]

Smith: No, I'm not saying—

***Daily Mirror* Journalist:** This is going on our rock page, which is ostensibly to sell records. And the first [*thing*], and I'll admit, that's a good story, the girl comes out and says, "Do not buy my record."

Smith: . . . Well they can buy the album. [*Laughs with journalists.*]

Kaye: Buy the album instead!

Smith: No, I mean, really, they should order it from America. Order the single, you know. Really, they should contact Wartoke [*Smith's publicity firm —Ed.*], you know? And, and Jane [*Smith's manager, Jane Friedman —Ed.*] is gonna figure out a way to distribute it herself. I mean, we'll do . . . Listen, I'd do anything to get, like, cool things across. You know, we made our own single. How we started was by making our own single.

Unidentified: "Hey Joe."

Smith: "Hey Joe," and we couldn't press any more because, you know, it was like, you know, in my contract I couldn't press any more. So, good! Accidentally lose the master on a subway and have some kids take it over. It was made for the people. We were the people when we did it, we gave it back to the people. You know? That's how I feel when I see bootlegs, you know. I don't feel ripped off when I see bootlegs, and as long as the bootlegs are cheap and the kids don't have to pay up the ass for them, I think they're cool. I buy bootlegs. When I see a Stones or Dylan bootleg, man, I'm there with my bucks. You know, it's like, we have a bootleg. In fact, we have a bootleg in the States that's better distributed than our single. [*Laughter.*] Really, I've gone to record stores. I can't find our single, but I can find our bootleg. It's called *Teenage Perversity and*

Ships in the Night. It's really cool. Yeah, it's like a bootleg from one of our Roxy shows. And since, see I think that that's important. I'm honored by this, and I'm also pleased, because we improvise every night, and because, you know, I'd say a third of our show is improvised and always lost in space, much like Najinsky's leaps [*Russian ballet dancer Vaslav Nijinsky —Ed.*] or anything that's lost in space.

Unidentified: So bootlegging is fair game to you, Patti?

Smith: Well, it's like this. I don't want it . . . I wouldn't want it to hurt—

Kaye: We'd like to draw a difference, though, between bootlegging and counterfeiting.

Smith: Yeah.

Kaye: Counterfeiting records I feel is a high crime because that's just thievery. Bootlegging is actual preservation of material that would otherwise not get released.

Smith: No, it's like this. What I'd like to see, if kids want, I mean, I don't, I can't make a big stance about this, but what my stance basically is, if like you tape an artist, and you know you've caught a magic moment, a long improvisation or something totally magic, if you're the only one that's preserved that moment, and it's worthy—I don't think that every piece of shit an artist does should be bootlegged, you know, but—I think if there's like magical moments that no one else has captured, then it's worthy. I mean, look, *Underground Live '69*, the *Velvet Underground Live '69 in Texas* [1969: The Velvet Underground Live —*Ed.*] to me is one of the top ten rock 'n' roll albums, and it was essentially a bootleg. I mean, RCA bought it, but it was essentially a kid that taped it on a Sony, and he captured some really fantastic moments in the history of rock 'n' roll. But I think that bootlegging, too, should be selective and tasteful and for a specific service to the people. I mean, bootlegging, too, can be a ripoff if you're just gonna like, you know, just because it's the Stones, every piece of shit, every time the Stones lay a fart you're gonna bootleg it.

Unidentified: Mmm.

Smith: I mean, these are sort of . . . I mean, you know, some people might think we're cutting our own throats, but I mean, I believe in this stuff, you know, and, uh, I think it's real important. I also think that some things are within public domain. I mean, the *heart*, I don't think that you should like, I mean, I've been like, the only time I've felt ripped off in my life, is like, when people have like snooped around in my personal, really, really personal life and exploited it. That's the only thing that hurts me.

Unidentified: How is that done, Patti?

Smith: Well, things like, you know, trying to like delve into like, you know, my life with . . . For instance, I'm in love with someone, but every time I'm with a guy in public, you know, I talk to Bob Dylan and they blow it up. Things like that, which is just like [*gossip columnist*] Rona Barrett kind of bullshit, you know, which to me doesn't belong in rock 'n' roll. Finding things about my past that, you know, could hurt my family, and you know, exploiting them. To me that has nothing to do with, like, the spirit and the heart of rock 'n' roll. I try to expose myself as much as possible. I talk about controversial things, you know, which is still socially unaccepted, you know, to talk about, just like Wilhelm Reich did. I talk about masturbation and things like that, not for shock value but because I think there are things that people can exploit to help develop themselves and their consciousnesses that they shouldn't feel guilty about. And I'm [not] talkin' about the stuff that I talk about in my interviews to be like some, you know . . . some shocking cunt or something. You know, I don't do anything for shock value. I think shock is a bore. I talk about things, you know, I mean, I don't say "Jesus died for somebody's sins but not mine," you know, to shock the Catholic church or the Christian church. I say something like that because I believe that people shouldn't, you know, that we form our own lives, you know, that when I do evil or if I do something socially evil or something, I know I'm doing it. *I* do it by my own free will. Someone else isn't going to accept the blame or accept the rewards of what I do. It's not because, you know . . .

Unidentified: Are you going as far, are you saying in fact what Robert Redford said when he was in London. He said, "All I owe the public is a performance; I owe them nothing of my life at all."

Smith: No, I don't say that, because I give a lot. What I'm saying [is] a lot opposite. I expose, I give my performance and I also expose myself quite a bit, in interviews, in performing, 'cause I talk a lot, I try to relate to people, and there are only a few things in my life that I prefer to remain private—very few things. I think I give, like, around seventy percent of myself, and the thirty percent of myself that I don't give mostly out of respect to other people I think should be left alone. You know, that's . . . I don't think that's a lot to ask. [*Indistinct comment from unidentified journalist.*] Yeah, I mean, Dylan exposed—I mean all these people, you know? It's just like, the Stones have done so much for us, why, like, try to snoop around and see if he's gonna get a divorce or this and that? You know, it's just that kind of stuff should really be left to, like, their in-crowd, or like each other, you know? That kind of stuff, you know, is, that kind of stuff to me is very cruel. It doesn't belong. I mean, I've read stuff about myself that . . .

Unidentified: But people want to know it all the same, Patti, don't they?

Smith: Yeah, well they want to know it, but there's so much exciting stuff to know, and to know . . . I feel, I mean, I don't want to get overdramatic about this, but I just feel that rock 'n' roll and the world, and the atmosphere that rock 'n' roll is creating and imploding, exploding and becoming, is giving people so much space that we shouldn't dirty it up with a bunch of petty crap, you know? I mean, it is, it should be a very conspiratorial thing. I mean, I don't feel like I'm competing with other people in rock 'n' roll. I mean, I think there's room for everybody, but I see groups all the time hurting each other, you know, like, being mean to each other, you know, the opening act gets treated like shit, things like that. It's just, I mean, you know, it shouldn't be like that.

Unidentified: There's one thing I wanted to ask, which is that people like Morrison and Brian Jones seem to bring up cosmology, and whether you regarded them as sort of sources of vitality or it ever occurs to you that there's some necrophilia in true rock?

Smith: No, I think they're just a part of all our . . . they're a part of all our cause. . . . It's our family tree. It's that simple, you know. I mean, as a performer and being so committed to what I'm doing, and being with my group so much, I mean we're together more than I'm with anybody else. It's almost—I mean, I still love my family, but I just don't . . . I mean, I see Lenny almost every day. I see my mother twice a year. I see my brother once a year. So, you know what I mean? He's like my new brother. It's like, the boys in the band are like my brothers and Jane's my sister, it just goes on and on from there, and rock 'n' roll has, like, become so heavily integrated in my system that, um . . . you know, it's like when I think of, like, my family tree, I don't, I mean, I don't relate to my grandparents. I hardly knew 'em, and the ones I knew I didn't like, you know, they were a drag. But what I do relate to as far as hereditorial trying to figure out who I am are the people that have inspired me and I branched out because of. I mean, I can look inside myself and see more, see more Mick Jagger traits than I can Uncle Bob traits, you know what I mean? . . . Uncle Bob meaning that I actually have an Uncle Bob, not "Uncle Bob" anybody else. [*Laughter.*] I mean, it sounds dumb and all, but all I'm trying to, it doesn't exactly answer your question, but—

Unidentified: But just, those characters are generally—

Smith: Well, they're the greatest, man! Like, you know—

Unidentified: But those are the subjects of politics, you know, sort of living on the brink. [*Indistinct.*]

Smith: Well sure, it's just like Artaud, or just like Rimbaud, or just like Manet, or any of those guys. I mean, you know, it's like, since I was like eleven years old and quit religion, art has been my whole—you know, except, including the people I love, or excluding the people I love—art has been my whole life. And people that I've celebrated are artists. If you would have talked to me when I was sixteen, I wouldn't have mentioned anybody, but it would have all been Modigliani . . . Rimbaud, Modigliani, and all them guys who also lived on the brink and also died young and also blew it out, you know.

Gold: I think Rimbaud is a bit different, because he stopped what he was trying to do, didn't he?

Smith: Yeah, but he went into something else that was like just as excruciating, just as painful. I mean, he was like, to me he went into something heavier. The whole idea of like, there's no white people in Ethiopia, maybe two traders, one guy who traded coffee and a couple explorers. He went into Ethiopia, home of Haile Selassie, you know? The mecca of the Rastafarians, he went in there first and stayed there ten years helping develop it, exploring, exploring different possibilities, becoming the greatest horseman, you know. I mean, just the fact that he became one of the greatest horsemen in Ethiopia, land of like—and Ethiopians are pretty big and beautiful. I mean, they were like supermen, and he was regarded as one of the heaviest horsemen in all of Ethiopia. I mean, to me that's like, fuck the poetry! I mean, it's like that . . .

Gold: Somebody once said he helped exploit it.

Smith: I mean, you know, it's like, um, I mean he blew apart the word, you know. He blew it apart and made it perfect. He went beyond Baudelaire and he went about I think as far as he could've at that point. And I understand that. I mean, I went through, if somebody was into my drawings, I was really into art, really into painting and drawing, then all of a sudden at twenty-two, I stopped and never did it again. Once in a while I'll do something, but essentially as a commitment and as a rhythm of my life, I stopped it. Just all of a sudden it was through. I was finished. I was onto a new thing. And people, like—it really tore people apart that were, like, into me or, like, my friends that were used to me as being this artist, I mean they couldn't understand it, like how one day it was gone after being into it for like ten years. And I just felt a complete sense of relief. It wasn't that I *quit*, it wasn't that Rimbaud quit, he transcended. He moved into a new rhythm. And to me, the main tragedy is that he actually returned to it the last few months of his life, you know, when he was really suffering when they amputated his leg and he was taking all this opium in a siphon. He started hallucinating and babbling and sitting in front of his window playing the oud, and, like, singing these songs. Part of them his sister recognized as being *Illuminations*, and part of it was new stuff, and part of it was Arabic that she couldn't even understand. It was like essentially this whole different rhythm. I mean, if we had only had a tape recorder. Who would've known what new plane he was on, as far as—but like, he was too far gone, it was like he knew he was dead. Probably some of his best writings, his greatest writings, there's still talk of that he had written all this stuff in Ethiopia. The lost notebooks of Rimbaud is one of the greatest sadnesses of my life, you know. They talk about him writing late into the night and nobody knows where the stuff is, 'cause he left it with his servant boy, and his servant boy was killed in the revolution that happened. So there's like really no way of knowing, but an artist doesn't stop, you know. An artist transcends a genre. Does an actress stop being a great actress 'cause she's directing? You know, it's like people are very hung up with that stuff, 'cause they're afraid of change. People got very upset, you know, when they thought I moved into rock 'n' roll and stopped being a poet and started being a rock 'n' roller. But they forget that the first time I ever performed poetry, I was with Lenny and he was playing guitar. The first time I ever experienced speaking poetry was with Lenny. The second time was with Sam Shepard. He was playing drums. I've actually never really experienced poetry without something behind it.

Unidentified: It's always been like a performance art, your written work.

Smith: Yeah. I mean, and like, it just grew. It flowered. It transcended. I mean, to me there's nothing more exciting than change. Sometimes frightening, but infinitely more meaningful, you know.

Kaye: The most salient part of that is that we've never planned our changes. We've always let 'em happen to us. We've never planned what we wanted in the group, we never planned members, we never even directed our sound, just whatever came along, you know? So that was the big—when it was just me and Patti and DNV, our piano player, and it became clear to us after a while that we needed another instrument, and decided to get a guitar player. We had—we went through hundreds of guitar players, 'cause we didn't know what we wanted. These guys would come in and want to be a great boogie guitar player, or be a great jazz genius, you know, whatever. And when Ivan came in the room and played, it suddenly struck us that we didn't have to sort of mold anything artificial to what we do, that we can retain our sound. You know, that we can do what we always do and we don't have to put it into any kind of formula.

Unidentified: Did you have any surprises on this tour? The sort of intensive touring you've been doing here, and sort of going across America.

Smith: What was the question?

Unidentified: Have there been many surprises?

Smith: Every night's a surprise. I mean, every night I'm amazed, you know. I mean, every night I'm still . . . well, every night is different. Some nights, some nights are a total struggle, you know. Some nights are a fight, and you come out winning, and it's great. You have this fantastic feeling of a battle won. Sometimes it's like a Blue Öyster Cult show, where the kids immediately spark up and it's real exciting. The kids scream and you just sail, you know, it's really fantastic. But within ourselves, there's always surprises because we improvise so much. Sometimes we totally blow it, but we blow it and then get on a new rhythm. Some nights, I'll be trying for a stream, but we'll disconnect, and it'll self-destruct, and it'll be like a moment of total pain. You can hear a pin drop. Kids are wondering, "How are they gonna get out of this? They've really blown it. They really fucked up." And usually I run to Lenny. Or I have to get on my knees to one of them. We'll just let anything happen, get ourselves out of the jam, or into a certain kind of ecstasy. I mean, there's always that—

Unidentified: Well, sometimes it's good to sort of embarrass yourselves.

Smith: Well, anything. We don't care. The thing is that to me, performing, worrying about being embarrassed, you just can't worry. When I was younger, all I cared about was being cool. I was very, very into cool, very, very into being cool. That's all I cared about. [*Indistinct question from a journalist.*] What?

Unidentified: Was that like masking your feelings?

Smith: Well, in a way, but not that heavy. I mean, I was like walking good, your image—"hey, man"—just being cool. Dancing in a certain way, it was all . . . And like when I first started, I was always very, very into that *Don't Look Back* syndrome of like being cool, but this is, like, this ain't the '60s anymore. It was in the '60s, it was all being cool and being paranoid and being suspicious, and that was groovy for the '60s. Now we're in, I mean, we're approaching the '80s, now. To me, it's like, *discovery*. What do I care about being cool. Sometimes I blow my cool and then I get into a whole new stream. I mean, does a dervish when he's spinning around worry about blowing his cool by falling on the ground? If he falls on the ground, it's because he's like hit some new bottom, you know? And then he crawls across the floor and then he starts whirling again. I mean, you know, if you worry about being cool all the time, you're gonna cut yourself off from a whole new level of experience. I mean, sure, it's painful sometimes. Sometimes I really blow it and I really feel like an asshole, you know. And I get up. You have to get up again. If Muhammad Ali or if a fighter makes a wrong move, do they sit down on the floor and say, "Well I give up?" You can't. You're under pressure. There's all these people watching. You've got to keep it going, show 'em what's going on and all that kind of stuff.

PATTI SMITH: MISPLACED JOAN OF ARC

Michael Gross | August 1976 | *Blast*

Caffe Reggio, still standing at 119 MacDougal, is a Greenwich Village landmark, a favorite gathering place for Kerouac, Ginsberg and the Beats, Bowie, Dylan, Dalí, and Warhol, rumored to be the first place in New York City to serve cappuccinos. Countless interviews have taken place there, in part for its rich history of nurturing the avant-garde, in part because the place has *ambience*. Michael Gross, a prolific rock writer and editor-in-chief of *Rock* magazine from 1976 to 1977, met Patti Smith there for this evocative conversation in between the release of *Horses* and *Radio Ethiopia*.

Smith goes deep on her early childhood miseducation, from youth gangs to discovering Dylan. She also gives an account of her life with Robert Mapplethorpe in Room 1017 of the Chelsea, the hotel's smallest room, back when the two were hitting the scene at Max's Kansas City hoping for a break. "I was half rock and roll and half literature," Smith said. And like a 1970s New York Rimbaud, she knew how to bring her own rhythm to her dreamlike vision of the city. "I want to make my own mythology," she explained. "I know I'm real good at that." —Ed.

There's a scrawny scarecrow of a girl standing on the stage. Her hair is ragged. Her tits swing slowly to a 4/4 beat under a Rasta t-shirt, over black pegged-legged pants.

The girl has Style. She can out-chameleon Bowie, out-Junkie Keith, out-sultry Ann Margret and out-smolder Dylan. She's black and white rock and roll in all its contrasting glory. Over-hyped by the press, stereotyped by the image makers (that chick from New York who thinks she's Brian Jones) and advertised to death by her record company and still, you know, when the shouting's over, she'll outshine 'em all. At a show in a ratty club on Long Island, Patti is asked "How's Dylan," by a kid in the audience and shouts "fine" in her mike before kicking her "boys" into a new song. She seems to say "I'd rather not bother," but you know she will. Pearls before swine? No, just a new voice commanding an army of cynics. It's her attitude, her conviction that gives her style. It's her talent that keeps her moving. It always has been.

She calls herself a "misplaced Joan of Arc," a bad bicentennial bitch. It's an exercise in exorcism every time she opens her mouth. She says the Bicentennial is America's chance to clean up its act, let the prisoners free. She says Patty Hearst should have a new trial, alone, in a locked room, so she can find out where it's at. She's still uncomfortable on a big stage, asking the lights to be dimmed, talking to the crowd without a mike, thinking it's a club she's in when thousands can't hear her. Stage-shy is appealing. It's as if she's saying, "Help me, this is a two-way street."

Who Is Patti? She's an American Woman. Where does she come from? Listen. She'll tell you.

PLACE: The Reggio Caffe, MacDougal Street, New York.

Also Present: Jane Friedman, Smith's manager.

Tell me your life story.

Everybody has heard it. I don't have much of an imagination. Just ask me the questions, and I'll answer you.

Where did you grow up?

I was born in Chicago. I lived in Chicago for a while and then I went to Tennessee, Chattanooga. Because my granddaddy had a farm there. Then we went to Philadelphia and lived in an Army barracks for a while, and I had a gang in Philadelphia called the COOL CATS—no girls allowed—the only girl allowed in my gang was my sister, Linda. She was the nurse. We used to fight the Irish kids.

Did you have a place where the gang played?

We had two refrigerator boxes. I cut holes in the side of the refrigerator boxes and it had "No Girls Allowed" in big words. What happened was eventually I was the leader of the gang. The guys got hip to the fact that I was a girl—I think their mothers told them I was a girl—and they kicked me out of my own club. The club was called Behind the Green Door. Remember that song, 'The Green Door'? The door was green. They kicked me out of my own club because I was a girl.

Did they let your sister stay?

Yeah, but she was only a nurse. So I wreaked revenge on all of them. I beat the shit out of all of them. I was a regular kid who played Flash Gordon and Giant Squid. I think one of the ways I started to get interested in music and performing was I used to set up a game like 20,000 Leagues Under the Sea. We acted it out and I would be the hero and I would have to wrestle the Giant Squid. That was all play; to get into it, I needed a sound track, so I would make up a sound track. "Don ta da—ooooo—ooooo." I would have all the kids standing there and going "tan-tan-da—da daf" and I would perform my slaying of the Giant Squid. Then we moved to New Jersey, the big turning point to my life. We moved to South Jersey, right near this pig farm, and it was rural. Is that the word, rural?

Yes. Rural.

I'd never lived in a rural area. I always lived in big cities, basically, so it was sort of scary. There were swamps and everything. In fact, one of my friends got caught in a quick mud and almost went down on Easter. There were wild pigs and stuff, but the other thing I didn't know about was I wasn't aware of races. I was sort of slow in certain things. I was about seven or eight years old and I was taking a walk one day. There was a little shanty-town area called "Jericho," and there was all these people living in little space, like living in refrigerator boxes. My club house! They were living there and they kept calling me "white cracker," and I had never seen nothing like that. I didn't know what was happening. I kept going there every day until they stopped. At first they threw stones, and then they threw dirt and then they started getting curious, and I started hanging out with them.

You kept going back and eventually they . . .

Like right now anybody could beat me up but when I was a girl I could really fight. That was a big turning point in my life because where I went to school was almost all black kids, and that's where I learned 3/4 of what I know. Like how to dance good and how to move and my taste for music. It all came out in that period of my life, that eight-year period in South Jersey. By the time I was 16, I was a great dancer.

Was it still Army barracks?

Not anymore. We had this little house. My mother got a Household Finance loan. H.F.C. was always banging on the door, and my mother would say, "Tell them I'm not home," and I would say, "My mommy's in the bathroom—but she's not home." That was a great period of my life because I was learning a thousand rhythms. The school I went to was a real experimental school. It's like a weird school because it was one of these new kind of experimental schools where they sent special children, geniuses. High-strung geniuses whose fathers were head of M.I.T. or something. Retarded kids and lots of Spanish-speaking people. There were a lot of epileptics. It was one of the schools that accepted epileptic children and had a regular program for them, [in] my school nobody was weird. Everybody was special in their own way—so like, you know, I never got a sense of myself being any different than anybody else. I was sort of like a beatnik kid, but so what?

Was this mid-way '50s?

Late '50s, early '60s. I graduated in '64—but, I mean, that was one of the biggest influences in my life, going to the school. It was like New York, but then all South Jersey isn't like that. It was just this school where I was. Then I went to this teacher's college. It wasn't like that anymore, and all of a sudden everybody thought I was weird. I was real naive— I was really a good girl. I didn't curse and I was a virgin and I didn't drink or nothing when I went to college. I was real good, but I got a real bad reputation as a doper and a weirdo. I had these fantasies about New York. Then I got this job in a factory. I worked in this factory in the summer, to get clothes for school. They started giving me a bunch of shit, so they fired me and when they fired you in '63, you didn't get unemployment. I just got the hell out of there with my money: $19.00, think, for two days' pay. I didn't know where to go. I wasn't going to school anymore.

You weren't living at home?

I was sort of bumming around, so I got on a train with my $19.00. I went to New York City and I had nothing with me after I paid my fare.

Back up for a second. When did you first hear Dylan?

My mother was actually responsible. I'd heard all the records like "Freight Train" and *The Times They Are a-Changin'*, but I didn't like protest music. First of all, I didn't like white music. That's how I was. I missed out a lot. I hated the Beatles and the Beach Boys. I like them all now, but I just didn't like that stuff then. I liked James Brown and Marvin Gaye. I thought all that stuff was jive. I really liked Dylan but I couldn't understand why. Then my mother got me this *Another Side of Bob Dylan* album at the supermarket. She said, "Patricia, I thought you would like this fellow because he's wearing all black," and he had a turtle neck and all. I said, "Yeah, I know who this guy is." I put it on and something happened to me. It was like the first time I saw the Rolling Stones. I was totally wiped out. He was having a concert in Forest Hills.

I went up there and then I just sort of kept making money and going back and forth to New York and I was sort of all mixed up when I got to New York. I was so harassed in Jersey. My mother was a waitress, and I would go into the fountain and all they would say was "Who's the weird one?" My mother would be ashamed that it was her daughter and I just couldn't stand it. I would get to New York and nobody would give a shit about me. I was walking around and I felt that I was invisible. It was neat. I mean it was just like I never got paranoid here. Nothing bad has ever happened to me in this city. I never got robbed or mugged or anything and I would walk around at three in the morning. I think it's because I have no fear. It's like when I'm riding in a car. I'm a bad girl. "Go faster!"

So you got to New York.

I was reading all the romantic books about the life of the artists so I went to Pratt, in Brooklyn, where all the art students were. I figured I would find an artist and be his mistress and take care of him. I found this guy, Robert Mapplethorpe. He was about 19. He was real cute and he had hair like yours. He was an artist so I got a job in a bookstore and he taught me. I used to do art, too, but I was sort of shy. I read poetry and I was sort of shy about it. The kids I hung around with in school had to be tough. I was always smart, but you really couldn't show it too much. Basically, you had to just be a good dancer and give your teachers trouble. Then for the first time I was in an environment which was art-oriented. You didn't have to act tough. Those people influenced me a lot. Robert started teaching me because he was going to school. He started teaching me discipline and structure to put my creative stuff in and then what happened? I lived there for a while. Oh, I went to France. That's what happened. I lived there for a couple of years, until I came into a lot of dough. So I took my sister, we are real close, and I took her to Paris. I had all these fantasies about Paris, and that is actually one reason I wanted to sing: Edith Piaf and my idea of street singers and being down and out, that's why. I loved being down and out. I think it's great. I've always had fantasies about being tubercular in a gutter in Paris and Tangier, so I never felt fucked up. I used to sleep in the subways in the city for weeks, but I was always so happy. I thought "Gee, I'm down and out." That's how I was. I thought it was great. I was struggling. I hated the country so much. I like the ocean though. So, anyway, me and Linda went to Paris and we started hanging out with these musicians and we met all these really cool people like jugglers. In '67 and '68 [Charles] de Gaulle was still the president and there was still this real romantic feel about Paris. It's not there no more, it's gone.

I was there during elections, too, and I saw de Gaulle's Last March. So sad. We met all these people and I wore this little black dress and I would sing all these little songs. My sister's real cute. She looks like the newsboy. She wears this old cap and passed the cap. We worked with the fire-eater. We made a lot of dough and then I came back to New York and, while I was in Paris, Robert had become a semi-hustler. He met Jane Friedman and all those Warhol people. We didn't know anybody. I came back from Paris and he said, "I met the people. Now we're going to make it. We're going to make it real fast." This was about *six years ago*. I was starting to get rock and roll fantasies. Actually, what it did was "Light My Fire." I was getting all these things going in my brain but Robert and I decided we wanted to make a lot of dough, so we pooled all our money and we lived in the Chelsea. A little tiny room. All we had was one bed and we had to pile all our stuff on the bed. I don't even know how we lived in it. It is the smallest room in the Chelsea: 1017, it's still there, I'm sure. That's how I met Jane. We were hanging out at Max's [Kansas City]. I said, "I found this place and you have to go there after midnight and you are supposed to just look cool," and I always used to act up a lot. Robert said, "Be cool, just be cool; don't start," because I used to like to do Tex Ritter imitations and funny stuff and it can't be funny. You have to be cool, so me and Robert hung out in Max's every single night until like three in the morning trying to get a big break. I don't even know what we were trying to get a break for. I guess we thought we'd go in the movies. We hung out there every night for about six months and nobody ever said hello to us. We would just sit there and we never had any money. I don't mind telling the story. I think it's real cool, you know? I can remember because when I was on the stage there I got this wave of nostalgia about coming in there all nervous. It's a whole circle. I learned I could go in there looking like a total creep. I'd walk in there and put barrettes in my hair with a pony tail and look like a housewife because it didn't matter. When it mattered, boy did I flash out. I used to wear black corsets and bras and tight black silk skirts. Leather outfits and stuff. I really didn't do nothing but now I work. It is part of the growing up process. It's a phase.

Some people never grow out of it. They are still there every night, sitting and waiting.

That's their whole thing, though—it's like Rona Barrett—only they don't have a TV show. That is what some people do. There are so few people in the world that develop skills. I feel like I'm developing a skill, singing, which takes me out of that bracket. I don't put nobody down for that kind of stuff because I got pleasure out of it for years. I see these new kids coming in and I look at them and I feel a real sense of fondness for them because I know just what they're thinking. You can see that nervousness and that sense of excitement. I can almost tell which girl's a virgin or which girl just lost it or which guys are going to lose it to what guys. What else? New question.

When did you first start thinking about performing?

Well I've been performing all my . . . I am basically a show-off. I was a show-off until I learned a skill. I always performed. I performed at school, after detention. You waited for the detention bus. I used to do acts. I always entertained my friends, that's how I got to be popular. I wasn't the best-looking kid in the world. Like I really did do a great Tex Ritter imitation—that was my claim to fame. When I was 14 years old, every-body in South Jersey knew about my Tex Ritter imitation. It's true. And then I was in a couple of La MaMa plays and I used to always act tough.

How long ago were you in those plays?

Five years ago. I played a gun moll. I didn't know nobody there. I just did my job, you know. I don't like to get to know theatre people. All I care about in the theatre is the stage. I used to want to be a school teacher, because you always have an instant audience. I didn't start really performing or nothing until February 10, 1971. I remember it real good because February 10th is Bertolt Brecht's birthday. Oh, I know what it was, I was writing a lot of poetry then, a real rhythmatic kind of poetry. I met Bobby Neuwirth and he really loved the poetry. To me he was a real hot shit. *Don't Look Back* and all that, and I was really in love with him. I thought he was the classiest, sexiest guy. I'll tell you. It was 1970 and that guy had dark glasses. I just loved guys in dark glasses. He was one of the few. He could really sport dark glasses. Bobby started me out . . . tried to inspire me with the poetry. He built up my confidence.

Treated me like a prodigy. He'd say, "Don't treat Patti Lee like a groupie, she's a poet." I never got laid because people don't think poets fuck. He taught me how to drink tequila, too. I got in my rock and roll period then 'cause I was hanging around his friends. Janis Joplin was alive then and Hendrix was around. I lived at the Chelsea and every night was a fuckin' party. Someone was always fighting or Nico was slashing some person. I got into that.

Did it keep up that way?

I met a playwright, Sam Shepard. He was a writer and a drummer. He was an inspiration to me. He was real rhythm-oriented, too. We pooled our resources and wrote some plays and all that shit. Men give me a lot of confidence. If I have a man who believes in me and pushes me, I can do anything. I'm just that kind of girl, y'know. If I'm protected I feel good. I got this poetry reading at Saint Marks. I was half rock and roll and half literature. I never thought I was a real literary poet. So that's how music got in. Lenny Kaye came along and he was real sympathetic. I did this show and it was real cool. I did this stuff about boys in stock cars and Jesse James's women. Everyone really liked it and I've been lucky cause everyone's given me the confidence. I've been like the rock writer's little bird. People that came to all my shows weren't really normal audiences. It was people like managers and rock stars and it gave me a lot of confidence.

Then came the record contract?

That was two years ago and since then it's been homogenizing the energy. When Jane found me two years ago I was onstage alone with a toy piano. I used to do a lot of cosmic-starry-eyed-motherfucker-poetry which was sort of teenage, but Jane knew I'd go through all the changes. Even though I'm sort of old, I'm a real late bloomer. I mean, I could be 18. I'm good when someone lets me go through all my stuff and lets me find out. In the process of finding out what was right and what was wrong, I learned a skill, singing, and when you got a skill, nobody can take that away from you.

What about image?

I created all my own images and my own thoughts. I want to make my own mythology. I know I'm real good at that. It's one of the things I do best. Nobody's gonna tell me I could be a great leather queen. I know what I'm great at. I need people to give me confidence, not tear me apart. Like Alfalfa. The teacher never told him he had a bad voice . . . she told him, "You're great, you sing real loud." It was terrible, but at least he felt good. Like Trudeau said, "I trust the universe is unfolding as planned." [*Canadian Prime Minister Pierre Trudeau quoted poet Max Ehrmann's "Desiderata" on election night in 1972 when he went to bed believing he had lost, only to discover the next morning that he had eked out a minority victory —Ed.*]

PATTI SMITH: PATTI CRACKS NOGGIN, RAPS ON REGARDLESS

Vivien Goldman | February 5, 1977 | *Sounds*

Most of the interviews in this book were live in person, but this short and sweet conversation took place over the phone—the reason being that Patti Smith was badly injured. On January 23, 1977, she was on stage in Tampa opening for Bob Seger, "spinning like a dervish," and spun herself right off the stage, fracturing several vertebrae in her neck. Less than two weeks into her recovery in bed, Smith was in good spirits, having "seen the angel of death" and won. *Radio Ethiopia* was behind her, but *Easter* was on the way, and Smith was ready for a resurrection.

    Vivien Goldman was still at the beginning of her career, first as a rock journalist for *Cassettes and Cartridges*, then doing marketing for artists including McCoy Tyner at Transatlantic Records, then as features editor of the London-based magazine *Sounds*. By the end of the '70s, Smith would be a touchstone for Goldman's own acts of feminist punk defiance as an architect of post-punk, part of the new wave with duo Chantage and as a member of the avant-garde collective the Flying Lizards. Later on, she became an academic and scholar of punk, Afrobeat, and reggae, bringing the spirit of revolt to NYU; the BBC affectionately dubbed her the "Punk Professor." But none of this had happened yet back in 1977 when the phone rang. —Ed.

Patti sounds plaintive, fragile, over the transatlantic wire. If you can imagine a voice sounding wan, you're near the mark. Reason being—"A swan dive. And there wasn't a pot to catch me." Rock's Queen Poetess dove off a 14-foot-high stage in Tampa, Florida at a gig in a huge amphi-theatre. Being a support act, the band hadn't received adequate time to get used to the dimensions of the stage. . . . "I didn't have my terrain worked out. Like, it was a new situation for us, a new stage set up. But I have all my faculties together."

But there you go, despite broken vertebrae in her neck, a cast separat-ing head from shoulders, and the prospect of eight weeks in bed, things could be worse. For a start, it sounds as if Patti's the centre of much love and affection. Her brother Todd jumped straight down the 14' drop onto the concrete after her, so from the moment she hit ground she wasn't alone. Her boyfriend Allen Lanier is with her, and when he has to go on the road with the Blue Oyster Cult again, the guys in the Smith band are rallying round in shifts to keep her company.

"I'm so *lucky,*" she kept repeating, "the doctors can't *believe* it! 'N I feel just like the Field Marshall, down in the line of duty. I know I'll be standin' soon, and in the meantime, just tell the troops to keep fightin' . . ."

Patti asked me what I was wearing. She told me that she was lying in bed wearing an Ethiopian blanket, a grey sombrero, and her neck brace.

"And 22 stitches in my head. But I got a hard head.

"I feel like I've done it. I've seen the angel of death, and wrestled with it. Maybe the other guys wrestled and lost and I won . . . it hap-pened when I was spinning like a dervish—you've seen me do that—and just as I stopped spinning, I reached for the mike, and just went off the stage. It was the most amazing thing that's happened to me. I'm like the kind of performer that courts risk, I court death, but the way I kept it together was totally relaxed. I saw, like a spiral tunnel of light, and I felt my consciousness draining through it.

"I felt myself going and I said—GET BACK HERE! I gripped my consciousness by the throat . . . the biggest battle was in my head, and I won.

"This is all physical shit, I can handle that. And the mental shit is all fine. I'm really happy to be alive, it's great. And, y'know, when they put those 22 stitches in my head, they couldn't use an anaesthetic, so

I just, like, pretended it was the Civil War, y'know? I pretended I was Robert E. Lee.

"You know how Lenny found out I was alive? I'd just written a poem for Tapper Zukie, it's called 'Tapper the Extractor.' It's the best poem I've written for a real long time. Tapper's poem kept me from losing consciousness, it's all about 'the thread of return'—tell him I'm gonna be sending it to him over the weekend, Lenny's coming over later to type it out for me. Yeah, the thread of return kept me here."

Patti's also happy that Ivan Kral is back playing piano with the band. The family's back together again. They've had a coupla weird incidents, like being banned from Boston and New York radio just the same time as the Pistols had their spot of media trouble, cos Patti said "fuck" on the airwaves. Now kids are picketing the stations to get them to play Patti's discs again. . . .

"This thing has brought us back together, and when I'm up we'll be stronger than ever, WE'RE GONNA COME ON LIKE TANKS!"

DELICATE DELINQUENT

Legs McNeil (Transcribed by Steve Taylor) | February 1977 | *Punk*

It was the summer of 1976, and twenty-year-old punk chronicler Legs McNeil was at the legendary Record Plant Studios at 321 West 44th Street, where Patti Smith was recording her much-anticipated follow-up to *Horses*. McNeil takes us behind the scenes with the entire Patti Smith Group and legendary producer Jack Douglas, fresh off the release of Aerosmith's *Rocks*. It was published a few months after the album, *Radio Ethiopia*, was released to mixed reviews. Appearing in the February 1977 *Punk*, only its seventh issue, this interview captures the manic energy that went into the making of the album.

To truly experience *Punk*, you have to see the original. So much of what made *Punk* punk was its aesthetic—its irreverent illustrations by cofounder John Holmstrom, Peter Bagge, and Bobby London; its handwritten, comic book–style text; its gonzo photos where you can almost feel the sweat; and its overall punk energy. Holmstrom called the magazine the "print edition of the Ramones," and it turned the dial up to eleven, helping define the subculture it enlivened. The covers alone were defining—Frankenstein Lou Reed in the first issue; Joey Ramone in the third; rabid Monkees in the fifth. Smith was on the cover of this one, headbanging and strumming an air guitar. Holmstrom has preserved some of the magazine's gritty glory in *The Best of Punk Magazine* (It Books, 2011), a coffee-table book with full reproductions, but this interview is not included.

When Smith's green-sleeved twenty-year-old interlocutor came down to the studio, she and the group had fun taking the piss out of him as they tried to guess his first name in a punk game of Rumpelstiltskin. McNeil was twenty years away from publishing *Please Kill Me: The Uncensored Oral History of Punk*, his and Gillian McCain's essential telling of the punk story from the perspective of the people who lived it. Smith declined to be interviewed for that book. But in the '70s, she was more open to *Punk*. This interview was originally published opposite Smith's "translation of W. B. Yeats poem Crazy Jane and the Bishop ['Crazy Jane Talks with the Bishop'] from English to future century American." Smith calls herself a "delinquent debutante," inspiring the piece's title. Yarns are spun and liberties taken, but there is a deeper truth in the hazy atmosphere. "Why should you read interviews?" Smith asks McNeil. "I never read interviews. I look at the pictures!" The pictures aren't here, but this one's worth reading. —Ed.

Starring: Patti Smith, Legs McNeil, Lenny the Kaye, Richard DNV (Death in Venice) Sohl and Jack Douglas.

Transcribed by Steve Taylor"

Legs is very nervous and has a lot of trouble getting tape recorder to work—Jack Douglas has to fix it.

Noise of tape recorder being started.

Patti – Yeah, . . . y'know, y'know Jack . . .

Lenny – How's the tape recorder, Legs?

Legs – It's O.K., it's workin'!

Lenny – Yay!

Male voice – Okay Jay? (In the background we can hear Jay Daugherty drumming around)

Jack – Awright it's gonna be acoustic guitar turning (indistinguishable)

Patti – What?

Jack – Acoustic guitar . . . Fender Rhodes . . . Stereo . . .

Patti – He's gonna play acoustic . . . guitar?

Jack – Acoustic guitar, yeah . . . on the basic he says he wants to overdub the other stuff.

Patti – Oh, no no no no no no no no, there's no basic track for this song, you tell him to play . . .

Voice – Wow! It could be really neat, I mean if he plays lead and rhythm with the acoustic.

Patti – I know . . . but the thing is . . . is that . . . we're . . . it's supposed ta . . . we have no structure for this song.

Lenny – Yeah, right, he knows that.

Patti – No . . . it's like . . .

Lenny – Y'think he's gonna screw around with the acoustic.

Patti – . . . Because he wants to put a boring rhythm guitar part and he's gonna think out this . . . and he's gonna—

Jack – Well, let's see then.

Patti – I know what he's gonna do . . . it . . . because it's . . . how'm I s'pose ta improvise. . . .

(Patti's voice goes off mic. Drumming and noise in background, humming, Donald Duck noises)

A Voice – Hello little Panasonic . . . you on?

Lenny – What do you think the guiding philosophy of your magazine is?

Legs – What?

Lenny – What's the guiding philosophy of your magazine.

Legs – We don't know what we're doin' . . . so . . . y'know . . . We keep goin' . . . ta do somethin'!

DNV – That's cool.

Legs – I dunno.

DNV – We don't know what we're doin' either.

Lenny – How'd you get the name "Legs"?

Legs – Uh . . . we were drinkin' in the car . . . y'know . . . we were drivin' around . . . I'd just did a movie for . . . a promotional film for this school for retarded . . . so uhm . . . we were drivin' back from signin' the contract, we were all drunk . . . and uh . . . so y'know, we're all dru . . . . and we were fantasizin' about . . . and . . . uh . . . that's where I came up with the name . . . I named it. *Punk.*

DNV – I'm talkin' about "Legs" y'know.

Legs – Well . . . that . . . we were sayin' . . . y'know . . . we were . . . I thought . . . y'know . . . yeah, if we call it punk we would be like gangsters—

DNV – How long have you been called Legs?

Legs – Well . . . is thinkin' . . . uh . . . something' like Bugsy, y'know.

Lenny – What's Holmstrom's name?

Legs – What?

Lenny – "Arms."

Legs – (Laughing) No . . .

Lenny – "Heads."

DNV – Hey, man . . .

Legs – Right!

DNV – Look at these pecs! They should call you "Pecs."

(Silence)

Legs – John just said . . . why no— . . . y'know . . . why not call you "Legs" . . . I thought it was funny 'cause it had no meaning at all. . . .

Lenny – What's your real name?

Legs – Ed.

Lenny – Ed?

Legs – Yeah. (Laughter)

Lenny – Edward?

Legs – Yeah . . . well . . . I dunno. I've had lotsa names.

DNV – What's your middle name?

Legs – Edward.

DNV – Edward Edward?

Lenny – Edward's your middle name too.

Legs – What . . . no . . . uh . . .

DNV – What . . . wha . . . wha—

Legs – Wha . . .

Lenny – "Will."

Legs – What?

Lenny – "Ed Will" is your name.

Legs – No, no—I have another first name . . . but . . . uh . . .

Lenny – Aww, c'mon, man, tell us, man!

Legs – Naw—no one knows that.

Lenny – Mergetroid?

Legs – No . . . no . . . it's worse than that!

Lenny – Randy!

DNV – Aloysius—

Lenny – Sandy!

Legs – No . . . don't try to get . . . 'cause yer not . . . ya won't get it outta me!

DNV – C'mon . . . c'mon, man. Tell us . . . please . . . please?

Legs – No one knows it. There's like three people in New York City that know it.

DNV – Who?

Legs – What?

DNV – Who knows it?

Lenny – How 'bout if we know it, how much'll you pay us not to reveal it?

Legs – Why? You know it?

Lenny – Maybe I do.

DNV – Maybe he doesn't.

Legs – No . . . you're not gonna fool me . . . you're not gonna . . .

Lenny – I . . . I know it, "Legs."

Legs: You do??

Lenny – I looked at your whole . . . we had a dossier on you put together.

Legs – Naw!

Lenny – Yeah! . . . to see whether you're . . . part of the problem or part of the solution.

Legs – Oh yeah? And what am I?

Lenny – Well, I don't know, that might . . . involve revealing your real first name!

(Long pause)

DNV – Go ahead, Lenny . . . tell 'im!!

Lenny – No.

DNV – It's (*Bleep!*) God . . . I don't believe it!

Legs – Is . . . uh . . . Aerosmith . . . playing . . . on-on . . . any . . . on this album?

Patti – (Who has returned from wherever she went) What??

(Lenny and DNV laugh)

Legs – Somebody told me to ask you . . . that . . . if . . . whether Aerosmith was playing on this album . . .

Patti – Ain't no fuckin' Aerosmith on the record whaduhya talkin' about, is Aerosmith . . . I . . . we . . . we're ourselves—

Lenny – Yeah . . .

Patti – Would you ask Aerosmith if, if, if, . . . uh—Blue Öyster Cult was playin' on their record . . . I mean . . .

Legs – Don't yell at me! They told me ta ask you! Y'know I didn't wanna ask ya!

Lenny – Who told ya ta ask us?

Patti – It's a stupid question.

Legs – Yeah it is. I agree.

Patti – I mean, they can't even . . . uh . . . my boys play better than Aerosmith. What do I need Aerosmith for?

Lenny – Awright!

Patti – We've Aerosmith's producer.

Legs – Oh. Okay.

DNV – Can you sing better than Little Stevie?

Patti – Except whatsisname . . . Stevie Tyler . . . Steve . . . oh I thought it was Stevie Paley . . . I was thinkin' of yer . . . of another one. . . .

Legs – Do you have a potato chip on ya? Anybody gotta potato chip on 'em?

DNV – No, but I gotta goober!

(Laughter)

Patti – Now, yuh . . . Legs—ya have ta turn yer tape recorder off while they're . . . while we're workin'.

Legs – Are they . . . are you starting to work now?

Patti – No, but, wh-when I leave . . . then . . . I mean . . . nothin's happenin' . . . you can ask—yer questions.

Legs – Did you really get beat up in the ladies' room of the . . . did you work in a pipe factory?

(Laughter)

Patti – No, I lied all 150 times I said that every time . . . every single time. A writer came in across . . . the . . . America 'n' asked me the same fuckin' question I th— . . . I . . . I . . . consistently lied.

Legs – Oh.

Patti – Never happened. I've never worked in a factory I . . . I'm—actually I had my coming out . . . (laughter) in Washington, D.C., my father's an admiral, I'm like a . . . I'm, I'm a delinquent debutante.

Legs – Didja really get beat up??!

Patti – No, man. I'm a delinquent deb . . . I've never been beat up, 'n' I've never been hit, I've never had a bruise, . . .

Jack – Playin' the Rhodes—

Legs – I used to work in a hypodermic needle factory.

Jack – Set up the vibrato the way you want it, O.K.?

DNV – Does she want vibrato?

Jack – Yeah, even if it's real soft.

Legs – What's the, uh, album about . . . what's on it?

Patti – Oh, it's, um, it's all, it's a . . . it's a . . . uhm . . . the album is . . . uh . . . mostly a . . . uh. . . protest against the, uh . . . against the . . . the, uh . . . burning of the poppy fields in Taiwan and—uh—where else . . . Istanbul.

Legs – In China?

Patti – Istanbul . . . no . . . burning of the poppy fields—

Legs – Yeah.

Lenny – I have ta smoke some (obscured) for this one.

Patti – All right.

Lenny – Have ta wig out! What's—what's— (Off)

Patti – (Snapping fingers) I—I—I, I knew Ivan . . . I knew I just knew . . . I just knew it!

Legs – Wh—what's the song "Chiklets" about?

Patti – It's about Alexander the Great's coke dealer.

Legs – What are some of the other songs on the album?

Patti – There's a song . . . uhm . . . lemme see what it sez. There's a song about this girl in Haight-Ashbury . . . that got run over on the strip . . . she was thirteen years old 'n' she was on acid 'n' she got run over by . . . a . . . uh—black Corvette Stingray . . . there's another song about . . . uhm.

Legs – Didja know her?

Patti – No . . . y'know . . . she was like the "groovy" of New York. . . . Remember when groovy . . . yer probly too young . . .

Legs – Yeah.

Patti – But this kid "Groovy" got in a basement—

Legs – I read about that in a book in high school . . . in English.

Patti – Yeah—that's a true story . . . yeah. (Laughter) She was like the "Groovy" of the strip . . . this girl that I'm talkin' about was named Angel and she . . . like . . . had this thing that angels were callin' her and like Andrea . . . Andrea Whipps . . . she had this vision that angels were callin' . . . she just walked right into this Ferrari.

Legs – Yeah? Were you hangin' around then, when all that stuff was goin' on?

Patti – I wuz a world correspondent.

Legs – Oh, yeah? For who?

Patti – (Laughing) *Rock Scene* . . . alright . . . remember that magazine "Eye."

Legs – Yeah.

Patti – Yeah, "Eye" . . . "Eye" . . . "Eye" . . . E-Y-E.

Legs – What else?

Patti – What else is on the album?

Legs – Yeah.

Patti – I don't know. We haven't made it yet. (Long pause). There's a song appealing to youth of America to buy Getty Oil. (Laughter) I dunno. (To Jack Douglas) You know what the first question he asked? "Is Aerosmith playing on this album?" (Laughter)

Legs – I—y'know—they told me ta come up here and ask you this!

Patti – They did? Y'know what they were tryin' . . . they wanted you ta' get abused. That's why they told ya that . . . that was a stupid question and whoever gave it to you wanted to see you abused . . . 'cause if I was in a bad mood . . . if I was like really feelin' . . . I . . . I . . . was . . . like . . . really . . . like tombstone teeth [*"Tombstone teeth" refers to a line in "Chiklets," a bonus track on the 1996* Radio Ethiopia *reissue. —Ed.*], you'd be out on yer ass!!

Lenny – Who's "they."

Legs – I dunno.

(Laughter)

Patti – But yer lucky I like ya' mostly 'cuz ya remind me of Richard Meltzer. . . . Now there was a boy. . . . Doesn't he remind you of a young Richard Meltzer?

Lenny – Yeah.

Patti – You should wear a baseball cap.

Lenny – Tim Considine on *My Three Sons*

(Laughter)

Patti – Y'should wear a baseball cap. First time I ever met Richard Meltzer I was workin' at Scribner's book store.

Jack – Where can I get this magazine with the hot pictures?

(The infamous *Daily Planet* nude shots of Patti)

Patti – Oh . . . ya wanna see 'em, Jack?

Jack – Oh, yeah! Sure!

Patti – Jack, what'd ya— what d'ya wanna see pictures o' me . . . when ya got the real thing right here?

Legs – Patti, what's happenin' with that?

Patti – With what?

Legs – With that . . . y'gonna sue 'em or somethin'?

Patti – Yeah, we're gonna sue 'em.

Legs – D'you think they'll ever come out again?

Patti – Well, we're gonna sue 'em or if . . . if nothin' happens all I'll do is wait for about ten years and one day that guy's gonna . . . turn . . .

Lenny – Send some a' yer mob after 'im.

Patti – In about ten years . . . I'll be cool about it, but one day that guy's gonna turn the wrong corner.

Lenny – Right on!!

(Laughter)

Legs – Can I quote you?

Patti – Have one less . . . yeah—well, I'm sayin' it, ain't I? . . . one less chance of bliss. I mean, y'know, I don't give a shit, I mean I ain't ashamed of my body, y'know. It's just that guy was, I mean he was a bastard, y'know? I mean, I—I'm an artist's model, man—I'm not ashamed of my body. I—I've posed nude for a lotta great artists. It's just . . . the guy was an exploitative sh— . . . the only reason that I don't . . . that I'd . . . I—I chose not ta see those pictures wuz outta respect for my old man, y'know? I mean y'know?

Legs – What's that?

Patti – At's my boyfriend Allen Lanier— ♪ da duh dah da! ♪ (Much laughter) And he's in the Blue Öyster Cult.

DNV – I'm proud of ya, Patti!

Jack – Is that tape runnin' 'cause he wouldn't believe it.

Patti – He's in the Blue Öyster Cult!

Lenny – Yeah!

DNV – Awright awright awright!!

Legs – Yeah . . . you used to . . . you did some on their—

Patti – Best rock 'n' roll band . . . American rock 'n' roll band—

Lenny – Amen!

Patti – Without a girl singer.

Lenny – So very much is at stake!

(Laughter)

Legs – D'you like that song Helen Wheels did for them?

Patti – What song—"Sinful Love"?

Legs – Yeah.

Patti – It's a great song—mostly 'cause it's gotta great drum . . . good drummin'!

Lenny – !! (Yells something affirmative about Albert Bouchard) !!

Patti – Actually it's got good words. . . . It's got good words. I know—I know why yer askin'. Supposed ta be about me. . . . But it's not really about me—it's prob'ly about . . . it's about, uhm, what'shername, Shirley Temple. . . . (Laughter.) I-I don't care who it's about if it's gotta good basic track. . . .

Jack – What's that static?

Legs – Oh, sorry, would you, . . . uh, would you act . . . ya hafta excuse me . . . 'cause I don't read a lot . . . I'd rather watch T.V.

Patti – (Laughing) You're excused . . . Should we excuse him?

Legs – Well, I don', . . . y'know, . . . like I ra—y'know ya' think, uh, I mean, I don't read I watch T.V., y'know.

Patti – Why, why do ya hafta read? What are ya talkin' about?

Legs – Well, y'know, it, all the other . . . I mean I don't read interviews y'know.

Patti – I don't, like . . . why should you read interviews?

Legs – Well—

Patti – I never read interviews. I look at the pictures!

Legs – I was gonna ask you about "Piss Factory," but I thought you were gonna start yellin' at me because, uh, in every other interview, you prob'ly say . . .

Patti – I just don't feel like talkin' about tha stuff, y'know? . . . It's just like old . . . it's like we did "Piss Factory" two years ago.

Legs – D'you watch T.V.?

Patti – No, I watch it but I turn the sound down.

Legs – Oh yeah?!

Patti – Turn the sound down and . . .

Note – From here on in a great deal of the conversation is obscured by the sounds of the acoustic guitar and drumming which is being piped through the control room speakers—it's a pity because most of what can be heard sounds rather interesting although not terribly important—some of the more notable remarks by Ms. Smith include something about a fellow who she describes as a celestial Jerseyite—from whom a great deal of inspiration has come and been introduced into the making of *Radio Ethiopia*. Much more is obscured and too bad as both Mr. McNeil and Ms. Smith seem at the peak of animation in their dialogue. Ms. Smith endeavors to enlighten Mr. McNeil by giving him a brief but concise clarification of the word "Fresco" all of which somehow escapes Mr. McNeil who can seemingly only relate it to a soft drink.

We then hear a discussion on an individual whose foremost contribution artwise would seem to be encasing dead animals in jello—in his refrigerator—Patti describes him as a great Dadaist. Mr. McNeil is obviously thrilled to hear a word that he can relate to. Dada's not clear but at least it's hip.

Everything else is all but indistinguishable except a small bit at the end where Patti says what a great honor it is to make a record and how terrible it is that thousands of recordings containing so much uncommitted garbage come out each month and how she resents it and a whole bunch of bullshit like that.

OFF ART!

Love, Steve

ZIGZAG ARTICLES

John Tobler | April and June 1978 | *ZigZag*

ZigZag magazine cofounder John Tobler met Patti Smith in London in October 1977 when she was in Europe for a poetry reading in honor of Arthur Rimbaud, who was born October 20. Elvis had just died that August, and Smith reflected on what it meant for rock 'n' roll now that "the King is dead." Part sneer and part sublimity, Smith ping-ponged between pithy one-liners and reflections on mortality in the interview, which would be published in two parts across *ZigZag*'s April and June issues.

She had finally recovered from the accident that left her bedridden and unable to perform for most of 1977, and the trip was a trial run for a more strenuous European tour in the spring of 1978 in support of her as-yet-to-be-recorded new album. That album was *Easter*; she already had the title, which she explains here. The accident had threatened to derail her career, but she bounced back and was "more crazy than ever," she said. "If God wants me he's gonna wait until I have a platinum record." *Easter* didn't quite go platinum, but it did go gold in France. —Ed.

Horse Latitudes: The Possession of Patti Smith

This interview with Patti Smith took place last October when she stopped off in London for a day en route for Europe. We were saving it to coincide with her recent British visit. Trouble is, the mag's late (as usual) and she's been and gone—that's the trouble with being a monthly. So we ain't gonna give you an account of the tour, 'cos you've probably read about it already in the fun-loving music papers. Just this interview, which sees

Patti in high spirits—her October European jaunt was a sort of trial run to see if she'd be fit to do the tour she's just done, and it was working out okay. S'not dated—she talks about her fall, her new book and talks at length about some scary experiences she's had with her dead heroes Jim Morrison and Jimi Hendrix (shudder). Read on. . . .

Your accident was in January and it seems to have taken a long time for you to get over it—was it more serious than you first thought?

Yeah, well what happened was pretty serious. I broke a lot of vertebrae in my neck and stuff, and I hate to reveal this but the reason that didn't seem serious was when I talked to all the press I was pretty drugged out by doctors, and I was feeling great. I was lying there and I was in a cast and in a brace and in traction, on the phone telling everybody, "Oh yeah, I'm feeling great, I'll be back." And Germany was calling up and asking me if I was gonna be able to tour and I couldn't move and I was saying, "Yeah, everything's cool, I'll be in Germany in a couple of weeks." I got my agents and everybody in a lot of trouble 'cos I was feeling great; meanwhile I couldn't even get out of bed. Also I'd never been injured before, so I didn't understand. To me it was like having the chicken pox. It was a lot worse than I thought, but a lot less worse than my doctors said. They gave me a year and half, but it's only taken me eight months, and like I told the kids—"out of traction, back in action"—that's how it looks.

Is it going to affect your performance—are you gonna be more careful in future?

Well, it's a double answer. The one good thing that happened is that I had to go through real rigorous physical therapy so I could perform again, and in the process of doing that I got stronger; my mind is sharper, I got more disciplined, I'm like ten times stronger than I was before my accident. I'm almost glad that it happened. We did a trial run—we called it basic training. We did nine nights at CBGBs to get me back in the rhythm of things and I thought, "Well, I'm gonna get more conservative, I'm gonna be cooler," . . . and I don't know if I'm sorry to report that I'm more crazy than ever. I got on the stage, plugged in my amp, grabbed my guitar, and immediately raped my guitar, immediately kicked in my amplifier, immediately was jumping out. I didn't do everything good at first, but every night I got stronger and I feel crazier now than ever. The strength I now have compensates for the mania I've developed. I didn't learn my lesson.

It must have been really hard for you during that eight months—like you couldn't go out.

It was a really great period for me. I'd been touring so hard that I'd never had a chance to sit down and look at myself and what I was doing. I was able to clean up a lot of loose ends and best of all, I wrote a book—which I'm real proud of—and I think it'll be an inspiring book, and I worked on my drawings for my gallery. I was able to do a lot of work I hadn't been able to do for a long time. And also I had some trouble with my hands—I worked on special physical therapy, I had to keep my hands moving constantly—so I started working on piano, and it's great, it's like I've found a whole new world of expression—and I hate to say it, but I feel like a punk Puccini!

You said you wrote a book, but you've written lots of books before, haven't you?

Yeah, but the other books were like very spontaneous efforts, which I did, like, in '71. I did one in '71 and one in '72, but I haven't published anything since early '73, because I was so intensely involved in perform- ing and verbal expression that I lost contact with the word on paper, and, like, this book is entirely different. Firstly, it's mostly prose pieces, they're longer and there's much more voyage, my early works were very sporadic and very rhythmic, and I found . . . actually, I had a big chal- lenge, because a lot of kids write to me and send me their poetry. I get about three or four hundred poems a week, and a lot of them seem to be inspired by my early work, and, in fact, they're doing better work than I did, which I'm really happy about, but, having a little bit of Jesse James in me . . . I mean, I immediately got competitive, and had to try and work harder. I had to extend myself because I'm really proud of the fact that I was able to inspire people to do better work than I did, but,

I thought, on the other hand, that meant I had to take . . . part of the responsibility of being a potential leader is to try to keep moving one faster than the people, so then they catch up with you, then you have to leap beyond them, and I think that this book will give them new territory, new fields, plus I just think it's . . . I wrote a lot of it in a very unusual state of mind, because I had special prescriptions from doctors, so I think that it's, um . . . it deals with a very subliminal landscape.

There's a number of names that you've variously reported you're very keen on and, one of the things about many of these people is that all of them died before they were 30—this has been said to you before, I'm sure. We're talking about Brian Jones, Hendrix, Jim Morrison, Rimbaud . . . why do you think it is? Do you think they had the desire to destroy themselves?

No, I think . . . first of all I would like to clarify that I don't love these people 'cos they're dead. I've a great fondness for life, which I think that my present state of being would suggest, but I think it's because these people, not because they desired to destroy themselves—I don't think any of them were self-destructive, but I think they desired to communicate with higher beings, whether it be the angels, whether it be gods, but they desired to communicate so fast, so hard and didn't pace themselves. It was their desire to communicate with all that's celestial, not their desire to excommunicate. I mean, trying to communicate with God on Earth is a very dangerous thing. I won't get really mystical with you unless you're interested. . . .

I'm interested, in view of the amount of blasphemy that appears on your records.

Well, I mean, trying to communicate with God . . . I spent all my life as a child . . . I mean, God has always been my biggest hero and the person I've sought the strongest to communicate with, but I'm earthbound. I'm an earth person, and I desire to communicate in the flesh. I feel very pissed off about the fact that he sent Jesus around back then. Why not now? He's the kind of guy I really could get into, you know.

Don't you believe in the Second Coming, which is scheduled for soon?

Well, I also have been notified that the Second Coming might be female!

Who told you?

Aah, Joan of Arc isn't the only one who hears voices, you know! But . . .
I've learned a lot from those people. Even my fall . . . one of the reasons
I fell was for the same thing. I wasn't spaced-out, or a mess, or stoned
out. I was strong, intense. I was doing my most intense number, "Ain't It
Strange," which is a song where I directly challenge God to talk to me in
some way. It's after a part where I spin like a dervish and I say, "Hand of
God, I feel the finger, Hand of God I start to whirl, Hand of God I don't
get dizzy, Hand of God I do not fall now." But I fell. But I think one of
the reasons that this happened to me is because I was seeking, just like
these other people are seeking, for very intense communication, but not
in a disciplined fashion. I've no desire to join these guys in heaven, I've
work to do right here and I'm not going to stop communicating with
God. It's just that I'm calling to collect next time! [*It seems the meaning
here was in fact "calling collect." —Ed.*]

*Do you think He was actually saying: "You say 'I'm not falling,' hey you
watch it!"?*

I think that . . . I mean, if I wanna really get in that frame of mind I
would say that he called my bluff. It seems strange to talk about it now
'cos it was a long time ago, but I was losing consciousness, I was going
through a tunnel, I felt like a warm flood of light, I felt that the whole
sense . . . having what you read about in Freudian books and stuff, the
great hand pulling me in. It was exactly like being inside the black tube
that I talk about in *Horses*. In *Horses* [*specifically in "Land" —Ed.*] I
was investigating the death of Hendrix. It says, "How did I die? I tried
to walk through light." Well, when I fell, I felt myself losing consciousness and walking through light, and I said to myself, "This is it Patti,
this is when you make your decision whether you're gonna go, whether
you're gonna stay." Well, perhaps all these people had this chance, perhaps Hendrix, perhaps Morrison had the chance, and maybe their life
was so painful that they chose to go, but I have a really great life and I
really love Earth. I have no bitterness and I have no sorrow . . . I love
my work and I think that I have a lot of important work to do. Perhaps
these people peaked or felt that they'd said everything that they could

on Earth and they wanted to release themselves to a higher energy . . . but I'm not done yet, I'm far from done.

Do you think Jim Morrison's dead, 'cos I don't?

I've a real weird feeling about Jim. It's like . . . it's real hard to talk about 'cos I feel like we're talking about all these deep moody subjects and I'm in the middle of feeling very ecstatic and alive, but, being as you're asking I'll try and talk about them best I can, but . . . I have a real weird thing about Jim Morrison, it's hard for me to talk about. . . . I've been to his grave several times. I've been to other people's graves where I've felt they were there. . . . I know Brian Jones is dead, I feel his death, I know that he has gone someplace, I know Hendrix has gone to some high place, but if Jim Morrison isn't dead he's in a hell of a purgatory because I really feel his presence. In fact, I had a very horrifying experience when we were touring. We were in Paris at the Pavilion . . . the slaughterhouse . . . and as we were going into "Horses" . . . and, of course, I can't not think of Jim when I'm in Paris . . . and I realised I was in the slaughterhouse for horses, and I was gonna do "Horses," and then I remembered "Horse Latitudes," so I sort of went into a drift, going into the leather raft carrying the to-be-slaughtered-horses of "Horse Latitudes," and then I got a really weird feeling that I was being taken over, and I started crying, and my voice has changed. I don't care what anybody says, I don't care if they think I'm full of shit, first it happened to me in the studio when we were doing *Radio Ethiopia.* If you listen to "Poppies," there's several voices, voiceovers like on "Horses." There's one voice that came out of my mouth that scared me, 'cos it's not . . . I'm like a little 100-pound girl, you know, I just like, "if you wanna go, go, if you wanna see, if you wanna go as far as me you must look God in the face. I'll adjust. I'll adjust God. God, he's just another outer-space man, he's just a movie star," but the voice in it sounds just like Hendrix, and I felt just like I was being taken over. It scared me. I don't scare easy, believe me. Even after I fell the first thing I was doing was instructing my band they were not to go with Linda Ronstadt. I was already giving orders . . . but that scared me. When I was performing in Paris I had a really weird feeling that Jim was there, there with the people, it scared me and it made me angry too. I don't think he's alive like a human being but I don't think he's dead in a completed high stage, like the other guys are. See I don't think his work was done. I think that Hendrix did perhaps the greatest work he could in his performing. I think Hendrix was the greatest there ever was, but Morrison, I think, had work to be done, mostly in writing. I think he'd a book to write, he wanted to leave his greatness through poetry. Morrison had this obsession about poetry, and he never completed himself, and I feel him, I feel him bugging me, really it's like, it bothers me sometimes, and I don't like to seem to be taking a responsibility that might not be merited to me, but it's not a responsibility that I want, it's just something that I intensely feel, and a lot of kids came up to me in Paris and said (adopts French accent) "Patti, I feel Jim Morrison was here, do you feel this?" and I did. It was a real feeling.

I talked to Iggy [Pop] a few weeks ago and Iggy thinks that he's . . .

Iggy has the same affliction, only worse than I do. Iggy's is like . . . mine is like an affliction that comes to me very seldom and usually when I'm performing, especially when I'm improvising, but Iggy's is something that he seems to carry around like a responsibility. I think that maybe Jim'll leave me alone and talk through Iggy (laughs), but I definitely think there's a part of him that wants to seek a voice on earth.

———

High on Rebellion: Patti Smith Speaks, Part 2

We join Patti Smith and John Tobler mid-conversation one day last October, when Patti was on her way to Europe to do her annual poetry reading in honour of Arthur Rimbaud's birthday. The jaunt was acting as a test run for the tour of Europe she's just done. That's about all you need to know. . . .

There's a group called Mars on it, yeah?

Yeah, they're working with Mars now. We have a Tapper Zukie record coming out (*Man Ah Warrior*), and there's a group in France . . . I guess really the first great fanzine to me was *Rock News* in Paris, and it was run by Michelle Esteband [*Michel Esteban —Ed.*] and Lizzy Mercier [Descloux], who really have done a lot for the New Wave—they really travel internationally to spread the word to each country, and now they've started a little band, and I'm gonna produce them myself because they're really deserving, and Lizzy is a great poet . . . so she's my project, and I might also . . . I was thinking of doing a solo guitar record, something that certainly no one else would want but Mer.

I believe that first single, "Hey Joe" and "Piss Factory," is coming out on Sire?

Yeah, well, one of the reasons that happened is, we wanted to start the Mer label. When I had my accident we really felt like we wanted to keep working and I wasn't able to work, so we felt like we would get the label going, we needed some funds, and Sire was the only label that would take it, and, it seems strange that nobody would want it now everybody saw us, but Seymour Stein was the only person who really had the foresight, and he also gave us enough money so that we could start our label. So our first little record had to be sort of the sacrificial lamb . . . the sacrificial lamb chop . . .

Mer is going to be an ongoing thing, it's not just a temporary thing that you would do when you're not doing anything else?

No, see . . . what we want Mer to be is a label where groups that we think have a lot of promise and really care can have a springboard. It's the same as it always was, it's for their formative period, it's for when their work is still on the borderline of art and noise. We're not trying to break anybody's career, all we wanna do is break even hopefully and give kids a shot, help them get some kind of confidence, give them a piece of product that they can be proud of, and a good demo so maybe they can keep going forward. We don't wanna tie up anybody. We're just interested in people's first efforts. . . . I listen to "Hey Joe" and it makes me cry almost, it's like we were completely innocent when we did that record . . . and rock 'n' roll is really tough, not just because of the business end of it but touring you go through a lot of pain and you age very quickly, and you develop a lot of scar-tissue, so I look at Mer as a pre-scar-tissue label, it's to catch things at their most innocent, it's more of a documentary label than anything else, although William Burroughs . . . I'm gonna produce William Burroughs. I'm gonna play guitar. We're gonna do some of *The Wild Boys*. We've talked about it—he happens to think I'm a great guitar player! Better than Jimmy Page, he said! How do you like that, coming from the master! [laughs].

I've read that your next album, which we ought to be expecting before long . . .

We go into the studio November 7. See, truth is I had again to get an okay from my doctor. I tried to go into the studio last month and I hurt myself. It's nothing dramatic but because it's my neck and it has to do with my motoring sensibilities I just couldn't do it, but I'm ready now.

"Rock 'n' Roll [n-word]"?

That's one of the cuts. It's not the title. The title is *Easter* because, first of all, the first time I got out of bed at all after five or six months in bed, the boys carried me. It sounds real dramatic but it was real great. It was real cool like Pasolini's *St Matthew* or . . . I don't know, it was Pasolini's big Christian effort which was on TV. Everybody in the country was watching Pasolini's version of Christ, and I was watching, and I was filled with . . . it was like a big event in America, everybody, was watching this on TV, and it was Easter and we were going to perform midnight at CBGBs. It was my first performance and I didn't know how I was going to do it. I jumped the gun again. One stoned night I said, "Oh yeah, I can do it," but the boys came for me and I was still in the cast, and they said, "How you gonna do this?" I said "I'll do it, just get me on the stage." I was really nervous, but it was jammed, and all our kids were there, there was so much energy in the place. The place was filled with light. I mean, it was Easter, we were in the same space, everybody thought . . . everybody was a Christ figure that night . . . or at least Mary Magdalene, and there was just so much energy, and for the first minute . . . I hadn't even walked around, I was rickety, and they went into the first chords and I got shot with energy . . . all the people, everybody . . . it was like being shot up by 500 people or something, it was so fantastic.

We did this show and it was so great, I felt cured of something. 'Course I had to go right back to bed, but it was like after that my . . . uh . . . my . . . when you get better what's that called?

Recuperation?

My recuperation. It was almost instantaneous. It was such a breakthrough and I was filled with so much energy and I got a lot of confidence that it got me up ten times faster. Doctors, nobody could believe it, they couldn't believe that I did it, and it was very symbolic to me. You know, Easter's a great time, so that's what it's going to be called.

Somewhere I once read that you used to always try out your new material in Europe before you went to America to play it to people who really mattered. Now, forgetting whether this was an insult or not do you . . .

I don't believe what I said really mattered, cos I love Europe. I can't believe that I said that. I mean, it's quoted badly. What I probably said is that you have more space in Europe to break stuff. I feel more artistically free in Europe, in countries where there is a complete language barrier, because art is a very European thing. The presentation of art has existed in Europe, and America almost killed it. . . .

Yeah, I think I probably misunderstood the quote. . . .

Yeah, cos Jimi Hendrix is a classic example of somebody who was too heavy for America, who had to go to England to be accepted as a band, as an artist. I've always been more honoured in Europe than I have been at home. It's been a bigger struggle at home, because basically America is more middle class and I came from a very working-class situation, and it's been difficult for me in America because the mood has shifted. It's not the Stones any more, it's like the Eagles and Linda Ronstadt and all that stuff, which I don't really identify with that much . . . but I think that stuff's on its way out, I'll tell you, and with this new record it's *really* gonna be on its way out. One of the reasons I started in rock 'n' roll was to get rid of this junk—maybe not get rid of it, but move it over a little, part the Red Sea, and I'm not stopping. If God wants me he's gonna wait until I have a platinum record. . . .

But when you started in rock 'n' roll these people we're talking about—the Eagles and Linda Ronstadt—were very minor league.

Ah, but things were even worse then. I don't like to say that stuff—there's no reason to put people down, everybody works hard—but I have no desire to spend the rest of my life listening to the Doobie Brothers, Allman Brothers, that kind of stuff; the laid-back in America's never been my favourite. I like action. I like really frontal aggressive attack. To me, we're a warless country. There's never been, apart from the Civil War, we never have war in America and . . . in the history of the world, since this nuclear stuff, it's hard to have war, it's hard to be a serious soldier, because the era of the foot soldier and the guerilla soldier is pretty much dead in civilised really Western countries. But that desire's still in us. It's years and years and years of heritage. I have American Indian in me. I wake up every day and I'm half Apache. It's like I have nowhere to put my tomahawk, so I have to scalp with my electric guitar. My guitar is my instrument of battle. That's why I like rock 'n' roll—it gives a little 100-pound monkey a chance to be a soldier. It's the only machine gun I ever got to hold. I can't help it, we were born out of violent times. I'm a war baby, I was born out of war and never got a chance to be a soldier myself, except now in rock 'n' roll, and my fight is to keep rock 'n' roll alive and to continue rock 'n' roll, now more than ever. When Elvis Presley died . . . I know he'd been out of the limelight a long time, he got fat and everybody says mean stuff about him, and once again he's almost prehistoric—he's like Rembrandt—but when the news came over the radio I thought, "Oh God," I didn't know what to think, he's been sorta dead for a long time, then all of a sudden it hit me. Rock 'n' Roll is what I believe in more than anything in the world, and he's the King of Rock 'n' Roll and the King is dead. And now the King is dead the People will rule. And, you know, it's true, the King died in the midst of a time when the people are starting to rule again, but we have to . . . there can't be total anarchy. To me, constructive anarchy is important, but we must keep producing, and we must continue or it'll be gone, and I'll tell you, I don't raise children or anything, but I had a kid once . . . I have a kid someplace that's 12 years old, I might never see it, but I don't want my kid growing up eight to ten years from now in a world without rock 'n' roll.

You talk about Elvis, it could be Mick Jagger in ten years if the Stones go the same way as Presley did, and there's nothing really to stop them . . .

You're gonna make me cry. I mean . . .

I saw Mick Jagger in 1962 and he is very, very tame now. I mean, when America first saw him he was pretty tame. I saw them when they played three hour sets a night, total Chuck Berry-Bo Diddley all the way. [In 1964, Chuck Berry and Bo Diddley recorded Two Great Guitars *together. —Ed.] They were amazing . . .*

Well, I don't care what anybody says about Mick Jagger. If Elvis Presley was the King I think Mick Jagger was the Crown Prince, and I still have yet to see anybody cut him. He might not be able to cut himself anymore but there hasn't been—apart from perhaps myself in rare moments—I have not seen anybody else cut Mick Jagger. The kid who cuts Mick Jagger, I'm gonna be his first groupie boy! Very first.

IT'S HOT: A PATTI SMITH INTERVIEW

Peggy Thompson | May 12–19, 1978 | *Georgia Straight* **(Canada)**

This interview was originally published in the *Georgia Straight*, a Vancouver alt-weekly, and later reprinted in the underground newspaper *Berkeley Barb*. Patti Smith was rocking the Commodore in Vancouver on May 8, 1978, and Peggy Thompson met her at English Bay beach overlooking the city. Thompson had a reputation for getting subjects to open up in offbeat interviews. "Around the same time," she told me, she went shopping with the I-Threes, the vocal trio backing Bob Marley. "Somehow we ended up in the fanciest store in Vancouver (Holt Renfrew) where they tried on fur hats while smoking spliffs."

Here, it was Fudgsicles on the beach. Smith discussed her teeth, reggae singer and deejay Big Youth's teeth, and the possibility of a role in a never-produced film adaptation of William S. Burroughs's first novel, *Junkie*. And her relationship with the beach itself. —Ed.

On Sunday afternoon I interviewed Patti Smith at English Bay. She wanted to see the ocean. After a loping run along the sand Patti stopped at a log, spread her American flag over it and we sat and talked. For me, meeting Patti Smith was hot.

I've been a fan ever since I saw her on the Mike Douglas show about a year and a half ago. She looked like Keith Richards and I think she sang "Gloria." [*Smith made two appearances on* The Mike Douglas Show: *January 19, 1977, and April 19, 1977. —Ed.*]

Mike's middle-aged groupies froze and so did Mike. Patti was electric, moving like a Jagger-dervish she gave it her all. Hot music. Luke warm applause.

Patti sat down beside Mike, beamed him a big warm smile and croaked, "I just want you to know that bein' on your show it the biggest thrill of my career so far."

Mike's not sure if she's jiving him, but he goes for broke. "Why is that?"

Patti: "'Cause my mother loves you, she watches you every day. All my life you've been the good guy. And I've been the bad kid. And now the bad kid is on the good guy's show, and my mom's real happy."

Patti smiles beatifically and slouches down in her chair. The audience of mums and dads bursts into spontaneous applause. Cut to commercial. Cut to English Bay.

Peggy: "Is it true that you were cloned from a piece of Keith Richard's tooth?"

Patti (eyes moving on the water, a half smile): "No, it's not true at all." She considers the possibility. "It could be true, 'cause my teeth are in really bad shape. If I have any of his blood in me it's certainly coagulated around my gums. I have some problems . . . I'm getting them all done in gold."

Peggy: "There's a reggae singer in Jamaica called Big Youth. . . ."

Patti: "Yeah I know him. . . ."

Peggy: "He's got three stones in his teeth."

Patti: "Yeah, I have a picture of me touchin' his teeth. We were talking and I was so attracted to his teeth that my finger touched them, and we both started laughing. . . ."

Peggy: "In Jamaica?"

Patti: "Nah, it was New York. In Central Park."

Peggy: "Does he smile a lot? He sounds like he smiles a lot."

Patti: "Yeah he smiles a lot. All those guys smile. They get stoned and read the Bible. That leads to a lot of smilin'."

Patti's rep from Capitol Records in Vancouver, Peter Taylor, arrives with popcorn and fudgsicles.

Patti: "Oh no . . ."

Fudgsicles are distributed and passed around.

Patti: "MMMmmm. God that's great."

Peggy: "So Patti, how long have you been into health foods?"

Patti: "Actually I eat very well. I don't usually allow myself to eat this kind of shit. It's just that I can't resist it. I tend to eat a lot of fish, a lot of raw fish. That's what I'm gonna have tomorrow. It's very good for you. I'm really interested in seeing what's going to happen in this town. It's like the psychic," she searches for the right word, "It's like I feel this town might have a lot of good psychic energy in it. People around here apologize for being relaxed, that's okay. I mean apart from being oppressed middle class you've got nothing to worry about. I mean I expect a lot of physical anarchy tomorrow night but it's like here," a sweeping hand motion encompasses the water and mountains and sky. Her voice trails off into silence.

Peggy: "What bands do you like?"

Patti: "Blue Oyster Cult. The Clash. Television."

Peggy: "Tom Verlaine's in Television, right?"

Patti: "Tom Verlaine *is* Television. I like the Sonic's Rendezvous Band. That's Fred Sonic Smith's band and they operate mostly around Detroit. But they'll probably come around here."

Peggy: "I hear you got a thing for Detroit City."

Patti: "Yeah. Well the Sonic Rendezvous Band's a great band and where there's a great band I get into the city."

Peggy: "Detroit's got a great history for music."

Patti: "Oh yeah. I was really into the Supremes. I like Diana Ross. I like, uh, who else do I like?"

Peggy: "The Chiffons, The Ronettes . . . ?"

Patti: "I like them all. But I don't think about them too much any more. Except Diana Ross. I think she really kept going. I think Johnny Rotten's great."

Peggy: "Did you see the Sex Pistols?"

Patti: "Nope. Saw 'em on TV. I think he's great."

Peggy: "I hear you've been signed to be in the movie *Junkie*, the book by William S. Burroughs. . . ."

Patti: "Well," she clears her throat, "Uh, I have my part. And I have my script. But they're going through some copyright problems. It will happen and when it does happen, if it happens under the jurisdiction of Mr. Burroughs, I'll be in it. My part kept shifting. . . ."

Peggy: "There's not too many women in the book."

Patti: "I think I'm the only girl in the movie. At least right now. I play a lot of different women in one woman."

Peggy: "All women are a lot of different women in one woman."

Patti (laughs): "Yeah, but not all of them play 'em. They don't all play their parts."

Peggy: "So who's producing the film?"

Patti: "Well, this is the problem. All I can do right now is sit tight and hold on to my script and hold on to my belief that it'll happen sometime. Because it really is one of Mr. Burroughs' dreams to see that book realized into a real hard-driving fifties Hollywood movie. Taking the turn of the decade, from the forties into the fifties and having it documented properly. You know . . . Sam Fuller should direct it. Yeah. He directed *Pick Up on South Street* and lots of stuff. Yeah. You know, every time I come into a new town I get a new idea. We've been trying to figure out who should direct this movie and I think Sam Fuller would be a good guy. 'Cause it's a good American tale . . . *Junkie*."

It's getting cold. One last question.

Peggy: "What do you think of the ocean?"

Patti: "I love the ocean. This is a real teeny one, littered with mountains. That's one thing I do love about the east coast is the ocean. No matter how bad I feel, uh, if I just feel like shit, I got the ocean. Sometimes me and a friend go to Coney Island. At five o'clock in the morning. We take the subway, it takes about an hour. We get off and like Coney Island's littered with all this trash. And all there are, are trash-guys. And we just get a bottle of wine or a couple of joints and fall asleep. And then when we wake up there's ten million people on the beach. But yeah, it's nice to be able to leave your hotel room and see the ocean. Even if it is just a baby ocean. Let's go."

On the way back to the car, I see a friend walking toward us. Lorraine is nineteen and sometimes calls herself a punk groupie. She thinks Patti Smith is "hot." "She's hot," says Lorraine. Lorraine phones AM request lines and asks to hear Debbie Harry. Vancouver frustrates Lorraine sometimes.

"Hey Lorraine, How ya doin'."

Lorraine's feelin' no pain. It's Sunday afternoon, she's walking beside Patti Smith on English Bay Beach, late night AM is playing "Because the Night," and Monday night Vancouver's going to rock it up. Lorraine smiles. "It's hot," she says.

GUEST DEEJAY PATTI SMITH

Howie Klein | May 14, 1978 | *KSAN*

Patti Smith achieved Top 40 success in 1978 when "Because the Night" rose to number thirteen on the *Billboard* Hot 100 and number five in the UK, but she didn't lose her commitment to the little guy. As FM radio slowly began to shift to a Top 40 format in response to corporate demands, she remained fiercely loyal to the holdouts perpetuating a model rooted more in antiauthoritarianism and sonic diversity beyond the hits. San Francisco's KSAN embodied this aesthetic, hosting America's first regularly scheduled punk radio show, *The Outcastes*, from 2 to 4 AM. Greil Marcus once called the station "the heart of rock 'n' roll radio in America," where renegade deejays Beverly Wilshire, Glenn Lambert, Richard Gossett, Howie Klein, Norm Winer, and others committed themselves to "opening the airwaves to outrage, farce and surprise."

On May 14, 1978, future president of Reprise/Warner Bros. Records Howie Klein, Beverly Wilshire, and the KSAN listeners experienced one such surprise when Patti Smith and Lenny Kaye paid a visit to the studio at Sansome and Sacramento Streets. Smith had rocked Bill Graham's Winterland Ballroom the previous night and was still coming down from the high of slaying at the fifty-four-hundred-seat venue. "I'm talkin' as if like everybody went to the concert is listenin'," she said on the air. Maybe they were. She talked over the music—Ike and Tina Turner, the Doors, Blue Öyster Cult, Jefferson Airplane—telling wild stories of her experiences of and with the bands, occasionally pausing to read public service announcements and critique the commercials. Later on in the broadcast, she also discussed a plan to publish a report in *Billboard* of all the stations that played a track from *Easter* with the n-word in the title. "I was fighting to take a term that was used in such a defamatory way and to take it as a badge for outsiders, artists, of any gender, any color," she told *New York Times* columnist Maureen Dowd in 2019. She never recanted the song, but has stopped performing it, recognizing that "the pain that people feel because of past injustice is real" ("Rock Star Patti Smith, Making Paris Swoon" by Maureen Dowd, September 19, 2019).

This excerpt shows Smith at her most uncensored and ecstatic—"I've never been happier in my life," she said at the end of the broadcast—encapsulating a cultural moment when, to some, the fate of FM radio seemed like the most important thing in the world. —Ed.

[*"I've Been Loving You Too Long" from* What You Hear Is What You Get: Live at Carnegie Hall *by Ike and Tina Turner plays in the background.*]

Patti Smith: I was so thrilled. I was like, I mean I hadn't, it was like one of my dreams since I was sixteen years old to see an Ike and Tina Turner show, and for *free* . . . and to go for free? And they took me to this show, and it was like in an armory, and like, there was hardly anybody there and it was all white kids, and it was really . . . they got on that stage, and they were so great, and people were just standing around. They were just standing around. I mean, it was like, when I went to concerts, when I went to concerts and saw, like, James Brown or the Marvelettes or, uh . . . who else did I see, Smokey [Robinson], when I saw, we didn't like throw stuff at the people, and we didn't . . . what we did is we just went *out*. It was like going to a Baptist church, you know? It's like when you're singing to Christ, you're singing to God—*sing out*, you know. You don't hold it in. I was watchin'—she was so great . . . she was so great. I went *nuts*! You know, I really went nuts, and I showed her how I feel, and you know what? She came up and she looked at me. [*Laughter.*] She did.

Howie Klein: I love it.

Smith: She came up and looked at me. I swear to God. I am not making this up. She came up, and I was like, I was just little Patti Smith from wherever I was. I was just like, she didn't look at me because you know, 'cause I had three records or something or whatever else I'd done. She looked at me 'cause I was . . . I was great out there; I was dancing with her. I said, "Tina, you are *fine*, but like, check this out, baby," but like in a cool way—to inspire her, not to challenge her. I wanted her to know that I was with her, you know? It was, like, it was pretty great. It was really . . .

Klein: Did the rest of the crowd start moving then?

Smith: Yeah!

Klein: Ayy, all right!

Smith: Well, what happened is, I'm very good at that. I did that at Earl's Court once, when I seen the Rolling Stones. We were playing at the Boarding House—uh, no, where was that?

Lenny Kaye: Roundhouse.

Smith: Roundhouse. It was like the Boarding House. No, it wasn't at all like the Boarding House. It was like the Longbranch. I always mix them up. I always, like, sometimes I want to say Longbranch, and I say Boarding House by mistake, because Longbranch is such a weird . . . it's like CBGB's; it's like this cowboy name? When I think of that place, I think of motorcycles, and that title, Longbranch, is so weird. I always hated CBGB's name, too, though, but now it's so much in my heart, I got used to it. But country—what's the words—for like blue grass or something . . . Lenny and I, me and Lenny really, really, I feel that, like . . . I mean . . .

Klein: Oh, by the way, Patti Smith and Lenny Kaye are here.

Smith: That's Lenny. Ike Turner. Sometimes I'm Tina, sometimes Lenny's Tina. [*Klein laughs.*] And I stand back and say, "Okay, baby. Bend for me." And he becomes—I mean, that's the core—that's the difference, though, between us. It's like they have their specific roles, uh huh, which are really good, and they done them the best. A whore and his pimp—her pimp—you know, it's like me and Lenny are as good as any whore and any pimp, only we also have like the slipperiness and the flexibility to switch our roles around. It's like, uh, he'll [*repeating Ike Turner line in the track playing in the background —Ed.*] "try anything." See what he's saying? Ike? He is really great. [*Klein laughs.*] But it's amazing that you should put this record, because, see how—that's really like one of our secret things that we don't talk about. It's like, when me and Lenny are alone and psyching each other up, you know, and we go to the bathroom before we go on stage, we get into this thing. It's like, you know, that's who we are, to me, only like, you know, not only . . . [*Laughter.*] My way of doing that is laughing. Did you ever see me laugh on stage?

Klein: Yes.

Smith: The reason I'm laughin' is I'm usually pissin' myself. The first time that ever happened to me was at the Longbranch. I was *so* ecstatic. Do you remember that night? I was so ecstatic, I couldn't believe it. That's really where I learned a lot of the kind of physical energy, and it was like I peed myself and I didn't know *what happened.* [*Laughter.*] I thought I had a kidney disease. I got hypochondriac. I thought like I had something the matter with my kidneys, but it was just, it wasn't piss at all. It was, like, another female excretion. [*Laughs.*]

Beverly Wilshire: It's 5:28. You're listening to KSAN in San Francisco. Lenny Kaye and Patti Smith. Patti Smith and Lenny Kaye so nicely came down. The weather's pretty nice right now.

Smith: Do you know what, I'll tell you. As far as like giving live concerts, you know, what's that, KZEL?

Kaye: KZEL.

Smith: KZEL in Eugene, Oregon, is the most progressive in America. But as far as like stoppin' by and visiting deejays, I'd say you guys, like, this is really the most fun I've ever had at a radio station.

Wilshire: Yeah, you've been by and talked to Richard a couple of times.

Smith: Well, I don't even remember Richard. I only remember what's *this*, happening now.

Wilshire: [*Laughs.*] We have a couple messages. Be right back.

[*Ad for Proctor and Bergman followed by an ad for* Making of Star Trek: The Motion Picture *by Gene Roddenberry and Susan Sackett.*]

Wilshire: And I got to tell you that [*rifling noises*] . . . where is that tag? Here it is. Everyone, start getting your costume ready for the World of *Star Trek* festival. Woohoo.

Smith: Oh yeah.

Wilshire: All you people from Venus, don't miss this one, and that's gonna be at the Oakland Coliseum on Saturday, May 20. This is KSAN in San Francisco. Patti Smith, Lenny Kaye are here, and—to talk and visit—

Smith: Well, I've got something to say just about your commercial. I've just recently got into *Star Trek*. I have to admit. I'm like the kind of person that rebels against stuff when it first comes out. You know, and then like a couple years later I get into it. [*Indistinct interjection from Wilshire.*] It's just like pot in the '60s. I waited till the '70s. You know, I waited to the *late* '70s to take acid. You know what I mean? And I haven't even started on beer yet. [*Laughter.*]

Wilshire: Save that for the '80s.

Smith: But I have to tell you that, like, I started watching a lot of television, like in my period of immobility [*after she had the accident on January 23, 1977 —Ed.*]. First, I got into Roger Moore's *The Saint* [*sings theme*], just because he was a guy that was invincible. He was like subtle Frank Sinatra way, but he was a lot like Captain Kirk; ultimately, nothing could harm him, you know. He could go through all these idealistic and perverse voyages. I mean, he was idealistic, Captain Kirk, but he also made all those chicks. You know what I mean? It was like, you always knew that he was gonna get a chick, you know. You always knew that like even the fourteen-year-old ones, no matter what age. [*Laughter.*] I mean really—I mean, he was a lot like Jimmy Page or somebody, or like one of those guys. Well, anyway, that's all I had to say.

Wilshire: About *Star Trek*. Here's "Volunteers of America."

[*"A Song for All Seasons" from Volunteers by Jefferson Airplane plays in the background.*]

Smith: What's this station call number?

Wilshire: 95.

Smith: Oh, this is KSAN!

Wilshire: Jive 95. [*Laughs.*]

Smith: I'm sorry I didn't come by yesterday when I was supposed to, but I was really . . . I sorta . . . I had to get ready for my concert. You understand.

Wilshire: I understood totally.

Smith: I had to figure out what to wear and things like that. [*Laughter.*]

Kaye: Yeah, lotta things to wear, too.

Smith: Yeah, that was my new outfit for San Francisco. I got pieces of that all over my American tour. It was like, I was like, it's like I wanted a certain thing out of last night. I wanted a point where something was gonna be revealed to me. The solidarity of an image, or you know, because I'm struggling toward something that I don't quite have the total definition for. You know, it's like I'm real happy because I feel more in focus than I ever did, but, like, I look to each night, each performance as another revealing. And like last night, I really had fun getting ready in my hotel room. I figured that was a new outfit, that's like my Marvel . . . that's like my Marvel Comics. It's like a person that, like, works for God, you know, but is like a Marvel . . . like an animated, you know, like, twenty-first century. I don't want to be like old-time worker for God, you know, and like . . .

Wilshire: The Salvation Army.

Smith: Yeah, but you know, I like the Salvation Army. In fact, when I get rich, you know, which if things keep going the way they do and I keep having Top 40 hits, I'm gonna give like, I'm gonna give a lot of my money to the Salvation Army.

Wilshire: And get 'em to buy new outfits like what you were wearing last night?

Smith: Oh, the Salvation Army is good for the people. I never toured much of America. We mostly have toured Europe, you know. But this being our first true American tour, I got to see places like Indianapolis, and Louisville, and all these places, as well as New Jersey, where I'm from, like South Jersey, where the Salvation Army and the Volunteers of America did a lot and do a lot to help us people that just can't [*quietly*] get our shit together. That's your segue into the next song, "Volunteers of America" by the Jefferson Airplane. . . . Oh, is it already on?

Wilshire: Yeah.

Smith: Is it on?

Wilshire: Isn't it? You gotta put your headphones . . .

Smith: I didn't hear it. Oh, I forgot my headphones. This is like . . . look at this, I'm not used to this place. Oh, they're around my neck. [*Laughter.*] Well, what do you know? I'm revealing a little more than I wanted to reveal, here. What part is this? This isn't "Volunteers of America."

Unidentified: It's coming up, I guess.

Smith: But I didn't ask for this song. I love the Jefferson Airplane, but not everything they do. I don't like country music.

Wilshire: It did sound *very* country.

Smith: That sounds like Hank Williams. Well I'm gonna do a Hank Williams song, then I'm gonna break into the country market.

[*"Meadowlands" from* Volunteers *by Jefferson Airplane plays in the background.*]

Kaye: You know which one?

Smith: What?

Wilshire: There's some real weird bands on this record. Is this it, do you think?

Smith: This doesn't sound like "Volunteers of America."

Unidentified: It's the last cut on side two.

Smith: Are we on the air? [*Jokingly*] People are really hearing you like this incompetent?

Wilshire: Loose radio.

Unidentified: It's like free-form, you know? [*Laughter.*] Look, you don't care about advertising, right?

[*"Volunteers" from* Volunteers *by Jefferson Airplane plays in the background.*]

Smith: Oh, this is it. My headphones are cutting out. Does that matter? They aren't cutting out to the people, right?

Wilshire: No.

Smith: [*With a raised voice*] Listen, if your headphones are cutting out, just put on the "Volunteers of America" by the Jefferson Airplane. [*Laughter.*] Am I still talkin' to them?

Wilshire: Do you want to not talk?

Smith: No, I want to talk all the time. I'm really having a great time. This is a great song, yeah. I like to do this song, like I'm trying, that's like, I figure, "Till Victory" [*track from* Easter —*Ed.*] is. "Ask the Angels." This is a really great song. This really did influence us a lot in the, uh . . . what's goin' on. Are you leaving?

Klein: I've got to get another record.

Wilshire: Don't go.

Smith: Did Lenny request something? Oh, okay. Well this is, do you know what? Can I tell a nice story about Grace Slick?

Wilshire: Sure.

Smith: Because I don't get really to tell this story too much, 'cause I always forget it. But being as I'm in San Francisco and everything, we'll keep it rural, you know. When I was like about seventeen or somethin', or eighteen, and . . . "White Rabbit," remember that one, and what was the other one—"If You Want Somebody to Love" [*"Somebody to Love," by Jefferson Airplane —Ed.*]—I could *not* believe a chick singin' like that. That really, 'cause you know that I'm mostly into guys. I mean, sexually and spiritually and on every level. It's just, like, I'm into guys, you know. But every once in a while, a chick'll really . . . I mean really, the way she was . . . and I got really, it really made me . . .

[*Tape stops, restarts. "Baba O'Riley" by the Who is playing in the background.*]

Smith: I always used to put that on and sing at the top of my lungs, and I never could finish the song 'cause she was too good. You know what I mean? Well, let me tell you somethin'. I practiced a lot on that Debby Boone song, and I think I might, I'm gonna try it again, but I might be able to tackle, like, a Grace Slick song pretty soon. I think she's really . . . I don't know what she's doin' right now, but she was really somethin', I'll tell you.

Klein: She's still okay. She did a good solo on that new album. What was that one about Esso oil or somethin' like that?

Wilshire: Uh, is it . . .

Smith: I like her. I don't know her personally, but like, uh . . .

Klein: She gets down. She drinks. She's cool.

Wilshire: Well she's givin' it up.

Smith: She should give it up. She was gettin' a little fat there. [*Laughter.*]

Klein: Well she lost the weight, so she's drinkin' again.

Smith: Oh, I like this one. Listen. Listen to these words. Now I don't listen to lyrics too much.

Wilshire: Don't you?

Smith: No. Really. I could care less.

Klein: What song?

Smith: Huh?

Wilshire: Should we let Howie hear some of this?

Smith: This is another one. This is another one. [*Chanting along with Pete Townshend —Ed.*] *Fields.* "Out here in the fields." That one's a good one. I sometimes think of this song, it's like, you know, I thought of this song a lot. Like when I had my period of immobility, you know it's like I really felt like the thing that made me not get depressed more than anything, was like feelin', whether it's fantasy or you know, or like illogical projection, kids givin' me my title. I was the Field Marshall; I was out in battle; I got wounded in the line of duty. And that's like, that made me feel really happy, you know. It's like, it was a cool thing to get into, just like I got into lookin' like Keith Richards in 1971.

Klein: You don't look like Keith Richards right now.

Smith: Well, no, I'm a field marshall now. [*Everyone laughs.*] I look like a field marshall. But I used to like this. "Out in the fields." You know, it's like, I watched what was goin' on, and it's like, all these kids, and please . . . how many people are we talkin' to?

Klein: Oh, twenty thousand.

Smith: Twenty thousand ain't bad.

Klein: Five million.

Smith: This station should go out to millions. This is a great station that you have here. But like, because this is like a last holdout, boy. And I go to radio stations all over America. They're tryin', though. I'm tellin' you that things *are* gonna change.

PATTI SMITH: STRAIGHT, NO CHASER

Nick Tosches | September 1978 | *Creem*

When the late Nick Tosches interviewed Patti Smith for *Creem* in 1978, Smith allegedly told him, "Hell, Nick, you know me. Just make it up." So what follows should perhaps be taken with a grain of salt; it could Patti Smith fan fiction à la Tosches. In this freewheeling piece, published shortly after the release of *Easter* and Smith's first hit single, "Because the Night," the literary bête noire shows his newly minted hit-maker interviewee was still punk.

Tosches wrote about the darkness within like no one else, and as a provocatively libidinal interlocutor, revealed that Smith's sartorial darkness was more than skin deep. A kind of rock Virgil to her waifish Dante, Tosches ferried Smith from dive bar to dive bar, through irresistible circles of hell as they got more and more drunk. There were a few colorful cameos—a nihilistic bartender and Al "Reverend" Fields, a pianist who frequented the Bells of Hell, a legendary Village haunt originally opened by writer and political firebrand Malachy McCourt. Four years later, Tosches would publish *Hellfire*, his 1982 biography of Jerry Lee Lewis that has been called one of the greatest rock biographies ever written—and "the Killer" himself gets a callout here.

More than anything, Tosches conjured a scene—what it might have been like to amble through Manhattan day-drinking with Patti Smith in 1978, evoking a kind of rock nostalgie de la boue for a time when New York was at its gritty worst, but the sounds emanating from CBGB's offered a kind of apropos salvation. —Ed.

We are sitting in the Tropical, the darkest bar in New York. Outside on Eighth Avenue it's late afternoon. In here it's midnight on the outskirts of Mayaguez. There is a day-glo Madonna next to the cash register.

Above her head is a sign: Absolutely No Credit This Means You. Patti orders tequila and I order gin. Since we are speaking English and are not drunk, we are the object of many crypto-Hispanic stares. The barmaid pulls at the hem of her brassiere through her t-shirt, then pours herself a shot.

"*No importa nada mas que toma licor,*" she says, and the bar stirs with rheumy laughter.

Patti lifts a quarter from our change and goes to the jukebox. A moment later, Tom Jones is singing "The Young New Mexican Puppeteer." Several customers begin to sing along in phonetic approximation.

"I heard you got divorced," Patti says.

"Yeah," I say.

"The Virgin Mary's face is chartreuse," she says, gesturing with a toss of her chin toward the icon that guards the till. "They should have the Holy Ghost on the other side of the register, where that cerebral palsy can is."

"Color-coordinated, of course," I say.

"Yeah. Black and red. Black for sin. Red for defloration. The colors of salvation. They were my high school colors, too. I used to dream about getting fucked by the Holy Ghost when I was a kid. Black and red. Christ, what a shitty football team we had."

"You could always fuck Jerry Lee. I guess that's about as close to the Holy Ghost as a girl can get these days," I counsel.

"It ain't the same," Patti says. "We need a new cosmology. New gods. New sacraments. Another drink. I wanna go to Alexandria, to the grave of Ibn al-Farid." We settle for Corby's Bar, on Sixth Avenue.

I first saw Patti Smith perform in 1972, at a poetry reading in St. Mark's Church on the Bowery. A few months earlier, Telegraph Books of Philadelphia had published her first, slender volume of poems, *Seventh Heaven*. But Patti wasn't like the other creatures of slender volumes who were there that night. It was not the fact that she had never read Pindar that set her apart, but rather a more visible fact: she had brought an electric-guitarist with her, and he was standing there, plugged-in. Her and Lenny Kaye, two skinnies from New Jersey, out to recast poetry with the nighttime slut-gait of rock 'n' roll. The other poets, being mostly wimps whom rhythm never knew, didn't like this at all. You might say they feared it, for none of them, once they had seen Lenny's amp sitting there like a dark Homeric vowel, wished to follow Patti's performance, and she was asked to close the show. So we sat there, Richard Meltzer and I and two girls who didn't seem to enjoy our company, sniffing lighter-fluid (the audience sat in pews, so there was privacy enough for one to douse one's hanky with the juices of the blue-and-yellow can) and waiting. Waiting while poet after poet bared his soul, which invariably turned out to be a dead mackerel. Then, as we sat knee-deep in the detritus of bared souls, Patti and Lenny came on, and Lenny struck the first notes of the Midnighters' "Sexy Ways," and Patti opened her mouth and loosed the ratted-hair rhythms of her poem "Sally."

> *you been messing around sally*
> *and you ain't been messing with me*
> *torn pants*
> *torn pants*
> *and juice all down your dress*
> *you been ripping it up with someone*
> *I think you better confess*

When she started to do "Rape," many of the gathered poets packed up their souls and departed.

> *I'm gonna peep in bo's bodice, lay down darling don't be modest*
> *let me slip my hand in. ohhh that's soft that's nice that's not used*
> *up. ohhh don't cry. wet what's wet? oh that, heh heh. thats just the*
> *rain lambie pie. now don't squirm, let me put my rubber on. I'm a*
> *wolf in a lamb skin trojan. ohh yeah that's hard that's good, now*
> *don't tighten up. open up be-bop. lift that little butt up. ummm*
> *open wider be-bop. come on.*

As I said, this was 1972. CBGB's, which would soon exist a few blocks farther down the Bowery, did not yet exist. (The new owner, Hilly, had bought the place the year before, but didn't yet know what he was doing with it. Before he ruined it, it was one of the last great skid-row bars. Ed Sanders had wanted to buy it and leave it in its original state. Hilly's first alteration was to paste a sign in the window declaring that the joint no longer wished the patronage of bums.) The Bowery was still for bums and poets, not for people who knew the words to "Stupid Girl." [*From the 1966 Rolling Stones album* Aftermath. *—Ed.*]

Soon there was another book, *Witt*. The band began to grow: piano, another guitar, then later drums. In the spring of 1974, Patti's friend, the photographer Robert Mapplethorpe, financed her first record, a version of "Hey Joe" coupled with "Piss Factory," a wrathful song about her days at the Dennis Mitchell Toys factory in south Jersey. Patti named her record label Mer, which is both an Indogermanic root meaning "to die" and an Old English word for the sea.

Less than a year later, Patti signed with Arista, and her first album, *Horses*, was released late in 1975 and received massive attention from the eyes and ears of the media. *Radio Ethiopia* came the following year, and it did not receive massive attention. There was no Patti Smith album in 1977, and toward the end of the year there were rumors that Arista had dropped her. But in the spring of 1978 there came *Easter*, one of the most successful albums of the year, and the single "Because The Night," Patti's first hit.

In Corby's Bar there is, for a reason known only to God and Corby (neither of which are here to explain), a faded map of the solar system taped to the mirror behind the bar. A man of indeterminable age, whose physical appearance lends much credence to the medieval theory that all life is born in a dismal swamp, sticks his face in mine and shouts, "Hey, wise guy, where's Pluto? I'll tell ya where it is, wise guy. It's in the upper left-hand corner." Then he turns and informs the rest of the bar in a loud voice, "Fuckin' guy don't even know where Pluto is." The clientele, which seems to have been there so long that its faces are the color of the floor's once-white linoleum tiles, waves him away and groans the groan of Job.

"This place is even worse than I remember," Patti says.

"At least they know where Pluto is," I say.

"And now we do, too," Patti says.

"Some people say you have a messiah complex," I say.

"Aw, fuck them. Goddam psychiatric doubletalk. Why can't they just say they hate my guts or something? People who need reasons to hate somebody are fulla shit. Buncha creeps. Who said that, anyway? —Hey, look, that guy was wrong. It ain't in the left-hand corner, it's in the right-hand corner! This whole goddam joint is *nuts*."

A few hours later, we are in the Bells of Hell, a couple of blocks from Corby's, on Thirteenth Street. I go take a leak. When I come back to the bar, I find Patti in dialogue with Al Fields, the Bells piano-player whose legend extends in rays for many blocks, if not as far as the cold planet Pluto.

"Hey, [n-word]," Al, who is himself the only patron of color in the establishment, calls to the bartender, "this girl don't believe I was raised by nuns. You tell her, am I right or am I wrong. I'm Al Fields, girl, I don't lie. Shit! Is a pork chop greasy?!"

Patti goes to the jukebox. "Hey, they got my record. No 'New Mexican Puppeteer,' though." She plays two Rolling Stones records.

"Hey, you ain't related to her, are you?" Al Fields asks me in his typhoon whisper. "What is it, she got somethin' against nuns? Shit, I'm Al Fields, the Village Legend. You know what I'm talkin' about. Am I right, am I wrong? No, really, she's a very nice girl. She come to hear me play?" He excuses himself and heads towards the men's room. "I gotta go pay my water bill."

"What was it like opening for the Stones in Atlanta?" I ask Patti, recalling the poets who had feared to follow her onstage a few years ago.

"It was great. When I used to open for all these acts, most of 'em usually made me carsick. I used to think how great it'd be to open for the Stones. One of my dreams. Now all I wanna do is open for Rimbaud."

"He doesn't play the States too much, though, does he?" I say.

"There hasn't been the right promoter," she says.

"What do you figure will happen now that you're Top Twenty? Are you gonna clean up your act for the bigger crowds?"

"Nah. Bein' top-of-the-pops just makes crowds more docile. Look at Jim Morrison. He just kept gettin' weirder and weirder. King's new clothes, y'know?"

"When are you gonna start makin' movies?"

"I don't know. There ain't that much I'd really be interested in. A Muslim Star Wars, maybe. *The Paul Verlaine Story*. I'd like to do one about an international plot to assassinate MOR [*"middle-of-the-road"* — Ed.] singers. Get all these Debby Boone-types and wimpy country singers to play themselves. Bang, bang, eat lead, dog of mediocrity."

"What's the next record gonna be like?"

"Very Plutonic. Liner notes by the Holy Ghost. They'll love it in Corby's."

THE PATTI SMITH GROUP

Andy Schwartz | June 1979 | *New York Rocker*

On Saturday, April 7, 1979, the Patti Smith Group performed at the Vassar College Chapel, a Romanesque building with vaulted ceilings. *Wave*, the Patti Smith Group's fourth studio album, produced by Todd Rundgren, would not be released for a month, and the concert was meant as a trial run for the new material in advance of a major tour. They played in front of an enormous American flag backdrop, part of the ironic set, and by all signs, there was no religious fervor, no patriotic zeal on stage or in the crowd. By the end of the night, some people had lost faith. Smith called the audience "bizarre" and said, "I can't get into singing tonight." Two articles ran in the *Miscellany News*, Vassar's student newspaper. One described her performance as "beyond wasted," while the other grappled with what felt like an existential crisis. "Patti Smith gave a bad concert the other night," wrote Susan Bruno. "Some people were bummed out about it. For some people, a hero fell. Some other people thought it was a good show—it was a thrill to see someone falling apart in front of them. As for me, I keep trying to find all kinds of excuses to make it better. It made me feel bad to see a woman who is such a talented poet, who can move so many people, who once had such a tremendous amount of energy, become so much less than she could be." If *Easter* had made people believe in Patti Smith, this cast doubt. What happens when someone we idolize reveals herself to be less than perfect—and so unbearably human? How does the audience cope when a hero has an off night?

Andy Schwartz was there that night, and as a former worshipper at the altar of Patti Smith, the seeds of doubt had already been sown. To Schwartz, "she *was still* a favorite and an inspiration, for all her rhetoric and her fuck-ups, which was precisely why A. had taken on this story." Writing in the third person, imbuing the piece with the probing detachment he felt wrestling with Smith's recent work, Schwartz's "A." interviewed each member of the group looking for some kind of explanation—only to inspire more questions. Was she immune to criticism? Hostile to it? "I think that a true hero can only be criticized by himself," Smith said. "A true hero is his own highest critic. What he needs is support, he needs confidence, he needs the energy and the strength of the people. He doesn't need criticism."

Ultimately, this series of encounters with the Patti Smith Group is a meditation on fandom, of hoping for so much, and through inevitable disappointment somewhere down the line, not losing faith. Little did her fans know, they would have to wait awhile—it was Smith's last tour before a sixteen-year sabbatical. —Ed.

A. was lost. He pulled the Toyota over to the curb, parked, and flicked on the overhead light to check his road map. Should he have turned right or left? At the second light, or the third? He looked up from the map and spotted a gaggle of co-eds crossing the street ahead of him. Ah, Vassar woman, bearer of knowledge. They pointed him back about a half-mile, to the green lawns and imposing stone walls of the campus.

Outside the college chapel, a line of fans had formed in the chilly twilight, thirty minutes or more before showtime. But it was, after all, the first-ever appearance by the Patti Smith Group at this college, and one of a short series of trial dates prior to the release of the group's fourth album *Wave* and a major spring/summer tour.

Inside, A. was surprised and delighted to find the amps and drums set up right on the altar before the massive pipe organ. It seemed particularly appropriate to this band—the stained-glass windows and rows of wooden pews. And in less than a minute, a whole catalogue of memories unfolded behind his eyes. . . .

Patti, on a bitter-cold day in a Minneapolis bookstore, autographing copies of *Seventh Heaven* for the half-dozen fans who'd bothered to show up.

Patti, in that *Blonde on Blonde* tab-collar shirt and neat black suit, not quite drunk enough to cover her nervousness, burning through "Jesse James" or caressing "Dylan's Dog" while an equally inebriated Tony Glover plunked away on a battered electric guitar.

Patti, stumbling off the plane on that first *Horses* tour, seemingly embarrassed by the small but worshipful crowd that had gathered at the terminal gate, later confessing her love over a local radio show; on stage that night, so proud and happy over her hot new band, the way their beat and energy could cut through the years of safe, dull, fake rock music.

Patti, on stage in Central Park last August, tormented and confused, with a "show" that dragged A. over a crazy-quilt emotional terrain and left him weary and depressed.

Patti, on stage at Max's for a private celebration of *Easter*, among friends, yet arrogantly commanding, "If you're not with me, then get the fuck outta here!"

A. wondered at that moment what it meant to be "with" Patti Smith. He'd been a Stones fan since the age of 12, but that didn't make *Goat's Head Soup* a good album. He admired the writings of Jack Kerouac, but thought himself capable of distinguishing the author's best, most illuminating prose from his worst, most self-indulgent blather. And having made these distinctions, he didn't mind speaking his thoughts. He couldn't see what made another favorite and inspiration like Patti any different. And she *was still* a favorite and an inspiration, for all her rhetoric and her fuck-ups, which was precisely why A. had taken on this story. Genuinely curious and interested, he wanted a closer look.

"Backstage" was a choir rehearsal room in the chapel basement, where a Yardbirds tape played while the band (Richard "D.N.V." Sohl, Lenny Kaye, Ivan Kral and Jay Dee Daugherty) prepared for the soundcheck, smoking, talking or picking at the cold-cuts and Chinese food buffet. Soon, everyone filed upstairs and on stage, laughing and jiving as they tried out bits of the Abyssinians' "Satta Massagan-na" and Manfred Mann's "5-4-3-2-1." Suddenly, there was Patti, in a loose, wrinkled shirt and blazer, testing the mikes and offering a few exploratory whangs on guitar. She looked pretty good, too: clear-eyed, confident, erect. The whole group ran through a few measures of "Inna Gadda Da Vida," a huge horrible hit from the late '60s for which A. felt not the least nostalgic.

Back in the dressing room, A. was nervous, his face flushed even before he'd switched on his cassette recorder. She'd made her statement with *Wave* and was enjoying the privacy of life in Detroit with guitarist Fred "Sonic" Smith, he of MC-5 and Sonic's Rendezvous Band fame. But the ever-accommodating Lenny had paved A.'s way, and with introductions made, the Inquiring Reporter and the Wary Subject sat down to talk.

It took a while. In response to A.'s not-terribly-original opener of "How's your general state of mind?" it seemed to take Patti a lot of "uh"s, "like"s, and long pauses to answer, "Indescribably happy."

A. was glad to hear that and said so, noting that the last time he'd seen her on stage—that strange, sad night in the Park—she hadn't seemed that way at all.

"Well, I was on the brink of . . . on the brink of . . . of leaping into—well, not leaping, but . . . Well, I was in the preparatory stages of the stage that I'm in now. So how it appeared didn't matter at all, whether the show was good or bad didn't matter at all. What mattered was that something was happening, and instead of avoiding it through professional slickness, or paranoia, or laziness, we all confronted it: myself, the band, the crew, the people. We were going through something together; we knew it was tough, but I think the fact that we were going through it together made it a worthwhile evening for everyone."

Her feelings that night—did they have anything to do with her launch into the charts with "Because the Night"?

"No, no, I wasn't talking about anything but the moment, not a lot of external dialogue. But I don't expect you to be presumptuous enough to know what I was going through. . . ."

(There was something about that last bit that A. didn't like—a tinge of haughty disdain—but he let it pass.)

". . . It had nothing to do with the business, nothing to do with anything. It's just an artist goes through various stages of awareness or coldness as he attempts to pierce further into the realm of high communication. It's like . . . well, uh . . . it's . . . well, y'know, all wondrous voyages have their hazardous moments. It's like the Seven Voyages of Sinbad. What makes each voyage so marvelous is that usually he's defeated some unspeakable monster. So that aspect of intense struggle is often the hallmark of a process of a certain act of creation."

With a new album on the way and the attendant need for publicity, was she really not going to give interviews?

"No, I said I talk to very few people now. The only reason I'm talkin' to you is because your newspaper and yourself have been carefully screened by Lenny Kaye. I don't talk to most press people 'cause they don't care anymore. I wanna talk to somebody that cares, that isn't interested in writin' a bunch of gossip and bullshit and their own twisted ideas of what we're doin' . . ."

In the creation of *Wave*, had her hit record created a kind of shadow, a commercial achievement to be lived up to or repeated?

"No, no, we don't worry about things like that. If you really knew anything about our band or about myself, you wouldn't even ask me a question like that. Those kind of things don't even enter our consciousnesses."

Well, it was a pressure that had brought a bear on a lot of talented performers. . . .

"Are you kiddin' me? If it's a pressure, it's a pressure I've brought to bear on myself. I like *all* our records to become hits. We had pressure on *Radio Ethiopia* 'cause I wanted it to be a hit record—*me, I*. Clive Davis wasn't trying to make it into a hit record, it was me. And the only thing it hit was bottom. . . .

"One of the things I tried to do on this record was write a little song that everyone would love, that people would like to hear while they were ironing, or fathers would like to listen to on the way to work, or kids would like dancin' to. That's one of the pressures I put upon myself, to write a song like that. And that's 'Frederick.' It's not a pressure, it's a goal. This band don't get pressured . . .

"Lemme tell ya something, son. If this band had the same kind of crass motivations as other rock 'n' roll bands, they would've got another lead singer years ago. This band don't need me to be successful and rich rock 'n' roll stars. We don't deal with that kind of pressure, and we don't get it either."

Okay. At the time of *Radio Ethiopia*'s demise . . .

"It never demised. Only I'm allowed to joke about my records."

Well, you would've liked to have heard more of it on the radio. . . .

"Even one cut would've liked made me happy!"

At that time you made a lot of strong statements about the lack of energy and innovation in rock radio. Now that you've been accepted by a lot of programmers . . .

"I *haven't* been accepted. I've said this many times and I'll say it again: When I'm Number One, I'm accepted. Anything else is just 'so what?' 'Because the Night' was only 13, it wasn't 1. When I have a string of hits, then I'll know that I'm accepted by radio. Or when we're played every single day. Not just a single that's 13—that's nothing to me."

In the heyday of the Bee Gees and Foreigner, didn't Patti think those were unrealistic expectations?

"I dunno. In my day, I remember when James Brown used to get played every hour. Maybe there's too many squares in the world these days; maybe people better turn around, check themselves out. The hipper the people get, the hipper the radio'll get. And I have a feelin' that kids of the future are no squares. . . . I don't know anything. . . ."

(A. was almost ready to agree with that. But what bugged him was that he was sure she *did* know: that she was smart enough to know all about the world of rock 'n' roll and more, but persisted in dealing in myths, historical acknowledgements, and a concept of pure visionary artistry that A. just couldn't swallow, try as he might. Yet at the same time he couldn't forget the profound effect these same words had had on him just three or four years before. Was he smarter now, or just more cynical?)

"I just have a feeling. . . . This is America, America is basically a sincere country, a country that might be fucked up and sorta square, as is pretty obvious by our TV, but a country made up of people that have—I mean, it was built up through idealistic guerilla tactics. The Revolutionary War guys were guerillas in the most illuminated sense, and we're the children."

An invocation of our radical heritage—was that what "Citizenship" was about?

"'Citizenship' is just a song talking about what it was like in 1968, when Ivan Kral escaped from Czechoslovakia to America and Patti Smith escaped from New Jersey to New York City. It's when I met Robert Mapplethorpe—I mean, it doesn't matter what it's about. We all have personal things from 1968, certain impressions—at least some of us do. . . . It's just a reflection."

Hmm . . . "Hymn"?

"Lenny and I writ it. . . . Lenny's playin' the autoharp. . . . He was lookin' at the psalm in the Bible that 'Rivers of Babylon'—that's a psalm out of the Bible that they just set to music. It was like seein' a famous person, y'know? And I told him it would make me very happy if we had a psalm, and Lenny, Lenny . . . always, always . . . well, I mean . . ."

Her voice trailed off. Everyone was stoned, except A., who was merely uptight. Why *Wave*?

"It's a real nice word . . . What I was tryin' to do was soften the aggression of a salute, and what was the friendliest extension of a salute? A wave. It's like, really—I don't have any time to waste. I mean, the world might as well know that I don't have any time to waste. And I expect for us to, y'know, get it on or miss the comet."

Was it *Wave* as in "New Wave?" Was that a favorable connotation? Did Patti still feel a kinship to the new bands?

"Oh, absolutely . . . I don't know what the definition is, but I have a definite appreciation for . . . the level of intelligence and the energy they're putting into this work. I expect people to work hard, and as they work harder, they'll build up a lot more self-respect. . . . I like that new Johnny Rotten record [*Probably* Public Image: First Issue *by Public Image Ltd., released December 8, 1978. —Ed.*], and I like *Street Hassle* [*the Lou Reed album —Ed.*]. We've always been supporters of the Clash—I seen 'em years ago, I'm sure they'll just progress. I like Bob Dylan.

"People can't be afraid of the hero syndrome. I know it's not a fashionable syndrome, but there's nothin' wrong with havin' some heroes. It makes life a lot more exciting and pleasurable, even for a short period of time."

A. thought so, too. The only trouble with heroes was their seeming immunity to criticism, the pedestal upon which they were placed.

"I think that a true hero can only be criticized by himself. A true hero is his own highest critic. What he needs is support, he needs confidence, he needs the energy and the strength of the people. He doesn't need criticism."

But if they were talking about rock 'n' roll singers—they're not supermen.

"I'm saying that someone that truly evolved can certainly see within himself his own faults. He's that blessed by God, God will certainly give him the knowledge of understanding his own faults. . . . I'm not saying they can't or shouldn't be criticized, or that they're beyond criticism—I'm saying they *don't need it*. All it causes is new pain and self-conflict."

Could Patti see herself doing something entirely different from now in, say, five years' time?

"Anybody can. I have a tremendous imagination; I can see, like, Alfa Romeo giving me their fastest model and me beating everybody at Indianapolis. I can see anything if I get into it. I can see myself bein' the mid-1980's sex symbol of the movies, or I could see myself goin' into some monastery and drinkin' wine for the rest of my life—with Lenny! (*laugh*) I probably won't do any of those things, but I don't think of stuff like that."

Close friend and stage manager/tambourine player Andi Ostrowe came into the room and wrote on a convenient blackboard: "PATTI—FRED IS HERE." Yes, Sonic Smith himself was here, not Vassar but New York City at least. Patti brightened, did her best to keep her mind on A.'s questions. He'd failed to bridge the gap; his face was burning, and he felt as though he'd been speaking in a foreign language. His next question didn't help matters much: Did Patti think that, in the past, her songs or statements had glorified things like heroin to a young and impressionable audience?

"I've never written a song about heroin. I mean, did you have hidden knowledge about one of my songs, that it's really a heroin song? The only heroin I've ever written about are female heroines. Even in 'Poppies,' it's a song against shit on the radio, but I was disguising it as a drug song, since it seems to be more accepted to take drugs than to talk against the radio. I was disguisin' my anti-radio song as a habitual blues song. But when I was thinkin' of poppies, I was thinkin' more in the *Wizard of Oz* sense—that kind of opiate is a drug that children are blessed with."

Had the band been approached to play for any of the anti-nuclear activist groups or other political cause?

"Oh, we always play for a political cause—every time we play, it's for a political cause. . . . We aren't entertainers, y'know—we're not a boogie band. Every time we play, we're truly alive and truly aware of the moment that we're dealing in. We're truly aware of the foundations that this country was built on, of freedom of speech . . . We're playin' CBGB on Bob Dylan's birthday—that's a political cause. It's a cause against Billy Joel."

Showtime was drawing near. A. made one last stab at making everything clear to himself. Was there any way Patti could summarize what she was trying to put across? Ideas? Ideals? Emotions?

"It's like real simple. To put it in the most common denominator terms at this time: I'm wavin' to everybody. I just want them to wave back. That ain't askin' for so much."

The show itself was a maddeningly up-and-down affair. Some tight, driving, passionate rock and roll—"Be My Baby," "Because the Night," "Redondo Beach," and others—was offset by a lot of self-indulgent, sloppy jams and an almost total lack of pacing. Lenny Kaye sang Buddy's "Oh Boy" [*Buddy Holly song —Ed.*], Ivan did "5-4-3-2-1" (Patti changing the chorus to "5-4-3-2-WAVE!," and the whole thing rolled and tumbled along to its conclusion with "My Generation." And though the concert offered something for everyone (from "The Star-Spangled Banner" to "Seven Ways Of Going" to a truncated version of "Tomorrow," from the musical *Annie*), A. was often bored, and left the hall with no more of a buzz than he'd brought to it.

———

Later that week, he hopped a West Side subway up to Lenny Kaye's place. Unlike some observers, A. didn't have any doubts about Lenny's credentials as a rock and roll musician rather than critic. But he had often wondered how anyone so knowledgeable and perceptive about the music could so often forego what A. saw as basic principles of directness, economy, and mere tunefulness. They began by talking about the current single, "Frederick," and launched from there into the whole question of Art vs. Commerciality.

"When we sit down and put together something, our concern is not whether it's commercially valid but whether it's artistically valid," Kaye explained. "To us, matters of form are not as important as matters of content. People tend to look at us in terms of form, i.e. do we have more poetry than rock and roll, have we made a transition from Patti as chanter over a minimalist background to quasi-heavy metal rock and roll. That's like the shells around what the core of our art is; what we've tried to do is create a situation for ourselves where we can utilize any form with validity. We can move from the precision that's required for a hit single, and it's not required in just a pure business sense, but because it's what people like to hear. When they're driving in their car, y'know, they don't want to hear twenty minutes of dirge-like music—which is all right, I mean, everything has its place. But on the other hand, you don't want to make just car radio music, if you have aspirations for something higher—which we do.

"We consider ourselves very much in a collective improvisation trip this year. I mean, I'd love it if we had a string of ten hit singles. But I wouldn't be satisfied with that, and neither would Patti, neither would the boys in the band. That's not why we started. . . .

"I don't think that we're not a commercial band—I think we're very listenable. . . . But we haven't basically changed our mode of approach over the last eight years. The things that fire us are still the things that guide us. We're a very idealistic band. 'Cause if we wanted to sell out and make a lot of money, we could have done it a million times over. . . . But in the context in which we're dealing now, with an artist the stature of Patti, we have no choice but to become great artists."

A. didn't offer his own opinion about the Vassar show, but asked Lenny to run down the group's performance ideology.

"We want to give everybody who comes to see us a different show. Now, that's pretty difficult, and obviously you're not going to be able to get it totally different. . . . But I think we try to gear ourselves around moods so much, and Patti gravitates so spectacularly from level emotion to level of emotion. . . . I mean, really, when we do something, sometimes we don't know where it's going to, how it's going to end, what ground is going to be covered, whether we're going to have fights on stage—it's a very organic type of situation that we're attempting to set up between us and the audience, and the audience is as much a part of it as we are, by necessity."

It wasn't, A. pointed out, a method of operation much in vogue today, though certainly not without precedent in rock and roll. He mentioned the Grateful Dead, Quicksilver Messenger Service, and Television. (He *didn't* say that, to his own ears, collective improvisation was perhaps something best left to Art Blakey's Jazz Messengers or the Ornette Coleman band.)

"In a sense," Lenny pointed out, "we've always worked at crosscurrents with those trends in many ways throughout our lives—which is why, I think, we occupy kind of a weird middle position. We're as much, in some ways, an 'old wave' band as a 'new wave' band, as a 'no wave' band. But that's the kind of freedom we're interested in getting: the freedom of being anything, of putting on any kind of skin. You know, Patti said on the first album, 'beyond politics, beyond gender, beyond . . .' Because when you get locked into something, you're there, you're stuck. It's like getting stuck in *Go Johnny Go* or *Rock, Rock, Rock*—where could Jimmy Clanton go? He couldn't become a member of the Grateful Dead."

Kaye had a point there. At other times, his statements seemed either admirably far-reaching or just plain silly in the context of rock and roll:

"'Seven Ways' was originally about the Ninja of Japan, who were these 16th-century assassins, like a martial arts offshoot in Japanese medieval times. They wore black, and they developed these techniques where, for instance, they could walk in the snow without showing which direction they were walking in, or they could go against that wall and become that wall. That kind of transformation is really what we're into. 'Cause I think, for the types of music that we've attempted and succeeded at, we can do anything.["]

The criticism they'd received in the press—was it all entirely groundless?

"No. But the fact is, the press has the ability to be as wrong as the artist. . . . The way we feel about it—because we don't swallow all the good things people say whole—I find that of our favorable criticism, most of it is as wrongheaded as the unfavorable. People generally don't tend to know what we're about, what we're doing, what our motivations are—"

But that was because the group preferred to leave these questions wide open!

"Which is true, and that's good—I don't mind that."

For example, A. suggested, who could say that the use of the American flag backdrop on stage was not just a gesture of jingoistic patriotism?

"Okay! That's again a question of people dealing with forms. Because it's tough to get into what a band's really like, especially a band that I feel is as complex as ours. . . . What you see, when you see an American flag—it's not a political animal. But look at the ideal of what the American flag is, what it represents, the revolution out of which it was born. To me, that's a very important thing.

"What I would expect is that when writers write about us, they try to write about us from inside us, instead of—to try to find out what it is we're doing, what it is we say. . . . I don't mind if I see the person's trying, at least, to see what we're doing. But I do mind it when I see they're just following, like sheep, the critical thing in the wind. If nothing else, give us a pat on the back for trying to outdo ourselves, for not taking the easy way out. Because when you look at the new wave bands that are making it, most of them are making it on the terms of the old order. We're still mavericks."

Lenny was proud of *Wave*. As for the choice of producers, he still loved Jimmy Iovine, "but for this album, Todd was the right one. I think it turned out to be a very good collaboration. He helped us out when we needed help, when we would run into an arrangement that wasn't working or we didn't know where to put a chorus, and more importantly, he left us alone. Todd's whole position as a producer is that he wants to make the record that you want—the more well-defined your objective is, the happier he is."

A. now asked Lenny, just as he had asked Patti, if there were a way to sum up what this band was really about.

"It's like a door—that's what we're trying to provide. A door that you open, and it unleashes a landscape of limitless possibility. You could take two steps into it, and be entertained. You could take another few steps in, and you find a little bit more—maybe some lyrical things which intertwine with each other and reflect on another song, or some kind of interconnection, some kind of archeological move. . . . We try to provide levels of depth. I think we're an entertaining band, but we try not to just be an entertaining band. As deep as people want to get into us, I think they can get into us on that level—as heavy as they want to make it, or if they just want to go out and have a party some night."

After the tape was shut off, they chatted some more and listened to records: Jimi Hendrix doing "Gloria," some great demo tapes by the Sidewinders (with Andy Paley) that Lenny had produced "on a four-track in a classroom at M.I.T." Then it was time to go, and A. stepped out into the crowds on Broadway with a lot more to think about.

The foyer wall of Ivan Kral's West Village pad was hung with as many pictures of Keith Richard [sic] as of Ivan, his girlfriend, or his own group. Kral, an amiable chap with what's called a "ready grin," had joined the Patti Smith Group four years ago after several frustrating years of projects that failed to pan out: a New York band called Luger, a brief sojourn to LA. to back 16-year old Shaun Cassidy in a pubescent glitter-rock act, an early version (with Cars drummer Dave Robinson) of Arista labelmates The Pop. He'd worked at the New York office of Apple Corps in that company's final years and "met all of them, except Paul." He'd done his share of scuffling; been broke, cheated, and disappointed; and was still thankful to be where he was today, despite his sometimes sharp differences with Patti or other members of the group. He had been mildly disappointed in Todd Rundgren. "There was no pre-producton period, and I missed that—the time before you actually go into the studio, when the producer comes to rehearsal, listens to the material, and you sort of get to know each other. And I just felt there were other times when Todd should have been there, and he wasn't—both mentally and physically.

"I guess I got too spoiled by Jimmy Iovine. He was around all of the time, or most of the time. . . . I guess Jimmy had a busy schedule and it just didn't work out this time, but I would love to work with him again."

In another contrast to Patti, Ivan seemed more responsive to the commercial pressures of his job.

"I can't speak for Patti, but I'm sure anyone would feel pressure. You need to push the album unless you are—who's that group that did *Aja*?—yeah, Steely Dan, or Pink Floyd or somebody. We *do* need a single, and we *do* need to sell records . . . If you want a band to survive and have the faith in themselves and build up the self-confidence to get up there, you have to sell records."

Was he aware of a kind of critical backlash that had formed against Patti in recent times?

"It is a trendy thing lately. . . . But it can help you, and I always think about it, no matter how bad it is. I mean, sometimes you get very closed up and bitter inside yourself, but I think it's very helpful. . . . There are people who loved *Horses* and I think it will always remain that way, but where Patti's going really depends on how she feels, how her life is. Like I said, she's the boss, just like Bruce Springsteen is the boss."

Had "the boss" changed since her serious accident and subsequent recuperation?

"I would say that at first, I didn't know if she would fully recover. And she's still—you know, she has pains and needs a doctor, a chiropractor. She was much more, I felt, cheerful before, on the road and in general. There was certainly a shock, and there's been a change.

"You have good quarrels and bad quarrels; sometimes it's helpful, sometimes harmful. You scream at each other, but then you say 'I'm sorry'—sometimes not as fast as you'd *like* to say it, but then you think back four years ago, and where you were then. . . . 'Citizenship' went through a lot of changes, also because of Todd. He put it more on the edge—it started like a more mellow song.

"I still think Patti is an original. There's no female that can compare with her on stage—that's why she draws people. I don't think it's 'new wave'. . . . Quitting? No, I never thought of it. I've always felt I had to fight for whatever I had to get, and it was mainly on musical ideas. I think one of my biggest fears was during *Radio Ethiopia*—there were a lot of changes in songs like 'Ask the Angels,' in the music I wrote. I have certain set ideas—this is the main part, this is the hook, this is the break. . . . You have, like five different ideas people tell you, but you have already set one idea. It was really hard to get used to it, but now I'm used to it.

"Patti and Lenny have been together so long—I'm like a newcomer, kind of. I feel I haven't accomplished a lot yet; I have a lot to go. Yes, sometimes I feel angry about things. Other times, I think, 'Thank God, I've seen the world and played big stages, and people liked what I was doing.'"

A. didn't know where this band would be without Jay Dee Daugherty. He was the anchor that held even their spaciest jams down to earth, and, with Ivan Kral, seemed to form the traditionalist wing of the Patti Smith Group. But his outside productions of singles by Mars and Lester Bangs indicated an intense interest in the music's radical fringe, and at home he listened to everything "from Mozart to the Contortions."

They met in a West 4th Street coffeehouse, and sat at an oil cloth–covered table beside a trickling artificial fountain. Was Jay pleased with the album he'd just made?

"Well, no one's ever really happy with any one thing that they do, I don't think. . . . Considering the way we went about the album, I'm actually pleased with it. We spent less time on this one than on any of our other records, even though it took longer from its inception to its completion. . . . We just went into the studio with no preconceptions. The last album was very meticulously planned, and of course, we're always trying to make the latest album different from the last one. So we just said, 'Fuck it, we're going into the studio' and we did—without any pre-production work with Todd or anything."

Did he miss that pre-production period?

"I actually enjoy it, because it enables me to get my bearings. So that by the time we get around to recording, I have an idea in my head of some sort of thread that runs through the work. That wasn't the case on this album—we really approached each song as an individual contribution."

Some cynics had termed "Frederick" "Because the Night, Part II," or pointed out that you could almost sing Springsteen's "Prove It All Night" to the tune. Had the comparison occurred to Jay?

"It really didn't—it still doesn't. I was playing it once on the piano, and it did sound a little like 'Because the Night,' but that's only because it has the same base chord structure. Big deal—'Prove It All Night' sounds like a dozen other songs; how many new chord combinations can you come up with? To me, 'Frederick' sounds more like a Motown song. We never intended to capitalize on any similarities; it's purely incidental."

Was A. wrong to place Kral and Daugherty at the more traditional end of the PSG spectrum, or Lenny and Patti at the more experimental end? (He didn't know where to put the mysterious D.N.V.)

"Well, I wouldn't go so far as to say we were polarized to that extent. Ivan's and my tastes tend to be more compatible, running to more conventional things than other people in the group. But that's the good thing about the group. There's five individual personalities and styles, and we've all learned from each other. . . . It's not necessarily compromise. We wouldn't be doing what we're doing if there were, you know, two different camps or something like that going on. It would just never work, it would be obvious, it would show."

Was the Patti Smith Group a democracy?

Daugherty laughed. "Well, Patti's sort of a benevolent despot. . . . It *is* called the Patti Smith Group, and she has the final say. This particular album, she was very very much in the forefront. This one was really strongly influenced by Patti, where the last album was probably the most democratic one we've made—it was like five people with pretty much an equal voice. But Patti had definite ideas about this album and that's the way we chose to follow through on it."

Did he have a response to former fans who felt the group was no longer forging the cutting edge of old?

"Well, I don't know what you can really say about it. It happens with all groups, basically—they'll be saying it about the Clash two years from now. I still think we're highly relevant to a lot of things, and that a lot of this criticism has come from really narrow-minded quarters. Obviously, for a lot of people, the thrill is gone. But we're always trying to

do something different, and I think every one of our albums is different
. . . It would've been very easy to do *Horses* Volume II, III, and IV. But
that would be dishonest. We're just trying to keep up with ourselves."

A. had heard about the possibility of the band playing Woodstock
II this summer. He thought it sounded like a terrible idea.

"I wouldn't be surprised if that happened, but we haven't heard anything. Our booking agent is that agent for that festival, and we know a few
other people involved. I sort of have mixed feelings about (*laughs*)—the
whole idea of it makes me want to throw up, actually. . . . But it just
might turn out to be a good thing. It really depends on what other acts
are going to be on. If it's just going to be a super-group extravaganza,
I'd rather steer clear. But if they're interested in exposing newer talents,
and giving other types of music a break, I'd be more than willing to play
for something like that."

Jay had "looked over" that week's pan of *Wave* by Julie Burchill in
New Musical Express. "I'm not surprised. They've always given us bad
reviews. The English press are the worst scumbags in the world. I hate
them. I wouldn't even talk to any of them. This whole English journalism school—I mean, look what happened to the (New York) *Post*. It's
become like a cheap, shitty London tabloid.

"Even though the English press was responsible for a lot of good
exposure, a lot of times . . . they liked us for the wrong reasons. We were
the new thing to latch on to—they didn't really get to the heart of it."

A. was chewing on the ice cubes left over from his cappuccino, and
the interview was winding down. Could Jay sort of sum things up?

"We're sort of feeling our way. The last album, I think a better title
might have been *Flux* rather than *Wave*. But Patti's in a really good
frame of mind as far as working goes. . . .

"The reason Patti and Lenny started was because they didn't like the
way that rock 'n' roll was. Let me tell you, anything that Patti says is very
heartfelt and she really means it. She's one of the most honest people I've
ever met in my life. She's virtually uncompromising. She would never
say anything for effect. As controversial as a statement might be—you
or I may not agree with it—she means it."

A. went home and listened to *Wave* many times over in the week that followed. Always a sucker for a good hook and a snappy arrangement, he liked "Frederick" and "Dancing Barefoot" right away. "(So You Wanna Be A) Rock 'n' Roll Star" confused him. Was it an angry, ironic diatribe against the rock-star system or a celebration of it? He heard Patti invoke "the age where everyone creates" but couldn't catch the rest of her words as the music overcame her. Well, at least it rocked along, with Rundgren's production providing both a certain gloss and a good deal of punch.

The rest didn't get to him at all. He began to think (especially after reading John Rockwell's plaudits in the *New York Times*) that his ears were plugged, that he wasn't opening his mind to the images and ideas. Maybe it was because he found much of the music turgid and confused; there didn't seem to be much "rock and roll" on *Wave*. "Seven Ways of Going" still sounded like much manic ado about nothing; "Citizenship" was strident and tuneless; "Broken Flag," a Long March to nowhere.

Yet the title track—that eerie, wind-blown mini-drama that closed the album, that abject object of Julie Burchill's derision—that song touched him in a soft place. It really seemed to capture some of the gentleness and vulnerability he'd once treasured in Patti Smith. A dumb conceit? Maybe. All A. knew was that "Wave" made him stop talking and thinking about anything else when he heard it play.

He knew his story wouldn't change a thing; he hoped it wouldn't lose him the casual friendship of the band. They weren't going to start making albums of three-minute hits, and he certainly wasn't telling Patti Smith how to write poetry. But as times got tougher, the country got crazier, and he grew older, A. hoped to see more of his world reflected in her words and music than he found today. He'd seen it there once before, where now he saw mostly images of Patti. But if their paths had now parted, he hoped that somewhere down the line they would meet again, and embrace.

WHEN PATTI ROCKED

William S. Burroughs | March 1979, published April 1988 | *Spin*

Somewhere between the time when William S. Burroughs pseudonymously published his 1953 debut novel, *Junkie*, and when he appeared on the cover of *Sgt. Pepper's Lonely Hearts Club Band*, he became a patron saint of rock. Steely Dan took their name from a dildo in *Naked Lunch*; Lou Reed described Burroughs as the one who "broke the door down." Visiting his loft at 222 Bowery was a rite of passage—Mick Jagger, Joe Strummer, and Madonna all came. That sphere of influence was significant enough that it has inspired multiple books. Victor Bockris's *William S. Burroughs: A Report from the Bunker* documents conversations the *Naked Lunch* provocateur had with the likes of Allen Ginsberg, Andy Warhol, and Susan Sontag; and in 2019, Casey Rae's *William S. Burroughs and the Cult of Rock 'n' Roll* puts it all in context.

Patti Smith counted Burroughs as a friend and teacher. For this interview, she met him in the Bunker for a frank reflection on her place in the rock industry shortly before the release of *Wave*. A Top 40 artist after the release of "Because the Night," Smith now found herself in a "psychic kind of war" with the people she described here as her "investors." The importance of artistic control had been a theme throughout her career, and her recent success meant it had inevitably begun to erode.

For much of this interview, she focused on corruption—of art, of the soul, and of the planet. The term "global warming" had only been coined four years prior in 1975, but Smith's environmentalist streak set in early. The fight to maintain her integrity, to "communicate with myself," seemed to be another preoccupation. Smith had already moved to Detroit to be with Fred "Sonic" Smith and left the "emotional tabernacle" she had built in New York. Yet sometimes a spiritual journey means leaving it all behind.

Six months after meeting Burroughs on this particular day, Smith concluded her last major tour in 1979 before her sixteen-year sabbatical. In *Just Kids*, Smith wrote of her frequent visits to the Bunker in the days when the East Village was still gritty. Winos and trash-can fires lined the Bowery. "You could look down the Bowery and see these fires glowing right to William's door," she wrote. In this, one of her last interviews before leaving the scene, her uncertain future must have been on her mind as she followed the line of fire. —Ed.

Patti Smith has been on the rock 'n' roll scene forever: first as a serious fan off in the wilds of New Jersey, later as a hipster in San Francisco, a writer collaborating with artists like Sam Shepard and Tom Verlaine, an *enfant terrible* on the New York poetry scene, and as a journalist for *Creem.* Her interview with Keith Richards is a classic: she asked him one question, then picked up her gear and split.

By 1973, Patti was performing poetry on stage with the likes of Anne Waldman and Dick Higgins. While they stood stock-still, intoning their verses with the monotony of high school English teachers, Patti came on like a cross between Tristan Tzara and Little Richard, swinging what hips she had, tossing her hair, and singing her poems like there was a Motown beat there, just behind each line.

When she added Lenny Kaye on guitar, the poetry turned to physical song, mineral song, and she turned the downtown poetry and music scene on its head, sacrificing nothing, but expanding the temple, letting light in through the windows, and opening the door for the likes of Chrissie Hynde.

Her independent single, "Piss Factory," recorded while she was still working, stocking books at the Gotham Book Mart, inspired the first generation of punks, seers, and methedrine mystics and led to her signing with Arista Records.

Horses, released in 1975, remains one of the bright spots of the Seventies and defined a moment with a sense of joy, anger, and freedom. None of her subsequent records (*Radio Ethiopia, Easter, Wave*) lived up to that wild moment, but each was filled with a daring and a vision that remains unmatched and unchallenged.

This interview was conducted in William Burroughs' loft in the Bowery, two blocks from CBGB's, in March of 1979. Burroughs' place (affectionately referred to as The Bunker because it had once been a YMCA locker room, and was still bleak and devoid of windows or light) proved a good confessional, and Burroughs an excellent Father Confessor.

Burroughs had first met Patti in 1974, when he returned to NYC after living outside the U.S. for twenty years. Theirs is a fond, respectful friendship that's endured to this day. It was conducted at a time when Patti was questioning the music industry and her place within it, and at a time when she was taking serious stock of her life and her work. Up until that point they had been one.

This was Patti Smith's last interview before leaving the music business.

In March of 1980, she married Fred "Sonic" Smith, formerly of the MC5, and moved to Detroit to begin a new life.

Smith: When I entered rock 'n' roll, I entered into it in a political sort of way, not as a career. I don't know if this is off the track, but I entered it because I felt that rock 'n' roll, after the death of a lot of the Sixties people, and after the disillusionment of a lot of people after the Sixties and early Seventies, people really just wanted to be left alone for a little while.

I didn't panic at first in 1970–71, even '72. I felt that maybe people were recharging. But when '73 came around, and early '74, it was just getting worse and worse, and there was no indication of anything new, of anyone regathering their strength and coming back to do anything. I felt that it was important for some of us that had a lot of strength to initiate some new energy.

Because I hadn't done anything in the Sixties, but worked privately, I felt that it was a time for me to do something. All I really hoped to do was initiate some response from other people. I didn't have any aspirations of a career, or anything like that.

I look at the world, I get very broken-hearted about what happens in the world. I hate to see people hurt. I see what's happening with Iran, and I'm mostly worried that Iran will lose its culture, or that somebody will destroy [Sufi poet] Rumi's grave. I worry about things that are not, I suppose, really so important to anybody.

But the things that I was involved with politically in America, were very simple things having to do with the minds of teenagers, and how they were being shaped. I feel that when I was a teenager, I was very lucky. I grew up out of the John F. Kennedy, Bob Dylan, Rolling Stones era, and there was a lot of food for thought in those times. There were a lot things that inspired me, not so much activistly [sic], but my mind was constantly fertile. And I felt that in the early-middle Seventies, there wasn't much happening at all to stimulate the minds of the new generations. The radio was like the Fifties again, the alternative radio that we had built up in the Sixties was becoming very business-oriented, and programmed like a glorified Top Forty. And there was no centralized communication ground for the youth of the future, no sense of unity at all in the country, and I felt that—

Burroughs: Do you feel that there is now?

Smith: I don't feel so much there is now, but I think there's more possibility for it to happen. I think that there's a re-awakening of the spirit of the kids. I mean, I'm not a nostalgic person. I've no desire to look back and moan about the Sixties. I look forward to the Eighties and Nineties.

But I think, simultaneously, kids are getting stirred up. I feel that in my own way, I was able to at least put a stick in the coals a little. Now it's '79 and I'm still involved in this thing, but it's come to a point in my life that, like you said, I have to stop and say, "What am I doing?" It's getting to the point now where, after having a hit single and having certain amounts of success and having people gravitate towards me because I have a success potential—it's time for me to really try to understand exactly what I'm doing.

'Cause I didn't start doing what I was doing to build myself a career. And I find myself at a time in my life when, if I'm not careful, that's exactly what's gonna be built for me. Or what I could find myself working for is other people's ideas of my career.

On the other hand, I'm a very strong person. I mean, all these things happened, but I feel like I've just pulled out of a time of temptation. I don't feel like I've ever sold out or done anything that I'm ashamed of, but I feel that I have entered into a period of temptation. And that's why I've been very quiet for about a year, because I've had to think about what I'm doing. Initially, all I wanted out of life was to communicate with myself and most of all, to achieve perfect communication with another person—as well as doing great work. To do great work, and thus communicate with myself, but most of all, to be able to honestly communicate with another person, totally . . . totally. Telepathically, or whatever.

I've no desire to be like some movie star and leave a trail of husbands behind me, you know?

Burroughs: Yeah.

Smith: I feel like I don't want to bullshit the people, and I don't like to be bullshitted either. I don't like any abstract, cow-like adoration for no reason. But I've often said, and I still find it the best way to describe it, it's like a very ecstatic, mutual kind of vampirism that you have to have with the people. Sometimes, I need their energy, and especially after my injury, when I was first trying to learn how to be on the stage again, I was not only afraid, but my energy . . . I couldn't really move around so much. I mean, you were at one of those performances when I was starting to get back [CBGB's, 1977]. I hadn't been out of bed for a few months, and I was addicted to pills, or whatever, and had to be carried on to the stage. . . .

I remember getting on the stage and I was thinking, "This was crazy, to do this show. I can't even walk, I'll have to sit." And I had them put a chair on the stage and I thought, "Well, they won't mind if I sit on the chair." Their energy, their psychic and spiritual, as well as physical energy, lifted me up.

Burroughs: Would you say it contributed to your recovery?

Smith: I felt that it did. These doctors told me, "If you're not operated on, you'll never perform again." Well, I refused to be operated on. I didn't believe any of that stuff, but I was on so much Percodan and things . . . And it was getting to a point after a couple of months where I really started wondering, having never injured myself before . . . I couldn't even get to the bathroom.

Well, those nine days that I spent with the people [the "Out of Traction/Back in Action" shows], doing a couple of sets a night at CBGB's, around Easter time in '77, was the best therapy that I had. I took my [neck-brace] collar off by the end of it. I couldn't stand it. It was real. I don't quite understand it myself, but I don't find it overly mystical.

Burroughs: This injury occurred in Tampa, right?

Smith: Yes.

Burroughs: I had one of the worst performances of my life in Tampa.

Smith: That particular performance was the culmination of one of my three periods. Performing was something new to me. After the initial stage of performing, where like I said, my first aspirations were political, in my own kind of way, then I found it got beyond that. I went beyond, because my politics are very simple. Basically, I just wanted to inspire kids, get 'em off their ass, get 'em thinking, get 'em pissed off, as pissed off as I was. Get them to look around at what was going on, even in the simplest way. Just get them to ask a few questions. You know, interject a little extra joy and pain into their lives.

But after a while, I got very intoxicated with the ritual of performing. I have great pride that I feel that our group, more than any other group at this time—except for the new kids who are experimenting—as a rock 'n' roll band, had more guts than any other rock 'n' roll band. It's that we always attempt something beyond what we can do, every night, which is excruciatingly painful for most of the band. For me, it's a joy. For, I'd say for half the band, it's a joy, and half the band, it's total pain to have to shoot beyond themselves in that kind of pressure situation, in front of people. But that was part of the rules of coming into our band.

I mean, I formed the band with my eyes open, but each guy had to have his eyes open too—that we were going to attempt things that were perhaps not always the thing to do in order to perpetuate ourselves as rock 'n' stars. They had to understand that we were going for certain things that were sometimes going to be detrimental to our advancement in the social and business circles of rock 'n' roll. And it was very tough.

Burroughs: Well, the same question arises with painting, or with writing—

Smith: Yeah, but the thing is, when you're painting or you're writing, you make that decision, and it's your own decision. But in a rock 'n' roll band, you're involved in a lot of different people's lives. And a lot of money's involved.

Burroughs: You're involved in a whole organization—your agent, the members of the band, all kinds of people.

Smith: These have actually been the hardest years of my life, because I was so idealistic about rock 'n' roll. I loved it so much, and I thought it was like, you know, the people's art. I really believed that of it. And because I believed it so much, I wasn't prepared for—even though it is true that a lot of people tried to prepare me—I wasn't at all prepared for the corruption within.

Burroughs: Well Patti, that's certainly implicit in the large amounts of money involved. Wherever there are those sums of money involved, there will be corruption. That's just par for the course.

Smith: And I don't even feel bitter. I don't always blame the corrupters, I blame the corrupted as much as the corrupter. I mean, I would say the corrupters are usually stronger than those corrupted, that's why people get corrupted—but we still have the option not to be corrupted. And I've had that option, that's the one thing that I did do. And when I first got a record contract, my record contract was one of the most unusual contracts of its time [1975], because although I got a lot of money for what is called a poet in those days—not so much money as they give kids now, but at the time, it was a lot of money and a lot of faith put into me—but I also got full artistic control of what I did. I mean, I don't think even Bob Dylan had that, I mean, at the time [of his first contract].

And although all these years have been a fight, I still always in the end get what I want, if I can hold out long enough. The truth of the matter is, managers and record company presidents and everybody, all these people have offered me things.

For instance, this last record [*Wave*, Arista 1979] was done two months ago. It still isn't out because I had to have long discussions with the people who were involved in this aspect of my life. And some of them really cared about me, in their own way. But all of them have a very different definition of success than I do. That's made it very difficult.

See, I feel right now, it's like . . . how we're talking now is different than how I used to daydream that we would talk, you know—

But it doesn't really matter. Actually, I'm very exhausted, because I've just spent two months in almost a psychic kind of war, between myself and the people who are helping to perpetuate my records. And I actually have respect for these people, even though I fight them. A lot of people would call me naive because I respect these people that I have to fight, but I still respect the fact that these people are my investors. But they try to get aesthetically involved with what I do, and it holds up my work.

They might even be right in some of the things that they suggested, because what they're trying to do for me is make a lot of money, and make me what they say is a big star—and also make themselves everything, but they have my interest in mind.

Burroughs: That's their function.

Smith: But I must protect—I mean, I have to feel like I can stand behind the work that I do, flawed or not. I can stand behind a piece of flawed work that was done with integrity; sometimes it's tough, but I can take it, 'cause I know there's a future. I know that I'll do another piece of work, that sometimes a piece of work is a springboard to the next piece of work. I can accept that.

Burroughs: Well, you've spoken of that, and also of the fact that your orchestra is trying to do something that's just a little bit beyond it; well, this implies that you're going somewhere. If you talk of a springboard, you're going from here to here—or you talk of the band playing a little beyond, surely that means there would be something beyond that, and beyond that.

Smith: I look to my future with so much joy, because I am at the most wonderful . . . I mean, superficially, my whole life's on crazy ground. You know I've moved to Detroit. It's wrenching to—I mean, I've lived in New York City for twelve years. I've struggled and built a certain emotional tabernacle here, some kind of tabernacle that represents my work here.

And I'm very proud of the work I did here. I feel that I did good work in this City. And I love this City, you know. To leave New York was a very tough thing. But I did it with great joy, too—you know, like a pioneer. It's like you have to "Go West!" I've always been a very East Coast girl. I was raised in South Jersey—Philly, Camden, all the coolest cities. Actually, though, when I was a teenager I thought that the coolest city wasn't New York, it was Detroit—because I was from the Motown, and stuff. . . .

But the thing is, I'm very happy because I have met the person in my life that I've been waiting to meet since I was a little girl. I feel that I have met that person. I always believed that I would meet that person. It was my greatest dream, to meet the person who I recognized as my person. And it came late in my life, I mean later than I thought. I thought it would be the person I met when I was sixteen, you know. . . .

And that person is open to me. For the first time, I'm not pursuing—the person has opened up to me another way to express myself truly, which is music. And even though I've been dealing in rock 'n' roll, and always thinking of myself as sort of a spokesman kind of person . . .

Burroughs: Well Patti, just regarding me as someone who knows very little—as I do know very little—about music and what's going on now, just give me a little talk. Tell me what's going on, and where things are going.

Smith: There isn't anything to know. The Seventies basically were a period where different people were trying to take a throne, you see? The only people that were interesting at all—not always even anyone that I liked—were people like David Bowie. And I don't demean David Bowie, in fact some of his work has been inspirational to me, but he's still . . . he's not an American. You know, he doesn't move me. I don't want to say anything negative, because he does enough positive things that make him worthwhile to me. But he didn't excite me in the Seventies. I think what it was, was a hunger that we didn't know that a lot of us had. We all felt loneliness as a hunger for something to happen. As we thought we were lonely, a group like Television thinks they're alone. The boys that later became the Sex Pistols thought they were alone. All of us people that should have been perpetuating, or helping to build on, the Sixties, we were dormant. And we thought we were alone.

Our credo was, "Wake up!" I've said this before, but just to tell you, in case you haven't read or anything: I wanted to be like Paul Revere. That was my whole thing. I wanted to be like Paul Revere. I didn't want to be a giant big hero, I didn't want to die for the cause. I didn't want to be a martyr. All that I wanted was for the people to fuckin' wake up. That's all I wanted them to do, and I feel that that's what happened.

Burroughs: Well, as you say that this is what happened. You have the whole punk generation, essentially, who are anti-heroes. See, they're rejecting the old values, because having been woken up, they realize that all this nonsense that they've been brought up on *is* nonsense. And all these standards. And they're rejecting those standards. So we could regard them, if you will, as something that you have been instrumental in creating.

Smith: I still believe in genius. I don't give a fuck, I don't agree with these kids. I believe in heroes. See, I love these kids, but I think that I've spawned a lot of little monsters, though, sometimes. Because I don't feel the same way they do. I don't think it's cool to shoot yourself up with heroin at 21 years old and die. I don't think it's cool to die at 21, you know.

I don't want to be dead. I would exist forever. I love life, and I love being on Earth. I love being an Earthling. I don't revel in the death of these people. I don't love Jimi Hendrix because he died. I loved what he did when he was most alive, you know, and consulting the gods on stage. That's what I loved. I don't have any interest in him consulting the gods to the death. I couldn't witness that. I could only experience that.

I think that what people thought of the New Wave—after it became the New Wave—got to be such a media and fashion-oriented, imagistic kind of thing, that the initial reason for it got all distorted.

Burroughs: But do you feel, then, that the whole music scene is going to progress?

Smith: What's important is that there are, I hate to call it this, more imposters, than ever. I never think that anybody should do art unless they're a great artist. I think that people have the right to express themselves in the privacy of their own home, but I don't think they should perpetuate it on the human race unless they've really decided that it was something that would help in the advancement of the human race—at least in a pleasurable kind of manner.

You know what I mean. It doesn't mean I don't like reading Mickey Spillane, or pornography books. . . . It used to be that art was unquestionably art. And I think that we have to get back into that frame, but that thing can only happen again by the eruption of like at least ten great people at once. I want to live in an illuminated time.

Burroughs: —But you know, everyone isn't as optimistic as you are.

Smith: Well, maybe that's my main gift, you know. I mean, I know that people aren't, especially men. I know that things have become so corrupt that the more . . . I also think that's the one card I have in being female. I'm talking in a gender kind of way, but only in a certain kind of way, not in the act of creation. I mean, I wouldn't talk to you about gender, if we were talking about performing properly, or the act of doing work. I understand that it's important to go beyond your gender in that process. But I'm proud to be the same gender as Anna Magnani, you know? I know that women, by the basis of our makeup, we perpetuate civilization, and we have to be optimistic. We have to believe in the future, or else . . . since we're the ones who bear the children of the future, we have to feel we're not setting them to light on a volcano. You don't want to bear a child and then drop it in a volcano. You want to bear a child and put him in paradise.

Burroughs: Yes, a lot of women do feel that way, I mean, they do feel that they don't want to bear children at this time.

Smith: But some of us have, you know. I, for instance, bore a child twelve years ago. This child's alive somewhere. I've a very Spartan feeling about it. I have no desire to meet her, or to raise her, or to have some kind of emotional reunion with her. But I would like for her to exist on a planet where there's space for her to develop her perceptions, I think that what can give more space is joy. I mean, I understand that, and I don't believe in having nine kids at this point. I'm not a Mexican Catholic, you know, I desire for the planet to go on, and not see swans go extinct, and all that stuff. . . .

But I don't have any desire to live on a planet that has no heroes, and no angels, and no saints, and no art. I'm not ashamed to say it. It's not very fashionable to think that way, I suppose, but the more unfashionable it becomes, the more angry, and the more strong I become in my position.

I was actually very heartbroken in the last few years, because I had to accept a lot of things about our planet and about, you know, realities. But still, like I said, just as we have the temptation to be corrupted, we have the strength to not be corrupted.

I like to think of those forty days when—I've talked to you about this before. The idea of Jesus. I haven't completely accepted that thing in my mind. I'm still, I can't just . . . the day that I totally accept Him is going to be a very wonderful day, if it happens, but I have to think about it still. I'm still exploring that guy. But one of the stories that I really like is when He, just at this period of time, went into the desert for forty days and wrestled with the Devil, you know, when they actually had a verbal and physical battle. Forty days of someone woodpeckering your spirit, is pretty . . .

Burroughs: Yeah, it's pretty harrowing.

Smith: And he came out of it. And so for me, whenever I think that I have it tough because I have to fight radio stations, or a record company or anything, I get pretty ashamed of myself when I think that this guy had to spend forty days without food or drink in the middle of a desert with the Devil . . . it doesn't seem like it's as painful as I make it out to be. But it does get to you.

PART II
1988-1996
Dream of Life

PATTI SMITH RESURFACES

Jim Sullivan | August 27, 1988 | *Boston Globe*

They say parenthood changes you, and when Patti Smith resurfaced in 1988 after vanishing for nearly a decade from the scene she helped define, the godmother of punk had become a mother. Smith had matured, and it was evident on *Dream of Life*—her first album since *Wave* in 1979—a collaboration with her husband, guitarist Fred "Sonic" Smith of the MC5 and Sonic's Rendezvous Band.

The youthful irreverence and spontaneous exuberance seemed to give way to a clear-eyed sense of obligation: there was the guileless optimism of "People Have the Power," a populist anthem that would remain a staple of her live set for the rest of her career; "Where Duty Calls," about the 1983 Marine barracks bombing in Beirut; and "The Jackson Song," a lullaby for her five-year-old son. The punk edge had been softened by years of provincial living in St. Clair Shores, a suburb of Fred's native Detroit. They kept a vintage boat in the yard where they whiled away the summer months listening to Tigers games. One day, lightning struck a weeping willow, the oldest in the town, resulting in a fallen branch and a backyard shipwreck. Yet even in the suburbs, the godmother of punk, who was always wary of the label, was still punk. And she still felt rock 'n' roll could change the world.

There would be no tour surrounding the album, but she wanted the broader public to know she hadn't merely disappeared; she was evolving, and had gained some wisdom staying in one place. "I was very happy not to be talking about myself," she told Jim Sullivan when they met at a Detroit hotel. "But I realize you have to communicate. I have gone through certain changes, and if I don't communicate them, people will keep me in one place. I have grown and shifted and have things I can, perhaps, share." —Ed.

DETROIT—"I'm still shaky from this," says Patti Smith, who's been driven by her husband, Fred Smith, through a hellish rainstorm and rush-hour traffic to make this late afternoon interview at a hotel. The traffic and the rain, Smith can bear. What's shaken her was driving past the aftermath of what looked to be an extremely recent, extremely violent, car crash in this Motor City. The more twisted the wreckage, the more fragile life looks. And, make no mistake, Patti Smith—wife, mother, poet, painter, writer, singer, artist—values life.

"I stand guilty of being positive and hopeful," she says, smiling. "I've always been optimistic. I mean, I've had my dark periods and certainly now I'm more worried about the condition of the planet than I've ever been, but I've always loved life and I've always been inspired by other people. I just saw *Empire of the Sun*. To see somebody do such a beautiful piece of work makes me optimistic. A new William Burroughs book, a new Jean-Luc Godard movie, a new Robert Mapplethorpe photograph. There's a million things that make me optimistic."

Smith, dressed in a black jacket, off-white blouse and faded black jeans, tries to compose herself, as she settles in to talk. Coffee helps. It's her only vice, she says, and she had to give it up during her two pregnancies. Now, she says, "I'm making up for lost time."

Smith—in the vanguard of New York's mid-'70s punk-rock/new-wave explosion, the co-author, with Bruce Springsteen, of the 1978 pop hit "Because the Night"—waved goodbye to the rock 'n' roll world in 1979. She married Fred "Sonic" Smith, former guitarist of the MC5, a revolutionary rock band of the late '60s–early '70s. She moved to Smith's home turf, Detroit, and had two children, a boy, Jackson, now 5, and a girl, Jesse Paris, now 2. Those details leaked out during the '80s. But Patti Smith—rock 'n' roller—was MIA. She resurfaced only this year with her fifth album, *Dream of Life*, and its first single, the power-of-positive-dreaming song, "People Have the Power."

Smith, who has no plans to tour, is doing selective interviews. "I felt really uncomfortable talking about myself again," she says of the process. "I was very happy not to be talking about myself. But I realize you have to communicate. I have gone through certain changes, and if I don't communicate them, people will keep me in one place. I have grown and shifted and have things I can, perhaps, share."

Changes . . .

Jump back to 1976: Smith and her group are on stage, playing—flailing, reclaiming—The Who's "My Generation"; Smith reworks Pete Townshend's famous "Why don't you all just f-f-fade away?" into something more vulgar, more angry, more punk-like; Smith rips the six strings from her guitar; Smith closes the timeless anthem with a shout, "We created it! Let's take it over."

"That was an inspired cry," Smith says now, about those days. "When we did that song we meant it; we did it with full heart. It's a young person's battle cry, and I think we really got it. There were plenty of bad performances, angry performances, and plenty of enlightened performances. But I was there. All my being was there.

"But I didn't miss it," she adds. "The day I stopped performing, that was it."

Smith regards herself, a dozen years ago: "I was a much younger person, young enough to get away with the fact that a lot of my energies were adolescent energies. I don't think I was negative or there's anything I should feel really bad about, but it's just that I'm 41 years old, the planet is going into the hands of people my age and a little older. Maybe it's being a parent. Having two children, it's become quite apparent to me, being a parent, that I have a lot more responsibility for my actions. I wanted to see myself as a person that was more caring about others and less preoccupied with myself."

Asked about her nine-year absence from public life, she laughs and repeats a joke she shared with guitarist Lenny Kaye, her former partner in the Patti Smith Group, comparing her missing years to Christ's or Cleopatra's. More seriously, she says, "I can say that it's been one of the best times of my life, really, in terms of self-growth. I was on such a fast pace, you never have time to think. You're going from one place to another and everyone's very preoccupied with your own situation. You don't really stop to think about what you're doing, who you are, how you're progressing as a person. Because everything is working toward a perpetuation of the situation—which at the time was the Patti Smith

Group, which I am infinitely proud of—but that constant, vigorous touring got me in a frame of mind where you lose judgment. Some things I wasn't happy with, both as a human being and an artist. So, all of a sudden I went from 98 speed to a much slower speed. I got to check myself out."

Smith wrote a novel (unpublished), painted, traveled, and wrote lyrics for the *Dream of Life* LP while husband Fred crafted the music. It's not, as Smith readily admits, a punk rock record. She says its aim is to be "universal." There's a terse quality to rockers like "Going Under" and "Up There Down There," but a positive tone flows freely through *Dream of Life*, from the anthemic, opening rocker "People Have the Power" to the reflective closer, the heartstring-pulling, mature nursery rhyme, "Song for Jackson."

"I'm well aware of the overly positive aspects of 'People Have the Power,'" Smith says. "Call it naive. I don't think being filled with hope and still having the desire and care and vision to dream is naive. The song is trying to give a little inspiration and hope in very troubled times. I don't see the point of just spewing negativity. If I wanted to put covers over my head, I would have never wed and had two children. If I'd wanted to put the covers over my head, I would have found some opium den and gone out in Cocteau-style."

She'd not have been the first. Some thought that might, indeed, be her fate.

"I might have thought it myself," she says, "when I was younger." She says she's envisioned a romantic death, "many, many times. I don't anymore because I can only die in my dreams. I have to get up and feed the kids and change the diapers and do the laundry. I have a lot of work to do. And Fred would kill me!"

Smith doesn't denounce her past. "I stand on it," she says. Still, she does distance herself from it. Smith says she views "Horses," her wild, beautiful, chaotic debut LP, much the way Picasso might look back on his "blue" period. "I'm not comparing myself to him," she says, "but you go through periods of work as an artist, where you look at it almost as if it were an abstract piece. I'm not the same person as I was back then.

I still feel for that persona and I feel for that work. But it's not for me; I've outgrown it."

Consider the way *Horses* opened, with "Gloria: In Excelsis Deo/Gloria (version)." The introductory line—"Jesus died for somebody's sins, but not mine"—was taken from a poem Smith wrote when she was 19, when she was heavily influenced by Albert Camus and Franz Kafka. Then, Smith wove her own sexual, stirring visions into a wired, pummeling remake of Van Morrison's "Gloria."

In time, though, Smith grew away from the song, stopped playing it live, and then wrestled with fans' demands to hear it. The last time the band played, in Florence, Italy, in 1979, Smith found a way out of her dilemma. The line became: "Jesus died for somebody's sins: Why not mine?"

She'd read a book about the views of radical director Pier Paulo [*sic*] Pasolini, who made the film, *The Gospel According to St. Matthew*. She became interested in the portrayal of a more intellectual, revolutionary Jesus, one closer to Smith's heart. It was hardly her first brush with religion or, as an artist, absorbing religious influences. Smith grew up a Jehovah's Witness, which is her mother's faith; her father, Smith says, is a "self-professed, spiritual atheist." She valued the scripturally oriented discipline of the former; the questing nature of the latter.

Smith, one of four children, was born in Chicago, but the family moved to Pitman, N.J., while Smith was young. A sickly child, she says she had every possible childhood disease and can be seen in family photo albums always "with a puss" on her face. As a child, she wanted to be a missionary. Her father talked her out of that, not wanting her to rob people of their culture. "Plus," says Smith, "with my luck I'd instantly get malaria." She then wanted to be an opera singer or ballet dancer; later a writer and artist. She got hooked on rock 'n' roll and became a fan of the Rolling Stones and Jimi Hendrix.

At 16, she worked in a Jersey factory and that experience led to her first recorded song, "Piss Factory," an enveloping tale of degradation, anger, and hopeful, eventual, fame in New York. The fame, in a manner of speaking, came to her—after sidetrips to college (Glassboro State Teachers College) and Paris. She moved to New York in 1968, and took a room at the Chelsea Hotel. She met and collaborated with playwright Sam Shepard ('Mad Dog Blues,' 'Cowboy Mouth'). She became a poet and, later, singer when Lenny Kaye began adding three-chord electric guitar to her readings.

"It was a stoned period, an exploratory period," she says. "There was a lot of self-indulgence. Just the intoxication—not even drugs—of just being on the stage and getting all this energy from the audience, the adrenaline, and then you go off on a stream of consciousness." That led to *Horses* in 1976 and *Radio Ethiopia* in 1977.

She began to shape her sound more cautiously by her third album, *Easter*, and its follow-up, *Wave*. The former yielded her only bona fide hit, "Because the Night." It reached No. 13 on *Billboard*'s chart, and she got a kick out of walking the streets of Manhattan and hearing the song blaring from the radios at Crazy Eddie's.

Now, as a writer, Smith says editing is most important to the process. "I finally got to the point where I can pretty much sit and concentrate and focus and say exactly what I want to say," she says. "I've somehow convinced clarity to come my way and stay there." Her husband's music conforms more carefully to the range of her voice, causing some to ask her if she'd taken lessons. "Is that a compliment?" Smith wonders rhetorically.

"The only thing I've ever wrestled with, through the years, in terms of art," she says, "was, 'Am I good enough? Do I deserve to call myself an artist?' Or when, I've had brief periods of the muse taking an extra-long vacation and you wonder, 'Did it go to Zanzibar and is it in some weird hotel, never coming back?'"

For Patti Smith, the muse is back. "I have so many things that I am extremely proud of," she says. "Fred, the children and the work that I do."

PATTI SMITH: THE POWER AND THE GLORY, THE RESURRECTION AND THE LIFE

Gerrie Lim | July 1995 | *BigO* (Singapore)

When Patti Smith returned again to public life in 1995, she had endured unspeakable loss. In 1989, she lost one of her closest friends, Robert Mapplethorpe, to AIDS. In 1990, she lost her longtime pianist, Richard Sohl. On November 4, 1994, her husband, Fred "Sonic" Smith, died of heart failure; a month later, her brother and road manager, Todd Smith, suffered a fatal stroke. This wasn't her first brush with loss. When she was seven or eight, her best friend died of leukemia. Smith made a point of visiting the graves of fallen idols like Jim Morrison, and others—Jimi Hendrix, Brian Jones, Arthur Rimbaud, and Joan of Arc—never seemed far from her thoughts. Yet it was not their premature deaths but their irrepressible life force, their spark, that she celebrated and kept aflame. We don't come to Patti Smith to experience what it's like to die; we come to her to experience what it's like to live. We don't come to her to experience what it's like to suffer through grief; we come to her to experience what it's like to survive it.

So in July 1995, when Gerrie Lim met Smith at Electric Lady Studios, itself a kind of shrine to its fallen creator, much of the conversation focused on mortality. Yet as raw as the loss still was, Smith seemed focused on appreciating every new day. She was making her first, as-yet-untitled album since *Dream of Life* in 1988, which would become *Gone Again*, in part a meditation on loss as she worked through it. Smith was recording "Dead to the World" in Studio A, which she explained to Lim matter-of-factly as "when you're in deep sleep, you're dead to everything around you." However, the song seems more about "when sleepers wake and yet still dream," to borrow a phrase from Yeats. Listen to the insistent rhythmic tambourine pulse on two and four, its buoyant melody, the jagged grain of Smith's quaking voice, and the lyrics: "Dead to the world, alive I awoke."

Her fans had waited a long time for her to come back to performing regularly—sixteen years to be exact. She was forty-eight years old, and had assumed a matriarchal role in absentia, at least in terms of influence, to artists like Courtney Love, Liz Phair, and R.E.M. Many people assumed, as we often do with celebrities made conspicuous by their absence, that she had simply disappeared. But perhaps what makes her so relatable is that sense that she was still out there, which she was, working every day, and living her life, just like the rest of us. After spending the better part of two decades out of the public eye, she granted very few interviews, and there was a lot of catching up to do. —Ed.

In art and dream may you proceed with abandon.
In life may you proceed with balance and stealth.

   —Patti Smith, "To the Reader," introduction to Early Work

Electric Lady Sound in New York, at 52 West 8th Street in once hippie-dippy Greenwich Village, is an unlikely location whose exterior resembles a bomb shelter and emanates perverse poetics. There's a sign right out-side, on the sidewalk, slung onto a lamp post, that actually decrees: "UNNECESSARY NOISE PROHIBITED."

An unused cinema lies next door, an optometrist next door to that, and a shoe store sits right opposite across the asphalt. It's so surreally nondescript, right smack in the middle of a busy block throbbing with pedestrians, that if you blink you'll easily miss it.

Yet Jimi Hendrix immortalised this place as Electric Ladyland, and on this swelteringly hot late July afternoon I'm sequestered in the con-trol room at Electric Lady's Studio A, spending some time with another legend, this one very much alive and well.

"This song is called 'Dead to the World,'" Patti Smith tells me. "It's about how when you're in deep sleep, you're dead to everything around you." I tell her it's not a bad state to be in—why, that's how R.E.M. got their name—and she laughs. "Yeah, it's pretty good," she agrees. She dons her headphones and goes down to the floor, where her band awaits. Lenny Kaye and Malcolm Burn, both on guitars, are co-producing this, Smith's first album in seven years. Tony Shanahan, who's played with John Cale, is on bass and Jay Dee Daugherty, still Smith's drummer for 20 years now, is playing synthesizer. Her voice is tremulous and deep, resonating with a rich and startling quality that I've never heard on record before.

The song itself is a dirge—a careening tribal march recalling "Ghost Dance," the Paiute Indian hymn from her 1978 album *Easter*—and it's in this spirit of invocation that history is being made right before my eyes. Smith is now five songs into this recording and the new album, still untitled, is slated for completion in September, for no other reason than that her two children then have to return to school.

That, in a nutshell, explains the so-called missing years of Patti Smith. Over a 20-year span, since 1975, she's made just five albums (*Horses, Radio Ethiopia, Easter, Wave,* and *Dream Of Life*)—all amazing works that have withstood the test of time—and while none of them have ever gone gold, the vagaries of rock stardom have never quite been her trip. Living legend? Perish that thought. On September 10th, 1979, the Patti Smith Group played their last show to their biggest-ever audience—80,000 in Florence, Italy—and in March 1980 she married Fred "Sonic" Smith, the brilliant guitarist of the Detroit band MC5 (and the man after whom Sonic Youth took their name), and retired to the suburb of St. Clair Shores, Michigan, where she still lives today with sons [*sic*] Jackson and Jesse.

That the New York punk rock lifestyle hadn't beckoned for so long did not particularly bother her, for motherhood had become her new-found vocation. This unwavering path, however, got detoured somewhat following twin tragedies late last year: Fred "Sonic" Smith died of a heart attack on November 4th—ironically the birthday of her best friend, photographer Robert Mapplethorpe, who himself had passed on from AIDS in March 1989—and, one month later, her beloved brother Todd died. Patricia Lee Smith turned 48 on Dec. 30, 1994, a celebration suddenly steeped in mourning.

But the Smiths had written some new songs together and so, in Fred's memory, this new record is being made. And there are two new books in the works—*Wild Leaves*, poems and prose in memory of her departed loved ones, and *The Coral Sea*, prose poems for Robert Mapplethorpe written shortly after his death. The former is still uncompleted, the latter will be published early next year by WW Norton, who recently issued a splendid compilation of her poetry, culled from books now virtually impossible to find, called *Patti Smith: Early Work 1970–1979*.

"I didn't really want to put it out," she tells me about *Early Work*, during a break in the recording session, "but it came to my attention that some people were selling copies of my old books to kids for a lot of money. I didn't think that was fair, so I agreed to have them compiled." That's Patti Smith the artist talking, one who's never ever done anything purely for financial gain. In fact, the very next evening, she does a free concert at Central Park, reprising a poetry reading she'd done there two years ago, though this time it's a campfire event, a gathering of "family and friends" to play some songs as well.

Just two weeks ago, on July 5th, she'd packed the Phoenix club in Toronto and played two electrifying sets. But this, at the open-air Central Park Summer Stage, is her first gig on home turf in a very long time. The *Village Voice* has her on its cover this week, a gorgeous color portrait of her in a garden with the coverline reading "The Return of Patti Smith," and the inside story headline proclaiming, after her best-known hit, "Because the Night."

Because that's why she still does it. Live rock is best a nocturnal thing, lest we forget, and she has not forgotten. She comes out at 9:15 pm and smiles at the massive throng below, several thousand fans who've been patient all these years, and her opening words are potent and poignant.

"I have not returned," she announced, "because I never went away." The crowd concurs and claps, and she grins. It's an oppressively hot and humid New York summer night, everyone is sweating, and a tall attractive girl in the front row has taken off her top and proudly stands bare-breasted. No one complains, of course, and the event is simply too historic for quibbles about the weather. Patti Smith has weathered the years well, with humour intact. She banters with the crowd, cracks jokes and mugs for the cameras. Flashes pop, amid song requests. Someone yells: "'Gloria!'"

"'Gloria,'" she yells back without missing a beat, "has been laid to rest in Singapore."

She then reads poetry for 40 mins, beginning with "Land of a Thousand Dances," which she dedicates to Robert Mapplethorpe, after which she brings out the band: Lenny Kaye, Tony Shanahan, and her sister Kimberly Smith (*the* Kimberly, incidentally, the song from the *Horses* album), all on acoustic guitars, and they play three songs—"Ghost Dance" (with the very apropos refrain *"We shall live again, we shall live again"*), "People Have the Power" (for which she saluted *in absentia* its writer, Fred "Sonic" Smith) and "Paths That Cross" (*"Paths that cross will cross again"*)—and then they leave.

Returning alone for the encore carrying an acoustic guitar, she sits on a stool and beings a monologue. "To many of you, I know I've been out of your eye for a while," she says. "And I can only explain that by saying that it was because I was privileged to have been the wife of a great man. . . ." Applause erupts for Fred "Sonic" Smith, and she plays a tender ballad of farewell, her voice cracking, and she stops and starts several times between stanzas, and leaves. I'm watching all this from the wings backstage, my pulse quickening. It's intense, a still-point, in the zen of understanding our own passage through this vale of tears. Between thought and expression, as Lou Reed neatly puts it. Between all that is the motherlode of memory, without which life is rendered useless.

Yet, never one to simply dwell on the past, Smith appears again the very next afternoon, taking the Lollapalooza second stage completely unannounced. Mere hours later, she signs books at Barnes & Noble on Astor Place in Manhattan. "It was exhausting. Hundreds of people showed up," she tells me over the phone the next morning. *The New York Times* has given her a glowing review, but she's not resting on any laurels. A car is already running outside her West Village townhouse, where Arista Records (whose big-hearted big cheese Clive Davis signed her to a US $750,000 seven-album deal in 1975) has her ensconced for the new album's recording, and she's off again. But not before giving me the phone number of a Toronto photographer and telling me that this piece I'm writing has her full blessing. "Call me, I'll be here all summer," she says, and hot-foots out the door.

But before the summer's over, I'll still be dwelling on the recent past, and one memory in particular. The same evening after I'd watched her record "Dead to the World," I spend an enjoyable hour browsing through bootlegs at Revolver Records, a supercool shop at 8th and MacDougal, and emerged to stroll past Electric Lady en route back to my hotel. From the street, it was noticeable that one light, Studio A's, was still on. The light's still on, I thought, which meant they were still in there, recording through the night. Which meant that Patti Smith, like her people, still has the power.

GERRIE LIM: *Well, I have the pleasure of telling you that we've voted your album* Horses *the #1 record of the last 20 years.*

PATTI SMITH: Thank you. That's really a great honour. I don't think it's ever been voted #1 before. It's been top five but I don't think it's ever been #1, so I thank you so much for that honour.

GERRIE: *I think the impact and the influence of that record has been just phenomenal and incalculable. When you think of* Horses, *what do you think of?*

PATTI: I think, one of the first things I think of is the camaraderie I had with my band. I think of all of our youthful hopes and dreams, all the things we put into it. Because a lot of the things that are in *Horses* I started writing when I was about 20. So *Horses* is, I think, a real extension of that great burst of youthful energy. It was really a period of strong idealism and physical energy and camaraderie, because it was when I banded with these people and had my first experience of having a rock 'n' roll band.

GERRIE: *You've made just five records in the last 20 years but they're such amazing records. Do you have a favourite one?*

PATTI: I can't say that I have a favourite record. I have favourite pieces. I really like "Birdland" (from *Horses*) and I really like "Radio Ethiopia" (from *Radio Ethiopia*)—that's always my favourite piece, that long one.

I hadn't listened to the records for a long time but lately I started listening to them again, and I enjoyed listening to "Dancing Barefoot" (from *Wave*) and "25th Floor" (from *Easter*). I'm really quite happy with the records because when I listen to them, every record we did exactly how we wanted. We never compromised any record for a company, we never compromised for money or career. So I don't have any bad memories when I listen to the music. When I listen to the music, I just think of all the hard work and the joy that went into them. I sometimes feel a little sad because some of the people that I wrote the music with have died. Things like that, I do feel a little sad. But the music, I still have nothing to be ashamed of. I have no regrets and I feel good about all of them.

GERRIE: Now you're recording again, and at Electric Ladyland too.

PATTI: Yes, where we did *Horses*.

GERRIE: And "Piss Factory."

PATTI: Yes, we recorded "Piss Factory" in 1974 here. And then we came back in 1975 to do *Horses*.

GERRIE: I was going through your newly-issued book of poems (Patti Smith: Early Work 1970–1979) and I noticed at the end of "Piss Factory" it says "Recorded at Electric Ladyland, June 5, 1974" and it struck me that this is like the completion of a circle going back 21 years. Do you see it that way? Is this a deliberate thing, to record again at Electric Ladyland?

PATTI: No. I didn't want to record uptown in New York where my husband and I had recorded *Dream of Life* because I thought it might be a little too difficult and sad. So I mentioned to Lenny [Kaye], "We should record downtown somewhere," and he said, "Well, we can go back to Electric Ladyland." And I thought that was a great idea. I didn't really realise, I hadn't thought about how long it had been or anything. It's an inspirational thing. Everybody's been so great here. It's wonderful to walk in because the room we're in has huge murals of Jimi Hendrix and all of Jimi Hendrix's gold records, and it has a really great spirit. You know, it's right off 8th Street in the Village. I go out, people say hello to me, it's got a good feeling.

GERRIE: *Why are you doing a record now, so to speak—I mean, at this particular time—after a lapse of several years?*

PATTI: Well, my husband and I, before he died, we were working on material to record. We wanted to record because we had things to say and we had ideas and also, you know, I have children—we have two children—and it's the way we make a living. (laughs) It was time. I'm very conscious of being a single parent and I want to make sure that I do a lot of work and get things ready for their future. So I'm doing it partially in tribute to my husband and also because it helps me to work. It makes me feel better and also to get things ready for my children.

GERRIE: *Is there a working title for the new album?*

PATTI: No, I don't have a title yet.

GERRIE: *You've pretty much kept the same band through the years excepting the* Easter *album when Bruce Brody replaced Richard Sohl on keyboards.*

PATTI: Yeah, because Richard was sick. It wasn't because he was out—he wasn't well. Richard passed away, after we did *Dream of Life*. He played all the keyboards on *Dream of Life* with my husband and then he passed away in '91, of heart failure. He was wonderful and I was actually quite heartbroken. I have a new keyboard player who plays very similar to Richard. He's from Detroit and his name is Luis Resto. And Lenny's playing guitar and Jay Dee Daugherty, who is a good friend of Lenny's, is playing bass. And we'll have other guitar players on this record—my old guitar player Ivan Kral and perhaps Tom Verlaine and certain other people might be guest-playing. I need to finish it this summer but we're going very well and I believe it will be completed and will be out in the fall. I'm not going to be touring too much because I have two children and it's very difficult for me. I might do special dates here and there. I really love the people I'm playing with. I think the sound is really good. It's a good strong sound, simple but really good.

GERRIE: *Do you ever think back on your place in the history of pop culture and on the whole idea of fame?*

PATTI: Well, I don't think about fame because, as Alexander the Great's servant told him, "All fame is fleeting." So I don't think about that too much. But influence is another thing. Fame, of course, is fleeting, and so is fortune, but influence is enduring. I'm really quite honoured when people say they've been influenced by me and the work my band did. Actually, a lot of people have said that and a lot of people I admire, so it really makes me happy. Because I think for an artist to have a positive influence on new artists, it's one of the great gifts you can give. Because so many people have influenced me. I was influenced by Jim Morrison and Bob Dylan and the Rolling Stones, and if I can keep the thread going and influence other people in a positive way, that's a great honour.

GERRIE: *What do you think of rock music today? Is punk still viable?*

PATTI: I think things are a lot more open than they were in the '70s. The field is quite wide and I'm really proud of a lot of the things that the new guard has done, all these groups from My Bloody Valentine to Nirvana. My son likes Green Day. There's a lot of energy in music right now. As far as what people call the "punk spirit," I think it doesn't necessarily have to take any specific form of music because it's really a spirit. And what the spirit is, I think, it removes itself or tries to repurify things when things get too convoluted or when they get too commercial. There's this resurgent spirit that people call punk that purifies everything again. Whether they call it grunge or punk or anything, it's the new guard coming in to purify, to let things renew and begin again.

GERRIE: *It sounds like you've been listening to what's out there.*

PATTI: Yeah, I like to see what's going on. I'm not always up on every-thing but I wish everybody well, you know. I think that everybody's done a good job. There's a continuing surge of new people that are trying to do things and trying to shake things up. I think that's important.

GERRIE: *What do you think of Courtney Love?*

PATTI: I think she's done some really good work. I don't know her personally and I hope that she takes care of herself. She has a beautiful daughter and I'd like to see Courtney take care of herself physically. But other than that, I think she's done really good work. I haven't seen her live but I saw the *Unplugged* show (on MTV) and I liked the *Live Through This* album. "Doll Parts" is a great song. I thought the *Unplugged* performance was really great. I think the band is really good and I think it's important for them to take care of themselves. They've already lost one band member, poor girl, and I just think it's important that for even artists that move toward the edge, you have to maintain some balance or you won't live. I think life is too great. I hate to see anybody throw their life away, so I hope that a lot of these younger people will try to maintain some balance.

GERRIE: How have you yourself managed to do that?

PATTI: Well, I've never really indulged much in drugs and things like that or anything negative. Most of my anger or, as they call it, angst or frustration, I've put into my work and not into a drug or into something negative. I've had a lot of anarchistic feelings and a lot of that kind of energy, and I've always put it into work. And even though I've tried a couple of drugs in my life and I liked to smoke pot when I was younger, I never got involved in it. I think that's really important. If one must visit a drug or want to see what a drug can do or use it as a tool for work, you have to be very careful. You have to respect drugs, 'cos drugs won't respect you. They won't respect you so if you don't respect them, you're gonna be in trouble. I'm just happy to be alive and I want to stay that way, and I don't flirt with a lot of stuff that will take my life away.

GERRIE: Speaking of death, I understand you're writing a book of poetry about your dead friends. Is that true?

PATTI: Well, I was writing a book of poems and stories and things that pretty much surrounded a lot of people that I had lost. Like my friend Robert Mapplethorpe, Richard [Sohl] and other people that I know. And also people that I admired—I wrote a poem for Nureyev and Genet and Audrey Hepburn, just different people that I really liked that influenced me. But when I lost my husband and brother—I lost my brother a month after my husband—I haven't been able to write much, so I've just set it aside for a while. But when I feel stronger I'll get back to it. I just find that I can't really write right now. But I have been able to write songs, and I am starting to feel a lot stronger emotionally and physically, and I think I'll be writing again soon.

GERRIE: Was that your brother Todd, who was involved in the that famous incident with Sid Vicious? (Free on bail two months after he'd stabbed his girlfriend Nancy Spungen to death at the Chelsea Hotel, Sid Vicious of the Sex Pistols slashed Smith's brother Todd in the face with a broken bottle.)

PATTI: Yes. That was actually quite frightening. My brother is a tough kid but he's very pacifistic. He was a real peacemaker type of guy. I think Sid Vicious was just crazy. He just went crazy in this bar and my brother almost lost his eye. He didn't provoke him or anything. But Sid Vicious was fairly out of control then, because he died soon after that. He was another kid who was really talented but he didn't keep his balance. That whole story is tragic. Both of them [Sid and Nancy] lost control and it's sad.

GERRIE: I've always thought that the interesting thing about punk rock is that there is a lot of anger that fuels the music and so it creates this energy, yet it's a very dangerous thing.

PATTI: Well, I think if they put more anger in the work instead of in their lifestyle, they'd be better off. I think a lot of times people put a lot of those feelings, those frustrations, into their lifestyle. These days especially, I think if one's filled with so much restlessness and anger, there's a lot of things people can do with that energy. I always tell people that if they don't know what to with themselves, go to an AIDS ward and see what it's like when people have no choice. Go to an AIDS ward and help those people out. Use some of your energy to help your fellow man. If you really think your life is tough because there doesn't seem to be a way out, go to see a person who has an illness that is so cruel they truly have no way out except that they're going to die. I think if people looked at other people's situations and saw what it's like for certain people, they'd feel a lot less sorry for themselves.

GERRIE: What are your own thoughts on death? Do you view it with any kind of apprehension and fear as opposed to a sense of fatalism?

PATTI: I don't have fears. For myself, spiritually, I look at death as a continuing journey. I don't wish to die, especially being a parent. I wouldn't want my children to be left without a parent. And I love life, love being on the planet. But I really think of death as part of a continuum. I think it's more of a Buddhist point of view. That's the way I feel.

GERRIE: *I only ask because there's been so much of it in your life. I've had people close to me die and every time that happens, it always makes you question your own mortality.*

PATTI: It does. It reminds me to try to take better care of myself, but also to appreciate every day. Sometimes I just feel ecstatic to wake up. I'm so lucky. My poor husband, he'll never wake up again. I just feel so happy to be able to see my children and to create and do work and just walk down the street and breathe the air.

GERRIE: *A lot of people consider you a feminist role model. How do you feel about that?*

PATTI: Well, I like to help people any way I can. I don't call myself a feminist. I don't call myself anything. I think it's important to take everyone's point of view. As soon as people get hardcore into one point of view, they snuff out somebody else's point of view. I think you have to be open to all people's needs. Like people would say, "Well, you came out to be a role model for girls." Well, I never did. I wanted to be something for everybody. I read in a magazine recently that a writer was really surprised because Michael Stipe had said that I was a viable model for him, and they thought it was unusual coming from a guy. I think that in our time, as we move into the future, future generations will be less prejudiced about gender, race, colour, and things like that. I just think that as we progress into the future, future generations will be less and less interested in those boundaries. Maybe I'm being optimistic [laughs]. But why not? Why not be optimistic? I've never been pessimistic. One can kick open a door but not because they're trying to destroy the door, but because they want to see what's on the other side. A lot of my work was just about exploring beyond.

GERRIE: Robert Mapplethorpe was a lot about that, too. There's a resurgence of interest in him now because of this newly-published book (Mapplethorpe: A Biography, *by Patricia Morrisroe), which just got a really savage review in* The Los Angeles Times. *The reviewer felt that the writer of the book was being unkind and hateful and spiteful towards him. I don't know if you've read the book yet.*

PATTI: I've read portions of it. I think the writer was more interested in a sensationalist point of view and I think that's a shame because Robert did have a very interesting life. Robert and I had similar philosophies. We didn't want to be in any particular boundaries. He didn't want to be known as a homosexual photographer. He's an artist and he did what an artist does, whether it's Picasso or Jackson Pollock or John Coltrane, it's to break boundaries. And create a new boundary for someone else to explore. I think that's what Robert was trying to do, amongst other things, and I think he was quite successful. But in the end, I think what was the most interesting thing about him was his drive, the drive that made him an artist. I'd known Robert since he was 20 and he always had that drive. He'd create art from morning till night. It was the thing that drove him the most. I think the book really makes it seem that the thing that drove him the most was money or sex or fame. And all these things were important to Robert, they were, but the most important thing to him was his work. That drive was the strongest thing in him. He was always trying to work. Even in the days before he died, when he could hardly see or walk, he was still trying to create and it was the thing that really drove him.

GERRIE: It strikes me that you're doing the same now with this new record, because it's been a while since Dream of Life. *Did you feel at any point in the last five or six years that it was time to do this again, that there was perhaps too long a lapse in between albums?*

PATTI: Well, Fred and I had been working. It's a lot more difficult to work when you have a family. We were very devoted parents and that was always our first priority. But we were always working at home. It wasn't like we sat at home not doing anything. We still wrote music. I wrote about four books which in due time I'll be publishing. I was doing a lot of studying and Fred was also. When he wasn't creating music, he became a pilot. He learnt all these new skills and we were interested in developing ourselves in various ways.

GERRIE: Well, it's not as if you don't have a record out so you don't exist!

PATTI: Right. I mean, sometimes people act like you've totally retired, disappeared or stopped working because you don't have something in public. But I work every day. I've worked every day for the past 30 years. I write every day or do something every day. I have my own personal work ethic.

GERRIE: You're now performing again. Do you still get the same charge from being in front of an audience these days?

PATTI: Well, I haven't done it too much, but I've always been the kind of performer that draws from the energy of the people. I don't just per-form at people or do like a stock show. I always think of it as a night that we all create together. I always draw something from the people, and so each night is always different and it's always exciting and energising.

GERRIE: There's always been a sense of invitation, of participation, in your music. A friend of mine said the other day, "Will you tell Patti Smith that the first time I heard 'Because the Night,' it made me want to go and touch myself?"

PATTI: [*laughs*] That's not bad!

GERRIE: Another friend of mine, she told me: "You listen to her version of 'Because the Night' and then you listen to Natalie Merchant's version, the difference is so huge. There's no sex in Natalie Merchant's version!"

PATTI: Well, I had written the lyrics to 'Because the Night' for my hus-band and we were quite in love then, so I'm sure there was some in it then! [*laughs*] It's a love song. The lyrics I wrote for Fred. We had fallen in love and it was intentionally like that. I was away from him and I was longing for him. It was written as a song for him and letting him know how much I wanted to be with him.

GERRIE: So Bruce Springsteen wrote the music?

PATTI: Yes. He wrote the music and the title is his, as well.

GERRIE: Springsteen's from New Jersey, as are you. But a lot of people still think of you as a New York artist, as opposed to New Jersey or Philadelphia or Paris or Detroit, those other places of your life. Do you consider yourself a New Yorker?

PATTI: New York is really where I formed the basis for my work and I love New York. . . . I relate more to New York. I live in Michigan with my children, I lived there with my husband, but I don't consider myself a Midwestern person. I'm more of an East Coast person. I was raised on the East Coast and there's regional differences, but as an artist one hopes to achieve some kind of globalness or some more universal quality to their work. I wouldn't even want to be called a New York artist. I just want to be called an artist. If I can achieve that, that would be great.

GERRIE: Is there anything you'd like to say to your fans and followers overseas who have over the years been anxiously awaiting a new record from you?

PATTI: Tell them that I am well. And that I wish them all well. And tell them how deeply honoured and touched I am that they would think of the work that I do with such regard. It means a lot to me. It's one reason I'm doing this interview. I'm not doing any press right now, I'm not doing any American press, and I told the record company that I didn't want to do any press but when they mentioned this to me, I certainly wanted to do this. It is an honour and it's not an honour I take lightly. It might seem small or obscure to some, but to me the fact that I'm even thought of so honourably from so far away, it's inspiring. I'm certain of it, and I don't take it lightly. I have to go in soon and do my vocal and I'll take that inspiration with me. So tell the people I'll be thinking of them as I sing my vocals. Give the people a salute for me.

GERRIE: People have the power! You've made my day.

PATTI: No. You've made mine.

PATTI SMITH

Thurston Moore | Winter 1996 | *Bomb*

If you believe in spiritual transference, there is a direct line from the Rolling Stones to Sonic Youth. Once, when Patti Smith saw the Stones, she grabbed Brian Jones's ankle; once, when Thurston Moore saw Patti Smith, he grabbed her ankle. In an interview, sometimes it's obvious when interviewer and interviewee are on the same wavelength, as is the case here. Growing up, Patti Smith was to Moore what Rimbaud was to Patti Smith. After dreaming of meeting her "for nearly 20 years," they were finally, and it seems inevitably, friends, confidantes, and mutual admirers. After all, Sonic Youth was named for Fred "Sonic" Smith.

They met in Lowell, Massachusetts, the birthplace of Jack Kerouac, to perform at a benefit for the Kerouac Foundation. Smith opened up to Moore about her early romance with the original Sonic, her pet fishing lure named Curly, seeing John Coltrane in Philadelphia as an underage teenager, her devotion to the work of the Dalai Lama, and developments in rock after her sabbatical. "I feel like Rip van Winkle who fell asleep in the '70s and woke up in the '90s," she tells him. It was all punctuated by a visit to Kerouac's grave site and their Saturday night performance, in which Smith read the lyrics to "High on Rebellion" from *Easter*, dedicating it to Sonic Youth. The interview took place first in a hotel room and then in a car, but sometimes the most profound conversations happen in the most mundane locations. —Ed.

Patti Smith was, and is, pure experience. . . . Her reign in the '70s as a street-hot rock & roll messiah seemed to exist from a void. No past, no future—"the future is here," she'd sing. I'd hear tales of romance, the girl with the blackest hair hanging out at recording sessions writing poetry. But I didn't know her. I could only embrace the identity I perceived. I was impressionable and she came on like an alien. The first time I met her was in 1975 in a magazine. It was two poems about three wishes: rock & roll, sex, and New York City. Her photo was stark—no disco color flash. It was anti-glam, nocturnal staring eyes, black leather trousers. She was skinny and smart. She posed as if she were the coolest boy in the city. And she was. I could only imagine her world through her poems: telling, truthful, dirty, hopeful. I wanted to meet her and take her to a movie, but she was so unobtainable and fantastic I could only entrust my faith to the future. The future would allow me to have a date with Patti Smith or at least hang out with her. And the future seems to have come. It seems to be happening, it's happened. It's here.

Patti grew up in south Jersey in the '60s. As a teenager she became involved in a succession of religious experiences: "Catholic lust," an intense relationship with the Jehovah Witnesses, and a full-on romance with Tibetan Buddhism. She completely immersed herself in the genius of Bob Dylan and Arthur Rimbaud. She loved (and loves) rock & roll with an unbounded passion. It instilled beauty and vision to a complex life of dreams.

Patti moved to New York City late in the decade. I've met people who knew her at this time and I'll stare at them as if to somehow transport myself through their memory to see her. She was skinny and exotic. She had Keith Richards's haircut. She was sexy and manic. She worked at book stores and wrote and read poetry and did art. She co-wrote and acted in *Cowboy Mouth* with Sam Shepard. She was muse and lover to Robert Mapplethorpe. They were writers, artists, and rock & rollers—they were young and had any which way to go. Years moved by.

She and Lenny Kaye jammed poetry and electric guitar at St. Mark's Church. Patti would touch her chest and pronounce, "Jesus died for somebody's sins but not mine. . . ." Word was out that an amazing woman with a wild, intellectual positivism was tearing it up downtown. Local news programs and the *Village Voice* would begin to monitor her moves. She wrote amazing, celebratory record reviews for *Rolling Stone, Rock Scene* and *Creem*. Rock & roll was the sounding tool for modern prayer. She went to hear Television at CBGB and joined forces with Tom Verlaine and Richard Hell. They amplified the influence of Burroughs, Genet, Hendrix, Dylan, Stooges, Dolls and reggae.

Patti and Television spent 1975 at CBGB creating a forum for an excited and completely distinctive sensibility. "We created it, let's take it over," she'd shout and brought serious sounds to the people away from the arena-mind of the corporatized music/youth culture. Revolution was necessary. The Ramones came in, Blondie came in, Talking Heads came in. Entrepreneurs hyped the Sex Pistols and a subculture was begun. Its current status as a valid mainstream format is just a commercial of its sublime expansion. By 1979 Patti split to Michigan with Fred "Sonic" Smith (legendary guitarist of Detroit's high energy prophets the MC5) and got married. They had two kids and did a lot of fishing. She was out of the scene and out of sight. A second generation of artists and musicians had come to New York City and began to make noise in an explosion of punk rock inspired enterprise. The strongest and most original force in the music's history had been a woman. And this fact alone exacted upon the "punk" culture a situation in which women were empowered and encouraged.

Patti reappeared in the late '80s with the affirming "People Have the Power." The song's video showed a distinguished, serious Patti at home in proclamation amongst images of spiritual leadership. She and Fred played at a celebration for Dylan and another for Jackson Pollock.

Fred passed away in 1995 as did Patti's brother and close friend, Todd. Robert Mapplethorpe had also passed away.

Patti doesn't drive. In 1977 she fell off the stage and her eyesight was damaged. Survival in Michigan is difficult and lonely without Fred. She wants to play. As soon as her 13-year-old ends the school year she plans on moving back to New York. She has no set design on a professional life but she loves performance. And teaching. I could only interview Patti in conversational mode. She speaks with humor and thoughtfulness, her words are at once searching and prosaic.

I flew to Boston to meet her and Lenny Kaye where we were to drive to Lowell, Massachusetts for a benefit for the Kerouac Foundation. She asked me to play guitar on three songs: one she had written, one by Jerry Garcia and Robert Hunter, and one an improvisation to a poem by Kerouac. We did a show in Lowell and two in Boston, all three in these cool churches. We spent Saturday visiting the haunts of Kerouac's Lowell. Patti took Polaroids of my hands for a Sunday exhibit at a friend's gallery in Jamaica Plain. She'd frame the photos with broad white frames and write around them vignettes pertaining to the subject. I was friends with someone I had dreamed of being friends with for nearly 20 years.

This conversation was recorded late night in a hotel in Lowell, October 6, and the next day in the back seat of a car driving to Boston.

Stone Hedge Inn. Lowell, Massachusetts.

Thurston Moore
How would Lester Bangs have conducted this interview?

Patti Smith
Lester wrote a really nice article about us a long time ago called "Stagger Lee Was A Woman." [*Referring to Bangs's review of* Horses *in the February 1976 issue of* Creem —*Ed.*] But then he turned against us because he felt we sold out with *Radio Ethiopia*. Everybody thought we sold out. They thought we had turned heavy metal. They found lyrics like "pissing in a river" offensive, they found experimentation offensive, definitely too sonic.

TM
It was for its time. It seemed like a very MC5 influenced record. There was nothing like it at the time.

PS
Lenny introduced me to their music. I had never heard of the MC5. *Radio Ethiopia* was influenced by "Black to Comm." When Lenny introduced me to Fred, it was March 9, 1976, almost 20 years ago. Fred was standing in front of a white elevator in a navy blue coat—the coat which appears in "Godspeed." "Walking in your blue coat, weeping admiral," that's Fred.

TM
I remember a little item in *Rolling Stone* back then about a love letter you sent Fred.

PS

I sent him a telegram: "Light and energy enclosed." I couldn't believe they found out about that.

TM

How are your children?

PS

I really love my kids, I like having them around me. They can drive you nuts and they're such a responsibility but it's like a movie you can never see again. You watch it as it's happening and you think it's always gonna be like that and then . . .

TM

And then you go see *Kids* [*referring to the 1995 coming-of-age film —Ed.*].

PS

Or one of your kids turns into *Kids*. Too much reality for me. I've lived reality, so why go see it on the movie screen?

TM

What do you think of the whole debate on censorship—parents being offended by pornographic lyrics? [*Most likely a reference to the Parents Music Resource Center, cofounded by Tipper Gore —Ed.*]

PS

I think they have the right to be concerned. Some of the stuff pawned off as freedom of expression, let alone art, is just trash, just jerking off, with no real duty attached. No seeking to elevate. No self-censorship. No conscience. Things seem too open to me now, children are being robbed of their childhood. I don't know. Somehow I feel like Rip van Winkle who fell asleep in the '70s and woke up in the '90s. When I was a child we were much more cut off from the adult world. What I think is, "Toyland, toyland . . . once you pass its portals you may never return again." (*laughter*)

TM

What's the first record you ever bought?

PS

Shrimp Boats by Harry Belafonte, Patience and Prudence doing *The Money Tree*, and, embarrassingly enough, Neil Sedaka's *Climb Up*. [*Sedaka's "Stairway to Heaven" was sometimes known as "Climb Up." Harry Belafonte never recorded "Shrimp Boats." It was recorded in 1951 by Jo Stafford. –Ed.*] My mother bought me a box set of *Madame Butterfly* when I was sick. I always got great records when I was sick. I got Coltrane's *My Favorite Things*. My mother was a counter waitress in a drugstore where they had a bargain bin of used records. One day she brought this record home and said, "I never heard of the fellow but he looks like somebody you'd like," and it was *Another Side of Bob Dylan*. I loved him. You see, I had devoted so much of my girlish daydreams to Rimbaud. Rimbaud was like my boyfriend. If you're 15 or 16 and you can't get the boy you want, and you have to daydream about him all the time, what's the difference if he's a dead poet or a senior? At least Bob Dylan . . . it was a relief to daydream about somebody who was alive.

TM

Did you ever see John Coltrane?

PS

Yes. Once in Philly in '63 when *My Favorite Things* came out. There were two jazz clubs right next to each other, Pep's and the Showboat. You had to be 18, so these people helped me get dressed up, trying to look older. I was basically a pigtails and sweatshirt kind of kid. So I got in for 15 minutes and saw him and then they carded me and kicked me out. He did "Nature Boy." I was in such heaven seeing them, Elvin Jones and McCoy Tyner, that I wasn't even disturbed that I got thrown out.

TM

I suppose youth culture was very familiar with jazz at that time.

PS

It was a small culture. Kids who were too young for the beat thing and too old for the Beatles got into jazz.

TM

Do you remember your first guitar?

PS

I saw this really old Martin in a pawn shop, it had a woven, colored strap and I loved it. I saved my money, but when I went back to get it it was gone. So I bought a little Martin. I didn't know anything about tuning. I could never understand why my chords never sounded like the songs in my Bob Dylan song book. And then I met Sam Shepard and he showed me. He bought me this '30s black Gibson, which I still have. It's the same kind of guitar Robert Johnson plays.

TM

Are you aware of these bands which are referred to as "riot grrl" bands?

PS

Now I know they exist but I couldn't tell you anything about them. Is it a positive thing?

TM

Yeah, its main focus and agenda is the communication of self-help and social issues to young women. It's a network and very band-oriented, fully inspired by punk rock.

PS

Well, that's heartening to know. I hope there's lots of them.

TM

When you guys would come out and say, "Fight the good fight," I was 18 and I thought, "That's cool, that sounds right, I'll take that over the other."

PS

Well, we did one or two things right.

TM

You guys were a nice band, you didn't cop a lot of attitude.

PS

We were nice. We shared whatever we had, because we didn't have anything. No opening acts then. Sometimes I'd do poetry, or we'd show our
home movies, footage of us when we were younger, on the road, having
fun with each other. I remember once, when we were in Austin, staying in
the Lyndon Baines Johnson suite, and this interviewer asked me, "What is
the future of rock?" And I said, "Sculpture." Then he asked me about the
future of art, and Richard's lying there beached, eating cheesecake, and
says, "The computer. It will take over everything."

Want to hear about my fish story? Did I ever tell you about my pet
fishing lure named Curly?

TM

No.

PS

It was purple and had a little curly-q tail. I would cast it and we would
have telepathy. I would get into such in-depth conversations with this lure
that I would actually see inside the water. I could see fish lurking. It was
like Herbert Huncke's poem about Jack Kerouac and his notebook. This
lure was an extension of me. I love that lure. If you ever come to Michigan
I'll show you Curly. You know how people say certain lures catch fish, this
lure never caught nothing. But we used to have the greatest thoughts. He'd
tell me things like how he once went fishing with Arnold Palmer. I much
preferred going out with Curly and catching nothin'. I always meant to
write a story about him, I forgot about it till right now.

TM

When did you first meet Bob Dylan?

PS

Backstage at the Bitter End. We didn't have a drummer yet. It was just the four of us, we hadn't been signed yet.

TM

Did you see him in the audience?

PS

No. Somebody told us he was there. My heart was pounding. I got instantly rebellious. I made a couple of references, a couple of oblique things to show I knew he was there. And then he came backstage which was really quite gentlemanly of him. He came over to me and I kept moving around. We were like two pitbulls circling. I was a snotnose. I had a very high concentration of adrenaline. He said to me, "Any poets around here?" And I said, "I don't like poetry anymore. Poetry sucks!" I really acted like a jerk. I thought, that guy will never talk to me again. And the day after there was this picture on the cover of the *Village Voice*. The photographer had Dylan put his arm around me. It was a really cool picture. It was a dream come true, but it reminded me of how I had acted like a jerk. And then a few days later I was walking down 4th Street by the Bottom Line and I saw him coming. He put his hand in his jacket—he was still wearing the same clothes he had on in the picture, which I liked—and he takes out the *Village Voice* picture and says, "Who are these two people? You know who these people are?" Then he smiled at me and I knew it was all right. The first time I ever heard him was way back in 1964. I went to see Joan Baez. She had this fellow with her. Bobby Dylan. His voice was like a motorcycle through a cornfield. . . .

Saturday: Driving from Lowell to Cambridge: We stop for Polaroid film and Patti buys a present for my daughter, Coco. Then we head on to the grotto where Kerouac used to write, and light candles for Fred. From there, we go to Kerouac's memorial, granite slabs with lines from his Dr. Sax *carved into their surface. Patti leaves her guitar pick at his grave.*

TM

You know, I grabbed your ankle once at a concert. It was during an encore when you were doing "My Generation." There was mayhem and you were real close and I reached up and grabbed you. But I got freaked out as if I was going too far and I let go.

PS

You were sonic youth.

TM

When we named ourselves Sonic Youth the word sonic wasn't so common. "Sonic boom" was a technical term; but in rock & roll I only knew of Sonic Smith.

PS

Fred loved that. He always said, "They got that from me!" I'd say, "Well, you don't know that." It was a source of pride for him. He *was* sonic.

TM

The only other time I saw you was in Bleecker Bob's in the '70s. You walked in eating pizza and wearing aviator glasses and Bleecker Bob showed you an Ian Dury picture sleeve and you said, "I don't listen to music by people I don't wanna fuck."

PS

(*laughter*) Yeah, that was me.

TM

One time I went to see you at CBGB and it was totally packed and you guys were wearing these black leather pants, you were totally bad-ass. It was a pretty intense scene, I was standing there biting my lower lip and you looked at me and bit your lip right back at me like, "I'll show you how to bite your lip. Kid."

PS

I was kind of mean. I'm so glad I'm nice now.

TM

Well, I didn't think you were mean.

PS

Well, I spotted you.

TM

That night William Burroughs came to the gig.

PS

I remember that. I was in heaven that night. Afterwards, he said to me, "Patti, you are a remarkable chanteuse." He was wonderful and so handsome. I had dinner with him recently and he's still handsome, such a good dresser, like he had the lead in *Guys and Dolls*.

I grabbed Brian Jones's ankle once. It was in 1964 and they were playing with Patti LaBelle and the Bluebelles in a high school auditorium in South Jersey. There were only about 450 people and folding chairs. The American flag and the school flag were up. I had never seen the Rolling Stones. The weird thing was that the only other time I'd seen any white rock concerts was Joan Baez. We went to see the Motown Revues. They didn't have white rock concerts, at least not in South Jersey. You went to the airport, it was five dollars a carload and the Motown bus would come in, and in one day you could see Little Stevie Wonder or Ben E. King. It was called the Airport Drive-In. So, anyway, I was sitting in this auditorium, with mostly other white girls. Everybody was sitting there politely during Patti Labelle, nobody danced or anything—it was kind of square. And then the Rolling Stones came on and all of a sudden girls started screaming and ran towards the stage. I had a front row seat. And I had no choice, they just pushed me into the edge of the stage. I had never seen anything like this ever. I was so embarrassed. They acted like such freaks, screaming. One girl broke her ankle. It was some kind of collective hysteria they had learned reading about people going to see the Beatles.

TM

They must've rocked when they came out.

PS

Mick Jagger looked very nervous. The funniest one was Keith because he was really young and nervous and his ears were big and he had pimples and his teeth were kind of bucked and cute. But I loved Brian Jones. He was sitting on the floor playing one of those Ventures electric sitars, and these girls kept pushing me and pushing me. They pushed me right on the stage and then I felt myself going under and I was gonna be trampled and out of total desperation I reached up and grabbed the first thing I saw; Brian Jones's ankle. I was grabbing him to save myself. And he looked at me. And I looked at him. And he smiled. He just smiled at me. (*sigh*) My Brian Jones story.

TM

"Brian, Brian, I'm not cryin' . . ."

PS

". . . I'm just tryin' to reach you."

TM

I used to really love that poem.

PS

Where did you and Kim [Gordon] meet?

TM

Through a mutual friend. I was in a band called The Coachmen and we were coming out of the no-wave scene.

PS

What's "no-wave?"

TM

Contortions, DNA, Lydia Lunch, Mars . . .

PS

Oh, I missed that.

TM

It was the next generation of the downtown music scene, all these new kids from art schools moving to New York and taking over the scene. Blondie became radio-friendly and they created this real harsh, nihilist music called no-wave. It was atonal, chordless, noise rock played by these weirdo personalities.

PS

Sounds like I could've got a job.

TM

It was total anti-rock. The Sex Pistols were supposedly destroying rock & roll, but they were just playing Chuck Berry chords a little faster and sloppier and louder.

PS

They were a pop band. Pop music used to be derogatory, but, especially since Pop Art, the word has been redefined. Pop is something, at its best, both pleasurable and inspiring.

TM

Do you have a lot of friends in New York?

PS

Yeah, I have a lot of new friends, a couple of old ones. A lot of my friends from New York are gone. My main friend in New York was Robert (Mapplethorpe). He was my best friend. And I really loved Richard Sohl. Whenever I came to New York after I moved to Detroit I'd always get excited as I'd see the skyline because I knew somewhere in that city they were working or cruising or whatever. I like coming back to New York. I love walking around, I'll pass cafés and people will say, "Hi Patti," just like when you've grown up in the neighborhood.

Are we lost? (*We ask for directions at a gas station.*)

TM

You wrote a poem for the Dalai Lama.

PS

Yes, I have always cared for him since I was a kid in 1959 when the Chinese invaded Tibet and he disappeared. I prayed for him constantly. In September I was asked to work with him at The World Peace Conference in Berlin. Every time I saw him all I could do was smile. At dinner I sat across from him but I couldn't say anything, I just waved and smiled. I felt so . . . young. So happy. For my young girl self so deeply loved him.

TM

You studied Tibetan Buddhism and the Dalai Lama when you were 13?

PS

Before then . . . 11, 12. I was leaving the Jehovah Witnesses so I was studying other religions. My frame of mind was that if you left a religion you had to find another one. I realized after time that that wasn't necessary. I fell in love with Tibet because their essential mission was to keep a continual stream of prayer. To me they kept the world from spinning out of control just by being a civilization on the roof of the world in that continuous state of prayer. The prayers are etched on wheels, they feel them with their hands like braille and turn them. It's spinning prayer like cloth. That was my perception as a young person. I didn't quite understand the whole thing but I felt protected. We grew up at a time when nuclear war seemed imminent with air raid drills and lying on the floor under your school desk. To counterbalance that destruction was this civilization of monks living high in the Himalayas who were continuously praying for us, for the planet and for all of nature. That made me feel safe.

TM

Buddhism has become a socially recognized religious philosophy for Americans, whereas it used to be considered an exotic religion.

PS

When I was a child, Jehovah's Witness was a completely misunderstood religion. We used to go door to door, and people would throw buckets of water on us and curse at us. It was awful. I don't agree with the dogmas of any church. They're just man-made laws that you can either decide to abide by or not. Buddhism is a lot like the truest aspects of Christianity. It's based on caring for one another. Like Jesus gave to us an 11th commandment: "Love one another." You can have aesthetic, scientific or philosophic differences, but if you saw somebody in trouble, wouldn't you give them a helping hand?

TM

Giving and forgiving.

PS

Wait a minute . . . Do you have this thing where you start thinking something and your mind takes it over and it's not in a language that you can translate yet so you're sitting and waiting but your mind's like . . . it's like in those movies where the computer starts talking to itself and locks the guy out. Sometimes I sit here and I feel like a shell harboring my brain and my brain is faxing different thoughts to other parts.

TM

(*whispers*) Look, a Dunkin Donuts.

PS

Is there? Oh man, I'd love some coffee and a French cruller with chocolate.

TM

Here, let me get it for you.

PATTI SMITH: SHE IS RISEN

Holly George-Warren | May 1996 | *Option*

Gone Again, Patti Smith's sixth studio album, was a month from its release when Holly George-Warren published this lengthy feature. She met Smith at the Java House, a favorite coffee shop in St. Clair Shores, the suburb of Detroit where she made her home with Fred "Sonic" Smith and their two children, Jackson and Jesse Paris. *Gone Again* is an elegy to her late husband and the many losses she had suffered, but reflecting on the album, it's clear that she carried his legacy with her. Smith revealed that in the last months of his life, her husband gave her guitar lessons, evidence of which can be found on the album's closing track, "Farewell Reel." It's just Patti, alone with her acoustic guitar, delivering the song's pivotal lyric: "We're only given as much as the heart can endure."

In this interview, beyond coffee, there was a car ride through Smith's suburban town, listening to the masters for *Gone Again* and how Bob Dylan inspired it, an impromptu jam session her kids have at the house, and the phone ringing with record executives on the other end as Smith gears up to get back into the swing of life on tour. It is a brief window into a "segment of life," to use one of Smith's expressions, a life in transition captured on the page. —Ed.

"I was feeling sensations in no dictionary
He was less than a breath of shimmer and smoke
The life in his fingers unwound my existence
Dead to the world alive I awoke."

"I never did miss fame," says Patti Smith. "What I really missed was a good cup of coffee." Sipping a double latte at the recently opened Java House near her home in suburban Detroit, Smith is talking about the reclusive life she's led since leaving New York in the late 1970s. Though her name is etched forever in the rock 'n' roll annals, her reputation here amounts to little more than her daily order of a cinnamon bun and two double lattes. The cafe's proprietor used to offer her free food, assuming from her usual attire—old jeans, work boots and a baggy shirt—that she was broke. Only when he spotted Smith on MTV with Michael Stipe did he realize his most loyal customer had been famous in a previous life.

"In the '70s I actually enjoyed the privileges and the excitement and some of the danger of being a rock 'n' roll star," Smith says. "It was very intoxicating at that time in my life. But it wasn't enough."

In fact, Smith has lived several completely different lives over the past five decades. Growing up in small-town South Jersey, she escaped to New York City at 20 with dreams of becoming a painter. She soon began pouring her energy into writing and performing her brand of visceral, hallucinatory poetry—inspired equally by French symbolists, the Beats and the Rolling Stones. Fronting the Patti Smith Group, one of the most visionary rock bands of the '70s, her lyrics mixed mystical poetry, sexual imagery and populist politics, which she delivered in a raspy voice that contained more fury and abandon than any female rocker had ever dared.

Raucous stints at downtown dens like Max's Kansas City and CBGB earned Smith a loyal following and a deal with Arista, and her 1975 debut, *Horses*, captured the rapturous anarchy of Smith's live shows. Three years later, her third album *Easter* contained the hit "Because the Night" (co-written with Bruce Springsteen), and rocketed Smith from cult artist to pop star.

Then Smith chucked it all for love. She moved, in 1979, to the home-town of her paramour, ex-MC5 guitarist Fred "Sonic" Smith. The Smiths married in 1980 and had two children, Jackson, now 14, and Jesse, eight. And while Patti Smith talks about life in Detroit with obvious fondness, the past seven years have been wracked with pain. In that time she has dealt with a string of deaths that began in 1989 with the passing of Smith's longtime soulmate, the photographer Robert Mapplethorpe. The death of her friend and former pianist Richard Sohl followed the next year. Then, in November of 1994, her 44-year-old husband died of heart failure, and a month later her younger brother Todd also passed away.

Resurrection, however, has always been a theme in Smith's work, and 16 years after largely vanishing from the public eye, she has returned. Along with original Patti Smith Group guitarist Lenny Kaye and drummer Jay Dee Daugherty, her old friend (and former Television guitarist) Tom Verlaine and several others, Smith spent the past year recording *Gone Again* (Arista), her first album in eight years, a collection of urgent, emotional songs that capture the sadness of Smith's struggles as well as her intense will to live through it.

In addition, Smith recently published *The Coral Sea* (W.W. Norton), a lengthy, imagistic prose poem dedicated to Mapplethorpe. This summer, she plans to move with her children back to New York City. And during the past year she has begun to perform again, making a surprise appearance at Lollapalooza last summer, an emotional homecoming in Central Park, and opening for Bob Dylan on his ten-date tour last December.

"I perceive that there's a lot of people who have their own troubles, whether they've lost a friend or a lover or they don't know what to do with themselves," she says, sounding more like an ex-hippie than a punk provocateur. "Maybe together we can have a good night, rise up and have a treaty on troubles, then hopefully go back a little more energized to get through another segment of life."

Sitting in the Java House on a warm May afternoon, Smith carries herself with a compassionate, maternal air. She openly reflects on her life during the past 16 years, particularly the carefree, reclusive days when she and Fred Smith embarked on their life together.

"We set certain tasks upon us and achieved them," she says. "Mine was to develop my prose writing; Fred wanted to study navigation and aviation. I like to write by the sea and was working on a character study of a man who just roams the beaches. So Fred charted all the places where he could take flight lessons at small airports along different seacoast towns. In the early '80s, when Jackson was small, we'd pack up the car and go up and down the coast and stay in little motels. We lived very frugally. I wrote; he studied aviation and eventually flew. It was a happy, J. G. Ballard existence—if a J. G. Ballard story was ever happy."

Though they shared the same name even before they were married, Smith and Smith were in many ways opposite in character. "Fred was gifted at driving motorcycles, race cars," she says. "He had great instincts, he was quick, the same way he was on guitar. If he put himself into a weird corner, he'd get out of it in ways other people wouldn't even think of." She, on the other hand, is scared of heights and is often stricken with motion sickness while flying. In the decade and a half she's lived in the Motor City suburb of St. Clair Shores, Smith never learned to drive a car. "I have that syndrome where I have to school myself about which is left and which is right," she explains. "I have to write my name in the sky and look to see which is my right hand."

The couple recorded one album together, *Dream of Life*, in 1988. "Fred wrote all the music," says Smith. "He was so prolific musically and had a lot of complex patterns and preferred to write his own music. He loved my lyrics and was real supportive of my writing. Quite often, he chose the title and concept of a song, then I wrote the lyrics. The song 'People Have the Power' was really important to him. That's where Fred and I really entwined in a song. The concept and title was his, then—as I'm wont to do—I brought in a biblical reference. Fred had a lot of ideas for more politically oriented songs. He liked to remind people that each individual is of worth and that their collective powers are infinite."

Smith gave birth to their daughter Jesse around the time of the album's completion, and the couple chose not to tour. "We took Jesse and Jackson through their formative years and were very close-knit," she explains. Though *Dream of Life* featured "Power" and other memorable songs, including the upbeat "Looking for You," the bittersweet "Paths That Cross" and "Jackson Song," the album was a commercial failure. Perhaps that experience fueled her husband's bitterness toward the recording industry. "He was cynical about the music business and business in general, but he had a lot of faith in people in the abstract," she says. She describes her husband as "a private man who could be difficult," but, with watery eyes, adds that "he was a really wonderful father, and though he did keep to himself, he was extremely kind."

During the last months of his life, Fred Smith taught his wife to play guitar. "I really wanted to be able to write my own songs, and I only knew how to play sounds, feedback," she explains. "I wanted to learn chords so I could sit down and write melody lines. So he gave me guitar lessons every night after the kids went to bed. I was slow, but he was very patient. He taught me chord after chord and how to structure songs."

She pauses and laughs at the memory. "He used to tease me, though, and tell me I wasn't allowed to tell anybody! I'd play a song really poorly and I'd say, 'I can't wait to tell people my guitar teacher was Fred "Sonic" Smith!' and he'd say, 'Don't do that, Patricia!'" When Smith died, he had already begun making plans for the couple's next recording. "Fred wanted us to do a rock 'n' roll album," she says. "I didn't want to do that because I was starting to write songs on acoustic guitar and I was feeling more reflective. But it was funny, he really felt I did rock 'n' roll well."

After Fred's death, Patti's brother, Todd—who worked on the Patti Smith Group crew in the '70s—came to her aid. "He tended to everything. He got me back on my feet," she says softly. "He said, 'You're going to do it, you're going to work yourself out of this, people will help you, they'll make you feel better. I'll be there.' Then he passed away within days of telling me all that."

She stops and stares off. "The interesting thing about it is that I could go two ways: I could think of him and go into this sea of complete desolation, or dip into the positive, that joy he exuded and the self-confidence that he developed in me. Instead of focusing on the loss of individuals, I've found that it's very helpful to consider one's privilege to have had those individuals in your life."

Smith's positive outlook was apparent when she performed before 9,000 people in New York's Central Park on a hot July evening in 1995. Joined by Kaye, bassist Tony Shanahan and her sister Kimberly Smith on acoustic guitar, it was a powerful reunion for Smith and her audience—which contained everyone from yuppies and middle-aged ex-punks to riot grrrls and green-haired boys who were toddlers during Smith's heyday. "I've always found New York the most friendly town I've ever been in," Smith says. "That night, the response brought tears to my eyes."

It also encouraged Smith's decision to return to the studio and the stage. During live shows she often performs poems and songs inspired by departed loved ones. It's an emotional experience to hear her proudly introducing "Babelogue" as her brother's favorite or dedicating the poignant "Farewell Reel" to her husband or improvising the verses to "About a Boy," declaring "this was writ for Kurt Cobain and a multitude of others—and the boy within us all."

These impassioned gestures communicate not so much grief, but strength. If Patti Smith's stage persona in the 1970s was remarkable for its raw fury, in the '90s her performances are just as powerful in their calm reflections on loss. "What I most like about performing at this stage of my life," she says, "is to be in a place with these people and it's a meeting ground, instead of an arena for rock 'n' roll stars. I like how it's evolving so that we get to spar a little. We communicate."

Nowhere was this more apparent than during her gigs opening for Bob Dylan at New York's Beacon Theater in December, 1995. After Smith's 40-minute set, she joined Dylan for a duet on "Dark Eyes" that was likely one of the most inspired performances either musician has ever given. "Getting to sing with him was one of the most treasured moments of my life," Smith says. It was Dylan's music, in fact, that helped her get through the bleak days following her husband's death. "I was playing [Dylan's 1993 album] *World Gone Wrong* over and over," she recalls. "It was the theme music of my life at that time. It actually inspired a lot of the songs on *Gone Again*. By listening to it, I started writing songs myself."

———————

Patti Smith is cruising through the streets of St. Clair Shores, listening to the final master of *Gone Again*. "Turn it up! Can we hear that one again?" she asks excitedly from the passenger seat as the hallucinatory

"Fireflies" comes through the car stereo. "That's Tom Verlaine playing his guitar with a screwdriver!"

Passing rows of tract houses on the way to a Middle Eastern restaurant, Smith gets so caught up in the music she forgets to give directions. Her thoughts are focused on the album's upcoming release. It's still undecided which song will be the first single, but Smith is thrilled that the choice is between "Gone Again" and "Summer Cannibals," two rockers written by her husband. "This obviously isn't the record that Fred and I were going to do," she says. "But he got his word in, though, because the two real rock songs on the record are both his—the last songs he wrote."

Strangely, the title track was a last-minute addition to the album. "Fred and Patti had worked on 'Gone Again' the summer before he died," relates Lenny Kaye, who co-produced the album with Malcolm Burn. "But we lost the tape and constructed the album without it. At the last minute, Patti was feeling agitated one day, walking around the house, kind of restless. She opened up a drawer and there was the 'Gone Again' tape as if by magic. We recorded it quickly, and all of a sudden it seemed to be the glue around which everything else could find its place." Kaye mixed into the track a rough tape of Fred Smith singing the melody line, audible in the background of the finished song as a kind of primal, chanting drone.

The genesis of the playful, spirited "Summer Cannibals" dates to Fred Smith's days as leader of Sonic's Rendezvous Band in the '70s. "He'd written part of it but never recorded it," Smith recalls.

"Like 'Gone Again,' he had the title and the music and told me about the concept. When I sing it, it's as if I'm him—it's his attitude toward the music business, although I've tasted the same kind of lifestyle. For him, the whole business was people shoveling drugs, champagne, promises of fame, money, just to keep them working so people could make money off of them. He really perceived the whole journey into fame, which he had tasted when he was younger, as very destructive. It's dangerous to work for those kinds of ends—fame and fortune will turn on you. If there's anything negative on the album, it's that song. But it's got a sense of humor, in the way I sing it, because I survived it all. It didn't have an unhappy ending for me. It's a survival song."

Throughout the album, Smith expresses her will to survive in a cornucopia of voices, from lush, resonant singing to a scratchy growl—often all in one song. Instrumentation varies too, from the eerie sound of a musical saw on "Summer Cannibals" and the effervescent vocals by Jeff Buckley on the atmospheric "Southern Cross," to Verlaine's imaginative guitar work on four tracks and sister Kimberly's mandolin trills on "Ravens."

Family is the most important thing to Smith, and she includes members in her work whenever possible. Just home from school this afternoon, her lanky 14-year-old son plugs in and works up the guitar line from Deep Purple's "Smoke on the Water" on his mom's Fender Duo Sonic, while his sister races to an old upright piano to join in. Riffing away gloriously, the two look like junior versions of their parents.

At the same time the music is cranking, the phone rings off the hook with calls from record company honchos asking Smith to make decisions about tour itineraries, video directors and various upcoming TV appearances. Rather than being overwhelmed by all the attention, Smith seems to be enjoying the excitement. Having survived the death of so many loved ones, life is clearly something she relishes. The afternoon light is fading, and even though she's tired, Smith's blue-gray eyes still sparkle. "I think the key to everything is to just wake up each morning and think, 'I'm alive, I can feel the blood in my body,'" she says. "Just take it from there."

THE ATN Q&A: PATTI SMITH (PARTS 1 AND 2)

Michael Goldberg and Jaan Uhelszki | June 1996 | *Addicted to Noise*

It was the fall of 1975, and rock journalist Michael Goldberg saw the Patti Smith Group when they played the Boarding House in San Francisco and the Longbranch in Berkeley. Between November 17 and 23, he saw them in all five of their Bay Area appearances, and it's safe to say that it was revelatory. "I felt like I had seen the Messiah," he later wrote of the experience.

Horses had just been officially released, but it hadn't quite made it into record stores. Goldberg and his future wife Leslie Robinson were covering the shows for the legendary *Berkeley Barb*, a scrappy alt-weekly that published cerebral takes on rock gods and goddesses and socialist activists opposite risqué classified ads. Their interview with Smith, published as "Patti's Pre-Tower of Babel Rock Language," was nothing short of ecstatic: "Patti reaches beyond narrow subjectivity vis-à-vis Joni Mitchell and grasps, with a visionary acuity, universal life forces which are sometimes manifested as myth and ritual, or what Ezra Pound described as 'the whole and the flowing.'"

Fast forward two decades. In 1994, after spending ten years as a *Rolling Stone* staffer, Goldberg created *Addicted to Noise*, a pioneering online music publication launched from his bedroom that was one of the first to embed multimedia content in its articles. *ATN* published work by leading rock writers like Richard Meltzer and musician-journalists like Lenny Kaye, during a time when the World Wide Web felt so full of possibility and hidden corners. Readers could access the piece in Hi-Fi or Lo-Fi, depending on their modem speed.

In March 1996, Smith was about to release *Gone Again* when she played San Francisco's Warfield Theatre on March 18 and 19. On the second day, Goldberg sat down with Smith in her hotel room with Jaan Uhelszki, the trailblazing *Creem* cofounder who, along with writers like Ellen Willis and Lillian Roxon, helped break the gender barrier in rock journalism. Gone was Smith's youthful naivete; she now had a sense of what she described to them as "comfortable plagued-ness," in which "I often feel dogged yet most of the time I feel blessed." In this excerpt, Smith showed she was older and wiser, but she hadn't lost her edge or ability to inspire that first captivated Goldberg right before she burst onto the scene. —Ed.

Nearly 18 years ago, at the peak of her creative powers, Patti Smith married one-time MC5 guitarist Fred "Sonic" Smith and turned her back on rock & roll. Now she's back with one of the best albums of 1996.

San Francisco

It's the same old Patti. Slouched in a chair in her hotel room, a block from where I'd last seen her perform, at Winterland, in May of 1978. Same old Jersey accent. Same passion in her voice when she talks about the things that excite her. Same cool I-could-care-less brush-off when Jaan Uhelszki or I ask about something that bores her.

A leather bomber jacket on the bed. Books. Notes. A raincoat. Somehow, as usual, Smith has managed to take a sterile hotel room and make it feel like an artist lives here.

We all go way, way back. Jaan first met Patti in the *Creem* magazine days, when they were both in Detroit, when they were both writing for the rock mag that first Dave Marsh, then Lester Bangs edited. For an example of Patti Smith, rock crit extraordinaire, check out her review in *Rock She Wrote*, the collection of writings about rock by women published last year.

I met Patti in '75, when I interviewed her for a now-defunct magazine a month or so before her debut album, *Horses*, was released. Then, as now, she answered questions in a very unique way. At times her answers were straight, normal, but at others she drifted into poet mode, not exactly speaking in tongues the way she sometimes did back in the

'70s, but certainly talking on a level far above the mundane banter one gets from some musicians.

Jaan and I interviewed Patti in late March of this year, at a San Francisco hotel in the early afternoon a few hours before she delivered the second of two knock-out performances at the Warfield Theater, where she performed a mesmerizing dose of material from her new album, *Gone Again*.

Michael Goldberg: The first line of your first album was one of the most powerful openings of any rock & roll album. "Jesus died for somebody's sins but not mine/ My sins, my own, they belong to me." Can you still relate to that?

Patti Smith: Not really. I mean, it's not that I don't relate to it. It's just not a preoccupation of mine. I wrote those lines when I was 20 years old and I wrote them really because I had such a Christian conscience. I was raised Christian. I was deeply religious as a child. But as I wanted more artistic and personal freedom, I was trying to sort of cut the cord with my . . . You know, I imagined that if I was going to explore, both artistically and personally, [then] if I did anything wrong, I'd take the blame. That was really my idea. I'd take the blame and I didn't want Jesus to have to worry about me. And I didn't want him to be responsible for my choices.

It's a very adolescent anthem. At this point in my life, it's not a preoccupation of mine. I'm not an adolescent, for one thing. And I actually find the idea of someone with the intelligence and the spectral vision of Jesus sort of hovering over me or being in my camp or (my) being part of his camp, comforting. In fact, the last time I did that song was in Florence in 1979 at our last job and the line that I sang then was: "Jesus died for somebody's sins/ Why not mine?"

So I guess I had already gone through quite a shift by then. I actually developed a much different take on Jesus actually through Pasolini because I read this interview with Pasolini when he was doing the movie *The Gospel According to Saint Matthew*. And he saw Jesus as a very revolutionary man. A man that came upon the scene, the true outsider, the true rock & roll [*n*-word], the true person outside society who drew to himself the lepers and the whores and the thieves and helped them reclaim their position in heaven or just their dignity as human beings. So I started finding him a lot more interesting.

It's sort of like when you're a kid and the only thing you learned about George Washington is he supposedly never told a lie and chopped down the cherry tree. And then as you progress through life, you find that he was an extremely interesting man with very fine ideas and things. He wasn't just an icon or somebody on a dollar bill. Jesus has become for me someone more than an image on a holy card.

Goldberg: Are there a lot of ideas that you articulated in songs in the past that you now see in a different way?

Smith: Not necessarily. I don't even see things, I'd say, a lot of things, in a different way. I've just evolved. I haven't really thought that much about it lately because I haven't really spent a lot of time listening to my records so I couldn't really give you any specific thoughts about that. What I have been thinking about being back on the stage after so many years is I am finding out who I am in relationship . . . . [phone rings] Hello, yes, uh-huh. Talk to him, don't bug me about this shit. OK? [hangs up] Sorry. They want me to pay $100 for cleaning a room, fumigating the smoke out of a room. I don't even smoke . . . oh man.

Goldberg: You were talking about what you were discovering about performing live again.

Smith: I really didn't know what to expect as a performer. I imagined that I had changed quite a bit, becoming a wife and mother and withdrawing from public life for so long that I would be a lot quieter on stage. I imagined that I would just be sort of straightforward and dignified and somewhat folky. And I was kind of amazed to find that [that's not the case.] There's certain things that have changed. I am older. I have less agitated adolescent energy. But in place of that, I have another kind of energy. Different strengths. Instead of a real aggressive sexuality maybe a different kind of sensuality or something. It amuses me to find, right in the middle of the song, I think, yeah, I know that person, I remember this, I still got that and I'm still like ready to kick a photographer in the face. Things haven't changed all that much.

In terms of philosophies, my priorities have shifted. In the '70s, I was very concerned with censorship and things like that. I'm not that concerned with censorship right now. I'm more concerned with more global concerns: the environment, communicable diseases, what we can do to help educate the youth about things like AIDS, about the environment, about nutrition, how we can help people who are HIV-positive or have developed full-blown AIDS, how can we help them, things like that. I don't really give a shit, truthfully, about whether people are allowed to say "fuck" on the radio anymore. I don't really care. They probably are allowed anyway. Those things aren't so important to me. I think that's more youth's games, it's their fight.

But lyrically, I really can't think of anything that I've changed my attitudes about. Except for the fact that perhaps in the '70s, before there were incurable sexual transmittable diseases and things like that . . . What I'm trying to say is, I feel more responsibility right now about the kind of world I might project. But I don't feel apologetic about the world that I helped project in the '70s. A lot of the landscapes that I helped build within art were riddled with sexual imagery, some drug imagery, but it *was* art. I still feel like art should be an open terrain. I do feel that we have to take a certain amount of responsibility for the kind of lifestyles that we seem to be projecting as romantic for the sake of youth. I try now to remind people, through my writing or if I'm talking in person, that art and life are two different things. In art we can perceive with more abandon. In life we have to be more guarded, be more aware. So those are the kind of things I think about. I think that where art and life merge is in the creative process, in the actual process.

Goldberg: That's pretty interesting that you really are separating life from art.

Smith: Well, you have to. I mean, I've been everything from a murderess to a rapist to some type of Trocian whore, all kinds of things in my art which I wouldn't do in real life. And I feel that in art, in my writing or in the arenas that I create in my work, that I should be able to slip in and out of different personas, different ages. It's one's imagination, you know, the articulating the deep terrain of the imagination. I'm very AIDS conscious, obviously, because I've lost so many close . . . well, we've all lost a lot of close friends but I lost my very best friend to AIDS, so I'm very sensitive to it. And having children of my own who are entering a world that has a fatal communicable disease, I think about these things. My conscience is torn sometimes about projecting sort of a science fiction sexual lifestyle in work, which I don't even do anymore, but I did in the '70s. I don't do it anymore just 'cause I outgrew it. But I did in the '70s. And again, I can't feel apologetic about that. But it does make me think. It does make me . . . I would like, if people are gonna read passages in "Babel" or listen to "Poppies" or certain things that I've done, I wouldn't want those same people to go out into the world and commit the acts that the characters in those pieces do. That's actually cerebral work. It isn't a manifesto for one to go out and completely abandon themselves philosophically and morally to the ravages of the world. I think, if somebody's going to do that, then they will. But I'm not urging them through my art to do that. My work in the '70s was a lot of cerebral voyaging.

Jaan Uhelszki: I wanted to ask about your decision to stop doing rock & roll. Why was Florence your last show? Were you aware during that show that it was going to be the last one?

Smith: Yeah.

Uhelszki: That was the turning point? What snapped?

Smith: Well, nothing snapped. Just touring and being parted from Fred became unacceptable, so I ceased to tour. And when I decided to do it, then I did it. I didn't do it with any particular fanfare because I don't believe in that. I really dislike these farewell tours or these comeback tours or one-last-time tour. I don't like that concept so when it was time to disseminate—is that the word?—or disintegrate, I just did it. I didn't want to prolong it or exploit it. That's a classic thing to do, to go out and exploit your farewell to the public. Also, it wasn't a conscious decision that that was the end. It was that at that point in my life, it was a decision. I didn't say that I was never going to set foot on a stage or make a statement about it. I just stopped.

Uhelszki: Fred was back in Detroit then.

Smith: Well, we were both living in Detroit. I was already living in Detroit, so every time I had to tour, we had to be parted. And like I said, that became unacceptable.

Uhelszki: You had enough of being a rock star? Did you want to shed that persona?

Smith: I don't think of things really that consciously. I had one directive. I didn't want to be parted from Fred. And I've always considered, even if it's sort of egotistical, I've always considered myself as an artist. Never shed that. I was, I suppose that I could say, I was a rock & roll star briefly. That was something I was honored to have the opportunity to do but I didn't . . . People have written all kinds of things like that. I stopped because I couldn't take the pressure, because I was taking drugs, because I . . . Or, whatever their take on it was. But it wasn't any of those. I've never had a drug problem. I've never had any drug dependency problem. And, it wasn't that I was sick of anything. I love my band. I had a great band of some of my closest friends, my brother ran the band and the camaraderie was divine, really.

Uhelszki: The priorities shift. You know love is love. I mean, how many times does it come? You've got to go with it.

Smith: Well, also you can't . . . I always admired Arthur Rimbaud for that. He was the greatest poet of his time. I don't know what would have happened. I like to imagine he could have taken over the world right from the streets of Paris. But he turned his back on it and he went to Ethiopia and became a coffee trader. I think it takes a lot of courage to shed a complete skin and to move on. But it also makes life infinitely more interesting.

Uhelszki: Right. It makes your life . . . Like with Rimbaud, it makes his life his art.

Smith: Also, I appreciate the repetition. The performing, there's a lot of repetition involved. In repetition, sometimes one loses the heart, starts to lose the heart or starts to lose the feel for what one's doing. There could have been some of that involved too. I mean, now I can . . . I couldn't even bear doing certain songs anymore. Now I can come back and do songs that people want to hear. I can do "Land" or "Rock & Roll [*n*-word]" or "Redondo Beach" with a fresh mouth and actually with some humor or with some, even, desire and give the song some new life, where before I was starting to resent my own work because the repetition of performing the same songs, even though we always tried to make varied shows, was really too much. I've always tried to make performing every night its own creative process. But that is also quite exhausting.

Uhelszki: Right. What about writing in those years. I mean, you didn't give up writing, you just gave up performing. Were you still writing a lot of poetry?

Smith: Always. Mostly prose. I've written quite a bit in the '80s. I haven't published much of it. Hardly any of it. But I worked quite a bit. I did a lot of studying. Fred and I both studied. Fred got a private pilot's license. He studied aviation. He studied golf. He studied various types of . . . the metaphysical sciences, or what is it? Physics. He studied physics. So we were studying quite a bit. I liked to study different periods of literature. 16th century Japanese literature or . . . So we studied quite a bit and did some traveling before we had Jackson and Jessie. Went to French Guiana and Surinam and Devil's Island.

Uhelszki: I could see him studying golf. He definitely had that Zen personality.

Smith: Yeah. That's exactly how he looked at it, as a Zen study. And, he was quite an athlete as well.

Uhelszki: Yeah, he always looked like one.

Goldberg: Sure. You talked a little bit about this earlier, but during your first period of performing, you were really seen, I think anyway, as kind of a wild female spirit of rock & roll. And now, on your return, there's kind of a Saint Patti kind of a thing with U2 and R.E.M. and all these bands who obviously were inspired by you and look up to you.

Smith: That won't last. [smiles] They'll be after me soon enough. You're only allowed a small bit of sainthood. I don't mean those groups but I mean the press and everybody, I promise you, will be turning on me soon. But, I don't mind. I don't really care about all that stuff. I don't think about that kind of thing really. When I started doing things . . . my initial motivation was to pump some blood into the arena of poetry and poetry performance and that sort of fanned out into the arena of rock & roll. I didn't really have any specific intentions for myself. I just wanted to urge and inspire and push and overturn others. I just always figured I was sort of an agitator or a visitor. I didn't really think that I had my own specific role other than that. Like I've often said, I always compared myself or the band more to Paul Revere. I imagined we were like the people that were like telling people to wake up and something was comin', wake up and be ready for it and be a part of it. I didn't necessarily think that it was me or I'd be part of it. I just felt like I wanted to get people agitated and ready. I wanted them to do something, especially after a while in rock & roll because I really perceived that rock & roll was in a down time in the early '70s, that we experienced a great period in the '60s with very strong individuals. Some of these individuals died. Other people sort of were laying low. And, I felt what was happening . . . we were getting more of a . . . it was becoming more of a corporate glamour . . . what's that word . . . with the big shows?

Goldberg: Stadium rock?

Smith: Well, you know. They had things like glitter rock and Kiss and David Bowie and all those big shows. . . .

Goldberg: Glam rock.

Smith: That type of thing where it seemed like the trappings were more important than the actual energy, the actual communication. That might have been presumptuous of me, but that's how I felt. I felt that rock & roll was being taken away from the streets, from its roots, from the people and being more taken over by people with money and more show business or theatrical aims. At that time, that was unacceptable to me so I was really trying to turn the tables. But in terms of my own identity and all that or where I sit in that or my importance in that, I really couldn't tell you. You'd have to ask other people.

Goldberg: But you know what happened was your performances were incredible. I know 'cause I saw a bunch of them when you played the Boarding House here and the Longbranch. The kind of connection that you made with your fans is very strong. There's people who waited the 9, 10 years for *Dream of Life* and who then have been waiting for another album from you. It's a very strong thing that you . . . in terms of your communication.

Smith: Well, it might be because I talk to them directly. Not each individual. It's not like I want to get into a thing where a guy starts thinking "she just met me" or a girl thinks . . . It's not like that. [laughs] But I comprehend and feel the fact that there's a human entity, a living entity out there that I'm communicating with. Like when we have a night like last night [Smith performed the first of two nights at the Warfield Theater in San Francisco the night before this interview], to me, I look at performance as a mutual responsibility. We're all there together. They're giving their time. I'm giving my time. And we're creating our own atmosphere, our own night, our own energy. And save the fact that there's certain technological things that have to go right, we're creating our own night. I've always felt that.

I've always felt that. I'm not an entertainer. I know sometimes I'm entertaining, but I'm not an entertainer. I don't sing at people. I don't talk at people. If I can't really feel something . . . for instance, last night I was on a roll but at the end, I was getting kinda tired. We were on stage for over two hours. I was tired. We were doing "Not Fade Away" and I like to improvise or take people on a journey, but I didn't have nothing left. I just didn't. So what could I do but within the song just tell them I don't got nothing left. I even feel like a jerk right now. I feel sort of . . . I'm sort of tired and I feel kind of . . . so we make that part of it. I think everybody feels like that sometimes so they can get into it and sometimes people help me turn it around or we got to live with it . . . that's part of the night. I used to suffer more when those moments happened in the past. They don't really bother me because I figure, after all the things I've seen in my life, it's not the worst thing in the world to feel like a jerk on stage for five or 10 minutes. I can live with that. My goal, the thing that I really want to do is something that Fred and I talked about. If I could make a good enough living with my records, which I haven't quite been able to do yet, but if people like 'em and I can make a good enough living for me and my kids, I'd like to start, if when I perform, every cent other than if I have to pay lighting people or the sound people or a musician or two, all that money go for others. You know, go towards AIDS hospices or the homeless or whoever needs it, whoever locally needs it the most that you can find. So that when I'm on stage, I'm no longer doing it for personal gain so that I become even more like the people. That's my goal: that I'm not profiting by being on stage. Because if I can go on stage and not be profiting one cent, then I'm just like the person there. We're all sort of the same and we are really making the night together and we're making the night together to benefit another. So if the night is great and fiery, fantastic. If it's beautiful and quiet . . . No matter what it is, it won't matter. What'll matter is we all had this night together and we made some money to help another. That's my goal. Then I'll feel like I've accomplished something as a performer.

Goldberg: If you do that, that will be an absolutely revolutionary thing within the confines of rock & roll, as you know, because no one else has that. . . .

Smith: I don't know why. To me, it seems obvious. I find it amazing that really rich groups . . . There are a lot of really great people out there who are really rich. I don't mean sort of rich, I mean who have maybe $100 million. They're making a lot of money out there and I don't think there's anything wrong with that but they don't need all that money. They don't need it. And I think we should all be doing it, the ones who . . . I mean, I'm not in that position, but if I get in that position, I can't wait. If I never get in that position, maybe somebody else can take the idea and do it. But I think it would be a very liberating thing for any performer. I know it would be liberating for me. And why not? Who needs all that dough? I mean, how many houses can you have? How many cars? How many collector guitars? How many Diego Riveras can you own? And I don't mean give $50,000 . . . . I mean, fucking *give* the money away. If you're going on a tour and you're making $11 million, give $9 million away if you can't bear to give it all. Who needs more than $2 million? Give it away. Not sort of give it away. Not like sign a t-shirt or give them your old motorcycle. I mean the lion's share. But it's just an idea.

Goldberg: Working on this album, has it felt different than when you made albums in the past?

Smith: Well, working on this album was unique, uniquely difficult because I expected to be working on this album with Fred. So I couldn't even begin to tell you what working on this album was for me personally. But the joyful parts of it of course was working with Lenny again and Jay. The first time we practiced a song and I heard Lenny and Jay playing together, there was a certain familiar thing there that just brought tears to my eyes. But I liked working on the record. I did a lot of wrestling. [laughs] Musically, it's different because I wrote, I'd say, three quarters of the music on it. I don't usually write music. So the music, a lot of it's fairly simple. I don't know. I liked recording it. I guess it's just, like I was talking about performing, got in the studio and a lot of it was familiar again. Some of it was a relearning process. Jeez, I'm not saying too much. You'd better ask me. . . .

Goldberg: Did you amaze yourself at all when you listened back to what you'd recorded?

Smith: No. I think my voice has gotten stronger. I don't know if it translates completely on the record. But I think a lot of that has come from Fred. I learned a lot about music from Fred. I found new voices. There are certain things on the record . . . the things that amaze me on the record are subtle things, just things that I can do with my voice now for whatever reason because it came out of grieving, because I developed my voice through Fred, whatever. So there are certain things that I found interesting. I'm learning what I can do. I'm learning that I can do things that I didn't know I could do. I'm not saying that they're great or anything or I've become a great singer. It's nothing like that. It's just that I'm able to articulate my ideas vocally in some new ways. For instance, I did that song, it's not on the album, but Oliver Ray wrote that song "Walking Blind" for the *Dead Man Walking* soundtrack and I think the vocal on that is more indicative of the kind of thing I'm talking about. I don't really know what kind of singing it is. It's some weird hillbilly blues crossover. I don't really know what it is. Or, South Jersey blues. I don't really know exactly what kind of singing I'm doing because I wouldn't be presumptuous to call myself a blues singer. But I'm doing something that . . . Michael Stipe calls it "porch singing." That's how he describes my singing, porch singing, so I guess that's pretty good, you know.

Goldberg: Is he on the album?

Smith: No. How would he be on the album? His encouragement is within it because he is very encouraging but he's not singing on it or anything. We talked about things like that and I think it would be really nice for us to collaborate sometime. But I felt that, it's my duty . . . This record was my duty. And I know that perhaps it might have more commercial viability if I had my friends come and join me on a track or two but that's not the goal of this record. This record was really my responsibility to record as Fred and I had planned, so perhaps on another piece of work.

Uhelszki: Do you feel that the album is a departure from vintage Patti Smith stuff?

Smith: I think it's different. I wrote three-quarters of the music, I've never done that before. Again, having Fred's spirit with me, I imagine. I don't know how. Fred taught me how [to] play some acoustic guitar. In the last few months he was giving me my little guitar lessons, and he taught me enough so I could write my own songs and I did write several of the songs. I really don't know how, I'm in some ways so out of touch with things that I have no idea where it fits, where it sits, what people will think about it, I can only say that it's an honest effort. Every record I (sic) done has been an honest effort. *Dream of Life* was really more Fred's record: It was all of Fred's music, Fred's philosophy, "People Have the Power," Fred's concept, the titles of a lot of the songs were Fred's—even though I wrote all of the lyrics, a lot of the titles and the concepts of the songs were Fred's. The title of the album was Fred's (laughs) so it was really Fred's gift to me. He really crafted that record for me. This particular record is really my record with Lenny's touches. But it pretty much reflects myself. I don't know what to say about it. I think one couldn't place it—it doesn't have any particular, you couldn't [say] it's any particular kind of music 'cause I don't really think it sits anywhere. I just think it's something people will like or not. I can't ever promise to give people what they want or what's in current favor. All I can promise them is an honest effort. I don't have filler stuff, I don't just throw stuff together. Everything that I do, I work hard on. Then it's up to the people whether they like it or not. It doesn't have any curse words on it.

Uhelszki: Well you have kids now.

Smith: It just happened that way. Actually, *Dream of Life* doesn't either. But I think all those things weren't even thought of, they just came out as they did. I'm anxious to do another record. This record really does reflect, Fred's in it, a lot of thoughts about losing Fred, whether abstractly or directly. I had to write that, I had to do that. And then the next record I believe I'll really find out what I'm thinking about.

Uhelszki: You have to pay homage to him. Somehow or another you will always be singing a Fred song.

Smith: Always. Always. I've always been singing them. I don't think people even realize how long I've been singing Fred songs. From "Because the Night"—all these songs. "Twenty-Fifth Floor," "Dancing Barefoot," and "Frederick." I've written so many songs for him long before people even knew I knew him.

Uhelszki: When did you meet him? Weren't you intrigued with him before you met him?

Smith: Well, I just met him. I only was from the first time I met him. I didn't know anything about him when I met him. I met him one day, it was March 9, 1976. And we met in front of the radiator in front of that hot dog place, the Coney Island place. Lafayette Coney Island.

Uhelszki: I remember you once threw a press party there, I didn't know why at the time.

Smith: Lenny introduced me to this guy, and I just looked at this guy. I heard that his name was Smith and my name is Smith. We just looked at each other, and I was completely taken by him. And I had no idea who he was, or anything about him until afterwards, when Lenny told me. I was taken by him from the moment I saw him. Lenny introduced me to him and said, "he's one of the great guitar players." And I said, "Perhaps you'll want to play with us tonight." And then he said, "Maybe so." Then he left and I said to Lenny, "so he's good?" And Lenny said, "the best." And that was the first time I met him. So I was playing with him that night. I had a lot of bravado in those days, you know. I didn't care who came on my stage, I didn't have respect for anybody. But I totally submitted to his reign. He came on the stage and started playing and I remember after a while, I just set my guitar down, and let my guitar feed back, and let him just take over because I had felt that I had met my match, that I had met the better man.

Uhelszki: It's such a highly charged love story. Did you feel that you had to take those years off to build the relationship?

Smith: I've never regretted, I only regret that he's gone. I don't regret nothing else. I have never ever once—never!—regretted anything. Not from the very beginning. I mean I missed my friends, I missed the camaraderie of the band, I missed certain things, but I never regretted a thing. To me it was—even sometimes it was difficult—it was a privilege to be with him.

Uhelszki: And there are your two children.

Smith: Yeah, and they're great. I've been pretty lucky in my life, and I've known really good people. The two most important relationships I had was with Robert and Fred. And they're both gone, but I feel magnified by them. I feel like when Mary said my soul is magnified by the Lord. I feel like my soul is magnified by them. And I feel actually still, even in losing them, pretty lucky.

Uhelszki: You were going to put a song about Jerry Garcia on your new album?

Smith: I didn't. But he [does] permeate the album. When we were recording, the night of the day that he died, that night we recorded a song by Robert Hunter called "All of My Friends," a song that he and Jerry Garcia wrote, I think [*Grateful Dead's "Black Peter"* —Ed.]. And we did record that, not for the album. We recorded it for Jerry, we might use it for a B-side of something, but we just recorded it for him. We did have his picture hanging up in Electric Ladyland through the rest of the recording, and we all said hello to him everyday. We ate the Ben and Jerry's Cherry Garcia ice cream that night. And when we are performing we do "Not Fade Away" in his memory. So we do, he's there spiritually.

Uhelszki: Did you have an affinity with Jerry Garcia before he died?

Smith: I really think we all owe something to him, many of us have an affinity. We opened for them and they were wonderful people. Lenny had a deep affinity with the Grateful Dead and with him. My affinity is more through others but I have a happy affinity with them. Certainly they weren't as pivotal for me as somebody like Bob Dylan, but I have good memories of them and a good feeling for them.

Uhelszki: You've spoken about Fred teaching you a lot of things. What'd you teach Fred?

Smith: I couldn't presume to answer that really. Thank you for asking though.

Uhelszki: That's OK. I hadn't seen Fred for a really long time after I left, you know. He was always an amazing character in my personal history. You were moved by Nirvana and Kurt Cobain. You wrote that song "About a Boy." Did you like their music?

Smith: Yeah. And it was typical of me to finally find a band I liked and then their leader should pass away, but that was quite a blow. Because I really didn't know anything about the group. I really liked their music. I was taken with them. I felt a certain kinship with their music and Fred did as well. He really liked them. And so it was quite a blow. Mostly what worried me at the time was I worried about young people and how they would take that. I know how it feels. I know when I was younger, I looked to people to help me get through difficult times. You know, I can't imagine how I would have felt if Bob Dylan would have committed suicide. It would have been . . . . Because I believed he had so much vision and so much strength and so much urgency and so much life. When I felt less than that, he spurred me on and I'm certain that many young people looked to Kurt Cobain to help spur them on and [it] must have been quite a blow and quite painful.

Uhelszki: It's different than Jim Morrison because it wasn't out and out suicide. Or Jimi Hendrix.

Smith: Yeah, none of them are pretty deaths but Jim Morrison was closest because Jim Morrison did drive himself to death through alcohol and drugs, which was also deeply unfortunate and stupid. But Jimi Hendrix was a pure accident. I don't think he was on that plane at all. And he had lots of plans. Jimi Hendrix built Electric Ladyland studios. I saw him right before he died and I was pretty young and I was at a party for him in 1971, I think, at Electric Lady and sat on the steps with him. He was talking to me. I was a kid and he was telling me his plans. I was calling him Mr. Hendrix, your studio's really great, what are you going to do? He was really nice to me. He said he had to go to England and do some things and he was going to gather some musicians and he was going to go upstate New York and he was going to start sort of a tribal musical experience with all different musicians from all over the world. He wanted to get into a sort of global rock jazz, not fusion, but a crossover and like a co-mingling of all these different forces and all these different types of music, more in the Coltrane type of line. So he had a lot of plans, but you can't be stupid, and mixing sleeping pills and alcohol [is] stupid. He had a stupid death.

[Part one ends; part two picks the conversation back up. —Ed.]

Jaan Uhelszki: I think 1996 is your year.

Patti Smith: That's what my mother says. It's curious that you say that. My mother said to me, even with all the difficulties I've had, she took my hand one day, still at the end of '95, and said, "Patricia, I just have a feeling that 1996 is going to be your year."

Uhelszki: You've been returning to performing in a cautious manner. You weren't so cautious the first time around.

Smith: The first time around I evolved. I didn't have any designs about what I was doing. I had a mission. I felt like I had a mission. My mission started out on my own. And then Lenny [Kaye, Smith's guitarist, and long-time friend] became part of this mission. And then we grew as a band. But I never, ever dreamed I'd have a rock & roll band. I never planned it or designed it. My ideas were to first of all, to hopefully inject some revolutionary energy into the world of poetry. At the time, which I thought was pompous and dead, around 1970–1971. That was my first mission. Then it developed into, it was developing through a lot of talks I had with Sam Shephard [sic] about the state of rock & roll. Which I thought was getting questionable by 1971 or '72. You know, we'd lost Hendrix and Morrison and Janis Joplin. And Bob Dylan and the Rolling Stones were sort of like at a different place. And I just felt like a lot of the direction that rock & roll was taking, was getting corporate, was getting show business, was technical, glamorous, and that the idea of the street and heaven were being lost, and I really felt that someone needed to come and save it. I didn't presume myself to be that person, but I thought that if I, I just felt like, I've said this before, but it was always I used to talk about it with my people. I thought of us sort of like Paul Revere and we were like letting people know the revolution was coming. Or something was coming. I didn't think that we'd be part of it, or anything. I just wanted people to wake up. So I felt we were a wake-up call, and I gleaned that the people that would really turn things around would come after us.

THE REBEL: PATTI SMITH

Ben Edmonds | August 1996 | *MOJO*

On March 23, 1996, Patti Smith was at the 1,850-seat Wiltern Theatre in Los Angeles; on March 25, she was at the five-hundred-seat Roxy in West Hollywood. She was back on tour in earnest for the first time since 1979, when the Patti Smith Group had played their biggest audience ever, eighty thousand at the Stadio Comunale, a soccer stadium in Florence, Italy. She sang "Gloria" on all three occasions, but twenty years after the release of *Horses*, the song that largely made her reputation no longer represented her; she was more mature, and her perspective had shifted. Smith had finally come back, the same but different.

Ben Edmonds witnessed that new outlook at the Roxy that night. Smith's son Jackson performed "Smoke on the Water" on stage, which—if you're reading this book in order—you'll notice he rehearsed at Smith's house outside Detroit in Holly George-Warren's interview. Edmonds's encounter with Smith took place over two conversations at her St. Clair Shores home, which he describes as a "small castle" with turrets. It wasn't quite as whimsical inside, he writes, but more lived in, freighted with memories of her late husband, which come flooding out as she waxes nostalgic. A lot of her new album, *Gone Again*, had been written in that house.

Smith lets us in on what motivated her to get back out there—not just words of encouragement from Bob Dylan but a deep social consciousness and an ardent belief in the power of rock 'n' roll as equipment for living, as a rallying cry against the nihilists. "When I say that the Rolling Stones got me through this, or Bob Dylan got me through that, *they did*," she said. And maybe she knew that her work had done the same for countless others. —Ed.

This album [referring to Gone Again *—Ed.] is unique for you in that it has so many solo songwriting credits.*

Fred was giving me guitar lessons. He had taught me some chords, basically so I could write songs. We studied song structure and things I didn't know a whole lot about. He taught me enough on the guitar that, after a lot of practice, I could write simple songs. When he passed away . . . I just . . . um . . . I used to spend a lot of time by myself at night with the acoustic guitar just making up little songs. A lot of the songs on the record—"Farewell Reel," "About a Boy," "Ravens," "Dead to the World," "Wing"—were written that way late at night. They're all in waltz-time, 3/4, which is the only time signature we worked on so it's the only one I know.

The version of "About a Boy" you played at the Roxy is already far beyond the album version.

That song has really grown in performance. It's the closest thing to anarchy—controlled anarchy—that we have right now, because we let the song completely open up at the end. I always like having a piece where everyone goes out but then returns. That was the beauty of John Coltrane, and what separated him from the noisemakers and indulgent jerk-offs. He would go out there and stay out there as long as he could, but he always returned. That's what we strive for.

When Kurt Cobain took his life, Fred and I were extremely disturbed about that. Both of us liked his work. We thought it was good for young people. I was happy that there was a new band I could relate to, and looked forward to watching them grow. He had a future. As parents, we were deeply disturbed to see this young boy take his own life. The waste, and the emotional debris he left for others to clean up.

I was also concerned how it would affect young people who looked up to him, or looked to him for answers. I guess that's the danger of looking to anyone else for answers, but I perceived that he had a responsibility. To himself, to the origin of his gifts, to his family, to the younger generation. So I wrote the song for two reasons. One was as a well wish, even after what he did, that his continuing journey be beautiful. But it was also written with a certain amount of bitterness. The chorus says "About a boy/beyond it all." One way of looking at it is that he's beyond this particular plane of existence. But it's also a wry statement, a frustrated refrain. It relates to my sorrow for the various boys we've lost. Whether it be Jim Morrison or Brian Jones; any of these young, gifted, driven people who *do* feel they're beyond it all, that they can completely ravage and ruin their bodies or have no sense of responsibility to their position and their gifts. We all were pioneering some kind of freedom, but I don't think what's been done with it is all that constructive.

When you were that age how did you deal with those feelings?

All young people feel sometimes that they can't take it, that they'd rather die than get up out of bed. But there was always something that reminded me, it could be anything. The handiwork of man. I could be feeling totally desolate and then look at a beautiful prayer rug or a Picasso, and that would be enough to make me want to live. That's what other people's work did for me. When I say that the Rolling Stones got me through this, or Bob Dylan got me through that, *they did.* That in itself is a motivation for working. The act of creation is a beautiful thing. That belongs to the artist; he's got that moment of illumination, when a kernel of an idea erupts and blooms. But after he creates it, it ceases to be his. It's really for other people.

What brought you back to New York to record?

I love Electric Lady, which is where we cut *Horses*; it's intimate but highly developed. It's right on 8th Street, so you can walk out at three in the morning and there are people on the streets. It's a good energy. I don't require privacy and silence when I'm recording. It's the first recording studio I was ever in. The first time I ever went there was also the first rock 'n' roll party I'd ever been to. Jane Friedman invited me to this party for Jimi Hendrix because he'd just opened the studio up. I was so excited because I'd never been in a recording studio before. But when I got there I was too nervous to go in, so I sat on the steps. Then Jimi came up the stairs. He was incredibly beautiful; tall, very . . . he was *Jimi Hendrix*, y'know? A great-looking man. But really shy. He came up the stairs and I was sitting there so he sat down next to me and just talked.

He asked me why I wasn't going down and I told him I was too nervous. He said, "Me too, I'm too nervous to stay." Then he told me some of the things about the studio, and how he wanted to work on a more global kind of music. He said that he was going to London, but that when he came back he was gonna go up to Woodstock with new musicians and then bring them into Electric Lady to record. But of course he never came back from London. . . . That was a great moment for me. So when Robert Mapplethorpe gave us money to do "Piss Factory," even though it was not much money I *had* to go to Electric Lady.

The equipment has been updated, but it's got a lot of the same things—the late '60s psychedelic paintings and bad murals of Jimi Hendrix playing right-handed. It didn't really occur to me how cyclic it was until I was in the middle of it. I was standing by myself in the hallway looking at those murals, when I remembered standing in that same spot in 1975 and Robert Mapplethorpe taking a picture of me and John Cale. Lenny came out and stood next to me and said, "Amazing, isn't it?" It was like he could feel what I was feeling. The first time we were back in the studio, just hearing those Lenny guitar tones and Jay on the drums, it was so . . . from the subconscious. It triggered so many memories.

How was this one as a recording experience?

This album was both joyous and heartbreaking to do. We were 80 per cent done with the record and I had to stop. I couldn't take it any more because . . . I just really missed Fred. It was so difficult, and I was so emotionally depleted. So we stopped for a while. When we did that little mini-tour with Bob Dylan I was supposed to be finishing the record, but I still couldn't face it. But I got a lot of energy and positive feelings from the Dylan experience, and then we went in and completed the album. Those dates gave me my confidence back.

Do you know what made Bob reach out to you?

What I gleaned from Bob is that he felt it would be good for me to come back out, that he thought people should see me. I wouldn't presume to speak for him, but he has been so highly influential that he knows probably what it tasted like to be influential and then get shuffled around somewhere. I guess he felt I could use some encouragement.

We weren't prepared, but I wanted to do it so badly that we prepared ourselves practically on stage. I think we had about five hours of rehearsal. But all of us had pretty much played together, and we all pooled the things we could do. The first night was pretty shaky, but after that I felt like I was back in familiar territory. My mission on that small tour was to crack all the energy, crack the atmosphere and set the stage for him, to get the night as magic as possible, so that when he hit the stage—'cos he hits a lot of them—that maybe it would feel a little more special. I think we did a pretty good job and I know that he was happy.

Had you been in touch with him over the years?

No, not really. I met him back in the '70s, before we even had a record deal. It was at the Other End on Bleecker Street in the Village. I was told he was in the audience, so I made a few obscure references that I knew the crowd wouldn't get, but would let him know that I knew he was there. It was kinda presumptuous, but that's the way I was then. I was thrilled that he was there, but I wasn't gonna let him know it. When he came backstage I was kinda snotty. "Any poets around here?" he said, so I said I wasn't into poetry anymore—Poetry sucks. Can you believe I said that? But he was very gracious, and even put his arm around me to have our picture taken. The next week it was in the *Soho Weekly News*, right on the cover, and seeing that was definitely one of my best moments ever. But it also made me kinda sad, 'cos I knew I hadn't treated him well and I felt like I'd kinda blown it, y'know?

A little while later, I was on 4th Street and I saw him walking toward me. I tried to shrink but he saw me anyway. And he was really nice. He pulled out that picture and said, "Who are these two people? Do you know them?" And he gave me this beautiful smile, just to let me know it was all right. So he's been incredibly generous and understanding toward me from the very beginning.

I've admired Bob Dylan since I was 15 years old; he's been an important part of my life for two-thirds of it now. So to have someone like that give you encouragement is . . . beyond words. [On the tour] we sang

"Dark Eyes" almost every night, and singing with him was just like being in heaven. I was so happy. I kept thinking . . . sometimes it made me think of Fred, because Fred really liked and admired Bob too. He often said that there were only two people that would be able to pull him out of his self-imposed retirement, Keith Richards and Bob Dylan. He'd say, "Now if Keith or Bob call and want me to play with 'em, I might have to come out." So how could I not answer the call? It was a great experience.

Do you still regard Bob with a fan's awe?

Meeting him again, I can't say I'm in awe of him. The way I relate to him at this point in my life is that he's a man that has a fine presence, a very noble presence. He's an extremely attractive man. When I talk to him I still feel sort of like a schoolgirl, but also like a friend and a colleague.

After Fred passed away, the record I most listened to for solace was Bob's album *World Gone Wrong*, which is all those great old blues and other songs from the trove of his knowledge. I listened to that almost continuously. Once again he helped me through a difficult time with his music. And then to have him reach out to me as a human being . . . I'll be forever grateful.

And this gave you the confidence to finish the record.

We'd pretty much recorded everything; most of the vocals on the record are the live vocals. It was just a question of pulling all the threads together and presenting the record. But I just . . . I just needed time to think about everything. We had pretty much everything cut except the title track "Gone Again," which we did right before we came out here. That was Fred's last music and . . . um . . . I just wasn't able to . . . write the lyrics. And finally I . . . I marshalled my energies and did it. Lenny had a lot to do with making certain "Summer Cannibals" and "Gone Again" came to light. We had a lot of cassette tapes with Fred playing acoustic guitar or chanting or giving some direction . . . to me, 'cos he often made tapes like that so I could write lyrics. Lenny had to lovingly piece those songs together.

So many people haven't yet discovered Dream of Life, *which I think is your best album after* Horses. *People are going to be discovering that album for years.*

I hope so, because it's the only real document we have of Fred's range, though it's still only a partial account. It's pretty much his album; I look at *Dream of Life* as his gift to me. He wrote all the music, arranged everything, a lot of the song titles, the album title, the concept of the songs, especially "People Have the Power," were all Fred's. I told him we should call it by both our names but he wouldn't. But he had promised me that on *this* album he would sing on it and we'd put both our names on it. So I was really looking forward . . . I thought this was going to be a great album because people would see his face, hear him sing, and he was getting interested in performing live again. But . . . ah . . . it didn't happen. Which has been the heartbreaking part of making this album for me.

There was one thing released under both your names: the atmospheric piece "It Takes Time" that you did for the Wim Wenders film Until the End of the World *in 1990.*

Thank you for remembering that one! I love to hear it, because Fred's reciting poetry. Again, that's almost entirely his piece. Not only did he write the music and some of the poetry, he actually dictated how he wanted me to read my parts. Oh yeah, we had some friction, some healthy friction, in the recording of that song. He was the suggester in the family. He was clearly the boss, although he liked to pretend that he wasn't. . . .

How did you first meet him?

It was March 9, 1976, and we met in front of the radiator at that hot dog place, Lafayette Coney Island, in Detroit. The Sonic Rendezvous Band was opening for us, but I didn't know anything about him. Lenny introduced me to this guy. I heard that his name is Smith, and my name is Smith. We just looked at each other and I was completely taken by him. I had no idea who he was or anything about him until afterwards when Lenny told me. Lenny introduced me to him and said, "He's one of the great guitar players." I said, Perhaps you'll want to play with us tonight. And he said, "Maybe so." Then he left and I asked Lenny if he was really any good, and Lenny said, "The best". So I was playing with him that night, and I had a lot of bravado in those days. I didn't have respect for anybody. But I totally submitted to his reign. He came on the stage and started playing, and after a while I just set my guitar down and let it feed back. I just let him take over because I felt that I had met my match, that I had met the better man.

As I understand it, the original plan you'd developed with Fred called for you to begin re-emerging now anyway.

Yes. This would've happened. It was according to plan. A couple of years after *Dream of Life*, Fred wanted us to go out with just a percussionist, Richard Sohl, him and I. It would have been more spoken art, more poetry with them doing interpretive things behind me. Fred really wanted to do that, but then Richard died suddenly. It really broke his heart, 'cos Fred was really close to Richard. So we withdrew from that idea.

Then, after a time he really felt it was time for me to walk back on stage. In his own way he had a somewhat competitive nature, and he was watching how the arena of female artists has really widened. The girls have done a great job. Now, I don't consider myself a female artist—I'm just an artist—but Fred had that bit of competitiveness. He wanted me to take a stand, I think. I actually was the one who was reticent. He felt it in me before I did.

We were gonna do pretty much what we're doing now: do a record, do dates in the summer, do things when we could. But he was . . . actually *(her voice slows down)* . . . looking forward to . . . that. So . . .

Are any of the songs from that period on this new album?

Two. I didn't do a lot of them, just because I couldn't. It was just too painful. Even doing those two . . . They're two rock songs. Fred really wanted me to do rock songs again. For all the knowledge and sophistication that Fred had acquired over the years as a musician, he always said there was always room for one more great rock song, and he never stopped trying to write it. It's just so happened to work out that the pivotal rock songs on the album are the two that Fred and I wrote together.

It's funny, but I really always wanted *him* to go back out. I would've been happy staying at home taking care of the kids. I really wanted the world to see him. I really loved his work, and I do regret that people didn't get to see his full range. But he was his own man, he did what he wanted. He wasn't a guy *trapped* in a family situation. He wanted a family deeply, and he committed himself to his family . . . to a fault, I think. He was a great father.

One of the main reasons that I'm able to feel no guilt, nothing but pride when I'm performing, is that I know he wanted me to do it. I never regretted my decision to stop performing. I spent the '80s study-ing and writing, and becoming a far more facile writer. I learned quite a bit about everything from sports to cooking, whatever I needed to learn at any given moment. And I really treasure those years. I didn't yearn for or regret the past. I didn't even think about it. I was too wrapped up in our present.

What I often did was to wake up early and write from five to seven or eight when the kids got up. I always allowed myself a time, and continued the work ethic that I had developed with Robert Mapplethorpe. No mat-ter what was happening, even when we were sick, Robert and I always worked. Every day. It was sort of a pact we made, and I've kept to that. I've learned that I don't need to smoke pot all night and then at three in the morning write my poem. I had to learn a whole different system of creation. If I have from five to seven to do my work, then that's when I'll do it. I've completely grasped the fact that it comes from within me, and I take it wherever I go. Whether I'm in a prison in French Guyana or in my laundry room. You don't have to be the victim of inspiration. I learned a lot of things from Fred. . . .

The recent Mapplethorpe biography [Mapplethorpe: A Biography, *by Patricia Morrisroe —Ed.*] *painted you as a prisoner of Fred's tyrannical whims.*

Oh, please . . . I made a decision about the kind of life I wanted to live. *I* made it, and I have never even once—*never!*—regretted making it. I mean, I missed my friends, I missed the camaraderie of the band, I missed certain things. Even though sometimes it was difficult, to me it was a privilege to be with him. I only regret that he's gone. I don't regret nothing else.

It was a treat to see Bob Neuwirth at your Roxy show.

I met Bobby around 1969 at the Chelsea Hotel. I was still kinda hoping to be a painter at that time, but it was beginning to become clear to me that it wasn't my beat and so I was writing quite a bit. I was in the lobby of the Chelsea and I had a notebook. "Hey poet," I remember him saying. "Well, you look like a poet. Do you write like one?" Defiant, very challenging. I thought, Whoah, *Bob Neuwirth!* He was in *Don't Look Back.* That's his leg on the cover of *Highway 61 Revisited!* So I gave him my notebook, and he read it and actually thought about it. He took me under his wing. He was a bit older than me, and really like a brother. He was very kind to me, but tough too. He taught me a lot, and helped me start to develop some sense of myself as a writer. At the same time he introduced me to a world that I hadn't been privy to. He introduced me to all kinds of people—Janis Joplin, the Grateful Dead—and introduced me in a way that they treated me respectfully.

After that I met Sam Shepard and he was the same way. He really felt that I was a good writer. He encouraged me to the point of conceit, nearly. He really made me feel good about myself, and made it seem important that I keep writing. He and Bobby did a lot to instill in me not only the desire to keep writing, but they made me feel that I *was* a writer. That's an important step. I had always felt different from other people, a misfit and an alien, but I never really gleaned myself as being special. Other people seemed to pull it out of me, whether it was Robert Mapplethorpe, Sam Shepard or Bobby Neuwirth. I've been very lucky in my life to have people perceive something in me that I didn't always perceive in myself.

When I called your hotel in San Francisco, you were out and they told me that Todd Rundgren had come by with his kids to pick up yours. That seemed like another nice full circle.

Yes. He was very important to me in those early New York days too. I think it was Bobby Neuwirth who introduced me to Todd. And Todd had been so good to Jackson. He let Jack play this beautiful Gibson of his on stage, and then let him take it on the rest of the tour. Todd's another person who really encouraged me. Todd actually thought I had a future as a comedian. I did too.

You mean we almost had Patti Lee Smith in stand-up comedy?

I had that daydream for years. I used to pretend that I went on the Johnny Carson show. He really liked me, and then he got sick and asked me to take over the show until he got better. And I did so well that when Johnny retired he gave me his show. It was one of my favourite daydreams. I still make use of my Johnny Carson studies, as you've probably realised. All the sparring I do, being able to take what hecklers dish out and one-up them, is from years of studying Johnny.

I wasn't really a '60s person. I had lived a fairly sheltered life in South Jersey. I came to New York in 1967, but I lived with Robert Mapplethorpe in Brooklyn. I spent that time working to be an artist or supporting Robert, and I really didn't go through all those '60s changes. I wasn't really involved in the political scene. I was frightened by the '60s, really. The masses of people and all the assassinations and the drug culture and the war in Vietnam . . . I found all of this overwhelming.

The one positive thing is that I *did* get a sense of the collective, that there was some sort of unspoken unity thing happening. Even though I was chronologically the same age, I felt younger because I was a bit behind. So I observed it from a slightly different perspective. What I like about it was how it produced its own networking tools, whether publications like *Crawdaddy*, *Creem* and *Rolling Stone*, or underground radio. Number one, of course, was the music itself, which was something new. Generations before us went wild over Benny Goodman or Frank Sinatra, but they didn't necessarily say anything. But our music was in concert with who we were.

So I did learn some good lessons from the '60s. I looked at the best of it, and what I thought would happen is that the '70s would come along and be even better. But then what I saw was the people losing interest, becoming more self-oriented, and I was very concerned. I was sort of disappointed with my own people. I didn't like what I saw, and that inspired me to do the kind of work that I did.

I understand it was Lenny and your brother Todd who helped you through the desolate time after Fred passed away.

Between Lenny and my brother, they wouldn't let me get too deep down. The minute Fred passed away, my brother got on a plane and came out. He devoted the rest of his life—which only turned out to be one month—to getting me back on my feet. Todd was one of those workaholic types who work around the clock and never take vacations, but he left work immediately and came and stayed with me.

Then at Thanksgiving we all went back to my parents', and I was having an extremely difficult time. We always went back to New Jersey for Thanksgiving, and this was the first time without Fred in 16 years. I could hardly even rise in the morning. So Toddie came in and said, "C'mon babe, get dressed," and he made me get in the car. He rolled down the windows—he actually had a car where you had to roll down the windows!—and put on a cassette of the *Natural Born Killers* soundtrack. Our song "Rock 'n' Roll [*n*-word]" is on that, and he turned it up as loud as he could get it, and we drove around to all our old hangouts and the places we used to play when we were kids.

Todd really loved that song, and he played it over and over, singing at the top of his lungs. He was going, "You're gonna be all right. You're gonna get back to work. Fred wanted you to and you're gonna do it and I'm gonna help you do it. Even if I have to quit my job to go on the road with ya, we're gonna pull everything up." He was so full of energy and love and enthusiasm that he made it difficult to disbelieve him. I wasn't familiar with that soundtrack, and he said, "There's another little song on it you'll like." So we parked in front of Hoedown Hall and Thomas's Field where we used to play, and this song came on. It was Bob Dylan singing "See the pyramids along the Nile . . ." ["You Belong to Me"]. Fred used to sing that song to me, and I sat there and cried listening to Bob sing it. We had been talking about Dylan and how great he was; again, Toddie would have loved being a part of that tour.

We talked and talked, and he stayed for another couple of days. He wouldn't let me not feel good; it was his mission. He said, "We're gonna spend Christmas together and we're gonna get back on our feet." Todd went back to Virginia, and right after that he suffered a stroke and passed away. Which isn't at all uncommon on my side of the family. It was really terrible, but after the shock of losing him I found that he had made me feel so good, and had brought up my spirits so much, that I made a decision. Since his last mission in life had been to get me feeling good, I wasn't going to have his mission be in vain. So even now when I feel . . . you know . . . I just think about that.

You have to let your loved ones go, even as you cherish their spirit as you move forward. Which is difficult, but very important. Then, because of the kind of person I am, I also feel it is my mission to do something in their honour. Like I keep working and collaborating with Robert. [*The Coral Sea*, her tribute to Mapplethorpe featuring many of his photographs, will soon be published by W.W. Norton.] I have many things to do for Fred, not only in terms of work but of course the lifelong mission of watching over our children. With my brother, my mission is to feel good, be happy and do my work. So in those ways . . . as deeply as I miss all of their earthly presences, they're still around. Very much around.

"Jesus died for somebody's sins but not mine" is a line that will forever be associated with you. How do you view it now?

I wrote that line when I was twenty years old. A lot of people misinterpreted it as the statement of an atheist, somebody who doesn't believe in anything. I happen to believe in Jesus. I never said he didn't exist. I only said that I didn't want him to take responsibility for my actions. Because I was young, I perceived myself as an artist, and the artist as a sort of cerebral criminal. I wanted the freedom to pursue all the things I imagined. Things within my art, not in life. In my art, I wanted the right to be misguided, misdirected, slightly criminal, utterly promiscuous, even a murderer. *Within the realm of my work.* I didn't want to be weighed down with such a conscience that I couldn't trample the earth, every junkyard *and* every cloud. I wanted to be free of conscience. I wanted free rein.

Over the years I got into studying Christ, reconsidering Him in Pasolini terms: Christ as revolutionary, a person who felt akin to our people. I found, as I got older and studied deeper, His roles, His ideals, His philosophies a lot more interesting. To the point that at our last show in Florence in '79, which was the last time I did *that* version of "Gloria," I sang, "Jesus died for somebody's sins, *why not mine?*" I probably would not sing that original line now. Not because I think there's anything wrong with it, just because I don't identify with it now.

You always operated from the belief that rock 'n' roll was a force for good. With all that's happened in the culture, do you still think that? Or has this belief in some way been perverted?

Well . . . I think everything gets perverted. But I'm not really concerned with how it gets perverted up in the mainstream, because that's business. I don't have the time or energy to pioneer against big business at this point in my life. Young people can do that.

I like the way young people are interacting globally. I like the alternative networking they're doing. I'd like to see them develop that, and start seeing what they can do collectively to better our situation on the planet. This planet is in deep trouble. What are we seeing? A resurgence of communicable diseases like tuberculosis, we have AIDS; the whole planet is becoming very *viral*. I'm not saying we can stop it, but only we can reduce all of these things.

Is music the same energy source for kids today that it was for us, or is it even possible that it can be?

I think there's so *much* stuff now. Look when we grew up. When I was a kid TV was black and white and there were three stations. They only had cartoons on Saturday morning. The records would come out, it's a big album, you have a *big* record player, you go home and put it *on* the record player, you *sit* and listen to it and really digest what the music's saying. It was its own experience.

Music is still a powerful force—if you have a powerful individual—but I think it's a lot more convoluted now, if that's the right word.

You and Fred talked about not doing anything for personal gain, that it would have to benefit someone else. How do you reconcile that with everything that's happening now?

With this little tour we're not making any money; we're pretty much breaking even. We did a benefit for an AIDS hospice in San Francisco, and benefits will continue to be a big part of our agenda. I have to get back on my feet, truthfully. If it starts building and things go well, I look forward to a time where I never have to take a cent for hitting the stage. I'm watching people in rock 'n' roll make millions and millions of dollars. I see a lot of my friends who've gotten extremely prosperous, and I think they should be doing a lot more. I don't mean giving an autographed guitar to charity. I mean, if you already have $20 million in the bank, take 10 million and find the people that are doing the strongest AIDS research and just give it to 'em. I would encourage performers to take the money they make on stage and give it to the people who need it.

When you first came around the mission was to keep alive and free a certain rock 'n' roll spirit. Is the mission this time about this different, though related, spirit? The responsibility that comes with freedom?

I think so. A lot of the things we attempted to do in the '70s were accomplished. Like T. S. Eliot said, each generation translates for itself. I done what I was supposed to do when I done it. It's not my place to do it now. I wouldn't even know *how* to. All I know is that the planet is full of hands needing to be helped, and I'm trying to see what I can do to get things motivated in a new way. I still think it has to be revolutionary. We still need to redesign stuff.

People are making comeback tours and farewell tours, they're going on *Unplugged* and they're picking up their lifetime achievement awards. But what are they *really* doing? I think we've gotten way too cute with all these tons of awards we're giving to each other. Too much bullshit, too much cute stuff. The Rock & Roll Hall of Fame. It's another money machine. I did appear at one of those to induct the Velvet Underground. I did that out of respect to the Velvets, and because that recognition meant something to them. But I feel about the Rock & Roll Hall of Fame pretty much the way Fred did: that we should be ashamed. The spirit should be the museum.

"Piss Factory" is still one of your more resonant works. But those women you described with such disdain—"these bitches are just too lame to understand/too God damn grateful to get this job to know they're getting screwed up the ass"—with all you've lived since, I'm wondering how you'd regard them now?

Oh, I'd be a lot more compassionate now. Not necessarily for their stupidity, because some of their rules and codes I would still rail against. But being hard-working women . . . maybe their husband's dead, or their husband took off and they've got six kids to look after. So yes, much more empathy, compassion. Much more *respect.*

When I was younger, I really felt completely *there* for the misfit, the person outside society. Artists, and people on the fringes, whether because of their philosophies or sexual persuasion or politics. And I still feel akin to those people, 'cos I'm still one of them. But I've been through so much . . . *life*—being a mother, being a widow, being a laundress, all the things I do—that I definitely feel more empathy, a more common bond with people. When I was younger I had so much intensity that it got to the point where I felt I was in a whole other realm. I don't feel that so much—I feel a lot more human these days.

JOHN CALE AND PATTI SMITH: HOW WE MET

Lucy O'Brien | August 25, 1996 | *Independent*

Here, Lucy O'Brien interviewed Patti Smith and John Cale for the long-running "How We Met" series in the *Independent*. Smith and the Velvet Underground cofounder re-create their tense collaboration on *Horses* in vivid detail. It started with a 4:00 AM phone call in 1975 and it ended with one of the most iconic albums in rock history.

On January 17, 1996, Smith gave the Rock and Roll Hall of Fame induction speech for the Velvet Underground at the Waldorf Astoria. She described the band as "the stark, elusive balloon that burst upon a deflated scene, injecting that scene with a radiance that connected poetry, the avant-garde, and rock 'n' roll," a legacy that galvanized Smith herself. Yet to Smith, "only one aspect [of the Velvets] can be truly romanticized: their work ethic." That band was enlivened by the alchemical combination of Lou Reed, Maureen Tucker, Sterling Morrison, and Cale, whom Smith said was "like a brother to me." It was a similar alchemy—and tireless work ethic—that gave birth to *Horses*. —Ed.

John Cale, 55, rock musician and composer, was born in South Wales, moved to New York in the early 1960s and became a founder member of the experimental rock group Velvet Underground. He went solo in 1968 and has since produced or collaborated on about 80 albums, the latest of which is *Walking on Locusts*. He lives in New York with his wife Risé and their two children.

Patti Smith, 49, rock musician and poet released her acclaimed debut album, *Horses*, in 1975. In 1979 she retired and moved to a Detroit suburb to raise a family. Since the death of her husband, guitarist Fred "Sonic" Smith, in 1994, she has been touring and recording again. She has recently published a book of poetry, *The Coral Sea*, and released her sixth album, *Gone Again*.

JOHN CALE

I first spoke to Patti on the phone from London, which is kind of when the energy started working. I got a call from her manager, Jane Friedman, who explained that Patti wanted me to produce her first album. She put Patti on, and this voice jumped down the phone at me. It was as if the conversation couldn't be contained in a phone call, it had to be done face to face.

When I got to meet her properly it was like boxing, quite combative in a playful way. I'd seen her perform at the poetry center near University Place in New York, and my first question as a producer was, how do I contain this energy? How do I capture it on a record? I had to take her physical presence into account, it's like putting Iggy Pop on record. There was a lot of power in Patti's use of language, in the way images collided with one another.

She struck me as someone with an incredibly volatile mouth who could handle any situation. She could also turn any situation around from a lethargic to an energetic one. But I think it was a very different experience for her going from being a band on-stage to working in the studio. It immediately throws you back on yourself. All her strength and instinct was there already, and I was trying to provide a context for it.

It wasn't easy. It was confrontational and a lot like an immutable force meeting an immovable object. Still, something creative came out of it. There was push and pull. She has a certain animal magnetism, but we were never sexually involved. I had more respect for her as an artist. It would have been difficult to enter the tight-knit circle of the band itself without undermining my position as a producer.

I didn't get on with Allen Lanier (a guitarist on *Horses*), her boyfriend at the time. He was a member of the band the Blue Öyster Cult and came in for the project as this great guitarist. He obviously thought that he was due a certain kind of treatment, and didn't feel I was granting him the space. It escalated and escalated until it got a little frightening. Confrontation with her was indirect, but with Allen it was sheer testosterone.

We toured a lot and went out on the road together after the album. I'd open the show with a few songs and play "My Generation" with her at the end of the set. Then we lost contact for a long time. Our lives went in different directions. We're both similar in that we do what we want to do. So, for example, she made a clear-cut decision to become a mother. She left rock 'n' roll for a while and just went and did it. I think that's really strong.

When I heard that Fred, her husband, had died, I knew that it would be a real blow for her. But when I heard that her brother died also, that was a shock. I don't know how she could have dealt with that.

I met up with her again eight months ago when I did my piano part on "Southern Cross," a song on her new album, and I wanted her to come and read on a record I was doing with the Nouvelle Polyphonic Corsican Choir. I'd built a little section for her to read on a track called "Desiree" [*it's unclear what song Cale is referring to here —Ed.*], and invited her over. It was the dead of winter and she came and had dinner one night with her family. She seemed a much sadder person. It was obviously a time when she was unraveling certain things in her mind. I felt I had to reassure her, make her feel at home, because there was a certain nervousness about how much of the past was really present. The old Patti was not going to come at you in the same way it did, yet I wasn't worried about her because I felt there was this inner strength that was never going to go away. The *spirit* was there.

Now we have a lot of fun. My daughter Eden, who's 11, has spent time with Patti's daughter, who's 10. Patti and I have a shred [*sic*] passion for doing things and not thinking about them. The pure instinct of just doing. She was a poet who wanted to be a rock 'n' roller, and I helped her in both fields. I'm glad she's back on the road now, showing her strength. From here, it can only expand.

PATTI SMITH

I met John when he was going to produce my *Horses* album in 1975. Truthfully, I had lined up another producer first. I didn't know anything about producers and just picked Tom Dowd because I admired him. But he was on Atlantic, and Ahmet Ertegun (former head of Atlantic Records) was really against me. At the time I was deeply into John's records and did everything to try to find him. Finally we wound up on the phone. There was a time difference and it was four in the morning for him, he was half asleep. It was the start of an unfolding nightmare for him.

I knew nothing about recording or being in the studio. We'd already done a single, but I didn't know anything. I was very, very suspicious, very guarded and hard to work with, because I was so conscious of how I perceived rock 'n' roll. It was becoming over-produced, over-merchandised and too glamorous. I was trying to fight against all of that. We had a big, hard battle. John did everything he could to fight our fight for us, even in his sleep. But I made it difficult for him to do some of the things he had to do.

I had all these ideas, and no one before or since has ever been as patient about them as John. I'd have seven different poems I'd want to put on different tracks, sometimes I only wanted three words from one, or two lines from another. I was creating a sort of William Burroughs cut-up. Instead of throwing his hands up or being pissed at me, John got even crazier and more obsessive. It was like having two crazy poets dealing with showers of words. It was a great experience. I drove us all crazy but I think we can look at it and say, we did this body of work together, it's intact, there's no compromises in it. There's a certain beauty in it that wouldn't have happened without John.

Other things. I didn't know how to sing, I don't know about pitch. But the band's adolescent and honest flaws—I wouldn't say weaknesses—John always left them in. But if he could subtly teach us to enhance what we were doing, he did that. He saw that we were improving and sometimes maybe we hit strange notes or hit a very explosive place, but he let us fly. It was a very beautiful, tortuous excursion. Sometimes we'd be all excited, John and I would have a really happy moment together hugging, then at other times we'd have tears streaming down. One time we drove John so crazy that he was falling asleep at the control board and banging his head on it trying to stay awake.

When I first met him I thought he had the most beautiful voice, the most beautiful Welsh accent. He was kind and very warm. We didn't always communicate, but instead of fights, his struggle was in always trying to figure out how to understand me. I was pretty young and volatile. I don't really remember conflict between him and my boyfriend at the time, but I know there was some jealousy. Truthfully though, I have so many memories, I try to remember the most positive aspects. I'll cherish even the tragic things—like the death of my husband and my brother two years ago—but I won't hold grudges. I only have time for comedy and tragedy in my life, I don't have time for the middle ground.

When we met I knew instantly that we would be friends. It was a new time, a struggling time, a discovering time and he helped us in the birth of ourselves. I'd never thought of doing an album or being involved in rock and roll. I wanted to be a painter or a writer, so it was all completely foreign territory to me. I didn't have any sense of the music business, I didn't want to know about it. I just wanted to do my work. John was too young to be a father figure, but he was like a brother to me, a brother who gave me a helping hand.

PART III
1997–2009

Blakean Years

IN THESE VIRAL TIMES: AN EXCLUSIVE INTERVIEW WITH PATTI SMITH

Laurie Fitzpatrick | November 1997 | *A&U*

A&U magazine, short for *Art and Understanding*, was founded in 1991 by David Waggoner in the wake of the loss of peers and collaborators from the arts community to AIDS. Patti Smith was on the cover of the November 1997 issue of "America's AIDS magazine" in a series of penetrating photos shot by photographer Steven Sebring, who went on to direct the 2008 documentary *Patti Smith: Dream of Life*.

Artist and AIDS activist Laurie Fitzpatrick interviewed Smith about her ongoing work as a fellow activist and her coming to terms with the disease that in 1989 ultimately would take her best friend, Robert Mapplethorpe. In the interview, she discussed *The Coral Sea*, a poetic precursor to *Just Kids* that she began writing immediately after his death, and what it really means to be a friend, especially in what she called "these viral times." Smith characterized this fraught cultural moment, not unlike our current viral times, as plagued by an insidious anxiety, "some kind of acceleration that is not akin to panic." Instead of giving in to fear, though, Smith felt "it's a really great time for us to claw our way back to each other." —Ed.

The endurance of Patti Smith is much needed good news. For punks and rockers who emerged as a result of the cultural work she helped pioneer, she shows us a future in aging, maintaining one's art, building a family and raising children. For kids of the MTV generation, Smith offers wisdom that is tried and true, and a poetic language she's been perfecting over the years.

Smith's new album, *Peace and Noise*, was meant to be the stage for her comeback, but its creation and release was interrupted by the death of her husband, Fred. She reemerged instead with *Gone Again*, an album of remembrance not only for Fred, but for her brother Todd, her pianist Richard Sohl, and her best friend Robert Mapplethorpe. With *Peace and Noise*, Smith picks up where she and her husband left off and tackles the dark side and disappointing aspects of the American Dream. Despite the fact that we're bogged down in materialistic, viral times, Patti Smith see great hope.

Laurie Fitzpatrick: It appears to me as if you've gotten fame on your own terms. Is this accurate, and if so, how do you think you've accomplished this?

Patti Smith: Well, I don't exactly know, I think the kind of recognition I have is pretty much from people. I lived a pretty simple life in the last sixteen or seventeen years and returning to do public work I found that people treat me very respectfully in a way that they didn't treat me in the '70s. But it's not on a commercial level because I don't sell many records. So the way that I've communicated with people or why I'm given a certain amount of respect I suppose is for the quality of the work because it isn't for the quantity. Courting fame is dangerous and as it's been said that all fame is fleeting but one's work has the possibility of enduring. And if one does good work, perhaps they'll be remembered, or counted on, or sought after for some word or some council through the power of their work.

Is there an overall theme for your new album *Peace and Noise*?

I think it's a very positive album. It addresses human difficulties, human pain, human concerns, and a lack of spiritual content in our society, but on the other hand it also addresses spiritual hope.

There is something poignant in your song "Blue Poles" that really moves me. What are the blue poles?

Smith: It's a very simple American song about the Depression and the Dust Bowl. It's a very optimistic song, you know, the girl is writing her mother to tell her that her husband died along the way out West. They lost everything but she's still hopeful for the future and able to watch the sun rise and set. Overall it's about people traveling across America in hopes of something better, and the blue poles are just a symbol of hope. "Blue Poles" is actually the title of a Jackson Pollock painting, and that's why in the beginning of the song it says "Hopes streaking, hopes dashed, immortal hope, hope streaking the canvas sky, blue poles." Also, whenever you see old pictures or movies of people journeying across America they show the long rows of telephone poles to indicate distance. I always thought the image of the telephone pole was quite beautiful. It's like a big crucifix.

So were you thinking of the hope of the American Dream?

Well, yeah. Human hope.

"Death Singing" is another song that strikes me deeply because it has some really wild images. Stuff like, "His throat was smooth as a lamb. . . ."

"Yet dry as a branch not snapping." I was inspired by this fellow named Benjamin who is from Atlanta and he has a group called Smoke. Benjamin [*Born Robert Dickerson —Ed.*] was once friends with my keyboard player Richard Sohl who passed away. Benjamin was quite a beautiful young man and quite a writer and singer, and he has AIDS. He did a farewell performance in New York in a little club called the Cooler and Oliver Ray and I went to see him. I didn't know what he'd be like and I found his band and his performance extremely moving. I just immediately wrote the song. I rarely write whole songs. That's why in the end of the song it talks about, "He sings of youth enraged, he sings of Atlanta burning, he sings of these viral times. . . ."

The images are so strong.

Well it was a very strong image to see this young man who was once quite beautiful, still very interesting looking but ravaged by AIDS and time, sitting in a chair in an old raincoat with a cigarette.

It makes me think of all the artists who have been lost to AIDS.

Well, I could say it's unprecedented, but of course in the nineteenth century we lost many great artists to syphilis, you know—Baudelaire, Rimbaud, Verlaine. Countless artists, from one viral situation to another. For me it's been not only a personal loss but it's heartbreaking to see people taken in their prime with so many ideas and so much energy.

I've been hit by this a number of times because I've interviewed many artists who have AIDS, and what strikes me the hardest is when people my age, you know, in their early 30s, are ill or have died. It's the worst thing when you're 31, 32, 33 and you start hitting your stride, then you have to leave.

Well, there's no good age, really. Robert Mapplethorpe died when he was forty-two and he had done a tremendous body of work but he was also such a worker and was continually evolving. And then you have somebody like his patron, Sam Wagstaff, who was in his sixties and still that seems shockingly young for him to have died because he was filled with energy and was a very astute patron of the arts. I suppose with youth it does seem somewhat tragic, but then one can say where does youth begin and end?

Do you think American culture is in recovery right now from losing so many artists because of AIDS?

Well, I think that, in terms of art, the individual rules. We always have strong individuals with ideas and new people that are born with a calling and synthesize all that came before them and things they imagine for the future. So as heartbreaking as it is, I always have faith that new people will rise up and that's what it's all about. It would be sad to think there were no more artists left or that all the artists have been born. It's a continuous calling. Michelangelo was called. John Coltrane was called. Robert was called and someone else will be called.

I feel as if the idealistic rebellion of the late '70s and the early '80s has been kind of assimilated into this rather cynical zeitgeist. On the surface, it feels like things are okay or maybe getting better, but underneath I feel a growing sense of unease that we're experiencing some

kind of calm before the storm. Do you share this feeling, and if so, what do you think this storm might be?

We're in a very unusual time in history. We are obviously moving toward a new century and millennium, and I think people, even if they're not consciously aware of it, are being propelled or accelerated, or feeling something. And I think this will keep accelerating until we hit that 2000 mark. I can only think of the word acceleration. Not always positive or negative, not even with design. It's some kind of acceleration that is not akin to panic, but I believe it exists.

Could it be a kind of anxiety?

Well, I think it's anxiety, and I think that people either consciously or subconsciously want to make their mark, want to say their last words for the old century, try to feel out what their tasks are or how to approach the new century. And I think that can be a very positive thing but I think it can also be, like you said, a very anxiety ridden type of thing. I just feel that when we have landmarks as a people, we always want to make a resolution.

So it's a psychological threshold that we cross?

Yeah, and I think that a whole new millennium and a whole new century puts a beautiful but a very intense pressure on everyone. Instead of being afraid of it, though, I think we should grab the reins and say this is our chance to try to redeem ourselves or to open new forms of communication or to heal wounds. It's a really great time for us to claw our way back to each other.

Saying "claw our way back to each other" strikes a chord with me and brings to mind HIV among other things, things that separate people and instill fear. AIDS, specifically, took away the dream that Americans were living in a freewheeling, powerful society with terrific healthcare, where we could be sexually free, party and have a great time. AIDS really put the brakes on a lot of things.

Well, I think it's important to put the brakes on a lot of things anyway because we aren't a freewheeling society. Sexual freedom isn't important. It's important for us not to be burdened with intense dogma from other periods of history, but I don't think that indiscriminate sexual freedom is important, necessary, or healthy. It's unfortunate that we should have to examine ourselves in the face of such a tragic viral situation, but I think it was time anyway. I think what we were striving for in equal rights, or gay rights, whatever types of rights people were striving for in the '60s and '70s, the idea is that it's a human right to feel good about oneself, the right not to be discriminated against, the right to be allowed to be a decent person in the structure or persuasion one sees fit. But the idea wasn't to make life one big, indiscriminate party. I think perhaps it's always like the golden calf or the Gomorrah aspect of our society. We cross a line into a new freedom and instead of being responsible and treating that freedom with respect, we have a tendency perhaps to erupt. So I think it's good for us to question ourselves.

As a people we are naturally decent, and I think with all the prejudice with AIDS or anything else, eventually, as a society we find a way to take a deep breath and come together and help one another. We have a bigoted strain and an uneducated strain, but I think as a society when the people are educated and really spoken to, they usually respond in positive kind. We've learned a lot. I was living in Michigan in the mid-'80s and living a fairly isolated life raising my children when I heard about AIDS by reading an obituary of an old friend of mine who was only in his fifties. I was shocked and I thought "what is this?" You know, "what happened to him?" And then I looked into it and found this was indeed a very insidious plague that was starting to permeate the world of all my acquaintances in New York. And so I went to New York in '87 to spend some time with Robert [Mapplethorpe] and still was completely uneducated about AIDS. I was pregnant at the time and visiting another very close friend, Sam Wagstaff, in the hospital, and I actually went to a doctor and asked if it was alright if I could touch Sam. I'm a fairly educated person and a compassionate, loving person and here was a dear friend of mine, but I was also a pregnant woman and my natural instinct was to protect my unborn child. I wasn't sure if you could kiss a person with AIDS or touch them, or be afraid of their sores, and things like that, and I had to be swiftly educated. And Robert helped to educate me, very compassionately.

I've read in interviews that you have issues with the Morrisroe biography of Robert, how she focused more on the personal and trivial aspects of his life and really didn't discuss his art. But she had one scene in the book about the last day you spent with Robert. . . .

Yes, I told her about it.

It was very touching.

I talked to her at length—and why I took exception to the book was, first of all, she drew my personal life into it, and my family's personal life. Also, I spent hours and hours talking with her about Robert's calling as an artist and felt that all of the time I'd spent trying to explain the spiritual mechanism of an artist was wasted. But that last time I saw Robert, that's the way it was. And I actually was in contact with Robert until he went into his last sleep. They held the phone up to him and I listened to him breathing until when he practically stopped breathing. I mean, Robert was my best friend.

So much has been written about your friendship that it's become legendary.

If it's legendary that's because it's a fine example of friendship. Robert and I went through a lot of things. We met when we were twenty. We experienced puppy love. We were girlfriend and boyfriend. Robert opened up and found himself to have a calling more toward homosexuality and we went through that together and stayed close. We collaborated together, we went through many artistic processes together and remained loving, caring friends until his death. I think any story of an everlasting friendship is worthy of legend.

Your book *The Coral Sea* was very lovely. It read to me like a dream portrait of someone you loved deeply.

Well, I knew Robert so well. I wrote that the same day Robert died. He was in Boston and I had my children and I couldn't go. I was sitting up all night in vigil because I knew he was dying and his brother called me at 7:30 in the morning to tell me that he had finally passed away. I was watching the opera *Tosca* on A&E, and they were doing the aria to life and art and I immediately began to work. I really believe that in lieu of tears, *The Coral Sea* was part of my grieving process for Robert. What I was trying to do was conjure up a portrait of Robert as I knew him, in a way that I knew him.

I felt that I had a privileged, insider's view, like I was standing there right next to him and experiencing things the way he did.

Well, it's very much like Robert. The Uncle who appears is a little homage to Sam Wagstaff, and I'm woven in and out of there. But even with any flaw it might have, I'm still very happy with it because when I read [*The Coral Sea*] I definitely see Robert. And I know he would see himself in that little piece.

What it did for me is it helped me understand the luminosity of his photographs.

Well, thank you.

What have you been teaching your kids about sex and HIV?

Well, my son knew Robert and my children know that I've lost many friends through AIDS. My son is fifteen years old and he's extremely knowledgeable and looks at these things with respect and maturity. My daughter is ten years old and she has many friends who have HIV in her school. She feels like it's sad but she sees them playing and she plays with them. I want her to be aware of certain things but I also want her to have a childhood, and I don't think the deep, intense instruction of children is necessary. If you're just direct with children, you can say things as simply as this person has something and it won't affect you. It's something that they have to deal with and you have to help them be strong. But you also have to feel free to laugh and have fun because sometimes in our pursuit to educate, we burden young children with more than they need to know. We can't just start explaining to them things about disease and viruses. We have to start right at the core of things, that we respect one another. Physical relationships are something to be respected and not taken lightly and something to be given deep thought about for various reasons. For love, for pregnancy, for respect, for disease.

My editor saw you last year at the Quilt playing to a small audience and he really loved the intimacy of that performance where he felt like he was among friends. Why did you decide to perform at the Quilt?

Well, I do a lot of benefit work. I mean, why not? I do as much as I can. I've done a lot of AIDS benefit work in so many different capacities. You never can do too much of it because it's ongoing. People act sometimes like these causes are fads, you know, like "oh that was last year's cause" or something. But it's a cause until we get a cure and even beyond that. It's a cause because people need money for their medical assistance.

That's how I feel with the new protease inhibitors. They're wonderful but . . .

Who can afford them?

For one thing, and they don't necessarily work for everyone. And the bottom line is that protease is not a cure.

And I think we just have to keep struggling. I also find the ways that human beings remember each other are quite beautiful. Certainly *Gone Again* was a remembrance record and in every record I've done I've always had some form of remembrance for someone or some idea. In *Peace and Noise* that remembrance resounds. So, whether it's the Vietnam wall, or leaving flowers by a gate, or saying prayers, visiting graves, lighting a candle, the way human beings pay homage to each other is beautiful. The AIDS quilt [*AIDS Memorial Quilt* —Ed.] is another fine example.

I've seen it a number of times and it's always emotionally overwhelming to me.

Well I have many friends woven within that quilt. And even the ones I know who aren't in the quilt, they're there anyway. It's symbolic and if every name isn't on the quilt, just the fact that it's been done means they're all in there. They're all in the weave and the cut of the cloth.

How does your performing energy feel different from your "High on Rebellion" days and today?

Well, some of it is nearly identical. There's certain energies that are completely attuned and I guess they're ageless. And then there are other levels of communication, other levels of performance that I never knew before. There are also ones that I know are gone or at least dissipated or shifted into another skin. I mean as human beings we're continuously shedding skins, we're evolving and so . . .

To me it's not an issue of age, it's an issue of depth of experience.

Personal evolution. Certain aspects of age might come into it because of how one is doing physically, but a lot of that has to do with how one takes care of oneself. The other component that's important is the people. And certainly when I was performing in the '70s I was performing to different people. At this time in my life the people that I'm performing before or performing with—because I always think of performance as a mutual experience—seem less specific, they seem like all walks of life, different ages, not any specific aesthetic or race or gender. I think in the '70s the people that I courted were more the people who were obviously misfits. But at this time in our history, the misfit is not so clearly defined. You can't recognize a misfit by the way they dress or the kind of music they listen to as a society. Many across the board people feel some misfit, so there's not any specific camp. And I like that.

Is this proof of progress?

In a certain way, yes. People always have their style thing and that's actually enjoyable, one's style, one's cool, one's aesthetic look, but it's not the most important thing. It's just one aspect. We have a common bond as human kind and these stylistic things are just sort of tribal type things, and they're not enough for people to fight for or band against each other for. These things should be heralded and celebrated but they shouldn't separate us.

THE PROGRESSIVE INTERVIEW: PATTI SMITH

John Nichols | December 1997 | *Progressive*

If *Peace and Noise* was Patti Smith's most overtly political album to date, then this 1997 interview, framed around its release, is the most overtly political interview in this book. Published in the Madison-based *Progressive* and conducted by Wisconsin native John Nichols, a gimlet-eyed observer of the American political scene who went on to become the National Affairs correspondent at the *Nation*, the conversation feels particularly prescient considering the political shifts in the decades to come.

Smith discussed a range of related political issues: the role of the artist as citizen; the wealth gap she witnessed between inner-city Detroit and affluent Grosse Pointe; how the materialistic culture that remained from the '80s distracted and divided people from any meaningful unity; and the inconvenient truths of being a responsible steward of the planet. She was aware of the limitations of artists to enact policy changes. Still, even if rock 'n' roll couldn't make the changes, it could be a "vehicle to share ideas or to incite people," and cause what she called a much-needed "reverberation." –Ed.

"To me, rock 'n' roll is a totally people-oriented, grassroots music. But it's not ours anymore."

Almost thirty years have passed since Patti Smith burst out of South Jersey, with a poem—"Piss Factory"—that declared, "I'm going to be somebody, I'm going to go on that train and go to New York City, I'm going to be so bad, I'm going to be so big, I'm going to be a big star, and I will never return."

Smith did become a star. She published critically acclaimed books of poetry. She traveled in the circles of Warhol and Mapplethorpe. And she did what no woman had done before.

Relying on male icons—the teenaged French poet Arthur Rimbaud, American Beats Allen Ginsberg and William Burroughs, rock stars Keith Richards, Jimi Hendrix, Jim Morrison, and Bob Dylan—she fashioned a rock-star persona that made the Patti Smith Group an icon for a whole generation of young rockers.

Smith defined the punk aesthetic, wrote a hit single ("Because the Night") with Bruce Springsteen, released four stunning albums, and performed before crowds that numbered in the tens of thousands. Then, in 1979, she "retired" to raise a family in Detroit with legendary MC5 guitarist Fred "Sonic" Smith. Over the next fifteen years, she brought up a daughter, Jesse, and a son, Jackson. Though she continued to write poetry and songs, she published only sporadically and released just one album.

In 1994, as she and her husband were preparing to record new music, a wave of tragedy hit. Fred died of a heart attack, as did Smith's brother, Todd. [*Todd Smith died of a fatal stroke on December 4, 1994. —Ed.*] In the wake of those deaths, Smith has forged a comeback. Haunted and fragile on last year's album, *Gone Again*, she emerged this fall with *Peace and Noise*, which *Billboard* magazine declared to be "as potent an artistic statement as Smith has ever crafted."

Peace and Noise is Smith's most politically charged album, with songs that address Tibet, the Heaven's Gate suicides, AIDS, memories of Vietnam, and anger at the lingering hangover of the Reagan era.

For all of its politics, however, *Peace and Noise* retains the reverence for poetry and the faith in rock 'n' roll that has always underpinned Smith's work.

On the eve of a series of concerts in New York, where she now lives, Smith met me at a cafe in Soho. We ate French toast and watched Jesse draw pictures of clouds. Then we wandered over to Patti's house—a venerable 150-year-old structure on land once owned by Aaron Burr.

On a wooden table in the kitchen sat a copy of Walt Whitman's *Leaves of Grass*.

Q: As an artist, did you feel you had to pick up a guitar and form a band to get your message across in an age where there are so many voices competing for attention?

Patti Smith: I've always loved the format of rock 'n' roll. I remember, as a child, watching rock 'n' roll develop. I grew up with it. I was certainly comforted by it, inspired by it, excited by it.

Then in the early 1970s, when I really felt that rock 'n' roll was losing some of its strength—when it just seemed like a format people were visiting for some kind of glamorous lifestyle, or to take a lot of drugs, twist people's minds, make a lot of money, and then exit—I reacted. Maybe I overreacted. But I really felt that rock 'n' roll was going into a bad place. I actually worried that it would just disintegrate.

I had never had any aspirations toward being a musician. I'm not a musician. I'm not really much of a singer. I wasn't brought up in a time where females even thought of things like that. In terms of female performers, we had memories of Edith Piaf, Billie Holiday, jazz singers, then you had Janis Joplin coming up, and Tina Turner. But in terms of a singer-songwriter leading a rock band, there really wasn't anyone I could think of. So I just didn't think about it.

It wasn't my intention to be involved in all this. I really wanted to be a painter, but I just didn't quite have the stuff to be a painter. Parallel to that, I always wanted to write.

But I seemed to have some kind of a natural calling to be a performer, to speak. I always felt comfortable and I had a desire to speak. When I was younger, I thought I'd be a missionary, or a preacher or a teacher. I went to teacher's college. I always liked the idea of talking to people about things, whether it was *Moby-Dick* or the environment or making them laugh. And it turned out that rock 'n' roll was the place for me to do it.

Q: You've been at it for a quite a while. Is the soul still there in rock 'n' roll?

Smith: I don't worry about that so much anymore. I think the soul is there, if you look for it. Luckily, a lot of young bands and new performers have gone the independent route. They exchange ideas through vehicles that I'm not even really schooled in—through computers and the Internet. There's a huge independent-music scene in recording, in performing.

But the music industry is worse than ever. It seems to me a lot like it was in the 1950s. I look at it now and the doors need to be kicked through because it's just as bad as any other time I can remember. Radio is more formatted than ever. Music TV is really a disappointment. They never took advantage of the potential that was there. They took advantage of how powerful they could get, and how much money they could make, but what I thought might be the prime directive—communicating in a serious way—they sort of forgot about that. Now they're just a big business.

All the communication that comes out in formatted radio and music television is token. It's really a shame. And I think that people are going to have to fight. We have to demand something more, something better.

I'll do what I can, say what I can. But it's got to be new people, new guard, who are going to have to fight and say they're not going to stand for this. I'm not just talking about musicians and artists. It's got to be people working at radio stations, people at the college level. It's got to be people across the board. People have to decide that they want to take over again.

I remember that the B-side of our first single, "Gloria," is "My Generation," recorded live in Cleveland. We said on there, "We created it. Let's take it over." To me, rock 'n' roll is a totally people-oriented, grassroots music. It came up from the people, from the blues. The roots are deep. It came from the earth. It's our thing. Rock 'n' roll is great because it's the people's art. It's not an intellectual art. It's totally accessible. The chords are totally accessible. The format is totally accessible. But it's not ours anymore. Right now, rock 'n' roll belongs to business. We don't even own it.

The people have got to wake up and reclaim what belongs to them. The music business should be working for us; artists should not be working for the music business.

It's the same with America. The country belongs to us. The government works for us. But we don't think of it that way. We've gotten all twisted around to a point where we think that we work for the government.

Q: You set out to address this a decade ago, with the song, "People Have the Power," which touched a lot of activists. How did you come to write it?

Smith: "People Have the Power" was Fred's phrase. I was sitting in the kitchen, literally peeling potatoes, and Fred came into the kitchen and said, "Tricia, people have the power—write it." And I said, "All right."

I had been reading the Bible, as I often do, and I had just reread the section about how the meek shall inherit the Earth. I was thinking a lot about all this, and he and I spent several days talking about what we were going to try to communicate through this song—we often did that, he'd have an idea and a philosophy but he'd ask me to write the lyrics.

"People Have the Power" was the perfect song for the two of us to write. He had protested the Vietnam War, he had supported the civil-rights movement. His band, the MC5, was a very political band. I also had addressed these things. I did it in my way, which was more biblical. He was more politically articulate. So we just merged all of our ideas.

A lot of different things were on my mind. The first verse abstractly addressed the state of the environment. The second verse was actually about Afghanistan—Russia had invaded Afghanistan—and I was imagining these Afghani shepherds and the Russian soldiers just lying together on a hill at night and looking at the stars and talking about things, instead of fighting. It was a vision.

That song came out in an election year, in 1988, and I saw Jesse Jackson delivering speeches and I felt like, if I knew his phone number, I'd call him and say, "I have a song for you." His speeches, the concepts he was addressing, were very similar to the lyrics in the song.

We still perform that song. I think it's a very important song.

Q: Almost twenty years ago, you wrote a song called "Citizenship." But it seems to me your ideas have evolved. Can you describe your sense of the role of the artist as citizen?

Smith: My feelings about that are mixed. When I was younger, the last thing I wanted to be was a citizen. I wanted to be an artist and a bum—what Genet would call one of "the sacred bums of art." That's pretty much all I wanted to be. I was concerned about certain things—about censorship, about nuclear power, about the Tibetan situation, and the famine in Ethiopia. I did have concerns, but still, as an artist and a human being and an American, I was basically self-centered. I didn't really have an understanding of what it was like to be a citizen.

In 1979, when I moved to Detroit to live with Fred, my life changed drastically. I came to understand George Washington's quote after he left the Presidency, when he said, "I have resumed my life as a citizen." I took comfort from that, because I actually became "as a citizen."

We had children. We had a house. We faced financial struggles. We lived very simply. We did everything ourselves, whether it was clearing our little piece of land or—because we lived on a canal that often flooded—sandbagging in the middle of the night. I had to wash diapers and clean toilet bowls and nurse sick children and find time to do art.

I had to get up at five in the morning and write before the baby woke up. My art didn't suffer. My work actually flourished in that period because I learned new disciplines. I had to become much more focused in those time periods when I could work.

I gained a lot of respect for people. It's not my bent. I'm just not a middle-class person. I don't have middle-class sensibilities, desires. But I would never again be so snooty about the middle class and middle-class struggles.

Q: Has that changed your sense of art? Do you feel different responsibilities?

Smith: I think the artist's first responsibility is to his work, to the quality of his work. An artist must concern himself with what's motivating him, whether it's a spiritual motivation, or a vision thing, an abstract principle, or something totally intellectual.

An artist must concern himself with the quality of his work. What it does out in the world is not always of the artist's choosing. I don't think it's the artist's duty to be political. It's the artist's duty to do good work. If that work inspires people—if he's a politically articulate artist—that's great. But the main thing is to inspire people or to comfort them or to touch them in some way, which may or may not be political.

Some artists become political just because what they're doing is revolutionary. Picasso was revolutionary because of the way he looked at the world. Jackson Pollack was not a political revolutionary; he was a very meditative man, but he seemed revolutionary because of the nature of his work.

An artist's role in society is often decided by the people. The people decide how they want to use the work of a certain artist, or how the work of that artist affects them or their ideas.

Q: That said, *Peace and Noise* contains a great many statements of a political nature. And those statements are, in many ways, refinements of messages you have delivered throughout your career.

Smith: I intentionally do that. I'm not a pure artist. I would like to be, and I would like to think that occasionally I write a pure poem or a pure prose piece. But, in terms of rock 'n' roll, I never set out to be a purist. Again, I'm not a real singer. I'm not a true musician. I had things to say, and I felt that it was my right to say those things in the format of rock 'n' roll. I took it as my right. I've always seen rock 'n' roll as a vehicle to share ideas or to incite people. I've really never considered—especially when I was younger—that my work itself was that important. What I thought was important was that I had a certain amount of energy, and I seemed to affect people in a certain way, and so I wanted to use that power to get people who were more articulate than me, more motivated, to take the next step and do things.

I've always wanted to make people think. We've got plenty of entertainment happening in America. There's plenty of people writing the kind of songs or singing the kind of songs or developing the sort of image that will entertain America. That's not my real interest.

I like people to have a good time when I'm performing. I like to see people laugh. I love to make people laugh. But I'm not there to entertain people.

Q: Perhaps the most powerful song on *Peace and Noise* is "1959." It's about Tibet, which is a trendy cause now, but for you this is an expression of a very old concern, isn't it?

Smith: I got involved in the Tibetan situation as a young girl. In the late fifties, when I was a schoolgirl, we all had to pick a country to do a year report on. We had to take things out of the newspapers. I picked Tibet, which I had learned about in the library. I was very taken with the Dalai Lama and his philosophies. My teacher said to me, "Patti Lee, this country you've taken is so obscure. You'll never be able to fill a scrapbook with newspaper articles about this country. No one's ever heard about it." And I said, "No." I insisted on keeping Tibet. And much to my shock, in March of 1959, the Chinese invaded and all of a sudden this country that I adored and was so obscure was suddenly all over the newspapers. It was heartbreaking. The Dalai Lama, they thought, was dead, and they didn't know what had happened to his family.

I was devastated by this. My father had fought in World War II. I was pretty much raised with the idea that the great wars were settled and the world was free. I just couldn't understand how this could happen in Tibet. And what I really couldn't understand was how no one seemed to mind. I've been baffled by the Tibet situation since 1959. I've thought about it a lot. I've written little pieces. But this was the first time I really addressed it in a song.

Q: There is anger in "1959," and in a number of the other tracks on the new album.

Smith: Certainly. There's a lot to be angry about. When you look around, when you open your eyes, you see things that make you angry. It's like when I lived in Detroit and I would drive through Detroit on this road called Jefferson. You drive through downtown Detroit, a once-proud city that's trying to build up, and then you drive through deeper downtown—which is pretty much boarded up. Then, a block away, there is one of the richest communities in America, Grosse Point. It's flabbergasting.

We have had so many great opportunities in America to make things right, and we still have them, but we just let the opportunities go by. It's almost like everything has just become a CNN soap opera. We look at children in Somalia dying on TV and then we just flip the channel and put on whatever sitcom we want to see.

What ended the Vietnam War, as much as anything, was a handful of photographs looking at the atrocities in Vietnam. A handful of photographs just incensed the people so much that we just couldn't take it. We couldn't take the guilt. And now people seem like they just can take anything. I just think, right now, we're preoccupied. We're too busy. Our heads have been turned. We're getting, unfortunately, on a real materialistic ride right now. And I hope it's a phase.

Q: You recently visited the grave of Walt Whitman for the first time. What drew you there?

Smith: When I was a teenager growing up in South Jersey, I was allowed to take the bus to Camden, and when I got off the bus there was the Walt Whitman Hotel. I was very taken with Walt Whitman. I felt proud that I was living in a state where they had things honoring Walt Whitman. But I don't think I realized that he was buried there, or I would have gone sooner.

I have always admired Walt Whitman. And the people I have admired have admired Walt Whitman. Allen Ginsberg's *Howl* is extremely Whitmanesque.

When Allen was dying, I went to his loft, and I spent time with him. One of the most memorable things was that there was a very peaceful portrait of Walt Whitman by his bed. That picture of Allen sleeping and quietly dying beneath Walt Whitman's portrait rekindled my thoughts about Whitman. Simultaneously, I got a letter from the Walt Whitman Cultural Center in Camden, asking if we might consider helping them. Camden is a struggling city, and they had seen me open up for Bob Dylan in Philadelphia and send a salute to Camden, New Jersey, and they thought I might be open to this. So I felt I had to go. I went to the Walt Whitman Cultural Center and did a benefit for them. We toured his home and his grave site, and it was all very moving. His grave is just beautiful; he designed it himself and it's very simple—slightly overgrown, very peaceful, right across from an old abandoned factory.

Q: Whitman is such a dramatic figure, yet he is so often taught in our schools today as a stodgy remnant of the nineteenth century. In truth, there's nothing stodgy about him. He really was, and is, a very radical figure.

Smith: He was the first true modern American poet. Certainly, he was the inspiration for the Beat movement. The Beats were also informed by his openness concerning his sexual persuasion, which was a radical thought in Ginsberg's time, let alone Whitman's. And Whitman's descriptions of the Civil War—which come from having been there, having nursed soldiers—are some of the most informative and beautifully written pieces I have ever read.

He had a strong sense of himself. He had a benevolent ego—he had a huge ego, but he loved mankind, and he loved people of all walks of life. Whitman intentionally communicates with us in our time. He says in his poetry that he is speaking to you—to you personally: To the poet who is reading this, 100 years from now, 200 years from now, I am thinking of you, I am telling you that I did all these things, suffered all these humiliations, went through these particular joys and illuminations, just as you are, and I am with you.

That is such a great thing—to speak across time. Right now, however, we're in a very quick-gratification time. We're not looking for the messages that poets have left for us. People want things quick, and their attention span is short. They want answers, and by the time they get those answers they want something new. This is because we have a myriad of ways to be entertained in these times. We're not really being spoken to, or informed, or drawn together.

Basically, right now, we're all being distracted. And what are we being distracted from? Unification. We're being distracted from finding some kind of common ground, from mobilizing, and getting things done. We're being distracted from what we need to be doing: deemphasizing material acquisition and finding some common beliefs on which we can rebuild our country.

Q: You've been very engaged with people like Ginsberg, who have tried to make America live up to its promise—in a variety of different ways.

Smith: Allen, really, was filled with a lot of joyful, conspiratorial energy. He really had that sixties thing right to his death. It's really a shame to lose him because I can't think of anyone else who brought so many people together, which was completely obvious at his deathbed. In his loft, through his dying process, coming to visit him or going in and out were all of these different types of people: young poets that none of us knew but that he had encouraged, the Buddhist community and his Buddhist teacher and the monks chanting, and all of his Jewish relatives who were flabbergasted at this whole monk scene, librarians from New Jersey. Allen's death was a lot like Allen's life—it was filled with people from various camps and he found a way to get along with all of them, and to try and pull everyone together.

Q: That's what you're talking about in a sense, isn't it? To get America and Americans more connected?

Smith: That's right—the sense that this country can be about something more than just the gratification of the individual. That's the thing I really didn't like about the whole Republican era in the eighties. Being a good American isn't being a flagwaver or having idealistic parades and all of that. The real American thing, to me, is first of all charity. This country should be built on charity. And it should be built on the idea that, while all of us should find our individual strengths, we should also promote a certain sense of equality. One can't say we are all equal in every way, I know that. We are different as people. We have different callings. We are not going to have equal lives. We are not going to have equal joys. But there are ways where we are equal. We are equal because we are all human. We are equal because we all have breath. And we're all going to die. We all enter life, and we all are going to have a story. And I think it's our duty to find a way for each of us to have the best story possible.

How do we do that? We do that by living as decent human beings. By thinking of others. By going through life and doing what we need to do and what we want to do, but also do enough that reverberates some good around us.

All of that reverberation is connective tissue. That's how we pull together a world that is good, that seeks to achieve good. It's not our inalienable right to have a car, or a nice house. Those things are great. But those are not our inalienable rights. Our inalienable rights are much purer, much more important than that.

What got instilled in the American population in the eighties was this sense that it's not only our right but our duty to better ourselves materially; in the way that we dress, in the way that our house looks, in the quality of our furniture, in the quality of our Wranglers—now you have to have this type of dungaree that costs four times as much and if you don't have it you're jive or something. There's so much attention not only on material things, but on image and on the way that people look.

Q: It's hard to break through the apathy that seems to go hand-in-hand with the entertainment culture, isn't it?

Smith: Very hard. People hear a lot of warnings. We're constantly being warned about things—about the environment, about health issues, about these new viruses. We're constantly being warned that we're taking chances with the planet that are dangerous, or that are too extreme.

To respond to those warnings requires us to cut back on things that make life easier. There's a lot of resistance to that. But it's not impossible. For instance, we know that if everybody would just stop buying Pampers and just wash diapers, it would make a big difference for the environment. Well, I'm a mother. I had small children. I washed a lot of diapers, and, yes, that's a drag. It's not the end of the world, though. If we all did it, there would be tons and tons and tons less of that kind of pollution.

There are so many things we could do that wouldn't hurt us at all and that would make a huge difference in all of our lives. There are all these things that we could do that could send out a reverberation, make things better—not just for ourselves, but for everyone.

Q: Is creating that spark, causing that reverberation, what motivates you as an artist?

Smith: I would hope so. I do work hoping only for that. I don't have the vocabulary, nor the energies, nor the organization skills to do the things that have to be done. I can do benefits and speak for things and be of some help. I just try as an artist to do the best that I can. And I try as a person to do the best that I can, to be maybe some kind of example. Because the example of somebody living their life in a certain way can cause a reverberation. And so I try to pass it on.

PATTI SMITH RETURNS TO GROUND ZERO

Fred Mills | January 30, 1998 | *Goldmine*

If all of Patti Smith's records are remembrances, as she has said, sometimes the albums—and her interviews about them—become remembrances for the lost loved ones of the listener. Such was the case when Fred Mills called Smith on the phone in 1997 for a cover story in *Goldmine*.

"That's one of my favorite interviews I ever did," Mills told me. "At the time of the interview, in the fall of '97, I had moved for a few months into my mom's house after her death in order to clean it out and prepare it for sale. I told Patti a story about how the final time I was able to spend extended quality time with my mom before she died was during a beach vacation when I was also obsessing over *Gone Again* and working on a review of it—and how I will always associate that album with Mom. Patti genuinely seemed moved by the story, and somehow Patti became, at that moment, a shoulder I could lean on, while surrounded by memories of my mother in her house."

Mills was a longtime fan. He first met Smith on January 21, 1977, when he snuck backstage the night the Patti Smith Group played Memorial Hall at the University of North Carolina at Chapel Hill. The show constituted a "turning point in my musical consciousness," Mills tells her here. It was a high-water mark for the band as well.

Mills was struck by the group's dynamism on stage in 1977, and as a testament to the Patti Smith Group as a collective, he interviewed Lenny Kaye and Jay Dee Daugherty alongside Smith for the '98 article, though only the discussion with Smith is included here. They touched on the group's first single, "Piss Factory"—an "experiment to see if that intensity we were generating live could be transferred to a disc," Kaye said—in addition to the influence of Albert Ayler, the missing *Horses* masters, and the serendipity that brought the group together at a specific time and place. The result gives a compelling portrait of an iconic group at the outset of an unlikely second act. —Ed.

The one-of-a-kind rock poet and her longtime sidemen tell their story in their own words

Leave it to one of Patti Smith's musical progeny to sum up perfectly the punk doyenne's impact.

"Patti Smith was, and is, pure experience," wrote Sonic Youth guitarist Thurston Moore, in a '96 article for Britain's *Vox*. "Her reign during the '70s as a street-hot rock 'n' roll messiah seemed to exist from a void, no past, no future," continued Moore, then concluding with severe certainty, "The strongest and most original force in the music's history had been a woman."

Not only original and influential—just ask Michael Stipe, Bono, Courtney Love or P.J. Harvey—but remarkably consistent of vision over the years. Consider:

In 1978, Smith told *Rolling Stone*, "Solidarity is not a myth, not some pathetic dream. The important thing [is to] wake up kids and inspire them to action."

Then again in 1989, in *Pulse!*, she said, "It is time to make things better. We have to help our fellow man. We have to clean up this world. The album [is] designed to motivate people to make things better."

And finally in 1987, to this writer, Smith commented, "One of the things I like to do in my work is to inspire people to do their own work . . . I think as a people, we need to strip down and work on ourselves and our self-respect, our respect for each other, and our respect for the planet. If we collectively come together, I think there's no limit to what we can do as a people."

Patti Smith was born on December 30, 1946, in Chicago. Her first exposure to rock 'n' roll came six years later while attending church, appropriately enough. As she recalled the incident in *Alternative Press*,

"Some kid put on 'Girl Can't Help It' by Little Richard. I'd never heard music like that, and I remember being in my little dress, my little brown shoes. I felt electrified and thought if my mother looked down she'd see rays coming out of me. It was so instantaneous, and that music articulated energy I couldn't express."

Bitten by the bug hard, Smith would often find solace in rock 'n' roll (Dylan in particular) and in poetry (Rimbaud), spending her teen years in Woodbury, New Jersey, where her family had moved when she was nine. By 1967 she was ready to hit the streets running New York City, and it is there that the fates of association began nudging her towards center stage.

In short order, Smith would meet photographer Robert Mapplethorpe, who would help get Smith her first poetry reading in 1971, finance her first single ("Hey Joe" b/w "Piss Factory") in '74, and provide the documentation that would be crucial in elevating her to visual iconic status over the years; rock writer Lenny Kaye, who would join her at that reading on guitar and go on to form the nucleus of her band; playwright/actor Sam Shepard, with whom she'd write the off-Broadway play *Cowboy Mouth* in 1972; Blue Oyster Cult's Allen Lanier, leading to her writing lyrics for several B.O.C. songs; and the rest of the movers and shakers of the thriving early '70s NYC downtown arts/music scene, where she immersed herself in writing record reviews for *Creem*, *Rolling Stone* and *Rock* magazine, as well as assembling material for her first two volumes of poetry.

But it was the Kaye connection that would prove the most significant. The duo continued to collaborate on guitar/poetry happenings, eventually adding a pianist, Richard Sohl, in '73, then guitarist Ivan Kral and drummer Jay Dee Daugherty, both in '74. The word quickly got out about this band fronted by a charismatic poetess who cast grand, surreal, sometimes profane visions of sex, death, drugs, religion, into the rock 'n' roll melting pot. Not long after a residency at punk watering ground CBGBs, the Patti Smith Group was signed by Arista Records. Debut album *Horses* appeared in January of '76; two decades later, this explosive marriage of primal rock chord progressions and free-jazz aesthetics is still considered a watershed release.

The band kept its profile high all year, releasing a second album, *Radio Ethiopia*, and touring extensively. But the next year was as quiet as '76 was busy. A tumble off a Florida stage and Smith's subsequent recuperation from fractured neck vertebrae pushed the band out of the public eye. The slingshot effect of '78 made up for lost time, however, as third album *Easter* yielded the Smith/Bruce Springsteen–penned hit "Because the Night." Now considered "real" stars by industry standards, the Patti Smith Group did what every other band does: record a fourth album (*Wave*), tour the world—and hang it all up in front of 85,000 Italian fans on September 10, 1979. Smith had fallen in love with MC5 guitarist Fred "Sonic" Smith and opted out of the business in order to pursue a family life.

For the bulk of 14 years, as it would turn out. Marrying in 1980, the two Smiths lived quietly in Detroit, raising two kids, Jesse and Jackson. They surfaced unexpectedly in 1988 with the album *Dream of Life*, then retreated just as quickly. And if Patti Smith had chosen to remain "that former rock singer who lives down the street with that former rock guitarist" to her Detroit neighbors, only the perennial "Where Are They Now?" series that journalists dredge up would have disturbed her domestic tranquility.

That, of course, was not the path upon which the fates had any intentions of shoving her.

In 1989 Smith's old friend Robert Mapplethorpe died from AIDS, then the following year keyboardist Richard Sohl died of a heart attack. Then tragedy for Smith struck even closer to home in '94: husband Fred and brother Todd died of heart failure within weeks of one another. A less resilient human would've gone into seclusion for good; Patti Smith, instead, returned from the edge with a burning need to pass along what she'd seen.

Here's esteemed writer Paul Williams commenting in *Crawdaddy* on a '95 performance by Smith:

"As good as I've ever seen her, and I saw her and PSG in 1975–76, in her prime, her glory. She's still in her prime. She threw open her arms and her heart to us, the other people in the room, with sincerity and humor and intelligence and energy and subtlety and sweetness and, yes, profundity, all night, more than two hours . . . There aren't many performers this good, and it was terrific to see her so relaxed and willing and full of her native power . . . She's back in the saddle, for however long this visitation is meant to last."

1996 became Ground Zero, Mk. II, for Patti Smith watchers. First recorded evidence: "Walkin' Blind" on the *Dead Man Walking* soundtrack. Then came a collection of lyrical prose honoring Robert Mapplethorpe, entitled *The Coral Sea*. R.E.M. issued its *New Adventures In Hi-Fi* album with Smith provided backing vocals and appearing in the video for "E-Bow The Letter." Finally, the first Smith album in eight years was released. *Gone Again*, with its contemplative glow and numerous acoustic-based songs, may have been differently textured from its predecessors but was no less powerful in its emotional depth and resonance. Smith and her band—Kaye, Daugherty, bassist Shanahan and young guitarist Oliver Ray (plus, on occasion, Tom Verlaine guesting on guitar)—didn't tour extensively, mainly hitting Europe during the summer, although they did make a number of guerrilla runs in '96 and on into '97, including appearances on "Saturday Night Live," the Leno, Letterman and Conan O'Brien shows, numerous benefits (Neil Young's annual Bridge Concert, an Allen Ginsberg memorial, the Tibetan Freedom Concert), and the PBS series *Sessions On West 54th*.

Last October saw the release of *Peace and Noise*, a logical follow-up to *Gone Again*, harder-edged, musically, and lyrically, too, aiming a thick strap at society's fat backside. (Interesting to note: the vinyl edition of the album was withdrawn at Smith's request; she reportedly was dissatisfied by the mix, which was different from the CD, and the plan now is to reissue it with a new mix—and as a two-LP set featuring bonus cuts.)

The band toured the East Coast during December, followed up by a January West Coast trek. Prior to that, Smith & Co. took up residency at an old haunt, New York's CBGB's, for four nights in October.

We caught up with Smith one evening via telephone, from her home in New York City, a few weeks before the CBGB's shows. (Interviews with Kaye and Daugherty took place a few weeks after the gigs.)

Goldmine: *The Patti Smith Group came to Chapel Hill, North Carolina, on January 21, 1977. I managed to pass myself off as a temporary crew member so I could get in to the soundcheck, meet you, talk to you, score autographs. I still think of that concert as a turning point in my musical consciousness, and no doubt for a lot of other people there, too.*

Patti Smith: That was a great night! In fact, we'd refer to it sometimes—often, when we'd done a good job, we'd say, "It was almost like Chapel Hill."

It set a high standard. I remember how nice you were to the people too—the crew was going to kick out these two girls who came down to give you flowers, and other kids who'd slipped in the side doors for soundcheck, and you told them to let 'em hang out. At the time, for a lot of us our only contact with "rock stars" was the big arena scenario, so to have the band treat us as something other than just paying schmucks, that seemed pretty special.

Yeah, well, that's often where we have our fun, y'know? At the end of a job, sitting on the edge of the stage, playing clarinet or something, seeing what's on people's minds. It's a good time for communication, you know? One-on-one. That was always the kind of band we wanted to be, how we wanted to work. I don't like having this abstract wall between myself and the people because we're all workers and we're all trying to do things. Especially at a concert—I feel like the people that come to a concert are working as well. We're all working for the night to be really great. So the idea is that the people have come there and they're giving you their energy, and then you have to take it within you and spew it back again. It's a real exchange.

I take it that remains true: that you wouldn't have returned to the stage if it wasn't still a charge for you.

Well, for me I like to think that hopefully we'll have a great time. Or at least an interesting or memorable time. And I like to think of our band and myself in some ways as public servants. Because the issues we're talking about and expressing within the context of rock 'n' roll. And also I found, within the last couple of years—I had a rough couple of years—that the energy of the people, and their enthusiasm, was very encouraging for me. I felt, truthfully, I had went back to performing with a lot of [laughs] rust on my feet! But emotionally, not at my strongest. Part of my healing process was my working. And people were very, very patient with me. They were patient in allowing me to go through certain things I had to to get back on my feet—as a human being and a performer. So it's been very helpful to me.

A lot of the reviews for Gone Again *spoke in terms like "comeback." I like to think of the '77 to '79 period as a continuum with a couple of vacations in there along the way.*

It's a continuum until you're dead! And then, who knows what that whole new journey or voyage is all about! While we're on the planet there's no reason to feel, y'know, that one has to feel isolated or, um, not plugged in to things. The work I do is just for whoever needs it, and for whoever wants it. At this point I'm 50 years old, I've seen a lot of things, but I'm healthy and have, I think, a pretty positive spirit and have things to say. But I don't have any specific age group or aesthetic/ hip group—I don't know who I'm talking to! At this point I just try to do my work and, hopefully, it will be of some avail to somebody. I don't have any prejudice or presumptions as to who I'm talking to; I just do the work at this point.

There's also a consistency for you over the years. In a '78 interview for Rolling Stone *your quotes were remarkably similar to what you said in a recent* Billboard *piece, about waking people up and inspiring them.*

Yeah. The only difference is back in '78 I *was* a kid, waking up! [laughing] I mean, now I have kids of my own! But yeah, I've always been concerned with the state of things, whether it be the spiritual state of people or the state of the environment or . . . there are so many different things to think about and care about. And it's not even a negative thing. Because after all the things I've seen, people I've loved passing away for health reasons or AIDS or Vietnam or drugs—I've lost a lot of friends and loved ones from all types of scenarios, and I feel really happy to be alive! I feel really lucky and grateful to be alive and having these things to confront.

We who have survived—and hopefully we've survived well!—we have a lot of work to do. We have to do our own work and remember those we've lost, and we have to remember to take new generations by the hand who really don't have a clue what to do. Partially because they're not getting any guidance; the kind of examples that are being set for young people today are material. That seems to be the driving force in America right now, material gain. That's the way people measure themselves. And it's getting like that all over the planet.

Young people right now are also going through economic shock: wondering if they're gonna have a bank account when they're 50 or 60.

I'm not saying they shouldn't be concerned about this, but often I find that they skip a lot of steps, y'know? I've met a lot of people who say they want to make it in the music business, they wanna be a rock and roll star and get a record contract. I ask what are they trying to do in their work, and they say, "Well, that will come!" But the thing is to focus on one's work. All of these things, if we're meant to have them, or if they're meant to happen, you know, we'll evolve towards them. But the most important thing is working on oneself. This is my great concern, really. I think as a people, we need to strip down and work on ourselves and our self-respect, our respect for each other, and our respect for the planet, y'know?

Is it tough to translate that kind of thought into a song lyric without . . .

Sounding preachy? Like I just have? [laughs] I'm sorry, I could go on . . . [laughing]

Some people do want their music and words to be very pretty and not have a message.

On *Peace and Noise* sometimes I'll do it subtly. For example, "Don't Say Nothing" is really about, amongst other things, the environment. The environment, the bomb, all the things we're doing to our planet and just sitting around letting it happen. This sort of abstract little song that says "don't say nothing" but is really saying, "Say something!" The narrator, myself, is just hanging out, looking out the window at this party, there's litter everywhere, dead cat floating in the river, and imagining some nuclear testing with the sky turning orange—and we're just sitting around saying nothing, y'know? So in that song I address things in a more subtle manner.

A song like "Last Call," it's more direct. That song is really inspired by the Heaven's Gate suicides. The counseling at the end of that song is more direct. It's not judging the people who committed suicide, because obviously they really believed in what they did and they were trying to have a better spiritual life. But what it's criticizing or counseling about, in one's pursuit of spiritual things, or anything in life, be careful and listen to your own inner voice. Be careful who you follow. Respect your fellow man—but you don't have to follow him. The tragedy of the Heaven's Gate situation is that these people followed a leader who I gleaned with a lot of study and examination was unqualified to lead. That, to me, is tragic. Like that fellow Jim Jones, down in Guyana.

False idols, false heroes, false gurus?

Yeah. Then other songs, like "Whirl-away," are addressing urban violence, how spiritually bankrupt young people are and how they're fighting and killing each other over coats and colors and codes and all these *things*. How people are more interested in material things.

So there's a lot of things addressed directly on the record—hopefully in not too preaching a manner.

You've never shied away from saying exactly what you think, albeit not in the same language as, say, a politician. Getting at something you mentioned a second ago, have you ever felt as if the shoe were on the other foot, that people were coming to you as their personal hero or guru?

No, I think I'm much too flawed an individual. I don't try to set myself up like that. When I was working in the '70s I constantly said in interviews, or when onstage, I petitioned people that if they're inspired by our band, great—but then go out and do your own work. When I'd go to radio stations, I say, "You don't need to play my song, here, play this one, this is a band you've never heard. Or let's listen to Jimi Hendrix or something." I mean, one of the things I like to do in my work is to inspire people to do their own work! Nothing makes me happier than when they say something like, "Oh, I listened to your CD and actually, I didn't even hear the end of it because I started painting and got involved with my painting so I had to put it on again . . . " I like to hear that our work inspired people to action: "We went out and started a band when we heard your band." So I've never gotten the feeling that people got so wrapped up in me or my work that they couldn't find their own way. The rare instance of that would be if the person was "troubled." I don't really invite that, though.

It's very seductive, however, for people to create their rock 'n' roll heroes. Especially when there's no one in the adult world to look up to.

Well, I understand that, because that's how I was when I was younger; I pinned my hopes on Bob Dylan. I pinned my hopes on him—but then I went and did my own work. He meant the world to me and helped me get through my adolescence; I thought there was someone there speaking for me. But then I went off and did what I had to do. I just think, in the face of that, if that's true, then more than ever, if people are involved—another thing that makes me sad, is that in the music business (I hate to even use that phrase), musicians and artists, all artists, should try to serve as an example. Because if we are in a time when people feel shafted by their political representation, and if they are going to artists for some real communication, then artists more now than ever, if they can't become politicians, they should be as truthful as possible.

But I think it can be dangerous!

Getting back to the new record, where do you think it stands in relation to what else is contemporary?

I'm very proud of this record, but I mean, I was told that the way things are in the music business now, there really isn't a place for it. It's too issue-oriented, the radio people don't want to hear this kind of record and don't want to be confronted or bothered with that kind of record. They are very afraid of what they call "issue oriented" work. But it's really important, and rock 'n' roll is a great format to communicate things! I mean, great love songs, but all kinds of things, too. And it's not a mindless format. It's a very strong, emotional format and I think all manners of ideas should be passed through it.

But it is the kind of record I do. And I don't believe that—and even if that was true [conspiratorially] what better time to do something people don't want to hear than when they don't want to hear! [laughs]

In Billboard *they have a full-page ad for Dylan's new album, talking what a great songwriter he is and the issues he addresses.*

He actually sent me a test pressing of it, so I was able to hear it, y'know, a little before it came out, and I just knew people would like this record. I had a feeling that people would like it. Which is nice for him. He's worked so hard and so long for us, but the last few years and the last few records he might have thought he was working in a void. So I think it's gonna be very nice for him to receive so much interest. And it'll be nice for us, too, because it'll open him up a little bit.

Do you still get excited when a record from one of your favorite artists is about to come out? Rush down to the store on Tuesdays for the street date release . . .

Well, I was excited when I walked into a store and saw our CD next to Dylan's new one—they both came out on the same day and just happened to be racked next to each other. That was exciting!

Unfortunately a lot of stuff I really like is stuff that was done a long time ago. But I got real excited when they put out this four-CD Coltrane box, live at the Village Vanguard, and I'm telling you it's really, really great. Sometimes you get these things and they're repetitive, but not this one. Every once in a while there'll be something of interest. I like some weird little bands . . . there was this one I saw called Smoke, out of Atlanta, that I really like. And I like Flying Saucer Attack [Bristol, England] a lot too. [laughs] So every once in awhile I find something.

You've been on a pronounced creative roll for about two years now. How long can that cycle last? Would you take another break?

Well, with music, I think I'm still on a roll. I mean, now I have enough material almost for another album already. It's like what Bob says on his record: "Now I'm on everything but a roll." [loud laugh] No, I *am* on a roll! I never worry about that, because if this particular thing subsides, I'll do what I always do, which is go back to writing, working on a book. Or some area of study: I really like studying. I'll pick something like Mexican mural painting and study it. I really love to sit and study. So I never fear having a dry period, creatively, because, thank God, so many great artists have produced things that you can look at and be inspired by. I can go and reread Walt Whitman—there's so much work out there to look at.

How about a live album? There are certainly enough Patti Smith bootlegs out there to tweak the record company.

Actually, we're playing live at CBGB's for a week, Halloween week, four nights, and we're gonna record all four nights. So we should get enough; that should make a really great album. It'll be fun. And we recorded some European stuff, and some places in New York when we were playing with Tom Verlaine. So we have a lot of work to consider.

When my brother passed away, I went into his room and was looking at his record collection. He had 32 bootlegs of ours! I only had at that time five albums! I thought, "Gee, it looks like the people have been more prolific than me!" [laughs] I sort of have the Grateful Dead attitude to it, that a lot of times it's the people who keep you alive. I mean, one keeps their work alive. An artist has to do his work himself, has to be responsible for his work. But a performing artist really does depend on the energy of the people, so if they want to sometimes make these, ah, "pirated salutes" [laughs], you have to, yeah, in some ways, have a sense of humor.

What's your take on the music industry in general over the last year? It can be a cold, cynical business these days.

Well, it's hard to give a simple answer to that. For me, obviously, the main thing I was involved with was the creation of *Peace and Noise* so that was my focus. In terms of how I relate that to the music business, I know that a record like that is gonna depend on our band really fighting for it and word of mouth. Because even though I believe it's a record that could be of some service, it just doesn't fit. Aggressive formatting, even of college radio, is really a detriment because it takes away from the possibilities of a cultural communication ground. TV, you know, we have music TV that's completely sponsor-oriented. I don't think it properly serves, culturally or politically, our people. And I think that radio could be. Radio *was* it in the '60s, you know? Radio was where you could go for new ideas, where you went for some political truths. It was a communication network. But I'm not just willing to stop fighting. Right now, public radio is one of our last holdouts. We have to do what we can.

There are pirate radio stations—micro transmissions—popping up around the country now too, helping retake some of the airwaves.

Oh yeah, I've heard about some of those. If they put their skull and crossbones flags up where I can see them, I'll visit!

Last question: Any comments on, or wishes and predictions for, the coming year?

Well, my wish is that people will get the scent of the new century coming and we'll start regrouping, reexamining, themselves and what they're doing. In a positive way. And start making some strong resolutions—not for a new year, but for a new century. I mean, can you imagine if everyone on the whole planet decided, hey, we have a new century coming, a millennium! How they are going to turn themselves around as human beings and try to do something for the good of the planet. Whether it's cutting down on their litter or material acquisitions, or going to a pediatric AIDS ward and reading to some children—there are so many things that we can do. I know what it must sound like . . .

It might sound to some like hippies at Woodstock chanting to stop the rain, but—who knows? You get a zillion people with the force of their minds . . .

Yeah, who knows? And you look at the scriptures, that's how people turned things around. God telling Jonah he's gonna destroy a city because the people have not handled themselves well, and by the collective prayer and the collective energies or efforts of the people God spares the city. Now, I know it could be like a "Bible Story," but it is telling us something. It's telling us, just like the Tower of Babel story, these people using one mind were almost able to penetrate God's realm. Using one mind, and one language. But of course this angered God in the story [laughs] so what did he do? He scattered everybody's mind and everybody's energy and language, and it proves that when the people are divided, they can't do much. But when they come together, they can practically pierce heaven.

We don't need to pierce heaven. But if we collectively come together, I think there's no limit to what we can do as a people. We limit ourselves. We have such complex minds and brains and spiritual outlooks and a sense of vision, yet we don't even touch upon it. We created everything on this planet, cathedrals and the Empire State Building and cures for terrible diseases and spaceships—we're an incredible people!

In any event, I'm always optimistic. I have a lot of faith in the future I look at things that people do. Look at somebody like an actress, Audrey Hepburn. Really beautiful, charming actress. She found she had cancer but didn't sit at home moping or mourning over her age and beauty and cancer. She went to Somalia, lobbied to get food, helped mothers feed their dying babies, she helped them bury their dead children—that one woman, beautiful woman, went over and made a lot of difference to people. Like Mother Teresa—individuals can do so much.

PATTI SMITH TALKS ABOUT *GUNG HO*

Jody Denberg | January 21, 2000 | KGSR

Jody Denberg conducted this interview with Patti Smith in advance of the release of her 2000 album *Gung Ho*. At the time, Denberg was working for Austin-based KGSR, which was owned by LBJ Holding Company, the business founded and run by Lady Bird Johnson. Smith had fond memories of its sister station, KLBJ, and of Austin in general, and called her stay in the LBJ Suite at the historic Driskill Hotel her "happiest American hotel memory." For a touring musician, that's quite a superlative.

The album is Smith's eighth and last album under contract to Arista as "a loving thorn in Clive's side for these twenty-five years." Here she discussed her writing process and her late father, World War II veteran Grant Smith, who appears on the cover. She also delved into her views on gender politics, the Detroit Tigers right fielder Al Kaline, why New York felt like a small town to her, and how she remained gung ho about life. "I think that our heart is continuously being replenished," she said. "Even by the people we lose." —Ed.

Q: Patti, I wanted to wish you a belated Happy New Year, Happy New Decade, Happy New Century, Happy Birthday. I wasn't sure if those traditional ways of looking at time mattered to you.

A: I enjoy a revolutionary point of view that breaks tradition apart, but I also do love tradition. I love history and I saluted the new century joyfully. So I'll go along with it.

Q: The last major work that you did was in 1998. It was a compilation book called "Complete." And now you have a new album called Gung-Ho, so now "Complete" isn't complete anymore.

A: Well, it's (laughs)—yeah, it's incomplete. I'll have to do one called "Completed." We did update the paperback with as much of Gung-Ho as I had ready at the time. And what we will do is, on the new album, include all of the lyrics for those who want them. So I did the best I could to get them in under the wire for the paperback.

Q: The album title Gung-Ho, it has so many implications. What were you trying to communicate with the title?

A: Well, it's got two things. One, it's a play on words, because the title cut called Gung-Ho is an overview of the life of Ho Chi Minh, looking at what drove him as a patriot and a person who foresaw and worked all his life on creating an independent Vietnam. He was a very special man, but he was also a very common man. And I thought of him sort of like Gunga Din, who had those qualities. And so it has that "gung-ho" sort of play on words. But also, when I was a kid, my father fought in World War II and my mother always used to use that term, "gung-ho". It was used for someone who was putting their whole heart and really believing in what they were doing and going into even a difficult task with positive idealistic energy. And I decided that I wanted to enter the new century like that. We have so many things that are wrong, so many difficult things. I wanted to go into the new century in a positive, work-oriented frame of mind.

Q: There's also the fact that "gung-ho" is a Chinese expression. And you've been so outspoken in trying to preserve Tibet's cultural heritage and return the Tibetans from exile. I know people talk a lot about this cause of late, but your interest in Tibet began when you were really young, I heard.

A: When I was about 12, I think I must have seen the movie about Shangri-La when I was a child. And ancient civilizations and ancient religions and Buddhism has always interested me since a child. And I started doing a report when I was 12. And I was in school and the teacher said, "Everyone can choose a country. You must spend a year doing a report." And I chose Tibet. And she said, "You can't choose Tibet. Nothing ever happens there. You have to have current events. You have to cut out articles in the newspaper. No one knows about Tibet." And I said, "I want Tibet." It was January of 1959. And the kids were laughing at me and teasing me, but I stood my ground and just couldn't find hardly a thing. And I used to pray, "oh, will something please happen in Tibet so I could write my report." Well, in March of '59, they were invaded by the Chinese. And the Dal[a]i Lama, who I had gotten very attached to in my studies, was feared killed. And it was not exactly the news that I was praying for, and—but I became very aware of their situation. But what really struck me, was, my father had fought in World War II. He explained that he had fought in it to set an example and help the world be free. And I couldn't understand how my father had done all of this work and I thought all the wars were over. I couldn't understand why a country's freedom was being taken away and nobody seemed to care. So it's been on my mind for a long time. When I was a 12-year-old girl, I prayed for his holiness. I prayed for the safety of the Dal[a]i Lama. Never in my life, as a skinny 12-year-old with a passion for Davey Crockett did I ever think one day I would be doing even some small help for the Tibetan people, but also I had the opportunity to meet and talk with His Holiness. And it just shows, you know, life—it's unbelievable, life. If you stick around long enough, the most wonderful things will happen to you.

Q: Calls for activism and awareness in your music are nothing new. We could go back to Till Victory, People Have the Power. On the new album, you continue that tradition. The first song on the album, One Voice . . . there's Upright Come. Do you feel that it's your calling as an artist to try and inspire righteous change?

A: Well, I'm not a politician. I'm not articulate, politically. But I do find that I seem to have a calling to at least speak out. But then I'm an American citizen and that's part of the responsibility, I think, of being an American. We're free. We have freedom of choice and—we have a responsibility to that. And also, I look around at other people and the work that they do. For instance, One Voice, was very inspired by the work that Mother Theresa did. I look at this little woman, you know, this one small woman and the tremendous impact she had on thousands and thousands of people. Not only with her hands-on work, but the way she inspired others to perform simple acts of charity throughout the globe that will mean so much to a person. And that's why it says in One Voice, "every action"—you know, I can't remember the words, even. But great or small, the idea is that they're all appreciated.

Q: The first song we heard from Gung-Ho a few minutes ago, was called Glitter in Their Eyes. I read it as kind of a rage against this rampant consumerism that's going on right now. And, Patti you seem to live a relatively austere life. What inspired you to write Glitter in Their Eyes?

A: Well, actually, Glitter in Their Eyes, I co-wrote with Oliver Ray. And it was actually Oliver's concept based on things that we talk about all of the time. And pretty much exactly what you said. The concept of the song was—well, it's actually addressed to young people to, as it says, "look out kids, the gleam, the gleam." It's sending out, both a warning and both just a caring salute to young people who are constantly being exploited by business. They're targets. Young people aren't—children aren't children anymore, they're a demographic. And they're a consumer demographic. And that's one of the things, like you said, is the rampant consumerism. But not just on the part of the consumer, but on the part of people who see people as potential consumers. It goes through every phase of life. Oliver and I were recently in Cambodia. And we were looking at the temples of Ankgor Vat. And the beggar children who by the hundreds sell little souvenirs for a living. Right now, Ankgor Vat is being targeted by Korean businessmen, who see it as a big money-making tourist attraction. And what they want to do is come in, get rid of all these beggar children, of course. And they're already starting to build huge hotels and have their own souvenir stores. It's like they're the people with the glitter in their eyes.

Q: Along with the external-looking songs that we were talking about on Gung-Ho, there are also songs that look within. The next song we're going to hear is Lo and Beholden. I was wondering if this was your own current romantic situation set behind some poetic veil?

A: Well, it's not, not really. What, what this song is—this is a real classic Patti Smith/Lenny Kaye song, I think in, because the music is so much like Lenny. It's taken from the point of view of Salome, who has been exploited by both her father-in-law, King Herod, and her mother. Her youth and beauty being exploited so that they can—King Herod because he's after a piece of her youth and beauty. Her mother because she wants the head of John the Baptist. So this beautiful girl has forever been tainted. She's known as one of the villainesses in the Bible because she was always a simple, beautiful girl, asked to dance and used by her mother to get the head of John the Baptist. That's what it directly is, applies to. But indirectly, how we're also exploiting youth and beauty these days. Girls are being exploited terribly. And people are being exploited because of their desire for celebrity and things like that. They're being exploited by these talk shows like Jerry Springer and stuff. They'll reveal anything about themselves or make up things about themselves to seem important. And everybody's important. You don't have to do something like that to make yourself important. Just by being alive, we're important.

Q: Patti, there's a beautiful harp on the song we just heard, Lo and Beholden. For the last 25 years, for the most part, you've played with the same core group of musicians. Is it simply a matter of loyalty for you or is the idea of being in a long-term rock-and-roll band part of what gets you off?

A: I never came into recording as musician or anyone with any train-ing or even any desire to do records. I really came into recording as a performer who was concerned about the state of rock and roll. My only concept of performing was that people had a real group, like The Rolling Stones. And I thought, when you have your group, that's your group. The only reason I've made changes in my group at all in time was if a person was ill . . . had to leave for a while. In the Patti Smith Group, we had our core group. And to me, that was a rock and roll band. That's what I had, a rock and roll band. There was no pretenses of us doing anything else. And I was completely untrained and just going on instinct and also sort of an idealistic idea of what a rock and roll band was, which includes the loyalty, the camaraderie and, you know, the struggle. That meant more to me than trying to make things technically perfect or having the optimum guitar player or something. I just liked the people that I worked with. We all believed in the same things. Lenny Kaye and Richard Sohl and I started together. And Richard Sohl was a very gifted piano player. He was classically-trained. And just a wonderful person to work with and improvise with, who I thought I'd work with my whole life. And he died of congenital heart failure in '91. Which was really difficult for me to lose him. Jay Dee Daugherty is the only drummer I've ever had. Lenny Kaye has always been my most avid supporter and continues to help in all different aspects of the work. And he brought in Tony Shanahan when I did Gone Again. He's a very gifted musician and has some of the musical temperament that Richard had, even though he's a bass player. And Oliver Ray, who has, who has a real revolution-ary spirit, who's a poet and also brings youth into the group. And we, we started struggling together on Gone Again. And believe me, it was a struggle because we were at all different levels of experience. And I hadn't played for like 15 years. But we have struggled in the past few years and this is our third album together. And I really feel like now we're a true rock and roll band. And that's really all I want—is just a true rock-and-roll band.

Q: *Except for a couple of songs, most of the songs on Gung-Ho are co-written with one other band member. I was curious how you decided which of your band members you were going to bring a lyric to to col-laborate on?*

A: I rarely write lyrics first. I improvise in the practice room. Lenny brought the music to Lo and Beholden and the band played it. And I just improvised, and the song, whatever, how the song felt, is what I gleaned from it. Gung-Ho was written because I was studying Ho Chi Minh. I had read several books about him, read, read all of his works. I walked in the practice room and they were riffing—you know, the band had this riff and I listened to it and I loved it. And it just drew me to the microphone. And I started improvising what became Gung-Ho. That's pretty much how I work.

Q: *Parts of Gung-Ho are a little more fleshed-out and full than the approach of Peace and Noise and Gone Again. Was that a result of working with Gil Norton, who had worked with Counting Crows and the Pixies and how did you choose him to work with?*

A: Well, I think it's two things. First of all, Gil Norton and his engineer, Danton Supple, are great. They're really great to work with. They're highly respectful. They allowed for us to be who we were, but give us, you know, their expertise and ideas about sound. But they never were invasive. They just enhanced everything that we did. Working with them was a really great experience. It was tough, but really great. I think the other thing—why this record sounds better and seems even more fully realized, that now we, as a band, have spent four years together. Gone Again was made just as best we could, because Fred passed away, I was greatly dispirited, I didn't really have a band and it was hard for me to even want to record. So that was really an act of a lot of people coming together, keeping my spirits up. Lenny. Tom Verlaine came in on it. All of the same band members. And Peace and Noise, I was still getting my feet back on the ground and re-learning how to record and perform myself, as everyone else was learning. And we were learning to play together and knowing each other as people. Now, we've been through all kinds of things together and I think this album reflects, the trust and the strength that we've built, with a lot of struggle. I think it reflects that. But much, much credit to our producer and engineer.

Q: *Before your late husband, Fred "Sonic" Smith, left in '94, he was giving you guitar lessons. But you held and manipulated a guitar onstage since the early days. And then I noticed you wrote two of Gung-Ho's songs by yourself. So I'm thinking you're still keepin' up with the six-string.*

A: In the '70s I got very involved in the sonic aspects of the electric guitar. And I worked really hard. I wasn't interested in chords. I didn't bother learning chords in the '70s. I was totally interested in feedback, sound. And Fred actually helped me with that. He helped me wire a Fender Twin in a special way, 'cause he was the king of feedback. But that was my essential interest in electric guitar, was sound. In '94 I really had the desire to write my own little songs, because, like sort of these little

Appalachian-style songs were coming into my head or I would—I would sing them a cappella. But I had the desire to try to work them out, 'cause often I'd forget them. And he promised me he would show me chords if I practiced hard. And I had an old '30s Gibson, an acoustic guitar, which I still have. And he showed me every chord, except we ended and I never got a B chord. But I know all the other chords. That was the last thing that Fred taught me, was, rhythm, getting a good rhythm, and my chords. And since then I've written actually several songs. And I always think about that, you know, it was like the last gift he gave me. And I've used it well.

Q: Are you keeping up with your clarinet playing?

A: Oh yeah I play a lot of clarinet and I play in the band structure a lot of clarinet. I'm actually really proud of my clarinet playing. Fred, also, of course, introduced me to clarinet. Bought me my mouthpiece and gave me my first clarinet lessons.

Q: You've explored so many avenues of expression over the years, besides poetry and music, beginning in the early days with theater and photography, drawing, painting. I also heard you were working on a novel at one point. Does alternating media keep you fresh?

A: In some ways it's also very difficult, because—I'm very lucky to be able to express myself in a lot of different genres, but it's also—I have a restless nature going from one to another and it makes it harder to finish things. So it's a mixed blessing. The one great thing about it, I've found, is that if you work hard on one skill, it will often permeate the other. You know, I find if I'm working on the clarinet quite a bit, it helps my singing, it helps my breathing. It takes a lot of discipline for me to finish all of these lyrics and go through the whole process of making an album. But it proves to me, again, that I can finish something. So then when I go to a book project, when I get dejected or I get, you know, bored or demoralized, I can access the fact that I can finish things if I stick to it.

Q: It seems that the artistic vibe also is permeating in your household and in your family. The last album's title Peace and Noise was conceived by your daughter Jesse. I think I read that she plays some piano. And

the next song we're going to hear, Persuasion, your son Jackson, plays
guitar on. I was wondering how old Jesse and Jackson were now, and
is it by watching you that they became inspired to make their own art?

A: Well, first of all, Jesse's 12. She's a 12-year-old girl, and she's exploring
many things. She writes. She's really looking at the whole world right
now. And she's curious about the whole world. Jackson is 17. And he
really picked up guitar after his father passed away. He was about 12
years old. And Jackson actually has a lot of his father's gifts. He didn't
know that he had them. He didn't show any real interest in music until
after his father passed away. He really wanted to be an ice cream man
for a long time. But he has his father's gifts. And he spends a lot of
time, you know, studying different guitar players and different styles of
music. Everything from Renaissance music to Danny Gatton. But he's
very involved in the playing of the music and learning. He's not interested
in the music business or anything like that. I really think that the things
that Jackson and Jesse do or find will be by their own volition. They
were well brought up, and there were a lot of different types of things
open to them musically and artistically. But I think that both of them
will make their own decisions. I as their, you know, surviving parent,
can only influence them so much. I really am more interested in—of
being an influence in how they take care of themselves and how they
treat other people. In terms of their work, they'll make those decisions.

Q: Patti, the song we just heard, Persuasion, it features your son, Jack-
son, on the guitar solo. But it's credited "Smith/Smith." Did Jackson
co-write that or is that a song that you wrote with Fred a while back?

A: Fred and I wrote that song for Dream of Life originally. We were still
addressing record album time, so we had too many songs for Dream of
Life so we never actually recorded it. So for this particular album, because
it was the last recording that I was going to do in the 20th century, I
wanted Fred represented one more time. And I always thought it was a
really great song. So we put it together as a band. Oliver one day said,
"You know, it's Fred's song, we should have Jackson play the solo on
it." And Lenny Kaye, who would have normally played it, was delighted

to step aside and have Jackson play the solo, and he did a great job. Just came in and did it.

Q: The vision I have of you during the writing process is a spartan one. I think it's brought about by the cover of your last album, Peace and Noise, because there's that black-and-white picture of you. You have pen in hand, you're writing on paper, resting on a book on a bed. The room is totally unadorned, except for a rosary hanging on the wall. (Right.) So is my vision accurate or am I forgetting about your typewriter? Have you moved on to a computer?

A: I do most of my writing by hand. I'm not computer friendly, yet. And I do have a couple of acoustic typewriters—I have a couple of really old typewriters. But mostly, I write by hand. In that shot, I was writing. Oliver Ray took that shot, and, I didn't even realize he was taking the picture, I was deep in my writing. But mostly I write in notebooks. And when I'm writing for the band, like I said, a lot of it starts out improvised, and then I go off with myself and start struggling with the connective tissue of the song—right up to the last minute. I'm sort of a slight nightmare for everyone because it's at the last moment, I'm still, you know, writing lyrics or improvising in the studio. I almost never have lyrics finished. It's just every once in a while. There's just a handful of songs that I actually have had finished lyrics for. It's always right to the wire.

Q: Whether it's lyrics or poetry, what motivates you to write? Is it the process? Is it the end result? Is it the immortality of the work?

A: It's always different. I mean, I've always written, as long as I can remember. I fell in love with books; it was like love at first sight. I've loved books since I was a small child. As soon as I learned that one could write a book, that one could write their own book, I became interested in writing. I read "Little Women" and there as—Jo was the writer, and it occurred to me, yes, I can do that. I've been writing all my life and it's—I write for various reasons: In reaction to things, out of sorrow, out of joy or I record my dreams, or out of duty. I mean, I have all systems of reasons why I write.

Q: Is there any of your work that you feel the closest to or that you feel represents you the best?

A: Well, I really feel this particular album well represents me because I think I'm at the top of my game in lyric writing. There's always a song or two where I feel like I failed lyrically, because I wasn't ready or the words didn't come. I feel extremely proud of this particular work. Like probably all artists, I can get pretty hard on myself. But I've allowed myself to be happy about this album.

Q: I understand that your dad is on the cover of Gung-Ho? And I know that you're very close to your family. Your sister, Kimberly, makes an appearance on the new album. Your late brother Todd was the head of your road crew. (Yes.) Your mom has been known to correspond with your fans. There's a beautiful ballad on the new album. It's called China Bird. And I—I could be wrong here, but I get the feeling that there's a family connection in that song.

A: Yes, there is. My father actually passed away in late August and I was very close to my father. And Oliver wrote the music to China Bird, and—several months before my father passed away. I heard the music . . . he was playing acoustic guitar and it was the most beautiful music and I, I said, "I have to have that music. Please let me write some lyrics to that." And I had been struggling with it because sometimes music is so beautiful it seems like there are no words for it. And I went home to see my father. And, my father had a china bird collection. And it was you know, a little shelf and he sent away every month and they would send him—he sent his check and they sent him a new porcelain bird. My father loved birds and fed birds all the time. And I looked at the china bird collection and I was just moved to, to write . . . something. I was moved by my father's little bird collection and I thought of my father, because it's the style of song that he likes. His way of unconditional, abstract love, is part of the theme in that song. And it also is a love song. But also I thought of my daughter, as well. Often two or three people will be within a song. So that song incorporates a few people that I love in one little song. And we decided to put my father on the cover because I had this great shot of my father in towns in Australia. In World War II, because he served in the Philippines and New Guinea, just a great shot of him in his late 20s. You know, idealistic, ready, gung-ho as my mother would say, with his black beret on. And the beautiful thing is, because he's so young, I could see my brother. He so resembles my brother. And it's really like having both my brother and father on the album cover. And both of them were highly supportive of what I do. So I thought it was a nice positive salute.

Q: That was China Bird. It's from Gung-Ho. It's Patti Smith's new disc. It's her eighth album in 25 years. Patti, there was a period of almost 17 years, between 1979 and 1996, when you only released one album and that was Dream of Life in '88. And you said, I guess one of the reasons was that you were raising your young family at the time. But it's also part of the artistic process to like absorb and then give, right?

A: Oh, yeah. And also, it's always humorous to me when people say to me, "Well, you didn't work in the '80s, right?" And, you know, I worked harder in the '80s than I ever did in my life. Not only tending to children and washing diapers and all of the different things that one—all the human tasks one performs in raising a family. But I spent hours and hours developing my craft as a writer, studying so that I would have new points of view, new things to say, a better understanding of humankind. I mean, I even studied sports. I didn't know anything about sports. I learned everything about sports. I watched many Masters tournaments. I knew everything about golf. I learned about basketball. I went through all the Piston's wins. You know, I did all kinds of things. I learned about subjects that I wouldn't normally be interested in for the sake of comprehending, what our society likes and what they do and who they are. And studied various aspects of art history, religions, the Bible. So I spent the '80s, really, as you said, replenishing myself as an artist and also evolving as a human being, because there is nothing that will stunt one's growth more than staying too long in just being a rock-and-roll star. And I thought it was time for me to actually—I'm not talking about growing up, I'm talking about evolving as a human being. And so I did a lot of work on myself and on my skills in the '80s.

Q: *In light of the fact of what we were just talking about, absorbing and then giving, how do you account for your current prolificness because Gung-Ho is going to be your third album in four years?*

A: One thing is my children have gotten to a point, where, you know, they're old enough where they don't need as much tending to, so I have a lot more time. I've always been a prolific person, but basically privately prolific. I do a lot of work that no one sees. But I think the real reason is because I've had a lot of input and energy from other people. Doing albums, for me, is . . . has always been a collaborative effort. And even though I enjoy being respected—having my name respected, my body of work as a person who does records, has been basically been collaborative. And I'm working with, right now a very energetic situation. I had a very difficult period before I began Gone Again. My children were young, my husband was ill. We were struggling, in various ways. Not only with our difficulties such as that, but you know, financially. I had a lot of responsibilities. I've had a lot of support from '95 on—from friends and colleagues and people I didn't even know. People like Michael Stipe. And it's just been—you know, it's been a really good period. I mean, even somebody like Bob Dylan, who I greatly was influenced and admired from afar, invited me to open his tour in, I think, late '95 or '96, I can't remember. Probably '96. And I sang with him and he also gave me words of encouragement. And so many people have really put so much belief in me to help me get back on my feet. I could do nothing but produce work to earn all of their support, all of their energy and all of the belief that's been put in me.

Q: *Well, now that Jackson and Jesse are a little older, do you think you might tour more than you have over the last few years?*

A: Probably. Not like Metallica or somebody (laughs). I'm not gonna— I can't do that, nor do I have the desire to do that. The way that we perform, every night is different. We really collaborate with the people and the energy of the night. I improvise a lot and it's physically taxing work. But certainly, we'll tour probably more than the last two albums.

Q: Here's a selfish question from someone from Austin, Texas, because I saw your last show in there. I think it was 1979. I'm certain it was the Wave tour. And that's the last time you visited us. So I'm hoping that if you do do some shows in the near future, you will come our way.

A: Well, I have to tell you that I have a very cool booking agent. I know that the term "booking agent" is like, it's—even he knows, it's not the greatest term. But I told him—his name's Frank Riley. I said, "I want to go"—I told him the places that we often go that I like; I said, "But the place I really want is Austin, Texas. Get me—can you get me to Austin Texas." And he said, "That's a great town." And I said, "I really want to go back to Austin, Texas." And I have three concrete reasons. One is because the people were great. I have the greatest memories of Austin, Texas, because in the '70s, they had a revolutionary and I felt responsible and caring radio station. And you gave me the name of it earlier. We talked—

Q: Right. It was KLBJ.

A: KLBJ. And didn't Lady Bird Johnson, that was her station? But the people, they were given a lot of freedom. And those people still cared about radio as a communication and cultural base, And that was fast fading at the end of the '70s and I really felt that Austin, Texas, was holding on to, you know—you know, keeping the torch burning. And also, I have my happiest American hotel memory staying at the LBJ Suite at the Driskill, which it was just really great. I just felt like I was on the top of the world then. So I have really, really happy memories of Austin. So I hope that the people will want us to return so that I can get a job there.

Q: I don't think that that's a problem. I think they've been more or less begging for you to come back. And just so you know, the station that we'll be airing this interview on KGSR, we are a sister station with KLBJ and we are still co-owned by the Johnson family.

A: Well, great. And I hope you'll—if you have time, you'll invite me—you know, invite me over if it's possible.

Q: Will you come play on the air?

A: Yeah.

Q: All right.

A: You have my promise. As long as I don't have to play a B chord. I'll bring my acoustic guitar and sing. I'll be really happy to.

Q: One other Austin question is that people used to tell me to "Ask Patti if the white dress that she wears on the Wave cover—someone said she bought that in Austin." Is that true?

A: Yes, my brother, Todd—actually, my brother, Todd, bought it for me. I always liked white dresses. And I mentioned that I wanted to wear one on my next album, if I could find one. And my brother found one. You know, it was like an old-fashioned, looks like a—sort of like a prairie, prairie girl dress. You know, it was like a really thin white cotton. I still have it. It's folded up in a little chest and I still have it.

Q: We're in New York City. And I guess it was about the time of Gone Again that you moved from Detroit, where you had lived with Fred, back to New York. Why did you move here and has the move been good for you?

A: Well, I moved here because—well, basically, I'm an East Coast person. I was born in Chicago, but I spent most of my life on the East Coast. And I wanted to come back to the East Coast to be near my family and my friends. And also I had a lot of support on the East Coast. And I felt I would be able to work. And it's been, it's been great for me. I mean I've always loved New York City. I left New York City because, you know, Detroit was Fred's home. So I migrated to the Midwest, for his sake. And I was happy there. But, being out on my own with my kids, I wanted to go back where I knew best. Also, I don't drive, so New York is pedestrian friendly. And it has a lot of great cafés—you can get a cup o' coffee anywhere. I've always loved New York. It's really like a small town, really, for me, because I can walk down the street and everybody just says hello to me. You know, a cop goes by on a motorcycle and says, "Hey, Patti." And you know, the guy—the trash man goes by and gives me a wave, and I feel good on the streets of New York.

Q: Well, moving to New York also put you closer to the record business, for better or for worse. Your whole career you've been with one label,

*Arista Records, (Yep.) and with Clive Davis. How would you charac-
terize your relationship with Arista and the music business in general?*

A: Well you know I'm not really music business oriented. I've pretty
much done what I wanted. I've been a, you know, a loving thorn in
Clive's side for these 25 years. He's always tried to direct me in a certain
way and I usually go the other way. But he's always put out my work
untampered, just the way I wanted, shaking his head the whole way,
but I've done what I wanted. My company hasn't always understood, or
rarely understood what I do. But they've always put it out—untainted,
untouched. And that means more to me than anything else anyone else
could give me. And I also am proud that I stayed with one company,
because again it's the loyalty factor. This is my eighth and last album in
my contract with Arista. And I feel like Al Kaline. I did my stretch like
he did with the Tigers. Through good and bad, he was a Tiger. And I
did my albums, my eight albums, and did them the best I could on the
label that took a chance on me. I mean, when Clive signed me up, he
saw somethin' in me. I wasn't much of a singer. I didn't really know
anything about music or the music business or making records. I just
loved rock and roll. I had, and still do hopefully, a revolutionary heart
and had things to say. And he gave me the arena to say it in. So whether
or not we agreed or saw eye-to-eye, I said what I had to say.

**Q: One thing that Patti Smith did was make the issue of a woman's
gender meaningless in rock and roll. And then the Lilith Fair came and
made it an issue again. Did you feel like that was a step backwards,
in some ways?**

A: That's not mine to judge. I'm sure they did a lot of positive things
for women performers who find it important to be known as a woman
performer. That's an important thing to people. For me, I mean, I'm an
artist. And I feel like I don't want to be genderized as an artist. People
don't genderize male artists. You know, they don't call them "male artists." I've said this over and over, but we don't call Piccaso a male, white
painter. I don't want to be known for my—in terms of my work: my
gender or my race or anything. The work stands on its own. But that's

how I look at things. And I can't presume my philosophy on other people. But I'm not going to change mine.

Q: Figures from the '60s are often asked if their upheaval really changed anything. Do you think that the mid-'70s punk scene changed anything?

A: I can't really answer that. It's not really—it's not my beat. For myself, I wasn't even trying to change things. What I was trying to do was make people aware of things, to wake people up. I think before you can change anything, you have to be awake. And that was always what I felt my responsibility was. There's always change. Some change is for the better. It seems like in everything, whether it's issues on censorship or race or gay rights or hunger, all the things that we're constantly trying to make strides in, we keep going back a little and then we make strides and we go back a little, because there's always new generations, new people who have their own opinions of things and their own way of interpreting things. So I can't really give you a specific sociological answer, because I'm just an artist.

Q: As an artist, you're getting ready to release this album Gung-Ho. You want it to communicate to people. Is there a hope that radio stations are going to open their airwaves to this record?

A: Well, I hope so. But I'm always optimistic. I always think that radio stations are going to like certain songs. I don't see how they can resist some of the songs that we do. And certainly not on this album. People make the decisions. I'm hoping that people will embrace some of the ideas on this album. And also, I think that, for me more than any other album, it has beautiful sound on this record. I don't know exactly why some things sound better. Obviously, we had a very brilliant engineer and producer. But I really make records for people. I don't make them for the music business or for radio stations. I make them for people and they'll make the decision.

Q: I did not read it, but there was a recent unauthorized biography written about you that I heard you didn't approve of. What was it about the book that upset you?

A: That it was unauthorized. You know, if I'm ready to go though my whole life and share it with people, I'll do it on my own.

Q: *You grew up having your share of heroes: Bob Dylan, Jimi Hendrix, Jim Morrison, to name a few. How does it feel now that you're a hero to people when they come up to you and tell you how you changed their lives?*

A: It's an honor when people do that. Sometimes it's embarrassing, you know, but not in a bad way. What I always hope is that . . . I've done some kind of work or done something that's inspired people or made them feel less alone. And they can use it and then discard it and go do things on their own. I wouldn't want people, you know to be so obsessed with, you know, what I did or what my band did that they didn't have their own life. I think they should use it to their advantage and go and be the best they can of themselves.

Q: *There was a song you did in 1996 called Farewell Reel and you wrote, "We're only given as much as the heart can endure." And you've suffered a lot of losses since 1989. Do you still believe that statement is true?*

A: Well, I think the human spirit's pretty resilient. I mean, I'm determined to always feel that, because I'm determined to go on as long as . . . you know, I love life. And I'm determined not to let anything beat me down so much that I no longer love it. Also, I think that our heart is continuously being replenished. Even by the people we lose. I mean, my heart felt extremely dark at a point after my friend Robert (Mapplethorpe) and Richard (Sohl) and then Fred (Smith) passed away. But when my brother (Todd) passed away right after Fred, after I, you know, experienced the initial shock, what I experienced was that my heart felt light and beautiful and joyful, because that's the kind of guy my brother was. And I felt filled with him. So he helped replenish my heart to get it ready for other things it would have to experience. So I guess the answer to your question is yes.

Q: *You also once sang in 1978, "Outside of society, that's where I want to be." And now you're 53 and you've got two kids is that still where you want to be?*

A: Well, it seems like often that's where I am, anyway. I'm just that kind of girl, you know.

Q: *Patti, I was thinking of this conversation or of calling it "One Common Wire". And that's a line from your song Grateful. I'm assuming that's about Jerry Garcia.*

A: It was inspired by Jerry. You know I was, learning of course to play the acoustic guitar. And one day I was feeling a little blue, because I was being teased about my newly-sprouting gray hairs. And usually, those kind of things don't bother me. But this particular day it, it sort of made me blue. I had sort of tears in my eyes and I was standin' alone. And I shut my eyes for a minute to regroup. And I saw Jerry! I know that it sounds really funny, but I saw Jerry Garcia. He smiled, and he tugged on his long, wiry, gray hair and just gave me a wink. And I opened my eyes and this little piece of music came in my head. And I took my little acoustic guitar . . . its one of those rare songs that I wrote right off. I wrote the music and I wrote the words without any struggle. And it made me feel better. And after I'd finished it, I was really grateful. And so I decided to call it Grateful in honor of Jerry. And—and I am, very grateful.

PATTI SMITH ON ALLEN GINSBERG

Jerry Aronson | February 15, 2001 | *The Life and Times of Allen Ginsberg*

Patti Smith's relationship with Allen Ginsberg began when he bought her a sandwich. Ginsberg was writing an elegy for Jack Kerouac, who died October 21, 1969—probably the poem "Memory Gardens." Smith was a young poet living with Robert Mapplethorpe in the Chelsea Hotel, and she hadn't encountered Ginsberg in person or on the page. The Beats did not quite make it into the Pines, the area of Southern New Jersey where Smith grew up.

Their friendship, and her appreciation for his poetry, deepened over time, until Ginsberg became one of the poets she read most. On February 16, 1995, Ginsberg was appearing at a benefit concert in Ann Arbor, Michigan, for the Jewel Heart Buddhist center, and he convinced Smith to perform. She was living nearby in St. Clair Shores and still grieving; Ginsberg was a galvanizing force in bringing her back into public service.

This 2001 video interview, edited by filmmaker Jerry Aronson from a longer conversation, is part of the special features in Aronson's award-winning 1993 documentary *The Life and Times of Allen Ginsberg*. When Ginsberg saw it, he remarked, "So, that's Allen Ginsberg." Ginsberg passed away on April 5, 1997, and Smith paid her last respects at his home. Here, she describes his death at 70 as a "nice death," most likely a reference to Albert Camus's *A Happy Death*, which she has claimed as an inspiration.

Ginsberg may have died too soon, but his spirit lives on. Five months after the great poet's passing, Smith released *Peace and Noise*, which includes "Spell," Oliver Ray's musical adaptation of Ginsberg's "Footnote to Howl." She performed this loving tribute to her friend on May 14, 1998, at an Allen Ginsberg memorial at the Cathedral of Saint John the Divine, blocks from where Ginsberg first studied at Columbia University and met his Beat Generation coconspirators. During the memorial, Smith felt Ginsberg's spirit. It somehow seems fitting that if the spirit of Allen Ginsberg were to possess an inanimate object, it would be a clarinet. —Ed.

Patti Smith: How I met Allen, I was in Horn & Hardart's, there used to be a Horn & Hardart's on 23rd Street, near the Chelsea Hotel. And I was really broke and it was winter and I had a big overcoat on, long hair and, like a cap like this, and I had some change, and they had just upped the price of cheese sandwiches in the automat. And I was short like a dime or fifteen cents. And I was just standing there, like . . . actually I was trying out the, if you know, automats—the sandwiches behind the glass thing. So I was like, checking, to see if anybody had like, you know, put some money in and didn't open the thing, see if I could get me a sandwich.

And I was pretty dejected, and I heard this uh, voice, this somebody say, "Are you hungry?" And I turned around, it's this guy, and he had, like, he had an overcoat on too and a camera around his neck. And um, I might've known it was him, I can't remember anymore. I mean, this was like 1969 or something, '70, you know, it was a long time ago. And I just nodded. And so he got me a sandwich and said, "Come on," and we sat down. I still hadn't said a word. So I'm just like eating the sandwich and he's talking and then he's looking at me, and then I start talking and then he starts laughing, and uh, the reason he was laughing is he thought I was a, a guy, you know, a boy, you know. Hopefully a nice-looking one. And uh, we start laughing about this and I said, "Well, can I still have the sandwich?" And he said, "Sure." That was my first encounter with Allen.

I mean the way that I would explain my relationship with Allen is, it's like bookends. That was the beginning of our friendship: he asked me if I was hungry and he fed me. And we you know, we just like peripherally, you know, moved in and out of each other's world. You know with—respectfully. But it wasn't until uh, well at the end of '94 my husband passed away, and then my brother passed away a month later. And I was pretty—it was probably the lowest point of my life, and I was living in uh, outside of Detroit. And I hadn't performed or been in the public eye for years, and I got a call, and it was Allen. And I hadn't heard from him, or seen him, maybe, at least in a decade. And he had heard of that, of what had happened, and uh, his voice was comforting. I think he heard it from William [S. Burroughs], because William and I still remained close. And he said to me, "You must," he said, "in the Buddhist tradition you must try to let go of the spirit of your departed. And of the departed, and uh, continue your own life celebration, or to celebrate your own life," and he said "the best way to do that is to begin to work right away and to serve others." So he was doing a benefit for the [*Buddhist organization —Ed.*] Jewel Heart Foundation, for Rimpoche, his teacher Rimpoche, Gelek in Ann Arbor, Michigan. So he asked me to join him. I thought it would be a good thing to do, but I, I was very afraid. I felt very vulnerable to be in front of people after such losses. I felt really naked, and I was afraid. But I knew that he would shepherd me through it. But I didn't even know how much he would shepherd me through it till it happened.

Well, I was really surprised when Allen introduced me at Jewel Heart, because I hadn't seen him for so long. And I had no idea at all. I mean, I was actually honored that he chose me, or really happy. But he introduced me, and I had not seen him, in, in all this time. He, he gave this introduction that went, you know in the true Allen spirit, it kept going on, and on, and on, and on, and it was uh, it was quite flattering. But, I was, the more it went on, the less I felt that I could possibly live up to the introduction. It was like, I just went [*groans*] . . . time to go home.

I don't know, how can I go on after that? I mean, after that introduction. I mean, it's like the person that he presented to them, I, I thought, I'd like to meet that person myself. But he was really kind to me—very, very kind.

The last year that he—right before he died—he was at Carnegie Hall and he was ill. And he took me aside and told me that he was quite ill, and just, you know, very straightforwardly said, you know, "I think I still have a couple of months, though."

We got a call. He called me, and I was working. I was out working, and I came home and my daughter said that Allen called. And then I called back, but he had already, uh, slipped in a coma. And it was, it was like on a Thursday or something, I can't remember the exact days or anything, but I talked to a few other people that he really cared for and he, he made a bunch, of, it was a lot of phone calls, you know. And mostly, he was calling people to see if they needed anything, you know. Like you know, I'm sure, "Do I have anything you want?" or "Are you in need of anything?" And so Philip Glass actually called and said that, you know, they were having a vigil. That uh, that I should come.

You know, in the room, you walked in, and it's a very big room, and all the books or, all his library, all his books were there and, and there were Tibetan monks chanting. You know, all beautifully, you know, arrayed, and they were chanting in the way that he wanted. His teacher was there scurrying about. And his relatives were there, just horrified and dismayed in a way, but also being—trying to be very gracious about the presence of these Tibetan monks.

There's his brother, you know, distraught and dignified, and you know, there's like yarmulkes and, and, and, and, and Buddhist's fragrances and smoke, and then all the different people in Allen's life, you know. Some people like Larry Rivers coming in, and Gregory Corso was there, and Peter Orlovsky and all these people in Allen's life. And you know, new poets and people that just adored him and uh, people I didn't know, a lot of his relatives. There was just all—just a steady stream of all kinds of people from all different worlds. Some really square people, you know, some totally wasted people, some very scholarly people, and all kinds of relatives, and of course Buddhists and uh, you know. . . . It was just, I thought it was great, and having seen different deaths in my life, um, you know, younger people dying of AIDS. Some very difficult, unhappy deaths, I looked at all of this, this sort of, kind of celebratory and edgy energy going on. And then walked into the back room where Allen was lying peacefully, you know, within all the chaos, the beautiful chaos, that he has sort of designed in his life. Lying very peacefully beneath his favorite photograph of Walt Whitman.

He was in his last sleep for quite a while. It was actually so, such a nice death, or such a nice dying that I actually, um, brought my children. Um, so they could see, you know, a nice death. I mean, they didn't see him die, but they came, they knew him alive and they both really liked him, so they got to say goodbye to him without being afraid. You know, that this is a, a dying person, but it's, it's alright, you know, this is part of the process of human existence.

I'd say that it was a very, very nice death, with—not without humor. And the thing that—the most heartbreaking moment for me of the whole thing was like about like one in the morning. Gregory Corso was sitting by him, and then he just sort of like [*sighs*] sat like this and he just said, "Oh my Allen . . ." It was just, that's, I just . . . I, I, I still hear that in my ear, especially now that Gregory is gone. It was interesting because, uh, Oliver and I went to see Gregory before he died, when he was quite ill. And over Gregory's bed, where Allen had Whitman, Gregory had Allen—pictures of Allen taped to the wall.

We all have Allen visitations. But I had a very specific one that left its mark on me. After Allen died, I don't know exactly when, but they had a big memorial service, or a tribute. I guess it was a memorial service at Saint John the Divine. Great, beautiful church, and uh, a lot of people spoke and read poetry. And my band, which is—my band, uh, we do, we began to do "Footnote to Howl," and Oliver wrote music to it, and we call it "Spell." And I play clarinet to it, and I just, I improvised on clarinet, and we performed it there. I was playing clarinet, and I was trying to end because there was also a time frame, because the next person had to come on. My clarinet would not stop playing. And I was playing it, and it was like really—and I took it, I stopped playing and it, like, jerked in my mouth—to keep playing. And it jerked in my mouth and hit my tooth and actually chipped my tooth, and I saw the piece of my tooth fly in the light. And I kept playing, and as I kept playing and I saw that piece of tooth, just a little white piece of ivory float in the air, in the light, I thought—it's Allen. I knew it was Allen. And um, I was just, just filled with this vigorous, vigorous, vigorous energy, this dance of life. I knew it was Allen. My once perfect teeth, my only vanity, uh, my front tooth is now chipped. And I always think that's my last, or one of my last gifts from Allen. [*Laughs.*]

PATTI SMITH STRIKES A STRONG NOTE FOR A PEACEABLE KINGDOM

Ed Masley | June 6, 2004 | *Pittsburgh Post-Gazette*

On June 9, 2004, Patti Smith was playing the Three Rivers Arts Festival in Pittsburgh, hard on the heels of the release of *Trampin'*. It was her first album in four years, and her first album for Columbia after working with Arista on the previous eight. Smith caught up with longtime pop critic Ed Masley before the concert, shedding some light on the new material: "Radio Baghdad," a twelve-minute-plus improvised screed protesting the 2003 invasion of Iraq; "Mother Rose"; and "Peaceable Kingdom," her take on what that biblical concept might mean in the wake of 9/11. The songs all seem to have some connection to Smith's mother, Beverly, who passed away in 2002.

Motherhood is the key theme here: no matter how wide the cultural divides, we all have mothers. And as a mother, Smith got to collaborate with her daughter on the album's title track, a spiritual she had first heard as a child growing up in Philadelphia. —Ed.

When Patti Smith emerged from CBGB's with "Horses," a punk-era classic that married the primal abandon of '60s garage to Beat-inspired poetry, she was merely responding, she says, to the state of the world as she knew it.

"When I was doing 'Horses,'" she says, "I was reading 'Wild Boys' by William Burroughs. I was concerned about the state of rock 'n' roll. I was mourning the loss of people like Jimi Hendrix and Jim Morrison. And all of those things are reflected in 'Horses.'"

"Trampin'"—a stunning new effort that finds her lashing out at the Bush administration in "Radio Baghdad" and quietly reflecting on her mother's passing in the understated "Mother Rose"—was similarly inspired by current events both personal and universal.

"I was very concerned about and opposed to the [military] strike in Iraq, so that found its way into the record," Smith says. "My mother passed away, and she found her place on the record. These are things that are happening within and around my life."

Her mother's death inspired more than just that one song, shaping the mood of the entire record.

As Smith says, "She was very active and high energy and optimistic and resilient. And I think a lot of that energy is in the record."

You can definitely hear her mother's sense of optimism, from her hope that one day we'll rebuild the Peaceable Kingdom in her haunting musical response to Sept. 11 to her vow that "doves shall multiply" to vanquish the circling hawks in "Jubilee."

"I think that if people decide they want a better world," Smith says, "they can build one. I just think it's up to us. It's not up to our government. They're not gonna do it. . . . It's up to the people and I always have faith in the people. So I guess I am optimistic."

That extends to her hopes for ousting President Bush in November.

"It's up to the people," she says "That's why it says, 'Come on people/ Gather round/You know what to do' [in 'Jubilee']. That's really appealing to the people to gather, register and vote. The same as in 'Gandhi' where it says, 'Awake from your slumber and get 'em with the numbers.' That's the way we'll overturn the present regime. With our numbers."

Even the freewheeling spoken-word epic "Radio Bagdhad," with its outraged attacks on the war in Iraq ("You sent your lights/Your bombs/ You sent them down on our city/Shock and awe/Like some crazy TV show"), was in many ways shaped, she says, by the death of her mother.

"I address it from a mother's point of view," she says. "The narrator is an Iraqi mother who is singing her children to sleep and also reminding them of their history and who they are as the Americans are bombing overhead. So even that is not so much from a political point of view as from a human point of view.

"It seems like the mother imagery does find its way through a lot of the album. In 'Jubilee,' the American mother is saying 'We have a beautiful country, it's beautiful out, we have a lot to celebrate.' But then she also senses trouble in her land, and so in that way, both of these females are put in the position of both heralding their country and also being concerned with its welfare and their children's welfare."

As for those who would find her concern for the welfare of her country—her dissent—unpatriotic, Smith says, "That's because those people haven't read the Declaration of Independence lately. The Declaration of Independence not only guarantees us the right to dissent, it also appeals to us and counsels us to constantly be vigilant and question our government. So I think that it is more patriotic to ask questions than to just sit as sheep. We were a country built on revolution and we have to guard our freedom. We have to make certain that it isn't being drained from us by insidious laws."

So what would she have done if she were Bush in the wake of Sept. 11?

"Well, I'm hardly qualified," she says, "but I think what I would have liked to have seen our president do would have been to reach out to the world community instead of making military strikes on Afghanistan and Iraq. . . .

"We had so much good will on our side globally after Sept. 11. Everyone was horrified. And now this good will has completely been demolished. There's more hatred for our country than ever. Since Vietnam . . . I think that we could have made this tragedy into something. We could have built global communication instead of fear and retaliation, which has a domino effect.

"Everywhere you look, there is much more aggression in the world because we've permitted it and because we're supposed to be an example for the rest of the world, and the example we've set is one of aggression instead of one of compassionate leadership and communication."

And aggression, of course, is no way to rebuild a Peaceable Kingdom.

"I'm not even thinking of Utopia or the Promised Land," Smith says. "My first hope is just a rebuilding process. A Peaceable Kingdom is basically, to me, people co-existing and allowing each other to coexist but also taking responsibility."

Weighing in on world situations with her music is a natural for Smith, who grew up a child of the '60s.

"I felt like music in the '60s was a real backdrop for revolutionary ideas and political ideas," she says. "I don't really feel that so much now but I guess musicians will decide, or artists will decide, what their role is.

"It seems to me that we're at a very materialistic point. We're living in a very sexualized, pop-oriented, youth-exploitive culture. We just have to reassess things. But I always think that things will shift. There's always cycles. And I always hope for the best."

If "Trampin'" finds her acting on ideals more often heard in '60s music, Smith is quick to note that believing we can make the world a better place is not "a '60s thing" so much as a human response to troubled times.

"I don't feel nostalgic," she says. "And I don't feel as if I'm trying to recapture the '60s. We're trying to build on our own times and respond to our own times. But you think of somebody like Neil Young. The Kent State tragedy happened and he wrote the song that night and it was on the radio two days later. That response to things, I think, is healthy. So I try to learn from those examples."

"Trampin'" takes its title from and ends with a Negro spiritual learned from growing up on Marian Anderson.

"I was raised in the Philadelphia area and listened to her all my life," she says. "And that little song, especially after my mom died, always made me feel hopeful. I just really like it and my daughter plays piano so I asked my daughter if she would perform it with me and it just seemed like a good theme song for the record."

And her daughter, she's pleased to report, "really committed herself to the song. We went to the Philadelphia Free Library and got the sheet music, the same sheet music that Marian Anderson's pianist used, and she learned the piece from the sheet music. I was really proud of what she did."

Asked if she feels a connection between the songs on "Trampin'" and her early records, Smith says, "Well, I mean, I'm the same person, so I still feel connected with certain work I did in the past. And other work, I don't. Sometimes, I can taste what it was like to be 7 years old or 27 years old or now 57 years old. I can access all my different times of life. But I'm a present-oriented person. So I'm most connected, of course, with the present album.

"We just performed at a radio conference in Louisville and we had an hour, and we only did songs from two records 'Horses,' and 'Trampin'.' And I felt comfortable with both. I just moved back and forth between them without any trouble."

AN INTERVIEW WITH PATTI SMITH ON *AUGURIES OF INNOCENCE*

Lawrence French | November 2005 | KUSF

"Well, I hate to be redundant and I've told that story many times," Patti Smith told Lawrence French in 2005, when she was in San Francisco. "Actually, my mother was really good at telling stories, because even if she told the same story over and over, she always told it from a slightly different angle and with so much enthusiasm, that you always felt like you were hearing that old Nat King Cole story for the first time." That is often the case with interviews—interviewers invariably ask for the same stories. Yet in this interview, as far as I can tell, only a few of the stories are repeated elsewhere in this collection. There are even details about the making of *Horses* I haven't found anywhere else.

Here, Smith certainly presented a different angle on herself than most of the rock-centric interviews; French shifted the focus back to Patti Smith the poet. This makes sense—French is a longtime devotee who runs the "Patti Smith Poet" group on Facebook. The interview centered around the recent publication of *Auguries of Innocence*, Smith's first book of poetry since *The Coral Sea*, her 1997 collection of prose poems dedicated to Robert Mapplethorpe. According to Smith, in some ways it was her first collection since *Babel* in 1978.

This lightly edited interview excerpt is eclectic and surprising. Smith touched on William Blake, the source of the book's title; the cover image she shot herself at an abandoned club in Hamburg, Germany; and how the migraines she suffered were not as bad as Virginia Woolf's. She somehow yoked together Robert Louis Stevenson, Diane Arbus, the death of Pope John Paul II, a lost poetry manuscript that resurfaced years later, and '80s kung fu films. She got polemical on the invasion of Iraq and prescient; then a minute later, she was talking about the time she communed with crepuscular frogs in Namibia.

Here's French: "In 2005, I talked with Patti Smith at KUSF radio in San Francisco, during her thirtieth anniversary tour of *Horses*," he told me. The interview took place November 13 or 14. "She also was promoting her first book of poetry in several years, *Auguries of Innocence*. This is what she said." —Ed.

LAWRENCE FRENCH: Tonight in San Francisco, you'll be doing your first full-length poetry reading since your new book of poems, *Auguries of Innocence* has come out.

PATTI SMITH: Yes, and the Victoria Theatre show [*On November 13, 2005 —Ed.*] was something we added at the last minute, and I think it will be really fun. Lenny will come by and we'll read poems and do some songs and things. Lenny and I are here celebrating the 100th anniversary . . . (Laughter) I mean the 30th anniversary of *Horses* and because I have a new book out, we've been lucky enough to visit all these cool places. I haven't really read the *Auguries of Innocence* poems out loud too much, only a couple of times, so it will be really interesting for me to get the opportunity to read them here tonight.

LAWRENCE FRENCH: I haven't seen too many reviews of *Auguries of Innocence*.

PATTI SMITH: No, as far as I know, there haven't been any reviews. But I'm very happy with the book, although I actually had an argument with my publisher about the cover. I said, "why does it have to say 'Poems' on the cover. You don't put 'novel' on a book's cover." So we compromised by making "Poems" real tiny. Originally it was real big.

LAWRENCE FRENCH: Where did you take the cover photo of *Auguries of Innocence*?

PATTI SMITH: That's a Polaroid I took when we were on the road and playing a big club in Hamburg (The Grosse Freiheit 36). [*The venue is more likely to be the Docks Club, where Smith played on July 15, 2004. —Ed.*] I went exploring and I noticed this door that led to a tinier club that was all boarded up within the big club. I went in there and it was really dark and dusty, it was like being in *The Twilight Zone*. It had these old tables and chairs that had been there for years and they were all covered with dust. But along the wall, for no reason I could comprehend, there where these friezes of cherubs. I guess they were sculptures, except they were carved into the wall. I couldn't really see them, because it was so dark, but I lit a match and was able to get enough light to take Polaroids of these two children. They really fascinated me, and while I was staring at them a little poem came into my head. So I writ this little poem, *The Oracle*, while I was looking at the children who are on the cover of the book.

LAWRENCE FRENCH: The title *Auguries of Innocence* fits in nicely with how William Blake spoke out against child abuses in his time, such as the use of small children as chimneysweepers. In fact, that's something alluded to in Roman Polanski's beautiful film of Charles Dickens's *Oliver Twist* [*released in 2005. —Ed.*]. In the movie, the young Oliver Twist is horrified when he is almost sold into indentured servitude as a chimneysweeper.

PATTI SMITH: Well, many little lads gave their whole life to the task of cleaning chimneys in England during the 18th century. Can you imagine these little children, who because they were small and very poor, being used as chimney sweeps when they were only 6 or 7 years old? They would be prodded and shoved up hot sooty chimneys, and nobody even cared. Most of them only lived to be nine or ten. While walking the streets of London, William Blake would see these children in their raggedy old coats, half starved and it broke his heart, seeing children in that condition. He couldn't imagine what was in the heads of people who would not only do this, but who would allow it to happen. But there was one day a year when the chimney sweeps had a holiday, and that was on May Day. It was their one shining day, when they would have a big parade. But because their heads were always singed from the burning coals in the chimneys they would put on these white wigs and cover themselves with gold and silver paper and be very festive and joyful, for one day out of the year.

LAWRENCE FRENCH: Of course, you speak about today's exploitation of children in several of the book's poems.

PATTI SMITH: Yes, because today, in our society, we're allowing all kinds of things to happen to children, and we should just think with the same clarity, and the same horror and the same innocence of William Blake. He looked at these children and wondered, "Why? Why do we let this happen?" So I chose the title, *Auguries of Innocence*, not only because of the Blake connection, but also because the theme of childhood is addressed quite a bit in the book. And another reason I chose it was because when I was a teenager, there was a spread in *Vogue* magazine of Diane Arbus's photographs of children and the article was called "Auguries of Innocence." [*This article was actually in the December 1963 issue of* Harper's Bazaar, *p. 76–79. —Ed.*] I cut it out and had it for a long time and I always wondered who this one specific child was. It was a very haunting photograph of a little girl in a nightdress with her black hair blowing in the wind. Recently, I met that little girl grown-up, and it was Diane Arbus's youngest daughter. So that was another reason why I decided to call the book *Auguries of Innocence.*

LAWRENCE FRENCH: And the poem *She Lay in a Stream Dreaming of August Sanders* references Diane Arbus.

PATTI SMITH: Yes, that was written with thoughts of Diane Arbus. It addresses the dark end of Diane Arbus, who despite the gifts that she had within her, and having children, found a place in her own heart so dark that she took her own life. I recently saw a great show of her work (at the Metropolitan Museum) [Diane Arbus: Revelations *ran May 8–May 30, 2005. —Ed.*], called *Revelations* and it is truly that.

LAWRENCE FRENCH: What was the inspiration for the poem *Fourteen*?

PATTI SMITH: I writ that after I read about the Elizabeth Smart kidnapping. She was just a nice little girl who was stolen from her house in Utah by these people and defiled in many ways. Luckily, they didn't kill her and she was returned to her family. But it's just one more example of the way our children are abused and misused and exploited.

LAWRENCE FRENCH: The first poem in the book is titled *The Lovecrafter*, but it's actually more about Johnny Appleseed than H. P. Lovecraft.

PATTI SMITH: Well, Johnny Appleseed is one of my favorite people in American history. He was a very simple man whose father fought in the American Revolution and his mother died when he was only about two years old. He was a very humble man and he's best known for loving apples and apple trees and wanting to share that with everyone. As a boy he worked on an apple orchard and he would keep apple seeds in a little leather bag, and go out for walks and plant the seeds. Then when he got a little older he'd go and look, and lo and behold, there would be apple trees. He decided that this was what he was going to do in life, and that's what he did. He walked across America with a little leather sack and simply planted apple trees. And the trees grew and people had something to eat. Everyone always loved him. The animals loved him, the Indians loved him and he just trod through the American landscape until his death. I always liked the story of Johnny Appleseed because it illustrates how little seeds become such great things. I was re-introduced to Johnny Appleseed through Ralph Nader, because Ralph has a great affection for Johnny Appleseed. So I was studying Johnny Appleseed and decided to write the poem as a sort of salute to Ralph. I was actually on a plane going to a political rally for Ralph Nader, and as I was sitting on the plane I looked over and saw a vision of Johnny Appleseed, just floating about in the plane. I don't know what he was doing on North-west Airlines, but I thought "well I saw Johnny Appleseed on the plane, it's best to write about it." So I wrote this poem on the plane. But in the center of it, I wound up also reflecting a bit on H. P. Lovecraft, because there is something of him in Johnny Appleseed, as well. Something of his generous obscurity. So Ralph Nader, Johnny Appleseed and H. P. Lovecraft all find their way into this little poem. I'd be happy to go to the prom with any of them.

LAWRENCE FRENCH: I found the *The Lovecrafter* to be especially effective because it has a kind of universal theme that can be very moving, even if you don't fully understand the words of the poem.

PATTI SMITH: I think it's also the voice in the poem. When I was a child I loved Robert Louis Stevenson, and I think some of the poems in the book reflect that. It's a voice that will universally touch some youthful, childlike chord within us. So perhaps it's the voice.

LAWRENCE FRENCH: That also applies to *The Long Road*, where you open the poem with a quote from Robert Louis Stevenson's *Garden Days*, (Chapter 8) [*A Child's Garden of Verses, initially published in 1885 —Ed.*]:

Here we had best on tip-toe tread
While I for safety march ahead
For this is that enchanted ground
Where all who loiter slumber sound.

PATTI SMITH: Well, *The Long Road* is sort of the main poem in the book, and I wrote it for my brother and sister, so it has a certain aspect of Stevenson's rhythms from *A Child's Garden of Verses*.

LAWRENCE FRENCH: Actually, I was quite surprised when I found out you liked H. P. Lovecraft, because he was always one of my favorite horror story writers. I really got into his Cthulhu Mythos stories in the seventies.

PATTI SMITH: So did I, and I just got into him again. Actually, I was into him in the sixties. It was just one of those things where I used him up in the sixties, then I just happened to find an old Arkham House book of his and I was looking at it and I tried to remember his stories. I was so immersed in him at one time in my life, but I couldn't remember one damn thing I had read! So I thought I better re-read him, because sometimes for me, I get so immersed in what I'm reading that I don't even remember what I've read. So lately I've been re-reading him and really enjoying his writing and his whole thing. I love all his Randolph Carter stories: *At The Mountains of Madness* and *The Silver Key*. I used to have a crush on Randolph Carter, because I imagined him as a young William Burroughs.

LAWRENCE FRENCH: The longest poem in the book is *Birds of Iraq*, which alternates viewpoints between the bombing of Iraq and Virginia Woolf.

PATTI SMITH: I remember quite well when I started working on that poem. It was around March 18th and there was a full moon out that night. I started thinking about it then and started writing it on the first day of spring, March 20th. I woke up that morning and the Americans had just invaded Iraq. We had gone into Baghdad and the TV was on and I could hear the news, and I could also hear the birds chirping outside my window and I wondered if the birds were chirping in Iraq on the first day of spring, while we were bombing Baghdad. This thought kept looping through my mind. But I also had this really terrible migraine. Getting migraines is really a nightmare, because they can go on for 18 hours. You really have to stay centered or else you'll go mad. So one of the things I did to keep my sanity while I had this migraine was to work on this poem. At the time, I was thinking of a couple of different things. First, the news reports kept filtering in, and also my mother's birthday had just passed, and my mother used to get these horrible migraines as well. So I was thinking about my mother and I was also thinking about Virginia Woolf, who also got these migraines, but for three weeks at a time. So I thought, "I'm really lucky, because this is only going to last 18 hours, so it will only last as long as a flight to Japan." Then sometime afterwards, I was talking to a journalist who was imbedded with the soldiers in Iraq, and I asked him what it was like that first day in Iraq. He said, "It was the strangest thing. They have millions of these little sparrow-like birds in Baghdad and you always hear them chirping, but on that day the birds were silent." They could feel it coming. So that's how I writ *Birds of Iraq*.

LAWRENCE FRENCH: I just hope that George Bush is going to have a continuous migraine for starting such a completely unnecessary conflict. Anyway, *Birds of Iraq* actually alternates between four separate viewpoints: Virginia Woolf, your mother, yourself, and the invasion of Iraq. I think knowing that really helps the reader to have a fuller appreciation of the poem. . . . [*The original article includes a lengthy excerpt from an early version of "Birds of Iraq" here —Ed.*] *Auguries of Innocence* is actually your first book of poems since *Early Work* came out in 1994.

PATTI SMITH: Well, *Early Work* was a compilation I put together of work I did in the seventies. I did write *The Coral Sea* (1996), which was prose poems for my friend Robert Mapplethorpe, but *Auguries of Innocence* is my first book of published poems really, since 1979.

LAWRENCE FRENCH: Since it's been over ten years since *Early Work*, I'm wondering if writing a poem takes a long time for you, as it did for Sebastian, the gay poet in Tennessee Williams *Suddenly, Last Summer*? It took him nine months to finish a single poem—"the length of a pregnancy."

PATTI SMITH: Actually most of the poems in the book are fairly new. I have a lot of unpublished poetry, but almost all of these poems were written in the past year or so, except for a couple of them. *The Writer's Song* I wrote in the eighties, and *Written by A Lake* is about ten years old. But most of them are quite recent. In fact, there's a very simple one, called *Three Windows* that is probably the last one I wrote before the book was published. I wrote it in St. Peter's Square the night John Paul II died in April of 2005. I was standing in the square and there were thousands of people there and I was told that these three lighted windows was where John Paul II was lying in his compartment, and that when the lights went out in the windows, that meant he had died. So I wrote the poem when the lights went out.

LAWRENCE FRENCH: You also wrote the title track to your album *Wave*, when Pope John Paul the first passed away in 1978.

PATTI SMITH: Yes, I had seen John Paul I on TV and there was just something about him that seemed truly beautiful. He seemed like a truly pastoral man. He really exemplified and radiated Christ's teachings, in their best form and unfortunately he died only 33 days after he became pope. So I wrote *Wave* for him and what it was about, was me imagining I'm walking along the beach and who do I see walking on the beach but my favorite Pope.

LAWRENCE FRENCH: You mentioned *Written By A Lake* being ten years old, and I believe you debuted the poem here in San Francisco.

PATTI SMITH: There's a funny story about that. I had written it, but I only had one copy of it, and after playing San Francisco, I had gone down to the Roxy Theater in Los Angeles and I guess I left it on the stage there, so I didn't have it for a few years. But someone who found the manuscript on the stage was kind enough to send it back to me, so I was finally able to publish it.

LAWRENCE FRENCH: If you hadn't gotten the manuscript back we could have probably reconstructed it from a bootleg tape.

PATTI SMITH: Oh, that could have been helpful. [*The original article includes the full text of a live version of "Written by a Lake" here —Ed.*]

LAWRENCE FRENCH: You said that *The Writer's Song* was written in the eighties.

PATTI SMITH: Yes, *The Writer's Song* I writ in the late eighties, when I was living in Michigan. I had a lot of tasks raising my kids in the eighties, but my one private time from all of my domestic tasks used to be on Saturday afternoons. Every Saturday afternoon there were these two shows I loved to watch, *Kung Fu Theater* and *Martial Arts Theater*. They used to show these old martial arts movies, one right after the other. One guy was dressed like Bruce Lee, and he'd say, "Today Shaolin monks will be flying through the sky." So I used to get a little jar of sake and some cheese and crackers and sit there in the afternoon and watch my martial arts movies. That's when the kids couldn't bother Mom, because it was *Kung Fu Theater* time. And then one Saturday I got my sake and was all ready, and I turned on the TV and *Martial Arts Theater* wasn't there. Another episode of *Cheers*, or something else was on. So I thought, "alright, I won't be greedy, I'll just wait for *Kung Fu Theater*." So I waited, and there's no *Kung Fu Theater* either. It was gone. There was some infomercial for one of those vacuum cleaners that only weighs six pounds. I can't tell you how upset I was that it wasn't there. But I wasn't just upset that it wasn't there, I was really upset that the week before they didn't tell us. Then I waited the next week just to see if maybe something was wrong, but they never came on again, so there was no closure, and the guy in the Kung Fu suit didn't ever say, "Patti, and everybody else who is watching, happy trails . . . " It was just over. I was really heartbroken, so I had to sort of dream my Kung Fu movies, and I wrote *The Writer's Song*.

LAWRENCE FRENCH: What was the inspiration behind *Death of a Tramp?*

PATTI SMITH: That's a poem I writ in Belfast, we were on tour there and I read this little thing in the Belfast newspaper about how a tramp was murdered in the hills, and what a kindly tramp he was. It was such a touching piece of reporting, because it said no one knew who killed old Willie or why, but the people missed him, because he had such a ready smile.

LAWRENCE FRENCH: Was *To His Daughter* written for Jesse? [*Smith's daughter, Jesse Paris Smith. —Ed.*]

PATTI SMITH: No, it was written for my niece Simone after my brother, Todd, passed away. The poem I writ for Jesse was *The Pride Moves Slowly*. I was talking about how Jesse has arms like her father.

LAWRENCE FRENCH: *The Leaves Are Late Falling* was written for Jackson?

PATTI SMITH: Yes, about him losing his father. Before we buried Fred, Jackson placed his favorite guitar upon him, which is why it says, "folding a guitar placed by our son."

LAWRENCE FRENCH: You quote William Blake in *Worthy the Lamb Slain for Us*. What was the idea behind that poem?

PATTI SMITH: I wrote it in response to the mass slaughter of lambs in England. I saw a photograph of a farmer in Wales who had to slaughter all of his lambs because of fear over hoof and mouth disease. I guess that had to be done, but this picture showed a huge cremation pile of all the lambs being burned and beside it was this farmer who was weeping. I found that to be very touching.

LAWRENCE FRENCH: I know you're a big environmentalist and recently Prince Charles was in San Francisco warning about global warming and speaking out against the destruction of the environment.

PATTI SMITH: Good for him.

LAWRENCE FRENCH: It's rather alarming that so many species of animals on the planet are in danger of becoming extinct. Was that part of the idea behind your poem for the Dodo bird?

PATTI SMITH: Yes, the little Dodo poem resonates right now with all of our concerns about the environment, and all the different animals, fishes and birds that are dying out from abuse. Because of the destruction of our environment, all these animals no longer have homes or they no longer have the food chain that they need to survive. And the story of the Dodo bird is so heartbreaking, because they were a very kindly bird; very family oriented, and were vegetarians. They lived on Mauritius Island, off the coast of South Africa and they were very specific to this one particular island. They were just a big lumbering bird with a huge beak, just like you saw in (Lewis Carroll's) *Through the Looking Glass*. Then when the Dutch and Spanish and other new people came to this island, they found them so hilarious and so clumsy they just killed them off for sport, because they really weren't that tasty. In fact there were very bad reviews written in the 17th century about Dodo meat, saying it's very fatty and unappetizing. So they eventually just wiped the Dodo bird out, slaying them for sport, this sweet, friendly bird. So I wrote this little poem, *Sleep of the Dodo*, in memory of the Dodo bird.

LAWRENCE FRENCH: Pablo Picasso's painting, *Guernica* was the inspiration behind one of my favorite poems in *Auguries of Innocence* and it also harks back to an earlier poem you wrote, *Picasso laughing*.

PATTI SMITH: Yes, I wrote *Picasso laughing* back in 1973, right after Picasso died. It appeared in my book *Witt*. But I always loved *Guernica*, so when I was young, I would go to visit it at the Museum of Modern Art in New York whenever I had the two dollars to get in, and I'd just sit and look at it for hours. [*Guernica was housed at the MoMA until 1981, when it was repatriated to Spain, as per Picasso's wishes that the painting remain outside his birthplace until Spain was free from fascist rule. —Ed.*] Then I was sort of heartbroken when they took it back to Madrid, although I knew that's where it was destined to be [*at the Museo del Prado —Ed.*]. But last year, when I played at the Festimad in Madrid [*alternative rock festival in Madrid founded in 1995 —Ed.*], I visited the Reina Sofia Museum and really contemplated *Guernica* again, and while I was there, I thought about Picasso in the act of painting *Guernica*. Then I wrote the little poem, *The Geometry Blinked Ruin Unimaginable.*

LAWRENCE FRENCH: Of course, the incident that led Picasso to paint such an enormous canvas was the bombing of Guernica during the Spanish civil war.

PATTI SMITH: Yes, it was on April 26, 1937, when a massive air raid by the German Luftwaffe all but leveled the Basque town of Guernica. 100,000 pounds of bombs were dropped on this peaceful little village, killing a third of the population. It was a major and tragic milestone in the Spanish Civil War. It inspired the grieving Picasso to respond by painting his masterpiece. Picasso had such an emotional grasp on the aftermath of the air assaults on the citizens. It's a really great painting that still serves as a prophetic vision of war as well as an international plea for peace. His work draws one to contemplate the events of August 6 and 9, 1945, the atomic bombing of Hiroshima and Nagasaki. We must continue to remember and be diligent. A lack of diligence and misguided nationalism led to allowing the Bush administration to invade Iraq. We must remember it was not a war. We invaded them with manpower and technology that they were powerless to defend. We brought that country down, destroyed its infrastructure and killed thousands of citizens. We cannot ignore that fact.

LAWRENCE FRENCH: In his book, *Our Endangered Values: America's Moral Crisis*, Jimmy Carter notes it really isn't a war in Iraq, because outside of the soldiers there, nobody in America is really being asked to give anything up, or sacrifice something, as every American did during World War II, or even during Vietnam. Instead, under Mr. Bush, we've been told we can have a nice big tax cut! So it's a completely absurd situation, spending billions of dollars in Iraq and having a tax cut which results in a 7 trillion dollar deficit. [*Excised here from the original transcript is brief further discussion of the US bombing of Hiroshima and Nagasaki and the preemptive invasion of Iraq under the Bush Doctrine, leading into a lengthy excerpt from "Nagasaki." —Ed.*]

You were in France after the riots broke out there in 2005, to play at a benefit peace concert that was broadcast on the Arte TV channel on December 29, 2005.

PATTI SMITH: Yes, I was in Paris, but I didn't actually see the riots, other than some smoke off in the distance. But this young guy who was about 22 was driving me to the airport, so I was curious about what a 22-year old French boy would think of this situation. I asked him, and he understood that in some ways it was futile and even wrong to create so much destruction, but his take on it was he thought one of the main reasons these young people were rioting was because they wanted people to know they exist. So it was a declaration of existence. Now, for some young people, picking up an electric guitar can be a declaration of existence, which I always thought was one of the beauties of rock and roll. I think America is a potentially great country, but to have a nationalistic government and a nationalistic President as we do, and to have this sense that we should be number one, and be the greatest country in the world . . . I mean, why should we be promoting that, when there are people all over the world who feel like nothing. And there's a big difference between being number one and being nothing. That's what we slowly have to become cognizant of: That the people who feel like nothing aren't going to stand for it anymore. We have to communicate with all our fellow men, or they're going to fucking burn it all down! For myself, I can't stop thinking about the Indian–Pakistan border, where there are hundreds of thousands of people that have no home or food after the earthquake. Their children are dying in their arms and that's their daily life. I don't know what we can do about it, and right now we're not doing anything about it, but we can at least be aware that they exist. They're a people in trouble and their strife is so much deeper than ours. We just can't help everybody, but we can at least be aware that these people exist. [*Here the original transcript includes lines taken from an improvised rap about the widening divide between the rich and poor that Smith delivered during a live show in San Francisco the night after this interview took place —Ed.]*

LAWRENCE FRENCH: You went to Africa to play your clarinet in a neo-dadaist film, *African Twin Towers*, directed by Christoph Schlingensief.

PATTI SMITH: Yes, I was in Namibia, but I was there as an amateur, because I'm not an actress, and I don't even know exactly what everyone was doing, I just had a belief in it and I wanted to be part of the common energy. I spent most of my time using my camera to take Polaroids of the work process, and of the earth and the people. Then while I was up near the Angola border, I was in a tent one night with heavy mosquito netting and I woke up around 2:00 am in the morning to go to the bathroom, and in the middle of this very eloquent squat, I noticed the moon through the mosquito netting. It was very full and blue so I thought, "That's really pretty, the moon is blue in Africa." Then I realized that the moon wasn't full, because it had been full a week ago, and there are no street lamps, so what was this? Then I saw another golden thing in the sky and I wanted to inspect what it was, so I unzipped my tent and sitting there was the biggest, ugliest frog I'd ever seen. I thought, "if I step on this, the wart will be so big!" so I said, "get away," and I started playing my clarinet at it . . . my legendary playing that will send animals flying. Then I went outside the tent and it was really dark, with trees everywhere so I couldn't really see the sky. I had to walk around to get a clearer view and you wouldn't believe what I saw. I can't imagine any acid trip being better than this, but this is a true story. I could see the curve of the earth and the sky with millions of stars in it, but also this round blue globe that was Venus, and it looked like a small moon. Then there was a smaller golden-yellow star that was Mars and a third planet that was even smaller, that could have been Saturn. It was really beautiful, and it was really there and I just stood there and thought, "Oh my God!" I was by myself and it was so overwhelming, I yelled out, "help!" before I realized it was coming out of my mouth. I don't know why I did that, because there was nobody around. But it was truly one of nature's wonders . . . just nature giving us her opera.

LAWRENCE FRENCH: That's quite an interesting thing to ponder, because the moon and stars have inspired artists throughout the centuries, and in *The Pythagorean Traveler* you note that Lord Byron was seeing the same moon, ocean and clouds in Italy that we still see today, which made me think about all the historical people who were inspired by the moon and the stars, from Pythagoras and Jesus Christ, up through William Blake and Pablo Picasso.

PATTI SMITH: Yes, and not only those things but also all of the other rare celestial phenomenon that take place, such as the transit of Venus. Before 2004, the last transit of Venus occurred in the winter of 1882 and it was most certainly witnessed by Arthur Rimbaud, as he paddled his intoxicated craft through the Milky Way.

LAWRENCE FRENCH: I see you've contributed an essay to this new book *Jerry Garcia: The Complete Artwork.*

PATTI SMITH: Yes, I actually forgot I had written something for it, but it's a really nice book of Jerry's paintings. I think Jerry would have been very proud of it.

LAWRENCE FRENCH: Of course, Jerry Garcia was the inspiration for your song *Grateful.*

PATTI SMITH: Well, I hate to be redundant and I've told that story many times. Actually, my mother was really good at telling stories, because even if she told the same story over and over, she always told it from a slightly different angle and with so much enthusiasm, that you always felt like you were hearing that old Nat King Cole story for the first time.

LAWRENCE FRENCH: What Nat King Cole story was that?

PATTI SMITH: Well, my mom was a really good jazz singer in the thirties, long before we were born. She had this great voice, but it was destroyed by cigarettes and she got throat cancer. It didn't take her down; it just took her voice down. She doubled as a hatcheck girl and a singer. And one day these Mafia guys took a liking to her and said they were going to take her down to Atlantic City, where they were taking a look at a piano player at one of their clubs. So they went to Atlantic City and my mom went into this club and said the piano player was one of the ugliest fellows she ever saw. So she listened to him play and she said he was really good, that he just radiated a specific kind of confidence. So after about an hour, it was about 2:00 in the morning and people started drifting away, and he started singing. He sang some little song, like *Tangerine*, and my mother said to him, "what are you doing playing piano for, you should be singing. You're one of the greatest singers I ever heard." He was very self-effacing and said, "oh, no, I'm just a piano player." She said, "No, you're a fantastic singer!" Then, later on, this guy she said was the ugliest person she ever saw, ended up becoming Nat King Cole.

LAWRENCE FRENCH: So your mother encouraged both you and Nat King Cole to become singers!

PATTI SMITH: Yeah, and I can clearly remember my mother's voice when she sang to us, putting us to sleep, and my father whistling *Deep Purple*. I also remember my first gramophone. It was just a little bigger than a shoebox. My first two records were *Tuby the Tuba* and *Big Rock Candy Mountain*. I loved to watch them whirl while I was dreaming. Then, when I was 9, my family moved to South Jersey and my music teacher loved Opera. He would bring these albums to class and play Verdi and Puccini. I was also really impressed by the singing of Maria Callas—her emotional intensity and depth. At that time I was dreaming that I would become an opera singer—but I just didn't have the talent for it, the body structure or the needed discipline.

Later on, I dreamed of becoming a jazz singer, like June Christie or Billie Holiday, with a mournful voice. But the song that left the greatest impression on me, that fascinated me the most, was *Tutti Frutti* by Little Richard. That's how rock and roll was born in my life. But I never ever dreamed that I'd be singing in a rock and roll band. Anyhow, the Jerry Garcia story happened when I was living in Michigan and various things were occurring in my life and I was a little blue. My hair was starting to turn gray, and I knew I would get old, but watching one's hair turn different colors is weird. So I went to the doctor and said, "something's wrong with my hair. I think I have iron deficiency anemia or something, my hair's turning silver." The doctor said, "yes, it's called getting old."

So I was having a bad laundry day, and feeling a little down, and all of a sudden out of nowhere I saw this vision of Jerry. I know this sounds like people who say they see Jesus in a potato chip, but this actually happened. I saw a distinct vision of Jerry just smiling at me with a twinkle in his eye. Then right after that, this little song came into my head. I don't write that many songs by myself, but this whole song just came into my head, so I sat down and writ it and when I was done, I decided because Jerry seemed to give it to me, that I'd call it "Grateful." And as I've often said, I truly am.

PATTI SMITH DISCUSSES *TWELVE* ON *WORDS AND MUSIC*

Rita Houston | April 11, 2007 | WFUV

Patti Smith has demonstrated a love of good public radio throughout her career, and WFUV in New York is one of the stations she has supported. Owned by Fordham University, the NPR affiliate has been a strong alternative voice on the air since it began broadcasting in 1947. Here, Smith discusses *Twelve*, her 2007 covers album for Columbia Records, which includes music from the Rolling Stones, the Allman Brothers Band, and Jefferson Airplane.

Smith, at the time a recent inductee to the Rock and Roll Hall of Fame, approached the interview with humility. She didn't feel ready for a full cover album until then, she told WFUV deejay Rita Houston, and remained an eternal student. She was self-deprecating about her on-air performance with son Jackson Smith and Lenny Kaye, too, telling the station to mix her down. When she stood on stage at the Waldorf Astoria on March 12, 2007, for her induction ceremony, a group performance of "People Have the Power," which she cowrote with her late husband, Fred "Sonic" Smith, rendered her speechless. Keith Richards, Fred's favorite guitarist, was on guitar. —Ed.

Words and Music, April 11, 2007

[Theme music]

Patti Smith: I have pretty much seen the complete history of rock 'n' roll unfold in my lifetime, and just wanted to give a little salute. Really, just 'cause I wanted to. It's just, why not?

Rita Houston: Rock 'n' roll is as much about music and talent as defying expectation. Patti Smith has covered all three in her now Hall of Fame career, and adds a few more surprises on her new album, *Twelve*. Tonight on *Words and Music from Studio A*, a conversation and performance with Patti Smith.

Announcer: *Words and Music* is supported by BK Eyewitness Travel Guides. Information at travel.bk.com. The guides that show you what others only tell you.

Houston: Hi, this is Rita Houston. News of a covers album is also followed by some hesitance, wondering, why do we need another version of a perfectly good song? Or did the artist just not feel like writing? But when that artist is Patti Smith, history removes all doubt, and all you have to do is go back to that first track on *Horses* to hear why. True, the words to "Gloria" belong to Van Morrison, but the life, breath, and raw power are pure Patti. Fast-forward to her new album, *Twelve*, and Patti is once again immersing herself in the words of others. And a range of artists from Dylan to Nirvana, Hendrix to Tears for Fears was just one of the topics we covered in Patti's visit to WFUV prior to her recent shows in New York City. Her son Jackson and guitarist Lenny Kaye came along as well to perform a few tunes live and acoustic. But the electric guitars are needed on this track, so let's get rolling with this one from the CD, *Twelve*. Here's Patti Smith and "Gimme Shelter" on FUV.

[Patti Smith, "Gimme Shelter," Twelve *comes on.]*

Houston: Patti Smith from the brand new album, *Twelve*, and the Stones tune "Gimme Shelter," in her very capable hands. Hi, Patti Smith.

Smith: Hi, nice to see you.

Houston: Good to see you. You brought along Jackson and Lenny Kaye, too.

Smith: Yes, I brought my son, Jackson Smith, and Lenny Kaye, and it's nice to stop by.

Houston: We're glad to have you here. Um, love this new album. Made up entirely of other people's songs this time around. Tunes from the '60s, '70s, '80s, and '90s. First question: Why a whole album of covers?

Smith: Well, I always wanted to do a cover record. Always. I wanted to do one in the '70s, but really felt, um, I just wasn't familiar enough with singing and just didn't feel that I had the scope, the range, the experience to do a whole album, and so just at this time in my life, I feel that I do. My band does. I have pretty much seen the complete history of rock 'n' roll unfold in my lifetime, and just wanted to give a little salute. Really, just 'cause I wanted to.

Houston: Right, right.

Smith: It's just, why not?

Houston: Exactly. You kind of started—"Hey Joe" was one of your first, your version of "Hey Joe" was one of your first releases, so it's kind of an interesting . . . you never strayed far away, but I guess a whole record is definitely . . .

Smith: Well, I, uh, you know, I didn't enter into rock 'n' roll as a singer-songwriter. I entered it, you know, with Lenny Kaye and Richard Sohl, as a poet. And often gravitated toward other people's work because I had no real foothold in creating work myself. I learned how to write songs working with Lenny and Richard, and I'm still learning. So it's a pleasure to work with other people's songs who have devoted their whole life to writing songs. For me, it's part of what I do, so it's also nice to work with people's lyrics who say a lot very simply, something I'm still struggling with, so . . .

Houston: "Gimme Shelter" becomes a whole other tune when it's sung by a woman. Was that part of what drew you to it?

Smith: No, I don't see, I don't think that has anything to do with it. It's an antiwar song. I don't think it has to do with any gender at all. I mean, I think that the only thing that might shift it a little, is when it came out done by the Rolling Stones, it was such a magnificent dance song that perhaps it obscured the lyrics for some, myself included. And it wasn't until I sang the song myself that I understood the power of these lyrics. 'Cause basically, you know, uh, to me, Mick is saying, love is a kiss away, and war is a shot away, and they're equally attainable. And, you know, what do we do from there? So I don't think of it as a gender-oriented song.

Houston: I guess some are and some aren't. Some tunes change and some don't.

Smith: Well, I think it's not even that they change. I just think that on our particular album, we were extremely centered on the lyric power of the songs, and we stripped down a lot of songs, and opted to focus on the lyrics, and that was my intent and our collective mission was to focus on the lyric power of all these artists. And even though a song like "Everybody Wants to Rule the World," um, I did the song because that one sentence I thought completely summed up our, you know, our global condition. And that's the brilliance of a really good pop song, that quite a bit is said in a sentence.

Houston: Another tune that really grabbed me on the new record is "Boy in a Bubble," because again, like you're saying, the lyrical power of a song . . .

Smith: Well, yeah. We did that a hundred percent because of the lyric. I was never, I don't really like Simon and Garfunkel music, or I don't really, I'm not, I don't gravitate toward Paul Simon's music, but he wrote brilliant lyrics. He wrote a lyric in "The Boy in the Bubble" which completely reflects our condition now, with cameras moving in slo-mo, and the bomb in the baby carriage, and lasers in the jungle, and exploitation of young, so I think that, I just stepped aside and thought, it doesn't matter whether I'm a fan or not. The artist has written great lyrics, and I wanted to sing them, because they speak for, you know, like I said, they speak for our present condition.

Houston: Yeah, it's amazing how a tune can travel through time and still ring true.

Smith: Yeah.

Houston: Patti Smith is with us here. You guys want to play some live for us? What do you want to start with?

Smith: Well, the three of us just stoppin' by, but um, we thought it would be nice to do a couple of songs. We're playing acoustically. This song was written by Neil Young, and chose to cover this song just 'cause it's beautiful, a beautiful, touching song, and we actually had the opportunity to perform this song with Neil, and so it has some kind of special, we have a special personal attachment to it. So, "Helpless" by Neil Young.

[They play "Helpless" by Neil Young]

Houston: Sounds great, thank you.

Smith: Thank you.

Houston: That's Patti Smith, live on the radio with us here at 90.7 FM, WFUV. Where did you guys do that one with Neil Young?

Smith: Um, it was at his annual Bridge concert, which he has a school called the Bridge School [*a Hillsborough, California school for children with severe speech and physical impairments. —Ed.*], which it's a foundation and a school to aid handicapped children. Is that right, Lenny?

Lenny Kaye: Yeah, yeah.

Smith: And do you remember what year that was?

Kaye: Jeez, it was in the late '90s. That's what I remember. '98 or '99 or something.

Smith: That was really great. He does it every year. We were lucky to do it with, I think Pete Townshend was there, and David Bowie. And at the end, everyone, and Crazy Horse, and everyone was on the stage, and we did the song. And it's always stayed in my mind, and um, a lot of people have done versions of it; k.d. lang does a beautiful version of it. Ours is sort of a simple, late-night version.

Houston: Yeah, very nice. You were just part of a big, you know, everybody on stage to sing a song encore at the Rock and Roll Hall of Fame, and the song was "People Have the Power." What was that like for you? You want to tell us a tale of what that . . . what was your experience? It must have been pretty like, whoa . . .

Smith: It was actually really moving, because "People Have the Power" was essentially written by my late husband, Fred "Sonic" Smith. It was his concept. I did write the lyrics, but the title, "People Have the Power," and the idea was his. And I know, one of the reasons he wanted for us to write the song and record it was in hopes that it would become a touchstone for people trying to express both individual and collective rights and power of the people. And I just know that he would have loved to see everybody doing it, especially since Keith Richards was his favorite guitar player. And to see, I just stood there actually. I stopped singing. I stood there and watched Keith playing Fred's chords and soloing to Fred's song, and it was just a happy, moving experience.

Houston: And how about the whole ceremony and being inducted into the Rock and Roll Hall of Fame? Is that something that is, it's got to be meaningful, right?

Smith: Certainly. Because it's not an award, it's an acknowledgment of, you know, at least twenty-five, thirty years of work, and so for me it's an acknowledgment of the work that we've all done: my band, my crew, everyone that helped us. The people that have supported us through the years, the companies that shepherd us, so I feel that it's a collective acknowledgment, so I'm proud of that.

Houston: Yeah. That was cool. Uh, also recently in New York was the show at Carnegie Hall where a bunch of artists got together to sing Bruce [Springsteen] tunes, and of course your choice was a natural, "Because the Night." Tell us the story, Patti, of that tune. The writing of "Because the Night."

Smith: Well, I, um, actually I was asked to quickly sub for Jewel, who was ill, so we did a very stripped-down version of that song. Tony Shanahan played piano, and it was sort of a last-minute thing, and it's always great to play Carnegie Hall, and always grateful to Bruce for offering the song to me in, what year was it?

Kaye: '77 we recorded it. It came out in '78.

Smith: Oh, so . . . Lenny's the date keeper. [*All laugh.*] And I can't be trusted with dates. But, um, well we were recording *Easter* at the time.

I had just had a very serious accident and hadn't been able to work for some months. So we didn't have our usual timespan to work on songs. Bruce was in the middle of a complex legal situation and not recording. And he offered the song to me through Jimmy Iovine, who was producing our record. And, um, I had it in my possession for a little while, but I was really trying to, we really wanted to write our own songs. And, um, the truth of the matter was I was up all night one night waiting for my, the fella in my life, which was Fred, who was living in Detroit, and he told me he would call me at seven o'clock. And eight o'clock came, and nine o'clock came. And I'm just one of those girls that'll wait all night for a phone call. You know, I don't have . . . you know, I'm, I won't just like say screw him, and go out. You know? I sit and wait for the phone call. So I was gettin' really agitated, and I put on this cassette tape from Bruce, and I listened to the song, and I realized that, I mean, this was a great song. It was in my key, the key of A, it was already beautifully arranged. He had the chorus and a lot of mumbling, so I filled in the blanks, waiting for Fred to call, and that's why it says, "Have I doubt when I'm alone, love is a ring, the telephone." 'Cause I was waiting for that phone to ring, and it did, at three in the morning. It did finally ring, but by the time Fred had called, I had done my part in what became for us, was our most popular song.

Houston: And again, a song that a lot of people have also recorded over the years, too.

Smith: Yes.

Houston: Your version is fantastic, and your version with Tony Shanahan the other night at Carnegie Hall was just beautiful.

Smith: Well, it's, Carnegie Hall, it's so great to sing there. It's, uh, one can almost feel like a great singer there. It's got such great acoustics, so it's always a pleasure to play at Carnegie Hall. And I've played there many times. Always a benefit. So it's always a nice feeling stepping on the stage of Carnegie Hall.

Houston: Patti Smith is our guest here at 90.7 FM, WFUV. What song do you guys want to play for us now?

Smith: Well, we're gonna attempt another song on the record. We've never done this in this configuration, but we'll try it out. It's an Allman Brothers song. I chose this song because I just love it. I've always loved it. I reviewed it when it came out in, I think, 1970—on *Idlewild* [*South*]. Was it 1970, Lenny, you think?

Kaye: I believe so. [Idlewild South *was released September 23, 1970. —Ed.*]

Smith: And, uh, I reviewed it, 'cause I sometimes wrote rec reviews back then. And, uh, I met all the fellas, and they were really nice, and I just love the lyrics to this song. I relate to them personally. So we'll try it out, and that's all I could say.

[*"Midnight Rider," by Gregg Allman, plays.*]

Houston: That's great, thank you.

Smith: Thanks. That was my son Jackson playing lead. And we'll be coming to your town soon.

Houston: So what's the configuration for the tour? I know there are a couple dates in New York and then you guys are headed to Europe. What are the plans?

Smith: Um, Lenny Kaye and Jackson on guitar, Tony Shanahan on bass and keyboards, and Jay Dee Daugherty on drums. And so we're really looking forward to it. Tourin' the world, on a bus.

Houston: Jackson, it's got to be weird to go on the road with your mom, right?

Jackson Smith: Uh, not really.

[*All laugh.*]

Houston: All right, Patti, is it weird to go on the road with your son?

Smith: He's my son, you know. It's always an adventure. You're, you know, life, family life is always comforting and weird. You know, that's part of the equation. So I think, uh, I think we understand each other. We know how not to get in each other's way and how to support each other, so I think it'll be just fine.

Houston: [*Laughs.*] And how about these shows in New York, you're callin' 'em the Bowery Sessions [*on Tuesday, April 24, 2007, Smith performed three "Bowery Sessions" shows at the Bowery Ballroom in New York City —Ed.*]. What's gonna be happenin' that night?

Smith: Uh, the Bowery Sessions, I love it. I think somebody at our record company invented that very high-class name. Um, basically, it's just a nice get-together. It's really, without being cynical about it, it's to promote the record. We're, it's people buy the record, and they can come. They're about a half-hour long, and they're whatever we make 'em. It's not the full band, because our bass player, Tony Shanahan, is getting married, and he and his bride will be off somewhere special. But we'll be there, just sort of foolin' around, doin' songs, answerin' questions, reading poetry. It's really to hopefully get acquainted with new people, and, you know, say hello, see what they're thinkin' about, see what they want. It is like three half-an-hour, a little more, and it's just really gonna be gettin' to know each other, you know, without much pressure, and havin' fun.

Jackson Smith: May I add, too, if you buy the three-session ticket, you get a special seven-inch or somethin'.

Smith: Well, thanks, Jack. Well, I've seen the seven-inch that you get if you buy all three, and it's actually worth it. It's actually really nice, because the two cuts on it, they're, they were two songs that we cut the same time as the album. They're not stragglers, they're strong cuts. So I think people will be happy with 'em.

Houston: What are the cuts?

Smith: Uh, "Perfect Day" by Lou Reed and the Decemberists song, "I Dreamed I Was an Architect."

Houston: Beautiful.

Smith: And we just partially didn't finish them in time, and could only put so many songs on the record, but I think they're worth hearing.

Houston: Cool. And that's an old 45, right?

Smith: Yup.

Houston: A real 45.

Smith: Yeah, it's a real 45, with a record sleeve and everything.

Houston: The next question has gotta be, what was your first 45?

Smith: Uh, my very first 45 was "Big Rock Candy Mountain." And I still can see it. And on the B-side . . . no, it was "Big Rock Candy Mountain," part one and two. So that was my first single.

Houston: Wow.

Smith: And what was yours, Lenny?

Kaye: I bought four singles the first time I ever went out when I was a teeny kid. I bought "The Purple People Eater" by Sheb Wooley. "It's Only Make Believe" by Conway Twitty.

Smith: Oh. I love Conway Twitty, too. Yeah.

Kaye: [*sings opening to "It's Only Make Believe"*] "People see us everywhere . . . " Um, "It's All in the Game" by Tommy Edwards, and I think something by Cathy Carr, but I can't remember what it was.

Smith: I remember.

Kaye: "To Know Him Is to Love Him."

Smith: Oh, oh my gosh, what a great song.

Houston: Oh. A heartbreaker.

Kaye: Yeah, but since I didn't know it, I didn't get the Teddy Bears version, but it's a beautiful song.

Smith: Beautiful.

Kaye: In fact, we should do that sometime.

Smith: I remember, we went out, and singles at that time cost twenty-five cents. And it was a big day. We were each, my mother got a singles machine, and she was a waitress. And she took her tip money, and we were all allowed to get a single. And she got "Sunday Driving" and "Come Rain or Come Shine" by Jerry Lewis.

[*All laugh.*]

Houston: Jackson, your first 45?

Jackson Smith: It was a Nashville [*expletive bleep; Nashville Pussy —Ed.*] single, and I honestly can't remember the song, 'cause I bought it solely for the cover.

Smith: He's not on mic, is he? Can they hear what he's saying?

Houston: Yeah.

Jackson Smith: I'm sure they can hear me a little bit.

Smith: Did I pay for that, Jackson?

Jackson Smith: No, I used my Subterranean Records.

Smith: Oh, you paid for Nashville [*expletive bleep; Nashville Pussy —Ed.*] with your own money.

Jackson Smith: I did.

Smith: Good boy.

Jackson Smith: And then later in life, I got to play with them in part of their US tour. A band I was playing in opened up for them. So that was pretty cool. But not probably part of the type of music your target audience listens to.

[*All laugh.*]

Smith: Probably more than we know.

Houston: You're opening eyes.

Smith: But that's a beautiful story. To get a single, and to like somebody, and to get to play with them. I mean, those things are magical. Whether it's Bob Dylan or Nashville [*expletive bleep; Pussy —Ed.*]. It's a magical thing.

Houston: Part of the whole circle of life, if you will. You know, it's like—

Smith: It's everybody bein' into music, whether one calls themselves a fan or a player, eventually we all merge or cross over the border, so . . . that's nice, that's a nice story. I didn't know that.

Houston: Patti, you mentioned Dylan. Your version of "Wicked Messenger" is one of my absolute favorite just plain old songs, you know.

Smith: Thank you.

Houston: There is, for me, as a music lover, a real affinity between your work and Dylan's work. That's sort of the way I hear it, and love both of you. Do you get to talk to Dylan? Do you ever share work? Is there a connection that is sort of a professional one between you guys?

Smith: I have my own connection with him. He's a very private man, so I think that that says it all. And I always felt connected with him since I first saw him play with Joan Baez in 1963, so in my life, I've had, as Jackson experienced—you experienced somebody, through listening to their work or seein' them, and one day you get to sing with them, and you get to talk with them. And, you know, we're all human beings, and it's just, um, you know, Bob is a private guy.

Houston: And your take on like *Modern Times*, or *Love and Theft*? I mean, do you love the new Dylan records?

Smith: I like "Nettie Moore." [*On* Modern Times —Ed.] Of his last albums, there's always a song or two that makes me cry, on every album. You know, "It's Not Dark Yet." But the last album that I actually deeply, deeply loved was *World Gone Wrong*. I loved that record. I thought it was great. I listened to that record hundreds of times. And, uh, lately, I usually get "When the Deal Goes Down," but I love "Nettie Moore," that's a really great song.

Houston: That's one of the songs that's just like, what other song is like that song, you know?

Smith: Yeah, it's one of those songs that always make you wish you were Nettie Moore.

Houston: Yeah. "Oh, I miss you, Nettie Moore." Patti Smith is our guest here on WFUV. Uh, what song do you guys want to play for us now?

Smith: Well, we're gonna do a song that I writ when we were workin' on *Trampin'*. And it's called "My Blakean Year." I'm gonna play a little guitar with it, and hopefully they'll mix my part low. Anyway, thanks for havin' us. [*Sings "My Blakean Year."*]

Houston: Thank you. That's great, you guys. That's Patti Smith, live on the radio with us here at 90.7 FM, WFUV. Brand-new album just out on Columbia. The album is called *Twelve*. So titled for the twelve songs on it.

Smith: Well, yup. It's twelve songs, and I didn't realize this till it was done, but it was pointed out to me that it was also my twelfth record, so I guess it's aptly named.

Houston: Fantastic. Always great to talk to you, and throw a microphone in your hands.

Smith: Thanks a lot. Thanks for the opportunity.

Houston: We'll go out here with a guest deejay pick. You get to play deejay, and anything at all. Your choice.

Smith: Well, I'd like to hear anything by My Bloody Valentine.

Houston: Here it is. And thanks to Patti Smith. Playin' a guest deejay pick for Patti Smith. That's the band My Bloody Valentine, and the tune, "Only Shallow." And thanks again to Patti Smith, Lenny Kaye, and Jackson Smith for the visit. Today's studio session was engineered by Tommy Englehardt and *Words and Music* from Studio A is produced by Sarah Wardrop.

EXIT INTERVIEW: PATTI SMITH

Richard Rys | July 22, 2008 | *Philadelphia*

In the spring of 2008, Patti Smith opened *Patti Smith, Land 250*, an exhibit of more than two hundred of her Polaroid photographs at the Fondation Cartier in Paris, but for at least a day, her mind was in Philly. Having established her reputation as a South Jersey defector from the autobiographical "Piss Factory," here she takes a moment to reflect on some of the good things about the area and the nearby City of Brotherly Love. That May, she had proudly received an honorary degree from Rowan University (formerly Glassboro State College), where she was known as an artist and contributed illustrations to the yearbook. She dropped out before graduating, moved to New York in 1967, and the rest is history. Interviewer Richard Rys graduated from the school.

Sharon DeLano's revelatory 2002 *New Yorker* profile of Smith opened in Philadelphia at Independence Hall, a favorite landmark Rys and Smith discuss here, but in the pages of the *New Yorker*, Smith never weighed in on the one truly important question any Philly resident would have: Pat's or Geno's? —Ed.

Exit Interview and rock legend Patti Smith have something in common: both went to Rowan University (Glassboro State in her day). That's where the similarities end: Smith, a Deptford High grad, left the 'Boro to become a groundbreaking singer, artist, activist, and inductee into the Rock and Roll Hall of Fame; Exit Interview asks famous people stupid questions. The 61-year-old phoned from Paris to discuss the new biographical book and documentary *Patti Smith: Dream of Life*, and in the process revealed herself to be *way* more in love with South Jersey and cheesesteaks than expected.

What are you doing in France? I have a few days off, so I'm closing out my exhibition in Paris, then I'm going to Munich to see Waltraud Meier, my favorite opera singer, in *Tristan and Isolde*. Eventually I'm going to make my way to Beirut to start my tour.

I feel so insignificant. What was your childhood like growing up in South Jersey? I lived in the Deptford Township area. We moved from Germantown. It was very rural in South Jersey in the late '50s. I gravitated toward art, even as a small child. It was just within me. Although I had a happy childhood, I needed to be where there was more culture available to me.

So the lyrics to your song "Piss Factory"—"I'm gonna be a big star and I will never return/Never return, no, never return, to burn out in this piss factory" . . . That summed it up. [laughs] I was 16, working at a factory with no air-conditioning, minimum wage, and very grueling, repetitious work. A lot of people worked there their whole lives, either by necessity or design. I really didn't want to do that.

When you attended Glassboro State College, it was still known as a teacher's college. Did you want to be a teacher? I wanted to be an artist and a writer, but I didn't have the money to go to art school, so my alternative was Glassboro. I worked my way through three years, and I got a great education there.

Why did you drop out? I couldn't pass biology or the higher mathematics. I could get straight A's in art, writing and student teaching, but I didn't have the stuff to get through trigonometry.

So we have Glassboro's advanced math curriculum to thank for all your music. Otherwise, you might have become Professor Smith. [laughs] Well, there's no shame in that. They had a theater program, and I found I liked performing in front of people.

Did your honorary degree from Rowan University this year rank up there with getting into the Rock and Roll Hall of Fame? Yes! Of course!

For me, one of my proudest things in life was that at Deptford High School, I, in 1964, was Spartan of the Year.

[**Laughs**] To this day, that's very important to me.

[**Realizes she's not kidding**] **Wow.** It was an affirmation that people believed in what I was doing, even though I couldn't exactly say I knew what I was doing. [laughs] So when I look at the things of that type of importance, it was that, receiving a medal from the French Republic, being inducted into the Rock and Roll Hall of Fame, and getting a Doctor of Letters at the college I attended. They're all tremendous landmarks that I'm proud of.

They should build a Patti Smith wing at Deptford High or something. [laughs] No, no, no. I just loved my high school. To this day, truthfully, I don't know why they gave it to me. I wish I'd asked somebody: "Why me?" I wasn't an exceptional student. I subsequently lost my Spartan of the Year badge, but I still cherish the memory.

Your book and the documentary have been 11 years in the making. That's an Axl Rose pace. What's the deal? That's a little misleading. Steven [Sebring, the director/photographer] intermittently went on the road with me. It had no real design. It's really Steven's portrait of me and what I do, whether it's painting or protesting or taking care of my children.

In the process of Sebring discovering who Patti Smith is, did Patti Smith discover who Patti Smith is? I had lost my husband and my brother and my best friend and my pianist, and I was at a real low in my life. If there's any message in the film, it's that despite whatever we go through, if we stay positive and work hard, we'll prevail.

This is rather random, but have you ever eaten a cheesesteak? Well, yeah, about a thousand of them! I was there not long ago with my son, and we went to Pat's and Geno's and had a taste test. My son liked Pat's. I liked Geno's. When I go to Philly, that's the first thing I do. I want to visit Independence Hall, walk the historic streets, and have my cheesesteak. I like it without cheese and with lettuce and hot peppers.

It would blow my mind if I saw Patti Smith walking around the Liberty Bell with a cheesesteak. It's quite possible.

PATTI SMITH AND STEVEN SEBRING ON *PATTI SMITH: DREAM OF LIFE*

Anthony DeCurtis | December 29, 2009 | *POV*

"Life is an adventure of our own design, intersected by fate and a series of lucky and unlucky accidents," begins Patti Smith's voice-over at the opening of Steven Sebring's beautifully rendered 2008 documentary *Patti Smith: Dream of Life*. One of those lucky accidents was the meeting of Smith and Sebring, a noted fashion photographer who shot her for a *Spin* feature in 1995 and documented their deepening friendship over a twelve-year period. The film itself was a lucky accident as well; as he explained here, when Sebring began shooting footage on his 16-millimeter camera, he had no idea what it would become. It was his first foray into the medium, and it channeled the renegade spirit of Smith's *Horses*, where inexperience didn't mean inability but possibility—an "air of experience and aesthetic sophistication weaves in with the amateur aspects of it."

The film gradually took shape as a life-affirming visual tone poem, a nonlinear narrative tracking Smith's experiences and insights, which reflect "the rhythm of [her] life" at the time of filming. The multilayered film gives us a glimpse of Smith backstage on tour, a sense of her interior consciousness, and takes us into her bedroom. The bedroom was her inner sanctum that doubled as her atelier, where we can imagine *Just Kids* coming together—she often wrote in bed. Smith offered a modest plug for her then-forthcoming memoir, which she describes as "a book about art, life, friendship."

Dream of Life, Smith said, has blood. Alongside Sebring, she explained that and more to award-winning *Rolling Stone* writer, editor, professor, and Lou Reed–biographer Anthony DeCurtis in this frank interview, which aired as part of the film's release on the PBS series *POV*.

Synthesized from the original text transcript and the final edited product, these interview excerpts capture Smith's spontaneous energy and her total commitment to her art. "If you're doing a performance for four or five people, you do it with the same conviction as when you go on stage and there's forty thousand people," Smith told DeCurtis. "You don't do things by degrees. I mean, if one has a vision then one brings that vision into everything they do." The same applies to her interviews. —Ed.

Anthony DeCurtis: You know Steven I was struck by one of the things that Patti said in the movie which was, she was describing that things are not necessarily chronological, that you don't live your life in a linear way. Your perceptions of what you're hearing, what you're seeing, you're thinking about all come into whatever your experience of life is. And it seemed to me that that was kind of, almost the technique of the film, you know, and I wonder if you could talk about, you know from your vantage, you know what your sense was about creating a movie in that way.

Steven Sebring: Well number one, it was modge-podge of footage and so it was so periodically that we would film. It wasn't all the time. So, so really nothing was synced or nothing was slated in the film. So it had that, I think it just became this organic piece when we started editing, where it became nonlinear and it just sort of became its own animal, its own beast.

Patti Smith: It was born nonlinear.

Sebring: It was born nonlinear. It's, it's so true. There was no way to like, to keep it that way. And I didn't want to tame it either, I wanted it to be different. So not your typical documentary.

DeCurtis: Can you talk about, you know a bit about your background and how that affected the kind of work that you were doing on the film?

Sebring: Well, my background is fashion and I photograph a lot of artists as well. So for me moving to film was very easy for me because I think sometimes my fashion pictures can look a little bit like documentary style pictures. So for me just to put a camera in my hand it was pretty normal. But I never went to film school, so I just sort of learned. She was sort of my experiment to be honest with you. And that's what we, that's what we got out of it. I learned a lot about how to make a film at, at the end of the day. So.

DeCurtis: Can you talk about, the two of you, can you talk about you know how you met?

Sebring: Do you want to talk about that one?

Smith: Well after, I had, I hadn't performed or been in the public eye for about 16 years. And when my husband passed away, I was obliged to go back to work to take care of our kids, but also I wanted to do a record in memory of him. So we did *Gone Again*. And I had to be photographed and go back to doing articles and interviews, something I hadn't thought of. But also with the death of Robert Mapplethorpe, I had lost my main collaborator in taking photographs. So I really didn't know who to work with. So I had met Michael Stipe and he was such a kind person and extremely understanding and I asked him if he knew a photographer that could, that would come to Detroit where I lived, that would be child friendly, that would respect my home. And he suggested Steven. And so I asked for Steven and one day a knock came on my door and I opened the door and there was Steven and he's been like a brother ever since.

DeCurtis: Steven, can you talk about that day or getting this opportunity to go and shoot Patti? Had you been familiar with her work?

Sebring: I wasn't familiar with her much at all actually. When I was asked to photograph her, my wife was like, "Oh my god, Patti Smith." So I looked at some Robert Mapplethorpe books and stuff. And I did remember those pictures. And so when I went there I was sort of very naïve about it. And I think that she picked up on that.

Smith: He didn't know anything.

Sebring: I think she picked up on that quite quickly, you know. And but, I, I like not knowing too much about somebody that I'm photographing anyway too, because it's more of an experience for me to learn about them. But I really quickly realized that she was somebody really special.

And I do remember that door opening and the squeaky door. It's this really old door, and it's, *rrrrrr*. And here is this beautiful, very attractive girl just looking out. And I think you forgot I was even coming.

Smith: Probably.

Sebring: She…I think she was a little bit shocked, the fact that I actually showed up. So, but we immediately just hung out and I think that if I remember right, she had to remind me to take a picture because I think towards the end of the day we took some pictures and I think I only talked, took maybe ten rolls of film.

Smith: Yeah, he just fell in with family life. You know was helping me wash dishes, play with the kids. And he immediately, I could tell that he was a person that understood families and this also was very nice for my children who quite naturally in losing their father, craved, you know, a warm male attention. And they gravitated to him right away.

Sebring: It was a beautiful moment. And I won't forget that day.

DeCurtis: Well, look at what it's led to.

Sebring: And I thank Michael [*Stipe* —Ed.], I mean, Michael if he wouldn't have mentioned my name, I mean.

Smith: Well I trusted him as I always have.

DeCurtis: You know Patti you talk in this particular anecdote even about family a lot. And somebody might expect like a different scene to go . . . I mean obviously, you know, you're an important recording artist and had done poetry. And by that point your absence had almost made you a kind of even bigger in a sense in people's minds. And so you know you might have mentioned somebody coming who just only had that sense about you, without the family, without the kids, without the other stuff. I wonder if you could talk about the relationship between those two things, you know, a kind of identity you know out in the world that maybe it's one way, a day to day aspect of your life that maybe involves a lot of other things.

Smith: Well, I think it wasn't so difficult for me because I don't have two separate personas. I mean, when I'm on stage and working, I channel different things, you know, different styles or different aspects of aggression or anger or political fervor that I keep more balanced offstage. But I'm not really that different. And I've never really been interested in being like a celebrity style person. I just want to be able to do my work and I like conversing with the people. And I don't like a lot of fuss. You know, I don't want like, I didn't want limos and bodyguards and people fussing around me. So I've pretty much always stayed the same. And at home, you know, I was a mom. My kids didn't even know I did anything, except tend to them. Even now, I mean. They comprehend my work. They've worked with me. We've all performed together in front of thousands of people, but they still look at me as their mom, who's going to sew a button or, you know, tend to them if they're sick, or remember their father with them. You know, they don't look at me, they don't have a separate identity for me, and, and I don't want one.

So you know, I felt when Steven came we just all . . . The reason it worked is 'cause we're all humans. I mean he's a very, he's a humanistic guy. He's a, he's a couldn't, shouldn't say normal, because no artist is really normal, but he's human. And he related to our situation in a human way, in a compassionate way. He was great with my kids. And we, we just, you know, relate to people, to each other as, as friends. You know, we don't have this other area where one has a career or one's this or that—we're friends. And even like siblings, I could say. So, I hope that . . . .

DeCurtis: That perfectly answers the question, yeah, absolutely.

Smith: Sorry if I ramble, I'm a rambling kind of gal.

DeCurtis: You were born a rambling gal. In relation to walking into that situation and not really necessarily knowing a lot about Patti, at what point did the idea of doing a film start to come up?

Sebring: Oh, you know, I knew that there wasn't a whole lot of information about her when I started. And I periodically was interested in films, so I just kept asking her, can I come around and come by? And she really let me in in London, when she first started to tour. And I remember the band members just like shocked at the fact that—especially Lenny,

Lenny Kaye was like shocked that I was coming along to film Patti. He didn't know what to think of that. And I was just really not, the whole idea of me making a movie at the beginning, I didn't even think that. I was just thinking of just documenting somebody. And it didn't really occur to me to make a film out of it towards really late in the years, you know. 'Cause totally it took twelve years to put this film together. But not till the end. I looked at Patti and I said, "Well maybe we should do something with this footage."

And I came up with some more money and, and took all this stuff and got a great editor and sort of made this film. So I really didn't go with this intention of making a movie. And I think that's why the film is like the way it is, because we always say it's a lot like home movies. Like I was just documenting her parents, you know.

Smith: Home movies shot by an artist, though.

Sebring: You know it was like I shot it all in 16-millimeter. I didn't want sway to video or anything like that, I just wanted to do something and really learn about her. That's why I think that film is from my perspective of learning about one, because I never once asked her questions in the film.

Smith: I think the film really says as much about Steven as a human being as—I mean, I know that it's centered around myself—but when I watch the film I see a lot of Steven because another person would have done everything they could to find something mean-spirited in our operation, which they'd be hard-pressed to find. But he was, he's not like that. And if someone didn't want to be filmed or my children said "don't film me anymore," he didn't try to sneak a shot or cajole them, he just respected that. But I had actually another motivation for letting Steven film us. I think really after sixteen years of being out of the public eye, losing my friends and losing my husband, some of my confidence, I should say undermined, but it was, it wasn't stable.

And he made it fun. You know, I could pretend we were sort of doing sort of a little *Don't Look Back*. And his presence was not threatening. He told me if I never wanted the footage to be seen by anyone he would give it to me. So I had nothing to lose and everything to gain.

You know it was really and what I gained was his supportive energy and the supportive energy of his wife who sometimes was the one who was schlepping, you know, equipment or doing the sound because he essentially did everything himself.

And it gave us the spirit of a camp. Not, I mean, like a military camp, to have, you know, Steven with his heavy camera on his shoulder, and my kids, and the band. And it had such a positive, we were confronting the world in a positive manner. And so it really, the process helped me psychologically, I suppose, get my feet back on the ground. And then, I got used to him.

Sebring: I mean, she was so supportive of me, too, because, I mean, there's nothing more . . . . I didn't have a crew where somebody was loading my camera, you know. So there was a lot of times where I'm like filming something really great and I'm hearing the camera just roll out, you know. "Oh Patti, we have to stop now."

Smith: I'd be like Audrey Hepburn in *Funny Face.* Take the picture, take the picture. And he was like "aaah." On the ground with the black cloth over his head trying to shove film into this . . .

Sebring: It was really difficult at times, I have to tell you, because it was like, I don't have anything like this, you know. And unfortunately, I had to stop for a half hour just to load a couple magazine backs. The old-fashioned one.

DeCurtis: You know what's great is that all of that comes through.

Sebring: We're not trying to hide it.

DeCurtis: No. Well it's, but it really seemed like fun [. . .] It just seemed exciting, you know. And everything was fresh, everything was new, and the whole film has that feel of—just like kids making it up. Kind of like doing, "What are we going to do today?"

Sebring: That's nice.

Smith: Well, there's also another point. I was at one of the lowest points of my life when we started this film, except I had, of course, two great children. But so the film is not documenting a decline, it's documenting a rise up. It's, you know, these baby steps and then big steps up. It's a, it's a, it's a positive thrust. You know, it's not plunging into the darkness of despair and drugs and whatever else can happen. The worst that could have ever happened to me had already happened. And so the film is on the ascent. And I think that's, that gives it a nice spirit.

DeCurtis: You know, there are a couple of things that you talk about in the film, like when you were talking about your brother having died, and your sense of being kind of infused by his spirit. And also you mention Allen Ginsberg's call to you when Fred died, saying, you know, continue the celebration—carry it on. And I wonder if you could talk about that element of it, I mean, 'cause it . . . so often it seems when people think about death, I mean obviously it's a terrible thing, but you seem somehow to have found a way to take something from it and make those people part of your ongoing life and work.

Smith: I've, I mean I've had to. I experienced death as a child when my best friend, when I was about, well, seven or eight, died of lupus, leukemia. And just, I learned really early that we lose people. And I think that going through the death of Robert Mapplethorpe was so devastating and so difficult and all I could . . . The one thing that I did know is our friendship was so deep and, and his consciousness was so intertwined with mine because we bonded so young, that I knew he would still be with me when he died. And he was with me even more, it seemed. And that taught me. It didn't make things less painful for the the people I lost after Robert, but it so proved to me that our people are still with us if we keep our mind, ears, and heart open. It's nothing mystical, it just is. I mean, I've learned from Robert since he died. Argued with him. Walked quietly, saw him sitting. And each person that passes away, passes away differently. Your communication with them is different. With my brother, it's just, as I said in the film, it's a feeling of love. And sometimes I'll be sitting somewhere and I start laughing. I still, I can't even talk about him without, like—he just makes me laugh. You know, he makes me smile. And each loss, whether my husband or my parents, presents a different way that I communicate with them as I go through life—each unexpected, each unique. And there's a certain beauty in that. It doesn't take away the sorrow or the longing to see a person in their earthly state, but, you know, if we lose that possibility there is still a multitude of others. And sorry, this is taking so long. Pasolini said a beautiful thing about this. He said that it is not that the dead do not speak, it's just that we have forgotten how to listen. And that made a lot of sense to me. And we have to just let go of our expectations and just see how they talk to us, each person we lose will speak to us, but in a different way. Sometimes like I said, a flutter of feeling, and sometimes they'll bug you.

———

Sebring: When I was filming Patti painting that scene.

DeCurtis: Yeah.

Sebring: I, it was the first time, I think was the first time I think I miked her with a wireless. And as she was painting, I remember hearing it, hearing the sound and everything together and you could hear her heart beating.

Smith: Yeah.

DeCurtis: Oh, that's fantastic.

Sebring: And so then every time I watch that scene it's like I'm hearing really distantly, you have to be listening for it, but you can hear her heart beat if it's a really good sound system. . . . That was really, really cool.

DeCurtis: The other thing that was cool was just like seeing the mike on the back of your jeans, you know.

Sebring: We don't hide mikes in our operation.

DeCurtis: Yeah, it was just like, what are you going to do?

Smith: No, I'm a singer. I mean, I'm microphone friendly, that's what I was telling the fellow. You know people work so hard to hide microphones and I'm like, hey, it's . . . where would I be without the microphone, you know?

DeCurtis: It's just like television is so annoying, you know. I mean, like commercial TV, where everything is blocked within an inch of its life and it's just ridiculous.

Sebring: You lose all the spontaneity. There's a scene on the DVD where she turned the mike cord into fashion.

Smith: Oh, it's on the . . .

Sebring: I think it's in the DVD extras, right?

Smith: Oh yeah.

Sebring: Where she talks about, she has a black coat, moth-eaten coat. And . . .

Smith: I think I was wearing my shirt. It's just 'cause my pack, it looked really cool, it had the military look. You know, I had the big . . .

Sebring: With the wire coming . . .

Smith: Wires and the pack, the battery pack. And I looked at it and I thought, this is totally cool, you know in the '70s I would have been walking around with that.

Sebring: Oh yeah, you could see it really good in the, in the Washington protest where you got your hands in your back and there's a mike right there.

Smith: Yeah, I like that look.

Sebring: I zoomed in on that mike.

Smith: I always liked the military camp look you know carrying a walkie-talkie . . . the communication tools.

Sebring: Well, and we had, we had "Radio Baghdad" playing on the record player really loud, so we felt like communication had to be . . .

Smith: I'm not a wuss.

Sebring: Yeah, right, exactly, there had to be some communication in the scene.

Smith: I mean look, if, I can understand trying to cover the mike up if it's Ava Gardner or something, but who cares if I got a mike hanging out, you know.

DeCurtis: . . . One of the really interesting things about the film as well is that it's a kind of, in addition to all of the very kind of personal elements, there's a kind of almost, it's a portrait of an artist. And the idea that there's Blake and there's Jackson Pollock, and Rimbaud—these people all being talked about almost in that way that you just described, just kind of living things. It made me think about the quote that's on the back of *Radio Ethiopia* that "beauty will be convulsive or not at all," you know, in that tradition of artists that you are drawn to. I wonder if you could talk about what it was like the first time you read Blake, or the first time you read Rimbaud? The first time that you looked at a Pollock painting, and what you drew from that and how you use it?

Smith: Well, I remember all of these things actually. And the first time I read Blake, my mother, I was an avid reader as a small child and my mother gave me a copy of *Songs of Innocence*. So that was my entrance into Blake. And the, the first time that I saw art actually was when I was about twelve. My father took us on a rare trip because he, my father had worked in a factory, he had four sickly children. They had a lot of money problems. And we didn't go on excursions often. But there was a Salvador Dali show in the Museum of Art in Philadelphia—and *The Persistence of Memory*. And my father found his draftsmanship just astounding, so he wanted to see it in person. So he took us all, or dragged us all to the museum. And I had never seen art in person before. And seeing paintings, seeing Picasso, seeing art, seeing John Singer Sargent. Just any, anything was, I was smitten. I was completely smitten and dreamed of being a painter. And I just, especially Picasso, I just totally fell in love with Picasso. But, you know, all of these things, whether it's Pollock, every time I've seen art that I've responded to, what I'm responding to is something that Steven and I have always worked with, it's that moment of creative impulse. That's what an artist gives you. You know, you look at a Pollock and he can't give you the tools to do a painting like this yourself, but he can in doing the work share with you the moment of creative impulse that drove him to do the work. And, you know, that exchange, that continuous exchange, whether it's through, with a rock 'n' roll song and you're communing with Bo Diddley or Little Richard, or communing with Rembrandt or Pollock, is a great thing. And it's just these moments are what we long for, you know. And that's, it's something that you know, it was so nice working with Steven because we could look for these moments within ourselves or he was in, is interested in everything I was interested in. If I wanted to drag him to a graveyard in the middle of the afternoon, in the middle of London traffic to say hello to William Blake's grave, he was right there. It was fun, you know, and it was also beautiful for the spirit. And also we both wanted to share this with other people. A lot of people might love William Blake, but never get to go to visit his grave. So we wanted to take them with us.

DeCurtis: Steven, can you talk about your own kind of formative experiences and what first drew you to photography and what kind of things got you excited and got you interested in that kind of creativity?

Sebring: I don't know, my family has always been, all my family members are pretty much teachers in the arts. So I picked up a camera years ago when I was in high school. I didn't do well in high school. When I came to take photography class, I keep saying I failed the class and I did 'cause I was doing something that wasn't required. I was doing something beyond, you know, experimenting with it. But I was, I loved being able to capture moments. And it just led to doing it more and more and more. And fashion was sort of the angle for me, because I found it to be really incredible to see couture—you know, see pictures, seeing Irving Penn or Helmut Newton, how they did fashion, I was really intrigued by that. And so that's what led me finally here to New York City. And fashion's been really good to me because it was how I financed the film. And that's also, too, why it took a long time, because of the money. Plus, I wasn't, the main goal wasn't to make a film. But fashion has been good. And I like all media of fashion right now. You can do everything with it, you know. And it's been a really great outlet for me, you know. I'd like to do more of it in the future, but I've been hit with the idea of doing more film and collaborative works with Patti. I mean, we're always thinking about doing other cool short films, not twelve-year projects. But fashion was, in a high school way, I just discovered photography and I loved it. And growing up in Arizona, it was an outlet and it . . . I knew also too in my heart it was a way to travel. You know fashion in Arizona, there is not much of it. So it allowed me to go to Europe and Paris and Italy and live there and, and it's been good to me, so I'm very happy.

DeCurtis: What were your impressions of New York when you came here?

Sebring: I was blown away by it. I was really blown away by it. And it was different then, it was a lot different. It was in '92. It's changed a lot, as everybody says. But it was really . . .

DeCurtis: [People] always say that, no matter when it was.

Sebring: There's like something so alive about it, you know. I spent a lot of time in Times Square, like just like looking around. And I took a lot of pictures. A lot of my early fashion work was done actually in the streets of New York. I have so much stuff of like in Grand Central Station and Penn Station. And just the city streets because I found it so alive and sort of. . . . I love Hitchcock and I love Orson Welles and it just reminded me of the dark sort of flavor, you know, how men wore trench coats. And I would bring the fashion into that kind of realm. So it was very cinematic for me then. But I didn't ever film it. I never shot movie film of those days, but I wish I did. But New York was really an eye-opener for me, it really was. And then not too much later, I think in '95, that's when I met Patti. And then she took me on another ride, you know, which has been quite a journey actually, it's been a really great journey.

DeCurtis: And Patti I know you have your, you have a poem that read about, or recite about New York in the film. I wonder, even though you were obviously closer than Arizona, what did New York represent or symbolize to you?

Smith: Oh, I had the same. I was raised in rural south Jersey. And even though I had done time in Philadelphia, in south Jersey there was nothing cultural there. There was a small library and that was it. There was nothing. And I mean it was a . . . I loved my childhood. I loved my siblings. I loved being a child. But when I craved culture, once I saw art and I wanted to see more art and I fell in love with opera very young and I dreamed about going to the opera, there was nothing there. And the first time I went to New York City, I was in total heaven. I was in heaven. It was like probably I went to New York City in 1964 or something. And because I was made fun of a lot, 'cause I was like a skinny kid with long greasy braids and dressing like a beatnik and I didn't really fit in in my, where I grew up. I didn't look like the other kids. I didn't look like the other girls. I didn't have the beehive. I wasn't going to be a hairdresser. And I just didn't fit in. And in New York, I suddenly just blended in with everybody else. Nobody cared. I didn't get stopped by cops. I didn't, I wasn't, you know, yelled at from cars. I was just, I was free. And I think that's what New York represented to me more than anything was freedom. I could walk anywhere, I didn't have to be afraid. I've never felt afraid in New York City. I've always felt just completely at home. And it's a walker city—I don't know how to drive, so you can . . . it's on a grid, I didn't get lost. And also, I totally fell in love with the Empire State Building. So. But I love New York. But there's also something that's, that. . . . When Steven was talking about fashion and when he was a teenager, I was remembering how I, my entrance into photography was also fashion, looking at *Vogues* and *Bazaars* in the '50s. It's where I found a lot about art. That's where I found Jackson Pollock, I think, in an old *Harper's Bazaar*. And I saw Irving Penn photographs and early Diane Arbus photographs. And you know just . . . .

I found that there was an aesthetic that didn't exist in the *Sears* catalog. You know, that there was some other way of looking at things and I craved that. And I think that's the real beauty of fashion, especially fashion photography at its greatest in the '50s and '60s because it, fashion and art, high fashion and art were synonymous, you know. And it wasn't really a commercial way of. . . . I mean, I look at people that did high fashion photography, early Avedon and of course, like Penn was such a master. But there's so many—they were artists. You know, it wasn't like commercial photography—this was, we were seeing these gowns and dresses and gloves and hats in a way that could only be deemed as art. So I have my own salute to fashion no matter how I look.

DeCurtis: One of the themes of the film that gets talked about is the idea of generations and, generations of artists. But generation is also part of the kind of personal life that's depicted in the film. You know, your own children, you and your parents. And now you came of age, as I did at a time when, you know, the whole thing, it's kind of "don't trust anybody over 30 and you know like . . ." But you seem to have a very warm relationship with your parents. I wonder if you can talk about that aspect of your life?

Smith: No, I love my family. I mean my motto was don't trust anybody over eleven. You know, I always wanted to be a child. I was a real Peter Pan kid. I loved my siblings. My parents struggled very hard, they had three kids in quick succession, right after World War II. We were all sickly. My dad worked in a factory; my mother was a waitress. She did ironing. They had—they had a lot of strife. But my father was a dreamy fella. You know, he read Plato and Socrates and watched the Phillies games. And my mother, who was the real worker, did everything, everything for us. Always made any situation a happier situation. If there was no food in the house but potatoes, she would make a mountain of French fries and say, "We're going to have a French fry party." And we were like, "yay," you know and sit around eating French fries, not realizing that for her, she was a mother of four children who had nothing else to give her kids to eat. But she made it exciting and fun. And I have great respect for my parents. They, I got such beautiful things from both of them. And it doesn't mean that we didn't have our rough times, which we did. But they were, they were remarkable people. Open-minded. Great sense of humor, creative, and hard-working. And so they set really good examples for all of us. And I just, I do, I love my family. I know it's not normal, because when I came to New York, everybody thought I was crazy 'cause I would just tell everybody tales of my childhood and tales of my mom and dad and it was not, you know, the normal thing. I was looked upon as abnormal because I loved my family. But I did, I do.

DeCurtis: That's so funny. I mean, that is such a kind of characteristic of that time, was just "kill your parents," you know.

Smith: Well, I mean, I'm not saying that I didn't dream about it at times.

DeCurtis: Sure.

Smith: But the bottom line was, is they were really great people.

Sebring: She made good hamburgers.

Smith: My mom is like, my mother had at the end of her life a, sort of a shaky hand. And she's talking to Steven like this, like, "Oh so tell me about yourself." And he's looking, and there's, you know the, what is it? The . . . [*Makes burger-flipping motion with hand.*]

Sebring: Spatula.

Smith: The spatula, the hamburger on the spatula going [*shakes hand*]. And he's watching the hamburger go like this. And he's like behind the camera. And yeah, it was, we had a good time there.

Sebring: It was quite an experience—it was great.

DeCurtis: Can you talk about, Steven, just in the course of the twelve years of making the film, did your ideas about it evolve and did, how, what happened in terms of your relationship with Patti? You know can you talk about you know, obviously, twelve years is a long time in any relationship. And what, what was the nature of the changes that took place between the two of you, if any?

Sebring: I think we just grew to trust each other more and more over years. You know, most of the time I didn't even have a movie camera. We were just sort of hanging out and trying to get, getting to learn who each other was. But I think the trust was a really big thing. Just a good friend, somebody I can talk to. She talked to me a lot.

Smith: Yeah, you can't work on that scale without trust. I learned that from working with Robert Mapplethorpe. Trust is everything between two artists, or, you know, subject and model and artist. Or, two people working together, you have to have trust or there's no point—nothing good will come out of it.

Sebring: And over time, it just got more and more intense as far as trust factor. I mean just, in the film, which was a really beautiful time and I knew that we were, we really had a great bond at the time when we were in her bedroom in the corner of the room and she could talk about stuff, personal things, show personal things. And I felt that she was showing those personal things to me, not to the people that would eventually see it in the movie. 'Cause that was the time when we started editing film and it was like a year of editing this film. And I was like, man, I need to make sense of all this footage I have, you know. Israel, Japan, you name it, there was stuff everywhere. So I needed to ground the film—a thread, so to speak. And so that's when we were—over sushi one day—we were just, like, well . . . I was hanging out, you know, and the bedroom is the place where she works, in her bedroom. And the corner of her bedroom is this great chair and so that made perfect sense. So I just left the movie camera there for, what, a couple months.

Smith: Yeah, I was in . . . Well, I work.

Sebring: Just left it in there.

Smith: My bedroom is like a big room, but it also has my desk, my books, my favorite things. So it's more like a, like my little studio.

Sebring: Yeah.

Smith: And I'd wake up every morning and see that big ass camera, excuse me that, that camera looking at me. I'd wake up and, you know, have the cat sitting on me here and that camera sitting there. But . . . it was kind of cool though.

Sebring: It was one of those moments where it's like, finally, the fashion got serious, because you know, here we are in the editing room. I have a really great editor, Angelo Corrao. And so, it's sort of like the camera was in her room and we really realized that, wow, we're kind of actually really making a movie here, we're trying to make it make sense. And . . .

Smith: Ha, ha, ha.

Sebring: Yeah, and it was really fun and that's when, you know that's when Patti would say, "Well you know let's have Sam Shepard come by." Sam, you know, we like to play the guitars together. It was a natural thing, you know—it's a natural occurrence. So I was there, I had the camera on, the mike literally turned on the camera, and it was real life. And I think it's a great moment in the film that way. And it really helped the film out. And having that trust over the years, I mean, she could have turned on the camera and filmed herself. It would have been fine by me, you know. So that's, that really helped at the end of the day. And that's how I think we just grew and grew together.

Smith: You know, because we were working with improvising, my friend, Flea, he . . . We were all in California and I said, "I want Flea in the film," 'cause he's such a great guy and we all just met on the beach. We didn't talk about what we were going to do, we just said, "Well, let's hang out," and Steven filmed us hanging out. But in order to hang out with each other with someone filming you, you all have to have some kind of—there has to be some [mutual] trust. And we always had that.

PART IV
2010–2018

Devotion

JONATHAN LETHEM AND PATTI SMITH

Jonathan Lethem | November 3, 2010 | PEN America

Patti Smith met Jonathan Lethem at the Great Hall at Cooper Union on May 1, 2010, as part of the PEN World Voices Festival of International Literature. She wore jeans, boots, a white shirt, a black leather jacket, and pink socks; he wore jeans, a button-down, and Ramones-style Chuck Taylors. It must be hard to find the right outfit to interview Patti Smith in, but Lethem proved himself fashion-forward; she dug his shoes.

To Lethem, a MacArthur Fellow and the National Book Critics Circle Award winner behind the 1999 neo-noir novel *Motherless Brooklyn*, Patti Smith was an inspiration from his days of disaffected youth at CBGBs. There is a generational divide between the two—Lethem was born in 1964 and was barely old enough to catch the tail end of the first wave of punk—but as it turns out here, Smith looks beyond intergenerational warfare to find common ground with great art from any era. And *Just Kids*, which had just been released that past January, was at once inextricably linked to its era and a timeless portrait of young artists in love with each other and each other's art.

For much of this interview, Lethem and Smith reflected on what it means to be a collector—of art, literature, and other items of historical significance often discarded by the forgetful present—and what that meant for Smith's own art. There is the physical and digital media that some might now call outdated technology—in this case everything from a leather-bound book, to her MySpace page, to the CDs people gave her on tour. To Lethem, Smith's propensity to collect precious artifacts from the past and present went hand in hand with her work as a collagist or remixer of sounds and stories. As Smith told him, though, it's not just the objects but the experiences, even the seemingly mundane ones, that go into the patchwork quilt. —Ed.

JONATHAN LETHEM: Patti, I want to start by making you talk about being a book scout. One of my favorite things in your memoir Just Kids was not just the fact that you were scuffling for rare books to make money, but your descriptions of those books: you say the pages were lightly foxed, or all the plates were in place. It made me remember my own days as a book hound imagining what I could turn over some item for.

PATTI SMITH: Well, I grew up in the '50s when most people in America were getting rid of their old stuff. They didn't want their grandfather's or their parents' stuff. They didn't want the nice porcelain; they wanted Melmac. They didn't want these old leather-bound books; they wanted the Reader's Digest collection. So even as a child I would go to rummage sales or church bazaars and pick out books for pennies, for a quarter. I got a first edition Dickens with a green velvet cover with a tissue guard with a gravure of Dickens. You could get things like that. It has never gone away, my love of the book. The paper, the font, the cloth covers. All of these things are slowly dying out.

LETHEM: And did you work at rare book shops at one point?

SMITH: I only worked at one: Argosy Book Store, in 1967. Though I falsified my credentials as a book restorer. The old fellow who ran Argosy was very touched by me and he tried to train me, but I spilled rabbit glue all over a nineteenth century Bible. He said it was not really rare, though; it was just a trainer Bible. Still, he had to let me go.

LETHEM: And you still collect precious artifacts? You showed me a few amazing things earlier. Patti let me hold Arthur Rimbaud's calling card this morning.

SMITH: I have such nice things. I have a couple of letters of H. P. Lovecraft's, a watercolor of Hermann Hesse's, a page from Jim Morrison's last notebook. All of these things we don't really own; we have a guardianship of them for a while. I look at them, I play with them.

LETHEM: I always feel that the collector's role connects very strongly to something curatorial. You've been a collage artist your whole life: You've cut things up to make other things out of them, you've been an appropriator. In gestures as simple as recording "Hey Joe" and "Gloria" among your first songs—as a cover artist, you're a remixer. And to collect things is also to want to repurpose them.

SMITH: I know of people who own rare manuscripts and keep them in vaults. All my stuff is in my room. I look at my things, love them, let them live outside of a metal box. Sometimes I photograph them. That's my way of appropriating things like that. I did naughtily appropriate a nineteenth-century mathematics book of the Riemann Hypothesis for a collage, but it was falling apart anyway.

LETHEM: I've just read your gorgeous account of the origins of your collaborative work—and collaborative life, really—with Robert Mapplethorpe. You're known now as a musician and a writer, but you still take photographs. Do you still draw as well?

SMITH: Oh, yes. It's funny because I don't consider myself a musician at all. I can play a few chords on the guitar. I have no natural gifts as a musician. Obviously I sing, but I think of myself more as a performer. When I think of myself in terms of my real skills, I would think of myself as a writer and a visual artist before I would a musician.

LETHEM: Were you ever an art student in any capacity?

SMITH: I studied Art History at Glassboro State Teacher's College. And then I came to New York in 1967, and really I studied through Robert. I was drawing at the time. We sat for hours and hours, night after night, drawing. And I studied in my own way. One of my ideas when I came to New York in 1967 was to get a job at the Museum of Modern Art as a guide. I knew the story and history of every painting in the Museum of Modern Art, and I tried to pitch that as a job but they scooted me out. I, like you, was an unruly student, but I always dreamed of going to Pratt. I couldn't afford to. I couldn't get a scholarship, as I wasn't the best of students.

LETHEM: This is a generic question to ask, but I'd be interested in knowing what your writing process is like, how you put the book together, and whether you are working on another book like it, or want to write another book in the same mode.

SMITH: This book was very difficult because Robert asked me to write it. He asked me to write it on his deathbed. I wanted to write it. I have lots of sources, I have daily diaries. I know the date when I cut his hair, when I first chopped off my hair, when I first met Janis Joplin, when Robert went to a taxi dance. I have lengthy journals, I have his letters. But after Robert died I had to face the death of my husband, my brother, and my parents. And I found it very difficult to write. It's only been in the last few years when all these notes and pages and baskets of writings—I was able to sit and put them all together. And I made two rules for myself: One, that no matter what I remember or what I had, that if I couldn't see what I was writing about as a little movie then I took it away. Because I wanted the reader to enter the book like they were reading a movie. And the second: Robert was not much of a reader, he didn't read hardly at all, so it couldn't be boring or too digressional or he would just be agitated. He'd say, "Patti . . . " For instance, I had a two-page meditation on Nathaniel Hawthorne's desk in there, don't ask me why, but I knew it had to go. I can put it somewhere else, but I knew it would just stop the reader—and also agitate Robert.

LETHEM: I was talking about your art as collage, and in a sense this was a collaboration with your own past self. You were collaging these journals and notebooks and letters.

SMITH: And the book is filtered through our relationship. You asked me would I write another. And I didn't think I'd write another, but I couldn't stop writing once I'd become friendly with my voice in the book. I'm still writing, but what I decided to do is to write maybe a little trilogy of books that all are in the same time period, but from a different angle. I could write about that whole time period again, but not filtered through Robert and I—it would engage with other things: how I wrote songs, or other things that happened.

LETHEM: There are others who seem to become pivotal who you just allude to, like Sam Shepard.

SMITH: Right. Or I could write a whole chapter on William Burroughs. Both you and I love Bolaño's 2666. It's such a freeing book for a writer.

It suggests the idea of entering and reentering and exiting worlds. I thought it'd be interesting to expand the world that I began. If people want it. And it seems like they might. I like your sneakers.

LETHEM: Thank you. They're not vintage.

SMITH: Doesn't matter, they're classic.

LETHEM: That's the word. Speaking of my Ramones sneakers—I was ten years old in 1974. I went to CBGB's three or four years later for the first time.

SMITH: You went to CBGB's when you were thirteen? I'm sorry!

LETHEM: Oh, it's ok.

SMITH: I wasn't even let out of the house when I was thirteen.

LETHEM: Well it was only a subway ride. But the way that my friends and I received your career, which was already legendary to us in '76, '77, is that you had graduated—you and the Talking Heads would not appear in a small club anymore. We'd have to go to Winterland or some place.

SMITH: That's not true, I still went back right to the end. It's just that I was often on the road, that's all. It wasn't a philosophy.

LETHEM: We were more often in those little clubs seeing our own peers, high school students who had started bands were now taking over CBGB's. And we would see you guys in these little mini arenas. But the concept of punk was so formative for us. It was so powerful. It created a possibility for us as listeners, and as a subculture—we could claim our own rock and roll. And that also had an adolescent-quarantine aspect to it. Certain things were decisively "uncool" or unacceptable. We didn't let ourselves hear how great the music that preceded punk was. We needed it to be our own anthemic thing. Of course, reading your story it's amazing to see—it shouldn't be shocking, but it was because of the prejudices I find I still have from that punk identity—how completely continuous you see it with the earlier rock and roll: '50s and '60s, and even early '70s, Janis Joplin being a great example. The development of your role as a performer, as the singer in a rock and roll band, didn't come from sweeping the plate clean.

SMITH: I love hearing about this, because people like Lenny Kaye and myself, we were born in 1946. We saw, from childhood on, the entire evolution of rock and roll. So when we started performing in '73 and '74, we were not punk rock. We were guardians, we felt, of our own history. We felt that rock and roll was becoming more corporate, more glamorous, less a cultural voice. We wanted to remind people that it was a grassroots art. That it was ours, that it was revolutionary, that it belonged to the people. It didn't belong to rich rock stars, it didn't belong to the record companies, it belonged to the people. Please don't get me wrong, I'm not comparing us to Moses, but Lenny and I often thought that we saw the promised land, we saw the future for generations. We saw rock and roll as belonging to the streets. Just people playing in their garages. Anyone could play rock and roll.

We were more the bridge. The people that came after, like the Sex Pistols: I knew all those kids, they came to our shows. I knew the Clash. But for a lot of them, it was necessary, as you said, to turn their back on their past because of their method. They had to break through without us, and even despise us. And I understood that. But I'm not like that. To me, being part of the chain that includes anyone from Raphael, to Coltrane, to Allen Ginsberg, to Jimi Hendrix—to be part of this is something that I embrace. I wouldn't want to turn all of that over. But I have no quarrel with people that need to do that. It's up to the individual and how one declares her existence. Sometimes one has to disengage in order to declare. I did that with religion just like certain new groups did to my band or to the so-called dinosaurs of rock and roll. But it's all OK, as long as we keep the blood infused in the medium.

LETHEM: For a teenage listener you were on the side of revolution at that time. We would have placed your relationship to the dinosaurs of rock and roll as a very aggressive one. And the irony is that you have always been so engaged with your sources, whether it's William Blake or Van Morrison, you've always worn them on your sleeve and celebrated them in a sort of ecstatic way. By combining them with an image of renewal and revolution you can also become a guide back to those sources for someone. What is your relationship to present-day music making? Do you listen to a lot of contemporary music when you think about what kind of recording you might make?

SMITH: No. I listen to opera, really. That's what I listen to. And I listen to my son and daughter. My daughter is twenty-two years old, and she's composing all the time. I listen to her playing, I listen to her friends. My son is a guitar player. They stick stuff on my computer. I'm listening to my opera and then one day there's the Yeah Yeah Yeahs. So, ok, I'll listen to that. The other thing I do is I have a MySpace page, and I'm not so active on it, but I have all these friends on MySpace, and a lot of them create their own music and I listen to them, I see what they're doing. I tour; a lot of young kids give me their CDs. People ask me, "Who are the new people?" To me, the new people are the unknown people. The new people that I embrace are the people that we don't even know—the people of the future, the kids that are in their basements, or the group that's struggling out there in Brooklyn. It's an abstract thing, but they're the people I invest my love in.

LETHEM: You just mentioned your kids. One of the things I find so stirring, having grown up with your career as a fan, is that there is a mysterious period in the middle where you became primarily the member of a family.

SMITH: A housewife.

LETHEM: A suburban housewife.

SMITH: Wasn't quite suburban.

LETHEM: I thought I'd try. So there's Dream of Life as this weird signal coming out of that in the middle, this incredible album—and as we now know you suffered a period of losses and transformations, but you also came back to a time of fertile productivity. And you have this relationship to your grown children, who play music on stage with you at times. This is great for people who have an alienated romance that to be creative is to be outside of a family, to not have children—it's something only young people do and you have to make a choice. Well, the story of your choices is a stirring one—but it's also incomplete. We don't know how you felt about moving out of New York and out of the role that you carved for yourself in the career that you had here.

SMITH: Well, the role that I carved for myself we had accomplished. In terms of rock and roll, our mission was to wake people up and make new space for the new guard. The new guard came and, I hope, we created space for them. So I felt that I had accomplished that mission. And being on the road and starting to become quite successful—the demands and pressure of that, and the media—I felt that I wasn't growing as an artist at all. I wasn't growing politically, I wasn't growing spiritually. And I met a great person, Fred "Sonic" Smith. He had been in the MC5, he had gone through all of the things that I had gone through. And I had a decision: Did I want to carve a more difficult life with this man, or continue the way I was going? And I most happily went with him.

I missed New York City. I love New York City. I missed the coffee shops, I missed the camaraderie with my band. But it's a misconception that those were not productive years. This book Just Kids came from those sixteen years of developing a writer's discipline, of becoming, hopefully, a better human being, of having children and finding I wasn't in center of the universe, being more empathetic to my fellow man. I became more knowledgeable politically, just seeing how human beings toil. I had to do all the cooking and the cleaning and the washing of the diapers. We didn't have nannies or anything like that; we did everything ourselves. We didn't make a big income because we both withdrew from public life. But for me, the skills and disciplines that I obtained in those years have magnified all of my efforts. So they certainly weren't lost years.

LETHEM: That's a beautiful way to put it.

PATTI SMITH: WARRIOR POET

Paul Zollo | January/February 2011 | *American Songwriter*

Here, Smith peeled back the layers of her songwriting process. Songwriter Paul Zollo, the editor of the 1991 interview collection *Songwriters on Songwriting* and senior editor of *American Songwriter*, knew a thing or two about the subject himself.

In this in-depth conversation, Smith discussed the extensive research that goes into her creative work and her inspiration—whether a dream that demands interpretation or an event in the political zeitgeist that demands action. There are the songs that came to her in a sudden burst and those that were much more labor-intensive, songs that were entirely improvised on the spot and songs that required a sense of mot juste, songs based on imaginative projection and songs that she lived, songs that take us on a journey and songs that take us home. And then there are songs that do *all* these things.

It might be tempting to think of Patti Smith, the punk poet laureate, as an artist who simply writes a poem that immediately becomes a song, but it's really not that simple. —Ed.

Since she was a kid, she knew she was an artist, and a serious one, willing to go the extra mile. As early as 11, she approached her own art with a remarkable singularity of purpose that has persisted ever since. "When I was a kid, I wanted to write a poem about Simón Bolívar," says Patti Smith. "I went to the library and read everything I could. I wrote copious notes. I had 40 pages of notes just to write a small poem." Decades later, the process persists. She spent months reading every book she could find about Ho Chi Minh before spontaneously improvising "Gung Ho." She relies on her ability to shamanistically channel songs and poems, but never blindly; she deepens her well with information before delving into it.

Of course, she's more than a songwriter. She's an artist who recognizes that art needn't be restricted to any one means of expression. Like her great friend, the late photographer Robert Mapplethorpe, about whom she wrote the beautiful memoir, *Just Kids*, she's always been devoted to making art itself—whether a poem, a memoir, a novel, a record, a series of drawings, a play (with Sam Shepard she wrote *Cowboy Mouth*), or a song. As a child, art for her was both a refuge and a means of escape from the monotony of the everyday world. "I did not want to be trapped," she says. "I grew up in the '50s, when the girls wore really bright red lipstick and nail polish, and they smelled like Eau de Paris. Their world just didn't attract me. I hid in the world of the artist: first the 19th-century artists, then the Beats. And Peter Pan."

Unlike Mapplethorpe, however, fame was never a goal. When she made her debut album *Horses*, which remains the most visceral fusion of poetry and rock ever recorded, she never intended to be a rock star, and was happy to return to her job at the bookstore, writing poems and creating drawings. But she also recognized the unchained potential of rock and roll to speak not just to an assorted few at a coffee-house poetry reading, but to 40,000 people or more in an arena, all united by song. Though she certainly never left poetry behind (she's written twelve volumes of published poetry, and several more books of poetry and memoir that are unpublished), she embraced the electric promise of speaking to the whole world. "Even now, it's an opportunity to have a universal voice," she says, "because everybody, all over the world, loves rock and roll. It's the new universal language. Jimi Hendrix knew that. The Rolling Stones knew that. We knew that. People of the future will know that. What they do with it is up to them."

How is writing poems different from writing songs?

Poetry is a solitary process. One does not write poetry for the masses. Poetry is a self-involved, lofty pursuit. Songs are for the people. When

I'm writing a song, I imagine performing it. I imagine giving it. It's a different aspect of communication. It's for the people.

We always write a certain amount of poetry for the masses. When Allen Ginsberg wrote "Howl," he didn't write it for himself. He wrote it to speak out. To make a move, to wake people up. I think rock and roll, as our cultural voice, took that energy and made it even more accessible.

When I'm sitting down to write a poem, I'm not thinking of anyone. I'm not thinking about how it will be received. I'm not thinking it will make people happy or it will inspire them. I'm in a whole other world. A world of complete solitude. But when I'm writing a song, I imagine performing it. I imagine giving it. It's a different aspect of communication. It's for the people.

I write songs when I'm by myself, like walking along the beach, and a song comes in my head. Or I wake up from a dream, like "Blakean Year." I often write songs out of dreams, and take them to my musicians to help me. Sometimes I write melodies that are too complex and I can't find them on the guitar, because I only know about eight chords. So I take them to Lenny [Kaye] or [bassist] Tony [Shanahan] and they transcribe them into a song.

"Free Money" came to me walking down St. Mark's at three in the morning. It was pre-dawn, but it was so light in New York City, and it came to me and I sang it to Lenny. He structured it and found the proper chords, and we made a song. It was one of our earliest songs.

Other songs, they just come in my head and I sing them out loud, and the band finds the place, and they adjust it. For myself, the simpler format the better. "Gandhi" is nine minutes on one chord. It's an improvisation. "Radio Baghdad" was completely improvised. I didn't know the lyrics, but I knew I wanted to speak out against the invasion of Iraq. Being a mother, I freely entered into the mother consciousness of the mothers of Baghdad who were trying to comfort their children as they were being bombed. So these lyrics that come to me are self-perpetuated.

It's miraculous that you can spontaneously come up with such amazing work.

It's easier for me than to sit and write verse-chorus. Writing lyrics, some-times, is torturous. Because I make them too complicated, and sometimes burden a song with complicated language. But it's just how I work. So, for me, it's freedom just to go and focus myself and see where my horse takes me.

Are there times you didn't get there?

I have never been unsuccessful.

How do you explain that?

It's a channeling. Burroughs always called it a shamanistic gift. Some-times I feel I am channeling someone else. Part of it is experience from performing, and understanding that as a performer one has a mission, like Coltrane, to take your solo out to talk to God, or whoever you talk to, but you must return. So it has structure.

That's one way that I write. Others take quite a bit of labor. Often the simplest song is the hardest to write. "Frederick" was very hard to write. Because in its simplicity, I also wanted it to be perfect.

Yes. And when people hear them, they think they came out perfectly. But to get to that place is a lot of work?

Yes, a lot of work. But I find, in the past decade, I don't struggle with lyrics as much as I did in the '70s. I think that's partially because, you know, I came out of nowhere. I wasn't a songwriter. A lot of *Horses* was based on poems that I had written. For instance, "Jesus died for somebody's sins but not mine" came from a poem I wrote when I was 20. I had written it perhaps in '69 and we recorded it in '75. "Redondo Beach" I wrote in 1971 as a poem. But I struggled.

I always thought when we did *Horses* I would do a record—and I was really honored to do the record—but then I'd go back to work, working in a book store, writing poems or doing my drawings. It didn't occur to me that I'd be doing more records. Because I felt like I had said what I had to say. *Horses* was based on five years of work and performing and thinking about things, and suddenly when we had another record I found it very, very difficult because I wasn't skilled in writing songs. And *Horses* was such an organic process. So I was learning as I went along.

But now I understand the songwriting process and it's not so difficult. I mean, it is difficult but it's not as difficult as it was. I remember writing the lyrics to the songs on *Radio Ethiopia*. At that time I had performed so much I felt a loss of language and just got very involved with playing electric guitar and making sonicscapes. I was much happier playing feedback than I was in spewing language. But the language came back.

I had always assumed—wrongly, I see—that your poetry and songwriting were intertwined. That you'd write a poem that would spark a song, and maybe vice versa.

Well, that can happen. Anything can happen. I have started poems that seemed best-served as a song. But that's just one of those things that happened totally organically. It would be false to say everything is black and white, it's either one or the other. It's just that my process is different. My mindset is different. And I've destroyed many poems [Laughs]. Just lost the thread on a poem and then went back to them and found that it could be the germ of something else. But the initial process is a different process.

Why is songwriting sometimes torturous?

Because I had so much responsibility to others. If I was writing lyrics to someone's music, I had responsibility to that musician. I had to project beyond myself and beyond my world out into the greater world. Allen Ginsberg told me, "If you have trouble writing, just write what you mean" [Laughs]. And that's a good lesson when you're trying to write a song.

As an artist who has expressed yourself in so many ways, how is it to have written songs which reach so many more people who might never read poetry or books?

Smith: I think of my work as relatively obscure. When you look at a poet like Jim Morrison, who is able to write very complex lyrics like "The Wasp" but also write "Hello, I Love You," this to me is a real gift, to be able to have a span like that.

With my own work, when I wrote the lyrics for *Horses*, I had a particular body of people who I was speaking to, and that was the people like myself, who I felt were disenfranchised. The more maverick person.

I wasn't really addressing the masses. I didn't even think I had anything of interest to share with the masses. But I felt that I had something to share with people like myself. So my early work was really written to bridge poetry and rock and roll, and to communicate, as I said, with the disenfranchised person. And I think in that way it was successful. But in the '80s, when I stopped performing and I got married and had a family, I became more empathetic to social issues and the humanist point of view. And I think my lyrics had changed. I was speaking to a larger body of people. As a mother, you want to speak to everyone. Because everyone is potentially a son or daughter. So my goal shifted. A lot of that came from my husband, Fred "Sonic" Smith, who was very political and very concerned with the human condition. So a song like "People Have The Power" came from Fred. It was Fred's concept. Even though I wrote the lyrics, he wrote the title, and the concept was his, because he wanted to address all people. So I would say there has definitely been a shift in who I am speaking to, at least in my mind.

That shift seems to have come with the *Wave* album, with a song like "Dancing Barefoot."

"Dancing Barefoot" begins the shift. That album, *Wave*, came from falling in love. And opening up my perspective. *Wave* addressed the fact that I was here, I did my work, I hopefully contributed. And I found somebody who I loved, and now I was embarking on a new life. So, you're right, it's really the album *Wave* which starts that shift.

It took me a while to understand you have license to have abstraction in a lyric. As a kid, I loved dancing. It's very funny I should wind up a songwriter and have to write lyrics. Because as a kid I wasn't so involved with the lyrics, I just loved to dance. Hearing "Gimme Shelter," I didn't really break down what the song was about, I just loved to dance to it. Talking about songwriting is complicated 'cause there's so many kinds of songs. And so I might seem like I'm contradicting myself, but I'm not. When I wrote "Frederick," I tried to write a song that everybody loved and everybody danced to. It was consciously written to be a dance song. When I wrote "Radio Baghdad," that was the last thing on my mind. For me, that has always been such a conflict because I love natural songs.

I love that song "Get In The Groove." [Sings] "Hey, get in the groove." I mean, what's that about? It's such a great little song to dance to. It doesn't mean to say much of anything.

Which is a great thing about songs, that they hit us on different levels at once—our hearts and minds and bodies.

Yeah. And I think that's why songwriting, to me, has been such a mystery, and still something that I haven't completely cracked. How a poet—going back to Jim Morrison—could write such complex lyrics and complex poems and then say, "Hello, I love you, let me jump in your game."

Your biggest hit ever was one you wrote with Bruce Springsteen, "Because The Night." How did that come together?

I got a tape of it, everything completely produced, and the chorus was done. He needed words for the verses, which were mumbled. I listened to it. I sat up with it all night writing a song for Fred, who was supposed to call me from Detroit. And I'm the kind of girl who waits for the call. I listened to it over and over, trying to distract myself from waiting for Fred. And that's why in the lyric it says, "Have I doubt when I'm alone/ love is a ring, a telephone."

I've always wanted to write a song that everyone could love. That's the one thing that I feel I haven't achieved. Writing a song that when you hear it, everybody is happy. When we're in Italy and we break into "Because The Night" and there are 20,000 people singing, it just brings me to tears. So I know that people must experience a certain amount of joy. When it comes down to it, I might write poetry for myself or poetry for the gods of poetry. But I write a song for the people.

PATTI SMITH DISCUSSES *BANGA* ON WORDS AND MUSIC

Eric Holland | June 5, 2012 | WFUV

It wouldn't be wrong to call Patti Smith an elegist. So many of her songs are elegiac in tone or explicit elegies, and her eleventh studio album, *Banga*, released in 2012, has a few. "Maria" was for Maria Schneider, who starred in *Last Tango in Paris*, got to know the Patti Smith Group in their early years, and died in 2011. "This Is the Girl" was for Amy Winehouse, who also passed in 2011. The spiritually probing ekphrastic song "Constantine's Dream," inspired by the Renaissance painter Piero della Francesca, was, in a way, an elegy for the artist as well as Saint Francis. Even her first published poem was an elegy for Charlie Parker, who died in 1955 at the age of 34. Yet Smith's outlook has remained characteristically resilient—in the face of losing loved ones and iconic heroes, she teaches us how to "walk with them."

Another inspiration and touchstone of the elegiac was Frida Kahlo. Smith's photo of Kahlo's dress was part of *Camera Solo*, an exhibit of her photographic work curated by the Wadsworth Atheneum Museum of Art in Hartford, Connecticut. She had just performed at the Detroit Institute of Art for the exhibit's opening there, flanked by Diego Rivera's *Detroit Industry Murals*, and was still in a "Diego Rivera and Frida Kahlo consciousness."

Here, longtime WFUV deejay Eric Holland and Smith took a deep dive into the album and some of the questions, spiritual and aesthetic, that have animated her career. At the end of the conversation, Smith took a "pop quiz," answering questions like "Who did you wish recorded one of your songs, dead or alive?" Her answers are surprising. —Ed.

Patti Smith: In truth, I've suffered a lot of loss. And one has to find a way to happily traipse through life no matter what. Because life is the best thing we got.

Eric Holland: Patti Smith has never shied away from the deepest complexities in life and in art. Though tagged early on as the godmother of punk, she has proved herself for almost forty years as a true artist, unfettered and without category. Many folks with that long a career have showered listeners with countless releases. Patti, rather, has judiciously fed us a well-considered body of albums, with space in between, each a stepping stone to the next. Like breadcrumbs leading us to the truth, they bring us to her latest release, called *Banga*. It gave me a prized opportunity to speak with her, and you'll hear our conversation coming up here on FUV's *Words and Music* from Studio A.

Hi, I'm Eric Holland. Patricia Lee Smith was born sixty-five years ago in Chicago and was raised in New Jersey as a Jehovah's Witness. Though she departed that faith early on in life, religion has long remained a fascination to her, and an analogy, fueling many of her works. And there is its twin influence: her intense involvement with some of the bravest artists of her time, including the photographer Robert Mapplethorpe and Patti's husband, Fred "Sonic" Smith, both now long deceased. She has also kindled friendships with many creative luminaries, from Jimi Hendrix to Allen Ginsberg to Michael Stipe.

Patti is the real deal, an artist's artist. Raw in life and fearless in poetry, Patti's unique interpretation of the human predicament has grabbed our attention ever since her first single in 1974. Her stark blend of highbrow and lowbrow has been a hallmark all these years, deepening with the addition of her role as a mother to son Jackson and daughter Jesse, her experience of going back and forth from living in New York and Detroit, from personal loss to professional bounty. She summed it up well in her 2010 memoir, *Just Kids*, which won the National Book Award. And her new album, *Banga*, is just as meaningful and rife with stories. Patti Smith recently sat down with me for a generous conversation, and I asked her how she's feeling these days.

Smith: I'm great, thanks. I'm really happy. I'm really happy to be talkin' to you, and everybody out there in Radioland. Say hello.

Holland: Well, you look great, and it's very exciting to have a new album, your first studio effort in eight years.

Smith: Yes, I think so. I mean, actually, I didn't even realize that, but people keep telling me that, so it must be true.

Holland: And you went back to not only where you recorded your first album but your very first single, Electric Lady Studios.

Smith: Yes. It just happened that way. We didn't plan it. But release date for the album is the anniversary of when we recorded "Piss Factory" and "Hey Joe" in 1974. So it's sort of a magical day.

Holland: Absolutely, your debut single. And not only did you start your recording career there, but you were there at the opening of Electric Lady.

Smith: Yes.

Holland: And when I read about that in *Just Kids*, it really knocked me out. I was hoping you would share that experience with everyone.

Smith: Well, I was doing some poetry readings, and I was writing some music journalism, and so I was invited, because I did a lot of record reviews and things, and it was well known how much I loved Jimi Hendrix. I was invited to the opening, which was in August—I forget the date—of 1970. So I was very excited, and I dressed so carefully. Um, you know, I had this old straw hat, and I had these ribbons with musical notes on them, and I was just so excited. And so I went to Electric Lady, which as it still is, is right on Eighth Street, and I went down the stairs, and then I couldn't bear to go into the party. I just got, it was like stage fright. I was too nervous. I just felt like an attack of shyness or wondering should I even be there. So I sat on the steps and then the door opened and bounding up the steps were some people, and then, was Jimi Hendrix. And he had to leave, because he had to catch a plane I believe. He was going to the Isle of Wight, and he stopped and looked at me, and he said something like, "Are you going in?" Or I forget what he said to me, 'cause it was so long ago. But I just told him that I was too shy to go in the party, and he had such a soft, cool voice, and he was very tall. Very long, long hands. I remember looking at his hands. They were just so beautiful. Just as you could imagine, the kind of hands that could strangle the neck of an electric guitar, and he was so nice to me. He told me he was shy too, and that he didn't really like parties, and then he told me about what he was going to do with the studio. He said he had to go to London and do some concerts, and when he came back he was going to gather musicians all over the world, take them up to Woodstock, and he told me they were gonna sit in a circle, and all "do their own thing," as he said. They were gonna all just play in sort of an Ornette Coleman kind of cacophony, until they all merged, and whether it took a week, or months, whatever, they would merge into a common language which he thought would be the language of peace, and then he'd bring them all back and record them. And I thought, really, I thought that that would change the world. That he was going to do something that was going to elevate the consciousness of the world. But unfortunately, Jimi never came back, and uh, he died in London. And I never dreamed then that I would one day be recording then, at the same place. I never dreamed I would ever record. I had no aspirations to record, and so when I started performing and then when Lenny Kaye and I decided to make an independent single, that's where I wanted to do it. And we did, and we've done a lot of recording there since. We recorded *Horses* and *Gone Again* and *Twelve* and *Trampin'*, so we've done a lot of time at Electric Lady.

Holland: Yeah, it's a magical place, and I'm sure when you look around when you're in there, you feel Jimi a little bit.

Smith: Oh, I always feel him. And I feel myself as well, you know, my own history, my own youth, my own growth. But we always salute Jimi when we're there. Always.

Holland: It's a great space to be in, a place where you feel connected to your youth.

Smith: Yes, and connected to the people that inspired and taught you so much through their work.

Holland: We're here in New York City, the town where you moved, I think it was forty-five years ago.

Smith: Wow. Yes.

Holland: And you were here from '67 to, was it 1980?

Smith: Late '79, yes. And then I moved to Detroit.

Holland: But then you came back, and that was about ten or more years ago?

Smith: It was in '96, I think. Late '95, after the death of my husband. I stayed in Detroit with my kids, but since I don't drive, it was very hard. It was not only very sad to be there without Fred, but it was almost impossible, 'cause it's not called the Motor City for nothin'. You have to have a car. So I came back to New York, because it's pedestrian friendly, and had to, I was obliged, 'cause it's much more expensive to live in New York than Michigan, to return to my work, to make a living for my children.

Holland: Well, I'm glad that there was a happy result where you felt like—

Smith: It was a productive result, yes.

Holland: How does living in New York affect your art?

Smith: Um, it doesn't affect my work as much as it affects being in a place where I can find, where I have collaborators and a community of people and a base camp. Because I travel so much, I work everywhere. I take photographs everywhere in the world, you know, I perform everywhere in the world, and truthfully, what I really need when I'm writing or drawing is solitude, and I don't get a lot of that in New York City, so I tend to write more holed up somewhere else. But, you know, New York is a place that helped form me as a human being, and it's my neighborhood, so I can think of New York happily as just my neighborhood, but in terms of workspace, I work, you know, where I have the best opportunity to do what I must do. I really associate New York more with recording, because there's probably nowhere else I'd rather record than Electric Lady. But in terms of my other work, I like bein' on the move.

Holland: I thought of you when I was at MoMA [*Museum of Modern Art —Ed.*] recently, looking at Diego Rivera.

Smith: Yes, I was just in Detroit actually, for four or five days. I had an opening of my photographs at the Detroit Institute of Art, and my son Jackson and my daughter Jesse and I performed in the Diego Rivera court, with all the beautiful murals he did that resonated the birth of the auto industry [*Detroit Industry Murals, Detroit Institute of Arts — Ed.*], and so Diego Rivera's been much on my mind lately. And we just had a big concert in Mexico, in front of the Diego Rivera Museum. So it's been, you know, May was my—May and the beginning of June has been my time that I've been really in a Diego Rivera and Frida Kahlo consciousness.

Holland: Let's talk a little bit about the songs on the new album, *Banga*. The title track, I heard you use the word absurd to describe it. It seems like you're really havin' fun with that. I love "the golden commode." [*Laughs.*]

Smith: Yeah, it's just, you know, it's really, I mean, that song came to me in a burst of energy, and I knew, I wanted to write a song saluting the dog, because Banga is the name of a dog in, the dog, in Bulgakov's masterpiece, *Master and Margarita*. And I wanted to write a song about this dog because he seemed to epitomize love and loyalty. And then, it just turned out, it's really a song to do live. It's really a song to engage the people, it's a salute to my band and their loyalty, and it's really just a song for us to all, you know, be unified, but for not any specific cause except for unity itself.

[*Excerpt from "Banga" plays.*]

Smith: I like the song. There's no particular message in it, except, you know, like I've said, that we're all together.

Holland: Yeah, I love it. And you've really given us the second great song inspired by that book—"Sympathy for the Devil," by the Stones, also.

Smith: Yes, yes. Yeah, it would be an interesting show to just do songs inspired by books. I mean, look at all of, you know, Jim Morrison, "Hyacinth House." That title is taken from Anais Nin. There's a lot of Jim

Morrison songs that were inspired by books, and I'm sure all kinds of, I'm sure everyone has at least one or two songs inspired by a book.

Holland: Let's put that together.

Smith: That would be an interesting show.

Holland: And your son Jackson does the barking.

Smith: Yes, Jackson and his wife Meg have five dogs, and they live in Detroit, and Jackson can imitate all of them, so there's a plethora of dog barking. But he also plays great guitar on the record, too, especially on the song "Maria." Very, very physical, visceral, emotional guitar solo by Jackson.

Holland: Yes, Jackson married to Meg White, formerly of the White Stripes.

Smith: Yup.

Holland: And I remember seeing Jackson with you in Damrosch Park, maybe three years ago. Does that sound right?

Smith: Yeah, Jackson plays with us intermittently. You know, if he's around, or he'll stop by and do a couple of jobs. He's been on tour with me. These days, I spend more time . . . my daughter Jesse does a lot of work with me.

Holland: We were talking about Jackson, and you mentioned his playing on "Maria."

Smith: Yes.

Holland: A song that sounds like it grew from loss. It sounds like an elegy.

Smith: The music was written apart from me. Tony Shanahan, my bass player, wrote the music, and did a demo with it, actually with a drummer named Louie Appel, who sadly died not long after the sessions, of heart failure. And he was a great drummer. And, um, and I was listening to the demo, because we were trying to ascertain whether we should re-record it, and I thought, you know, this is the drummer's last work. We should honor it and keep the demo. And when I was sitting listening to it, um,

Maria Schneider had just died, and Maria, the actress on *Last Tango in Paris* and *The Passenger*, I knew Maria quite well in the '70s, and she even traveled with us a little when we first toured *Horses*. And I always think of that period. She's part of the images, the very strong images of that period of my life, and I just started thinking about her, but also that time. And I think of all the songs it's the most personal and the most, I don't like to use the word nostalgic, but it does resonate. Not only Maria, but a time. It's a very '70s song. You know, it's just sort of like an R&B style song, but it deeply for me resonates that particular time in my life, and, uh, I didn't set out to write—you know, I didn't really set out to write a lot of these songs. I didn't set out to write a song for Amy Winehouse. These things just happen organically. You know, they just, we're driven to do them.

[*Excerpt from "Maria" plays.*]

Holland: I'm Eric Holland, you're listening to *Words and Music* with Patti Smith at 90.7-WFUV. That's maybe one of the defining characteristics of your career, being able to take loss and channel it into art. You've done it a number of times when you've lost people—

Smith: Well, yeah, I'm sorry. I'm sorry. I was thinking about this, because some people like this, and some people criticize me for it. I don't know why. I don't know why anybody cares. You know, I think it's, I mean, the living are meant to remember the dead. That's how the dead [are] remembered, by the living. So, um, but when I was a kid, um, I suffered loss as a kid. My best friend died when I was about eight or nine years old. But when I was fifteen, my first published work was an elegy to Charlie Parker. Maybe I was less than fifteen. It was in 1959, and Charlie Parker died, and my father used to listen to Charlie Parker. So I writ a little poem and it was published, like in the, you know, the school paper or something. And it was called "Bird Is Free," and so that was my first published piece was an elegy. So I've been consistent. You know, *Horses* has an elegy to Jimi Hendrix and an elegy to Jim Morrison. And, you know, I'm consistent.

Holland: Well, I think it's brilliant, and the fact that not only can you work through grief, but you give everyone a chance to—

Smith: Well, I think it's important that . . . well, everyone has to know, I mean, we all have a limited time period on the earth, and it's up to us all to use it well, and we're all gonna lose somebody. We're gonna lose our parents or a friend or a loved one, or our dog, you know, we're gonna lose somebody, and we have to know that, and we have to find a way to reconcile that, you know, in our hearts, in our minds. And it's always gonna be painful. I mean, I lost my husband sixteen, seventeen years ago. I think of him every day. But the way that I operate, really, is I don't leave people in the past. I bring 'em along with me. I walk with them. You know, sometimes, I talk to my husband. You know, I don't . . . I talk to my mom, and, uh, you know, I talk to Robert [*Mapplethorpe —Ed.*], and we're like computers, so we maintain within our brains everything that we know about the people we lost. So it's not impossible to have an ongoing dialogue with them. And yes, we're going to suffer the pleasure of their physical company, but we don't have to, you know, we don't have to leave them behind. We can keep them informed. We can still be scolded by them. We can still feel love. And, um, that's been really helpful to me, because in truth, I've suffered a lot of loss, and one has to find a way to happily traipse through life no matter what, because life is the best thing we got. There's nothin' better than our own life, so, you know, we got to do good by it.

Holland: It's a great attitude, and we can all take solace in the music and some inspiration from that attitude. You mentioned the song you wrote for Amy [Winehouse], which you debuted at City Winery. Your daughter Jesse was there. Uh, "This Is the Girl."

Smith: "This Is the Girl." Again, a song I didn't plan to write. Um, when she died I was in Madrid, and I felt very badly. I felt badly for two reasons. One, because I greatly admired her voice. She had a very unique, authentic voice. She could sing songs of my generation with such authenticity, but also this modern spin, and I really looked forward to how she would evolve. But also, you know, as a mother, she's the same age as my kids, and you know, I was concerned as a fan and a human being, that her lifestyle was going to, you know, destroy her voice, be so bad for her health, and so of course, the worst of scenarios happened, and I wrote her a little poem. I didn't—I just wrote it, because I felt compelled to write it, and when we were finishing the album, my bass player, Tony Shanahan, presented me with some new music. And I was working on the poem and half listening to the music in Electric Lady's lounge, and I noticed that his music and my poem were the same. And I said to Tony, "Look, this is amazing." And I showed him. It went, "This is the girl for whom all tears fall. This is the girl who was having a ball." Everything fit perfectly, even, you know, I had the next section of the poem fit his chorus. So we decided to just go in the studio, and he showed everybody the chords, and it was Lenny and my son and Jay Dee Daugherty, our drummer, and Tony, and we just recorded it, very simply and without any embellishment. Some background vocals, just a little simple song. Little piece of, like a little bouquet for Amy.

[*Excerpt from "This Is the Girl" plays.*]

Holland: Religious imagery has been part of your work for your entire career. The first line on your first album, "Jesus died for somebody's sins but not mine." And this album has quite a bit of religious imagery on it. It feels to me like the climax of the album, and maybe even a culmination of a lifetime of thinking about religion in your life comes on the song that was inspired when you were in Italy. Please talk about that.

Smith: Well, "Constantine's Dream," the one you're speaking of, is, the lyrics are improvised over, around a ten-, eleven-minute track that Lenny Kaye composed. And the band recorded the track, and then we went to Arezzo, Italy, Lenny and I, where I had first the germ of this idea happened in Arezzo, where I had a dream that inspired the idea for the song, and I saw the painting, *Constantine's Dream* [The Dream of Constantine *by Piero della Francesca —Ed.*], and we had some musicians from Arezzo, an accordion player, a steel guitar player, a violinist play, do some overdubs to give the track atmosphere. And then we set the track away. And then I contemplated what I wanted to improvise on the track. I wanted to speak of the painting; I wanted to speak of our environment; I wanted to speak of exploration; I wanted to speak of

Saint Francis. Because he epitomizes, he's the ultimate human being. He could be a poster boy for our present environmental crisis, because he was so in tune with nature, and was able . . . he was a very rich young man, the son of a rich merchant. He was really destined to be a prince with all kinds of worldly goods. He shed everything. He shed everything to become more in tune with nature and not mar nature with any more material goods or pollution. Just a very good example for us in terms of perhaps sacrificing material things for the sake of our environment. All these things were in my mind, and I contemplated and studied, and then I went into Electric Lady to improvise the track, 'cause we always have one long improvisation. Usually I do it live with the band, but I wanted to try something different. So I listened to the track, and I only did two passes. I don't usually do more than two, because it takes so much mental concentration to improvise that long of a piece that sometimes I'll get migraines after. When we did "Radio Baghdad," "Strange Messengers," sometimes the next day I have a headache all day. So it's not a kind of thing you can do over and over. You have to deeply commit to it, and that's very nice what you said, because what came out was much different than what I thought would come. I thought that I was going to be more focused on Saint Francis and the environment. And I didn't think that it was going to be such a deeply personal piece, but in the end, it's, in some ways, one of the most personal things that I've done, because it addresses my deepest conflict, and the deepest question that I've asked. You know, it's the question of nature, art, and religion. And I don't mean God, I mean religion. Religion being the physical manifestation of spiritual ideology. To me, God and the idea of prayer or the essence of what religion teaches doesn't need art, churches, clergy. It's simply what Christ said: love one another. I mean, that simple . . . you know, he even said it. "If you can't deal with the Ten Commandments, I give you an eleventh: just love one another, and everything will be fine." And as simplistic as that is, it's absolutely true. If we just simply gave each other space, everyone on the planet respected one another, we could do anything. And um, but this constant questioning that I've had my whole life about the value of art, you know, how much, you know, anything we do, material, compromises our environment, compromises nature. You know, all of these questions, even "Jesus died for somebody's sins but not mine" was really a question in a way. I was just, it wasn't against Christ or Christ's teachings. It was against the idea of how religion interprets Christ's teachings. It was wondering, you know, what am I to do with my life? You know, if I have to choose between art and religion, what will be my choice? Or, I have to choose between art and being a public servant, what will I choose? You know, these are questions that I've been asking myself since I was a young girl . . . culminated in this piece, and as you said, and I never planned that at all. After it was done, you know, I wondered, you know, should I do it all again? And then I thought, no, this is what came out, and that's what I'll present.

[*Excerpt from "Constantine's Dream" plays.*]

Holland: You slipped in a truly punk phrase in that song as well. What was it, "Die on the back of adventure?"

Smith: Oh, he says, that's Piero della Francesca, the painter. He went blind at the end of his life, and Piero della Francesca, I learned in my studies, died at the same, it's like he died at the same moment, the same day that Columbus set foot in America, October 12, 1492. So I imagined Piero della Francesca, and of course, speaking for myself, he says, "Oh Lord, let me die on the back of adventure, with a brush and an eye full of light," because he was blind. And then God transports him right on the back of Columbus, and Piero della Francesca gets to see the New World, which of course is going to ultimately be destroyed by man.

Holland: Patti, I have at least three more hours of questions for you. [*Laughs.*]

Smith: Thank you for being attentive to "Constantine's Dream," and to comprehend something that, well, is so deeply rooted in it. Thank you.

Holland: My pleasure. Thank you for all the great music over the years.

Smith: Thanks.

Holland: Um, will you indulge us with a quick pop quiz?

Smith: Yes, yes.

Holland: You're very kind.

Smith: I'm terrified.

Holland: [*Laughs.*] Nah, this is easy. Here we go, it's the WFUV pop quiz, with Patti Smith. "Aside from gear, instruments, my band, I don't go on the road without . . . "

Smith: Oh, uh, a book. I always have a book. In fact, that's my greatest trauma. It's the thing that will make me, you know, late for my flight, is trying to figure out what book I'm gonna take. But I already know what book I'm gonna take on our tour, so I'm not gonna be late for my flight.

Holland: What's the book?

Smith: Um, I have the three-paperback set of Murakami's, it's *IQ84* [*1Q84*]. So I'm really in a Murakami period, and I like takin' a big, hefty book and, but my last big tour I took Bolano's *2666*, in the three-paperback, so this time I'm takin' Murakami.

Holland: What song do you wish you'd written and why?

Smith: Oh gosh. Of the nine million? Uh, jeez. I really like "Mermaid Turn the Tides" . . . "1985," is it?

Holland: In 1983?

Smith: Is it called "1985?"

Holland: You're talking about the track on [*Jimi Hendrix album* —Ed.] *Electric Ladyland*?

Smith: Yeah, yeah. Sorry, I keep forgetting, it's been so long. [*The Hendrix song Smith refers to here is "1983 . . . (A Merman I Should Turn to Be)."* —Ed.] But that's one of my most favorite songs, just because his vision . . . such a visionary, you know, well—it's visionary. But there is one . . . can I have two? On the other side of the coin is this little song "Today Is the Day," that Maureen Gray sings. It is such—it is a song, it's like the ultimate, I don't know if you would call it a pop song, it would be more R&B, early rock 'n' roll. But it is so exuberant, and it's such a sad song. You know, it goes somethin' like, [*sings*] "Today's the day that you're going away." You know, but she sings it with such exuberance. It's like the saddest teenage song in the world, sung with such exuberance. I have been listening to it since I was like fourteen, and it still makes me so excited and happy.

Holland: Who do you wish recorded one of your songs, dead or alive?

Smith: Wow. That's really hard. I mean, well, I always imagined hearing Dolly Parton sing "The Jackson Song." Um, the Jackson song my husband and I wrote for our son Jackson. But the range of it was a little difficult, even though we wrote it for me, and I always, when I sang it, I always thought, Dolly Parton would sing this perfect.

Holland: So random. I never would have guessed a Dolly answer. [*Laughs.*] What song would you sing in the shower but never in public?

Smith: Oh, when I'm in the shower, I always sing arias from opera . . . that sound really good in the shower, because, you know, I have like this tiled shower, and when the water's on, there's such a natural echo, and I do my best singing. I always wish there was some way that I could record my vocals in the shower, but the water would have to be on, because that adds to it. And I sing, um, a lot of arias. One of my favorites is the aria for the coat in *La Bohème*, and I like to do Pavarotti's version. In English, though. But I sound pretty good. Sometimes if I'm tired, though, I'll sing it in fake Italian.

Holland: [*Laughs.*] Gibberish Italian.

Smith: Well, you know, fake Italian.

Holland: What's the first album you bought?

Smith: Oh, the first album I bought. Well, when we were kids, we really didn't have the money to buy albums. Um, but my mother joined the Columbia Record Club. It was, you know, back in the '50s, or really early '60s, you could join the Columbia Record Club and get ten records for a dollar, and I think, if I remember rightly, I got an Olatunji record, like *Let There Be Drums* or something [*Probably Olatunji's* Drums of Passion, *released in 1960 —Ed.*]. I can't exactly remember.

Holland: The Nigerian drummer?

Smith: Yeah. Because you had to get records that were on the Columbia . . . I was pretty young, but we didn't have record albums then. We had singles. You know? I mean, probably one of the first singles I had was Little Richard's "The Girl Can't Help It." And but the actual first single I ever had was "Tubby the Tuba," part one and two. But you know, record albums, you know, for my family, they came far and far between. I remember, sorry, 'cause I don't have any straight answer to give you, because it was more like I had no record albums, and then when we could get things from the Columbia Record Club, I would get more albums, like, uh, you know, the first Bob Dylan album, and I remember Jimmy Smith albums, and you know, Roland Kirk albums, but I was deeply into jazz when I was young, so my first real albums were mostly jazz albums—and Coltrane—until I switched over to Bob Dylan. And my first rock 'n' roll album, I know what that was: *The Animals*.

Holland: All right.

Smith: *The Animals.*

Holland: Did you hear Springsteen do that crazy rant about the Animals at the South by Southwest?

Smith: No. I didn't hear it.

Holland: It's great.

Smith: I wasn't there. But I always loved the Animals, you know. They were the greatest.

Holland: Well, I'm getting many hand signals from various people. [*Laughs.*] And it kills me to let you go, Patti, but I guess I will have to say aloha. Thank you so much.

Smith: Oh, thank you. Sorry I couldn't give a one-thing answer.

Holland: Not at all.

Smith: So hard.

Holland: One thing is lame. That was awesome.

Smith: Thanks! Bye.

Holland: Bye-bye.

[*"House of the Rising Sun" by the Animals plays.*]

PATTI SMITH: I WILL ALWAYS LIVE LIKE PETER PAN

Christian Lund | August 24, 2012 | Louisiana Channel

This interview took place at the Louisiana Literature Festival at the Louisiana Museum of Modern Art in Humlebæk, Denmark, a seaside town about twenty miles north of Copenhagen. "We contain multitudes," Smith told festival director Christian Lund, quoting Whitman. There is an aspect of Smith's personality here that is not as present in the rest of this volume: Patti Smith the comedian. Elsewhere in this collection, Smith talked about her childhood dream of being the next Johnny Carson; here, she showed that she can deadpan with the best of them.

Her focus on rhythm in poetry, and what she sometimes refers to as a poem's "punch line" translates well to comic timing. And if it doesn't always translate to the page, so much is in the delivery. The audience laughter is not marked here, but the belly laughs were there throughout as she regaled the large outdoor crowd with tales of her childhood crush on Arthur Rimbaud and Robert Mapplethorpe's gold lamé pants. And she knows just when to tug on the heartstrings as she builds to a punch line. "I can still cry thinking of other things," she said of her lifelong friendship with Mapplethorpe, "but there was always a lot of laughter, which is important in life and important in any relationship." Who knew—if Patti Smith had ditched the other arts to become a standup, she could have killed in Denmark. —Ed.

Christian Lund: Welcome to Louisiana, Patti.

Patti Smith: Thank you. I'm really happy to be here. It's beautiful here. Really special.

Lund: When you are on stage, you are considered as the "Godmother of Punk." But when I read your books, it seems like I meet another Patti Smith. It's like you are expressing two different sides of yourself in two different medias.

Smith: Well, there is a lot more than two, because as Walt Whitman said, "We contain multitudes." And that energy that people later called punk rock, an energy I've had since I was a child, I still have. I'll have it my whole life. But I have many different energies and many ways of expressing myself.

So if I'm expressing myself, if I'm, you know, taking care of my children, if I am washing clothes, I am still the girl that can put her foot through the amplifier. I am the same person.

Lund: I would like to invite you to do a reading from *Woolgathering*.

Smith: Sure. Actually, this little passage talks about the year 1957. I think I was about ten years old, and it's the story of two important things: the birth of my little sister Kimberly, which I wrote the song "Kimberly" about, on *Horses*. And also about my dog, Bambi, who I, now, how many years from '57—wow, over fifty years ago, I still remember this dog with the most precious of loves . . .

[reads from *Woolgathering*]

Lund: Thank you very much.

Smith: You're welcome.

Lund: You've said you lived in a clan of Peter Pan when you were a child. Could you give some examples of what was that?

Smith: Well, as a child I cherished all my books. I loved *Little Women* and *Pinocchio* and *Alice in Wonderland*, but *Peter Pan* was really my favorite, because that was the atmosphere in the world that I most lived in. And really, I thought it was possible because it was in a book, that we didn't have to grow up. And when I was very small, I decided I didn't want to grow up. That I would stay about ten or eleven and that was good enough for me. And, uh, it was a big surprise for me—actually, I was heartbroken to find out that we didn't have a choice. I thought we were just put on Earth and then we could decide what happens in our life. And, but I've never let go of that feeling. You know, I have never really felt that I've grown up.

Lund: You describe how your family had their daily prayers and praying seemed like an important part of your childhood life. I connect that somehow maybe to your poetry . . .

Smith: Well, you know, to me prayer is the essential, that is, you know the essential way that we communicate with our loved ones and of course with our god. In my life, my last time I was in an organized religion was when I was twelve. I left my religion, but I never left prayer. You can pray anywhere. You can pray—there's beautiful cathedrals and churches everywhere, but at the sea or in a field or when you're falling asleep at night. You know, it's a way to stay in contact, sometimes just with yourself, sometimes with a higher energy, and sometimes with our loved ones. And prayer to me is just a natural part of being.

Lund: You had an early interest in poetry. Do you see there is a connection with you being brought up with praying and the interest for poetry?

Smith: Yes. I never thought about that really, but that's really a good thought, because many poems are like little prayers. My first book of poetry was called *Silver Pennies* and it was all poems that had to do with elves and fairies and mysticism and in that book, I read Blake, I read Yeats, and Vachel Lindsay—many poets that have stayed with me in my life, and a lot of them were like little prayers [*from "The Lamb" by William Blake —Ed.*]:

> Little lamb who made thee
> dost thou know who made thee

It's quite like a prayer. Yes, that's a nice thought. I think there is an absolute connection there.

Lund: You were also reading Arthur Rimbaud, the French poet when you were sixteen. That's quite an early age to discover French poetry.

Smith: Well, I discovered Rimbaud two ways. When I was fourteen, fifteen years old, I wanted to be an artist, and I was very skinny, and

I loved Modigliani, and I loved his paintings because they reminded me of the Sienese paintings. But you know, his models I could relate to, and I read a book about him, and he loved this poet named Arthur Rimbaud. And I didn't know who Arthur Rimbaud was, but I thought, "I have to read him if this painter liked him so much." And then I was in Philadelphia and there was a secondhand bookstore outside a bus station—books very cheap—and there was a book, and I saw it, and what attracted me was the boy, the face on the cover. I mean, I was fifteen, sixteen years old, and Arthur Rimbaud was really cute, so truthfully I was attracted by his face, and then I picked up the book and realized this was the poet that Modigliani liked. So that was very lucky that it just happened to be a very cute poet. So I fell in love with him, but not just his face. When I opened the book, his language I couldn't really understand at all, because poetry is sometimes like a secret language and sometimes takes a while to unlock. But I've never let that bother me. If I don't understand a poem right away but I'm seduced by its beauty, I just revel in the beauty of the language. So it took me a while to decipher Rimbaud, but I loved him right away, his words and his face. . . . Well, until I discovered Bob Dylan!

Lund: You left rural South Jersey when you were about twenty years old and went to New York City, and you described that you felt like a country mouse in the city. New York City back then is quite different from what it is today. Could you describe the atmosphere that you met at that time?

Smith: Well, I mean, first of all, for me it was fantastic because there was no real culture where I was raised. There was no libraries, no bookstores, no art museums. There were fields and pig farms and most of the culture was in my house, 'cause all my family were readers, so our house always had lots of books. But when you left my house there was, you know, nature, which is beautiful, but no culture. So New York City was a mecca for culture. But also, it was interesting because the architecture was very dense—it was turn-of-the-century architecture. It was a gritty city. There was all kinds of life. You know, if you went to Forty-Second Street, there were the sailors and the prostitutes, and then there was a lot of places where you could get voodoo things and Spanish and Mexican talismans, and there were bookstores everywhere. And you could live very cheaply, and it seemed just alive with, also, creative energy. Because at that time, the city was economically oppressed, so a lot of young people were coming there, 'cause they could live there very cheaply. I can't say that it was deep poverty, but it was a poor city, so it was exciting, and I felt at home there, and I never felt afraid because there were people everywhere. People would say, "Oh, it's a dangerous city," and I said, "No, there's people everywhere. They're out all night!" I was never afraid, nothing bad ever happened to me there. So it was like opening up Pandora's box except—only good came out of it.

Lund: Actually, you arrived being an artist or feeling like an artist. And you said that rural south Jersey wasn't so pro-artist, wasn't so favorable for artists.

Smith: Well, I mean, there was nothing to do. There was no center. There was no cultural center, and most of the people that I went to school with—the boys were sent to Vietnam, or the girls became wives or worked as hairdressers or worked in factories. There wasn't a whole lot of work. And truthfully, I went to New York City not to become an artist at first. I went to New York City to get a job, because I lost my factory job in Philadelphia. There was no more work. A big shipyard closed and like thirty thousand jobs were lost and there was no work for a twenty-year-old girl with only a partial education. So my first duty was to get a job because I had no money. There was no credit cards in those days—you know, if you didn't have money in your pocket you didn't eat. So I needed work. And New York City had so many bookstores, I figured sooner or later one of them would hire me, which they did, and I got bookstore jobs for the next seven years. So it was a good place at that time to get a job.

Lund: Could you please tell us about your first encounters with Robert Mapplethorpe, who was not a famous photographer at that time. . . .

Smith: He wasn't famous anything. It's very funny, though, because sometimes people read my book and they say, "Well you drop all these names, you seem like you ran around with all these famous people." And I say, "None of us were famous." Even Allen Ginsberg wasn't famous. I mean, there was a cult of people that appreciated him, but none of, most of the beat poets—Gregory Corso never had any money. Everybody was scrambling. Jim Carroll was just a kid. You know, the cult of celebrity was not so big then. Even rock stars that I met that lived in the Chelsea Hotel at the same time as us, they weren't much different.

But I met Robert by chance. I met him going to Brooklyn looking for some friends, and my friends had moved, and they told me to go in a room and ask the boy in there if he knew where they went. And so I went in the room and there was a boy sleeping. And I stood there and looked at him, and it was like looking at a shepherd boy sleeping, 'cause he had all these masses of dark curly hair. He was a slender boy, just sleeping peacefully. And he woke up and I was standing there and he smiled at me. And from that moment it just seemed like we were destined to be friends or destined to know each other. It's just, his smile was so totally welcoming. It held nothing back. I was just a stranger standing in front of him. And that was my first meeting with Robert.

Lund: The second meeting you had, or encounter, was in Tompkins Square Park.

Smith: No, that was the third. The second was, Robert also worked in a bookstore. He worked in this bookstore named Brentano's. He worked downtown and I worked uptown in the same bookstore. And he had some kind of credit slip, and he wanted to buy something, and he came into my bookstore uptown because they sold ethnic jewelry. And there was a Persian necklace there that I really loved. It wasn't expensive—it was very simple. But it seemed mystical to me, and I really wanted it but I didn't have the money to buy it. And so, Robert came in, and we said hello, and he remembered me. And he was there for like an hour looking at every single thing, and then he pointed to the Persian necklace and said, "I want that." And I couldn't believe he picked—'cause there were hundreds of things there—that he picked the one thing that I wanted. So I wrapped it up and gave it to him. And to this day I don't know how

I got the guts or the balls to say this but I said to him, "Don't give it to any girl but me." And he said, "I won't." And he left.

And then the next time I met him, I was in a funny situation because a week had gone by working. In New York City, you have to work two weeks before you get a paycheck. I didn't know that, 'cause it wasn't like that in New Jersey, and I was so hungry and I worked for a week, stood in line for my paycheck and they said, "No. Next week." And I was really crying. I was so, so disappointed. And then this guy asked me for dinner—if I wanted to go out for dinner. A strange guy, an older guy—[*lowers voice for comedic effect*] *thirty years old*—but he was kind of square, you know. And I was really nervous. I had never gone out with an older guy before, and my mother always said, "Don't take anything from strangers, 'cause they always want something in return—especially a guy." So I'm thinking, well, all right. But I was so hungry, I decided to go. So he took me to eat and I was nervous the whole time, and then we walked down to Tompkins Square Park, which was the East Village, the grittiest of the parks, and the coolest. That's where all the hippies slept and everything. And I was sitting there on a park bench with him and he asked me to come up to his apartment and have a cocktail. And I thought, "This is just what my mother told me about." So I was trying to figure out what to do and how to get out of this. And I was really nervous, 'cause it just seemed like such a difficult situation. And all the sudden, I looked and coming up the path was the boy, was Robert. And I didn't even know his name actually, he was just "the boy." And I saw him and I just impulsively ran up to him, and I said, "Ah, do you remember me?" And he said, "Of course." And I said, "Will you pretend you're my boyfriend?" And he said, "Yes!" So I took him over to the guy and I said, "This is my boyfriend, he's really mad." And I said, "So I have to go." And the guy was looking at me like I was crazy. And I grabbed Robert's hand and I said, "Run!" So Robert and I ran away, and then finally we sat on a stoop. And I said, "Oh, thank you. You saved my life." And then, I said, "Well I guess we should exchange names. My name is Patti." And he said, "My name is Bob." And I said, "Um, Bob. You don't really seem like a Bob. Can I call you Robert?" And he said, "Sure." So I called him Robert. And then, after a time, everybody called him Robert.

Lund: *Just Kids* begins with Robert dying, and it gives the story of your relationship, a light of intensity. It's a story of love, but it's also a story of loss.

Smith: Well, I think it's also a story of unconditional friendship. I think really, love and loss is framed in that, but the heart it is what true friendship is all about. I mean, Robert, you know, was my boyfriend, and it was heartbreaking for both of us to go through the transition of going from being so intimate to being friends. And naturally, this would break up most couples. But Robert and I had something so much deeper than things like, well, sex, and things like that. Which, all of these things are important—you know, living together, being true to one another, being physically intimate—they're all beautiful things. But the thing that we had transcended everything. And that was that we bonded through our work, and both us felt magnified by the other. Both of us completed our self-confidence and our belief in ourselves as an artist through the other and it was so strong that I still feel it today. If I falter, if I feel lacking in confidence, I can access that part of him that believes in me, and I feel stronger. And there was no reason to give that up. There was no reason to give up, you know, other things that we shared like our common laughter, 'cause we laughed a lot. And really, had he lived I know that we would have worked and collaborated and laughed till the end of our lives because we were only a month apart. And I always thought we'd know each other forever, and of course we do in a certain way, but I never imagined that he would die so young. But I cherish that thing that we nourished and that we saved. If we couldn't save our relationship as a couple, we saved something more precious. So I think that is at the heart of the book.

Lund: What strikes me when reading it is your ability to communicate the love and compassion that was in your relationship. It is so strong, it resonates, even after you put down the book. Even years after, it really resonates. It's incredible.

Smith: Well, I still feel it. It's like my dog, you know. I wrote that piece not long ago. And just reading it, it almost made me cry. I still love my dog as much as I did when I was eleven. I still—what we had was true love, me and my dog. And what Robert and I had is also true. It would have to resonate because it does resonate.

Lund: In your book, you say that Robert was the one asking you to write your story. Why do you think he wanted you to write your story?

Smith: Well, I think that, one—I was the only one that could write it. There weren't many people that knew Robert when he was so young. I met Robert when we were twenty, and we lived such a secluded life. And I think I probably in some ways, well, I knew his young self better than anyone, and he knew also that he could trust me. Robert really liked my writing. He knew that I would do well by him. And he wanted to be remembered. He was only forty-two years old. He was still evolving as an artist. He had all kinds of work to do. He didn't want to die. He did not go gently. So I think, truthfully, he wanted to be remembered, and I also think he was proud of our connection. So it took me a long time to write but I promised him I would, and I did.

Lund: How long did it take you to write the book?

Smith: Well, he asked me in March of 1989 and it came out in 2010. And it went through two publishers, but a lot of things happened in my life that made it difficult to write. First, just grieving for him. And then the loss of my pianist, my husband, my brother, my mother, my father. I suffered so much loss and also raising my young children that I didn't have the emotional energy to write it. And I kept shelving it. I'd write it and put it back. And write it and put it back. And then sometimes I'd throw it away and start it over. But finally, I got to a point where I felt around 2008 or '9 that if I didn't get it done then, I'd never do it. And I had a lot of responsibility—how I would portray other people, both living and dead. I wanted to make sure I was fair toward everyone. And also was able to provide an atmosphere of the city and there's a lot of responsibility. I think people write memoirs or autobiographies really overly concerned with themselves and don't realize how they impact other people's lives by writing about them—sometimes really vindictively. A memoir should not be a format to seek revenge on people. Because you're writing to give the people something inspiring, something interesting, something that hopefully they can identify with or that will take them someplace new. It shouldn't be a format for personal grievances. Books are too precious for that.

Lund: You write in the beginning of *Woolgathering* that the writing process took you out of melancholy. What did the writing process of *Just Kids* do to you?

Smith: It nearly killed me, that's what it did. It was not an easy book to write. It was difficult technically, it was difficult in many ways. I wasn't really comfortable talking about myself, especially when I started becoming successful. I felt a little uncomfortable. I had to really think about how to talk about that without seeming conceited or self-preoccupied, so there were a lot of challenges in that book. And it was also painful, sometimes sad. But the one thing I did like is sometimes it made me laugh out loud, because things that Robert and I did, some of them were really funny. And our arguments, 'cause we argued all the time about the stupidest stuff. And I don't know if this is in the book or not, but Robert around 1970 started designing his own clothes, and they were getting pretty, um, flamboyant, and he designed these like chaps like cowboys wear where they're around here, and he had like a codpiece, here, in gold lamé—these pants. And we're in a café and we're on our way to a poetry reading and Robert's wearing gold lamé chaps and a codpiece. And I used to like to have honey in my tea but they never serve it in restaurants—they would only have sugar. So I would carry honey in a little bag. So I pulled out the honey and I put it on the table, and I'm putting the honey in the tea, and Robert said, "Patti, why do you have to bring honey to a restaurant?" And he said, "You're drawing attention to yourself." I don't even think I said—I just looked at him. You know, he's like sitting there with like four necklaces, bandanas, a big thing of keys, and gold lamé pants for a poetry reading. And I said, "Yeah I'm just—you know me, I'm just a real exhibitionist." But they were more playful little bickerings or arguments, but these things, that was the part of the book that I enjoyed just, you know. I can still laugh. I can still cry thinking of other things, but there was always a lot of laughter which is important in life and important in any relationship.

I always think my mother and father, who fought all the time—we were pretty poor when I was young. They fought about money, they fought about . . . I mean, they were always fighting, but I never saw another couple laugh as much as those two. They would tell, retell, and tell stories about the Thirties and World War II stories but from the funniest angles and just be on the floor laughing. And I think it saved their marriage. It wasn't the kids. It was the laughter.

Lund: In *Just Kids* there is a description of your first performance at St. Mark's Church on February 10, 1971.

Smith: Yeah, it was Bertolt Brecht's birthday.

Lund: But that was your first poetry reading.

Smith: Yes, and it was Robert who helped me get it. Robert always thought I should have poetry readings, he really liked to hear me read my poems, and he always wanted me to sing and read poetry. And he got a poet Gerard Malanga, who was part of Warhol's factory, to let me open him and read for like eighteen minutes, and I really wanted it to be special. Mostly because I was really good friends with Gregory Corso, and I would go to poetry readings with Gregory and if the poetry readings were boring, which they were *always* boring—there was a lot of really boring poetry readings—and Gregory would go, [*nasal voice*] "Eh . . . no blood, no blood. Eh . . . shitty! You're killin' poetry." I would sit next to him and I thought, "Oh my gosh, if I do a poetry reading, it better be good, 'cause Gregory will heckle me the whole the time." So I was seeing Sam Shepard at the time. Sam Shepard and I were doing a play together that we wrote called *Cowboy Mouth*. And I said to Sam, "Um, I really want my poetry reading to have something special." And he said, "Well why don't you get a guitar player and maybe sing a little or something?" And so I had met Lenny Kaye and he was working at a record store, and I said, "I think that guy Lenny plays guitar." So I went and visited Lenny and said, "You play guitar, right?" And he said, "Yeah." And I said, "Wanna play with me at St. Mark's? You know and do some sonic stuff? A couple of songs. And then, can you do a car crash? Can you make your guitar sound like a car crash?" And he said, [*Kaye* *impression*] "No problem." Because the big finale was about a boy in a stock car race that like smashes against a wall, so I wanted there to be [*car crash sound*], sort of like feedback and car crash sounds. And so, he said sure, and so, you know, we put together eighteen minutes and we did our poetry reading, which began with what is now "Gloria." At the beginning of "Gloria" there used to be a poem called "Oath" that began:

Jesus died for somebody's sins but not mine
Meltin' in a pot of thieves
Wild card up my sleeve
Thick heart of stone
My sins my own

And so it began like that and went straight into the car crash. And it was, some people loved it and heralded it as a new thing and other people thought I should be arrested for desecrating the church which is not all that unfamiliar now, is it?

But in any event, Lenny and I weathered that, weathered all kinds of storms and we're still together forty years later.

Lund: Actually, you mention somewhere that your first song or your first poem, maybe it was your first song, was "Fire of Unknown Origin."

Smith: Yes.

Lund: That was part of the performance at that time in St Mark's Church, 1971, with Lenny. I would ask you please to read it so we can have the atmosphere. I'm not sure Lenny can do the car crash.

Smith: Well, Lenny and I haven't done this for a very long time, but sure, we could figure it out. Lenny, come on up. This poem, actually I wrote in memory of Jim Morrison. Well, we haven't done it in some years so if we fuck it up it's your fault. [*Laughs.*]

Lund: I'll take the blame.

Smith: This is scary. [*Laughs.*]

[*Smith and Kaye perform "Fire of Unknown Origin."*]

Lund: Beautiful.

Smith: Thanks, Lenny.

Lund: Thank you, Lenny. [*To Smith.*] Thank you.

Smith: You're welcome.

Lund: In *Just Kids*, you mention somewhere that you knew you wanted to be an artist, but you also said you wanted your work to matter.

Smith: Since I was a child, I wanted to be a writer. And then I discovered art. I saw art in person in a museum when I was about twelve and wanted to be a painter. When I say artist, I mean them all, not necessarily a painter or whatever creative expression I choose or one chooses. But people who have a real true calling, so it's not simply just expressing oneself, which is beautiful, but something more than that, something that sometimes you have to sacrifice deeply for. And I really, I wanted to be one of those people. I wanted to produce work that would be enduring, work that would inspire other people. When I read *Pinocchio* or when I read Murakami or Roberto Bolaño or the Songs of Solomon, anything that is given to us, it makes me want to give something in return for all of the . . . I mean, I'm a real bookworm. All the pleasure in my life, I would say at least I've spent over half my life reading, and so to give back something. You know, something worthy to be in that canon. Something that would give some people equal joy.

Lund: I noticed that you wrote about Andy Warhol saying that you "felt little for the can and didn't like the soup." That you preferred an artist not mirroring the world but transforming it.

Smith: Yes. Well, when I was young I truthfully didn't have an affection for Andy Warhol. As a human being, I thought that he was not a very generous or kind person. His work really didn't speak to me. Robert loved Andy Warhol though, and Robert believed he was a genius, and so I didn't dismiss him because I knew Robert knew things. I trusted in Robert's instinct. But when I was young his work just didn't speak to me. At this time in my life, I've found I've really gotten to appreciate what a genius he was, and I find if I'm in a museum and looking at contemporary art—I'm not so drawn to contemporary art—and I'll suddenly see something across the room and I think, "That's strong." And

I go over and it's Andy's. And the last works he did or some of the last works he did before he died, his "Last Supper" body of work, I thought was genius. It was quite moving. So I've learned to appreciate Andy's genius. I think part of it is I didn't have to deal with him as a human being. I could just look at his work. And really, it's important to . . . especially, I look at our times. We're so celebrity driven, and we expect, you know—one loves an actor or loves the work somebody does and then you expect them to live up to your expectations or want to know all about their personal life. In the end, the best thing any artist or any actor or people that do work—the only thing they owe us is their work. And if they do good work, their personal life should be their own and it's just that I kept colliding with Andy. You know, we all lived around the same area, but he was a great artist.

The reason I wrote that, too, was well, it was how I really felt. When I wrote that about Andy's work, I wrote that as a young—in the mind of a young person, because I've evolved to other places where I deeply, deeply appreciate him. You know, with Picasso, they're two of the most important artists of the twentieth century, so I understand his importance.

Lund: But what I think is important in the quotation about an artist either mirroring or transforming. I think what you do is you are transforming instead of mirroring what you see. It's two different conceptions of how to be an artist.

Smith: Well, I feel more drawn to the transformative in art itself. I'm not so drawn to nonfiction, but I also appreciate more and more someone that has the ability to mirror our times. I think that it's important that people do that, it's just, I'm not really that style of person. And but you know, we need everybody. We need all kinds of points of view.

I learned this lesson when September 11 happened. Where I live in New York City, I could see the towers from my stoop and I watched them come down, and then I went, I didn't live far from there, so I went and looked at the remains of one of the towers, the south tower, and it was an extraordinary—it was like a piece of sculpture. It looked like the tower of Babel. And I started thinking a lot about Andy then. I really missed Andy as an artist then because he would have known what to do as an artist, not to transform but to document this extraordinary thing that happened. I'm not talking about the pain or the loss of life or the political resonance. I just mean the physical event and these buildings and I know that he would have done a body of work and that it would have been extraordinary. And no one was doing it. So I had a little studio, so I made pictures and made silk screens and did a body of work of silk screens only to satisfy my need or longing to have someone do that, because in my whole lifetime, Andy would have done it. And I even did some of the images in silver to resonate Andy's silver hair and the silver pillows in his Factory. And I only bring that up not to speak about my body of work but to speak of how much I missed having an artist there who could reflect and animate what had happened. Even though I'm not that style of artist, I recognize the importance of that type of artist. But when I was young I was really judgmental! [*Laughs.*]

Lund: *Just Kids* is about many people, many friends. You write about you and Robert being surrounded by people all the time. And I think we heard from *Woolgathering* that you were surrounded by your siblings and your spirit dog, Bambi, and in your recent album, *Banga*, it's Amy Winehouse and Maria Schneider.

Smith: Yeah, I don't know why, but it's always been like that. The first poem that was ever published that I wrote was in—I was about fourteen years old, I think—and it was a poem dedicated to Charlie Parker. Charlie Parker died in 1959 [*Charlie Parker died March 12, 1955 —Ed.*], and my father used to listen to Charlie Parker's music and called him "The Bird," that was his nickname. So I wrote a poem called "Bird Is Free." Just probably a corny teenage poem, but it was the first real poem I wrote, was in remembrance to someone that passed. It's just part of what I do. I can't say why, I just do it. I didn't plan to write a song about Amy Winehouse. You know, she lost her life while we were working on the record and I just wrote her a little song. Maria Schneider, I had known in the '70s and felt very sad when she died because she wasn't that old—she was younger than me—and wrote one for Maria. But on the other hand, there's also a song, "Nine," which was written for Johnny Depp's birthday, and he's very much alive!

Lund: You call it your talismanic nature, right?

Smith: What?

Lund: You call it your talismanic nature.

Smith: I suppose—one of them. It's one of my natures.

Lund: I would like you to read a little from *Just Kids*. You talked about Robert, and actually, I would like at the end of the conversation for you to read the foreword.

[*Smith reads from the foreword to* Just Kids.]

Lund: In 2010, you won the National Book Award, and I saw on You-Tube from the award, you having tears in your eyes describing how you worked at Scribner's Bookstore, dreaming about one day writing your own book.

Smith: Well, I worked in bookstores for years, and my best job was at Scribner's Bookstore. And every year when the National Book Award happened, all the winners of the National Book Award, they would order a lot of copies, and then I had to wrap them in blue paper and put a little silver seal on it—and I hated this job. 'Cause I was a really bad wrapper. I mean, everything would look all crooked, and I'd get hairs in the Scotch tape, but when I would pick up these books they would all have a gold seal on them. 'Cause you would have to put . . . I would get like a big roll of gold seals from the National Book Foundation and it would say, "Winner of the National Book Award," and I thought that was so cool. And I used to daydream about writing a book and then I'd win the National Book Award, and then—somebody else would have to wrap them.

Lund: And now you are admired by many young people, not least many of the young artists and writers here at the festival who find inspiration in your book and in your life story. How do you feel about that?

Smith: It's inspiring. It's really, I never—I mean, my main goal was first to finish the book 'cause I promised Robert, and then give Robert to the people, because no one knew anything about Robert except the end of his life. And there was more to Robert, you know, than someone who broke new boundaries and died of AIDS. He was a holistic person, and I wanted people to know him as a human being. And that was my great hope, and I thought, well, maybe it'll be a little cult book and some people will read it, and so many people have read it and talked to me about it. And it makes me so happy. One, because it's so nice for Robert, but it's inspiring. It makes me want to write more books. A writer or any artist can't expect to be embraced by the people. I've done records where it seemed like no one listened to them. You write poetry books that maybe fifty people read. And you just keep doing your work because you have to, because it's your calling. But it's beautiful to be embraced by the people. Some people have said to me, [lowers voice] "Well, you know, don't you think that kind of success spoils one as an artist." Or, you know, "If you're a punk rocker, you don't want to have a hit record." And I say, you know, "Fuck you." [Laughs.] You know, it's just like one does their work for the people and the more people you can touch the more wonderful it is. You don't do your work and say, "I only want the cool people to read it." You know, you want everyone to be transported or hopefully inspired by it. But I am equally inspired, 'cause truthfully, I never thought I would write another book of nonfiction or another memoir, but so many people have asked me to write one that now I'm working on one. Because Robert asked for that one and the people have asked for another, so I'm working.

Lund: You made it all the way to here from rural south Jersey.

Smith: Yes.

Lund: Is there some advice you could give to a young artist who has a long journey in front of him or her?

Smith: Just work hard and be true to yourself and, you know, don't forget that the most important goal is to do good work. When I was really young, William Burroughs told me, and I was really struggling—we never had any money. And the advice that William gave me was, "Build a good name." You know, keep your name clean. Don't make compromises, don't worry about making a bunch of money or being successful. Be concerned with doing good work. And make the right choices and protect your work, and if you build a good name, eventually, you know, that name will be its own currency.

And, uh, I remember when he told me that and I said, "Yeah, but William, my name's Smith." [*Audience laughs.*] Just joking. But he gave me that advice, and it was beautiful advice and I tried to follow it. To be an artist, actually, to be a human being in these times, it's all difficult. You have to go through life hopefully trying to stay healthy, being as happy as you can, and pursuing, doing what you want. If what you want is to have children, if what you want is to be a baker, if what you want is to live out in the woods or try to save the environment, or maybe what you want is to write scripts for detective shows. It doesn't really matter, you know. What matters is to know what you want and pursue it and understand that it's gonna be hard because life is really difficult. You're gonna lose people you love, you're gonna suffer heartbreak, sometimes you'll be sick, sometimes you'll have a really bad toothache, sometimes you'll be hungry, but on the other end you'll have the most beautiful experiences. Sometimes just the sky, sometimes, you know, a piece of work that you do that feels so wonderful, or you find somebody to love, or your children. There's beautiful things in life. So when you're suffering, just, you know, it's part of the package. You look at it—we're born and we also have to die. We know that. So it makes sense that we're gonna be really happy and things are gonna be really fucked up, too. Just ride with it. You know, it's like a roller coaster ride. It's never gonna be perfect, it's gonna have perfect moments and rough spots, but it's all worth it. Believe me. I think it is.

Lund: One last question?

Smith: Yes.

Lund: Your children, Jesse and Jackson, they are at the same age, more or less, as you and Robert in *Just Kids*. What are your reflections on the world that they are meeting today as opposed to the one you are describing in *Just Kids*?

Smith: I think our world is . . . you know, I'm sure that each generation could say that their time was the best and the worst of times, but

I think that right now we're are at something different that I've never seen. You can say the best and the worst of times, but also, we're in a transitional time, something very unique to the history of mankind because of technology. Everything is shifting at a very rapid pace, and there's a lot of challenges, but I just think also, it's a pioneering time because there is no other time in history like right now. And that's what makes it unique. It's not unique because we have, like, Renaissance-style artists; it's unique because of the people. It is a time of the people, because technology has really democratized self-expression. Instead of a handful of people making their own records or writing their own songs, everybody can write them. Everyone can post a poem on the Internet and have people read it. Everyone has access, an access that they've never had before. There is possibilities for global striking. There is possibilities for bringing down these corporations and governments who think they rule the world because we can unite as one people through technology. We're all still figuring it out and what power we actually have, but the people still do have the power more than ever. And I think right now we're going through this painful sort of like adolescence. Again, what do we do with this technology? What do we do with our world? Who are we? But it also makes it exciting. You know, all the young people right now, the new generations, they're pioneers in a new time. So I say, stay strong, try to stay—have fun—but stay clean, stay healthy, because you have a lot of challenges ahead, and be happy.

Lund: Thank you very much.

Smith: [*To audience.*] Thank you for coming.

PATTI SMITH: MAKING THE PAST PRESENT

Daniel David Baird | March 2013 | *Border Crossings* (Canada)

Here we find Patti Smith the visual artist and photographer. This article originally appeared in the 2013 photography issue of *Border Crossings*, a quarterly cultural magazine based in Winnipeg, Manitoba. Daniel Baird met Smith at her hotel in Ottawa during a snowstorm when she was opening for Neil Young and Crazy Horse in the fall of 2012. *Patti Smith: Dream of Life* had recently aired on the PBS series *POV*, and her photography exhibit *Camera Solo* was traveling to the Art Gallery of Ontario in Toronto. Smith's photographs are stark, black-and-white Polaroids captured over the course of years as she toured the world. They are almost all objects, but not without significance. People are absent, but there is an undeniable, sometimes ghostly presence. She shows us Virginia Woolf's cane, Frida Kahlo's bed, Sylvia Plath's grave, her own father's chipped cup. And by seeing these seemingly mundane objects up close through the lens of Smith's camera, we can absorb her presence, get a glimpse of what it's like to view the world through her eyes.

Here, we get a sense of Smith's artistic process and the visual artists who have inspired her. For Smith, the border between the arts is porous; one discipline seems to just bleed into the others. "Sometimes I find myself so involved in the writing of a poem," she said, "that it actually ends up becoming a drawing as well." —Ed.

When many of us think of Patti Smith, we tend to think of one of two things. There is the Patti Smith on the cover of her landmark 1975 debut album, *Horses*, shot by her lover and lifelong soulmate Robert

Mapplethorpe. In that photograph, a desperately skinny Smith stands, decked out in a loose white men's shirt with its sleeves rolled up, thin tie draped down from her collar, jacket insouciantly thrown over her shoulder. The expression on her face is at once contemplative, cocky and intransigent, the background just a blank white wall slightly brushed with shadow. If *Horses* is one of the finest first albums in rock history, then the cover photograph is one of the most beautiful and evocative: here Smith is sensuous, romantic, edgy and somehow volatile. And then there is Patti Smith the furious possessed performer of the 1970s in storied venues like CBGB, part punk rocker part beat poet part shaman, shouting and spitting, whispering and purring her lines. "And when I look inside of your temple it looks just like the inside of anyone one man. And when he beckons his finger to me, well, I move in another direction, I move in another dimension," she murmurs in "Ain't It Strange" from *Radio Ethiopia*. "I was lost and the cost was to be outside of society," she snarls in her controversial anthem "Rock N Roll [*n*-word]" from her third album, *Easter*, a song that is about as close as Smith ever got to the confrontational iconoclasm of punk rock. "Jimi Hendrix was a [*n*-word]/Jesus Christ and grandma, too/Jackson Pollock was a [*n*-word]/[*n*-word] [*n*-word] [*n*-word] [*n*-word]/[*n*-word] [*n*-word] [*n*-word] . . ."

The Patti Smith I encountered when she opened her hotel-room door in Ottawa this past November, while she was in the middle of a whirlwind, eight-city international tour with Neil Young and Crazy Horse, was hardly the frenzied, spit-spraying performer she was in the 1970s—and, incredibly, still is. Hotel room strewn with clothes and open suitcases, books and room service trays, Smith, who turned 66 in December, was clearly exhausted and distracted, her voice hoarse from too much singing and too much dry airplane air, and she was going on stage at the Kanata Centre in just a few hours [*This concert took place November 24, 2012, at Scotiabank Place in Ottawa —Ed.*]. But once she plopped herself down in an easy chair beneath the room's window, an early snowstorm blowing outside, put up her bare feet and pulled her long, tangled, grey-streaked hair from her face, she was suddenly focused and eager to talk, not about the old times at the Chelsea Hotel or CBGB, but about art, poetry, music and ideas. And when Smith talks, her voice low and insistent, her long, bony, beautiful hands fly, punctuating the rhythm of her speech.

Patti Smith's 40-plus year career has been remarkable and in many ways wildly improbable, driven almost entirely by her innate fearlessness and the force of her sensibility. Born in Chicago, Illinois and raised in a working-class family in southern New Jersey, Smith moved to New York City in 1967 to become an artist and poet. She became a rock musician more or less inadvertently through performing her poetry with musical accompaniment and hanging out at Max's Kansas City, but once she got going in earnest in 1974, her ascent was meteoric, and four important albums followed in quick succession: *Horses* (1975), *Radio Ethiopia* (1976), *Easter* (1978), and *Wave* (1979). But after five years of relentless performing, Smith had fallen in love with the former guitarist for the Detroit proto-punk band MC5, Fred "Sonic" Smith, and was ready to give up the rock and roll lifestyle to raise a family. The Patti Smith Group's final performance was in Florence, Italy in the fall of 1979; when Smith arrived in Florence, the first thing she did was hit the streets in search of Michelangelo's unfinished *Slaves*. Soon after, Smith was married and had moved to a quiet life in the suburbs of Detroit, where she lived in semi-retirement for 15 years.

When her husband died suddenly in 1994, Smith revived her career and moved back to New York, and her re-emergence has, if anything, been more spectacular than her initial rise. There have been six studio albums, including the critically acclaimed *Banga*, which was released last year and contains some of her most powerful work since *Wave*. There have been books of poetry, like the ruminative *Strange Messenger*, 2003, and *Auguries of Innocence*, 2005, and the heartbreaking memoir of her friendship with Robert Mapplethorpe, *Just Kids*, 2010, which won the National Book Award for non-fiction. And there have been major exhibitions of her work as a visual artist: "Land 250" in 2008 at the Fondation Cartier pour l'art contemporain in Paris, which included work she made from 1967 to 2007, and "Patti Smith: Camera Solo," an exhibition of her photographs that opened at the Wadsworth Atheneum in Hartford, Connecticut in 2011. "Camera Solo" will be on view at the Art Gallery of Ontario through May 19.

"I've always loved drawing," Smith told me. "I've always felt connected to the idea of the written word and with the act of writing. When
I was young, I wanted to be an illustrator because I didn't really know
what fine art was, but when I was 12 years old my father took me to
the Philadelphia Museum and I saw a show of the work of John Singer
Sargent. As a young person I fell completely in love with Picasso—I was
just in Madrid, and I went to see *Guernica*, and especially the drawings he
did as studies for it. Drawings are intimate and they have a close relationship with the written word—you can do both with a pencil. Sometimes
I find myself so involved in the writing of a poem that it actually ends
up becoming a drawing as well."

Smith's drawings are both fierce and incredibly intimate and often,
at least in part, consist of frantically improvised text. In the early figu-
rative drawing, *Self Portrait*, 1969, which shows the strong influence of
the Willem de Kooning *Woman* series of the 1950s, Smith's smeared
head and face and truncated torso look like they are in furious motion,
a black cloud of words rising like smoke from her head. The hand-drawn
cover for her 1997 album *Peace and Noise* has text pulsing and swirling
in what looks like either the petals of a flower or a map of flowing rivers. The drawing does not itself form a full, coherent text, but is rather
an accumulation of words connected instant by instant and in various
directions; here, the words themselves are indistinguishable from the
marks, and seem the graphic equivalent of her well known vocal improvisations. Unlike Cy Twombly—whose work Smith admires but did not
know until later—where the focus is mostly on the act and form of mark
making itself, for Smith the verbal and the visual are completely intertwined. Other drawings are more wispy and lyrical. In *Orchid*, 1998, for
instance, both the lines and the elegantly drawn cursive writing move
in circles, form small, clustered islands, rise and curve and open. When
she wants, Smith can draw in finely rendered script, and she told me
that when she was young she loved copying things like the *Declaration
of Independence*. In an untitled work from 2006, the lines, pale and occasionally smudged with pink and lavender, drift shimmering across the
page as though over the surface of water. At one point there is a form
that appears to be a hand holding pencil to the paper, which suggests

that these drawings are as invested in their moment of creation as a saxophone solo by John Coltrane.

"I'm not a natural draughtsman," Smith acknowledged. "I'm not like some people, who can draw anything. I never developed those skills. When I was 19 I leaped forward immediately—I was into Picasso, Kandinsky, de Kooning, Pollock; the abstract expressionists have always been important to me. I tend to work in spurts. I can work on a drawing for months, and in order to do that, I need to be able to concentrate. The difficulty with being a performer is that I feel split down the middle: I've always preferred a solitary life, but being a performer is completely public, and it requires one to be completely present—when you're performing, there's no time to let the mind wander."

"The Polaroids have been a blessing," she continued, speaking of the black and white Polaroid photographs she takes with vintage Land 100 and Land 50 cameras and then has scanned and printed in editions, which is what will be on view at the Art Gallery of Ontario. "When you're on tour, you can be in 30 different cities in 40 days, and I can go out and take a couple of photographs in every city. I've always loved photography. I remember when I was a child in the 1950s I would see Irving Penn photographs in *Harper's* [*Bazaar*] and I knew they were different from the photographs in the Sears Catalogue, and later I went to the library and saw photographs by 19th-century photographers like Julia Margaret Cameron. I'm not technically very good, and anyway these days anyone with a cell phone can take a decent photograph. I wanted to take photographs that I can take, and what I can offer is my sensibility and also the access I have. One of the most recent photographs I took was of Sylvia Plath's grave in West Yorkshire—most people don't travel as much as I do and so would never have the chance to see it."

Smith has always been a romantic, a lover of poets, artists and musicians, and her work as a singer and songwriter, poet and visual artist is full of elegies, invocations and allusions to her heroes. The lovely *Virginia Woolf's Bed II*, Monk's House, 2003, is, for instance, a picture of Woolf's austere bed, cross stitched into the center of the stark, white bedsheet, shot at a low angle with swarming shadows and a flash of light in the upper left-hand corner. *Virginia Woolf's Cane*, 2011, on the other hand, is simply a picture of Woolf's old, wooden cane, shot in direct light from above. *Grave, Amedeo Modigliani and Jeanne Hébuterne, Père Lachaise, Paris*, 2010, is a shot of the tormented artist and his equally tormented— and pregnant—lover's grave, a long-stemmed white rose carefully set on top of it. Then there is *Headstone for William Blake, Bunhill Fields, London*, 2006, and *Roberto Bolaño's Chair 2*, 2010, and *Frida Kahlo's Bed, Casa Azul, Coyoacán*, 2012, shot with overlapping shadows, a skeleton set behind the bed. These photographs, which are notably devoid of people (apart from occasional self-portraits and pictures of her children, Smith rarely photographs people), are what Smith calls "third-class relics"; they are the places great artists have been, the things they have lived with, their final resting places. The sense is that by contemplating them we can absorb their presence.

"A lot of people might think I'm morbid," Smith admitted. "But that's really not the case. I don't think of these things and people as part of my past; they are part of my working life. I don't think of Robert Mapplethorpe or my husband as part of my past, and while I never knew Rimbaud or Blake or Bolaño, they are always with me, and they have made my life more inspiring." Not all of Smith's photographs are of relics of the great artistic visionaries of the past; some are more private and introspective. In *Self-Portrait, NYC*, 2003, for instance, Smith's head is tilted back against the wall, her face half in shadow, half in stark white light. *Jesse with Flower*, 2003, has her son's extended hand holding a small, shriveled sunflower [*This may be of her daughter Jesse's hand —Ed.*]; *Fender Duo-Sonic, NYC*, 2009, is a blurry snapshot of Smith's electric guitar, which she bought on time on the Upper West Side in the 1970s; and *My Father's Cup*, 2004, is a simple still life of her father's engraved coffee cup set on a shelf.

Smith has, from the beginning, had a powerful and ambivalent relationship to the spiritual traditions. This should come as no surprise: her mother was a failed Jehovah's Witness (she was never able to give up smoking) and her first book was the Bible, and to this day she seems to have the prophets and the gospels at her fingertips. Her two favorite poets, William Blake and Arthur Rimbaud, are both arguably religious poets, though in a heretical mode: *Marriage of Heaven and Hell* and *A*

Season in Hell are both steeped in a visionary tradition that descends from *The Book of Job* and *The Book of the Prophet Isaiah*. And while early Smith songs are sometimes aggressively iconoclastic—the famous refrain in the tellingly titled "Gloria (In Excelsis Deo)" goes "Jesus died for somebody's sins/but not mine"—her subsequent work is increasingly saturated with religious, and specifically Christian, allusions. Think, for instance, of "Ghost Dance" from *Easter* ("Here we are, Father, Lord, Holy Ghost/Bread of your bread ghost of your host/We are the tears that fall from your eyes/Word of your word cry of your cry/We shall live again we shall live again") or the same album's title song ("I am the spring the holy ground/I am the seed of mystery") or more recently in poems like "Eve of All Saints" in *Auguries of Innocence* ("*My dove*, your name is water in my hand/I will offer it with salt and bread . . .) And Smith's photographs reflect her enduring fascination with religion. *Cross with Mirror*, 2003, is a picture of an old stone cross set beneath a mirror, the cross's reflection receding back into the mirror's darkness. *Ghent Altarpiece (The Backside of the Mystical Lamb), Ghent, Belgium*, 2005, is an image, shot from an oblique angle, of Jan van Eyck's masterpiece.

Art and religion, the pure life of the spirit and the transfiguring power of the imagination, confront one another in Smith's stunning 10-minute song "Constantine's Dream," the high point of *Banga*. The song moves between, and ultimately beyond, Piero della Francesca's resplendent *The Dream of Constantine*, 1452, part of the fresco cycle *The Story of the True Cross* in the Basilica of San Francesco in Arezzo, Italy, and the life of Saint Francis. "When Robert [Mapplethorpe] died, we had a mutual friend named Dimitry, and he sent me a postcard of the troubled King," Smith recalled. "I ended up losing the postcard, but I spent years trying to find the painting in libraries—because of the armour on the guard, I assumed the painting was Spanish, so I was looking through books of Spanish art and at one point I even announced that I would search for the painting in every museum in Spain. Then I was in Arezzo on tour and I had this incredible apocalyptic dream of St. Francis receiving the stigmata. I couldn't shake the dream, so I went out onto the street and found myself in front of the Basilica of St. Francis. I went inside to say a prayer and, when I looked up, there it was—the painting I had been looking for."

"Constantine's Dream" opens with guitar and slow, heavy drums, but soon layers of other instruments join in to create a moody, swarming soundscape, Smith's voice low and moaning. "In Arezzo, I dreamed a dream," she sings, "of St. Francis who kneeled and prayed/For the birds and the beasts and all human kind/All through the night I felt drawn in by him/And I heard him call like a distant hymn." The song, whose text Smith improvised, was originally meant to be an account of her dream of St. Francis, but halfway through the song, her voice increasingly urgent and incantatory, the theme suddenly shifts. "But I could not give myself to him," she intones, "I felt another call from the basilica itself/The call of art—the call of man/And the beauty of the material drew me away/And I awoke, and beheld upon the wall/the dream of Constantine/The handiwork of Piero della Francesca . . . " For Smith, St. Francis, friend of birds and wolves, a saint whose spirit had achieved a serene relationship with the natural world, is a model of how we, in our era of climate change and mass extinction, should aspire to relate to the world; but St. Francis was not an artist, did not transform the material of the world into something beautiful. "At that point in the song, I encountered my dilemma about art," Smith said. "I don't think we should have an imprint on the earth at this point, but art is really about making an imprint. I was brought up as a Jehovah's Witness, which is a very austere religion. But when I saw art the first time, I knew that was what I wanted. I can't imagine a world without art, no matter how perfect it is."

"Still, I think prayer is the most important thing," Smith reflected. "But it's not always obvious what a prayer is—some prayers are asking for things, others are a form of praise. Think of Psalms. There's an aspect of prayer in all of the work that I do. In improvisation, you try to find a deeper form of concentration, you try to find the deepest and purest part of you and draw it up and send it out to someone, whether it's an ancestor or an archangel. You want it to come from a place that wakens God or the dead, and if you're doing that then you know you're doing something worthwhile. You can see that in a John Coltrane solo when he goes out to talk to God for 10 minutes and then comes back or in

Rilke's *Duino Elegies*. They are trying to find stepping stones to perfection." Whether moving fluidly between a poem and drawing and back again, or taking a Polaroid of a fork and spoon Rimbaud once ate with, or launching full force into her ecstatic love song "Dancing Barefoot" on stage at the Kanata Centre in Ottawa nearly 20 years after her lover and husband died, Patti Smith's art is powerful because of its incredible lack of self-consciousness, because it has a strange and furious kind of innocence and, most importantly, because it so obviously comes from a pure, deep place. She is, as the song goes, a benediction.

PATTI SMITH'S ETERNAL FLAME

Alan Light | Conducted 2007, published February 12, 2015 | *Medium Cuepoint*

"I'm so entrenched in the present, in the present-future," Patti Smith told prolific journalist and author Alan Light in this 2007 interview, unpublished in its entirety until 2015. What does it mean to be in the present-future? It seems an apt description of a visionary artist; Smith is so viscerally present, yet always one step ahead. She had just been inducted into the Rock and Roll Hall of Fame, and when Light asked why she'd never released a box set or career retrospective, the answer was obvious: "Well, I'm still working." Patti Smith lives in the progressive or continuous tense, maybe the future perfect.

She looks back, too, but her past doesn't always resonate with her present. *Horses*, the album that made her reputation, continues to inspire generations of people outside of society. "It's *for* them," she explained. "It's not really for me anymore." In hindsight, she had a searing clarity of vision in her self-reflection. At one point, she defined the "mission" of five of her records in under twenty words each. It wasn't until *Trampin'* that she recorded "my first real record as myself." She seems to know exactly what she's trying to do with each creative project, but as she evolves the goals change with her. And yet there's a sense of a core mission running through it all: to serve the people. —Ed.

"No matter what anybody thinks about any of them," said Patti Smith, "every record I've done has been done with the same amount of care, anguish, pain, suffering, and joy. We never threw a record together. Each record was done really seriously, as if our life depended on it."

In 1975, when Smith released her astonishing first album, *Horses*, she became the first member of the nascent CBGB crew to make it to

424 | PATTI SMITH ON PATTI SMITH

vinyl, helping set a global revolution in motion. Her sinuous, searing poetry—first unleashed on the influential independent single "Hey Joe" / "Piss Factory," which actually predates the album—didn't fit any simple definition of "punk," but its defiant outsider attitude sure did.

In 2007, I spoke at length to Smith on the occasion of her tenth record, *Twelve*, on which she covered some of her favorite songs by a wide range of artists, from Stevie Wonder to Nirvana to the Allman Brothers. She sat calm and still on a sofa in a Sony Music conference room; listening back to the tapes, we were both fighting colds. Our discussion of the album ran as a news story, but we also got into an examination of her full body of recorded work, none of which has ever been published.

She talked about her ambitions for *Horses*, and of her pain when *Dream of Life*—her 1988 return to the public eye after spending most of a decade living quietly in Michigan with her husband, Fred "Sonic" Smith, a former member of the MC5—was met with bad reviews. Since this interview, Smith has released only one new studio album, 2012's *Banga*, but she also wrote the magnificent *Just Kids*, a loving reminiscence of her early days in New York City, which won the National Book Award in 2010.

This year marks Patti Smith's fortieth anniversary as a recording artist. Though she's never had a huge-selling album and her only hit single was 1978's "Because the Night," co-written by Bruce Springsteen, she has become an international icon, an influence on artists from U2 to Madonna, an activist and author and, at age 68, a living, breathing, working connection to the fading spirit of a transformative era of music and poetry and commitment.

"My mission is to stay healthy and productive, and serve as a good example," she said. "That's what I can contribute. I haven't had the most thrilling lifestyle. I was a pretty good dresser, but I would have a pretty boring *Behind the Music*. So it's got to be the work, and I'm still working."

Smith had recently been inducted into the Rock and Roll Hall of Fame, so that's where our conversation began.

———

Alan Light: What thoughts did the Hall of Fame ceremony bring up for you?

Patti Smith: I'm so entrenched in the present, in the present-future, that if I didn't feel that I continued to contribute, I would have never accepted it. It's an institutional honor and I have thoughts about institutions—not all negative—and I have a strong regard for history, so it has its meaning for me. I'm proud to have the recognition. But it didn't really make me reflect on my life like I was dying, drowning and seeing my life go by. It actually made me think more of the future than of the past, because it made me feel like I've done this work and it's been recognized. Now what can I do in present-future to magnify that or to show that this faith was justified? Because it's not like I wrote the song in 1975 that changed the world; I didn't do that. I didn't have a record that sold 30 million copies and everyone was dancing to. So whatever contribution I've given is, to me, as valuable as the contribution I keep making.

Do you spend any time thinking about your catalogue, or is everything focused on looking forward?

Well, that's not the only body of work I have. I have poetry books and photography and drawings, being a mom, I have a lot of different aspects to look at. In terms of the records, I was an amateur. I wasn't a singer, I didn't know anything about what I was doing or how to make a record. I did the best that I knew how to do.

To you, does *Horses* sit in a different place from the rest of the albums?

Only because *Horses* was not so much a band project. *Horses* really stemmed from a lot of things that I had written as poetry. "Jesus died for somebody's sins but not mine" came from a poem I wrote when I was 20 in 1970. "Redondo Beach" from a poem I wrote at the same period. "Land," "Johnny" and all that came from my experiences hanging out with William Burroughs and reading *The Wild Boys*, so a lot of *Horses* came from my relationships with other poets, and my relationship with poetry and performing.

It's also different in that my mission on that record was really to speak to my own kind. I really didn't have a sense of the world at that time; I was concerned about the disenfranchised, maverick people who were looked down on because of the way they dressed or because they were homosexual or because they were artists or deadbeats, intelligent people but just people outside society. It was my way of saying "We're not alone, we are a community, we can find each other and get strong," reaching out to the people we found—Tom Verlaine and Richard Hell and Jim Carroll—and then people all over the world, like the Clash, the Dead Boys, whoever we found. But it was very specific.

I had only been on an airplane once in my life, and then I started touring and I realized that there's a whole world out there. So on subsequent records, in my mind I was speaking to a much broader audience. By the time of *Trampin'* I felt like the idea of the disenfranchised is no longer the artist or the poet, but people who are under the heel of corporations, of corrupt governments, of the imperialistic goals of our own government—we're all disenfranchised.

So *Horses* reflects my experience in life, which was not broad. I was still learning, I was not sophisticated, and I was looking for my people as I perceived them. That's why I think to this day, young people come up and tell me how much they like that record or that it's important to them, because it's *for* them. It's not really for me anymore. It was written by a young person for other young people, for people who felt they didn't have a place, that nobody cared about them.

So once your perspective opened up, where did the next records go?

So if on *Horses* I wanted to merge poetry and rock and roll, and to speak to the disenfranchised, on *Radio Ethiopia* I was developing poetry and improvisation and playing some electric guitar. On *Easter* I was expanding in another way and on *Wave*, I was sort of saying goodbye and writing love songs for my future husband. But in that period, the mission was to reclaim rock and roll from big rock stars and glamorous people—we had a mission, and we accomplished our mission. We wanted to create space for the new guard. And the new guard took over, and that was great, and I went my way.

Why was it time to re-enter the music world when you made *Dream of Life?*

Fred and I always continued to write songs at home. And then in the middle of the '80s, Fred wanted to make a record. I think an election was coming, so we wanted to make a statement about certain things. "People Have the Power" was originally written with the idea that if Jesse Jackson ran for president, we were writing him a song. He never used it, but Ralph Nader did, and I was very proud of that. MoveOn used it as well.

It was a strange time, because I became pregnant with my second child right when we decided to do it, and at the same time found out that my best friend had AIDS, so it was a time of real transition and we wanted to express that, too. "Paths that Cross" we wrote because another of my friends died of AIDS and I knew another friend was dying, and that really spoke of that. The record was really Fred's baby, and it was heartbreaking because it received terrible reviews, they just crucified the record. I don't mean like bloggers, these were major newspapers—the *New York Times*, the *Village Voice*—that were dismissive and cruel. I've never cared about those type of things, but Fred was so proud of the record and wanted people to hear it. But the cruelty—they called it a cranky, menopausal record. I was pregnant while I was doing it! Everybody has the right not to like something, but the personal vehemence against it was beyond not just liking a record.

Still, after that experience, you started releasing music more steadily.

In *Dream of Life*, the mission was to do a record with Fred and have the honor of working with him. And then on *Gone Again*, the mission was to remember Fred after he died. On *Peace and Noise*, to explore my thoughts and see where I was at, where things were at. *Gung Ho* reflects my studies at the time, I was studying about Vietnam and Ho Chi Minh and various things.

For me, *Trampin'* was my first real record as myself. I felt confident to speak out against the Bush administration's strike on Iraq, but to do it in a way that couldn't be dissected politically. "Radio Baghdad" is an improvisation, taking the point of view of a mother who was dealing with bombs falling on the night of Shock and Awe and comforting her children, telling them about their country, and if anything happened to her, investing her personal history and her people's history into her children. I was very proud of *Trampin'*, because for me it was like *Horses* in that I wasn't filled with self-doubt—*Am I good enough? Should I be here? Should I quit? Am I trying to make money? I didn't do this to be famous*—all the things Kurt Cobain spoke about, I know those conflicts and that schism. But *Trampin'*, I had things to say and ideas that I wanted to impart and I wasn't worried about all of that.

Doing [*Twelve*] was almost like a little commercial break—it was fun, it was sometimes torture, really interesting. I learned a lot of stuff, because when I'm doing records, writing lyrics is just so painful for me. Not having that responsibility, I could spend a lot more time getting to know my voice and giving more direction. I learned more things about my voice, new things I can do.

You've never done a box set or a big retrospective.

Well, I'm still working. Also, I never over-recorded—back then, you had a certain amount of money and you did your eight songs. We didn't have the kind of budget that allowed us to record 22 songs, so there's not a lot of hidden things. Probably the most interesting thing is when I've done improvisations, we might have done a few and each are different. On *Peace and Noise*, one improvisation of "Memento Mori" was just about the death of Blind Lemon Jefferson.

I feel like I'm still learning. I still keep thinking I'm going to do the great record, write the great book, but if some people think I already did it, and it was the first one I ever did, then how lucky am I that I was allowed to keep going? So whether they tapped into the consciousness of people or not, they were all done to do so. I keep thinking that if they're not universally appreciated, or if a lot of the songs are obscure, people will find them. They're there.

What do you think is the biggest misconception about you?

The thing that bothered me the most was when I had to return to the public eye in '95 or '96 when my husband died. We lived a very simple lifestyle in a more reclusive way in which he was king of our domain. I don't drive, I didn't have much of an income, and without him, I had to find a way of making a living. Besides working in a bookstore, the only thing I knew how to do was to make records—or to write poetry, which isn't going to help put your kids through school. But when I started doing interviews, people kept saying "Well, you didn't do anything in the '80s," and I just want to get Elvis Presley's gun out and shoot the television out of their soul. How could you say that? The conceit of people, to think that if they're not reading about you in a newspaper or magazine, then you're not doing anything.

I'm not a celebrity, I'm a worker. I've always worked. I was working before people read anything about me, and the day they stopped reading about me, I was doing even more work. And the idea that if you're a mother, you're not doing anything—it's the hardest job there is, being a mother or father requires great sacrifice, discipline, selflessness, and to think that we weren't doing anything while we were raising a son or daughter is appalling. It makes me understand why some human beings question their worth if they're not making a huge amount of money or aren't famous, and that's not right.

My mother worked at a soda fountain. She made the food and was a waitress and she was a really hard worker and a devoted worker. And her potato salad became famous! She wouldn't get potato salad from the deli, she would get up at five o'clock in the morning and make it herself, and people would come from Camden or Philly to this little soda fountain in South Jersey because she had famous potato salad. She was proud of that, and when she would come home at night, completely wiped out and throwing her tip money on the table and counting it, one of her great prides was that people would come from far and wide for her potato salad. People would say, "Well, what did your mother do? She was a waitress?" She served the people, and she served in the way that she knew best.

PATTI SMITH SAYS *M TRAIN* IS THE ROADMAP TO HER LIFE

Shadrach Kabango | October 15, 2015 | *q*, Canadian Broadcasting Corporation

In this interview with the Canadian Broadcasting Corporation's *q*, Patti Smith sat down with host and hip-hop artist Shad (Shadrach Kabango) to reflect on *M Train*, her 2015 follow-up memoir to *Just Kids*. For much of the interview, they considered what it means to let the mind be free, whether through daydreaming, journaling, or quietly observing the signs and patterns we might miss if we're not looking. These idle moments are central to Smith's writing process, and she had one right before the interview started. Studio *q* is home to Steinway D #271146, the rehearsal piano Glenn Gould used when he had an office at the CBC, and Smith spent time communing with Gould's spirit and playing a few notes at the bench.

Gould, in addition to a holy litany of other artists dear to Smith, makes an appearance in *M Train*. "I had no idea whether Bach's *Coffee Cantata* was a work of genius, but his mania for coffee, at a time when it was frowned upon as a drug, is well known," Smith wrote. "A habit Glenn Gould certainly adopted when he fused with the *Golderg Variations* and cried out somewhat maniacally from the piano, I am Bach!"

Coffee, another part of her writing process, makes an appearance here, too, as do her beloved detective shows. In her solitary writer's life, so diametrically opposed to her life on stage or collaborating in a recording studio, she seemed to revel in the space for rumination, a space she also carved out as a voracious reader. It's a space she lamented as ever-narrowing in the media-bombarded culture at large. When people spend all their time glued to a screen, she said, "their peripheral vision starts closing in. We're getting tunnel vision." —Ed.

Shadrach Kabango (Shad): Patti Smith is here with me in Studio *q*. Hello.

Patti Smith: Hi. Good morning.

Shad: Welcome.

Smith: Nice to see you.

Shad: I hope you enjoyed the piano we have here.

Smith: Oh my gosh. Seeing Glenn Gould's beloved piano and touching it. It's so silky. I mean the piano itself, and the keys. I mean, I'm not even a player, but I can feel—I can feel why he loved it, really.

Shad: And you're excited to come see this piano.

Smith: Oh yes. I love Glenn Gould. I listen to him like all the time so to see the piano that he loved is really special.

Shad: What strikes you about him?

Smith: Well, I mean, it's the same thing that strikes me about somebody like Bobby Fischer or H. P. Lovecraft. It's a certain level of genius that's inaccessible, but yet they produce work that gives us so much pleasure.

Shad: I want to get into this book a little bit. You describe it as a road-map to your life. What's the most important thing you wanted to show about yourself?

Smith: In this book?

Shad: In this book.

Smith: Well, I really, I had no real agenda when I started the book. I just wanted to write. I wanted to be unfettered by direction, by responsibility, and by any particular chronology or plot. Because *Just Kids* was so exhausting and had so much responsibility—to Robert; to New York City, and that it was a period piece; to the people living and dead who passed through the book. So I just wanted to mosey through a book with, you know, no particular place to go, as the song says [*"No Particular Place to Go," by Chuck Berry —Ed.*] and just see where I went. Also, I started it when I was almost sixty-six, so I was ruminating on what that actually meant. What does it mean to be sixty-six years old? As a human being, as a mother, as an artist. And I have to say of anything I've ever writ, it's really the most like me as who I am. And if you were wondering what she's like, if that was important to know, the book pretty much tells you the kind of person I am.

Shad: Did you arrive at any conclusions about what it means to be you at sixty-six?

Smith: Well, one thing I arrived at is life—whether you have no designs or not—there are patterns. You know, nature has patterns, even if they seem random. The book has symmetry. I had no plot, no outline, yet as life unfolded, patterns emerged, and it had a certain symmetry by the end. And I also learned that, I suppose, I like where I'm at. You know, as you age, you have a lot of challenges, some of them physical, but I like it. The mind, you know, the mind becomes to me expansive in a different way. Not maybe as technically proficient, but it's just empathetically expansive.

Shad: It seems that you still do love finding patterns. Has that been a lifelong obsession for you?

Smith: Well, yeah. Signs. There's this line, James Joyce, in a little poem he wrote [*"Bahnhofstrasse"* —Ed.], and the line is "the signs that mock me as I go." You know, we have all kinds of signs. It could be just that we see a piece of paper on the ground and it has a few words on it that seem to set up our day or a random number becomes a winning lottery number, or, you know, you pick up a card out of a deck. But sometimes we try to ignore signs, like Jonah. He wanted to ignore the whole thing. "I just want to be Jonah. I don't want to be tellin' people anything. Leave me alone, Lord." So he wound up in a whale for a few days to figure it out. And then went, "Okay, okay. I won't ignore the signs." But they're there.

Shad: I think especially now, people ignore signs.

Smith: Well, I think partially they ignore them because they're so preoccupied. You know, if you're constantly looking at a phone or a computer, constantly scrolling or looking at the same e-mails or looking for aspects of social media—which I'm not criticizing, I'm just saying we overuse it—people become addicted to it and they stop, their peripheral vision starts closing in. We're getting tunnel vision. You see people on the street—instead of daydreaming or instead of looking at the leaves chang-ing or something, they've got their nose in the phone. And I think we need to daydream more. We need more time for thinking.

Shad: What's the impact of that loss of daydream time? 'Cause you brought that up in an interview before. How you had all sorts of day-dreaming time when you were young, living in New York City with no phone, no radio, no TV. What's the impact of that loss?

Smith: Well, in daydreaming, we, a lot of creative impulses come through daydreaming. A lot of new ideas. Working out problems. Entertaining oneself. You know, it's important. It's important for children. And it's important for adults. You know, I remember riding on the subway, if you have a thirty-, forty-minute ride, maybe you have a book, but maybe you just sit there and just let your mind drift and see where it goes. And we don't want to lose that drift time. It's important.

Shad: Is that something you've had to be deliberate about as well?

Smith: No, I [*laughs*] . . . no, it's the opposite. I was always gettin' my head or shoulder tapped because of daydreaming in school or daydream-ing while I was supposed to be washing dishes. I'm a born daydreamer.

Shad: So even in this digital age, it's not a problem for you.

Smith: Oh no, it's not a problem for me. I daydream when I'm supposed to be doing digital stuff, so . . .

Shad: Okay, I want to get into some of the stories and journeys in this book. You make pilgrimages to the homes and gravesites of artists and writers. What does that mean for you?

Smith: Well, I suppose it's really proximity. For me, to go visit the grave of somebody I admire, it's like going to visit my family, or if I go to visit Proust or if I go to visit Sylvia Plath or Miles Davis, whoever's grave I go and visit, you know, it gives me a moment. I know that a part of them is underground. And it's the proximity. And I just like to, you know, it's not a dramatic thing. Sometimes I just go and stand there for a few minutes and thank the person for the work they've given us. And usually you don't meet these people in person, especially if they died a hundred years ago, so it gives me a chance to thank Baudelaire. It gives me a chance to think about all the people who have come. Like when I was young, I went to Jim Morrison's grave, and they didn't have his headstone up yet. This was in '73, and young French kids had graffitied all the tombstones and all the stones, and everything they could with white chalk messages to Jim in French.

Shad: Wow.

Smith: So you felt a sense of him, but you felt also a sense of all these people's love and prayers. It's like going to church. It's a nice place to be.

Shad: You describe these people like family to you, in terms of what they've given you, I'm assuming . . .

Smith: Yes.

Shad: . . . in your life. Is that the common denominator as far as what people make it into your personal pantheon?

Smith: Their work. It's usually work-based. When I was a kid, I remember seeing Arthur Rimbaud's face on a book cover, and I just like fell in love with him, or I fell in love with Bob Dylan seein' him first as, you know, a young girl's response to a cool-looking guy. But in the end, long-term devotion is really work-based.

Shad: First of all, Arthur Rimbaud, his birthday's coming up. It's October 20, just next week. You have a thing for anniversaries and significant dates. What do you get out of marking the passage of time that way?

Smith: Well, I don't think of it as marking the passage of time. In fact, that's one of the things in this book that I came across, was that all of a sudden, when I turned sixty-six, I thought, wow, that's a number. I had to really face my chronology, because I've always been a late bloomer. Never really concerned about my age, never worried about aging. And for the first time, I really thought about it. And I thought about it because I have children, and I have so much work to do. So it's something I really, really had to ruminate on. But people's anniversaries and people's birthdays, I just like to celebrate them, 'cause it's nice. I love my birthday. It's when I got to be alive. I love being alive, so I, you know, if it's Saint

Francis's birthday, or it could be Jeanne Moreau's birthday, I don't, I just . . . my friends always laugh, 'cause they'll say, "Patti, whose birthday is it?" And I'll tell them.

Shad: But you see significance in it? It's not to mark the passing of time. It's celebratory.

Smith: It's celebratory. Yesterday I did a book signing—well, last night. There were three people there—it was their birthday. I was so happy that they would spend their birthday at a book signing, in a reading. And I did sing "Happy Birthday" to all three of them. But it's wonderful.

Shad: How do you keep track? Do you just have a good memory for dates?

Smith: Well, I didn't at school. If I had a test, I could never remember any—when wars were fought or you know, battles in history—I was never good at dates. But I don't know why I remember people's birthday. I don't remember them all, but I have a lot. I'll just pass through and think, ah, today is November 28. It's William Blake's birthday.

Shad: It'll just pop into your mind.

Smith: Yeah.

Shad: I'm speaking with writer, poet, and musician Patti Smith. Her new memoir is called *M Train*. One touchstone, Patti, that some people might find surprising in this new book is TV detective shows. You write that "yesterday's poets are today's detectives." What do they have in common?

Smith: Well, I think they have the obsessional desire to get their man. Meaning for a poet to . . . all of the clues and the abstract language and all of the impressions, to get that to zero in and get the punch line of the poem. To make the poem, not abandon it, but make it whole. And detectives, they have all of these abstract clues and all of these seemingly unrelated pieces of information that they have to put together like a puzzle and in the end come up with a conclusion. But I do love detective shows. I don't like crime and I don't like gory stuff or looking at autopsies, and I don't like suspense. I don't like when stuff is scary. I just like the minds of the detectives.

Shad: The psychology.

Smith: Yeah.

Shad: And that obsessive nature also tends to draw detectives outside of their community a little bit.

Smith: Yes.

Shad: Maybe in a similar way that it does for artists?

Smith: Yeah, well I mean, also these detectives, some of them are so interesting, like Kurt Wallander, or Morse, both of them, you know, they don't eat right. They have dysfunctional lives, usually divorces, but they sit alone at night when can't sleep trying to unravel a case, listening to Maria Callas. You know, they love opera. They're usually loners, so, I don't know. I feel a certain kind of kinship with them.

Shad: A strong kinship in some cases. You wrote this about Detective Sarah Linden from *The Killing*. "Even as a character she is dearer to me than most people." What does she mean to you?

Smith: Well, I just love Detective Linden, because also, most of the great detectives are guys. And here's this little thing. She's not really that concerned with her appearance. She's not really, she has a dysfunctional life, just like many of the great detectives, but she has that obsessional energy, but being a female, she also has a rich intuitive sense. But that intuitive sense that one often uses in a family situation or with their children, she lavishes it on her victims, trying to comprehend what happened to them, trying to vindicate them, and I just like her obsessional, loner nature, and she drinks a lot of coffee. I just, uh . . .

Shad: There's a lot you can relate to there.

Smith: I, you know, how can you break down when you really love somebody. I just love her.

Shad: The knock against a lot of detective shows is that they're formulaic. What do you think about that?

Smith: That doesn't bother me. Agatha Christie was very formula oriented. I like, I'm a habit kind of person. You know, I have my little rituals. I like to get up at the same time in the morning, have my black coffee, write, roam around. I have, I'm ritualistic, and I don't mind that kind of repetition.

Shad: It can be part of the appeal.

Smith: Yeah, it's like, well you know what you're gonna get, you know? I'm not looking for suspense. I'm looking for unraveling puzzles.

Shad: What's the relationship for you between ritual and creativity?

Smith: Well, for me, maybe the two of those, why they're kin is just ritual for me has a lot to do with discipline. You know, and so that informs my creativity. I developed a lot of discipline as a mother, because I used to write all night or I lived around the clock, but when I had small children, I had to be much more disciplined, and I had to find a time for myself, so I started waking up at five in the morning. And from five in the morning till eight in the morning, when my children got up, was my time. And so that became sort of a ritual, which now that my children are grown, I still like to write early in the morning.

Shad: That's really interesting, 'cause a lot of people would probably assume that parenthood would take away from your creative energy, so to speak.

Smith: No, for me it just made me prioritize, and it made me become, sort of condense my creative time, but in a meaningful way. I did more work and evolved as a writer when I was, in the sixteen years of my marriage and being with Fred, because in order to do my work, I had to really buckle down, as they say, and do it every day, and be diligent and focused in a certain small time period. And I thought that it really strengthened me as an artist.

Shad: That's such an important word I think for any aspiring artist out there, the importance of that discipline.

Smith: Absolutely.

Shad: And focus.

Smith: People, they keep asking me, you know, "I'm a young artist," or I want to do this, or I want to make it in the world. They ask me all these questions, and really, in the end, start with the work. Don't worry about those things. Don't worry about fame and fortune and how many people like what you did. Be concerned with the work itself, because in the end, all that stuff will fall away. Nobody's gonna care about how many hits you got on YouTube or anything. What they're gonna care about in the end is the work itself, and that's what one has to focus on.

Shad: It sounds like it's a balance of that discipline, and then also allowing yourself moments like when you walked over to this piano to my right, and really kind of allowing for poetic moments and spiritual significance.

Smith: Well, you also gave me that moment, you know. I went over there. I felt free to have a moment. I know that you and I had work to do. But you gave me a moment, and it was a concentrated moment where I had real joy in just those few moments, to see his piano, to touch it, and to play a few notes, improvise a few notes. So it's, you know, I entered an atmosphere that allowed that.

Shad: Is that the key to staying inspired and creative?

Smith: Which?

Shad: The latter, allowing those moments to be free.

Smith: Well, you know, I'm lucky. I am free. I've struggled a lot in my life, and I've worked hard, and had a fair amount of strife, but at this time in my life, my kids are grown, they're happy, they're healthy, they're both musicians, they're out in the world. You know, I'm on my own. I have enough income that I can really do what I want. You know, if I just want to sit in my little house and write for the next year, I can do that. I live simply and for me, fairly prosperous right now, so I'm really lucky. But I also know it wasn't just luck. I've worked really hard to get there.

Shad: You said something very interesting at the outset about this particular memoir, that you wanted to work with fewer parameters. You wanted to be very free creatively. I wondered if projects for you sort of swing on a pendulum, between projects where you want to have a lot of freedom, very few parameters, and projects that are a little bit more focused.

Smith: Well, you'll understand this, of course. You know, *M Train*, it was my own. You know, it was my own. I didn't even have a book contract when I began it. I just wrote. And I didn't have any responsibility to anyone, really, except to the work itself. But also, soon I'll be doing another record, and I'm walking into a whole different world. I'll be responsible to the musicians I'm working with, to any engineer, all of these people will be part of the collaboration of doing a record. For me, since I'm not a true musician, I don't really play anything. I really depend on—and I'm not technical—I depend on a lot of people in order to do my records. And it's a real, true collaboration. Completely different atmosphere. But I walk into that willingly. But also, it's nice. I'm quite lucky to be able sometimes, to be able to walk away and just go off on my own, and, uh, just, you know, with a notebook and a pen, and that's all I need.

Shad: Thanks so much for your time today, Patti.

Smith: Oh, thank you.

PATTI SMITH LOOKS BACK ON LIFE BEFORE SHE BECAME THE GODMOTHER OF PUNK

Terry Gross | October 23, 2015 | *Fresh Air*

Fresh Air began in 1975, and has continued ever since with its perspicacious host Terry Gross at the helm. There has always been a searing clarity to Gross's interviews that delves a little deeper, mixed with an air of levity, and this conversation with Patti Smith exemplified that quality. Gross's husband, Francis Davis, is a leading jazz critic, and one of the hallmarks of her interviews is an ability to improvise. Interviewing is an improviser's art, and in her first *Fresh Air* encounter with Smith, in 1996, Gross asked her what songs she liked to sing around the house. Smith had a somewhat unlikely answer: the jazz standard "On a Slow Boat to China." Gross knew the composer, Frank Loesser. "I've always loved jazz," Smith said—her father listened to Ellington, Kenton, and Miles Davis, and she "kept moving" through Coltrane and Albert Ayler. And within a minute, Patti Lee was singing "On a Slow Boat to China" like she was Peggy Lee.

We can imagine Smith as a jazz singer, and part of this conversation explored roads not taken. What might have been if she had not given her first child up for adoption? What would have happened if she graduated from Glassboro State College and become an English teacher? Of course, that didn't happen, and Smith and Gross discussed some of the more poignant things that did. There was Smith's relationship with Robert Mapplethorpe as they come to terms with his sexuality; the iconic *Horses* cover photo he took of Smith that inspired stadiums full of black ties and white shirts; and "Paths That Cross," her elegy for Mapplethorpe which became an AIDS anthem.

This broadcast was adapted from two previous interviews with Smith, in 1996, when she returned to public life, and in 2010, on the publication of *Just Kids*. The passage of time became a theme here—"The idea that time heals all wounds is not really true," Smith told Gross. In its place, she offered a few of her own aphorisms. —Ed.

The singer joins *Fresh Air* for a conversation about her career and her relationship with photographer Robert Mapplethorpe. Smith's new memoir is *M Train. Originally broadcast in 1996 and 2010.*

TERRY GROSS, HOST:

This is FRESH AIR. I'm Terry Gross. Today, Patti Smith.

(SOUNDBITE OF SONG, "HEY JOE")

GROSS: That's Patti Smith's first studio recording, a single she made in 1974 in Jimi Hendrix's Electric Lady Studio. She created a hybrid of poetry and rock and developed a high-energy performance style that was sometimes aggressive, sometimes ecstatic. Before Patti Smith earned the name the Godmother of Punk, she was—well, that's the subject of our interview today, which we recorded in 2010 after the publication of her memoir, "Just Kids," which won a National Book Award. It's about growing up in New Jersey, moving to New York in 1967 and slowly evolving into a poet, songwriter and performer. The book revolves around her relationship with Robert Mapplethorpe, who she met just after she got to New York. They became soul mates, both aspiring to be artists. She became famous first. The cover of the album that made her famous, "Horses," has an iconic photo of her taken by Mapplethorpe. He later became known for his erotic and sadomasochistic photos of gay men. He died of AIDS in 1989. Patti Smith has a new memoir called "M Train."

(SOUNDBITE OF ARCHIVED BROADCAST)

GROSS: Patti Smith, welcome back to FRESH AIR. At the beginning of your memoir [Just Kids —Ed.], we get a glimpse of how different your life might have been. In 1966—when you were about 20 and you were going to Glassboro State College, which is now Rowan University, you were studying to be a teacher—you got pregnant by a boy who was 17, a boy you describe as even more callow than you were. So you were pregnant and you decided to have the baby and give it up for adoption. When you were trying to figure out what to do, what did you think your life would have been like at that time if you'd decided to keep the baby?

PATTI SMITH: Well, I was a lower middle-class kid. My family had no money. There was no room in our small house where there were already four kids, including myself, living. I would have had to get a job in a factory, ask my mother to help me and she was already overworked. She was a waitress. It would have been difficult for everyone I think. And the child would have had no father. I felt that I just wasn't ready as a human being. I wasn't prepared and that—although I knew that I would be responsible and loving—that I just was not equipped to embark on that path.

GROSS: I think that this pregnancy was a turning point in your life and contributed to your decision to leave college, give up on the idea of being a teacher and go to New York. It's in New York that you met Robert Mapplethorpe and, you know, you changed the course of each other's lives. Would you tell the story of how you met Robert Mapplethorpe?

SMITH: Well, our—my first meeting was very simple. I had some friends at Pratt Institute, people that went to my high school that had the means to go to art school. I was looking for them, hoping for a little shelter since I had nowhere to sleep that night. But when I went to visit them, they had moved, and the boy that answered the door didn't know where my friends had moved and said, well, go in there and maybe my roommate will know where they are. And I went in a room and there was a boy sleeping, lying on a little iron bed and just with a mass of dark curls. And as soon as I walked in, he awoke and looked at me and smiled. And then I talked, and he knew where my friends had lived. But the thing that I remember, the very first impression I have of Robert is waking up and smiling.

GROSS: Then he helped bail you out of a possibly difficult situation.

SMITH: (Laughter) Yes, he was my rescuer because—I mean, it might seem contradictory that, you know, a girl has the experience that I had would still be extremely inexperienced in a dating situation, but I was. I had very little experience. And I had never dated an older man. He was probably, like, under 30 but he seemed like a grown-up to me. And I was so hungry. I hadn't eaten in a few days and my boss was friendly with him. He was a science fiction writer, and he asked me to go to dinner after work at Brentano's. And we walked all the way to Tompkins Square Park and sat on a bench. I kept wishing it would just end. And then he asked me to come up to his apartment, which was nearby, and have a cocktail. And I thought, oh, man, this is it. I'm—you know, I was just imagining, you know, what's going to happen. I'm not going to be able to get away. You know, he's going to try to get me drunk. I'm going to get raped. I mean, this poor guy, I mean, I'm sure he wasn't so horrible. But I was just in a—well, I was afraid. And I was thinking about, what should I do? Should I run? And then I looked and, as if an answer to a prayer, here comes walking down the path this boy who I had just briefly met now twice, and walking alone, just dressed like 1967 in a sheepskin vest and a lot of love beads with long curly hair, looked a bit like Tim Buckley. And I just impulsively ran up to him and said, do you remember me? And he said yes, and I said, will you just pretend you're my boyfriend? And he said, sure. And I dragged him over to the science fiction guy and I said this is my boyfriend. He's really mad. I have to go home now. And the guy looked at me like I was crazy. And I said to Robert, run.

GROSS: (Laughter).

SMITH: And he grabbed my hand and we ran away. He did, he rescued me. In my mind, he rescued me. And he was my knight ever since.

GROSS: At some point, you realize that Mapplethorpe was gay. At some point, he realized that he was gay. And you found out in 1968, and he said to you that he was going to San Francisco and that if you didn't come with him, he'd turn homosexual. It sounds like he didn't want to be gay at that moment, that he was hoping you'd help save him from that.

SMITH: Well, I don't think it was that he wanted me to save him. I just—he just didn't want our relationship to end. I mean, I think that it was scary territory for Robert. But obviously he felt this in his nature. I had no inkling that Robert was suffering this conflict. I knew something was wrong and something was bothering him and that he had become increasingly moodier. And there was something that he couldn't communicate with me. And this frustrated me because we were so open with one another. But it was just too painful for him to tell me. And also, one had to consider a factor that he came from a very intense, Catholic, military family, and it wasn't easy for him to lay out his inner world to anyone.

GROSS: How did it affect his relationship with you when he came to terms with being gay and had lovers and eventually had a long-time lover? Were you able to stay as close, even though the relationship had changed?

SMITH: Oh, Robert and I always were just as close. I mean, we had to work out, obviously, the physical aspect of our relationship. And it was really me who, in the end, severed the physical aspect of our relationship because—well, for various reasons. Because I just tend to be monogamous, and there was always the concern about social disease. I mean, we had—I had gotten gonorrhea from him. And I—it wasn't even the social disease that horrified me as much as the needle regimen that you had to receive to get rid of it. And I had a terrible fear and phobia of things like that. And, you know, and in the end, we worked that out. I mean, because we were so close and our love for each other was so deep that the absence of—and we were still physical with one another. He was always very affectionate. Till the day he died, we were still affectionate toward one another.

GROSS: In your book, you write about how Mapplethorpe's work started to change and become more sadomasochistic in its imagery, which he became quite famous for. And you write that that imagery was bewildering and frightening to you. You write, he couldn't share things with me because it was so outside our realm and that you couldn't comprehend the brutality of his images of self-inflicted pain. It was hard for you to match it with the boy you had met. Can you talk a little bit about—a little bit more about your reaction to his images and what you found disturbing and incomprehensible about it?

SMITH: Well, they were disturbing images.

GROSS: They're meant to be disturbing, yeah, right.

SMITH: I'm just—I mean, Robert—I mean, a lot of my reaction was out of, first of all, negativity. I didn't know anything about that world. I still know very little about that world. And my protective instincts for Robert—they frightened me. I worried that he would be hurt or something bad would happen to him. But he was—always assured me that all of these situations were controlled, consensual situations. The imagery was brutal, and I'd never seen anything like these images. But I have to say, as always, after I felt that Robert was safe, I step back and look—looked at them as work and they were brilliant images. I mean, some of them—there was so much blood and disorder, they had an abstract expressionist look. I mean, there were a few of these images that I thought were actually brilliant. And so we were able, after I processed the subject matter, to talk to—to talk about these images as art. But I was never really curious to talk about them in any other way. And he respected that.

GROSS: Now, I found it really interesting that before you started, like, singing on stage, you acted in a few plays. You collaborated with Sam Shepard, who you were very close with. You acted in—you acted on stage in that, acted on stage in something else, and you finally realized that you were yourself on stage. It was hard for you to become somebody else. How did that realization lead to becoming a performer?

SMITH: Well, I know from an early age that I'd like—I have no—well, I'm very comfortable in front of people. When I was a young girl, I'd love giving book reports.

GROSS: (Laughter) That's great.

SMITH: I remember—I remember once I was—one of my teachers was talking about Moby-Dick and she—she was so boring. And, you know, most of the kids in my classroom were semi-illiterate, you know, and they're, like, spitting spit balls. And I was extremely restless, and she got fed up with me. And she said, Patti Lee, if you think you can teach this better, you get up here and teach it. And I said, sure. I was really happy. I went up there and I laid out Moby-Dick for those kids in a way that, like, they comprehended Moby-Dick you know? And I enjoyed that. And that's sort of what made me think I could be a good teacher because I really didn't know practically how to make money in the world. And I thought, well, I could have a job as a teacher 'cause I'd like talking in front of people. And I had no—I'd let—I did plays in college. I played Phaedra. I was in musical comedy. And I did very well, but the memorization killed me. I'm not good at memorizing and it gave me a lot of anxiety. I hated the makeup. I hated all that pancake makeup. I didn't really like dressing for parts. So I liked being on stage, I just didn't like the theatrical aspect of being in front of people.

GROSS: My guest is Patti Smith. We'll hear more of the interview after a break. This is FRESH AIR.

(SOUNDBITE OF MUSIC)

GROSS: This is FRESH AIR. Before we get back to our 2010 interview with Patti Smith about her life before she became the godmother of punk and about how photographer Robert Mapplethorpe became her soul mate, we're going to hear an excerpt of the interview I recorded with her in 1996 in which we talked about her first album "Horses," which was released in 1975. The iconic photo of Smith on the album cover was taken by Robert Mapplethorpe. Here's some of the title track of "Horses."

(SOUNDBITE OF SONG, "LAND")

(SOUNDBITE OF ARCHIVED BROADCAST)

GROSS: Now, you wrote for several years before actually performing in a rock 'n' roll kind of setting and performing with music. When you started putting the two together, did you have any idea that you could sing? Had you used your voice that way before?

SMITH: No, not really. I mean, I used to daydream when I was a kid about being an opera singer. And I loved Maria Callas, and my mother's a really nice singer. She, you know, had sort of like a '30s-style jazz voice. And my father had a nice voice. I think I sang in the school choir or something, but I didn't really excel or have any real gift. But what I did have, I think, always was—I've always, for some reason, been comfortable talking in front of people or performing in front of people. And I guess I got a lot of guts, but I never really had that great a voice. I think it's basically guts.

GROSS: Well, speaking of guts, when you first started reading, you've said that you were reading, you know, early on, often in bars, that weren't places you'd be very likely to hear a poet.

SMITH: No, they weren't.

GROSS: What kind of places did you read in?

SMITH: You know, I wasn't really accepted in the poet clique. I didn't have a lot of respect for poets, you know, and the more academic way of breaking into the poetry circle, it wasn't interesting to me. I didn't really relate to them and I thought most of the poetry readings I went to were boring, and it just wasn't my scene. So I started pursuing different venues to perform my poetry. And I just read anywhere that anybody would take me, usually for free, just to get the experience, or for $5 or $10. And sometimes I'd be the opening act's opening act.

GROSS: (Laughter).

SMITH: And so I'd play, like, in a bar that had, like, a little rock band and some little blues band and I'd go on before the blues band. Nobody was interested in what I had to say, you know? They weren't interested in hearing poetry or, you know, they wanted to hear music and they were half drunk. But I had figured if they told me I had 15 minutes or 20 minutes on that little stage, that was my stage and I was going to fight for it.

GROSS: Let me play the first track of your first LP. And this is "Gloria." What made you decide to rework this song?

SMITH: Well, truthfully in the beginning, it was just Lenny and I and then we brought in a piano player, who was Richard Sohl. He was quite young, quite gifted. He was actually a classical piano player, but he had a great sense of rhythm. So it was just the three of us—a guitar, piano and I. And we did very simple songs because the configuration was so simple. And we just chose songs that were basically three chords so I could improvise over them. I didn't really have any interest in covering "Gloria," but it had three chords and I like the rhythm. And we just sort of used it for our own design, the same as "Land of a Thousand Dances." "Land of a Thousand Dances" became, really, like a battleground for all kinds of adolescent excursions. And so that's why we picked songs like that. Our—I remember I had to write—I wrote the ad copy for our first album. And the ad copy I wrote for "Horses" was three chords merged with the power of the word.

GROSS: That's great, yeah.

SMITH: That was our philosophy.

(SOUNDBITE OF SONG, "GLORIA")

GROSS: We're listening back to an interview with Patti Smith recorded in 2010 after the publication of her memoir, "Just Kids." She has a new memoir called "M Train." After we take a short break, she'll tell the story behind the iconic photo of her on the cover of her debut album "Horses." It was taken by Robert Mapplethorpe. I'm Terry Gross and this is FRESH AIR.

(SOUNDBITE OF SONG, "GLORIA")

GROSS: This is FRESH AIR. I'm Terry Gross. Let's get back to my 2010 interview with Patti Smith, recorded after the publication of her memoir, "Just Kids," which won a National Book Award. It's about coming of age and slowly evolving into a poet and performer, and it's about her relationship with the transgressive photographer Robert Mapplethorpe, who she describes as her soul mate. He died of AIDS in 1989. She's currently on an international tour celebrating the 40th anniversary of the release of her first album, "Horses."

Robert Mapplethorpe did the very iconic photograph for the cover of "Horses." Would you briefly describe the photo?

SMITH: Well, it's a very classic photograph by Robert, very simple. I'm standing against a white wall with a triangular shadow, dressed in the clothes typical of myself then. And just an old white shirt—a clean old white shirt—sort of a black ribbon that symbolizes a tie or a cravat, black pants, jacket's slung over my shoulder, looking directly at Robert. It's—has a little bit of Baudelaire, a little bit of Catholic boy, a little bit of Frank Sinatra and a lot of Robert.

GROSS: (Laughter). What impact do you think that photo had on how people perceived you?

SMITH: Well, I—you know, I don't know. I (laughter), I know people really liked it. I know the record company didn't.

GROSS: They didn't? That's such a great photo. Why didn't the record company like it?

SMITH: 'Cause my hair was messy, because you know, it just—it was a little incomprehensible to them at the time. But I fought for it, and they did try to airbrush my hair, but I made sure that was fixed. People were very upset constantly about my appearance when I was young. I don't know what it was. You know, they just—it was very hard for them to factor. But I've always had that problem. Even as a child, you know, I used to go to the beach when I was a little kid and just want to wear my dungarees and my flannel shirt. And the whole time, people would be, why are you wearing that? Why don't you get a bathing suit, you know, why are—it's like, leave me alone. (Laughter) It's just, like, I'm not bothering you. Why are you worried about, you know, what I look like, you know? It's just—I'm not trying to bother anybody.

But people love the photograph. The people on the streets love the photograph. And it gave Robert some instant attention. I think it was his, you know, the—where he—it really helped, you know, launch his work into the public consciousness. And so we were both very happy about that. And the funniest thing and sort of the sweetest thing was, when I started performing after the record came out, I would go to clubs anywhere—it could be Denmark, it could be in Youngstown, Ohio—and I would come on stage and at least half of the kids had white shirts and black ties on.

GROSS: (Laughter)

SMITH: It was kind of cool. We were all—we all had suddenly turned Catholic.

GROSS: You say that until a friend suggested that you be in a rock 'n' roll band, it had never occurred to you. It was just, like, not part of your world.

SMITH: No, why would it? You know, I'm not a musician. You know, I don't play any instrument—I didn't play any instrument. I didn't have any specific talents. I mean, I came from the South Jersey–Philadelphia area. And in early '60s, everybody sang. They sang on street corners, three-part harmonies, a cappella. I knew—most of my friends were better singers than me. There was nothing in what I did that would give a sense that I should be in a rock 'n' roll band. Also, girls weren't in rock 'n' roll bands. I mean, they sang but, you know, the closest thing to a rock singer, a real rock singer that we had was Grace Slick, and I certainly didn't have Grace Slick's voice.

GROSS: You know, you didn't think of yourself as a singer, per se, that your friends had better voices than you did, but you created this new style, really, that was a combination of poetry and music. It wasn't about having, like, a perfect singer's voice. It was the style that you performed and the personality that you put into it—the kind of defiance that you had in some songs, the energy. Would you talk about what you felt you were doing early on that was different from what you'd seen other people do?

SMITH: I think my perception of myself was really as a performer and a communicator. You know, my—I had a mission when we recorded "Horses." My mission and the collective band mission was really, on one level, to merge poetry and rock 'n' roll. But more humanistically, to reach out to other disenfranchised people, you know, I—we—in 1975, the, you know, young homosexual kids were, you know, being disowned by their families. The kids were, you know, kids like me, who were a little weird or a little different, were often persecuted in their small towns. And it wasn't just, you know, because of sexual persuasion. It was for any reason—for being an artist, for being different, for having political views, for just wanting to be free. And I really recorded the record to connect with these people, you know, and also in terms of our place in rock 'n' roll, just to create some bridge between our great artists that we had just lost—Jimi Hendrix and Jim Morrison among them—and to create space for what I felt would be the new guard, which I didn't really include myself. I was really anticipating people or bands like The Clash and The Ramones. I was anticipating in my mind that a new breed would come—Television—a new breed would come and they would be less materialistic, more bonded with the people and not so glamorous. That's—I didn't—I wasn't thinking so much of music. I wasn't thinking so much of perfection or stardom or any of that stuff. I was thinking—I had this mission, and I thought I would do this record and then go back to my writing and my drawing, and, you know, return to my, you know, my somewhat abnormal normal life. But "Horses" took me on a whole different path.

GROSS: My guest is Patti Smith. We'll hear more after a break. This is FRESH AIR.

(SOUNDBITE OF MUSIC)

GROSS: This is FRESH AIR. Let's get back to my interview with Patti Smith. She's on tour celebrating the 40th anniversary of the release of her first album, "Horses." Our interview was recorded in 2010, after the publication of her memoir, "Just Kids," which is in part about her relationship with photographer Robert Mapplethorpe, who she describes as her soulmate.

(SOUNDBITE OF ARCHIVED BROADCAST)

GROSS: Robert Mapplethorpe was diagnosed with AIDS in 1986, and you say this is at the same time you found out you were pregnant with your second child. You were married to the musician Fred "Sonic" Smith. Then you'd moved to Detroit, where you were living. And Mapplethorpe's lover, his longtime companion Sam, died before he did. And you say that to comfort him, you wrote the lyrics—Fred—Fred "Sonic" Smith wrote the music—for the song "Paths That Cross"—"Paths That Cross Will Cross Again." It's a great song. And I'd like you to just—I'd like to play it, and I'd like you to talk a little bit about writing it for Mapplethorpe.

SMITH: Well, it's—well, the night that Sam died, I couldn't sleep because I knew that—I was in Detroit. Robert was in New York, and I could just imagine his suffering. I could feel him just— not just the pain of losing Sam, but, you know, the shadow that it also cast upon himself because he was counting on Sam to pull through—pull through because Sam was always the sturdier one. He was, like, physically, like, a god, you know, even though he was over 20 years older than both of us. He was never sick. He was virile, in perfect health. And I think that I could feel all of these things that Robert was feeling and thinking. And so I sat up all night and wrote this little song. And I tried to write an optimistic song—it is an optimistic song, I think—and write it in a sort of Sufi style, which—Sam loved the Sufi ideology. And it's interesting, I wrote this song for Robert to be comforted. I knew when I was writing it that one day I would be listening to it thinking of Robert. But this song had a long, long life after that. Many people who lost loved ones from AIDS played this at their funerals, their wakes. People have sent me pictures of their headstones of their loved ones with the words carved on the headstone. It really became, within a certain community, a song of comfort for a lot of people who lost their loved ones specifically through AIDS. And, you know, so I—you know, truthfully, when I wrote it I knew that I would listen to it thinking of Robert. But I never anticipated that I would also someday listen to it thinking of my late husband and my brother and Richard Sohl, who played so beautifully on it, on "Dream of Life." So the song has—it's seen a lot of loss in its wake.

GROSS: Let's hear that song "Paths That Cross." This is Patti Smith, as recorded on her 1998 album "Dream of Life."

(SOUNDBITE OF SONG, "PATHS THAT CROSS")

(SOUNDBITE OF ARCHIVED BROADCAST)

GROSS: That's Patti Smith from her 1998 album "Dream of Life." And that song was written to comfort Robert Mapplethorpe, who is the subject of her memoir, "Just Kids." You write that, you know, when Mapplethorpe died of AIDS in March of '89, the morning that he died you describe your feelings. And you say that you were shuddering, overwhelmed by a sense of excitement, acceleration, as if, because of the closeness that you experienced with Robert, you were to be privy to his new adventure, the miracle of his death. You say this wild sensation stayed with you for some days. Could you describe that? Did you know he was dying when you—had you gotten the phone call when you felt this? Or were feeling this, you know, without even . . .

SMITH: No, I felt that after he died.

GROSS: After he died . . .

SMITH: I had already received the call that he had died. I mean, we knew that he was dying. We knew that he was dying the last couple of weeks of his life. I talked to him—I talked to Robert in the last hour that he could still speak. And I listened to his breathing before I went to sleep. His brother called me and let me listen to his breathing. And he died that morning. So that sensation that I felt was his, you know, acceleration into his next place after death. I could really feel that. I've experienced a lot of death since Robert. I sat with Allen Ginsberg when he died. I was with my husband when he died, my parents. But Robert—the acceleration and energy I felt after Robert's death was unique. And it did stay with me for quite a while. And I think that each of us, you know, our energy leaves in a different way, according to the person, you know, according to the energy of the person, the way the spirit manifests. Each of us die differently. And we have, you know, I believe that—I believe we all have a unique journey, whether it's a journey of pure energy, if there's any intelligence within the journey. But I think each of us have our own way of dissipating or entering a new field.

GROSS: You say that one of the people who you were with when he died was Allen Ginsberg. And in your memoir, you mention some advice that Ginsberg had given you after your husband died. He said, let go of the spirit of the departed, and continue your life's celebration. Having experienced as much death as you have, is that good advice, do you think?

SMITH: Yes. I mean, I think that—you know, the idea that time heals all wounds is not really true. Our wounds aren't really ever healed. We just learn to walk with them. We learn that some days we're going to feel intense pain all over again. And we just have to say, OK, I know you. If (laughter)—you can come along with me today. And the same way that sometimes we start laughing at—in the middle of nowhere, remembering something that happened with someone we've lost. And, you know, life is the best thing that we have. We each have a life. We each have to negotiate it and navigate it. And I think it's very important that we enjoy our life, that we get everything we can out of it. And it doesn't take away from our love of the departed. I mean, I take Fred along with me in the things that I do—or Robert or my father or my mother. You know, whoever wants to come along, they can be with me. And—you know, and if I want them, I can sense them. You know, we have our own life, but we can still walk with the people that we miss or that we lose. And I think it's very important to not be afraid to experience joy in the middle of sorrow. When my brother died, my sister and I sat with his body, our beloved brother, and we wept. And then, I don't know what happened. One of us triggered laughter in the other. My brother and sister and I used to laugh so much that we would get sick. And my sister and I started laughing, sitting with my brother, as if he had infected us. And we laughed so hard that we were scolded by the funeral director. And—which—you know, my brother, who was so mischievous, I'm sure caused all of this. But it's all right, you know? We knew the depth of our sorrow, so it was all right for us to also, you know, experience some joy in his presence because, you know, that's what our life is, you know—it's the "fearful symmetry" of Blake [*from "The Tyger"* —Ed.], you know, joy and sorrow. You don't want to just feel one of them. They're both valuable to the spirit.

GROSS: Patti Smith, thank you so much for talking with us.

SMITH: Oh, you're welcome (laughter). Nice to talk to you, too.

GROSS: Patti Smith, recorded in 2010, after the publication of her memoir, "Just Kids." She has a new memoir called "M Train." And she's currently on an international tour celebrating the 40th anniversary of her first album, "Horses." I'm Terry Gross, and this is FRESH AIR.

PATTI SMITH ON *DEVOTION*

Margery Eagan and Jim Braude | September 28, 2017 | *Boston Public Radio*, **WBGH**

Boston Public Radio hosts Margery Eagan and Jim Braude made no attempt to hide their adoration for Patti Smith in this interview framed around the publication of *Devotion: Why I Write*. Every year, the Windham-Campbell Prizes at Yale have a keynote address given by a noted author on the subject "Why I Write," which is subsequently published by Yale University Press. Past speakers include Elizabeth Alexander, Eileen Myles, and Karl Ove Knausgaard. Patti Smith gave the lecture in 2016, and her slim volume, *Devotion*, was published the following year. Devotion is her answer and her core theme—devotion "to a craft, or to an art, to a calling."

Smith cultivates a state of grace in her devotion to the arts, and a sense of genuflection before her saints. Bob Dylan is high up in the order, and Smith discussed her performance at the award ceremony when he was given the Nobel Prize in Literature in absentia, when she "blanked out" on "A Hard Rain's Gonna Fall." What do we do when we falter? Smith keeps moving forward; this is another part of devotion. Smith aspires to write books that stack up to their shelf-mates, be they *Pinocchio* or *Moby-Dick*—to find a place in that holy canon. The key, she explained, is discipline. Her devotional practice starts early every morning, a habit she picked up when her children were young.

For the believers, seeing Patti Smith is like seeing a saint. Once, when Braude had a Smith sighting in New York—some might say it's one measure of a real New Yorker—he "vibrated for a week." I saw her shortly before the publication of *Devotion*, in McNally Jackson Books in SoHo, where she signed a stack, and I bought one. I didn't stop her, though; I wanted to respect her privacy. I wasn't vibrating then. But on September 11, 2017, the sixteenth anniversary of the attacks and the day before the pub date for *Devotion*, my partner and I were lucky enough to attend a book launch event at St. Ann and the Holy Trinity Church in Brooklyn Heights. It was part of the Brooklyn Book Festival, and the throngs of Patti Smith devotees stretched around the block. It culminated in the entire congregation singing "Because the Night" as the sanctuary reverberated in a come-to-Patti moment of collective rapture. Then I was vibrating. —Ed.

[*Theme music plays.*]

Jim Braude: Welcome back to *Boston Public Radio*. I'm Jim Braude. She is Margery Eagan. And in honor of Bob Dylan's Nobel Prize in Literature, at the awards ceremony, Patti Smith performed a profoundly honest and moving rendition of "A Hard Rain's Gonna Fall." In the *New Yorker*, Smith described that experience, writing, "I had somehow entered and truly lived the world of the lyrics." In her latest book, Patti Smith gives us a way to enter and live the world of her words. It's entitled *Devotion: Why I Write*. It's an exploration of the creative process, specifically hers. Patti Smith, of course, wrote the National Book Award–winning memoir *Just Kids*, the *New York Times* bestseller *M Train*, among so many other things. Patti, it's a thrill to meet you. Thanks so much for being here.

Patti Smith: Thank you. I'm happy to be here.

Margery Eagan: Yeah, thank you very much for coming in. So this is a wonderful, small book, but it's a wonderful book. And it's in several parts. And you start—you're kind of roaming around in Paris. And we want to get to the whole picture of it, but you talk about going to look for the grave of Simone Weil. And if I may be selfish, I've always been a huge fan of hers, and I think a lot of people don't know, but you obviously wanted to go see her small, modest grave. Tell the people who she is and why you were interested.

Smith: Well, she was a writer, a visionary, also a revolutionary. She died during World War II. She was a very precocious if not genius French girl. Her brother was also a mathematical genius. And she became, she evolved as a visionary, but at the end of her life, because she had Jewish blood, she had to leave France. And she went to England, and she wanted to join the French resistance, but she was very ill. She had consumption, and she was too frail to join the French resistance. And she died in a sanitorium in Ashford, England, and because the war was still raging, she had to be buried there. And she mourned not being able to be in her country, so while I was in France on publishing duties, I gathered some wild flowers, and I decided to go to Ashford, which is a bit out of the way, and find her grave and just deliver her some flowers and say hello.

Braude: Well, you would know about writers, revolutionaries, and visionaries, I should say, Patti Smith.

Eagan: And it was such a modest, just a small little plaque in the ground.

Smith: Yes, it was very difficult to find. In fact, it was raining, and I was a bit demoralized, but I did find it. And I was glad that I did because it just seemed, she seems so alone there that, uh, I just wanted to bring her back a bit of France.

Eagan: We're talking to Patti Smith. The book is *Devotion: Why I Write.* So this was about your going to talk to journalists about writing, and then you had this short story in the middle of the book about a young woman who is a very talented ice skater. Tell people about the story, which is of course a fictional story. It's not like other things you've done.

Smith: Well, I was supposed to be writing an essay on writing for Yale Press [*Yale University Press* —Ed.], and I'm not really an essay writer, so I thought what I would do was to write about my process, or to record my process, and then as a centerpiece, have a piece of work that was the results of process and also the comings and goings of my life. And I was reading Simone, and Simone was small, with very unique, cropped hair, and little round glasses, and she was slight of build, and she was brilliant. And I saw an ice skater, a Russian ice skater, on television, who was about sixteen, who had very dark, cropped hair, but her brilliance was expressed through her athleticism and the poetic aspects of her athleticism. Many Russian skaters have a particularly defined grace because many of them have studied ballet as well as skating. And I sort of put these two girls together in my mind. The genius—and Simone was also a polymath—so the cerebral genius of Simone with the physical genius of a young skater and made them one person.

Braude: And there's another person, too, an older man who becomes obsessed, becomes her lover, and that's at the core of this story in the middle of *Devotion*.

Smith: Yes, but the core of the story is devotion itself. Devotion to a craft, or to an art, to a calling, and also perhaps devotion to obsession. But I didn't plan to write the story; it just evolved. And after I had written the story and studied my notes, my diaries, just the things I had written in my journal, it was very easy to see where some of the impulses or some of the material came for this story, and I thought that that might be interesting for the reader to see the whole package, so to speak.

Braude: It is interesting to the reader, I should say.

Eagan: You talk about this—and I'm speaking with Patti Smith; her new book is *Devotion: Why I Write*—that people sort of thought, I don't know where I read this, but people sort of thought your previous work, *Just Kids, M Train,* kind of just came out of nowhere—but in fact you've been keeping voluminous notebooks for most of your life, ever since you were a kid.

Smith: Yes, I have, and when I left public life in 1979, I moved to Detroit, and I married and had children, and I was really out of public life for almost sixteen years. But I was not—I was working that entire time, mostly working on writing. I wrote every day. I struggled with writing every day. I developed my craft. Because it was the one discipline that I had that I was most able to devote some amount of time to every day while raising my children.

Eagan: Okay, let me ask you the question that people that are listening to you right now, that have aspirations to do some writing. Were you one of these people who get up first thing in the morning and did it before your kids woke up?

Smith: Yes, yes. I mean, I had to.

Eagan: Yup.

Smith: I mean, when I was younger, I didn't write like that. I would sit up all night and write. But once I had a child, I had to find a new discipline, a new routine, so I found getting up at five in the morning and writing till eight, which wasn't easy to do, but that was when I had complete time to myself, and so, after some months, I became more comfortable with that routine and I maintained it. I still write very early in the morning.

Eagan: Is it hard? Do you find the writing hard, or do you find it comes fairly easily?

Smith: Well it's always different. Some days you could write for hours, and other days, you know, if you write a sentence, you're lucky. And, you know, some days you can't write at all, so perhaps you might spend the lion's share of your time editing or studying or researching.

Braude: We're talking to Patti Smith. Patti, when I introduced you, I mentioned something that I've watched many a time: your singing at the Nobel ceremony where Bob Dylan was awarded the Nobel Prize in Literature. He did not show up. My understanding is you were booked beforehand, were gonna sing one of your own songs. When you heard Dylan was not coming, you decided to sing "A Hard Rain's Gonna Fall." Not only, in my opinion, is the rendition you do unbelievably beautiful, the moment when you stop is one of the most powerful things I've ever seen. Can you describe for people who don't know about it, what happened in the middle of your singing there?

Smith: Well, I was asked to sing a song for whoever the Nobel laureate might be, so I had a song of mine in mind that would seem to fit any writer, and then none of us knew that Bob Dylan would receive the prize, but when he did, I felt that it would be morally wrong not to sing one of his songs. And I chose one that I felt the language was so potent politically, poetically, just so beautiful. And I knew the song very well, but I don't know if it was a quality of nerves, I don't know exactly what happened, but I just completely blanked out. It wasn't that I forgot the lyrics, 'cause I knew them, it's just that I couldn't . . . I froze. And I never do that, 'cause I don't really get stage fright. So it was something that I'm really not accustomed to experiencing, and it was so profound. And you know, the king and queen and all the Nobel laureates were right there looking up at me. I was surrounded by an orchestra and also huge television cameras because it was being globally televised. And it was so profound, and I know I covered my face with my hands because I was just ashamed, really, because all I wanted to do was to represent Bob Dylan in the best possible way. And I just, I thought, you know, in seconds, I had to decide what to do, and I just asked if we could stop, start over, and I apologized and I told them the truth. I was nervous. And, um, and I've never had to do that. Only playfully. Maybe on stage, something happens and it's a rock 'n' roll concert, and you can just talk your way out or get by, but this was, this was, I had a tremendous responsibility, so I'm just thankful I was able to regroup, and everyone, everyone was so supportive and wonderful to me, not only that night, but the following day.

Braude: Yeah, I've read a lot about what you just described. What I haven't read, did you speak to Dylan before you performed or after you performed?

Smith: No, no.

Braude: Have you spoken to him since?

Smith: No. Um, Bob is a very private man. I mean, I know through certain channels that he was pleased with everything. I also know through certain channels that he said that no one messes up his lyrics as well as himself. [*Braude and Eagan laugh.*] So I think he was very pleased, and that, really, that's all I wanted, was to represent him well.

Eagan: You know, obviously, you're a famous woman for your music and for your writing, but you've talked about having that self-confidence issue—am I good enough to be an artist? Is that because you're female, or that's just your personality?

Smith: Oh, no.

Eagan: Your parents made you nervous? Or . . .

Smith: No, no. It has nothing to do with those things. My parents were very supportive. I'm very comfortable with my gender. My gender doesn't come into play when I'm doing my work. I don't even think about being any gender, whether I'm on stage or writing. I just do my work. It's really a matter of because I admire the work of others so much, and would hope to measure up, and it's just self-measurement. Am I good enough? You know, is this book as good as *Pinocchio*? Is it as good as—does it merit being on a shelf with *Moby-Dick*? Because I think of things like that. But it's not out of lack of confidence or anything. It's really scrutinizing the work and always wanting to do better.

Braude: You know, Mark Shanahan from the [*Boston*] *Globe* is a friend of ours, did an interview with you a couple days ago. And one of the quotes from you along the lines of what Margery says, you were talking about walking down the street and people recognizing you. By the way, I walked by you on East Eighth Street once when I lived in New York City, and I vibrated for about a week with excitement, I should say.

Smith: That's so nice.

Braude: Well it's true! I mean, it is true. But your response—"I really don't know what people see in me." When I hear that from somebody as celebrated as you, I often think it's phony humility. Now I know it's not. No, no, no, don't worry. I'm not gonna accuse you of that. I don't know you, but I know of you, but how can you possibly believe that? You are one of the most accomplished artists of our time. How can you say I don't know what people see in me or why they want to meet me or touch me?

Smith: Well the thing is, when I'm walking down the street, I don't walk around thinking about, you know, my various identities that the public might connect me with. I'm just myself. You know? Sometimes I get up, I'm cleaning out the cat litter box, and I'm taking care of this and that, and I'm trying to find my glasses under the bed, and I'm stumbling out, you know, with my hair sort of messy and a wash cap on, and just trying to get to the cafe and have a cup of coffee. And then, people, you know, are so excited, and they're shaking, and they want to take a picture, and I look at myself, and think, jeez, you know. That's what it is. It's really not, you know—I know my self-worth. I know that I'm a good worker. I know my abilities. But when you're just stumbling around your neighborhood, you know, I don't think about that stuff. My mind is, I'm just, I have the same kind of sensibility as any human being that has sometimes an awkward morning, or you know, you're just hoping nobody sees you because, you know, you have your pajama bottoms on and boots.

Braude: She's wearing her pajama bottoms right now, I want you to know, Patti Smith.

Smith: No, but I have been known to wear them. No, I have actual, real pants on.

Braude: Yes you do.

Eagan: We're talking to Patti Smith. The new book is *Devotion: Why I Write.* Many people know some of her previous bestsellers, including *Just Kids*, when you wrote about your young life. And you just wrote something in the *New Yorker* about Sam Shepard, with whom you had a fifty-year friendship. Tell us a little bit about your relationship with him.

Smith: Well, um, truthfully, it's still very hard for me to talk about Sam. Um, it's just, I'm so, it's so difficult for me to reconcile the fact that he's not here on earth among us. I mean, I always feel him, his presence. But he was just, from the very first, when I first met him, I always felt protected by him, artistically provoked by him. We read books together, you know, all through our life. Even at the very end of his life, still talking about Gogol and Proust and Bulgakov and Bruno Schulz. He loved books—we talked about books all the time. He was so well read. He roped cattle, he rode horses, he knew every tree on his land. He was just, he was just a wonderful man, a wonderful friend, and you know, I could talk about him forever, but I also, in a certain way, can hardly talk about him, because it's, it's just so hard to imagine that he's not here. But he handled the end of his life just like he's always handled everything—very stoically and very bravely, and also handsome, always handsome.

[*Bob Dylan's "A Hard Rain's Gonna Fall" plays in the background.*]

Braude: Was he ever. You wrote about him beautifully.

Eagan: Let me be my superficial self for a minute and say I don't even know how you could be in the same room with him when I just looked at pictures.

Smith: Well, Sam is just like me. He's just like . . . believe me. When Sam and I'd be walkin' down the street, we're just like me and Sam. You know, it's like, people, he was the same way as I am. He never understood. He'd say, "Why do people want my autograph? Why do people . . . " You know, if you're work-centric, you don't think about stuff like that.

Braude: Patti, thanks for your time. It's a thrill to meet you. We're really glad that you're here.

Smith: Oh, thanks.

Braude: Good luck with the book. It's terrific.

Smith: Thank you.

Eagan: Thank you very much. That was the voice of Patti Smith, writer, musician, performer, visual artist. Her memoir, *Just*—

Smith: Mother.

Eagan: And mother. And mother. That is right. Her memoir, *Just Kids*, won the National Book Award. Her latest book is *Devotion: Why I Write*. The Harvard Bookstore is sponsoring an event tonight with Patti Smith. Event tickets are sold out, but don't let that stop you from buying the book. Thank you so much for being here with us and thank you for listening to another edition of *Boston Public Radio*. Tomorrow, we're gonna be at the Boston Public Library for a tribute to John Coltrane with our own Eric Jackson.

Smith: Oh, wow. Cool.

Eagan: Emily Rooney and her famous list, Callie Crossley, *Under the Radar*, and tech writer Andy Ihnatko. Uh, tell us what's on television, Jim, please, Jim.

Braude: I can't tell you. I'm in awe. I can't even talk.

Smith: No, let's hear what's on. I love this channel.

Braude: Channel two? You love GBH?

Smith: Yes, I love it.

Braude: David Gergen's gonna be on tonight, and we're gonna talk about what's wrong with Donald Trump. Is that decent enough for you?

Smith: Well, I like when you show detective shows.

[*Laughter.*]

Braude: Patti Smith, great to see you.

Eagan: I'm Margery Eagan.

Braude: I'm Jim Braude.

Eagan: Thank you so much for tuning in. Please tune in again tomorrow and have a wonderful afternoon.

PATTI SMITH ON CLIMATE CHANGE AND THE ONE THING DONALD TRUMP IS AFRAID OF

Kristin Iversen | October 18, 2017 | *Nylon* (US)

The United States produces roughly 14 percent of global greenhouse gas emissions, second only to China. We are witnessing a historic moment. Will US climate policy shift toward a Green New Deal or continue further along the road to perdition? On June 1, 2017, less than five months after his inauguration, President Donald Trump announced the decision to pull the United States out of the 2015 Paris Agreement. As a climate-change denier and staunch capitalist, Trump claimed that mitigating the effects of climate change would hurt the US economy and thereby violated his nativist America First policy. As of this writing, all 197 members of the United Nations Framework Convention on Climate Change have signed the agreement, and 189 have ratified it, including the four top polluters: China, the United States, India, and Russia. Yet in November 2019, the US formally began the withdrawal process and is on the path to be confirmed on the earliest possible withdrawal date: November 4, 2020, one day after the presidential election.

Yet some youthful activists have taken a stand. Instead of retreating into nihilism and despair, voices such as Greta Thunberg have confronted the threat head-on in an attempt to stave off climate catastrophe. Inspired by the People's Climate March in 2014, Jesse Paris Smith, Patti Smith's daughter, cofounded Pathway to Paris, a global nonprofit initiative partnered with Bill McKibben's 350.org that uses music to promote renewable energy and raise social awareness of climate change by uniting artists, academics, activists, and politicians.

These grassroots movements have largely been led by young people, but Patti Smith, who has been at the forefront of climate activism for decades, has been a vocal supporter. On September 17, 2017, shortly before this interview with *Refinery29* deputy editor Kristin Iversen, Smith appeared at a press conference at the United Nations with her daughter; Pathway to Paris cofounder Rebecca Foon; May Boave, executive director of 350.org; and Jo Scheuer, director of climate change and disaster risk reduction for the United Nations Development Programme. In defining her role, Smith had a realistic sense of the limits of the artist as activist. "As an artist, I believe that we have a unique role, where we can excite, incite the people, rally the people, entertain the people," she said, "but real change of course is not really made by a handful of artists. It's made by the people themselves."

Nevertheless, the people need a rallying cry. To that end, on November 5, 2017, Smith appeared at Carnegie Hall in an all-star concert for Pathway to Paris. On the set list were Paul McCartney's "Mother Nature's Son," Emily Dickinson's "Nature Is What We See," and Neil Young's "After the Gold Rush." But there was of course only one song that could unite everyone for the finale: Patti Smith and Fred "Sonic" Smith's populist anthem "People Have the Power." Smith, Lenny Kaye, Michael Stipe, Joan Baez, Flea, Talib Kweli, Cat Power, and others belted it out from the stage, with Smith leading the entire audience in a resounding chorus. And suddenly, the future did not feel so bleak. —Ed.

"The saddest answer is we can't do anything until more and more people are personally affected"

On the mid-October afternoon I spoke with Patti Smith about her involvement with Pathway to Paris, the collective organization of activists and artists working to amplify solutions to the crisis of climate change, it was a humid 87 degrees in New York City. It felt like August—in Miami. Beyond that, the news was filled with stories of the horrific wildfires devastating California and the hurricane-ravaged conditions in Puerto Rico, the U.S. Virgin Islands, and Texas. So it felt beyond appropriate to be talking with Smith, who will be one of many notable musicians participating in a Pathway to Paris concert at Carnegie Hall on November 5 (along with Joan Baez, Michael Stipe, Talib Kweli, Cat Power, and more), about the perils of ignoring our changing environment, what we can all do to help, and how the younger generation must—and will—be the one to enact radical change. Smith feels this last thing deeply as her daughter, Jesse Paris Smith, is one of the co-founders, along with Rebecca Foon, of Pathway to Paris. Read our interview below to find out Smith's thoughts on what's going on in the world and why she maintains hope for change in 2020.

We're speaking at a time when wildfires are blanketing California, and New Yorkers still need air conditioners. I guess my first question is, what do you say at this point to people who are climate change-deniers?

I think that this is a subject that has concerned many of us for a long time. You go beyond America . . . as a traveler, everywhere I go people talk about this. They are concerned about the extreme change. It's not like, "Oh, it's warmer than usual," it's, like, so hot that you don't have the facilities to cool anything down. There's nothing in one's recent history to prepare oneself for these changes.

So I guess the simplest—or the saddest—answer is we can't do anything until more and more people are personally affected. I mean, we can do everything that we can do, but it seems that people are going to be in denial until they are so affected, that they become concerned. It's just like the war in Vietnam; we couldn't get people involved against the war that was so long and so terrible until so many people lost sons, so many people lost brothers. So many young men or so many young women realized they were going off to some war they didn't understand, and might never come back. This became so widespread, it was touching everyone, and then the people rose up and protested.

But I don't want to hope for that because, in hoping for that, we are hoping that things will get worse and worse, but they're already worse. They're already so bad everywhere you look. The air right now in San Francisco is the most toxic it's ever been in San Francisco's history because of all the fires in Santa Rosa. So, I don't know how much worse it can get except all these dots start connecting, and it takes a toll on human life, on human health, on human resources.

That's why for me this event is so inspiring. It's not really an event that's going to raise a lot of money or anything like that. It's not that kind of event; it's an awareness event. It's to do something high-profile and to really have good people gather together to raise some awareness about the situation.

This is something done by two young girls, and that is the other thing I find so extraordinary. Of course, one happens to be my daughter, but still, I'm in awe when I think about myself at her age. Yeah, I was speaking against radio censorship and I was concerned about the war in Vietnam at the time and, of course, Civil Rights, but the amount of activism that she's engaged in far surpasses anything I ever did as a young person.

So, for me, there are two things that make me want to be a part of it. One, is the support, the activism of our youth, and the other is because it's a necessity. Even though my daughter's concerns are my concerns, she has become the more articulate one. She has been the most active politically. She is the one going out there on the forefront, and so I'm not leading this charge, I'm following.

I think it's important that young people lead these charges. So that's why I'll be there. Because we're doing two things by supporting this concert: It's a learning experience, it's also entertainment. But we're not only supporting an idea, we're supporting the young who have taken an initiative. This initiative is far more reaching than the concert. The concert is one milestone or one stepping stone. I want people to come and know they're doing. They're learning, and they're also responding to this crisis, but also supporting the youthful initiative.

Something that stood out to me about Pathway to Paris is how it's really youth-led, which is really inspiring and also emblematic of the activism that I see in people who are in their 20s or in their 30s right now. But also it's great because it's drawing on different generations of people who have all been activists and people who can bring together the kind of audience that needs to be paying attention to this issue. It's fascinating to think of using activism techniques from the last 50 to 60 years, in order to try and effect change now for the environmental disasters.

Well, look at the people . . . I mean [Jesse] got in touch with Joan Baez, and Joan Baez responded. Fifty years ago, Joan Baez was walking with

Martin Luther King. Joan Baez has been working on behalf of the people, the environment, against war, against racism, in support of immigration. Here she is again coming to help a young girl who she's never met. I've met Joan Baez, and she's a wonderful person and I'm a big fan of hers. But she's coming from California to give support to this, and she believes in the same thing because that's what she did as a young girl.

This environmental crisis essentially is a human rights issue, and it's just going to affect everybody, but it's going to affect everybody in the world incredibly unequally. It's really easy if you live in a first world country and you're semi-protected by the infrastructure to think, *Oh I'll just have to use my air conditioner an extra couple months of the year,* **or,** *That's why flood insurance exist*s, **and not actually change your behaviors and your habits.**

Mother Nature knows no race, she knows no good or evil, she just exists. How we abuse our planet and abuse Mother Nature, and how she erupts because of it, is on us all. About 20 years ago, I think, a group of us were working with the Dalai Lama. We were sitting around, and Adam Yauch, who was in the Beastie Boys, asked His Holiness, "What is the number one thing that young people can do for Tibet?" The Dalai Lama looked at him and said, "The number one thing that young people can do is be concerned and vigilant about the environment." He said, "Not Tibet, not any place," he said, "we have to go beyond personal concerns."

We have to choose, if you're going to be an activist or if you're going to be active or aware; choose the thing that affects all mankind, not just the people of Tibet or any particular region. He said that close to 20 years ago, that's why you have to be attentive, because everything that we do, every atrocity that we perform upon the Earth environmentally to pollute our water, the dirt, fracking, hazardous waste, all of these things that are poisoning our water and our Earth, are going to eventually seep into the greater water system. It's going to seep into the drinking water. It's going to seep into the Earth. You're gonna have animals and bees and flowers filled with pesticides. Everything he said has come to pass. In terms of activism, the most beneficial to all mankind is the one that benefits and will protect and help all of mankind, and that's environmental awareness and what we can do to move from antiquated energy sources and going off of fossil fuel and developing renewable energy and transforming our cities. That's what we have to do, in city after city after city after city.

I guess what always shocks me is the inherent nihilism that goes along with not caring about the environment. You're preparing the world to end for your children and your children's children. It's so fatalistic.

People say, "Well, I have air conditioning," or "those fires aren't coming my way." There are always ways to feel like it doesn't affect you, but sooner or later, the dots will start connecting, and it's not just affecting your neighbor across, you know, three states. It's going to be your backyard. You know, it's not like doomsday things, these are things that are happening around us. I'm 70 years old, and I can't ever remember such extreme weather in so many places.

It's happening everywhere. What's your feeling about people who might be disillusioned or disheartened because of the monstrous human being who is now our president? Do you have any inspiring words?

Well, I feel the exact same way. Beyond being broken-hearted, there are all the things that go with it. Anger, a certain amount of fear, shame, all kinds of things, because again, as I travel, I see how the respect that people had for us and for Americans and for our country is so diminished. When you have someone for president, he becomes, whether you like it or not, a role model for behavior and police systems. And we have a person that doesn't seem to have any empathy, who is not qualified, is not knowledgeable, and it's like . . . his golf course wasn't affected by the storms. If it was he probably has the best insurance. Like he said in Puerto Rico, "Oh, you didn't lose thousands of people, it wasn't so bad." Thirty-four people died, and if 15 of them were his family members, how would he feel about that? Are those 34 people expendable?

I know for myself, it's very very hard. Every single day, it's a challenge not to get swept up in the worst of his behavior. So I try not to do that, and I try to just be as good of a human being as I can be, that's productive, and stay healthy. Basically, try to be even more positive than ever, even in the face of all of this.

I remember once when I was working for Ralph Nader, he said, "Pessimism and negativity breed nothing." You don't create out of pessimism, you don't create out of negativity.

So somehow, we have to stay optimistic and stay on our own course. We can't feel powerless; we can't let ourselves feel helpless. Like those at Standing Rock who stood and fought and fought until they bled, we can't give up. The best thing that we can do is unite. That's the one thing that we have and young people have in this present culture. This present culture is a lot more complex than things were when I was younger. But the one thing that this present culture has that we didn't have is the technological ability to unite almost instantaneously. And if young people just decided to take one initiative, which would hopefully be climate-involved, and decided they are going to globally take a stand—whether it's against nuclear weapons, whether it's against war—they can become the most thunderous voice in human history.

I think it's very very hard to think about what we can do to change things or be positive right now with [Trump] at the helm. But we are the people, and the people in the end rule. The people vote, the people march, the people can unite, and the only thing, when you think about Donald Trump—what fills him with anger, worry, and made him start to lie in the very beginning of his presidency—he didn't have as many people at his inauguration as Obama. Numbers are very important to him, and if we multiplied our numbers against him, numbers are the one thing he fears and cannot deny. I'm not talking about a thousand people, a million people. I'm talking about millions. We can do that. The youth of America has it in their power. The youth of the world, not just America. They just have to start developing a network. A network that has a plan and comprehends their potential power. Their potential positive power. Just about the best way I can answer is somehow in the midst of everything, stay healthy, stay strong, and don't let anybody beat you down.

There is power in truth and numbers and ultimately, there's a lot more of us who either already realize or are beginning to realize or are just on the verge of it that this just isn't a problem that we can ignore.

It's just gonna happen because even if it takes a while, in 2020, there's going to be another election. And 2020, when you think about it is "20/20," and what does "20/20" represent? It's perfect vision. It's, like, time for the visionaries to roll up your sleeves and get ready for 2020. We're all making little patches for the great activist carpet, we just have to get our little patches stitched together.

ALL THE POETS (MUSICIANS ON WRITING): PATTI SMITH

Scott Timberg | September 29, 2017 | *LA Review of Books*

Isn't it romantic to imagine the architects of punk as young bookstore clerks? And yet, to some extent, it's true. There was Richard Hell, Tom Verlaine, who took his nom de guerre from French Symbolist poet Paul Verlaine—and Patti Smith. "We all worked at the Strand," Smith told the late author and critic Scott Timberg. It wasn't that the job was great; they did it for the discount. Imagine CBGB's, that legendary punk incubator, as a favorite haunt of downtown bookworms, the 1970s New York equivalent of Paris's Left Bank in the 1920s. Inspired by literary trailblazers like Lou Reed, the city's unofficial poet laureate; William S. Burroughs; and Allen Ginsberg, Smith explained that the "first tier of CBGB's had a poetic nucleus."

Here we have Patti Smith the reader. She started reading when she was three and a half or so, and she never stopped. "The prospect of boarding a plane without a book produces a wave of panic," she wrote in *Devotion*, which had just been published when this interview took place. To Smith, literary language is intoxicating; so is the materiality of the book—its paper, its feel, whether a secondhand paperback or her signed first edition of *Finnegans Wake*.

Smith is hard on first sentences, but once she commits, she commits. "I'm a serial monogamous reader," she said. Here, she discussed some of her favorites: Camus, Genet, Modiano, Bolaño, Murakami. She is an avid reader of biography—of Rimbaud and other beloved poets, *The Fabulous Life of Diego Rivera* by Bertram D. Wolfe, and Nabokov's *Nikolai Gogol*. She even listed her favorite translators by name. This is Patti Smith, the "very, very experienced book clerk." —Ed.

After decades as a major force in punk rock—dating back to her shows at CBGB's and her 1975 LP Horses—*Patti Smith has earned a considerable reputation as a literary figure as well. She has introduced books of poems by Blake and Rimbaud [*Poems by Blake, *Vintage Classics, 2016;* A Season in Hell & The Drunken Boat, *New Directions, 2011 —Ed.], published several volumes of her own verse and song lyrics, and won the National Book Award for* Just Kids, *her 2010 memoir about her crucial early years with photographer Robert Mapplethorpe.*

Smith's new book is Devotion, *a slim volume that is—at once—an ode to her favorite French writers, a short story or fable about a mysterious young ice skater, and a meditation on the creative process. (It is based on a speech Smith gave at Yale and is part of Yale University Press's* Why I Write *series.)*

Smith spoke to me from her home in New York City.

SCOTT TIMBERG: So I want to talk to you about the new book and the inspiration that went into it. A lot of us who know your music have long been aware of your admiration for French literature, especially poetry—Baudelaire, the Symbolists, Rimbaud. I wonder what draws you to that. What does French literature do that nothing else can: English literature can't do it, rock 'n' roll can't do it, punk rock can't do it . . .

PATTI SMITH: Yeah, but Roberto Bolaño could!

For me, when I was young, it was all about language. Even though I can only read in translation, there are beautiful translations of Rimbaud, and not just Rimbaud but French literature in general. And it wasn't just French literature but film—you know, Godard, Bresson, and on and on. I was aesthetically drawn to French culture. And that also includes French fashion. In the '50s, when I was a kid, I loved looking at fashion magazines and the House of Dior and all the great houses, and then the films—Cocteau and Godard and Bresson—and the way they dressed, and the poets, the architecture. So a lot of it was, especially as a young girl, aesthetic.

The language within Rimbaud to me was intoxicating. And I admit, at 16 years old, I didn't always understand what I was reading, but it really didn't matter. The language to me was so beautiful, and I was just drawn to it. Of course the work was paramount, but I was also fascinated by the lifestyle of someone like Rimbaud . . . reading about all the lives of the poets.

I've always had an affection and felt an affiliation. As I got older, the writers changed—it became Camus, the movies became Resnais—but it was a continual mental dialogue between myself and much of French culture. And also, thinking about Paris in the '20s and going to Paris, there's so much history there. You can see it when you're standing on the street where Picasso painted *Guernica*, and all the streets are named after poets. It's wonderful.

Right, Victor Hugo and so on . . .

Yeah, exactly. It's a very romantic city. That perhaps has shifted, and it might not have the same deep romance. But, nostalgically, I still fall in love every time I go there, I still want to see the same things that I saw in the books.

So it never gets old for you?

No, I'm happy to see Apollinaire's head, and Boulevard Saint-Germain, happy to see a statue of Baudelaire or Victor Hugo, and happy to see La Coupole. There's just something in the fact that they haven't changed. I can still see my young self walking in the park where Marcel Proust used to walk. There's a connection—it's still the same and you can still feel all of that.

I wonder, when you were a teenager living in a small town, you weren't taking the train to whatever the cool club was in 1970, or 1965 . . .

Oh no, when I was young we had an armory down the street that once in a while had dances, and maybe if you were lucky they would have somebody come and lip sync and maybe do one song—it might be Cathy Young [*likely referring to singer Kathy Young —Ed.*], it might be Hank Ballard. Or you could go to the skating rink. But in 1965, I did save my babysitting money, I saved my factory money, and I saw Bob Dylan, I saw Joan Baez.

And that would have been an incredible time to see Dylan, too.

That's the first time I ever saw him. It was at Perrytown, New Jersey, or something, at a fair, and I went to see Joan Baez and she introduced Bobby Dylan. And then I went to see him in the Visions of Johanna period, in Forest Hills. I saved my money and I did get the train and go up there and see him. But just once or twice.

So you grew up in a small town, which I expect was pretty provincial, pretty Catholic. I imagine you growing up in Springsteen country, very blue collar.

No no, I'm from rural south Jersey. He's like mid-Jersey. It wasn't blue collar, it was rural. I'm from a rural area. When we moved there in 1957 it was mostly swampland, orchards, and pig farms. It was more of a lower middle-class area, places where GIs got little houses with their GI bill . . . My father was a factory worker and my mother was a waitress. So it's a whole different type of upbringing, and a different type of community.

So reading Verlaine and Rimbaud and so on must have been pretty exotic. Did it seem like a whole different universe to you?

I mean, I was an avid reader. By 16 I had read *The Fabulous Life of Diego Rivera [by Bertram D. Wolfe —Ed.]*, so I was also connected with Mexico and with Tina Modotti and Frida Kahlo. I've been reading since I was about three-and-a-half or four, and by the time I was 20 years old I was well acquainted with all kinds of scenes. But it was all work-centric. It was just feeling a connection or a kinship with workers of a certain generation, and seeing the architecture that they lived in, the streets that they walked on, the work that they committed.

As you were getting into French literature, you were also getting into Mexican art, and, at the same time, into Dylan, maybe Velvet Underground a few years later—did these things seem to have a lot in common? Or was French culture its own thing?

I mean, I was deeply into Rimbaud when I was a girl of 14, 15, 16, but then, when Bob Dylan came on the scene, the difference was—he had a very Rimbaudian look, in a certain way, and he was a poet, and he gave us a political awareness, but he also moved quickly through his work like Picasso. You know, it was like the Rose Period, the Blue Period, Cubism—you had to move quickly with him. But I think the difference was, for one thing, Bob Dylan was alive. And it was exciting to be drawn to someone who touched on all of art, travel, social awareness, and who was alive.

You couldn't go see Rimbaud with the Hawks at a club . . .

[*Laughs.*] No, I tried! Bob Dylan was alive and reacting immediately to our times. And you know, I was a young girl with a romantic imagination, and it was nice to have a romantic imagination about a guy who was living.

That brings me to the New York music scene of the mid-'70s. We think of it as being punk rock, as being raw and direct, but it was actually very literary. Between you, Richard Hell, Tom Verlaine, and Lou Reed in the background . . .

Well, the thing is, we didn't walk around saying that we were punk rockers. It never would have occurred to us. All of us were writers. And Richard Hell and I weren't even musicians, we were performers. Richard Hell was a poet, and I came to rock 'n' roll through poetry. Tom Verlaine is a really fine musician—he was an exception. And Lou Reed was also a poet. And we weren't just poets, we were people who loved poets, we were people who read all kinds of literature. We were all reading Paul Bowles and Baudelaire. And there wasn't much difference in age between us, just a year or two. And so the first tier of CBGB's had a poetic nucleus. And it just grew.

There were no rules that you were supposed to be . . . anything! Except doing your own thing. Developing original material and not being confined by anything. There wasn't any place to play for people who were off the grid. Unless it was a cabaret, but a lot of them had uptight rules. And the great thing about CBGB's was—we just did what we wanted.

And there were no expectations or restrictions. It was a really great place for us to develop a vision that sometimes was only half-formed.

I think a lot of artists, in whatever field, tend to operate through intuition—they know they want to do something but they can't quite tell what it is until they have a forum for it, an audience.

Well, I don't know, for me I just do my work. That's the first thing. It's just about the work, and where it goes comes second. Unless you have a particular target in mind. But for me my target has always been an imagined greatness: I want to do something really great, or I want to do something better than the last thing, or I want to get closer to doing something of worth. That's the first thing. And other things fall around it.

I interviewed Sonny Rollins once, and I asked him why, at age 82, he was still flying around the world playing when he could just hang out with his friends. I basically said: "Why are you still working this hard? Aren't you Sonny Rollins?" And he said, essentially: "Well, I am Sonny Rollins, but I'm not yet the Sonny Rollins I want to be."

Yeah, exactly, I can totally relate to that. It's like that Bob Dylan song "When I Paint My Masterpiece." You're always thinking: When am I gonna write this classic book that I have in my head? When am I gonna do this song that communicates the most to people? And sometimes we've already done it and we don't even know, and we just have to keep going. It's that kind of mental restlessness that keeps us going and keeps us working.

I wonder what makes the difference between people who continue to grow and people who don't. You mentioned Picasso, and there's also Dylan, Miles Davis. Is there a sense of not being satisfied with what you've done before, of being hard on yourself?

Well, that's part of being restless, you know? It's also curiosity. You can't stop your mind from thinking, reinventing. You go into a movie theater and you're watching it and your mind starts moving and redoing scenes, or you go to a concert and some melody line you're hearing somebody do produces words of a different nature. You go and see something and you want to photograph it. The mind doesn't stop moving just because you closed the books on a project on Monday. On Thursday your mind's already moving on to another one. It's just the nature of that kind of calling.

So you were hit as a teenager by the 19th-century poets. I'm curious about your interest in Camus. He has a whole different set of concerns—he's morally engaged in a different way from those earlier writers, who saw themselves as immoralists. What connected you with his work?

Well, first, just his literature—*A Happy Death*, which is still one of my favorite books. And reading *The Stranger* and his other works. So it began with literature and other aesthetic connections. There's just something about his language. There's something about French in translation that I just relate to. Maybe it's the starkness. It's both complex and simple at the same time.

I think sometimes I'm drawn to writers who reaffirm that I'm on the right track. I'm not saying that I'm as good as them or anything, I'm simply saying, "Yeah, I understand this, and I know why this is good, and I have a relationship to it."

There are whole areas of literature that I can't even read. I don't read a lot of contemporary fiction, I don't read a lot of American writers, I don't really like contemporary nonfiction or self-help books. I like fiction, I like biographies of people who are dead (I don't like any about people who are living). And it's funny, because I do write memoir myself, but I'm often writing about people who are departed. But I do like somebody like Genet, who crosses the line between fiction and nonfiction—they're so perfectly melded that you have your feet in both words. That's the type of writing that I aspire to, especially in the future. I like writing fiction. I haven't published much but I write a lot of it. I like the merging. I think Genet is, in certain ways, one of my favorite writers in terms of his process. That seamless process of fact and fiction. Sam Shepard does that a lot. There are certain writers who do that, Samuel Beckett does it.

Another Paris guy, too . . .

[*Laughs.*] A Paris Irishman. I go through phases, though. A couple years ago I went through a Murakami phase—I spent almost a year reading Murakami. And a couple years before that it was Bolaño. I'm a serial monogamous reader. I just get into somebody and that's all I want to read. When I was writing *Devotion* I was in my Patrick Modiano phase.

Modiano is a French writer whom a lot of Americans, including me, don't really know, aside from the fact that he won a Nobel Prize. Tell us a little about Modiano and why you sank so deeply into his work.

I discovered him just like I discovered Henning Mankell: in an airport, because I didn't have a book and I was desperate. I was looking for someone else, I don't know who I was looking for, another M writer, and I ended up finding Henning Mankell and I read all through the Wallander books. And I found Modiano the same way. I was looking for a new Murakami book and I couldn't find anything, and I saw Modiano. It was *In the Café of Lost Youth* or something. But the way I pick a book, I might just like the way it feels in my hand or I like the paper. I'll read the first couple sentences and I'm either in or out. Sometimes the first sentence will turn me off and I won't read the book.

I just got drawn into that one. And again, it's like an addiction. So I had read about 85 percent of Modiano when I was writing *Devotion*. He was much on my mind. There are a lot of references to him. It wasn't an intentional thing—I wasn't planning to write about him. It was because I was supposed to write an essay on writing. A long essay. I got this prize, you know—a prize connected with a bigger prize. I was chosen to write a long essay about the process of writing to introduce the recipients of the Windham-Campbell Prize.

This is at Yale?

Yeah. And so it's an honor in order to bestow another honor. But I'm not the classic essay writer—I don't have the kind of sustained analytical ability, or the vocabulary, to write an essay like Sebald or various other essay writers I like. I read Marguerite Duras's *Writing*, a very simple book, and shorter than *Devotion*. And I reread Virginia Woolf and other writers on writing.

I wasn't quite sure how I was going to approach the book, but when I was looking at all this material, as I explain in the book, I started thinking that instead of trying to describe process, I would just show it—show what I was thinking in the diary section, in the small essay pieces, and show it in the little piece of writing that I was doing while I was thinking about all this stuff. It's really a little book that's like a parable or a metaphor for process. It is process itself.

The part that startled, or pleasantly surprised me, is that middle section with the ice skater. And you said you've written fiction . . .

A lot of it. No one knows, because I wrote it mostly in the '80s, when I was out of the public eye, and I haven't published any of it. But I've written a lot of fiction. And it got waylaid by writing *Just Kids*. And I tried to experiment—*M Train* was an experiment. But I didn't expect to write that little story, it just came out.

It's sort of like a short story, sort of like a fable, sort of like a prose poem, it's intimate—I don't know what it is but it's really nice, whatever it is.

Yeah, I don't know what any of my work is.

Are you hoping to publish more character-based stories?

Eventually I will. Since I turned 70, I've really thought about what I want to do with the next decade of my life. And I think I'm going to devote it mostly to writing. Tour less, travel less, and just focus on writing. Because I have so much unpublished work, and so much I still want to do, you know? This little book came off the tail of finishing *M Train*, but I didn't set out to write it. I was supposed to be writing an essay. What gave me permission was, around 1946 or so, Nabokov was commissioned by New Directions to do a biography of Gogol. You know, a major biography.

And Nabokov wound up reading Gogol and taking notes and this and that, and instead put out this little book called *Nikolai Gogol*, which has biographical material and quotes, but it's Nabokov's take on Gogol. And it's a very small book, not the big heavy tome they were hoping for. But it's an awesome book. And again, it's a take on things. So I just thought, I've got to figure out a way to present the process of writing, but in a way I can handle, in the way that I write. And think. I thought that would have some kind of unique charm. [*Laughs.*]

It's like I was saying that, if *Devotion* was a crime, all around it was the evidence of the crime. It's like a crime scene. The little loosely kept diary of me traipsing around Paris and Ashford. There are a lot of things in it that just subconsciously came out in the story, whether it was a plate of eggs, or a skater, or Simone Weil's haircut. There wasn't any intentional thing, things just seeped into it. Usually those things are very far apart, and to have them running parallel was unique. I was able to see it all unfold before me. My own process.

I laughed at that section in the first part of the book where you talk about traveling and not having a book in your luggage. Do you have that compulsion when you're traveling, where you keep finding stuff that moves you and that you want to acquire, especially books, and you have to restrain yourself?

Well, yeah, all the time. But I have one that's even worse. I have a hard time restraining myself from buying books I already have and love. I see them again. I looked and I have four copies of Nabokov on Gogol. Because I was into it, and then I forget it somewhere, and then I see it in a bookstore and I'm hungering to read it again. I have three copies of Murakami's *The Wind-Up Bird Chronicles*, three or four copies of Bolaño's *2666*. You know, eventually, I'll give 'em to somebody, but I can't resist buying them again.

But I have some really beautiful books. Actually, my prize book is the first edition of *Finnegans Wake*, signed by James Joyce. And the way I got that was, I was traveling really light, and I had to do a poetry reading, a couple of them, in Ireland. And I got paid in cash—you know, like £300 here or there—and after about four or five of those readings I had, like, £4,000 I think. So it was a lot of money. In, like, a paper bag. And I was walking down Charing Cross, this street in London that I really love that has a lot of old bookstores.

So one of the stores I really like was going out of business. And there, in the window, like glowing [*laughing*], like the ruby of books, the crown prince of books, was this battered red copy of *Finnegans Wake*.

And the cover is red silk cloth, and the pages are all cut and raggedy—it was just so beautiful.

And I just went in, and the guy's packing everything up, you know, and I said, "Could I look at the *Finnegans Wake*?" And he lets me look at it. And I said, "How much is it? It must be a lot of money." And he said, "I know it's worth a lot of money, but I've had it for 20 years and no one's bought it, and I didn't pay that much for it 20 years ago. If I could get a good price, I'd sell it." You know, he said, "I'm leaving." And so I took out my envelope and I said, "I have £4,000 in this envelope. Will that do it?" And this book is worth at least twice that much. He took it and we shook hands! Shook hands on it. And I took it out into the street, not even in a bag. And it's one of my prized possessions. But I don't know why I told you that story . . .

No, every book buyer can identify with that, even if it doesn't always end as well.

Well, it could be anything! I've bought books for a quarter, when I was a kid. You know, a first edition of Robert Louis Stevenson's *A Child's Garden of Verses*, with a blue silk binding. And that's quite valuable now. But it just cost me a quarter—I mean, I had a good eye when I was a kid. I love books, I love every aspect—the paper, everything. But I'll love a battered paperback. My copy of Hermann Hesse's *The Glass Bead Game*, which I got when I was 16—a battered shitty paperback, all brown and crumbling—I still read it.

You're of mostly Irish descent. Has Joyce been a major figure for you for a long time?

Well, I'm not mostly Irish. My father was mostly Irish and English. So I have a good mix—I'm more Celtic. I have Welsh, English, French. But yeah, I've gone through many periods of literature. There was a time when all I was reading was Yeats. Sam—my friend Sam Shepard—loved Beckett, and I went through a Samuel Beckett period with him because that was his fella. He loved Nabokov and Beckett. I've read a lot of Joyce, but it's just that *Finnegans Wake* is more than a book. It's like it contains the world. You open it up and it's incomprehensible, a lot of it, but the language—it's like the whole of the world in this book. So owning it is like having the essence of everything. I feel like it might just as well be a Sumerian text. But I don't really care. I mean, I went through Ukrainian literature, I went through a Bulgakov period. It's not really country-based, it's usually person-based.

What's interesting about Joyce is that he's always so musical. In a different way from some of the people we're talking about—there's just that lilt to the language with him.

Yeah, there is. I mean, I'm not as drawn to Joyce as I am to other writers. Even his music isn't the music that I hear. I might read Beckett more, and I really loved Yeats as a kid. But for some reason I love reading books in translation. There's something about the clarity, if it's a good translator. Like with Bolaño, Natasha Wimmer. Bolaño's lucky he has great English translators. She's a genius, that Natasha Wimmer. And then you have César Aira.

French literature in translation is so straightforward. I know that people always say you're missing something because you're not reading the real French. But I'm thrilled to have the books that I have. I'm thrilled that there are great translators that let us read Genet or Murakami. I thank them—I include them in my prayers, great translators.

You mentioned Mexican literature . . .

It's more Mexican art. I can't say that I've read a lot of Mexican writers. The culture of Mexico is what I was talking about. Especially at that one period—Frida Kahlo, Diego Rivera. But Bolaño—I was just in Mexico City and read some poems dedicated to him, and he's much revered in Mexico, much revered.

There's something idealistic about the love of art and poetry in Bolaño's books, the sense that this is what makes life worth living, that romantic experience.

People, if they love their work—whether one is a baker, or a mother whose whole life might revolve around her children—it's all the same: if you love what you're doing, it's beyond romantic. There's a fervor to it. When you have a calling, it's like a beautiful obsession. You wake up in the morning, and that's just part of who you are, what you do.

I totally agree, but don't you think that, with some people, it can just disappear? People stop writing, stop painting—the inspiration is gone.

Yeah, but they might do something else. Or they might just want to live. One doesn't know why people do that—maybe it's because of a certain bitterness, or maybe it's a sense of completion. Maybe they feel they've said all they wanted to say.

I mean, Brâncuși just stopped at a certain age. He said he still had a million ideas but not the will to execute them. Some people, like William Blake, still scrawl on their deathbeds. I can imagine myself being like that, still writing. You know, the Angel of Death is right there, and I go, "Eh, I just gotta finish this one line. As soon as I'm done with this sentence."

One major writer we haven't talked about is someone you knew well, who just left us, Sam Shepard. Tell us a little about what his work means to you. I know it's probably impossible to . . .

Well, yeah, that's really impossible—I can't talk about Sam in such a general way. I'd been friends with him for almost 50 years. And you know, Sam loved books. He loved to read, he loved to talk about books, he cherished his books. We talked about a million things, but, as I said, there was hardly a conversation in our life that we weren't talking about some book, some writer, some idea.

He was an American writer. He loved the Irish writers, loved Beckett. He loved Nabokov, Bruno Schulz. He loved reading history. But in terms of what he gave us, he was an American writer. True American writer— that you can say: this person represents a great aspect of the American consciousness, high consciousness—not religious, or even spiritual, just the essence of America. The landscape, the roads, the people, the diners. The suffering, the joys of America.

I remember reading those 1970s poems in college, and *Buried Child* [*1978 play by Sam Shepard that won the 1979 Pulitzer Prize for Drama —Ed.*], and they were simultaneously completely bizarre and made perfect sense. It was the weirdest sensation.

Right, just like Rimbaud. That's how Rimbaud is for me. You've described exactly what it's like when you're drawn by pure language. You can be totally seduced by language, and just the music of it, the sound of it, the way the words form in your mouth, the way they look on the page . . . We evolve, but before evolution we have intuition. Just pure intuition. And we just sense things. We sense kinship, we sense the smell of kinship, blood that has nothing to do with blood.

I have one last question. You worked at a bookstore, the Strand I think, in the 1970s, maybe the late '60s. Can you tell us a little bit about that?

No, no, I worked at the Scribner's Bookstore. Well, I worked at Brentano's in '67, Scribner's from '69 to '72. And then, in '73, maybe a little later . . . well I was going to CBGB's when I was working at the Strand. And Tom Verlaine had worked at the Strand, and I think Richard Hell, too. We all worked at the Strand.

I worked in the basement. I had a really shitty job—I wasn't on the floor. And I was a very, very experienced book clerk, because I had worked at Scribner's for years and I was very good at what I did. But I was stuck in the basement. You know, just dusting off books and putting them on metal rollers to take to universities or something. It was a crappy job.

But the great thing about it was, back in 1974, they didn't have AbeBooks and all these book services online, and you had to come to a store. And the Strand was a gold mine of used books. I mean, I bought every single book on Rimbaud that there was in English. They were all battered—you know, *Rimbaud in Abyssinia* and all these French translations that were out of print. I filled my shelves, because they were all just a couple dollars and I got a big discount. That's why we all worked there. It was a shitty place to work. I mean, I still love the Strand, but I'm not gonna make out like it was a great place to work.

But it was a great place if you loved books. We didn't get paid much, but we got a really good discount. It was beautiful in that sense. Now many of those books are worth a lot of money, you have to find them online, but back then, you could get a library of the most wonderful books that nobody wanted! Nobody wanted Gérard de Nerval or stuff like that, printed in 1934. Nobody wanted them. Except us. And we bought them.

I'd say a large portion of people in CBGB's worked at the Strand, or at Bleecker Bob's, you know, when he sold records, or Cinemabelia, selling movie memorabilia. We did our time in those little shops. And thank god the Strand still exists. I love seeing it there, because so many of the bookstores are gone. I walk by it and I think, "Okay. We're still in business, we've still got the Strand."

PATTI SMITH ON "BECAUSE THE NIGHT" AT 40: HOW HER BRUCE SPRINGSTEEN COLLABORATION IS "A WHOLE LIFE IN A SONG"

Hilary Hughes | June 21, 2018 | *Billboard*

It seems a fitting coda to this book to end the way so many Patti Smith concerts have ended, with "Because the Night." Her only Top 40 hit, the song began as a discarded demo for Bruce Springsteen's *Darkness on the Edge of Town* and became the lead single on the Patti Smith Group's third studio album, *Easter*. Springsteen had the music and the chorus, but he entrusted the verses to Smith. The lyrics sprang out of her while she waited for a phone call from Fred "Sonic" Smith, then her long-distance boyfriend. Some songs would take weeks, but she began writing at around 7:30 PM, and by the time he finally called at midnight she was finished.

It's natural to wonder what it's like for artists to perform the same songs night after night, but it seems for Smith, a born improviser, the song is never quite the same twice. Moreover, it has evolved with her over its more-than-four-decade existence. It came into her life during a low point—she was living in a sixth-floor walk-up and had just recovered from breaking her neck—and it has been there as a balm to the soul through all the ups and downs ever since.

When the song was released in March 1978, it burst onto the charts with a carnal fervor that was not typical of mainstream radio. Smith recalls being told at the time that "only one female gets onto the top ten." It was the year of *Saturday Night Fever*, Olivia Newton-John and John Travolta singing "You're the One That I Want" on the *Grease* soundtrack, and Debby Boone's "You Light Up My Life." Listening to the hits of that year, and listening to the song now, Smith's ecstatic anthem honestly bears witness to sexual desire in a way usually reserved for male rock stars. Smith had agency and power—it was fierce.

Love is an angel, disguised as lust
Here in our bed, until the morning comes

The thing is, Smith has never wanted to be considered a great *female* artist; she is a great artist, period, and "Because the Night" is a great rock song that seems only more potent over time. Whenever it comes on, it still makes you want to sing along.

Attesting to this fact, it has now inspired several generations of artists and listeners everywhere, from U2, 10,000 Maniacs, and Michael Stipe to Garbage and Screaming Females, who covered the track in 2013. In 2018, Hilary Hughes made it new again with this extensive interview documenting the song's epic history. "The story is definitely a life highlight," she told me. And like Smith's best recorded work, it is a collaboration; Hughes spoke with Smith, Lenny Kaye, producer Jimmy Iovine, Bono, Shirley Manson of Garbage, and Screaming Females' Marissa Paternoster.

Some songs just seem to transcend their makers. "I would've loved [to have] written a song that captured the imagination of the people or the pulse of the people or the beat of the people," Smith tells Hughes. "If I knew how, I would. I haven't written one. But we did write that." —Ed.

Jimmy Iovine, Lenny Kaye, Shirley Manson, Bono and more speak on the significance of Smith's greatest hit—and the love and loss that continue to fuel it.

In 1977, Patti Smith pressed play for the first time on the tape Bruce Springsteen had scrawled "Because the Night" across. Instantly, she knew the song had transformative powers. She just didn't realize the full extent of them for decades.

Jimmy Iovine, future Apple Music titan and demonstrated hitmaker, was then an ambitious engineer helming his first album as producer with

Smith's third LP, *Easter*. He shepherded the star-crossed collaboration, which paired Springsteen's music and chorus with verses penned by Smith. She feverishly wrote while listening to the demo on a loop as she waited for a long-distance call from the boyfriend who would become her husband and the father to her children, Fred Sonic Smith, the guitarist of Detroit's rabble-rousing MC5. Set to Springsteen's building piano arpeggios and rising to an enigmatic chorus, her verses immediately bring us into Smith's room as she paces, waiting: *Love is a ring, the telephone.* She finished by the time he rang around midnight, the first sign that this song was different—that this love was different, too.

She and Iovine recorded the track immediately, and "Because the Night" served as *Easter*'s first single and Smith's first hit, with reverberations resonating 40 years after its peak at No. 13 on the Hot 100 (on the June 24, 1978 chart). Smith and Springsteen seldom perform the song together, but it's a regular highlight on both their setlists. They do stride onto the same stage from time to time, sometimes hand-in-hand as they did after an April 2018 performance in New York City. (When U2 performed it at the 25th anniversary concert for the Rock n' Roll Hall of Fame in 2009, Bono invited them both to join the band, and referred to the tune as "the song we wish we'd written.")

Numerous covers—including a 2013 collaboration from Garbage and Screaming Females, and a 10,000 Maniacs live version from their 1993 *MTV Unplugged* set, which peaked at No. 11 on the Hot 100—speak to the pop potency of "Because the Night." But for Smith, its staying power is rooted in its ability to evolve. Their children were young when Fred died of heart failure in 1994, but now they're grown, with son Jackson playing guitar and daughter Jesse playing piano in her band. Together with the rest of the Patti Smith Group, they perform "Because the Night" as a layered tribute for Fred and Patti's love, as well as the family and art that came from it.

Below, Smith, Iovine and Lenny Kaye, her guitarist and longtime collaborator, reflect on "Because the Night" and the path it forged over the last 40 years. Shirley Manson of Garbage, Screaming Females' Marissa Paternoster and Bono also spoke on their connections to "Because the Night," all showing how many lives are tied up in a single love song that began with one long night spent waiting for the phone to ring. *(Their answers, from individual interviews, have been lightly edited for clarity and length.)*

On the mend—and brink—in 1977

After her epochal debut LP Horses *launched Smith and her band out of the subterranean rock clubs of New York and into the national ether in 1975, and follow-up* Radio Ethiopia *further fueled her punk explorations in 1976, she fell off a stage in Tampa, Fla. and nearly killed herself in the process. The fall took Smith and her band out of commission, but before the end of the year, one that established their home of New York as punk epicenter and rock 'n' roll hotbed, the eager, hungry band met their match in an eager, hungry producer.*

Patti Smith: In January of '77 I had a very bad accident. I mean, I fractured my skull; I had several spinal injuries, so I was out of action for several months. We had done *Radio Ethiopia* and we were supposed to do another record, and I couldn't do anything. I was flat on my back for months. We had no money. It was one of these desperate situations.

Clive Davis gave me the opportunity to do my third record, but I'm not a prolific songwriter. I never wanted to be a songwriter. Some people can write 30 songs, you know; I would labor over a song for weeks. So we didn't have a lot of songs. In those days, you only needed eight; you only had 18 minutes a side. But the way that I worked, I looked at every song like it was a poem—it just took a long time.

Jimmy Iovine: I always respected Patti, but I didn't know her. I thought she was incredible. I walked into the Record Plant, and there she was. For some strange reason, she just said, "I want you to produce my next album." I said, "Yeah, but I just got fired from one." She said, "I don't care. I don't give a s--t about that." She recruited me, which was an incredible thing.

Smith: Jimmy had never produced a record, I don't think; this was his first production job. I had watched him work with Bruce Springsteen and John Lennon, as an assistant engineer, as an engineer. To me, he did all the work. I like workers, and Jimmy was a worker. He would work twelve hours. I thought, "This is the kind of person I want to work with. I don't want to work with someone of high standing who was a band psychologist or anything, or even a person with vision." I wanted to work with a fellow worker.

And so I chose Jimmy, which was controversial at the time, because my record company would've preferred if I chose someone with a track record. So I fought for Jimmy, and he had something to prove, and we had our material—some of it controversial. Jimmy worked really hard with us, but he really wanted to make a special mark on this record. He was good friends with Bruce, and Bruce had worked on this song.

Lenny Kaye: Jimmy was living on Central Park South—Jimmy always loved elegance—and I remember riding home with Jimmy one morning around dawn after we'd been in the studio all night. We were talking about how cool it would be if these two New Jerseyites, Bruce and Patti, could get together on something. We weren't really sure how that might happen given the fact that both of them are pretty solitary artists, in a certain way: they rely on their bands, and rely on their own sense of conception.

Then—and I really wish I had these tapes—I remember Bruce wrote a couple songs for Patti, but he wrote them in our style. It was funny— maybe he had them in his back pocket before that, but he was trying to write a Patti song, and he'd give 'em to us, and we'd have a listen. They seemed like neither fish nor fowl, as they say.

Iovine: I just had so much respect for the both of them, and I love them so much, their music and their lyrics, that I said "This should happen." People don't do a lot of things until they *do them*. No one said that to me, you know what I mean? Patti wasn't sure about it and Bruce was thinking about it and I was positive about it.

Smith: [Bruce] had the music. He had the chorus, but he was struggling with the verses, and he lost interest, I suppose. He was also embroiled in some legal matters. [*These kept Springsteen out of the studio in 1976 and 1977 when he and former manager Mike Appel exchanged lawsuits.*] Jimmy somehow talked him into letting me work on the song. We were in the same sphere; we were different kinds of people, but he trusted his song with me.

When Jimmy gave it to me, I really resisted . . . Bruce was already established, and I felt like I should write my own songs. Jimmy gave me this cassette tape—40 years later and we still laugh about this—and I looked at it, and I thought, "I really want to write my own songs." So I put it on my mantle in my little place.

Kaye: Jimmy did not let ["Because the Night"] out of his hands . . . I have to say, since it was his first hit production, that he had a sense of destiny about the song, and about his place in the music business. ["Because the Night"] would not have existed without Jimmy. I salute him for his fortitude, persistence and vision. He believed in the song. He believed in Patti as an artist.

He came to us at a time when we were crippled, you know? We weren't just rock poets anymore. We had the audacity to want to be a full-fledged rock n' roll band, with all that entailed, without losing our sense of creative energy and spirit and outlier status. Patti fell off the stage, and we were kind of down on our luck, especially in the moment when the two sevens clashed [*A reference to* Two Sevens Clash, *the 1977 release by Culture —Ed.*], and it seemed like the music we had championed and inspired and encouraged was starting to take over the world. We were unable to be there because we had to recover. He just came there and worked with Patti to make this really definitive album with a great, great single to be its spearhead.

"It's one of those darn hit songs."

As she healed and prepared for her return to performing, Smith was falling deeper in love with Fred Sonic Smith, who lived two Great Lakes and 600-odd miles away from New York. She soon found herself in a serious long-distance relationship, which came with a hefty phone bill—and unexpected inspiration thanks to one frustrated, delayed phone date.

Smith: Every day, Jimmy would call me and say, "Did you listen to the song yet?" I'd go, "Not yet, I will." He'd call me at night. "What are you doin'?" "Nothin', I'm writin'." "You listen to the song? Put the song on!"

"I will, I will, I will." We were getting very close to finishing the record. He'd call me or talk to me in the studio, and I'd say, "I will, I will."

We didn't have any money. To make a long-distance phone call then was really expensive. If you were making $32 or $40 a week, and your phone call was $7 or $15 . . . we only talked like, once a week. So Fred was supposed to call me at like, 7:30, and I looked forward to his phone calls more than anything in the world. There wasn't anything that could eclipse my phone call with Fred. 7:30 came; I guess something happened and he didn't call . . . Time was going by and I just was beside myself. I couldn't concentrate. As I was pacing around, I noticed that cassette sitting there. I can see it. It was a typical cassette. It might have said "Because the Night" on it—I think it did—in Bruce's hand. I thought, "Okay, I'll listen to the song."

So I get my little portable cassette player, and I put it on, and I remember looking at it, just staring at this cassette player, waiting for the phone to ring . . . it's in the key of A, my key; anthemic; great beat. I listen to it, and I remember it, all by myself, standing there. There are certain things in my past I can't remember, but this I can remember second by second. I stood there, and I shook my head, and I might have said it out loud: *"It's one of those darn hit songs."*

Kaye: Jimmy really wanted us to have a hit. Even though we had a lot of good material together for the album that would be *Easter*, Jimmy was always looking for something with hook potential.

Smith: I thought, "This is a moral dilemma for me: Here, he's giving me a song that's going to be very popular if I can deliver it. And so, thus, my first really popular song will be written by somebody else—or [someone] not in my band. Is that right?" It was because I didn't have any sense of being a singer. Now I know that people sing other people's songs all the time, but I was like, listening to Bob Dylan, Neil Young, Jim Morrison—people who wrote their own songs. I thought I was supposed to write my own songs, other than songs that I'm reinventing or interpreting. I thought, "Is this fair?"

Meanwhile, Fred hadn't called me, so I sat there and listened to it over and over. Of course, it's one of those songs where it's an immediate song—it's like the first time you hear a Smokey Robinson song; it's like potato chips. You want to hear it over and over.

Kaye: Patti played it for me over the phone . . . and that chorus is, like, just anthemic. There's no way that you could deny the power of that anthem, that incredible couplet: *Because the night/Belongs to lovers.* It was really great.

The song itself, in Bruce's demo form, had a really different feel—it was almost Latin in its movement. It was a little more like what Leiber and Stoller would do with the Drifters; it had that kind of sway to it. When we started working on it after Patti wrote the verse lyrics, we definitely, as the Patti Smith Group, put a sense of rock energy into it that wasn't there on the original. From there like topseed it just grew.

Smith: Fred didn't call me until almost midnight, but by midnight I had written all the lyrics. *All* the lyrics. It was like, done. I sometimes labor for months over the lyrics of a song, still, or I'll shelve a song. Only very rarely do they come in a night. Funny that it's called "Because the Night."

A "true marriage" on tape

Springsteen's fourth studio album, Darkness on the Edge of Town, *and* Easter *are spiritual cousins: they were released within months of each other, and Iovine, who engineered Springsteen's effort, can be found in both sets of production credits. "Because the Night" took shape during one of Springsteen's* Darkness *sessions, but the track needed her words as much as his music in order to strike such a resonant chord.*

Smith: Jimmy said to me, "You listen to the song?" I said, "Yeah, I listened to the song." He said, "What do you think?" I said, "It's one of those hit songs. It's a really great song." "Well, what do you *think?*" "Well, I wrote words to it." "You *wrote*—?!" We were in the studio that night, I think, recording it, or the next day.

Iovine: When the lyrics are that powerful, it's something you're attracted to and you want the whole world to hear it. That's how I felt about Patti. I just wanted to do the best I could to help everybody hear Patti Smith, because she was such an incredible person. Still is. I knew the song was [written for] *Darkness*, but [Bruce] wasn't gonna use it. I just thought Patti, a woman, singing those lyrics, at that time, would be very powerful. They're just great, powerful lyrics . . . It's one of the great rock records.

Smith: I took it to the band, and I had a band meeting—it was so serious. When I think about it now I have to laugh at myself, because I was so serious about everything. We had to have a discussion: "Well, I've received this song. It's a really great song. If we record it, it'll probably be very popular, but of course none of you have written it." I made such a big thing: "If anybody has any objection, tell me." They were all like, "No! Do it! Do the song." I'd been out of action; I'd been seriously injured and hadn't worked for months, so it was both a dilemma, but a thrilling dilemma to have.

Iovine: I remember playing it two hours after I mixed it for Bruce and [Jon] Landau [Springsteen's manager]. They just thought it was fantastic. They just loved it. I finished mixing it at 10 in the morning and I played it for them at noon.

Kaye: It was fun to record. It was great to see Patti sing it and soar over it. What I really remember most was when Shelly Yakus, the engineer, and Jimmy mixed it—they had all their hands on the faders, and when the drums came in, they just went, "*YEEEAAAH!!!*" and pushed the faders up. Those drums come in like thunder, Jay Dee Daugherty's drums. The next thing we heard was Vin Scelsa playing it on WNEW for about four times in a row on its release date, which is just about 40 years ago from this moment.

Smith: I have been at many crossroads in my life where I've been offered really big things, a huge amount of money or some kind of contract I've turned down because it wasn't right for me. It's not strange that I would have to think about it. But in this instance, we made the right decision. In the end, we were a good match for that particular song. I could have never written a song like that. I'd never write a chorus like that. All I'm saying is he gave us a gift . . . I would've loved [to have] written a song that captured the imagination of the people or the pulse of the people or the beat of the people—but one isn't good in everything. I have my gifts. That's a special gift. I really admire pop singers, people that make our hits. I love listening to hit songs. I dance to them; I listen to them. Sometimes people think that because I don't write them that I'm snobby about it. It's not that. If I knew how, I would. I haven't written one. But we did write that.

Iovine: There's a lot of respect between them. They're peers. They're from the same period of time . . . Patti and Bruce, they have very, very strong points of view on the world and life in general, you know what I mean? That's what I think you're feeling. You're feeling two very strong lyricists, not just writing about, "How do I have a hit?" They're not casual songwriters, let's put it that way. Patti and Bruce are writing to say something.

Kaye: We didn't hear much of Bruce's record when we were making it, and I don't think he heard much of ours, but we were in the same time and space. The world outside was the same. I would say they're parallel records in a certain way, but there was not a lot of specific interaction. Jimmy helped be the matchmaker. The musics of Patti and Bruce have perhaps some similar roots, but also come from different places in the human artistic psyche.

That, to me, is one of the reasons why "Because the Night" is such a special song: they each brought their fascinations into a single song, and thankfully they were able to complement each other in the same way that sometimes a great collaboration really enhances—like Leiber and Stoller, the Brill Building artists, Ellie Greenwich and Jeff Barry, Gerry Goffin and Carole King. It makes for a whole greater than the sum of its parts.

Smith: Some people think that I didn't do anything: "You stole that song from Bruce!" No, he gave it to me, and he trusted me with his verses—and I think the verses are good. I think it's a good marriage. And in fact, when we did it the other night, and he came and did the song with us at the [2018 Tribeca Film Festival], I said to him—he does perform it live, and he does his own lyrics—"Please, sing your lyrics on it!" And he goes, "No, no, I want to sing your lyrics." That was really nice. When we're together, he calls it my song. It's truly a Bruce song, but I infused myself into it.

Easter's rock resurrection

On March 3, 1978, Easter *saw its release (and subsequent controversy, thanks to its track list and, uh, armpit hair). Before long, Smith scored her first* Rolling Stone *cover and "Because the Night" became a slow-burning radio staple, eventually peaking at No. 13 on the Hot 100, her first hit on the chart.*

Smith: I was full of energy in those days. I couldn't wait to get back on the horse. I did a huge amount of physical therapy and just got back in action. Also, we didn't have any money, the band; I lived in a sixth floor walk-up in the East Village. We were about to experience some success. We didn't know that, but we were about to.

We went to Europe. The song was huge in Europe—America, it did really good, but Europe, we were always well-received . . . I was glad to be back. The only thing that was hard was that I didn't have all the mobility, and I never regained all my mobility, but I still had the energy to put my foot through an amplifier. [*laughs*]

Kaye: As a band we were not as radio-friendly as some. To actually hear the song and to tour behind it and see it move up the charts over the weeks was truly exciting. I remember [when] we were on tour that summer—we were in Kansas City or something like that—hearing it on the radio, and going out on the balcony of the hotel, and just taking it in, taking a deep breath and saying, "Well, we're in the air. Those radio waves are going over."

Bono: It was a sound everyone hoped one day they would hear, and a feeling they hoped one day they would feel. That ["Because the Night"] came together on pop radio made it feel like the radio was again a place for outsiders, like our kind of people had gatecrashed a party the mainstream rarely throws for us. Patti's voice was no longer crying in the wilderness. The wilderness was the only place to be.

Shirley Manson: To hear a woman talk about lust is so unusual. Women's sexuality is supposed to be covert and hidden somewhere—certainly back in the '70s when this was recorded. Women were expected somehow to not have sexual desire. That was such a taboo, and it's only men, really, that wrote about that kind of stuff back then. She talks about it in such blatant terms. It's so thrilling. Or at least when I heard it, it was like, "Whoa, she's talking about . . . " The inference felt so sexual to me . . . you could taste it and feel it. Powerful stuff.

Smith: The album was controversial for reasons I never even dreamed. I had armpit hair showing on the cover, which never even occurred to me. I had light armpit hair; I never shave my armpits—mostly out of fear! And my camisole is inside-out, and my label is sticking up. You wouldn't believe the controversy over the label and the armpit hair. People did not want to show the album cover in stores, and they couldn't turn it over, because one of the [song] titles was "Rock n' Roll N----r." So the album was problematic to show, especially in the South. It was a funny album, because it had our most popular, accessible song we ever did on our most controversial album. I guess in the end I'm just myself.

Kaye: ["Because the Night"] is on an album which, taken in context, is very much the resurrection of its title, with Patti's coming back from being off the road for almost a year because of her neck injury. We're gathering our energies. I think we felt our music was sometimes misunderstood in terms of its straightforward rock n' roll aspects. We wanted to make a very distinct statement about our strength as a band and about our confidence as artists. If you look at the many different songs on *Easter*, from "Till Victory" through "25th Floor," through "Our Black Sheep" and "Rock n' Roll N----r," or things like "Ghost Dance," to me, it's an album that really visits a lot of parts of our psyche, and one of those is the great hit single . . .

We always wanted to have the freedom to explore pure sound on sound, noise, distortion and lyrical imagery, and then also have a great hit single . . . We want that whole range of musical exploration to be ours. We've never limited ourselves to one thing.

Smith: In those days, I went to all these radio stations, and they all said to me, "It's a shame this song won't get on the top 10. Only one female gets onto the top 10." Debby Boone had the No. 1 song in the country, "You Light Up My Life," which was a great song. So, we were destined not to get any higher than maybe 11, but I didn't care. I thought, "That's such a stupid rule! What would you do if there were three big female singers at the time?!" I don't know if that was universal in America, but I was told that by many big, important DJs. It wasn't like a rumor; I was told it over and over again.

When people said to me, "You've sold out, you've done the song!" I just told them to go f--k themselves, really. I'd say, "I didn't do my first record for it to be played in the closet." The first record, I reached out to the people who were disenfranchised. I figured if 50,000 people liked it, it would be unbelievable. But if 500 million people liked it, it'd be even better. Because if you do your work—if you do work that you think is worthy, call it art, call it trade, call it anything—you hope it'll go to as many people as possible.

Kaye: Sometimes the music is so well developed that there's no surprises in it left anymore . . . CBGB's in the early '70s, all the bands were different. As Tom Verlaine once said, they're all different ideas. After the Ramones, a kind of template for punk rock was invented, and then they all became punk rock, which is great. I love punk rock—I'll go in the mosh pit anytime. But you know what it's gonna be. I like when lines are blurry. I like when things happen, when you put different seasonings into a piece of music and it has its own taste. I like the unpredictability of what comes out when musical minds meet.

I don't think that either Bruce or Patti understood the power of that song until it became a *song* and started riding up the charts, and then all of a sudden, we could feel a certain energy coming from these two force fields that intermingled—Bruce with his E Street Band, Patti with her group. And together we all made something that was greater than all of us.

Manson: I do remember listening to *Easter* in my bedroom in Scotland at home. And to be honest, ["Because the Night"] wasn't my favorite Patti Smith song at the time . . . I thought it was very commercial-sounding when I first heard it compared to some of the stuff that I'd been listening to. But of course, over the years, I've just realized what a genius pop song it is and I've started to sort of understand properly the longing behind it—which is universal and exquisite.

A legacy born "when hearts beat together"

"Because the Night" remains Smith's biggest hit, a fixture in her live show and a song that's been covered by musicians all over the world, from U2 and Garbage and Screaming Females to Italian electronic acts and Japanese singers. The musical bones and potent lyrics lay the foundation of its legacy, but its inspiration—Fred and Patti Smith's love story—is eternal, and its most faithful testament only gets better with age.

Smith: I was a pretty arrogant, independent kid back then. I mean, I am, still. People might say, "How could you do that? How could you not listen to it right away?!" Because I had thoughts about it: Was this the right thing to do?

Now, I'm grateful. That song really delivered me in time of great crisis. When my husband died [in 1994], we had no money. I had two small children. We lived very simply. We didn't have any big windfalls or anything. A couple of things happened that helped me: 10,000 Maniacs did the song, and Bruce put it on a live box set [1986's *Live/1975-1985*]. [*Springsteen also included the studio version of "Because the Night" on* The Promise, *the 2010 album of material recorded during the* Darkness *sessions*]. Because I get a certain royalty from it, it helped deliver me from a very difficult time. You know, I was really grateful for that. I was grateful that a choice that was made somewhat reluctantly when I was young helped me years later in time of trouble.

I love singing it. It's all written for Fred. I was so in love. Fred has passed away; we went through such difficult times and I lost him. But when I sing it, I can reclaim all of that youthful idealism and passion and belief. I enjoy singing it. I never *not* enjoy singing it.

Kaye: It's a true love song. To see it evolve and come of age with Patti's family, to see it tell the story of her life with Fred—it's almost like she reaches into the future. It's almost like Fred's legacy in a certain way, as well as Patti's. To see it evolve into a true tribute to the beauty of this family, which was just in its visionary stage when this song was done, and now to see Jackson and Jesse on that stage, you realize that this is what love is about. It's from the heart. It's from both of their hearts, which is really nice when hearts beat together.

Smith: The first couple of times we [performed it with Jackson and Jesse] I cried through the whole thing. I mean, first hearing Jesse play it . . . Now, my daughter plays those opening lines in a song about her father, and Jackson playing, it moved me so that I just cried. I had to stop, it was difficult. Now, I really enjoy it. I feel happy; I feel like we're doing this song for their father. Bruce was very kind to my children after Fred died. The song has evolved, not just like a love song to Fred, but it's a real family . . . Bruce, we're still here, both of us. We've both lost many people, but we're both still here, still working, we have our children, and so when I sing the song, what I said at Tribeca was the truth. These three men are in my mind: Jimmy, who forced me to do it; Bruce, who gave me the structure of the song; and Fred, who inspired the words. That's a happy meld, those three men, that will always be a part of my cosmology through the song. That's not a bad cosmology to, you know, have in one's memory and one's present.

One funny thing, though, is Fred really admired Bruce's songwriting abilities. Fred was such a musician, and he really liked Bruce's song structures. When he wrote "People Have the Power" [the single off 1998's *Dream of Life*]—I told this to Bruce the other night—Fred studied "Because the Night." He really studied its structure. Obviously, it's a political song, but he wanted it to have an anthemic impact like "Because the Night." At this point, the only song that has ever eclipsed "Because the Night" in popularity in every way has been "People Have the Power," which I think Fred would get a kick out of.

Kaye: To me, a great song can be covered in any number of different ways. Most of them stick pretty close to what the song is—Garbage/Screaming Females is a little more punk; [10,000 Maniacs]'s is a little more laid back and wholesome.

Marissa Paternoster: When you do covers, it's fun to do stuff that's a hidden gem from an artist's catalog. But for the most part, ["Because the Night"] is a joy for everybody, the audience and the performer . . . I feel like it's a song that lends itself to any musician—that's the beauty of it. It's just some chords and a really, really strong melody and really good lyrics. As long as you know how to play it, you can do it, and then you can siphon that through your own personal lens and personal style. That's the cool thing about a lot of Bruce Springsteen songs: if you're learning how to play music, it's a good place to start. There's that instant gratification.

Kaye: Sometimes, when we're performing it onstage, I like to look at the audience and think that the audience is doing the song, because we're singing it and playing along, trying to keep up with them. The audience rises up when we play it. What else could you hope for for a great song to energize the people and sing along with? It's the same thing I do. I've been to see Bruce, when I'm out there in the pit, when he's singing "Because the Night," I'm singing along. It all makes a great, beautiful circle.

"Same guy. I'm the same girl. Just a little older."

On April 22, 2018, the Tribeca Film Festival premiered Horses: Patti Smith and Her Band, *a black-and-white documentary that immortalized the final two shows of the tour celebrating that album's 40th anniversary. The band performed a brief set after the credits rolled, and Springsteen shocked the audience when he sauntered out to perform with them—an occurrence so rare it's only one of a handful of times both he and Smith have sung their verses together.*

Smith: I hadn't planned to do a film. We did this Horses tour, and my drummer, Jay Dee, was diagnosed with cancer. He's alright now, but those last couple dates were traumatic, because we found out. We had to sort of go off the road; Jay had to go through his treatments. He's been my drummer since 1975, so I wasn't going to do anything without him. Those two L.A. dates were our last *Horses* dates, and we had no idea we would be out of action because we didn't know what the prognosis would be with Jay. So at the last minute I asked Steve [Sebring, director], "Will you film this so we have something archived?"

Jimmy Iovine, once again—the same Jimmy that handed me that cassette—I love things like this, it's like fate again. He comes backstage at the last concert . . . He loved the concert. He was thrilled with it, happy, excited. He said, "I wish we filmed it. Why don't we do another?" I told him, "We can't do anymore—but we did film it; we sort of rag-tag filmed it." Steve and I had done all this backstage footage. He said, "You mean you have *this night?!*" I said, "Yeah, in our way."

He talked to Apple and they agreed to fund whatever it took to make it a film, which was a lot of technical work. We only had what we had, and that required a lot of editing. We agreed, Apple funded us, and really, it's a nice arrangement, so they'll stream it for awhile. Eventually it'll be our little film and then we'll do what we do with it. Because of Jimmy and because they gave us the resources, we were off the road, had to regroup and it gave our people some work to do.

Tribeca heard that Steven was doing this and asked if we wanted to show it, and that was exciting enough. Right at the last moment, someone from Apple talked to someone from Bruce's people unbeknownst to me, and it was a sort of a surprise for me. They didn't ask me! Believe me: Bruce works really hard. In fact, I was really pissed at them. I said, "This man works on Broadway, what, six days a week, and he has one day off, and you're gonna ask him to come here on his day off?!" They said, "No, he's in town! He's happy to do it!" I scolded them! They thought I was gonna be in heaven, and I said, "How could you do that to him?!"

Bruce came to the rehearsal that day and everybody was happy to see him. We did our rehearsal, and "People Have the Power" was going to be the next song, and I said, "Play on 'People Have the Power!' You've performed it!" I thought, I had one of those moments . . . *[She tears up]* I'm there onstage with my daughter, my son, and Bruce doing "Because the Night" and "People Have the Power," and I just know Fred would've loved to have been there playing—and I know his amp would've been just a little louder than Bruce's. Bruce's was the loudest, but I know Fred would've made his just a little louder. It started with a Horses moment, but it ended, as many things do, as a Fred moment.

It was great. I loved it because, the thing is, Bruce and I, our roots, no matter what successes he has and how we've evolved, we're just the same people. He sauntered on the stage and I can recognize who we are. Sometimes, people change. Same guy. I'm the same girl. Just a little older.

Iovine: They have an unordinary amount of respect for each other. I watched that Patti performance standing next to Bruce, the one at the other night at the Beacon. We both just looked at each other and said, "Wow. Man, she's great." And she is.

Kaye: It's great to have him there. It's a shared sense of wonder that 40 years after this song was part of Top 40 history that it was able to be celebrated in such a nice way. There's a lot of songs that don't get to live on past the six weeks they have to make an impact on the public, but here's a song that has been taken to heart for over 40 years. Hopefully, we'll still be sung along to for the next 40.

Smith: There are certain songs I listen to and they're themselves. When I think about them or I look at the lyrics, there's something very specific in the abstract or they reflect a moment in time when I was young. But "Because the Night"—not just because it's a collaboration with Bruce— when I wrote it, so many things had happened that the song traveled with me. I fell in love; I wrote the lyrics of the song for Fred; I left New York; I left the public eye; we had our children; and then he died, and I was obliged to come back and start working again to take care of my kids, doing the song again.

The song has followed me. When I look at my personal life, I can't sing the song without seeing the '70s on. I see it's a whole life in a song. I met Fred in '76. A lot of my memories in life and my hopes and dreams are tied up in that meeting, and are sort of embedded in the song. The song for me spans decades. It's not a song I used to do; it's a song that seems alive every time we do it.

ABOUT THE CONTRIBUTORS

Jerry Aronson is a retired senior instructor at University of Colorado Boulder in the Department of Cinema Studies and Moving Image Arts. He produced and directed *The Life and Times of Allen Ginsberg*, a winner of the International Documentary Association Award in 1993 and a finalist for a Peabody award, which has been exhibited in more than 250 international film festivals. His film *The Divided Trail* earned an Academy Award Nomination for best documentary short in 1978, won the Aspen Film Festival Grand Prize, and was broadcast in 1980 on a special PBS series in entitled *Matters of Life and Death*. His six-hour documentary miniseries *American Music: The Roots of Country* aired on TBS and TNT in 1996. He has won grants from the National Endowment for the Arts and the National Endowment for the Humanities. His other films include *Fun with Lines*, *Old Glory Marching Society*, *Superstars*, *Options*, and *Chasing Ice*, which won a National Emmy in 2014.

Daniel David Baird is a writer and editor focused on art, culture, and ideas. He cofounded the New York–based monthly the *Brooklyn Rail* and served as an arts editor, features writer, and columnist. He went on to become the arts and literature editor at the *Walrus*, where he was also a regular contributor. His writing has appeared in *Canadian Art*, *Border Crossings*, and *Eighteen Bridges*. Baird also contributed to *The Canadian Encyclopedia*.

Victor Bockris has published seventeen books, including *Warhol: The Biography, Muhammad Ali in Fighter's Heaven, With William Burroughs: A Report from the Bunker, Beat Punks: New York's Underground Culture from the Beat Generation to the Punk Explosion,* and *Transformer: The Complete Lou Reed Story.*

Jim Braude is the host of *Greater Boston* and cohost of *Boston Public Radio* on WGBH. He has worked with cohost Margery Eagan for eighteen years, first doing a TV show together at NECN then a radio show at WTKK. The duo came to WGBH in 2013. During law school, he ran a small retail business in Provincetown (HUBE—Help Us Break Even!). He started his professional career as a legal services lawyer in the South Bronx handling housing and prisoners' rights cases. He was the founder and first president of the National Organization of Legal Services Workers, a union representing staff in civil legal offices for the poor in thirty-five states. He then served as the executive director of TEAM, the Tax Equity Alliance for Massachusetts, a tax reform coalition, where he led many ballot campaigns, including the defeat of what would have been the largest budget cut on the ballot in US history. He published *Otherwise,* a magazine on American politics, and has served as a Cambridge city councilor.

William S. Burroughs was a founding figure of the Beat Generation. He wrote eighteen novels and novellas, six collections of short stories, and four collections of essays. These include *Junkie (Junky), Naked Lunch, The Nova Trilogy, The Red Night Trilogy, The Electronic Revolution,* and *Interzone.* He died in 1997.

Anthony DeCurtis is the author of *Lou Reed: A Life, The Soundtrack of My Life* (with Clive Davis), *In Other Words: Artists Talk About Life and Work,* and *Rocking My Life Away: Writing About Music and Other Matters.* He edited *Present Tense: Rock & Roll and Culture, Blues & Chaos: The Music Writing of Robert Palmer, Rolling Stone Illustrated History* *of Rock & Roll, Rolling Stone Images of Rock & Roll,* and others. He is a contributing editor at *Rolling Stone,* where his work has appeared for more than thirty years. He holds a PhD in American literature from Indiana University and is a Distinguished Lecturer in the creative writing program at the University of Pennsylvania. His essay accompanying the 1988 Eric Clapton box set *Crossroads* won a Grammy for liner notes and he is a three-time winner of the ASCAP Deems Taylor Award. He has appeared as a commentator on MTV, VH1, *The Today Show,* and others. In 1996 he served as moderator on the VH1 show *Four on the Floor* and as editorial director for the channel's nonfiction programming. He has served as a member of the Rock and Roll Hall of Fame nominating committee for more than twenty years.

Jody Denberg is coauthor, with Bob Gruen, of *See Hear Yoko.* He has been on the air in Austin since 1981—at KLBJ-FM, as program director for KSGR-FM, and currently on KUTX-FM. He is the founding producer of KSBR's *Broadcasts,* an annual fundraiser album with sales supporting local charities.

Margery Eagan is the cohost of 89.7 WGBH's midday program *Boston Public Radio.* She has worked with cohost Jim Braude for eighteen years, first doing a TV show together at NECN then a radio show at WTKK. The duo came to WGBH in 2013. Eagan was the Catholic spirituality columnist for the *Boston Globe*'s website, Crux. In 2015, she won first place for excellence in religion commentary at the Religion Newswriters Association's annual conference in Philadelphia. She has written for her hometown paper, the *Fall River Herald News,* as well as the *Standard Times* of New Bedford, *Boston Globe,* the *Burlington Free Press, Boston Magazine,* and the *Boston Herald,* where she wrote a column for twenty-seven years.

Ben Edmonds was a former editor of *Creem* and a contributor to *Rolling Stone, MOJO,* the *Detroit Free Press,* and other publications. He was coauthor, with Al Kooper, of *Backstage Passes* and author of *Marvin Gaye: What's Going On and the Last Days of the Motown Sound*, and *Kill City Revisited: Confessions of a Fool for the Stooges*, for which he won one of his two ASCAP Deems Taylor Awards. Edmonds was a two-time Grammy nominee for liner notes and funded and oversaw the demo tapes for what became Iggy Pop and James Williamson's *Kill City*. He worked as manager of the post–Jim Morrison Doors, and was an A&R executive at various labels, including EMI Capitol and Arista in New York, London, and Los Angeles. While at Capitol, he discovered and signed the band Mink DeVille. He died in 2016.

Laurie Fitzpatrick is an assistant professor of practice at the Fox School of Business at Temple University, where she received the Crystal Apple Award, given annually to a Fox School adjunct for teaching excellence. Her artwork has appeared in shows in Philadelphia, New York City, and elsewhere for more than two decades. She is the founder and executive director of Friends of the Garden of the Arts, which works to raise funds and promote the development and maintenance of green space in Center City, Philadelphia. She has edited and contributed to *Art and Understanding* and the *Swedish Colonial Society Journal*.

Lawrence French is the administrator of the "Patti Smith Poet" group on Facebook. He is the editor of *Visions of Death: Richard Matheson's Edgar Allan Poe Scripts*. His writing has appeared in *Cinefantastique* and he has been a cohost of the *Cinefantastique* podcast.

Holly George-Warren is the author of, among others, *Janis: Her Life and Music, A Man Called Destruction: The Life and Music of Alex Chilton, Public Cowboy No. 1: The Life and Times of Gene Autry*, and the children's books *Honky-Tonk Heroes and Hillbilly Angels: The Pioneers of Country & Western Music* and *The Cowgirl Way*. Her writing has appeared in numerous anthologies, as well as in *Rolling Stone*, the *New York Times*, the *Village Voice*, *Redbook*, the *Oxford American*, *No Depression*, and elsewhere. She has contributed liner notes to countless anthologies and box sets and is a two-time Grammy nominee. Her essay for the Gram Parsons anthology *Sacred Hearts and Fallen Angels* won the 2002 ASCAP Deems Taylor Award for excellence in liner notes. She has edited many books, including two editions of *The Rolling Stone Encyclopedia of Rock & Roll*, for which she won a 1996 ASCAP Deems Taylor Award. She teaches arts journalism at the State University of New York in New Paltz and has lectured at Cornell, the University of Pennsylvania, and CUNY, among other universities.

Mick Gold was a rock photographer and journalist from 1968 to 1978. His work appeared in *Let It Rock, Melody Maker, Sounds, Creem*, and *Street Life*, and he published a book of photo-essays about live music, *Rock on the Road*. His work as a television documentary director and producer includes *Europe After the Rain*, a history of Dada and Surrealism; *Watergate*, a five-part history of the downfall of President Nixon, which won an Emmy; and *Endgame in Ireland*, on the secret history of the peace process in Northern Ireland, which won a Peabody Award.

Michael Goldberg is a novelist, journalist, and pioneering digital-music entrepreneur. His writing has appeared in *Esquire, DownBeat, Creem, Musician, New West*, and *NME*, and he is a contributor to *Kerouac on Record: A Literary Soundtrack*. From 1983 to 1993, he worked for *Rolling Stone*, where he was first a senior writer and later West Coast editor. In 1994, he cofounded the first web music magazine, *Addicted to Noise*, for which *Newsweek* included him in its 1995 "Net 50" list of "the 50 People Who Matter Most on the Internet." He is the author of the *Freak Scene Dream Trilogy: True Love Scars, The Flowers Lied*, and *Untitled*, and is an animal-rights activist.

"Punk Professor" **Vivien Goldman** is the author of *Soul Rebel, Natural Mystic*, a biography of Bob Marley; *The Black Chord*; and most recently, *Revenge of the She-Punks: A Feminist Music History from Poly Styrene* to *Pussy Riot*. Her writing has appeared in *Interview*, the *Village Voice*, *Rolling Stone*, *Spin*, the *Daily Telegraph*, and *Harper's Bazaar*. Her television work includes coproducing and conceiving of *Big World Café*. As a songwriter, she has released tracks with Japanese symphonist Ryuchi Sakamoto, Coldcut, and trip-hop pioneers Massive Attack. She is a founding member of avant-garde pop combo the Flying Lizards.

Michael Gross, who began his career contributing to *Circus*, *Rock*, and other music publications, is the author of, among others, *New York Times* bestseller *Model: The Ugly Business of Beautiful Women*, *740 Park: The Story of the World's Richest Apartment Building*, *Rogues' Gallery: The Secret History of the Moguls and the Money That Made the Metropolitan Museum*, and most recently, *Focus: The Sexy, Secret, Sometimes Sordid World of Fashion Photographers*. He is a contributing editor of *Departures* and has written for the *New York Times*, *New York*, *GQ*, *Esquire*, *Vanity Fair*, and others.

Terry Gross is the host and executive producer of *Fresh Air*, which she has hosted since 1975. She began her radio career in 1973 at public radio station WBFO in Buffalo, New York. There she hosted and produced several arts, women's, and public affairs programs, including *This Is Radio*, a live, three-hour magazine program that aired daily. Two years later, she joined the staff of WHYY-FM in Philadelphia as producer and host of *Fresh Air*, then a local, daily interview and music program. Since 1987, a daily, one-hour national edition of *Fresh Air* has been produced by WHYY-FM. The program is broadcast on 566 stations and, in fall 2008, became the first non-drive-time show in public radio history to reach more than five million listeners each week. The show won a Peabody Award in 1994. Gross has been a recipient of a Gracie Award, the Corporation for Public Broadcasting's Edward R. Murrow Award, the Literarian Award, the Columbia Journalism Award, and the Authors Guild Award for Distinguished Service to the Literary Community. She is the author of *All I Did Was Ask: Conversations with Writers, Actors, Musicians and Artists.*

Eric Holland is WFUV's evening host and assistant music director. He spent time behind the microphone at rock stations like WAQY in Springfield, Massachusetts, WKGB in upstate New York, and KKLV in Honolulu, where he was program director and afternoon host. In Massachusetts, he continued on air at WZLX and WBOS and taught classes at Emerson College, where he later received his Master of Arts. In Tokyo, he cohosted a radio program called Henna Communication, which featured popular music from all over the world. He was the music reporter on NY1-TV from 2012 to 2017.

Rita Houston is program director at WFUV in New York. She has hosted hundreds of interview sessions and Marquee Member concerts. She also serves as executive producer of the FUV Live concert series, books the annual Holiday Cheer for FUV concert, and produces annual benefit CDs of performances from WFUV's Studio A. After years as a popular midday host, Houston shifted her on-air presence to create *The Whole Wide World with Rita Houston.* She is a two-time Radio & Records (R&R) Music Director of the Year and three-time designate of Gavin's Music Director of the Year and has been awarded the ASCAP Deems Taylor Award for Broadcast Excellence.

Hilary Hughes has served as senior editor at Billboard, editor at MTV News, and music editor of the Village Voice. She has been a contributor at *Esquire, Rolling Stone,* the *New York Times, NPR Music, Pitchfork, USA Today, LA Weekly, Nylon, Elle,* and more.

Kristin Iversen is the deputy editor for *Refinery29.* She has been the executive editor of *Nylon* and *Brooklyn Magazine,* and she has written for *Elle, Literary Hub,* and *Catapult.*

Shadrach Kabango, better known as Shad or Shad K, has released six studio albums since 2005. Four of his albums have been shortlisted for the Polaris Music Prize and he won a Juno Award for Rap Recording of the Year in 2011 for *TSOL*. He hosted *q* on CBC Radio 1 from 2015 to 2016 and hosts the International Emmy Award– and Peabody Award–winning documentary series *Hip-Hop Evolution* on HBO Canada and Netflix.

Veteran rock journalist **Robin Katz** has been published in *Disc*, *Sounds*, *Record Mirror*, *NME*, *Black Echoes*, *Let It Rock*, and numerous other publications, and edited Virgin's in-flight magazine *Hot Air*. Her radio work includes BBC Radio 4, Capital Radio, BBC World Service, and BBC Radio Scotland. She toured with Bruce Springsteen for *Street Life*.

Howie Klein is, alongside Norman Davis and Chris Knab, one of the cofounders of *The Outcastes*, the first "punk" radio show in America, on KSAN in San Francisco. In 1978 he, Knab, and Bruce Bridges cofounded the San Francisco new wave record label 415 Records. He was the founder and editor of *New Wave* magazine. He joined Sire Records in 1987, becoming general manager, and was president of Reprise/Warner Bros. Records from 1989 and 2001. He has taught at McGill University.

Jonathan Lethem is the author of the novels *The Feral Detective*; *New York Times* bestseller *The Fortress of Solitude*; *Motherless Brooklyn*, which won a National Book Critics Circle Award; *Gun, with Occasional Music*; and others. His nonfiction titles include *The Ecstasy of Influence: Nonfictions, Etc.*, *Talking Heads' Fear of Music* (for the 33⅓ series), and *More Alive and Less Lonely: On Books and Writers*. He is the editor of the 2002 *Da Capo Best Music Writing: The Year's Finest Writing on Rock, Pop, Jazz, Country and More*, *The Exegesis of Philip K. Dick* (with coeditor Pamela Jackson), and *Shake It Up: Great American Writing on Rock and Pop from Elvis to Jay-Z* (with Kevin Dettmar). In 2005, he received a MacArthur Fellowship.

Alan Light is the former editor-in-chief of *Spin* and *Vibe* magazines and a former senior writer for *Rolling Stone*. He has been a contributor to the *New Yorker, GQ, Entertainment Weekly, Elle, Mother Jones,* and other publications. He cowrote the *New York Times* bestselling Gregg Allman memoir *My Cross to Bear* and is the author of *The Skills to Pay the Bills: The Story of the Beastie Boys; The Holy or the Broken: Leonard Cohen, Jeff Buckley, and the Unlikely Ascent of "Hallelujah"; Let's Go Crazy: Prince and the Making of Purple Rain;* and *What Happened, Miss Simone?* He has been on the air on WFUV, as music correspondent on the NPR show *Weekend America,* and on Sirius XM. He is a two-time winner of the ASCAP Deems Taylor award for excellence in music writing.

Gerrie Lim is the author of *Inside the Outsider, Invisible Trade, Idol to Icon, In Lust We Trust,* and *Singapore Rebel: Searching for Annabel Chong,* among others. He has written for numerous publications, including *Billboard, Details, Elle, Harper's Bazaar, L.A. Style, Playboy,* the *Wall Street Journal,* the *Asian Wall Street Journal,* the *South China Morning Post,* the *San Diego Union-Tribune,* and Virgin Megastore Online. He was the US Bureau Chief for the Singapore rock magazine he cofounded, *BigO.*

Christian Lund is the director of the Louisiana Literature Festival at the Louisiana Museum of Modern Art in Humlebæk, Denmark, and the editor of Louisiana Channel. At the annual festival, he has interviewed Ai Weiwei, Karl Ove Knausgård, Anne Waldman, and others.

Dave Marsh has written or edited more than a dozen books about rock and popular music, including *Born to Run: The Bruce Springsteen Story, Before I Get Old: The Story of the Who,* and *The Heart of Rock and Soul: The 1001 Greatest Singles Ever Made.* He cofounded *Creem* and spent five years as an associate and contributing editor of *Rolling Stone,* where he was chief music critic, columnist, and feature writer.

Ed Masley has been covering pop music professionally since 1991. He is the pop-music critic for the *Arizona Republic* and formerly the *Pittsburgh Post-Gazette*. He is a musician and songwriter whose bands have included the Frampton Brothers and the Breakup Society.

Alongside John Holmstrom and Ged Dunn, **Legs McNeil** is a cofounder of *Punk* magazine, which gave the movement its name, and was its "Resident Punk." He is a former editor at *Spin* and editor-in-chief of *Nerve Magazine*. He is coauthor, with Gillian McCain, of *Please Kill Me: The Uncensored Oral History of Punk*, which has been published in twelve languages, and *Dear Nobody: The True Diary of Mary Rose*. He is coauthor of *The Other Hollywood: The Uncensored Oral History of the Porn Film Industry* (with Jennifer Osborne and Peter Pavia) and *I Slept with Joey Ramone* (with Mickey Leigh). He has appeared in numerous television documentaries, from the History Channel to VH1.

Fred Mills has contributed to *Billboard, Magnet, Harp, Stereophile, No Depression, ICE, Detroit Metro Times, Stomp & Stammer, Goldmine*, and others. He is the editor of *Blurt* magazine.

Thurston Moore is a member of Sonic Youth and other groups and was ranked thirty-fourth in *Rolling Stone*'s 2004 edition of the "100 Greatest Guitarists of All Time." In May 2012 *Spin* published a staff-selected list of the top one hundred rock guitarists and ranked Moore and Sonic Youth bandmate Lee Ranaldo at number one. He is the founder of the record label Ecstatic Peace! He is the author of, among others, *Alabama Wildman, Mix Tape: The Art of Cassette Culture*, and *Lion: Only Noise*.

John Nichols is the author of *Dick: The Man Who Is President, The Rise and Rise of Richard B. Cheney: Unlocking the Mysteries of the Most Powerful Vice President in American History, The Genius of Impeachment: The Founders' Cure for Royalism, The Death and Life of American Journalism:*

The Media Revolution that Will Begin the World Again (with Robert W. McChesney), *People Get Ready: The Fight Against a Jobless Economy and a Citizenless Democracy* (with Robert W. McChesney), and others. He is the National Affairs correspondent for the *Nation* and associate editor of the *Capital Times*. He has contributed to *In These Times* and the *Progressive*. He is cofounder, with Robert McChesney and Josh Silver, of Free Press. Nichols is a regular radio and TV guest of many liberal and progressive talk shows, including *The Ed Show* with Ed Schultz on MSNBC and *Up with Chris Hayes* on MSNBC.

Lucy O'Brien is the author of *Dusty, Annie Lennox, She Bop: The Definitive History of Women in Popular Music, She Bop II,* and *Madonna: Like an Icon.* She has contributed to *Q, MOJO,* the *Guardian, NME,* and the *Quietus,* and numerous anthologies including *Mute Records: Artists, Business, History* and *Voicing Girlhood in Popular Music: Performance, Authority, Authenticity.* She has appeared on Channel 4 and BBC2 and coproduced the Channel 4 documentary *Righteous Babes.* In 2002, she adapted *She Bop II* as a two-part documentary for BBC Radio 2.

Richard Rys is the editor of *Wharton* magazine at the Wharton School of the University of Pennsylvania. He has taught at Temple University and Rown University and has contributed to *Men's Journal, Elle, Cosmopolitan, Men's Health,* the *New York Times,* the *Boston Globe, Radar,* and others. He was formerly senior editor at *Philadelphia* magazine.

From 1977 to 1982, **Andy Schwartz** was publisher and editor of *New York Rocker.* He served as director of editorial services for Epic Records (a division of Sony Music) until 2000. He edited the program booklet of the Rock and Roll Hall of Fame induction ceremonies and later served as a research consultant to the Rock Hall's Library and Archive project. He is coauthor, with Scott Schinder, of *Icons of Rock: An Encyclopedia of the Legends Who Changed Music Forever.*

Susin Shapiro broke into rock 'n' rolldom at *Crawdaddy*, went on to the *Village Voice, Rolling Stone, Circus, Sounds*, and the *Daily News*, and in 1993 began a twenty-year stint at the *New York Times* as S. S. Fair.

Jim Sullivan is a former *Boston Globe* arts and music staff writer who has contributed to the *Christian Science Monitor*, the *Boston Herald*, the *Boston Phoenix*, WBUR's the *ARTery, Best Classic Bands, Rock and Roll Globe*, and the *Cape Cod Times*. He has hosted the monthly music and interview show "Boston Rock/Talk" on Xfinity On Demand.

Peggy Thompson is an associate professor at the University of British Columbia. Her 1989 short film *In Search of the Last Good Man* won the Genie Award for Best Live Action Short Drama. She won the award for best screenplay at the fourteenth Genie Awards in 1993 for *The Lotus Eaters*. Her other film credits include *Better than Chocolate, Saint Monica*, and *Bearded Ladies: The Photography of Rosamond Norbury* and the television series *The Beachcombers, Da Vinci's Inquest*, and *Big Sound*. Her stage plays include *Brides in Space* and *The Last Will and Testament of Lolita*. She is coauthor, with Saeko Usukawa, of *Hard Boiled: Great Lines from Film Noir* and *Tall in the Saddle: Great Lines from Classic Westerns*. She is a board member and founding president of Women in Film and Television Vancouver.

Scott Timberg is the author of *Culture Crash: The Killing of the Creative Class*, which won the National Arts & Entertainment Journalism Award in 2015. He was a staff writer for *Salon*, a staff writer for the *Los Angeles Times*, and a contributing writer to the *Los Angeles Review of Books* and the *New York Times*. He died in 2019.

John Tobler was a founder of *ZigZag* magazine alongside Pete Frame. His books include *25 Years of Rock* (with Pete Frame), *The Record Producers* (with Stuart Grundy), *MTV Music Television: Who's Who in Rock Video*,

The Buddy Holly Story, The Rock Lists Album (with Alan Jones), *Who's Who in Rock and Roll, 100 Great Albums of the Sixties,* and *Brian Wilson and the Beach Boys: A Complete Guide.* He has written numerous liner notes for record reissues and compilations. He runs the Road Goes On Forever record label.

Nick Tosches was the author of the novels *Cut Numbers, Trinities,* and *In the Hand of Dante,* and the poetry collections *Chaldea* and *Never Trust a Loving God.* His nonfiction works include *Hellfire, Dino, The Devil and Sonny Liston, Where Dead Voices Gather, The Last Opium Den, King of the Jews, Country: The Biggest Music in America,* and *The Nick Tosches Reader.* The *Observer Music Monthly* declared *Hellfire,* his Jerry Lee Lewis biography, to be the greatest music book ever written. His writing appeared in *Esquire,* the *Village Voice,* the *New York Times, Ring* magazine, *Fusion, Rolling Stone, Creem,* and *Vanity Fair,* where he was a contributing editor. He died in 2019.

Jaan Uhelszki is one of the illustrious gang of writers—Lester Bangs, Dave Marsh, et al.—who made *Creem* a rock 'n' roll household name in the '70s. Her writing has appeared in *USA Today, Uncut, Classic Rock, Rolling Stone, Spin, NME, Relix,* and elsewhere. She is the only journalist to have ever performed in full makeup with Kiss. She has written liner notes for Sony Legacy Recordings, Rhino Records, and Time-Life, and contributed essays for Rock and Roll Hall of Fame inductees the Pretenders, Lynyrd Skynyrd, Patti Smith, and the Stooges. Uhelszki appears as a music authority on VH1's *Behind the Music* and elsewhere.

Paul Zollo is the senior editor of *American Songwriter* magazine and the author of *Songwriters on Songwriting, More Songwriters on Songwriting, Conversations with Tom Petty, Hollywood Remembered,* and others. The former editor of *SongTalk,* he has contributed to numerous publications, including *Variety, Billboard, Oxford American, Sing Out!, Grammy Magazine, Playback, Boulevard, Acoustic Guitar,* and others, as well as writing each year for the annual Grammy Awards. As a songwriter, he has collaborated with many artists, including Steve Allen, Darryl Purpose, and Severin Browne. He released one eponymous album with his band, the Ghosters, and as a solo artist released the album *Orange Avenue*, which features a duet with Art Garfunkel.

CREDITS

I gratefully acknowledge the help of everyone who gave permission for material to appear in this book. I have made every reasonable effort to contact copyright holders. If an error or omission has been made, please bring it to the attention of the publisher.

"The Poetry of Performance: An Interview with Patti Smith," by Victor Bockris. Published 1972 by Red Room Books. Copyright © 1972. Reprinted by permission.

"Patti Smith: Somewhere, over the Rimbaud," by Susin Shapiro. Published December 1975 in *Crawdaddy*. Copyright © 1975. Reprinted by permission of Rock's Backpages.

"Patti Smith: Poetry in Motion," by Robin Katz. Published December 13, 1975 in *Sounds*. Copyright © 1975. Reprinted by permission of Rock's Backpages.

"Patti Smith: Her Horses Got Wings, They Can Fly," by Dave Marsh. Published January 1976 in *Rolling Stone*. Copyright © 1976. Reprinted by permission of Rock's Backpages.

Interview with Patti Smith by Mick Gold, May 10, 1976. Copyright © 1976. Printed by permission.

INDEX

A&E, 253

"About a Boy" (Patti Smith), 202, 220, 224

Abyssinians, The, 131

Addicted to Noise (or *ATN*), 205

Adventures of Pinocchio, The (Carlo Collodi), 396, 407, 455, 461

Aerosmith, 83, 88–89, 91

"After the Gold Rush" (Neil Young), 466

AIDS Memorial Quilt (or NAMES Project AIDS Memorial Quilt), 255

Airport Drive In, 32, 192

Aja (Steely Dan), 142

Alcott, Louisa May, 6

Alexander the Great, 175

Alexander, Elizabeth, 455

Alfa Romeo, 136

Alfalfa, 79

Al-Farid, Ibn, 124

Allman Brothers Band, The, 106, 329, 336, 424

Ali, Muhammad, 20, 69

Altamont Free Concert, 41

American Beauty, 50

American Songwriter, 373

Anger, Kenneth, 44

Ann Arbor, Michigan, 302, 304

Another Side of Bob Dylan (Bob Dylan), 74, 187

Apollinaire, Guillaume, 16, 475

Apple Corps, 141

Arbus, Diane, 312, 315, 358

Arista Records, 23, 27, 35, 49, 51, 126, 141, 148, 154, 171, 198–199, 271, 283, 298, 307

British, 53, 56–57, 60–61

Aronson, Jerry, 302

Art Gallery of Ontario, 414, 416, 418

Artaud, Antonin, 65

Astor Place, 171

Atlantic City, New Jersey, 48, 327

Atlantic Records, 242, 327

Auguries of Innocence (Patti Smith), 312–328

Ayler, Albert, 269, 440

Babel (Patti Smith), 312
"Babelogue" (Patti Smith), 202
Bach: The Goldberg Variations (Glenn Gould), 430
Baez, Joan, 190, 192, 340, 466, 469, 476
Bagge, Peter, 83
Baird, Daniel David, 414
Ballard, Hank, 475
Ballard, J. G., 200
Balzary, Michael "Flea," 362, 466
Banga (Patti Smith), 380–394
Bangs, Lester, 38, 143, 185, 206
Barrett, Rona, 63, 77
Baudelaire, Charles, xiv, 46, 66, 250, 434, 449, 474, 475, 477
"Be My Baby" (the Ronettes), 137
Beach Boys, The, 32, 74,
Beats, the Beat Generation, 70, 198, 258, 266, 302, 374
"Because the Night" (Patti Smith), 112–113, 123, 126, 132, 134, 137, 144, 147, 162, 166, 170, 180, 198, 218, 258, 272, 424, 456
  Bruce Springteen on, 162, 180–181, 198, 258, 272, 334, 379, 424, 488–506
  Lenny Kaye on, 334–335, 490, 492–504
  story behind, 334, 379, 488–505
Beacon Theater, 202, 505
Beatles, The, 26, 32, 74, 188, 193
Bee Gees, 134
Belafonte, Harry, 31, 187
Bells of Hell, 123, 127

Berkeley, California, 48, 205
Berkeley Barb, 108, 205
Berry, Chuck, 107, 194, 431
Best of Punk Magazine, The (John Holmstrom), 83
Big Youth, 108–109
Bird in Space (Constantin Brancusi), 55
"Birdland" (Patti Smith), 28–29, 50, 172
Billboard, 258, 275, 279
Bitter End, The, 23, 190
"Black Peter" (Grateful Dead), 220
"Black to Comm" (MC5), 185
Blake, William, 312, 314, 315, 321, 326, 355–356, 370, 397, 419, 435, 454, 474, 485
Blakey, Art, 139
Blast, 70
Bleecker Bob's Golden Oldies, 191, 487
Blonde on Blonde (Bob Dylan), 130
Blondie, 184, 194
Blue Öyster Cult, 35, 46, 68, 81, 88, 93, 110, 113, 241, 271
"Blue Poles" (Jackson Pollock), 249
"Blue Poles" (Patti Smith), 248–249
Bluebelles, 192
Boarding House, 115, 205, 214
Boave, May, 466
Bockris, Victor, xvi, 3, 4, 147
Bolaño, Roberto, 368, 392, 407, 419, 473, 474, 480, 482, 484
Book of Dreams, A (Peter Reich), 28
Boone, Debby, 120, 128, 489, 499

Border Crossings, 414
Born to Run (Bruce Springsteen), 30
Boston Globe, 461
Bouchard, Albert, 93
Bowery, 23, 35, 46, 48, 124, 126, 147–149
Bowery Ballroom, 337
Bowie, David, 48, 70, 155, 213, 333
Brancusi, Constantin, 25, 54, 55, 485
Braude, Jim, 455
"Break It Up" (Patti Smith), 28
Brecht, Bertolt, 77, 405
Brenda Starr, Reporter, 27
"Broken Flag" (Patti Smith), 146
Brody, Bruce, 174
Brooklyn Book Festival, 456
Brooklyn Heights, 456
Brown, James, 28, 32, 74, 114, 134
Bruno, Susan, 129
Buckley, Jeff, 204
Buckley, Tim, 443
Burchill, Julie, 145, 146
Burn, Malcolm, 169, 203
Burr, Aaron, 258
Burroughs, William S., xvi, 25, 45, 46, 104, 108, 111, 147–148, 162, 184, 192, 258, 304, 307, 368, 425, 473
Bunker, xvi, 149
first meeting with Patti Smith, 149
on writing, 376, 411

Caffe Reggio, 70,
Cain, James M., 5
Cale, Eden, 241

Cale, John, 169, 226, 239–241
Camden, New Jersey, 40, 155, 265, 429
Camera Solo, 380, 414, 416
Camus, Albert, 165, 302, 473, 475, 479
Captain & Tennille, 27
Carnegie Hall, 304, 334–335, 466
Carroll, Jim, 20, 21, 400, 426
Carroll, Lewis, 322
Cars, The, 141
Carson, Johnny, 233, 395
Cassettes and Cartridges, 80
Cassidy, Shaun, 141
Cathedral of Saint John the Divine, 302
Catherine the Great, 44
CBGB, 23, 35, 48, 97, 104, 115, 123, 126, 137, 149, 151–152, 184, 191, 198, 271, 273, 280, 307, 365, 369, 415, 423, 473–474, 477, 486–487, 500
Céline, Louis-Ferdinand, 9, 10
Cendrars, Blaise, 5, 10, 16
censorship, 54–55, 58–60, 186, 209, 262, 299, 468
Central Park, 109
Central Park SummerStage, 131, 170, 199, 201
Chandler, Raymond, 5
Chantage, 80
Chelsea Hotel (or Hotel Chelsea, the Chelsea), xvi, 3, 34, 45–47, 70, 76, 78, 166, 177, 232, 302, 303, 400, 415

Chiffons, The, 110
Clanton, Jimmy, 139
Clash, The, 110, 135, 144, 370, 426, 451
Coachmen, The, 193
Cobain, Kurt, 202, 220, 221, 224, 428
Cocteau, Jean, 164, 474
"Coffee Cantata" (Johann Bach), 430
Cole, Nat King, 312, 326, 327
Coleman, Ornette, 139, 383
Coltrane, John, 250, 279, 370, 376, 394, 418, 421, 440, 463
Columbia Record Club, 394, 398
Columbia Records, 40, 51, 307, 329, 341
Columbia University, 302
"Come Josephine in My Flying Machine" (Blanche Ring), 31
Commodore Ballroom, 108
Considine, Tim, 92
"Constantine's Dream" (Patti Smith), 380, 389, 391, 420–421
Contortions, The, 143, 194
Cooler, the, 249
Cooper Union, 365
Copenhagen, Denmark, 395
Coral Sea, The (Patti Smith), 170, 199, 235, 240, 247, 253–254, 273, 312, 319
Corby's Bar, 124, 126–128
Corso, Gregory, 305–306, 400, 405
Cowboy Mouth (Patti Smith and Sam Shepard), 3, 166, 183, 271, 374, 405

Crawdaddy, 23, 233, 272
Crazy Eddie's, 166
Crazy Horse, 333, 414–415
Creem, 38, 123, 148, 183, 185, 206, 233, 271

Dalai Lama, 182, 195, 264, 469
Dali, Salvador, 70, 355
"Dancing Barefoot" (Patti Smith), 146, 173, 218, 378, 422
"Dark Eyes" (Bob Dylan), 202, 228
Darkness on the Edge of Town (Bruce Springsteen), 488, 495
Daugherty, Jay Dee, 24, 28, 36, 84, 131, 143, 144, 169, 174, 199, 269, 271, 273, 288, 336, 389, 496
Davis, Clive, 23, 36, 49, 50, 56, 133, 171, 298, 491
Davis, Francis, 440
Davis, Miles, 433, 478
de Gaulle, Charles, 75
de Kooning, Willem, 12, 17, 417–418
Dead Man Walking, 217, 273
"Dead to the World" (Patti Smith), 167–168, 172, 197, 224
Death in Venice, 35
"Death Singing" (Patti Smith), 249
Declaration of Independence, 309, 417
DeCurtis, Anthony, 345–346
DeLano, Sharon, 342
Delehant, Jim, 48
della Francesca, Piero, 380, 389, 391, 420–421

Denberg, Jody, 283

Dennis Mitchell Toys

Deptford High, 342, 344

Descloux, Lizzy Mercier, 103

Detroit Industry Murals (Diego Rivera), 380, 385

Detroit Tigers, 161, 283, 298

Devil's Island, 212

Devotion: Why I Write (Patti Smith), xviii, 455–464, 473–474, 480, 482

Dickerson, Robert "Benjamin Smoke," 249

Dickinson, Emily, 46

DNA, 194

Doctor Sax (Jack Kerouac), 190

"Doll Parts" (Hole), 176

Don't Look Back, 43, 45, 69, 77, 232, 350

"Don't Mess with Bill" (the Marvelettes), 32

Doobie Brothers, The, 106

Doors, The, 34, 43, 76, 113. *See also* Jim Morrison

Doubleday, 16

Douglas, Jack, 83, 84, 91

Dowd, Maureen, 113, 114

Dowd, Tom, 242

Dream of Constantine, The (Piero della Francesca), 389, 420

Dream of Life (Patti Smith), 414–422, 424, 426–427, 452, 502

Dury, Ian, 191

Dylan, Bob, 10, 12, 17, 21, 22, 23, 26, 41–43, 45, 48, 53, 63, 70–71, 74, 135, 137, 150, 153, 175, 183, 184, 187, 190, 197, 199, 220, 221, 223, 225, 227, 228, 234, 258, 271, 278, 279, 300, 330, 339–340, 394, 398, 434, 455, 460, 476–478, 494

First seeing Patti Smith, 35, 49, 189

Nobel Prize, 456, 459

Performing with Patti Smith, 202, 226, 265, 295

Poetry, 32, 33, 34

Song book, 188

"Dylan's Dog" (Patti Smith), 130

Eagan, Margery, 455, 456

Eagles, 105–106

Early Morning Dream (Patti Smith), 25

Early Work: 1970–1979 (Patti Smith), 168, 170, 173, 319

Earl's Court, 115

Easter (Patti Smith Group), 80–82, 96–107, 113, 120, 123, 126, 129, 131, 148, 166, 169, 173, 174, 182, 198, 272, 334, 415, 416, 420, 426, 488, 490, 494–495, 498–500

Edmonds, Ben, 223

Electric Lady Studios, 23, 24, 167, 382

"Elegie" (Patti Smith), 23, 28

Eliot, T. S., 21, 237

Ellington, Duke, 440

Empire of the Sun, 162

English Bay, xvi, 108–109, 112

Ertegun, Ahmet, 242

Esso, 120

Esteban, Michel, 103

Eugene, Oregon, 116

Fabulous Life of Diego Rivera, The (Bertram D. Wolfe), 473, 476

Faithfull, Marianne, 10, 13

"Farewell Reel" (Patti Smith), 197, 202, 224, 300

Fear (John Cale), 50

Fender Duo-Sonic, 204

Fender Duo-Sonic, NYC (Patti Smith), 419

Fields, Al "Reverend," 123, 127

Fillmore, The, 48

Finnegans Wake (James Joyce), 473, 482–483

"Fireflies" (Patti Smith), 203

Fitzpatrick, Laurie, 247

"5-4-3-2-1" (Manfred Mann), 131

Florence, Italy, 165, 169, 207, 210, 223, 236, 416

Flying Lizards, The, 80

Fondation Cartier, 342, 416

Foon, Rebecca, 466, 467

"Footnote to Howl" (Allen Ginsberg), 302, 306

Ford, Mary, 31

Fordham University, 329

Foreigner, 134

Francis (Saint), 380, 390, 420

"Frederick" (Patti Smith), 133, 137, 144, 146, 218, 376, 378

"Freight Train" (Elizabeth Cotten), 74

French Guiana, 212

Fresh Air, 440–441

Frida Kahlo's Bed, Casa Azul, Coyoacán (Patti Smith), 419

Friedman, Jane, 34–35, 47, 76, 225
    managing Smith, 35, 40, 61, 71, 240

French, Lawrence, 312

Fuller, Sam, 111

Garbage, 489, 490, 501–502

Garcia, Jerry, 184, 220, 301, 326–327

Gaslight Café (or the Gaslight), 47

Gaye, Marvin, 74

Genet, Jean, 35, 176, 184, 261, 473, 479, 484,

George-Warren, Holly, 197, 223

Georgia Straight, 108

Getty Oil, 91

"Ghost Dance" (Patti Smith), 169, 171, 420, 499

Gibson, 188, 233, 290

Ginsberg, Allen, 17, 70, 147, 258, 265–266, 273, 302–306, 352, 375, 377, 381, 400, 473
    death, 453

"Girl Can't Help It, The" (Little Richard), 31, 271, 394

"Girl Trouble" (Patti Smith), 5

Glassboro State College, 165, 342–343, 367, 440–442

"Gloria" (Them), 28, 48, 141, 165, 330, 447–448

"Gloria (In Excelsis Deo)" (Patti Smith), xv, 53, 108, 165, 171, 420, 223, 236, 260, 330, 367, 406, 420, 447–448

Glover, Tony, 8, 130
Go, Johnny, Go!, 139
Goat's Head Soup (the Rolling
  Stones), 131
Godard, Jean-Luc, 43, 162, 474
"Godspeed" (Patti Smith), 185
"Going Under" (Patti Smith), 164
Gold, Mick, 53
Goldberg, Jeff, 3
Goldberg, Michael, 205–206
Goldman, Vivien, 80
Goldmine, 269
"Gone Again" (Patti Smith), 203, 228
Gone Again (Patti Smith), 167, 197,
  199, 202–203, 206, 207, 223–238,
  240, 248, 255, 258, 269, 273, 275,
  288–289, 295, 297, 347, 383, 427
Goodman, Benny, 233
Gordon, Kim, 193
Gore, Tipper, 186
*Gospel According to St. Matthew,
  The*, 165
Gossett, Richard, 113
Gotham Book Mart, 47, 148
Gould, Glenn, 430–431
Graham, Bill, 48, 113
Graham, Billy, 18
Grateful Dead, 139, 220, 232, 280
*Grave, Amedeo Modigliani and
  Jeanne Hébuterne, Père Lachaise,
  Paris* (Patti Smith), 419
Grease, 489
Green Day, 175
"Green Door, The" (Jim Lowe), 72
Greenwich Village, 23, 47, 70, 168

Gross, Michael, xvi, 70
Gross, Terry, 440–441
Grosse Pointe, Michigan, 257
Gung Ho (Patti Smith), 283–301,
  374, 427
Guys and Dolls, 192

Hamill, Janet, 7
Hammer, Mike, 9
Happy Death, A (Albert Camus),
  302, 479
"Hard Rain's Gonna Fall, A," (Bob
  Dylan), 455–456, 459, 462
Harrison, George, 43
Harry, Debbie, 112
Hartford, Connecticut, 380, 416
*Headstone for William Blake, Bunhill
  Fields, London* (Patti Smith), 419
Hearst, Patty, 48, 71
Heaven's Gate, 258, 277
Hell, Richard, 184, 426, 473, 477,
  486
Hellfire: The Jerry Lee Lewis Story
  (Nick Tosches), 123
Hendrix, Jimi, 23–24, 26–28, 31,
  33, 35, 37, 44, 46, 51, 78, 97, 99,
  102,105, 141, 165, 168, 173, 187,
  221, 225–226, 258, 277, 300, 330,
  370, 374, 381, 382, 387, 392, 415,
  441, 451
  death, 100–101, 156, 167, 222, 307
Hepburn, Audrey, 176, 282, 351
"Hey Joe" (Patti Smith), 23, 48, 61,
  103, 126, 271, 331, 367, 382, 424,
  441

Higgins, Dick, 148
"High on Rebellion" (Patti Smith), 102, 182, 255
Highway 61 Revisited (Bob Dylan), 232
Holden, Stephen, 49
Holiday, Billie, 259, 327
Holland, Eric, 380
Holmstrom, John, 83
Holt Renfrew, 108
"Horse Latitudes" (the Doors), 101
Horses (Patti Smith), xiv, 23–24, 30, 36, 39, 50–51, 53–69, 70, 83, 100–101, 126, 130, 142, 145, 148, 164–166, 169–173, 185, 198, 205–206, 223, 225, 229, 239–242, 269, 271, 307, 311–313, 330, 345, 374–377, 383, 387, 396, 414–416, 423–428, 446–451, 454, 474, 491, 503–504
    ad copy for, xiv, 448
    cover photo, xv, 415, 440–441, 446, 448
Houston, Rita, 329
Howl (Allen Ginsberg), 265, 375
Hughes, Hillary, 489
Humlebæk, Denmark, xviii, 395, 515
Huncke, Herbert, 189
Hunter, Robert, 184, 220
"Hymn" (Patti Smith), 135
Hynde, Chrissie, 148

I-Threes, 108
Icarus: Fly to the Light, xiii

Iggy Pop, 240
Illuminations (Arthur Rimbaud), 7, 15, 26, 43, 49, 67
"In-A-Gadda-Da-Vida" (Iron Butterfly), 131
Independence Hall, 342, 344
Independent, 239
Iovine, Jimmy, 140, 141, 335, 489, 490
Irushalmi, Risé, 239
"It Takes Time" (Patti Smith and Fred "Sonic" Smith), 229

Jackson, Jesse, 261, 427
"Jackson Song, The" (Patti Smith), 161, 200, 393
Jagger, Mick, 8, 11, 13, 18, 22, 31–32, 36, 41, 48, 65, 107–108, 147, 193
Jamaica Plain, Boston, 185
James, Jesse, 78, 98
Java House, 197–199
Jazz Messengers, The, 139
Jefferson Airplane, 45, 113, 118–120, 329
"Jesse James" (Patti Smith), 130
Joan of Arc, xvi, 9–10, 13, 71, 100, 167
Joel, Billy, 137
Johnson, Lady Bird, 189, 283, 296
Johnson, Robert, 188
Jones, Brian, 34, 43, 52, 64, 71, 99, 167, 182, 192–193
    death, 44–45, 101, 225
Jones, Elvin, 187
Jones, Tom, 124
Joplin, Janis, 45–47, 78, 222, 232,

259, 368–369
"Josephine" (Les Paul and Mary
Ford), 31
Judex, 14
"Judith" (Patti Smith), 11–12, 15
"Jumping Jack Flash" (the Rolling
Stones), 8
Junkie (William S. Burroughs), 108,
111, 147
Just Kids (Patti Smith), xiv, xvi,
xviii, 148, 247, 345, 365–372, 374,
381, 402–413, 416, 424, 430–431,
441, 448, 451–452, 454, 456, 458,
462–463, 474, 481

Kabango, Shadrach "Shad," 430
Kafka, Franz, 165
Kahlo, Frida, 380, 385, 414, 419,
476, 484
Kaline, Al, 283, 298
Katz, Robin, 30
Kaye, Lenny, xiv, 113, 163, 184, 203,
205, 287, 288, 291–292, 329, 330,
336, 350, 375, 383, 389, 466, 489,
498, 500
backing Patti Smith's poetry, 3, 23,
28, 32, 35, 39, 46–48, 53–69, 78,
125, 148, 166, 183, 222, 271, 331,
405
"Because the Night," working on,
334–335, 490, 492–504
Central Park concert, 201–202
early influences, 338, 370
on *Horses*, 23, 54–69
in the Patti Smith Group, 115–122,

131, 137–139, 169, 171, 173, 199,
269, 273
on *Wave*, 133, 137
Kennedy, John F., 150
Kenton, Stan, 440
Kerouac, Jack, xvi, 70, 131, 182, 185,
189
death, 190, 302
Kerouac Foundation, 184
KGSR, 283
Kids, 186
King, Ben E., 32, 192
Kiss, 213
Klein, Howie, 113
Knausgaard, Karl Ove, 455
Kodak (Patti Smith), 25, 47
Kral, Ivan, 23, 28, 36, 82, 131, 134,
141, 143, 144, 174, 271
KSAN, xvi, 113
KUSF, 313
Kweli, Talib, 466
KZEL, 116

La MaMa, 77
LaBelle, Patti, 192
*Ladies and Gentlemen: The Rolling
Stones*, 34
Lafayette Coney Island, 54, 218, 229
Laforgue, Jules, 21
Lake, Steve, 54
"Lamb, The," (William Blake), 397
Lambert, Glenn, 113
"Land: Horses/Land of a Thou-
sand Dances/La Mer (De)" (Patti
Smith), 28, 48, 49, 171, 448

Lanier, Allen, 35, 46, 47, 81, 93, 241, 271

Last Tango in Paris, 380, 387

Le Puits, the "Wishing Well," 43

Leaves of Grass (Walt Whitman), 259

"Leda and the Swan" (W. B. Yeats), 12

Lee, Peggy, 440

Lee, Robert E., 82

Left Bank, 473

Lennon, John, 56, 491

Lenya, Lotte, 3

Lethem, Jonathan, xvi, 365

Lewis, Jerry, 31, 338

Lewis, Jerry "the Killer" Lee, 123

Life and Times of Allen Ginsberg, The, 302

Light, Alan, 423

"Light My Fire" (the Doors), 43, 76

Lim, Gerrie, 167–168

"Little Girl Blue" (Janis Joplin), 47

Little Richard, 31–32, 148, 271, 327, 356, 394

Little Women (Louisa May Alcott), 6

Live Through This (Hole), 176

Lloyd's of London, 52

Loesser, Frank, 440

London, Bobby, 83

Longbranch, 115–116, 205, 214

"Looking for You" (Patti Smith), 200

"Louie Louie" (the Kingsmen), 32

Louisiana Literature Festival, 395–413

Louisiana Museum of Modern Art, 395

Love, Courtney, 168, 175–176, 270

"Love Song of J. Alfred Prufrock, The" (T. S. Eliot), 21

Lowell, Massachusetts, 182, 184–185, 190

Luger, 141

Lunch, Lydia, 194

Lund, Christian, 395

Lyndon Baines Johnson Suite, 189

M Train (Patti Smith), xviii, 430–439, 441, 448, 454, 456, 458, 481

MacArthur Fellow, 514, 365

Mad Dog Blues (Sam Shepard and Patti Smith), 45, 166

Madame Butterfly (Giacomo Puccini), 187

Madison Square Garden, 3, 18

Madonna, 147, 424

Magnani, Anna, 27, 157

Making of Star Trek: The Motion Picture (Gene Roddenberry and Susan Sackett), 116

Malanga, Gerard, 46, 405

Man Ah Warrior (Tapper Zukie), 102

Manet, Édouard, 65

Manfred Mann, 131

Manson, Charles, 51

Manson, Shirley, 489–490

Mapplethorpe, Robert, 134, 162, 179, 183, 199, 226, 235, 252, 258, 271, 273, 312, 319, 360, 374, 388, 395, 399, 419, 400, 441–444, 446, 451, 474

death, xvi, 167, 169, 170, 171, 176,

184, 198, 247–248, 250, 272, 300, 347, 352, 420, 451–452

financing "Piss Factory," 35, 48, 126

first meeting Patti Smith, 32, 42, 43, 75, 367, 442

living with Patti Smith, xvi, 3, 23, 34–35, 45–47, 70, 76, 78, 166, 177, 194, 231–233, 302, 381, 400, 415–416

photograph of Patti Smith, xv, 226, 415, 441, 448

Mapplethorpe: A Biography (Patricia Morrisroe), 179, 231

Marcus, Greil, xvi, 113

"Maria" (Patti Smith), 380, 386–387

Marley, Bob, 36, 50, 108

Mars, 194

Marsh, Dave, 38–39

Marshall, Charlyn "Cat Power," 466

Martin, 188

Marvel Comics, 118

Marvelettes, The, 32, 114

"Mary Jane" (Patti Smith), 9

Masley, Ed, 307

Max's Kansas City, 35, 48–49, 70, 76, 131, 198, 416

Mayagüez, Puerto Rico, 123–124

Mayer, Bernadette, 20

McCain, Gillian, 84

McCartney, Paul, 466

McCourt, Malachy, 123

MC5, 149, 161–162, 169, 184, 198, 206, 258, 261, 272, 372, 416, 424, 490

McKibben, Bill, 465

McNally Jackson Books, 455

McNeil, Roderick "Legs," 83–84

Melody Maker, 54

Meltzer, Richard, 92, 125, 205

Memorial Hall, 269

"Memory Gardens" (Allen Ginsberg), 302

Mer Records, 23, 48, 103–104, 126

Mercer Arts Center, 47

Merchant, Natalie, 180

Meyer, Russ, 52

Michaux, Henri, 9–10

"Mickey's Monkey" (the Miracles), 32

Middle Earth Press, 46–47

Midnighters, The, 125

Mike Douglas Show, The, 108

Mills, Fred, 269

Minnelli, Liza, 38, 46

Miscellany News, 129

Mitchell, Dennis, 126

Mitchell, Joni, 47, 205

Moby-Dick (Herman Melville), 259, 455, 461

Modiano, Patrick, 473, 480

Modigliani, Amedeo, 6, 17, 65, 398, 419

"Money Tree, The" (Patience and Prudence), 187

Monkey, the, 32

Moon, Keith, 36

Moore, Roger, 117

Moore, Thurston, 182, 270

Moravagine (Blaise Cendrars), 16

Moreau, Jeanne, 26, 435

Morrison, Jim, 46, 51, 64, 99, 100, 102, 128, 175, 221, 258, 300, 336, 377, 379, 385–387, 406, 451
death, 28, 97, 101, 167, 222, 225, 307, 434
Morrison, Sterling, 239
Morrison, Van, 28, 31, 53, 165, 330, 370
"Mother Nature's Son" (the Beatles), 466
"Mother Rose" (Patti Smith), 307–308
Motherless Brooklyn (Jonathan Lethem), 365
Motortown Revue (or Motown Revue), 192
MTV Unplugged, 490
Murakami, Haruki, 392, 407, 473, 480, 482, 484
My Bloody Valentine, 175, 341
My Father's Cup (Patti Smith), 419
My Favorite Things (John Coltrane), 187
"My Generation" (the Who), 53, 55, 137, 163, 191, 241, 260
My Three Sons (TV show), 92
Myers, Vali, 13
Myles, Eileen, 455
MySpace, 365, 371

Naked Lunch (William S. Burroughs), 147
Namibia, 312, 325
Nashville Skyline (Bob Dylan), 12
National Book Award, xvi, 381, 410, 416, 424, 441, 448, 456, 463, 474

National Book Critics Circle Award, 365
Natural Born Killers, 234
"Nature Is What We See" (Emily Dickinson), 466
Neuwirth, Bobby, 44–45, 77, 232
New Musical Express, 145
New York Dolls, 47
New York Post, 145
New York Times, 23, 49, 53, 113, 146, 171, 427, 456
New Yorker, 181, 342
Newton-John, Olivia, 488
Nichols, John, 257
Nijinsky, Vaslav, 62
Nikolai Gogol (Vladimir Nabakov), 473, 481
"1959" (Patti Smith), 263–264
Nirvana, 175, 220, 330, 424
no wave, 139, 193–194
Nobel Prize, 456, 459
Norton, Gil, 289
"Not Fade Away" (Patti Smith), 214, 220
Notting Hill, 53
Nureyev, Rudolph, 176
Nylon, 465

Oakland Coliseum, 116
O'Brien, Conan, 273
O'Brien, Lucy, 239
Ochs, Phil, 35
"Oh Boy" (Buddy Holly), 137
O'Hara, Frank, 17
Olson, Charles, 21

"On a Slow Boat to China" (Frank Loesser), 440

One Plus One, 43

Ostrowe, Andi, 136

Other End, The, 23, 26, 49, 227

Out of Traction/Back in Action shows, 152

Outcastes, The, 113

Page, Jimmy, 104, 117

painting/artwork, 25, 50, 55, 66, 153, 278, 280, 290, 353

Paiute, 169

"Pale Blue Eyes" (the Velvet Underground), 32

Pallenberg, Anita, 5, 13, 44

Palmer, Arnold, 189

"Parade" (Patti Smith), 15

Parents Music Resource Center, 186

Paris Agreement, 465

Parker, Charlie, 380, 387, 409

Pasolini, Pier Paolo, 104, 165, 207–208, 236, 353

Paternoster, Marissa, 489–490

"Paths That Cross" (Patti Smith), 171, 200, 427, 440, 451–452

Pathway to Paris, 465–468

Patience and Prudence, 187

Patti Smith: Dream of Life, 247, 342–343, 345–362, 414

Patti Smith Group, 23, 83, 129–146, 199, 201, 205, 223, 258, 269, 271–272, 274, 287, 380, 490, 495

Patti Smith, Land 250, 342, 416

Paul, Les, 31

Paul, Steve, 39, 46

Peace and Noise (Patti Smith), 248, 255, 257–268, 273, 276–277, 280–292, 302, 417, 427–428

"Peaceable Kingdom" (Patti Smith), 307–309

"People Have the Power" (Patti Smith and Fred "Sonic" Smith), 161–162, 164, 171, 184, 200, 217, 229, 261, 285, 329, 333–334, 378, 427, 466, 502, 504

People's Climate March, 465

Peppermint Lounge, 46

Pep's, 187

Percodan, 152

Persistence of Memory, The (Salvador Dali), 355

Phair, Liz, 168

Phoenix Concert Theatre (or the Phoenix club), 170

Philadelphia, 342

Piaf, Édith, 46, 75, 259

Picasso, Pablo, 25, 164, 179, 225, 263, 322–323, 326, 355, 408, 417–418, 475, 477–478

Pickup on South Street, 111

Pindar, 124

Pines, the, New Jersey, 40, 302

Pineys, 41

Pink Floyd, 142

"Piss Factory" (Patti Smith), xiv, 23, 35, 40, 42, 48, 94, 103, 126, 148, 165, 173, 226, 238, 257, 269, 271, 342–343, 382, 424

Pitman, New Jersey, 27, 40, 45, 51, 165

Plath, Sylvia, 414, 418, 433
Please Kill Me: The Uncensored Oral History of Punk (Legs McNeil and Gillian McCain), 83–84
poetry
  inspiration for, 36, 51, 198, 271, 292, 397–398, 474, 477, 484
  performance poetry, xiv, xv, 3–22, 27–28, 34, 39, 67, 75, 78, 96, 102, 124, 148, 170–171, 183, 213, 230, 240, 382, 405–406, 416, 447, 482
  writing process, 37, 46, 55, 146, 212, 258, 292, 319, 374–375, 377, 379, 395, 425–429
Poetry Project at St. Mark's Church, The, xiv, 3
Pollock, Jackson, 14, 17, 179, 184, 249, 355–356, 358, 415, 418
Pop, The, 141
Pope John Paul II, 312, 319
"Poppies" (Patti Smith), 101, 136, 210
Portobello Hotel, xvi, 53
Pound, Ezra, 21, 205
POV, 414
Pratt Institute, 32, 42, 43, 75, 367, 442
Proctor and Bergman, 116
Progressive, 257
"Prove It All Night" (Bruce Springsteen), 144
Public Image: First Issue (Public Image Ltd.), 135
Puccini, Giacomo, 98, 327
Punk, 83–84
Quicksilver Messenger Service, 139

Quilt, the, 255

"Radio Baghdad" (Patti Smith), 307–308, 354, 375, 378, 390, 427
"Radio Ethiopia" (Patti Smith), xix, 172
Radio Ethiopia (Patti Smith Group), xvi, 70, 80, 83, 91, 95, 101, 126, 133, 142–143, 148, 166, 169, 172–173, 185, 272, 355, 377, 415–416, 426, 491
Ramones, 53, 83, 184, 369, 451, 500
"Rape" (Patti Smith), 125
Rastafarianism, 51
"Ravens" (Patti Smith), 204, 224
Ray, Oliver, 217, 249, 273, 286, 288, 292, 302
RCA Victor Victrola, 31
Reagan, Ronald, 258
Record Plant Studios, xvi, 83, 491
Red Room Books, 3–4
Redford, Robert, 64
"Redondo Beach" (Patti Smith), 137, 212, 376, 425
Reed, Lou, 31–32, 46, 49, 51, 53, 83, 135, 147, 171, 239, 337
Refinery29, 466
Reich, Peter, 28
Reich, Wilhelm, 63
R.E.M., 168, 213, 273
Rembrandt, 106, 356
Reno Sweeney, 35
Renoir, Pierre-Auguste, 44
Reprise Records, 113
Resto, Luis, 174

Revere, Paul, 156, 213, 222

Revolver Records, 172

Richards, Keith, 18, 24, 36, 39, 108, 121, 148, 183, 228, 258, 329, 334

Rimbaud, Arthur, xiv, , 5–7, 10, 15, 17, 20–21, 26, 33, 36, 37, 43, 46, 48–51, 53, 58, 65–67, 70, 96, 99, 102, 127, 167, 182–183, 187, 211, 250, 258, 271, 326, 355, 366, 395, 397–398, 419, 422, 434, 473–477, 486

Rimpoche, Gelek, 304

riot grrrl, 188, 202

Riperton, Minnie, 28

Ritter, Tex, 76–77

Rivera, Diego, 216, 380, 385, 473, 476, 484

"Rivers of Babylon" (the Melodians), 135

Roberto Bolaño's Chair (Patti Smith), 419

Robinson, Dave, 141

Robinson, Leslie, 205

Robinson, Smokey, 17, 26, 28, 32, 114, 495

Rock and Roll Hall of Fame, 237–238, 239, 329–330, 333–334, 342–344, 423–425, 490

"Rock & Roll [*n*-word]" (Patti Smith), 208, 212

Rock News, 103

Rock, Rock, Rock!, 139

Rock Scene, 91, 183

Rock She Wrote: Women Write About Rock, Pop, and Rap (Evelyn McDonnell and Ann Powers), 206

"Rock-a-Bye Your Baby with a Dixie Melody" (Al Jolson), 31

Rocks (Aerosmith), 83

Rockwell, John, 23, 49, 146

Rolling Stone, 3, 23, 183, 185–186, 205, 233, 270–271, 275, 345, 498

Rolling Stones, The, 3, 17–18, 25, 34, 41, 43, 59, 74, 115, 126–127, 150, 165, 175, 182, 192, 198, 222–223, 225, 287, 329, 331, 374

Ronettes, The, 41, 48, 110

Ronstadt, Linda, 101, 105–106

Ross, Diana, 110

Rotten, Johnny, 110, 135

Roundhouse, 53, 115

Roxon, Lillian, 206

Roxy Theatre, The, 62, 223–224, 232, 320

Rumi, 150

Rundgren, Todd, 129, 141, 146, 232

Rys, Richard, 342

Saint, The, 117

"Sally" (Patti Smith), 125

Salvation Army, 118

Sanders, Ed, 126

Saroyan, Aram, 3

"Satta Massagana" (the Abyssinians), 131

Saturday Night Fever, 488–489

Scene, the, 46

Scheuer, Jo, 466

Schneider, Maria, 380, 387, 409

Schulz, Bruno, 462, 485

Schwartz, Andy, 129–130

Screaming Females, 489–490, 501–502

Scribner's (or Scribner, Charles Scribner & Sons), 16, 45, 92, 410, 486

Season in Hell, A (Arthur Rimbaud), 28, 50, 420, 474

Sebring, Steven, 247, 344, 503
On *Patti Smith: Dream of Life*, 345–362

Sedaka, Neil, 187

Sedgwick, Edie, 10, 13

Seger, Bob, 80

Selassie, Haile, 66

Selected Poems (John Wieners), 5

Self-Portrait (Patti Smith), 418

"Seven Ways of Going" (Patti Smith), 137, 146

Seventh Heaven (Patti Smith), 3, 8–22, 25, 46, 48, 124, 130

Sex Pistols, 53, 111, 156, 177, 184, 194, 370

"Sexy Ways" (the Midnighters), 125

Sgt. Pepper's Lonely Hearts Club Band (the Beatles), 147

Shanahan, Mark, 461

Shanahan, Tony, 169, 171, 201, 273, 288, 334–337, 375, 386, 389,

Shapiro, Susin, 23

Shelton, Robert, 53

Shepard, Sam, 3, 11, 45, 67, 78, 148, 166, 183, 188, 232, 271, 362, 368, 374, 405, 445, 462, 479, 483, 485

Showboat, 187

"Shrimp Boats" (Paul Mason How-ard and Paul Weston), 31, 187

Sinatra, Frank, 10, 117, 233, 449

"Sinful Love" (Blue Öyster Cult), 93

Sire Records, 103

"Skunk Dog" (Patti Smith), 13–14

Slick, Grace, 120, 450

Smith, Beverly, 41, 42, 65, 73, 165, 221, 271, 284, 294, 308, 312, 318, 326, 327, 355, 360, 393, 401, 403, 405, 419, 446, 454,
death, 307–308
employment, 40, 74, 187, 338, 359, 429, 442, 476

Smith, Fred "Sonic," 53, 110, 131, 136, 147, 171, 180, 182, 185, 191, 203, 210, 215, 219–220, 372, 379, 488, 490, 493–495, 501, 504, 505
becoming a pilot, 180, 212
collaborating with Patti Smith, 203, 216–218, 229–230, 235, 237–238, 261, 291, 329, 334, 378, 427, 466
death, 184, 190, 201, 218, 226, 228, 234, 240, 241, 248, 258, 272, 289, 300, 321, 352, 381, 384, 427, 454, 490, 502
first meeting Patti Smith, 182, 184–185
marriage to Patti Smith, 149, 161–162, 164, 166–167, 169–170, 179, 197–200, 206, 211, 216–218, 229–231, 235–238, 258, 262–262, 272, 291, 329, 334–335, 378, 416, 424, 427, 437, 451, 458, 466
teaching Patti Smith to play guitar, 201, 217, 224, 289–290

Smith, Grant, 37, 40–41, 45, 52, 89,
165, 264, 327, 355, 359, 387, 403,
405, 409, 414, 417, 419, 440, 446,
454, 476, 483
death, 293
World War II, 283–285, 293–294
Smith, Jackson, 162, 164, 169, 197–
198, 200, 212, 223, 233, 258, 272
performing and recording, 291–292,
295, 321, 329–330, 336, 381,
385–386, 393, 412, 490, 501, 502
Smith, Jesse Paris, 162, 169, 197,
198, 200, 258, 272, 291, 295, 321,
381, 385, 386, 388, 412, 419
Pathway to Paris, 465–469
performing with Patti Smith, 490,
501–502
Smith, Kimberly, 28, 34, 40, 171,
201, 204, 293, 396
Smith, Linda, 3, 40, 43, 45, 72, 75
Smith, Todd, 40, 81, 177, 201,
234–235, 248, 258, 293, 297
death, 167, 169, 184, 199, 201, 235,
258, 272, 300, 321
Smith, Patti
childhood, xvii, 27, 37, 40–41,
51–52, 65, 73, 89, 150, 165, 183,
221, 264, 271, 284, 294, 302,
308, 310, 358–360, 366, 374,
387, 393, 401, 403, 405, 409,
414, 417, 419, 440, 476
guitar, learning to play, 201, 217,
224, 289–290
drugs, 39, 136, 166, 176, 203, 211,
221, 231, 259, 271, 275, 352

education, 5–6, 40–41, 73–74, 77,
124, 165, 284–285, 342–343,
344, 347, 356, 387, 399, 435,
440–441, 446–447
employment, 6–7, 40, 42–43, 74,
89, 126, 165, 342–343, 399, 442,
476
fame, 165, 174–175, 179, 198, 204,
248, 374, 438
first meeting Fred "Sonic" Smith,
182, 184–185
first meeting Robert Mapplethorpe, 32, 42, 43, 75, 367, 442
first pregnancy, 42, 440, 442
injuries from performing, 80, 96,
97, 103, 117, 142, 151–152, 335,
491, 496, 499
marriage to Fred "Sonic" Smith,
149, 161–162, 164, 166–167,
169–170, 179, 184, 197–200,
203, 206, 211, 216–218, 229–
231, 235–238, 258, 262–262,
272, 291, 329, 334–335, 378,
416, 424, 427, 437, 451, 458,
466
move to New York, xvi, 3, 23,
32–35, 42–47, 70, 75–76, 78,
166, 177, 194–195, 231–233,
302, 381, 400, 415–416
move to St. Clair Shores, Michigan, 161, 169, 197, 200, 203,
223, 302
Paris, 34, 43–44, 75–76, 101–103,
165, 324, 342–343
photography, 418–419

raising children, 161, 163, 174, 178–179, 224 , 234, 291, 359 , 437, 460

religion, 19, 37, 99–101, 105, 114, 118, 165, 281, 284, 24, 370, 381, 389–391, 397, 419–421, 476

return to New York, 297–298

Smoke, 249, 279

"Smoke on the Water" (Deep Purple), 204, 223

"So You Wanna Be (A Rock 'n' Roll Star)" (Patti Smith), 146

Sohl, Richard "DNV," 24, 28, 35, 131, 174, 194, 230, 271, 288, 331, 447, 452

death, 167, 176, 199, 248–249, 272, 300

SoHo, 258, 455

Soho Weekly News, 227

"Somebody to Love" (Jefferson Airplane), 120

Songwriters on Songwriting (Paul Zollo), 373

Sonic Youth, 169, 182, 191, 270

Sonic's Rendezvous Band, 110, 131, 161, 203

Sontag, Susan, 147

Sounds, 30, 80

"Southern Cross" (Patti Smith), 204, 241

Soutine, Chaim, 6

"Spanish Harlem" (Ben E. King), 32

"Spell" (Patti Smith), 302, 306

Spillane, Mickey, 5, 8–9, 157

Spin, 345

Springsteen, Bruce, 30, 38, 41, 142, 144, 394, 476

collaboration with Patti Smith, 162, 180–181, 198, 258, 272, 334, 379, 424, 488–506

Spungen, Nancy, 177

St. Ann and the Holy Trinity Church, 455–456

St. Clair Shores, Michigan, 161, 169, 197, 200, 203, 223, 302

St. Mark's Church, 3, 124, 183, 405

Stadio Comunale, 223

"Star-Spangled Banner, The," 137

Steely Dan, 142, 147

Stein, Seymour, 103

Steinway D #271146, 430

Stevenson, Robert Louis, 312, 316–317, 483

Stewart, Rod, 22, 48

Stipe, Michael, 178, 198, 217, 270, 297, 347–348, 381, 466, 489

Stone Hedge Inn, 185

Stooges, The, 184

Strand Bookstore, 473, 486–487

Stranglers, The, 53

Street Hassle (Lou Reed), 135

Street Life, 54

Strummer, Joe, 147

Sullivan, Ed, 41, 60

Sullivan, Jim, 161

"Summer Cannibals" (Patti Smith), 203–204, 228

Summer Jam at Watkins Glen, 47

Supple, Danton, 289

Supremes, The, 110

Surinam, 212

Symbolist, Symbolism, 473

"Sympathy for the Devil" (the Rolling Stones), 43, 385

Talking Heads, 184, 369

Tangier, Morocco, 75

Taylor, Peter, 109

Teenage Perversity and Ships in the Night, 61–62

Telegraph Books, 3, 8, 124

Television, 110, 139, 156, 184, 199, 451

10,000 Maniacs, 489–490, 501–502

"This Is the Girl" (Patti Smith), 380, 388–389

Thompson, Peggy, 108

350.org, 465–466

Three Rivers Arts Festival, 307

Through the Looking Glass (Lewis Carroll), 322

Trampin' (Patti Smith), 423, 426–427

Thunberg, Greta, 465

"Till Victory" (Patti Smith), 120, 285, 499

Timberg, Scott, 473

Times They Are A-Changin', The (Bob Dylan), 74

Tobler, John, 96

"Tomorrow," 137

Tooth of Crime, The, 45

Tosca, 253

Tosches, Nick, 123

Transatlantic Records, 80

Travolta, John, 489

Tropical, the, 123

Trudeau, Pierre, 79

Trump, Donald, 464, 465, 471

Tucker, Maureen, 239

Turner, Ike, 113, 114, 115

Turner, Tina, 113, 114, 259

Twelve (Patti Smith), 329–341, 383, 424, 428

Twenty Thousand Leagues Under the Sea (Jules Vern), 72

"25th Floor" (Patti Smith), 173, 218, 499

Twitty, Conway, 338

2666 (Roberto Bolaño), 368, 392, 482

"*Tyger, The*" (William Blake), 454

Tyner, McCoy, 80, 187

Tzara, Tristan, 148

Uhelszki, Jaan, 206

Until the End of the World, 229

University of North Carolina at Chapel Hill, 269

University Place, 240

"Up There Down There" (Patti Smith), 164

Useless Death, A (Patti Smith), 25

U2, 213, 424, 489–490, 501

Vassar College, 129–130, 136, 138

Velvet Underground, The, 56, 62, 237, 239, 476

Ventures, The, 193

Verlaine, Paul, 128, 473

Verlaine, Tom, 28, 110, 148, 174, 184, 199, 203, 204, 250, 273, 280, 289, 426, 473, 476, 477, 486, 500

Vicious, Sid, 177

Village Voice, 35, 170, 183, 190, 427

Virginia Woolf's Cane (Patti Smith), 418

Vogue, 27, 315, 358

Volunteers (Jefferson Airplane), 117–119

W. W. Norton & Company, 170, 199, 235

Wadsworth Atheneum Museum of Art, 380, 416

Waggoner, David, 247

Wagstaff, Sam, 250, 252, 254

Wailers, The, 28

Waldman, Anne, 148

Waldorf Astoria, 239, 329

"Walking Blind" (Patti Smith), 217

Walking on Locusts (John Cale), 239

Walt Whitman Cultural Center, 265

Walt Whitman Hotel, 265

Warfield Theatre, 205–207, 214

Warhol, Andy, 21, 45–46, 70, 76, 147, 258, 407

Warner Bros. Records (or Warner Records), 113

Wartoke, 47–48, 61

"Wave" (Patti Smith), 146

Wave (Patti Smith Group), 129–148, 154, 161, 166, 169, 173, 272, 296–297, 319, 378, 416, 426

Wenders, Wim, 229

West Village, 23, 141, 171

Westchester, 42

WFUV, 329–330

What You Hear Is What You Get: Live at Carnegie Hall (Ike and Tina Turner), 114

Wheels, Helen, 93

"Where Duty Calls" (Patti Smith), 161

Whipps, Andrea, 91

"White Rabbit" (Jefferson Airplane), 120

Whitman, Walt, xviii, 259, 265–266, 280, 305–306, 395–396

Who, The, 36, 120, 137, 163

Wieners, John, 5

Wild Boys: A Book of the Dead, The (William S. Burroughs), 104, 307, 425

Wild Leaves (Patti Smith), 170

Wilde, Oscar, 17

William S. Burroughs: A Report from the Bunker (Victor Bockris), 147

William S. Burroughs and the Cult of Rock 'n' Roll (Casey Rae), 147

Williams, Hank, 119

Williams, Paul, 272

William, Tennessee, 319

Willis, Ellen, 206

Wilshire, Beverly, 113

Wiltern Theatre, 23

Windham-Campbell Prizes, 455, 480

Winehouse, Amy, 380, 387–388, 409

Winer, Norm, 113

"Wing" (Patti Smith), 224

Winnipeg, Manitoba, 414

Winter, Edgar, 39, 46

Winter, Johnny, 39, 46

Winterland Ballroom, 48, 113, 206, 369

Witt (Patti Smith), 25, 47, 126, 322

Wizard of Oz, The, 136

Wolcott, James, 35

Wolfe, Bertram D., 473, 476

Woman (Willem de Kooning), 12, 417

Wonder, Stevie, 21, 32, 89, 192, 424

Woodstock, 47, 145, 226, 281, 373

Woolf, Virginia, 312, 318, 414, 418–419, 480

World Gone Wrong (Bob Dylan), 202, 228, 340

World of Star Trek, 116

World Peace Council, 195

Wylie, Andrew, 3–4

Yale University Press, 455, 457, 474, 480

Yeats, W. B., 12, 84, 168, 397, 483–484

"You Belong to Me" (Bob Dylan), 234

"You Light Up My Life" (Debby Boone), 489, 499

Young, Neil, 273, 310, 333, 414–415, 466, 494

"Young New Mexican Puppeteer, The" (Tom Jones), 124

"You're the One That I Want" (Olivia Newton-John and John Travolta), 489

Zanzibar, 166

ZigZag, 96

Zollo, Paul, 373

Zukie, Tapper, 82, 102